Beatles Deeper Undercover

Kristofer K. Engelhardt

2010

We acknowledge the financial support of the Government of Canada through the Book Publishing Industry Development Program for our publishing activities.
Published by Collector's Guide Publishing Inc., Box 62034, Burlington, Ontario, Canada, L7R 4K2
Printed and bound in Canada
Beatles Deeper Undercover / Kristofer K. Engelhardt
 ISBN 9781-926592-09-1

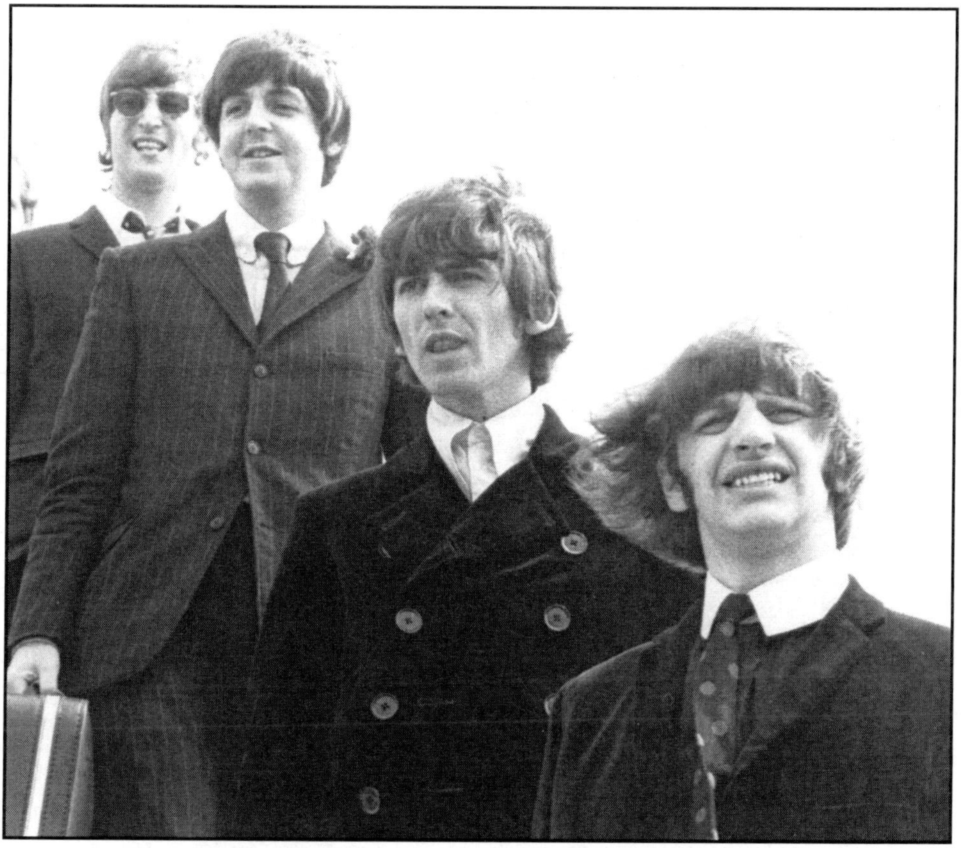

The Beatles arriving on August 11, 1966 at Boston's Logan Airport for the beginning of their final US tour. © and photo courtesy by Guy Greve.

Beatles Deeper Undercover

Kristofer K. Engelhardt

2010

Cover design is by Josh Long using portraits of The Beatles painted by the artist Gon'l in 1998. Gonl's paintings are owned by a number of celebrities including Ringo Starr.

Acknowledgements

Acknowledgements are a great part of what this book is all about. A very special thanks to the following (past and present) groups, musicians, producers, engineers, managers, agents, photographers and others who willingly and unselfishly gave of their time to personally help me achieve this level of accuracy: Dino Airali, Anya Alexeyev, Rusty Anderson, Rod Argent, Curtis Armstrong, Tony Ashton, John Askew, Brian Auger, Randy Bachman, Badfinger (Joey Molland & Mike Gibbins), Long John Baldry, The Band (Levon Helm & Rick Danko), Adrian Barber, Chris Barber, Mike Batt, The Beach Boys (Jeff Foskett, Bruce Johnston & Brian Wilson), The Beat Brothers (Howie Casey, Tony Sheridan & Roy Young), Barry Beckett, Cliff Bennett, George Benson, Lenny Berman, Tom Bert, Rodney Bingenheimer, John Bird, Cilla Black (Robert Willis Jr.), Billy Blanco, Graham Bonnet, Dan Bourgoise, Pattie Boyd, Delaney & Bonnie Bramlett, Peter Broadbent (Joyful Company Of Singers), David Bromberg, Gary Brooker, Joe & Samantha Brown, Jack Bruce, Brute Force (a.k.a. Stephen Friedland), Eric Burdon, T. Bone Burnett, Lori Burton, Johnny "Guitar" Byrne, Jim Capaldi (John Taylor), Eric Carmen, Paul Carrack, Johnny Cash (House Of Cash), Ernie Cate, Felix Cavaliere, Chantal (Michael Hofmann), Cheech And Chong, Clarence Clemons, Joe Cocker, Phil Collins (Annie Callingham), Billy Connolly, Lol Crème, The Crickets (Jerry Allison, Gordon Payne & Joe B. Mauldin), Steve Cropper, Crowbar (Kelly Jay), Charlie Daniels, Spencer Davis, Kiki Dee, Elle Denneman (International Tina Turner Fan Club), Lynsey de Paul, Johnny Devlin, Dr. John, Tymon Dogg, Lonnie Donegan, Terry Doran, Jack Douglas, Gus Dudgeon, Peter Dymond, Duane Eddy, Elephant's Memory (Wayne Tex Gabriel, Gary Van Scyoc & Chris Robison), Geoff Emerick, The Everly Brothers, Adam Faith (Alan Field), Marianne Faithfull, Fanny, Mark Farner, Horst Fascher, Dennis Ferrante, David Fishof, Mick Fleetwood, John & Robert Fogerty, The Fourmost, Les Fradkin, Peter Frampton, Kinky Friedman, Todd Rundgren (Eric Gardner), Kim Gardner, Georgia Satellites, Allen Ginsberg, Bob Glaub, Andrew Gold, Mark Goldenberg, David Gooch, Graffiti Band (Jim Ehinger & Bobby Tsukamoto), Grapefruit (John Perry, Geoff Swettenham & Pete Swettenham), Sylvia Griffin, Daryl Hall And John Oates, John Hanti, Roy Harper, Rolf Harris (Pat Lake-Smith), Ronnie Hawkins, Colin Hay, Jeff Healey, David Hentschel, Richard Hewson, Tony Hiller, Roger Hodgson, David Hood, Nicky Hopkins, Jim Horn, Larry Hosford, Mark Hudson, Ian Hunter, Steve Hunter, Jimmy Ienner, Neil Innes, Yusuf Islam (a.k.a. Cat Stevens), Ivory (James Duncan, Maxie Taylor & Derek Fields) Andy & Glyn Johns, Jimmy Johnson, Kenney Jones, Paul Jones, Michael Kamen (Zoe Lovell), Jubilee Action, Jim Keltner, Bobby Keys, Aashish & Pranesh Khan, Lee Kiefer, Ben E. King, Simon Kirke, Peter Kirtley, The Knack (Bruce Gary), Al Kooper, Larry Knechtel, Billy J. Kramer With The Dakotas (Billy J. Kramer & Mike Maxfield), Ulf Kruger, Jo Jo Laine, Greg Lake, Jon Landau Mgt., Mark Lapidos, Trevor Lawrence, Billy Lawrie, Viktor Lazlo, Will Lee, onovan Leitch, Julian Lennon (Annie Fowler), Jerry Lee Lewis, Mark Linett, Nils Lofgren, Jackie Lomax, Kirk Lorange, Nick Lowe, Steve Lukather, Lulu, Kenny Lynch, Liam Lynch, Vera Lynn, Jeff Lynne, Taj Mahal, Melissa Manchester, The Manhattan Transfer, Gered Mankowitz, Jimmy Markham, Gerry Marsden, Richard Marx, Dave Mason, Heather Mills McCartney (Renata Matijasevic), Mike McCartney, Hugh McCracken, Roger McGough, Ian McLagan, Terry Melcher, George Michael, Rusty Michaels, Adrian Mitchell, Zoot Money, Daniel Moore, Gary Moore (John Martin), Mortimer (Guy Masson), Jonell Mosser, Alan Moulder, Nervous (Justin Travis), Harry Nilsson, Don Nix, Rick Nowels, Yoko Ono, Barbara Orbison Productions, Buck Owens Productions, Hugh Padgham, Lindsay Pagano, Andy Paley, May Pang, Michael Parks, Van Dyke Parks, Jack Patrilla, David Peel & The Lower East Side, Richard Perry, Stan & Carl Perkins, Peter & Gordon, Tom Petty, "Papa" John Phillips, Vini Poncia, Duffy Power, Don Preston, Jim Price, P.J. Proby, The Radha Krsna Temple (Mukunda Goswami—ISKCON), Leon Redbone, Noel Redding, Martha Reeves, The Remo Four, The Righteous Brothers, Mark Rivera, Bruce Robb, Elizabeth, Ted & Kate Robbins, Andy Roberts, Todd Rundgren, Leon Russell, Roger Saunders, Michael Schenker, Timothy B. Schmit, Tom Scott, Frank Serafine, Ravi Shankar, Danny Sheridan, Glenn Shorrock, The Silkie (Sylvia Ramsden), Carly Simon, Nina Simone, John Sinclair, "Legs" Larry Smith, Sounds Incorporated, Roger Ruskin Spear, David Spero, Dave Spinozza, Splinter, Billy Squier, Freddie Starr, Prince Stash (Stanislas Klossowski de Rola, Baron de Watteville), Dave Stewart, Hamish Stuart, Bill Szymczyk (for

Rudy Romero), Bernie Taupin (Gilles Robigailles), John Tavener, 10cc (Graham Gouldman & Eric Stewart), Ron Terry, Guthrie Thomas, Russ Titelman, Doris Troy, Ruby Turner, Twiggy, Lon & Derrek Van Eaton, Tony Visconti, Mark Volman, Klaus Voormann, John Waite, Joe Walsh, Don Was, Pete Waterman, Cynthia Webb, Jimmy Webb, Paul Weller, Jerry Wexler, Alan White, Bobby Whitlock, Allan Williams, Andy Williams, Nicol Williamson, Mary Wilson, Wings (Denny Laine, Laurence Juber & Denny Seiwell), Edgar Winter, Johnny Winter, Steve Winwood, Ron Wood, Gary Wright & Shelly Yakus

Thanks to my fellow writers and researchers (past and present): Andy Babiuk, Keith Badman, Richard Barnes, Kathryn Bunting, Alan Clayson, Ray Coleman, Glen Dundas, Howie Edelson, Hans Gottfridsson, Gary Johnson, Stefan Granados, Arno Guzek, Bill Harry, Thomas Jones, Harvey Kubernik, David Leaf, Jeff Levy, Martin Lewis, Mark Lewisohn, Chip Madinger, Ross Myers, Peter Nash, Marc Roberty, Garath Powlowski, Mike Rapsis, Ron Scarlett, Ken Sharp, Neville Stannard, Eddie Veltman, Joe Viglione, Ronald Watson, Joel Whitburn & Allen Wiener.

Thanks to the following publications, organizations and record companies (past and present): Angel Records, AFM, ASCAP (American Society of Composers, Authors and Publishers), *Beatlefan*, *The Beatles Book*, *Beatles Unlimited*, *Beatletter*, *Belmo's Beatleg News*, *Billboard*, *Blue Suede News*, BMI (Broadcast Music, Inc.), British Equity, British Musician's Union, The Writers' Guild of Great Britain, Bug Music, Hal Carter Organization, *Cashbox*, CEMA, Cilla's Circle Of Fans, *Club Sandwich* (Paul McCartney's Fan "Fun" Club magazine), Country Music Foundation, *Disc and Music Echo*, *Discoveries*, East End Lights, East West Records, EMI Records, Guinness Publications, *Goldmine*, *Good Day Sunshine*, *The Harrison Alliance*, *Ice*, In Dreams, *Melody Maker*, *New Musical Express*, *The New Times*, New Zealand Wellington Rock 'n' Roll Revival Club, *Playboy*, PRS for Music, *Record Collector*, *Rolling Stone*, Screen Actors Guild, Del Shannon Appreciation Society, Stony Plain Records, *Strawberry Fields Forever*, *True Brit*, Westbury Music Consultants Ltd. & *The Write Thing.*

TABLE OF CONTENTS

Left to right: cover artist Gon'l, Ringo Starr and author Kristofer Engelhardt,
Pine Knob Clarkston (Detroit), MI June 11, 2000.
Photo by David Fishof, © Kristofer Engelhardt

Foreword

Beatles Deeper Undercover is by far the most comprehensive history and reference book on The Beatles' direct musical contributions to other artists' records, recordings and performances ever compiled. It is a greatly revised, updated and expanded edition of Kristofer Engelhardt's groundbreaking and critically acclaimed book *Beatles Undercover,* published in 1998. These books take their titles from the fact that The Beatles often had to resort to using pseudonyms or refuse credit for their contributions. Since then much new information has come to light and members of The Beatles have continued to make contributions to other artists' work. This book represents the culmination of nearly 10 years of his research and writing. It is not a price guide or a discography. It does not seek to expose the artists' personal lives or critique their work. You will be disappointed by this book if you are looking for tales of sex, drugs and self-destruction, but you will find a wealth of rock 'n' roll history, much of it uncovered for the first time. In short, this book is about The Beatles' admiration for, and generous support of their friends and fellow musicians who recount what it was like creating music with them. For anyone who thinks the music of John Lennon, Paul McCartney, George Harrison and Ringo Starr is confined to The Beatles, and their solo recordings, you are in for a very big and pleasant surprise because their contributions to other artists' recordings represent some of their best work.

Between 1989 and 2003 I produced the first eight tours for Ringo Starr's All-Starr Band. Many people in the music industry told me it would be impossible to put such a concept together for anything more than a benefit concert or a couple of dates; certainly not for an entire tour. However, I believed in the concept, so I took a chance and mortgaged my house in Manhattan, and put the first band together, which included Ringo, Jim Keltner, Dr. John, Billy Preston, and Levon Helm and Rick Danko from The Band, Nils Lofgren and Clarence Clemons from Bruce Springsteen's band and Joe Walsh* from The Eagles. On the fourth date, at the Garden State Arts Center in New Jersey, I was having dinner with the President of Radio City Music Hall who I was trying to convince to book the band. As we're talking, Clarence Clemons comes up and says, "Fishof, I quit! I can't take the fighting." I excused myself to see what was going on. As I approached the dressing room Nils Lofgren walks out and says, "Fishof I really appreciate the gig but I'm out of here. There's just too much fighting. The band can't get along. Joe Walsh and Levon Helm are fighting over the song list." I was scared to go into the dressing room. I certainly didn't want to get involved in any musical disputes. I went looking for Ringo to resolve the situation because it was his band, but he was nowhere to be found. The security guards told me I'd better go into the dressing room and resolve things. I was scared as hell. I walk in and see Levon and Joe fighting with each other. Levon's got a knife in his hand and blood on his face. Joe has a glass bottle in his hand and blood all over it. I started screaming at the top of my lungs calling them a bunch of babies. Levon grabs a glass bottle and smashes it over Joe's head! Joe grabs a knife and starts stabbing away at Levon and there's more blood. I was really scared. I was certain the tour was over! I started screaming at them again. They turned around, looked at me, stuck their tongues out, and started laughing their asses off! Then I find out Jim Keltner is videotaping the whole gag. Then everyone in the band starts to hug me. It was quite an initiation for a square like me who in all of my years in the business had never really spent any time on a tour with a band. It's my most memorable All-Starr Band moment, though it wasn't very funny at the time. I wanted other people to share the same experiences and fun I had with all of these musicians. I thought, "This must be what camp is like." From that I got the idea for the Rock 'n' Roll Fantasy Camp. Years later Levon and Joe shared this, and other stories, at one of my camps.

Every band sounded great. I don't think there was one tour rehearsal where after a few days Ringo didn't say, "OK we're ready to go." A lot of credit for that goes to Mark Rivera. Everyone got tapes and came well prepared – really well prepared. Everyone was very professional and wanted to learn everyone else's songs, including Ringo. Everyone wanted to sound great — for Ringo. I've worked with some big stars over the years and Ringo is the biggest, but he was the least demanding, which I find amazing.

Ringo is very sharp about life and has an incredible sense of humor. There were always a lot of laughs on tour. Joe Walsh said it best when he said, "We have a very democratic band. Whatever Ringo says we do." Being in the biggest band in the world, Ringo has amassed a tremendous amount of knowledge and life experiences. The greatest thing about being on all of those tours was how open Ringo was in sharing some of his amazing stories with everybody — from meeting Elvis to recording with John, Paul and George.

All of the musicians were grateful and honored, and some were in awe of playing with Ringo every night, especially when they realized that for Ringo it was just about being in a band with them and nothing more. He believes it should be a team effort. It isn't just about him, but about the guys in the band and being a band. He plays the best he can on their songs and they do the same for his songs. He tries to promote them and push their talent as much as possible, so everyone benefits. He's very unselfish that way. He's very appreciative of his band. I find that amazing in this business. He also has great concern for his band members' health and well being. Band members have to get a physical, and some have learned of potentially serious problems and are probably alive today because of that. Ringo is a great role model for these musicians because he takes care of his health by eating right and working out in the gym. These are just some of the many great lessons I learned from Ringo. I also learned from him the importance of surrounding yourself with good people because you have to live and work with them on the road. The last thing Ringo wants is a problem on the road. It's a priority to him to have people around that he enjoys on a personal level. Even though he knows it's important to sell tickets, he told me that in the long run having people around that he enjoys would translate into selling more tickets, and he was right! He also surrounds himself with some of the best tour support people, so things always went smoothly on the road.

All of the tours were great but that first tour is still my favorite, and then the British All-Starr tour. I toured with a Beatle, and those other great musicians, to Europe, Russia and Japan, which was an amazing growth and learning experience for me. Anyone who goes through the All-Starr Band experience receives an amazing education from a Beatle. Nobody had a negative experience. Everyone walked away with a tremendous high. It was great fun – great fun. However, I wanted to get on with my life, and dedicate more time to the Rock 'n' Roll Fantasy Camp, which I love because I'm helping change people's lives. I owe that to Ringo. I even learned how to have a happy marriage from Ringo. I owe him a lot.

Kristofer and his books have been inspirations and guides for me, and my All-Starr Band concept. So, read on and go deeper under the covers of his incredible new book to find out much more about The Beatles' other amazing musical story.

DAVID FISHOF
For more information go to
www.rockcamp.com

David Fishof and Kristofer Engelhardt, Meadow Brook Music Festival, Rochester Hills (Detroit), MI July 8, 1998.
Photo by Susan Long, © Kristofer Engelhardt.

Introduction

Early in their career The Beatles, in whole or part, didn't contribute much to other artists' recordings. Their contributions in those early days were mostly limited to Lennon and McCartney compositions being donated to other artists who were also represented by their management, Brian Epstein's NEMS Enterprises. With the creation of The Beatles' Apple Records in the late 1960s, it increased the opportunity, and necessity for them to contribute to artists signed to their label. Each Beatle had an even greater opportunity or desire to work with other artists following the breakup of the group. George produced a considerable volume of recordings for Apple and his label, Dark Horse Records. He also contributed several of his compositions to other Apple artists. Harrison, who was an executive producer and an owner of HandMade Films, also made cameos and musical contributions to some of that company's films. He frequently played his trademark slide guitar on other artists' recordings up until his death in 2001. Paul was the most active contributor to other artists' recordings while The Beatles were together. During most of the 1970s he devoted his musical time to his group Wings and to MPL (McCartney Productions Limited) projects. He also contributed to recordings by members of Wings, including his wife Linda. Following Paul's ending of Wings in the early 1980s he started working with a variety of well-known artists. He has also contributed to a number of film soundtracks, and classical and orchestral works. Ringo Starr has contributed to a wide range of artists' recordings, though primarily as a session drummer or as a part of his All-Starr Bands. John Lennon's primary contribution to other artists' recordings was as producer, and to a lesser degree vocalist or composer, particularly for his wife Yoko Ono, and friends such as Harry Nilsson and Elton John. Though Lennon was adequate on keyboards, and one of the steadiest rhythm guitarists in the business, he wasn't inclined to spend much time in studios. He was too busy filming nearly every event in his and Yoko's life to have much time to contribute to anyone else's film projects.

The Beatles and their solo recordings come from the same source. Therefore, their contributions to each other's recordings aren't considered *contributions* to another artist. Recordings by The Beatles' groups, or under assumed names, such as McCartney's Wings, Thrillington, The Country Hams, Twin Freaks and The Fireman, or Harrison's Traveling Wilburys are also considered solo Beatles' recordings, even if they don't feature a Beatle on a lead vocal. Under these assumed names, if a Beatle contributes something but doesn't sing lead vocals, the following are considered contributions: group recordings that were initially released under another group member's name; Ringo Starr's All-Starr Band recordings; Plastic Ono Band or John Lennon and Yoko Ono recordings featuring someone other than John as the primary vocalist, or composer on instrumentals (usually Yoko Ono); recordings released under the names of wives or family members that The Beatles contributed to are also considered contributions.

The majority of the entries in this book consist of those where members of The Beatles' contributed instrumental, backing vocals, production, arrangements, engineering assistance and compositions to the recordings of other artists. Contributions to other artists' musical performances in videos, films or soundtracks, including scores, are also included. Films that any of The Beatles had any other role in, such as director, producer, screenwriter or appearance in, are noted where appropriate, but not considered musical contributions. Also included are liner notes written by, photographs taken by, or drawings or designs made by any of The Beatles specifically for another artist's record. Many record releases with contributions by The Beatles (and many without) include photos of The Beatles, but the photos aren't considered contributions. Records only acknowledging, thanking or dedicated to The Beatles aren't considered a contribution. Interviews or dialogue by members of The Beatles aren't considered contributions unless purposely contributed by that Beatle. Samples of any of The Beatles' recordings aren't considered a contribution unless there is an additional contribution, even though permission is usually needed or granted for their use. Songs primarily featuring lead vocals by one of The Beatles, or a duet vocal of a song wholly composed by that Beatle, released by or co-credited to another artist, are not considered a contribution to another artist's recording. Duet vocals credited to a Beatle and another artist on a song not solely written by that Beatle are considered contributions to that other artist. Duet vocals with a Beatle released solely under another artist's name or record are also considered contributions.

Members of The Beatles have frequently contributed their compositions to other artists to record and release prior to their own release of the song. In a few instances the artist or record company has delayed a release by months or years, or not released the recording at all, sometimes at the request of the composer. Conversely, occasionally a Beatle will record one of his songs, and he, or his record company, will hold it from release for months or years, and give another artist a chance to record and release the song. If an artist recorded or legally released his version of a song before the composer did, it's considered a composition contribution. This is likely only possible if the composer had initially intended to contribute the song to another artist with the likelihood that the artist would release it first. If there is evidence that a record company released a recording by an artist before its composer, without the knowledge or consent of the composer, it is not considered a composition contribution. A composition recorded by an artist subsequent to its composer, but not released before the composer's version, is considered a cover version and not a contribution. There are exceptions to these criteria, but only in cases where there is substantial evidence indicating that the composition was originally intended by its composer to be released by another artist first. Subsequent re-recordings of the composition contribution by that artist aren't considered additional contributions and aren't noted unless other (new) contributions by a Beatle were made to it. Samples of any member of The Beatles' previously released composition aren't considered a contribution unless they made an additional contribution, even though permission is usually needed or granted for their use.

This book was written with the generous help and approval of those listed in the acknowledgements. All direct quotes were taken by me from those to whom they are attributed, unless credited to another source. I returned to my original notes and taped interviews used for *Beatles Undercover* for relevant new information and revisions. Two highly rewarding aspects of working directly with these people were the solid friendships that often developed and the opportunity to reunite many of them with long lost friends. Unfortunately, many have passed away since this project began, some while I was in the process of gathering information from them. I've used only those sources that have proven reliable, and have verified my information from as many sources as possible. Unfortunately, sometimes as I dug deeper the information became increasingly inconsistent and unreliable. Take young, impressionable musicians, sometimes under the influence of mind altering substances, put them in the presence of their idols, The Beatles, let decades pass with myth and misinformation polluting their memories, and you are often left with little reliable information. It was also unrealistic to expect that many of these artists would remember minute details. In some instances I was sure people were telling me what they thought I wanted to hear, as opposed to the truth. Well documented stories were often recounted to me in a degraded or self-serving manner. Sometimes they would contradict what they had previously told me. On many occasions I had to take what I was told with a large barrel of salt and disregard it completely. There is naturally less conflicting information when one artist, as opposed to a group, was involved. I've tried to present all sides of the story in the interest of objectivity. In an interview conducted by Allan Kozinn in 1995, Paul was asked if *The Beatles Anthology* film was the definitive statement. He felt that they had done their best to make it the definitive statement but also reminded us that there's no such thing as definitive. He explained one process by which the three surviving Beatles reached a conclusion during interviews for the film. He said that Ringo recalled that while The Beatles were in Paris, George had a sore throat. George recalled it was Paul who had the sore throat. Paul recalled that it was John who had the sore throat. Paul reasoned that if Ringo and George knew they weren't the ones with the sore throat, and Paul knew he didn't have a sore throat that it must have been John. Presumably Lennon would have remembered it being Ringo with the sore throat. There's even confusion concerning who first approached Yoko Ono with the idea of taking some of John's unfinished recordings and turning them into new Beatles' songs for *The Beatles Anthology*. Yoko says it was Harrison and Beatles' assistant Neil Aspinall who approached her. Paul thinks he first approached Yoko but isn't certain. When necessary, I also had to use a process of elimination to draw some conclusions.

The job of uncovering The Beatles' contributions to other artists' recordings was made more difficult because, particularly in the 1960s and '70s, they resorted to using pseudonyms or weren't credited. This was done primarily to avoid violating record contracts, paying fees or drawing attention away from the artist to whom a famous Beatle was contributing. All of The

Beatles created some rather clever but thinly veiled pseudonyms. Some of the most difficult information to verify was recording dates, studios and musicians involved for these contributions. Studio logs, tape boxes, diaries and union payroll sheets are useful but not always reliable. Record keeping and the atmosphere at many recording studios is often informal with musicians dropping in for a quick contribution. Sessions can also take place at a number of studios over long periods of time. Adding to the confusion are the multi-tracks used to record a song that may be omitted from the final mix, or songs are omitted from an album just prior to release, but the credits aren't amended. Much mystery and confusion is created when album credits are general and not specific for each song. In some unethical cases, records have falsely claimed or implied that a famous musician contributed to it. Pseudonyms have been replaced with their proper names but are usually noted in the text. Any misinformation (misspelled names, incorrect titles, composers, times, studios, dates etc.) on records or recordings has been corrected, or noted where known.

For many years, recordings have also been made on artists' personal recording equipment or at private studios where credits for the participants are left at their discretion. Many of The Beatles' contributions to other artists' recordings were made at one or more of their home or private studios in the UK. John had a makeshift studio in his Weybridge home in the mid-1960s. After he moved into his home in Tittenhurst Park, Ascot in the late 1960s, he had a studio built that he called Ascot Sound Studios (ASS). When Ringo bought the home in 1973 he renamed it Startling Studios (like one of his publishing companies) and made it available for hire. Ringo has had studios he calls RoccaBella at his homes for a number of years. George built a studio, known as FPSHOT, at his Friar Park, Henley-on-Thames home shortly after he acquired it in 1970. Paul has had makeshift studios in his home in St. John's Wood in London, at his High Park Farm house on the Kintyre peninsula near Campbeltown, Scotland called Rude Studio and in a barn there called Spirit of Ranachan. Many of his recordings over the past two decades have been made at his Hog Hill Mill Studios near his home in Sussex. Paul also built a replica (Replica Studios) of EMI's Abbey Road Studio 2 (where The Beatles did most of their recording) at his MPL offices in London. The Beatles, as a group and individually, also recorded at a studio they built in the basement of their Apple Corps Ltd. offices at 3 Saville Row in London.

Recordings don't lie, but they don't always reveal their secrets easily. When information was unavailable, or credits weren't specific to a song, experienced ears and a process of elimination were used to identify musicians. If one horn player is listed in the general credits and there are horns on a song then that musician is credited. There's always the danger of wanting to believe rumors that a Beatle made a contribution to a recording despite any "sound" evidence to support it. It's usually easy to identify a Beatle singing on a recording. Except for McCartney's infectious hooks and melodic writing style, most of the other Beatles' compositions aren't obvious. Paul's bass, keyboard and guitar work are unique but can't always be positively identified. John's piano playing and acoustic guitar picking are fairly distinctive. George's slide guitar solos are usually unmistakable. Ringo's steady off-beat and unique fills usually make his drumming recognizable but others also have a similar style.

Identifying technical contributions by a Beatle, such as arranging, mixing or producing, just by listening, is nearly impossible. The term and role of producer is not easily defined. Many well-known producers exercise complete control over artists by imposing their arrangements, distinctive style and sound. Other producers play a very passive role allowing the artist a good deal of control and decision making. Personal managers, arrangers, engineers, A&R (Artist and Repertoire) managers, assistants, friends, a spouse, group members and other musicians may contribute as much to the production of a recording as the designated producer, and may or may not receive co-production credits. Quite often a Beatle has assisted producers or engineers in mixing or arranging recordings for other artists, but isn't credited. Conversely not all recordings listing a Beatle as producer received their full, if any, attention. The term executive producer is more appropriate when referring to a managerial, financial or superficial role in production, and isn't considered a production contribution unless there is evidence of considerable involvement. If a Beatle is known to have mixed a recording it is only noted if someone else produced the song, as mixing generally falls under the role of producer.

Artist's given names at birth are noted, though middle names are omitted unless used as part of their professional or primary name. Dates and places of birth are listed when known for artists who have chapters on them. Some artists didn't want their date of birth published or quoted me a later year. As former

Record Plant owner, and Lennon's recording engineer and close friend, Roy Cicala told me, "This is an industry obsessed with youth." Without checking a birth certificate, determining the accurate date and place of birth for some artists proved challenging, especially given that some of their press releases also shave off a few years. It's common to find completely different dates and places of birth listed for someone. Part of the confusion arises from birth certificates, which list the legal locale (the hospital) where a person is born as well as where the person's family lives at the time of their birth, which are often different. Within greater city areas are smaller suburban communities, which may or may not be noted as a more specific place of birth in publications. Even birth certificates aren't always accurate. Apparently George Harrison learned that he was born around 11p.m. on February 24, though the time filled out on his birth certificate was a little over an hour later on the 25.

Record charts are still the primary measuring stick of success in the music business. Charts are generally listed in major music trade publications on a weekly basis. They don't always reflect the popularity or long-term sales of a record. Over the years, the methods, criteria, and organizations responsible for compiling and publishing chart and sales data have changed, and there are many variable factors. The results can be subjective or self-serving to the industry, and be easily influenced or manipulated. Brian Epstein was suspected of ordering large numbers of The Beatles' first single for his record store to influence that record's chart position. The chart positions and dates listed are taken from *Billboard* magazine's Hot 100 (singles) and the Top 200 (albums) charts. The highest chart positions are noted in the familiar categories of Top 40, Top 20, Top 10, Top Five, and number one or top of the charts. Songs that didn't chart but became popular are often noted. Over the years there have been a number of sub-genre charts such as R&B (rhythm & blues or black), classical, jazz, country, dance, alternative, video, regional charts and others. All chart information is for the US unless noted otherwise. British chart positions are taken from the Official Charts Company (OCC) and *New Musical Express* (*NME*) magazine. Dates for a record's highest chart position can be misleading as they don't reflect when the record first appeared on the charts or when it was first released. Dates for a record listed in the text refer to its release date or highest charting date, not necessarily when a contribution or recording was made.

This book is not a price or collector's guide, or discography of every record release (as opposed to recording) containing a contribution by The Beatles. That would be an enormous task and book. The highest fidelity format, usually a CD, DVD or LD, and most readily available or desirable record (such as a compilation), which include a contribution, is listed in preference to vinyl (often the original release) unless it is only available in that format, or on cassette or VHS tape. Unless noted otherwise, all records are CDs manufactured in the US. If the CD wasn't made in the US, or is extremely difficult to find, a more available foreign CD is listed. Both CD and vinyl releases are identified if there are important differences between them, or if the album package (jacket and contents) contain additional contributions. Extended versions, usually alternate mixes on 12" vinyl or CD singles, are noted but edited versions aren't. Remixed recordings aren't included unless identified as such and noticeably different, or contain an additional contribution. No distinction between mono and stereo mixes is made though the vast majority of records listed are stereo mixes. Contributions also available on DVD are listed in preference to the CD, but the CD is noted. This is also the case for LDs.

It is sometime difficult to determine the authenticity of a record release. Unauthorized releases are noted when known. Unauthorized record releases, or bootlegs and counterfeits as they are commonly known, are records that are not legally authorized for release by the artist or their record company. They are generally available only from private dealers in limited quantity, usually containing out-takes, demos, rehearsals and live performances, and usually with inferior fidelity. Some of the information and material contain on these records is erroneous, often deliberately, so determining their true origin (and country) is often difficult. These records are noted only if they contain a contribution not available on an authorized release. There are many live recordings of songs from a particular tour that include a contribution from a Beatle. Only songs that haven't been officially released, or those with a different musical lineup, or are significantly different from those released, are included. and then only one example is listed. Mastered CDs and DVDs are listed in preference to CD-Rs and DVD-Rs. [This book, its author and publisher do not sanction, or encourage the promotion, advertisement, manufacturing, sale or purchase of any unauthorized record release. Their inclusion is for reference purposes only.]

Throughout my research I have encountered countless rumors and claims that one or more of The Beatles contributed to another artist's recordings, but with no creditable evidence, or overwhelming evidence to the contrary. After thorough investigation I can say almost categorically that as yet none of The Beatles have contributed to the following artists' recordings: Herb Alpert, Tasmin Archer, The Babys, Stephanie Bennett, Gary US Bonds, Graham Bonnet, Brand X, Buffalo Springfield, The Byrds, Campbelltown Pipe Band, David Cassidy, Cerrone, Michael Chapman, Phil Collins, Cook & Moore, Suzy Cope, Culture Club, King Curtis, Bo Diddley, Fanny, Fresh, The Futz, Georgia Satellites, Johnny Hallyday, Jimi Hendrix Experience, Jools Holland, Chuck Howard, Hudson, Garland Jeffreys, Kanda Bongo Man, Klaatu, Viktor Lazlo, Buzzy Linhart, Little Village, Lord Sitar, Nick Lowe, The Mamas And The Papas, Melissa Manchester, The Masked Marauders, Christine McVie, Joni Mitchell, Rab Noakes, NRBQ, Elaine Paige, Michael Parks, Don Preston, The Raspberries, Rudy Romero, Tim Rose, The Rutles, Mike Sanchez Band, Shakespear's Sister, Gene Simmons, Nina Simone, Dave Stewart And The Spiritual Cowboys, Thee Image, Twiggy, Les Variations, Gene Vincent, Andy Williams or Karen Young. It is also highly unlikely that any of The Beatles have as yet contributed to the following artists' recordings (though in some cases they are personally thanked): Bad Company, Maggie Bell, Blackberries, Laurie Bogin, Keni Burke, Susan Cadigan, The Carpenters, Stewart Copeland, The DB's, Rob de Nijs, Michael Des Barres, "Mama" Cass Elliot, Eulenspygel, Everybody's Children, The Fifth Dimension, Phillip Goodhand-Tait, Guns And Roses, Jan Hammer, Alex Harvey, Tony Hazzard, Dick Heckstall-Smith, Hudson-Ford, Hummingbird, Alexis Korner, Linda Lewis, Lindisfarne, The Meters, Leslie Mills, Maria Muldaur, Randy Newman, Paladin, Professor Longhair, Martha Reeves, Kenny Rogers, Steward Saturn, Scorpions, Neil Sedaka, Split Enz, Stairsteps, Vivian Stanshall, Alvin Stardust, Steelers Wheel, Al Stewart, Barbra Streisand, Survivor, Topo D. Bil, Martha Velez, Wang Chung or Wishbone Ash. George Harrison is thanked for his support (probably financial) of ISKCON (International Society for Krishna Consciousness) worldwide projects on about a dozen albums. It is highly unlikely, and has never been suggested, that Harrison contributed musically to any of these albums.

All contributions by a member of The Beatles in the record or recording data are in bold, and listed first even though they may not be listed that way on the records. The following template is used for the book:

Artist/Group Name

Each (chapter) artist or group's official name, or as it is listed on the record, or what is known to be correct, is listed in the book alphabetically starting with the first letter of a group's name (excluding "The") or the first letter of the last name of an artist. In the case of a record with no specific artist listed, or a recording that is truly the product of a variety of artists, it is filed under "Various Artists" and then alphabetically by the first artist listed in the group or record title if there is no artist listed. Musical contributions exclusive to a film starring a number of people, are generally classified as "Various Artists" alphabetically by title. The exceptions are films with musical contributions that are billed as being by a particular artist, which are filed under the artist's name.

Title

Each record is listed by its official title as listed on the record, including alternate or subtitles, alphabetically (starting with the first letter of the title (excluding "The"). If there is a song contribution, but no record or record title [none] is listed. Artist or group names in brackets after the record title are those listed on the record, if different from the artist or group in the chapter heading. Various artists' records are noted in brackets.

Label, Catalog Number, (Alternate Media), Alternate Country, Release Date & Contribution to Record

Listed first is the record company label, and, or subsidiary, as stated on the label, jacket or package, or what is known to be the correct label (subsidiaries are always used in preference to the parent label). The vast majority of the subsidiary labels belong to one of the following parent labels: Universal Music Group (UMG), Electric & Musical Industries (EMI), Warner Music Group (WMG) or Sony Music Entertainment. In cases where a record is clearly intended to be cataloged or identified under more than one label, these are listed. Following the record label is the catalogue identification (letters and numbers) as listed on the label, jacket or package. The full catalogue identification, sometimes including the Universal Product Code (UPC), is usually listed. If the record has been issued under more than one catalog number by the label, or it is a package with multiple records, the second number (if known) is additionally listed in parenthesis. If there is no catalogue number, the matrix number (the manufacturing number stamped into the media) is used. If there isn't a record or catalogue number it is listed as [none]. All media except VHS tape (Vertical Helical Scan a.k.a. Video Home System) and cassette tape are referred to as records. All records are 5" CD (Compact Disc) albums unless noted otherwise in parenthesis following the catalogue number, such as a single or extended play, DVD (Digital Versatile Disc a.k.a. Digital Video Disc), 12" and 8" video LD (Laserdisc), or 12", 10", 8" or 7" vinyl albums, singles or extended play records. All records are manufactured in the US, unless noted otherwise in parenthesis following the catalogue number. Portions of a record package manufactured in other countries are noted. Also following the catalogue number in parenthesis is the date (month/day/year) that particular record was released. If a subsequent release date is listed, it is for the earliest know release of that record title anywhere in the world. Every effort has been made to determine the accurate date of release, usually the official record company release date. Songs broadcast on radio and TV, or in videos and films aren't considered released until they are available for purchase. Unreleased records are listed as [unreleased]. If a Beatle contributes to the record package, such as writing liner notes, taking photos or helping with the package design it is noted last.

Producer

This identifies the producer of the recording contribution as listed on the record package, which may not be the same as the producer for the rest of the record. If there is more than one contribution recording to a record with different producers, the producers are listed with the song data. If there are discrepancies, or there are additional producers not credited, they are noted in brackets.

Musician Credits

The musician credits are identified for each contribution recording when known. If there is only one contribution on the record or if the musician credits are the same for all of the contributions on the record, they are listed with the record. If there is more than one contribution song on the record and the musician credits are different they are noted with the song entry. Unfortunately, quite often musician credits are listed only for the record, and not for specific recordings, and often more than one musician will be listed for a particular instrument, complicating the process of making a positive identification. In these cases a "probable" or "possible" notation in parenthesis is used or an "&/or" is added. A "supposed" notation in parenthesis refers to reported involvement that is in dispute or is proven to be false. In some cases it was necessary to list the entire general musical credits of an album stating: "probably one or more of the following are involved." The musician credits aren't always complete, especially in regards to live finales during which many performers participate. In these situations only those who are actively singing or playing an instrument are noted. Instruments played are as listed in the credits or what is known to be correct. Types of guitars (electric, acoustic, etc.) and style of playing (lead, rhythm, slide, etc.) aren't always differentiated. A cross (†) after a musician indicates the studio and, or date the contribution was recorded is known, and also so noted.

Recording Site, Region & Date

Recording site, region and date identifies where a recording was made (usually a recording studio or a live venue), the city, state or country, and the date recorded. Recordings are only noted as "live" in brackets after the song title if made at a public performance. Unless noted otherwise, all recordings took place in the US. Studios or venues located in suburban communities of a major city are usually identified as being located in that major city. Over the years many live venues and studios have changed names, or relocated under the same name. When the specific studios and dates for a contribution aren't listed in a record's credits (or published elsewhere, or known) all of the credited studios and dates are listed. The dates or period listed identify when the recording was made. A specific date doesn't necessarily indicate the entire song was recorded then. A specific date could indicate the beginning of, or when the majority of the song was recorded, or the date the contribution was made. If the studio or date of the contribution are known they are noted by the cross (†) suffix. If there is more than one contribution song on a record, and it was recorded at a different site or date, it is listed with that song entry. Where there is uncertainty about the studios and dates a "probable," "possible" or an "&/or" is added.

Song Titles, Composers, Time, Track & (Date)

Listed in bold alphabetically below the record or recording data are the songs from that listing to which a Beatle made a contribution. The songs are spelled as listed on the record, or what is known to be correct. Alternate or subtitles are noted, but only in bold if part of the official title. If a Beatle is known to have made a contribution to a recording, but the title isn't known, it is listed as [unknown]. The composer is noted in parenthesis after the song title. The initial of the composer's first name and their entire last name is listed as it appears on the record or what is known to be correct. If the composer is unknown it is listed as [unknown]. A Beatle's composition is only in bold if it was a contribution. Lennon and McCartney didn't always co-write their songs credited as such, so only the actual composer is listed in bold. If a Beatles is known to be a composer but isn't legally credited, he is listed in brackets. The time listed is as stated on the record or what is known to be accurate. The number in parenthesis following the song time is the track where it appears on the record. If there are two numbers separated by a dash, the first number indicates the record number (for multiple record sets) and the second number indicates the track. If there are two numbers separated by a slash, the first number indicates the side of the record and the second number indicates the track. If there are three numbers separated by slashes, the first number indicates the record (for multiple record sets), the second number indicates the side of the record and the third number indicates the track. The use of slashes usually applies to vinyl records. If a date is listed it indicates the earliest known release of that recording anywhere in the world (earlier than the release date listed for the record).

Biography & Text of Contribution

The contribution data is followed by a brief biography of the artist or group highlighting their career. This is followed by a detailed history of The Beatles' working relationship and contribution to their recordings including contributions by that artist to members of The Beatles' records (excluding compilations unless unavailable elsewhere). An asterisk after an artist or group in the text references a chapter on them in the book. Official websites are listed for additional information.

Glossary

The following people, places and organizations are frequently mentioned or referenced throughout the book:

A&R	An Artist and Repertoire manager who is usually in charge of overseeing an artist for a record label.
Abbey Road	EMI-Abbey Road Studios in London where most of The Beatles' recordings were made, unless in italics, which refers to The Beatles' album *Abbey Road.*
Apple Corps Ltd.	The Beatles' company founded in 1968, which included (film, publishing, electronics, retail and record divisions), still functions as Apple Records and is referred to as Apple unless noted otherwise.
Neil Aspinall and Mal Evans	The Beatles' Personal Assistants and Road Managers in the early to mid-1960s, and later employees of Apple.
Dark Horse	Dark Horse Records formed by Harrison in 1971. Dark Horse has been a subsidiary label for A&M Records from 1974-1976, for Warner Bros. Records from 1976-1992 and for EMI from 2002 to the present.
DJ	A radio disc jockey.
EMI	EMI Records (The Beatles' parent record label on the subsidiary labels Parlophone in the UK and Capitol in the US).
Brian Epstein	The Beatles' manager from 1961 until his death in 1967. The Beatles and many other artists were signed to Epstein's management company NEMS (North End Music Stores) Enterprises.
HandMade Films	Formed in 1978 by Harrison and Denis O'Brien. Harrison sold HandMade Films in 1994 and was successful in his 1995 lawsuit against O'Brien for fraud and mismanagement.
Hits	Hit songs.
Allen Klein	Managed Apple and The Beatles (except McCartney who sued them to break up The Beatles) from 1969-1973. Under Klein's management company ABKCO (Allen & Betty Klein Company) most of Apple's artists were abandoned and Apple became little more than a holding company and record label for The Beatles, and their solo projects.
Mark Lewisohn	Author and noted authority on The Beatles. He has also served as an archivist for The Beatles and McCartney.
Liverpool	Liverpool, England.
London	London, England.
Los Angeles	Los Angeles, California.
May Pang	Assistant to John Lennon and Yoko Ono during the early 1970s. She and Lennon had a romantic relationship between 1973 and 1975.
MPL	McCartney Productions Ltd., a company Paul set up following the breakup of The Beatles in 1970 to handle his music and publishing.

NME	New Musical Express magazine, UK music trade publication
New York	New York City, New York
Ring O'Records	Formed by Ringo in 1975 and ceased issuing records in 1978.
Mark Roberty	Author and noted authority on Eric Clapton.
Derek Taylor	The Beatles' Press Officer in 1964. He was Apple's Press Officer in the late 1960s and early 1970s and from the mid - 1980s until his death in the mid-1990s. He was also an assistant to Harrison in the 1980s.
UK	United Kingdom (England, Scotland, Wales and Northern Ireland).
US	United States of America.

The terms artists, groups and musician, and film and video are generally used interchangeably.

Beatles Deeper Undercover

Anya Alexeyev

A Leaf
EMI Classics-CD LEAF 1 (single) (UK) (04/24/95)
Producer: John Fraser
Anya Alexeyev: Piano
St. James' Palace, London, UK 03/23/95

A Leaf (I Andante Semplice, II Poco piu mosso, III Allegro ritmico, IV Andante, V Allegro ma non tanto, VI Moderato, and VII Andante semplice [II]) [live] **(P. McCartney)** 9:56 (1)

Anya Alexeyev was born on March 21, 1972 in Moscow, Russia. She is an award-winning pianist and daughter of the renowned pianist Dmitri Alexeyev. She studied at the Moscow Tchaikovsky Conservatory with pianist Dmitri Bashkirov. Anya caught the attention of Paul McCartney when she received the Queen Elizabeth Rose Bowl Award in 1994, presented at Britain's Royal College of Music, from which she graduated, by the school's titular president Prince Charles.

McCartney agreed to help organize and contribute to a benefit concert for the college, including his classical composition *A Leaf.* The event was billed as *An Evening With Paul McCartney And Friends.* It included McCartney performing newly arranged versions of several of his Beatles' songs accompanied by Michael Thompson and the Brodsky Quartet, Elvis Costello*, Sally Burgess and Willard White performing portions of McCartney's *Liverpool Oratorio* (see The Royal Liverpool Philharmonic Orchestra & Choir and Choristers of Liverpool Cathedral) and Alexeyev. John Fraser, who has worked with McCartney on many of his classical music projects, produced a recording of the performance. Other portions of the event were available for promotional purposes only. For his efforts, McCartney was given honorary Fellowship of The Royal College of Music, Britain's highest honorary award to a musician, by Prince Charles.

Anya recounts, "I eagerly accepted when they asked me if I would perform *A Leaf*, Paul McCartney's first piece for solo piano, for the benefit concert. I didn't know then that my performance would be released as a single. I've enjoyed listening to The Beatles' music since I was a teenager, so it was very exciting for me to premier a work by one of the world's most famous musicians. I soon met with Paul and producer John Fraser in London to discuss the piece and play it for them. Paul seemed to like my playing. He was very friendly and approachable, and made me feel completely at ease. *A Leaf* is not as technically demanding as some pieces, and doesn't seek to be. It's quite melancholic, wistful and nostalgic; one can hear moments reminiscent of the familiar Beatles' cadences, but it is written in a very different style. It was very exciting to work with Paul and interact with people such as Elvis Costello and Prince Charles. I certainly wasn't expecting or aiming to be part of that crowd. Being young and having just graduated, it was very exciting. I'm very grateful to Paul and the college for providing me with such an opportunity. Afterwards, Paul sent me a nice letter of thanks."

Anya has been a soloist with the Royal Philharmonic, Moscow State Symphony, St. Petersburg Philharmonic, Belgian National Symphony, Vienna Chamber, Malaysian Philharmonic and many others. She currently serves on the Faculty of Music at Wilfrid Laurier University in Waterloo, Ontario Canada.

All Occasion Brass Band

In The Presence Of The Lord
MCA-MCA 362 (album 12") (xx/xx/74)
Producer: Jim Price for J.J. Productions (OM)
Ringo Starr: Drums; Klaus Voormann: Bass; Chris Spedding: Guitar; Jim Price: Horns; probably one or more of the following: Stu Blumberg, Jock Ellis, Jake The Rake, Dave McDaniels, C.B., Rev. D.S. Poncher; Steve Delaney, Carol Farhat, Ken Klinger, Chris Kimsey, Nat Seligman, Barbara Wood, Joe Zagarino, Dave Farrell: Greg Matheson
Olympic Studios, London, UK xx/xx/71

Oh Happy Day (E. Hawkins) 3:33 (1/5)

The All Occasion Brass Band was a Jim Price project. Jim Price was born in Fort Worth, Texas on July 25, 1945, and is primarily a session horn player. He was a part of the Delaney & Bonnie & Friends* tour in December 1969 that included George Harrison; and when they backed up John Lennon and Yoko Ono* at the Lyceum Ballroom in London included on the Lennons' 1972 album *Some Time In New York City*. The All Occasion Brass Band's instrumental album *In The Presence of The Lord* has musical credits that contain a number of obvious pseudonyms such as Pietro Frampini (Peter Frampton*), Christo Spedingo (Chris Spedding, who would later become a member of Paul McCartney's makeshift band in his *Give My Regards To Broadstreet* film) and Richard Starkey (Ringo Starr) who Price says plays drums on the album's song *Oh Happy Day*. The album also includes cover versions of songs from Harrison's *All Things Must Pass* album on which Price played. According to Price, *Oh Happy Day* is the only recording of his to which any of The Beatles contributed. Price appeared in a musical scene in Harry Nilsson* and Ringo Starr's film, *Son Of Dracula*. For more information go to www.jimprice.co.nr

The Alpha Band

The Arista Albums (The Alpha Band, Spark In The Dark & Statue Makers Of Hollywood)
Acadia-ACAD 8091 (UK) (08/22/05)
Producer: Steven Soles
Paramount Recording Studio, Los Angeles, CA probably 08/xx/77

Born in Captivity (A. Stahr) 3:44 (1-12) (09/26/77)
Ringo Starr: Drums; Steven Soles: Lead Vocals, Guitar & Percussion; T-Bone Burnett: Lead Vocals, Guitar & Percussion; David Mansfield: Mandolin, Dobro Guitar, Percussion & Steel Guitar; K.O. Thomas: Piano; David Miner: Bass; Matt Betton: Drums

You Angel You (B. Dylan) 2:44 (2-1) (09/26/77)
Ringo Starr: Drums; Steven Soles: Lead Vocals & Acoustic Guitar; T-Bone Burnett: Lead Vocals & Acoustic Guitar; David Mansfield: Electric Guitar; David Miner: Bass; Matt Betton: Drums; Cindy Bullens: Harmony

The Alpha Band consisted of John Henry "T-Bone" Burnett who was born on January 14, 1948 in St. Louis, Missouri, David Mansfield who was born on September 13, 1956 in Pittsburgh, Pennsylvania and Steven Soles. Burnett has worked with Elvis Costello*, Delaney Bramlett* and Roy Orbison* among many others. Ringo Starr's introduction to The Alpha Band was the result of their both performing with Bob Dylan's* Rolling Thunder Revue tour (see Kinky Friedman) at The Houston Astrodome on January 25, 1976. Starr contributed to the songs *Born in Captivity* and *You Angel You* on The Alpha Band's 1977 album *Spark In The Dark*.

Rusty Anderson

Undressing Underwater
Oxide-OXI-001 (12/17/03)
Producer: David Kahne
Paul McCartney: Bass, B. Vocals & Electric Guitar*; Rusty Anderson: Vocals, Keyboards, Acoustic & Electric Guitar; Abe Laboriel Jr.: Drums; David Kahne: Keyboards & Programmed Drums; Probyn Gregory: Flugelhorn; Brian Ray: Acoustic Guitar; Paul Wickens: Keyboards
Sunset Sound*, Oxide & Valhalla Studios, Los Angeles, CA probably 10/31/02†

Hurt Myself (R. Anderson) 3:21 (1)

Rusty Anderson was born on January 20, 1959 in Los Angeles, California. He began playing guitar at the age of eight and was forming bands such as Eulogy when he was 13. Prior to Eulogy's breakup in 1980 they had earned spots opening for The Police, Van Halen, Quiet Riot and other headline acts. In 1983 Anderson formed the band The Living Daylights who disbanded when he signed a solo deal with Columbia Records in 1987. Producer David Kahne had heard Living Daylights' recordings and asked Rusty to play guitar on sessions he was producing for The Bangles. [Since that time Rusty has contributed to about 100 albums including recordings for Elton John*, Belinda Carlisle*, Joe Cocker*, Little Richard*, Cat Stevens*, Ricky Martin, Animal Logic, Willie Nelson, Sinead O'Connor, The New Radicals, Dido, The Wallflowers and Rob Thomas.] By 1993 Rusty was a member of Ednaswap who released four albums before breaking up in 1999. Their song *Torn* became a major international hit for Natalie Imbruglia.

Kahne employed Rusty's guitar and vocal talents for his production of Paul McCartney's *Driving Rain* album in 2001. Anderson was part of McCartney's backing band at *The Concert For New York City*, which appeared on CD and DVD in 2002. Rusty became a member of McCartney's touring band in 2002, which produced the albums and DVDs *Paul McCartney Back In The U.S.* and *Party At The Palace (The Queen's Concerts, Buckingham Palace)*.

Rusty recalls, "We had a very short break in the 2002 tour before we headed to Mexico. I'd played Paul recordings for my album *Undressing Underwater*, which he liked. I asked him if he'd be interested in playing on it, and he said, 'Sure.' Because we had very little time to record, I was thinking I'd have Paul play on a track I'd already started, but then I thought it would be better to start a fresh recording with the whole touring band. I played my producer David Kahne a few tunes as possibilities and he picked *Hurt Myself*. Paul arrived at Sunset Sound Studio later, so the rest of us had a head start on learning the song. It was kind of cool and surreal watching Paul curse himself when he'd make a mistake playing bass on it because it made him so human — like everybody else, but he's such a talent. He had some amazing ideas for the song and also did some backing vocals on it. There was one section where he suggested there should be some unexpected musical element, such as horns — something orchestral, so my friend Probyn added flugelhorn to that section at my Oxide Studios. Then I went to David's Valhalla Studios and changed the vocals a bit. It's the only song of mine that Paul has contributed to, though once on a flight we started developing a melody to an unusual humming sound the engines were making. I recorded it on a hand-held recorder and Paul thought about using it, but never did. Obviously, he's an amazing musician, singer and composer. He's impulsive, and has great internal feel with his sense of time, pitch and taste, even on those super early Beatles' recordings. He knows so many tricks and techniques, such as playing the kick drum with his hand or using pennywhistles. He knows how to turn an accident into a hook. He uses a very light touch when he records his acoustic guitar on the more intimate stuff he's done, letting the microphone, and compression do the work to create a very inviting sound. It's hard to calculate the depth of his musical influence on me because it was The Beatles' music that initially got me interested music."

Rusty also contributed to McCartney's albums *Chaos And Creation In The Backyard* in 2005 and *Memory Almost Full* in 2007. He was also a member of McCartney's touring band in 2003, 2004, 2005, 2007 and 2009, which produced the 2003 album *Paul McCartney Back In The World Live* and DVD *Paul McCartney Back In The World Tour Documentary & Live In Rome*, the 2005 DVDs *Paul McCartney In Red Square (A Concert Film)* and *Live 8 UK*, the 2006 DVD *The Space Within US* and the 2009 CD and DVD *Good Evening New York City*. Rusty says, "It's pretty cool playing before 500,000 people in Rome or playing in the Garden of Buckingham Palace and meeting the Queen and Prince Charles, and many of my musical heroes. It's not something I really thought I would do – at least at such a magnitude. There was one very scary moment during the second show of the 2005 tour in Tampa, Florida. Paul was about to introduce me when he stepped back and fell into the deep pit that had just opened in the middle of the stage where the grand piano was to be hoisted from. I looked down in stunned shock to see him sprawled flat on his back, with his bass, on top of the piano. I thought, 'Holy shit! Is he alive?' I thought the tour was over. When the hoist with the piano reached the top of the stage he got off and launched into the next song. He wasn't even sore the next day!" Rusty continues to compose and record, releasing the album *Born On Earth* in 2009, and work with McCartney. For more information go to: www.rustyanderson.com

The Applejacks

Lennon & McCartney Song Book Vol. 2
Connoisseur Collection-VSOP CD 162 (UK/EEC) (05/31/91)
Producer: Mike Smith
Al Jackson: Lead Vocals; Martin Baggott: Lead Guitar; Phil Cash: Rhythm Guitar; Don Gould: Keyboards; Megan Davies: Bass; Gerry Freeman: Drums
Probably Decca Studios, London, UK probably 05/xx/64

Like Dreamers Do (J. Lennon-**P. McCartney**) 2:30 (18) (06/05/64)

The Applejacks' members Al Jackson, born Harry Llewellyn on April 21, 1945; Martin Baggott, born on October 20, 1947; Phil Cash, born on October 9, 1947; Don Gould, born on March 23, 1947 and Gerry Freeman, born on May 5, 1943 are all Birmingham, England area natives. Unusual at the time was their female bassist, Megan Davis who was born on March 25, 1944 in Sheffield, England. All but Jackson were members of the same scout troop growing up. They formed a musical group in the early 1960s and soon adopted the name The Applejacks. Their first single, *Tell Me When*, was a Top 10 hit in the UK in 1964.

The Applejacks became friendly with The Beatles during a 1964 TV rehearsal and were offered *Like Dreamers Do*, an early Paul McCartney composition The Beatles included in their live repertoire and recorded during their failed audition for Decca Records in early 1962. Ironically, The Applejacks' recording was produced by Mike Smith, who oversaw and was probably responsible for The Beatles being turned down by Decca, and it was likely recorded in the same studio. The Applejacks' keyboard laden arrangement of *Like Dreamers Do* was their only other UK Top 20 hit. They recorded a cover version of The Beatles' song *Baby's In Black* in 1965, and broke up a few years later. The Beatles' Decca audition of *Like Dreamers Do* was officially released on The Beatles' album *Anthology 1* in 1995.

Rod Argent

Ringo Starr & His All Starr Band Live 2006
Koch-KOC-DV-4543 (DVD) (07/08/08)
Producer: Brent Carpenter; Executive Producer: Ringo Starr
Ringo Starr: Drums; Rod Argent: Lead Vocals & Keyboards; Richard Marx: Electric Guitar & B. Vocals; Billy Squier: Electric Guitar; Sheila Escovedo: Drums; Hamish Stuart: Bass; Edgar Winter: Keyboards & B. Vocals
Mohegan Sun, Uncasville, CT 07/16/06

Hold Your Head Up [live] (R. Argent-C. White) 7:38 (24)
Additionally: Billy Squier: B. Vocals; Hamish Stuart: B. Vocals
[Also available on Koch-KOC-CD-4542-2 (15) (07/08/08)]

She's Not There [live] (R. Argent) 3:31 (10)
[Also available on Koch-KOC-CD-4542-2 (8) (07/08/08)]

Rodney Argent was born on June 14, 1945 in St. Albans, England. He took piano lessons as a youngster and sang in the church choir. At age 16 he was playing keyboards, and writing songs in his band The Zombies. The Zombies' 1964 Top Five hit *She's Not There*, and Top 10 hit *Tell Her No*, were composed by Argent, as well as their 1968 Top Five hit *Time Of The Season*, following the group's breakup. Rod next formed the band Argent who had a Top Five hit with his song *Hold Your Head Up* in 1972. When the band broke up a few years later, Rod carried on as a session musician for such artists as The Who (see Roger Daltrey, John Entwistle, Keith Moon), Gary Moore*, Nanci Griffith and Andrew Lloyd Webber. He also pursued a solo career and a deeper interest in classical music.

Rod was a member of Ringo Starr's All-Starr Band in 2006. He recounts, "I'd been asked to be in the All-Starr Band before – the one Peter Frampton* was in. I thought it was a great line-up, and I really wanted to play with Ringo, but I turned it down because I knew they wanted me to sing the hits I wrote, and I wasn't comfortable with that because I didn't originally sing them. They asked me again some years later. At that time I was working with Colin Blunstone, who sang on some of those hits, so they suggested we both join, and we agreed but then Colin backed out because he felt he wasn't up to playing guitar on all of the other artist's songs. I'd recently sung some of these hits I wrote in concert, and they had gone down really well, and Colin had no problem with it. My good friend Paul Carrack*, who'd been on a previous All-Starr tour, told me that if I ever got asked again, that I should accept it because Ringo was lovely and that everything on his tour was first class, so I joined the All-Starrs.

"I'd met George Harrison briefly. I'd met Paul McCartney during recordings for Roger Daltrey's album *One Of The Boys*, but I'd never met Ringo. I'd never met any of the other members of this All-Starr Band either. They were all terrific musicians. We were given each others' songs in advance, so when we got to rehearsals everybody did them pretty much like what we'd been given, except that Billy Squier decided to change his stuff quite a bit at every rehearsal, Sheila E did that sometimes too. But they were lovely people, as was everyone on the tour. Ringo's laid back and has a very dry sense of humor. He's a storyteller and very generous. On opening night I accidentally hit the wrong patch on my keyboard starting off *She's Not There* in the wrong key, so I had to stop and start over. Ringo was really cool about it later saying, 'It's live – this is what happens!' I also did *Hold Your Head Up* with Ringo on drums.

"I've always loved Ringo's drumming and what he brought to The Beatles. It has something of a 'swing' feel to it. However, Ringo underrates himself as a drummer, so he likes to have another great drummer playing with him, such as Sheila E. One particularly hot night in Florida, I looked behind me and suddenly Sheila had fainted and was gone, and then Ringo began to fly on the drums. No slight on Sheila, who we were very concerned about, but after the show, I told Ringo that he really needed to consider playing alone more. It was great to finally get to play with a Beatle." For more information go to www.rodargent.com

Artists United Against Apartheid

Sun City / Not So Far Away (Dub Version)
Manhattan-B50017 (7" single) (11/11/85)
Producer: Little Steven Van Zandt & Arthur Baker
Ringo Starr: Drums†; One or more of the following: Run DMC: Vocals; Grandmaster Melle Mel & Duke Bootee: Vocals; Afrika Bambaataa & Kurtis Blow: Vocals; Big Youth & All Rappers: Vocals; David Ruffin: Vocals; Pat Benatar: Vocals; Eddie Kendrick: Vocals; Bruce Springsteen: Vocals; George Clinton: Vocals; Joey Ramone: Vocals; Jimmy Cliff & Daryl Hall: Vocals; Darlene Love: Vocals; Linton Kwesi Johnson & All Rappers: Vocals; Bonnie Raitt: Vocals; Ruben Blades & John Oates: Vocals; Lou Reed: Vocals; Bobby Womack: Vocals; Jackson Browne & Bob Dylan: Vocals; Peter Garrett: Vocals; Nona Hendryx & Kashif: Vocals; Bono: Vocals; Zak Starkey: Drums†; Keith Le Blanc: Drums & Drum Programming; Tony Williams: Drums; Pete Townshend: Guitar; Stanley Jordan: Guitar; Little Steven Van Zandt: Guitar & Drum Programming; Doug Wimbish: Bass; Ron Carter: Acoustic Bass; Herbie Hancock: Keyboards; Richard Scher: Keyboards; Robbie Kilgore: Keyboards; Zoe Yanakis: Keyboards; Miles Davis: Trumpet; Clarence Clemons: Saxophone; Shankar: Double Violin; Ray Barretto: Conga; Sonny Okosuns: Talking Drum; Jam Master Jay: Scratcher; D.J. Cheese: Scratcher; Benjamin Newberry: Drum Programming; BLT: B. Vocals; B.J. Nelson: B. Vocals; Lottie Golden: B. Vocals; Tina B: B. Vocals; Daryl Hannah: B. Vocals; Kevin McCormick: B. Vocals; The Dunnes Stores Strikers: B. Vocals; Annie Brody Dutka: B. Vocals; Gil Scott-Heron: B. Vocals; Robert Gordon: B. Vocals; Steve Walker: B. Vocals
One or more of the following studios: Shakedown Sound, Hit Factory, Electric Lady, M&I Recording, Unique, Right Track, Soundworks & Power Station, New York, NY, Cherokee & The Outpost, Los Angeles, CA, Syncro Sound, Boston, MA; Eel Pie & Fallout Shelter, London, Startling†, Ascot, UK; Windmill Lane, Dublin, Ireland

Sun City [single version] (S. Van Zandt) 4:58 (1/1)
Sun City [Various Artists]
Razor & Tie/Capitol-RE 2007 (03/30/93)
Producer: Little Steven Van Zandt & Arthur Baker
Ringo Starr: Drums†; One or more of the following: Run DMC: Vocals; Grandmaster Melle Mel & Duke Bootee: Vocals; Afrika Bambaataa & Kurtis Blow: Vocals; Big Youth & All Rappers: Vocals; David Ruffin: Vocals; Pat Benatar: Vocals; Eddie Kendrick: Vocals; Bruce Springsteen: Vocals; George Clinton: Vocals; Joey Ramone: Vocals; Jimmy Cliff & Daryl Hall: Vocals; Darlene Love: Vocals; Linton Kwesi

Johnson & All Rappers: Vocals; Bonnie Raitt: Vocals; Ruben Blades & John Oates: Vocals; Lou Reed: Vocals; Bobby Womack: Vocals; Jackson Browne & Bob Dylan: Vocals; Peter Garrett: Vocals; Nona Hendryx & Kashif: Vocals; Bono: Vocals; Zak Starkey: Drums†; Keith Le Blanc: Drums & Drum Programming; Tony Williams: Drums; Pete Townshend: Guitar; Stanley Jordan: Guitar; Little Steven Van Zandt: Guitar & Drum Programming; Doug Wimbish: Bass; Ron Carter: Acoustic Bass; Herbie Hancock: Keyboards; Richard Scher: Keyboards; Robbie Kilgore: Keyboards; Zoe Yanakis: Keyboards; Miles Davis: Trumpet; Clarence Clemons: Saxophone; Shankar: Double Violin; Ray Barretto: Conga; Sonny Okosuns: Talking Drum; Jam Master Jay: Scratcher; D.J. Cheese: Scratcher; Benjamin Newberry: Drum Programming; BLT: B. Vocals; B.J. Nelson: B. Vocals; Lottie Golden: B. Vocals; Tina B: B. Vocals; Daryl Hannah: B. Vocals; Kevin McCormick: B. Vocals; The Dunnes Stores Strikers: B. Vocals; Annie Brody Dutka: B. Vocals; Gil Scott-Heron: B. Vocals; Robert Gordon: B. Vocals; Steve Walker: B. Vocals
One or more of the following studios: Shakedown Sound, Hit Factory, Electric Lady, M&I Recording, Unique, Right Track, Soundworks & Power Station, New York, NY, Cherokee & The Outpost, Los Angeles, CA, Syncro Sound, Boston, MA; Eel Pie & Fallout Shelter, London, Startling†, Ascot, UK; Windmill Lane, Dublin, Ireland

Sun City [LP Version] (S. Van Zandt) 7:10 (1) (11/18/85)

Sun City [The Last Remix a.k.a. Dub Version] (S. Van Zandt) 9:37 (8)
Additionally: Desmond Tutu: Vocals

Sun City [Version II] (S. Van Zandt) 5:43 (4) (11/18/85)

Artists United Against Apartheid was organized by Little Steven (Steven Van Zandt), long known for his association with Bruce Springsteen*. In 1985 Van Zandt organized a campaign to discourage performers from working in Sun City, a major international resort in Bophuthatswana, within South Africa. Bophuthatswana was one of several native tribal homelands set up by the white government of South Africa in an attempt to diffuse criticism of Apartheid (racial segregation) by allowing blacks autonomous self-rule. Sun City, unlike South Africa as a whole at the time, had the appearance of being racially tolerant and integrated, but most of the world's governments refused to recognize these homelands as independent nations. Sun City attracted many entertainers who normally refused to perform in segregated South Africa because they felt it was a step in the right direction. Steven and the Artists United Against Apartheid saw Sun City as a facade.

Steven organized some of music's top jazz, R&B, rap and rock performers to contribute to his project on behalf of The Africa Fund. Among them were Ringo Starr and his son Zak, who drummed on the backing tracks used on the four versions of the song *Sun City*. The *Sun City* CD contains three versions (all but the single version) of *Sun City*. Ringo and Zak also appear in the video release for the *Sun City* project. The *Sun City* project was also released on LD (IMG-1985 ID5150). Steven joined Ringo Starr's All-Starr Band during their performance of *With A Little Help From My Friends* at Radio City Music Hall in New York on July 20, 2006.

Ashton, Gardner & Dyke

The Worst Of Ashton, Gardner & Dyke
Repertoire-REP 4458-WY (Germany) (05/15/94)
Producer: George Harrison, Tony Ashton, Kim Gardner & Roy Dyke
George Harrison: Electric Swivel Guitar; Tony Ashton: Lead Vocals & Keyboards; Kim Gardner: Bass; Roy Dyke: Drums; Eric Clapton: Lead Guitar; Bobby Keys: Saxophone; Jim Price: Trumpet; Phil & His Boogie Brass: Horns
De Lane Lea Studios, London, UK probably 07/xx/70 &/or possibly 03/xx/70

I'm Your Spiritual Breadman (T. Ashton - **[G. Harrison]**) 3:16 (2) (09/28/70)

Ashton, Gardner & Dyke formed in 1968. Tony Ashton and Roy Dyke had previously been members of the Liverpool band The Remo Four*. Kim Gardner was born on January 27, 1946 in Dulwich, England. In 1964 he joined the band The Birds with Ron Wood. In 1967 they joined The Creation.

Ashton, Gardner & Dyke were a supporting act

for the Delaney & Bonnie & Friends* tour in December 1969, which included George Harrison and Eric Clapton*. Following the tour its members (excluding Ashton who was present) backed John Lennon and Yoko Ono* during their performance on December 15, 1969 at London's Lyceum Ballroom.

Several months later, Harrison and Clapton contributed to Ashton, Gardner & Dyke's song *I'm Your Spiritual Breadman* on the *The Worst of Ashton, Gardner & Dyke* album. The song's credits say "kneaded and leavened by George Harrison" and George is listed in the credits as George O'Hara Smith (a pseudonym he used on his 1970 album *All Things Must Pass*). Clapton is credited as Sir Cedric Clayton. According to Ashton, "I played the song for George and he liked it, so I asked him if he'd like to play on it and produce it. He said, 'Sure.' He was so good about it. He did the general production and helped with some of the lyrics in the middle eight. The song was originally going to be the A-side of the single, but that ended up being *Resurrection Shuffle* [a Top 40 hit], which our record company thought was more commercial." *The Worst of Ashton, Gardner & Dyke* album also contains the song *Sweet Pattie O'Hara Smith* in tribute to Harrison's wife, Pattie. According to Ashton and Gardner, *I'm Your Spiritual Breadman* is the only recording of theirs that contains a Beatles' contribution. Ashton laments, "Isn't it a pity my keyboard work on Harrison's recording of *Isn't It A Pity* wasn't credited."

Ashton, Gardner & Dyke broke up in early 1973 after several moderately successful albums. Gardner and Dyke went on to join Badger (see Jackie Lomax) and worked with Chris Barber* and other artists. Kim Gardner died on October 24, 2001.

Michael Aspel, Tracey Ullman & Paul McCartney

[None]
[Unreleased]
Paul McCartney: Vocals; Michael Aspel: Vocals; Tracy Ullman: Vocals
ITV Television Studios, London, UK 06/07/84

That'll Be The Day (B. Holly-J. Allison-N. Petty) 1:25

Michael Aspel was born on January 12, 1933 in Battersea, England. He began his career as a newscaster for the BBC in the late 1950s and has hosted a wide variety of popular UK TV shows since the 1960s including *Aspel And Company, This Is Your Life, Strange But True?* and *Antiques Roadshow.* He made his acting debut in the film *The Magic Christian* (see Peter Sellers, Terry Southern & Ringo Starr).

Tracey Ullman was born on December 30, 1959 in Slough, England. She first gained notice in British musicals before regularly appearing in UK TV comedy shows. By 1983 she had also found success as a recording artist with the UK Top Five hits *Breakaway* and *They Don't Know* and the UK Top 10 hit *Move Over Darling* all from her US Top 40 album *You Broke My Heart In 17 Places.* Her *Tracey Ullman Show* on FOX TV in the late 1980s made her a star in the US. She continues to have a highly successful film and TV career.

Paul McCartney and Ullman were guests on June 7, 1984 (broadcast on June 9) for the launching of ITV's show *Aspel And Company.* McCartney talked about his upcoming film *Give My Regards To Broad Street* in which Ullman made an appearance. McCartney had recently made a cameo in the video for *They Don't Know.* Ullman and McCartney joined Aspel singing a rendition of Buddy Holly's song *That'll Be The Day* to close the show. George Harrison and Ringo Starr appeared on the show on March 3, 1988 (broadcast on March 5). It was the first time since their breakup that more than one of The Beatles appeared together on TV.

Chet Atkins

Chet Atkins Picks On The Beatles
RCA-07863-53531-2 (01/30/96) (03/xx/66)
George Harrison: Liner Notes

Chet Atkins was born on June 20, 1924 in Luttrell, Tennessee. His father was a piano teacher. Young Chet became one of the most accomplished guitarists in the history of country

& western music. He won nine CMA Awards as Musician of the Year, 13 Grammy Awards and is a member of Country Music Hall of Fame. He contributed to dozens of recordings by some of the biggest names in music, including Hank Williams, Elvis Presley and The Everly Brothers*. Atkins, who served an executive role with RCA Records for several decades, was instrumental in developing and promoting some of the biggest names in country music.

George Harrison wrote five paragraphs of liner notes for the album of Beatles' cover versions titled *Chet Atkins Picks On The Beatles* because of his respect and admiration for Atkins. Like Atkins, Harrison used Gretsch guitars. Atkins also did cover versions of other songs by members of The Beatles.

Atkins played guitar on The Country Hams' *Walking In The Park With Eloise* along with Paul McCartney on washboard and bass, Wings' brief drummer Geoff Britton, and legendary country & western pianist Floyd Cramer, during Wings' recording sessions in Nashville in mid-1974. The song was composed by McCartney's father James. Atkins was featured on Paul McCartney's 1995 radio series, *Oobu Joobu.* Chet Atkins died on June 30, 2001. He was inducted into the Rock and Roll Hall of Fame the following year. For more information go to www.misterguitar.com

Attitudes

Ain't Love Enough / The Whole World's Crazy
Dark Horse-DH 10004 (7" single) (12/09/75)
George Harrison: Picture Sleeve Photographer

Good News
Dark Horse-DH 3021 (album 12") (05/05/77)
Producer: Jay Lewis & Attitudes
Ringo Starr: Drums; Paul Stallworth: Lead Vocals & Bass; David Foster: Piano & B. Vocals; Danny Kortchmar: Guitars & B. Vocals; Jim Keltner: Drums, Percussion & B. Vocals; Booker T. Jones: Organ; Tower Of Power Horn Section (Horn Arrangement by Greg Adams); Jorge Calderon: B. Vocals; Y. Rankin: B. Vocals
Probably Producer's Workshop, A&M &/or Sunswept Recording Studios, Los Angeles, CA probably 12/xx/76 or 01/xx/77

Good News (P. Stallworth) 3:45 (2/5)

Attitudes was conceived by Lee Kiefer and comprised of well-known studio musicians Dave Foster, born on November 1, 1949 in Victoria, British Columbia, Canada; Danny "Kootch" Kortchmar, born on April 6, 1946 in New York, New York; Jim Keltner, born on April 27, 1942 in Tulsa, Oklahoma and Paul Stallworth. Foster was a founding member of the group Skylark and is a noted producer. He has contributed to Paul McCartney, George Harrison and Ringo Starr's recordings over the years. Kortchmar has contributed to Starr and Harrison's recordings. Paul Stallworth has also worked with Harrison. Jim Keltner has been a backup drummer on countless recordings by Harrison, Starr and John Lennon. He came to their attention via Delaney & Bonnie & Friends*. Lennon added Keltner to his backing band Elephant's Memory* during his *One To One* benefit concerts. Harrison recruited him for his 1974 US tour. In 1989 Ringo included Keltner in his first All-Starr Band tour. He backed Ringo on *I Call Your Name* as a contribution to *The John Lennon Scholarship Concert* held on May 5, 1990 in Liverpool, which is included on the 1991 LD *The World's Greatest Artists Sing LENNON A Tribute.* Keltner also joined the All-Starr Band during their performance of *With A Little Help From My Friends* at Mandalay Bay in Las Vegas on July 1, 2006 and at the Greek Theatre in Los Angeles on August 2, 2008. Keltner was also the drummer for the Traveling Wilburys (see Bob Dylan, Jeff Lynne, Roy Orbison, Tom Petty), adding to his long list of credits playing with virtually every major name in rock 'n' roll.

Album credits for *Attitudes* (Dark Horse-SP 22008) gives "special thanks to Ohnothimagen," a self-deprecating pseudonym Harrison used at the time. The photo used for the picture sleeve for Attitudes' first single, *Ain't Love Enough*, was taken by Harrison. The title track for Attitudes' second and final album, *Good News*, features Ringo, and also gives "special thanks" to Harrison. According to Keltner, Harrison didn't contribute to any of Attitudes' recordings. He said the special thanks to Harrison was for his support of the group. For more information go to www.davidfoster.com,
www.dannykortchmar.com

Randy Bachman

The Best Of Ringo Starr And His All-Starr Band...So Far
Image-ID0828RO (DVD) (10/23/01)
Producer: Michael Drumm; Greg Delancy (music mixer); Executive Producer: Ringo Starr & David Fishof
Nippon Budakon Hall, Tokyo, Japan 06/27/95

You Ain't Seen Nothin' Yet [live] (R. Bachman) 3:39 (13) (12/08/97)
Ringo Starr: Drums; Randy Bachman: L. Vocals & Electric Guitar; Mark Farner: Electric Guitar; Zak Starkey: Drums; John Entwistle: Bass; Felix Cavaliere: Keyboards; Billy Preston: Keyboards; Mark Rivera: Acoustic Guitar
[Also available on *Ringo Starr And His All Starr Band The Anthology...So Far.* Koch-KOC-CD-8312 (2-10) (07/24/01) (02/05/01)]

Ringo Starr And His All Starr Band The Anthology...So Far
Koch-KOC-CD-8312 (07/24/01) (02/05/01)
Producer: Greg Delancy (mixer); Executive Producer: Ringo Starr & David Fishof
Nippon Budakon Hall, Tokyo, Japan 06/27/95

Takin' Care Of Business [live] (R. Bachman) 7:37 (2-9)
Ringo Starr: Drums; Randy Bachman: Lead Vocals & Electric Guitar; Mark Farner: Electric Guitar & B. Vocals; Zak Starkey: Drums; John Entwistle: Bass; Felix Cavaliere: Keyboards & B. Vocals; Billy Preston: Keyboards & B. Vocals; Mark Rivera: Saxophone, Percussion & B. Vocals

Ringo Starr And His Third All-Starr Band Volume 1
BlockbusterExclusive-0ERE4<5297>
RINGOSTARR ADFL (08/12/97)
Producer: Greg Delancy (mixer); Executive Producer: Ringo Starr & David Fishof
Nippon Budakon Hall, Tokyo, Japan 06/27/95

No Sugar Tonight [live] (R. Bachman) 4:15 (6)
Ringo Starr: Drums; Randy Bachman: Lead Vocals & Lead Guitar; Mark Farner: Electric Guitar & B. Vocals; Zak Starkey: Drums; John Entwistle: Bass; Felix Cavaliere: Keyboards, Percussion & B. Vocals; Billy Preston: Keyboards & B. Vocals; Mark Rivera: Percussion & B. Vocals

Randy Bachman was born on September 27, 1943 in Winnipeg, Manitoba, Canada. He is a founding member of The Guess Who (see Burton Cummings). Randy recalls, "The Guess Who always had a fascination with England and when the new Liverpool sound began its influence in Winnipeg, we radically changed our stage show to cover every track on every Beatles' album. We tried to write original material like The Beatles. The Beatles were everything to us."

Randy left The Guess Who in 1970, released a solo album and (with his younger brother Robbie and The Guess Who's Chad Allan) formed Brave Belt. In 1972 Randy's brother Tim, and Fred Turner replaced Allan and they renamed themselves Bachman-Turner Overdrive. Tim was soon replaced by Blair Thornton. In 1974 they had a Top 40 hit with *Let It Ride*, Top 20 hits with *Takin' Care of Business* and *Roll On Down The Highway*, and *You Ain't Seen Nothin' Yet*, which topped the charts. *Hey You* in 1975 was their last Top 40 hit.

When Randy left Bachman-Turner Overdrive in 1977 the group officially became known as BTO. Randy released a solo album and formed the group Ironhorse, who had the Top 40 hit *Sweet Lui-Louise* in 1979, before becoming known as Union in 1981 when Fred Turner joined. In 1983 the most successful line up of The Guess Who, which included Bachman and Cummings, briefly reunited for a tour that resulted in an album. Randy and Tim Bachman along with Turner regrouped and released an album in 1984.

Randy joined Ringo Starr's All-Starr Band in 1995 (Burton Cummings had been a member in 1992). Bachman remembers, "When my phone rang and the voice said, 'Hello, this is Ringo calling from Monaco. Welcome to the band.' It was a dream comes true. It was the ultimate rock 'n' roll bar band led by the world's greatest rock drummer." Ringo drummed on Bachman's performances of *Takin' Care Of Business*, *You Ain't Seen Nothin' Yet* and The Guess Who's hit *No Sugar Tonight.* Bachman says, "Every show was memorable. Playing guitar on Ringo's songs every night, and looking back over my shoulders and hearing and seeing him playing drums on my songs, was the highlight of my musical career. I don't see anything that will eclipse it. I would have done it for nothing. It was a privilege. For his birthday my wife and I had a newly discovered star named after him called 'The Ringo Starr.'" Randy continues to writing, record and tour with and without members of BTO and The Guess Who. For more information go to
www.randybachman.com

Magic Christian Music
Apple/Capitol-CDP 7 97579 2 (11/19/91) (09/09/70)

Carry On Till Tomorrow (T. Evans-P. Ham) 4:47 (8)
Producer: **[Paul McCartney]** & Mal Evans

Tom Evans: Guitar & Lead Vocals; Pete Ham: Lead Guitar & B. Vocals; Ron Griffiths: Bass; Mike Gibbins: Drums; George Martin: String Arrangement & Conductor
EMI-Abbey Road Studios, London, UK 08/22 & 26/69

Come And Get It (P. McCartney) 2:21 (1) (12/05/69)
Producer: Paul McCartney
Paul McCartney: Piano & Maracas; Tom Evans: Lead Vocals & Guitar; Pete Ham: Guitar; Ron Griffiths: Bass & B. Vocals; Mike Gibbins: Drums
EMI-Abbey Road Studios, London, UK 08/02/69

Crimson Ship (T. Evans-P. Ham) 3:42 (2)
Producer: [Paul McCartney] & Tony Visconti
Pete Ham: Lead Vocals, Guitar & Keyboards; Ron Griffiths: Bass; Tom Evans: Lead Vocals & Guitar; Mike Gibbins: Drums
Trident Studios, London, UK probably 08 or 09/xx/69

Midnight Sun (P. Ham) 2:46 (5)
Producer: possibly **Paul McCartney** & Mal Evans
Paul McCartney: (probable) Piano; Pete Ham: Lead Vocals & Guitar; Tom Evans: B. Vocals & Bass; Mike Gibbins: Drums
Probably EMI-Abbey Road Studios or IBC Studios, or possibly Trident Studios London, UK 08-09/xx/69

Rock Of All Ages (**[P. McCartney]**-T. Evans-P. Ham-M. Gibbins) 3:16 (7) (12/05/69)
Producer: [Paul McCartney] & Tony Visconti
Paul McCartney: Piano & (probable) B. Vocals; Tom Evans: Lead Vocals & Bass; Pete Ham: Guitar; Mike Gibbins: Drums
IBC Studios, London, UK 09/18/69

Straight Up
Apple-CDP 0777 7 81403 20 (05/25/93) (12/13/71)
Producer: George Harrison & [Todd Rundgren]
EMI-Abbey Road Studios, London, UK 06/xx/71 [unless noted otherwise]

Day After Day (P. Ham) 3:10 (9) (11/10/71)
George Harrison: Lead Guitar; Pete Ham: Lead Vocals & Lead Guitar; Joey Molland: Guitar & B. Vocals; Tom Evans: Bass & B. Vocals; Mike Gibbins: Drums; Leon Russell: Piano
EMI-Abbey Road Studios, London, UK 06/03/71

I'd Die Babe (J. Molland) 2:33 (5)
George Harrison: Electric & Acoustic Guitar; Joey Molland: Lead Vocals & Guitar; Pete Ham: Guitar & Keyboards; Tom Evans: Bass & B. Vocals; Mike Gibbins: Drums

Name Of The Game (P. Ham) 5:17 (6)
Pete Ham: Lead Vocals & Guitar; Joey Molland: Guitar & B. Vocals; Tom Evans: Bass & B. Vocals; Mike Gibbins: Drums; Leon Russell: Keyboards

Suitcase (J. Molland) 2:52 (7)
Joey Molland: Lead Vocals & Guitar; Pete Ham: Slide Guitar; Tom Evans: Bass & B. Vocals; Mike Gibbins: Drums & Maracas; Klaus Voormann: Keyboards; Leon Russell: Guitar; Kathie Molland: Tambourine
EMI-Abbey Road Studios, London, UK 05/31/71

Badfinger was first known as The Iveys when they formed in the mid-1960s. They consisted of Swansea, Wales' natives Ron Griffiths, born on October 2, 1946; Pete Ham, born on April 27, 1947; Mike Gibbins, born on March 12, 1949, and Tom Evans, born on June 5, 1947 in Liverpool, England. They were huge fans of The Beatles and did cover versions of their songs. The Iveys' manager, former bandleader Bill Collins, who knew Paul McCartney's father, got Mal Evans to convince the Beatles in July 1968 to sign them to Apple. *Maybe Tomorrow*, their first single late that year, fared well in Europe but the limited release of their *Maybe Tomorrow* album in 1969 delayed their chances for success. The Iveys were looking for a new name, so John Lennon suggested "Prix," and McCartney suggested "Home" and "Mama's Boys," which they wisely rejected. They settled on "Badfinger," naughty Liverpool slang, that had also been part of the working title for The Beatles' song *With A Little Help From My Friends*.

Paul McCartney took Badfinger under his wing and gave them his song, *Come And Get It*, about the financial woes at Apple, which proved to be perfect as the theme song for the film *The*

Magic Christian (see Peter Sellers, Terry Southern & Ringo Starr). McCartney auditioned each member during his production to determine who would sing the lead vocals. He told them that if they wanted a hit to stick strictly to the simplicity of his demo, and that if their version didn't measure up, he would release his version. Their recording was a Top 10. A version of the song with McCartney singing lead vocals backed by Badfinger appears on unauthorized releases. McCartney's demo of the song was officially released on the Beatles' 1996 album *Anthology 3*.

McCartney also arranged for Badfinger's songs *Carry On Till Tomorrow* and *Rock Of All Ages* to be included in *The Magic Christian Soundtrack*. There's confusion surrounding their production and that of Badfinger's song, *Crimson Ship*. The *Magic Christian Music Soundtrack* album and the first issue of Badfinger's *Magic Christian Music* album don't list a producer for these songs. Reportedly McCartney was attempting to downplay his involvement with Badfinger because they were being labeled as "Beatles light." The *Magic Christian Music* CD credits Mal Evans as producing *Carry On Till Tomorrow* and Tony Visconti as producing *Crimson Ship* and *Rock Of All Ages*. Visconti doesn't recall what he produced for Badfinger. According to Mike Gibbins, McCartney was involved in the initial production on these three songs but didn't want to be credited. Tom Evans has also stated that McCartney was involved in their production.

According to Gibbins, McCartney also helped write *Rock Of All Ages* and played piano on the recording. Evans has also stated that McCartney played piano on the track, and that he and McCartney did a take sharing the lead vocals but that McCartney decided against using it. Molland thinks McCartney contributed some backing vocals to the song though Gibbins disagrees. However, it does sound like McCartney doing his best Little Richard* vocal impersonation in the background. Gibbins and Evans have been the source for most of the information on McCartney's musical contributions to Badfinger's recordings as Molland was not a member at the time. The fade-out of *Rock Of All Ages* on the soundtrack album and Apple single is six seconds longer than on the Apple album. After these recordings, Ron Griffiths was replaced by Joey Molland, born on June 21, 1947 in Liverpool, England. Hamish Stuart* (who joined Paul McCartney's band in the late 1980s) was also considered as a replacement for Griffiths.

Apple initially rejected Badfinger's follow-up single *No Matter What*, suggesting they record and release the Ringo Starr composition *It Don't Come Easy*. The group (for their sake and Ringo's) wisely resisted, and *No Matter What* became one of their biggest hit singles. Evans and Ham ended up singing backing vocals on Ringo's first single success, *It Don't Come Easy*, in 1971. Ham also contributed to Ringo's 1972 song *Blindman*. Badfinger's members served as backing musicians for a number of solo Beatles' projects in the early 1970s. They played on George Harrison's 1970 album *All Things Must Pass* and Ham also took part in sessions for what would become Harrison's 1973 album *Living In The Material World*. Molland and Evans contributed to John Lennon's 1971 album *Imagine*.

Harrison began producing tracks for Badfinger's third album *Straight Up* in 1971 but after four songs turned production duties over to Todd Rundgren* because he was busy organizing *The Concert For Bangla Desh*. (As consolation, Badfinger was part of the backing band at *The Concert For Bangla Desh*.) Rundgren also worked on the four tracks begun by Harrison. *Day After Day*, produced by Harrison, and featuring his trademark slide guitar in unison with Ham's guitar, became one of the group's biggest hit singles. Harrison also produced *I'd Die Baby*, contributing rhythm and acoustic guitar, and *Name Of The Game*. Molland recalled Nicky Hopkins* playing piano on *Name Of The* Game but Hopkins didn't recall playing on any of Badfinger's recordings. Arranger John Barham, who was involved in Badfinger's recordings, says Hopkins contributed to The Ivey's recordings, which may explain some of the confusion. Gibbins said it was Leon Russell* who played piano on *Name Of The Game* (other sources suggest it was Gary Wright*) but Russell seems the likely candidate as he played on *Day After Day*, and *Suitcase* also produced by Harrison.

Ironically, Badfinger's biggest success came with Harry Nilsson's* mega-hit cover version of their song *Without You*. Except for The Beatles, Badfinger was Apple's most successful band but like most of its artists fell victim to the budget-slashing of Allen Klein. Badfinger left Apple disgruntled and disillusioned. It was no accident that their last three Apple albums were titled *No Dice*, *Straight Up* [your] and *Ass*. *Ass* contained a song called *The Winner* written by Molland about John Lennon who he felt was constantly complaining and angry in public.

Badfinger moved to Warner Bros. Records in

1973 but with little success. The band became embroiled in what would prove to be long legal and financial difficulties. On April 23, 1975 a distraught Pete Ham took his life. Badfinger disintegrated with the remaining member joining other bands. Badfinger, with Molland and Evans, released two albums between the late 1970s and early 1980s. Tom Evans suffered the same fate as Ham on November 19, 1983. Molland and Gibbins reunited in 1984 to continue the highly augmented Badfinger legend, but the two were been unable to sustain a long-term partnership. Mike Gibbins died on October 4, 2005. Molland still records and tours under the Badfinger name. For more information go to www.peteham.net, www.tomevans.info, www.mikegibbins.com

The Band

The Last Waltz [Various Artists]
Rhino/WEA-R2-78278 (04/23/02)
Producer: Robbie Robertson
Winterland Arena, San Francisco, CA 11/25/76

Ending Jam #1 [live] (The Band) 5:23 (3-9)
Ringo Starr: Drums; Robbie Robertson: Guitar; Levon Helm: Drums; Garth Hudson: Keyboards; Rick Danko: Bass; Eric Clapton: Guitar; Neil Young: Guitar; Dr. John: Keyboards; Ron Wood: Guitar; Paul Butterfield: Harmonica

The Last Waltz [Various Artists]
MGM/UA-1003426 (DVD) (05/07/02) (xx/xx/85)
Producer: Robbie Robertson

I Shall Be Released [live] (B. Dylan) 3:26 (33) (04/10/78)
Ringo Starr: Drums; Bob Dylan: Lead Vocals & Guitar; Robbie Robertson: Guitar & B. Vocals; Rick Danko: Bass & B. Vocals; Levon Helm: Drums & B. Vocals; Garth Hudson: Keyboards; Richard Manuel: Keyboards & B. Vocals; Eric Clapton: Guitar & B. Vocals; Neil Diamond: B. Vocals; Joni Mitchell: B. Vocals; Neil Young: B. Vocals; Van Morrison: B. Vocals; Dr. John: B. Vocals; Ronnie Hawkins: B. Vocals; Ron Wood: Guitar & B. Vocals; Paul Butterfield: B. Vocals; Bobby Charles: B. Vocals
Winterland Arena, San Francisco, CA, 11/25/76
[Also available on Rhino/WEA-R2-78278 (3/1/8) (04/23/02)]

Ending Jam #2 [live] (The Band) 11:42 (chapter: 3 #2)
Ringo Starr: Drums; Robbie Robertson: Guitar; Levon Helm: Drums; Garth Hudson: Keyboards; Eric Clapton: Guitar; Neil Young: Guitar; Dr. John: Keyboards; Ron Wood: Guitar; Paul Butterfield: Harmonica; Stephen Stills: Guitar; Carl Radle: Bass
Winterland Arena, San Francisco, CA 11/25/76
[Also available on Rhino/WEA-R2-78278 (9:10) (3/1/10) (04/23/02)]

The Band originally consisted of Ontario Canada natives Jamie Robert "Robbie Robertson" Klegerman, born on July 5, 1943 in Toronto; Eric Garth Hudson, born on August 2, 1937 in Windsor; Richard Manuel, born on April 3, 1943 in Stratford; Rick Danko*, and American, Levon Helm*. They were first known as The Hawks when they backed Ronnie Hawkins* in the early 1960s. The Hawks split with Hawkins in 1963 and became Bob Dylan's* folk-rock, backing band in 1965. In 1968, simply know as The Band, they released their legendary album *Music From Big Pink*.

The Band also continued working with Dylan and went to the UK to perform with him at the *Isle Of Wight Festival* on August 29, 1969. George Harrison was a huge fan of The Band, so The Beatles (minus McCartney) attended the event and spent much time with The Band and Dylan during their visit. More critically acclaimed albums followed, along with hits such as *The Weight*, *The Night They Drove Old Dixie Down*, *Rag Mama Rag*, *Life Is A Carnival* and *Up On Cripple Creek*.

The Band (minus Manuel) contributed to Ringo Starr's 1973 album *Ringo*, and Robertson contributed to his 1974 album *Goodnight Vienna*. The Band gave a farewell concert on Thanksgiving Day 1976 at Winterland Arena, where they first performed as The Band. The concert was the centerpiece of Martin Scorsese's documentary film *The Last Waltz*. The concert included guest performances from old friends such as Ringo Starr, Eric Clapton*, Dr. John*, Ron Wood*, Dylan, Hawkins and many others. It did prove to be the last time all of The Band's original members would perform together. Unfortunately, none of the video releases feature *Ending Jam #1*, which includes Ringo, at the end of *I Shall Be Released*. Varying portions of it are included on all of the audio releases. Eleven minutes and forty-two seconds of another jam, *Ending Jam #2*, which also includes Ringo and many of the musical guests, is included on the DVD releases. The

The Band VIP pass, courtesy of Levon Helm.

entire 12:27 of *Ending Jam # 1* and 17:28 of *Ending Jam #2* are available on the unauthorized release *The Complete Last Waltz* (Cool Daddy Productions-CD-001/2/3/4).

The Band reunited in 1983 and by 1985 included all of its original members except Robertson who never rejoined. On March 4, 1986, while on tour, a road-weary Richard Manuel took his life. The Band marched on adding several new members along the way. In 1989 Danko and Helm were part of Ringo Starr's All-Starr Band tour and were joined by Hudson on one occasion. In 1993 The Band released *Jericho*, their first album since *The Last Waltz*. Ringo Starr and the All-Starrs are listed in the album's credits under "project support," though Helm says Ringo didn't contribute to the album. The Band was inducted into the Rock and Roll Hall of Fame in 1994. The 1995 *Authorized Video Biography of The Band* includes appearances by Harrison and Starr. The Band's 1996 album, *High On The Hog* also thanks Ringo but again without his participation. Rick Danko died in 1999 and along with him The Band. The multi-instrumentalist Hudson continues to be a much-in-demand session player for a wide range of well-known musicians. Since 1976 Robertson has been involved in film soundtracks, acting, composing, producing, recording and performing.

Band Aid

Do They Know It's Christmas? [Various Artists]
Columbia-44-05157 (12" single) (12/14/84)
Producer: Midge Ure & Trevor Horn
Paul McCartney: Spoken message; vocals and, or messages by: Adam Clayton, Bob Geldof, Steve Norman, Chris Cross, Paul Young, Tony Hadley, Glenn Gregory, Simon Le Bon, Simon Crowe, Marilyn, Keren Woodward, Martin Kemp, Jody Watley, Bono, Paul Weller, James Taylor, Peter Blake, George Michael, Martin Ware, John Keeble, Roger Taylor, Sarah Dallin, Siobhan Fahey, Peter Briquette, Francis Rossi, Robert "Kool" Bell, Dennis Thomas, Andy Taylor, Jon Moss, Sting, Rick Parfitt, Nick Rhodes, Johnny Fingers, David Bowie, Boy George, Holly; John Taylor: Bass, B. Vocals & Message; Phil Collins: Drums & B. Vocals; Midge Ure: Keyboards & B. Vocals; Gary Kemp: Guitar; Jens Langhorn: Drums; Adam Clayton: Bass
Sarm West Studios, London, UK 11/25-26/84

Do They Know It's Christmas? [Remix] (B. Geldof-M. Ure) 6:16 (1/1)

Feed The World (B. Geldof-M. Ure) 4:15 (2/2)

By the fall of 1984 Ethiopia, which had seen years of drought and war, was in the throes of a massive famine. Bob Geldof, of the band Boomtown Rats, recruited an array of UK rock stars dubbed Band Aid to record two songs and use the proceeds to assist in the famine relief. Some artists, such as Paul McCartney, who were unable to attend the recording sessions, contributed a prerecorded message. Geldof's efforts led to a worldwide outpouring of support and contributions for which he would later receive a Nobel Prize and be knighted by the Queen of England (see: Various Artists-Live Aid). All of the recordings on the 12" single *Do They Know It's Christmas?* are included on the rare 1985 Japanese CD *Band Aid Special* (Mercury-32PD27).

Band Aid 20

Do They Know It's Christmas?
Mercury-0249869413 (single) (Canada) (11/29/04)
Producer: Nigel Godrich
Paul McCartney: Bass; Bono: Vocals; Danny Goffey: Drums; Thom Yorke: Piano; Jonny Greenwood: Guitar; Fran Healy: Vocals & Guitar; Justin Hawkins: Guitar & Vocals; Dan Hawkins: Guitar; Charlie Simpson: Guitar & Vocals; Daniel Bedingfield: Vocals; Natasha Bedingfield: Vocals; Keisha Buchanan: Vocals; Mutya Buena: Vocals; Heidi Range: Vocals; Vishal Das: Vocals; James Bourne: Vocals; Matt Willis: Vocals; Chris Martin: Vocals; Dido: Vocals; Dizzee Rascal: Vocals; Ms. Dynamite: Vocals; Skye Edwards: Vocals; Estelle: Vocals; Neil Hannon: Vocals; Jamelia: Vocals; Tom Chaplin: Vocals; Tim Rice-Oxley: Vocals; Tim Wheeler: Vocals; Beverley Knight: Vocals; Lemar: Vocals; Shaznay Lewis: Vocals; Katie Melua: Vocals; Roisin Murphy: Vocals; Mark Richardson: Vocals; Grant Nicholas: Vocals; Taka Hirose: Vocals; Gary Lightbody: Vocals; Paul Wilson: Vocals; Jonny Quinn: Vocals; Nathan Connolly: Vocals; Tom Simpson; Vocals; Rachel Stevens: Vocals; Joss Stone: Vocals; Robbie Williams: Vocals; Will Young: Vocals; Olly Knights: Vocals; Gale Paridjanian: Vocals
Air Studios, London, UK 11/14/04

Do They Know It's Christmas? (B. Geldof-M. Ure) 5:05 (1)

Band Aid 20 was organized by Midge Ure to re-record his co-composition *Do They Know It's Christmas?* on the 20th anniversary of the Band Aid* charity song's release to raise money for Sudan's troubled Darfur region. Its producer, Nigel Godrich, was also producing Paul McCartney's album *Chaos And Creation In The Back Yard* at the time and asked Paul to play bass on the recording. McCartney and Bono are the only artists who performed on the original Band Aid recording. McCartney also appeared in the video for the song. Like the original, it became the biggest selling single of the year in the UK.

Chris Barber & His Band

The Songs Lennon and McCartney Gave Away [Various Artists]
EMI-NUT 18 [0C 054-07 003] (album 12") (UK) (04/13/79)
Producer: [Paul McCartney], Chris Barber, Giorgio Gomelsky& Reggie King
Paul McCartney: Keyboard, Catcalls & B. Vocals; Chris Barber: Trombone; Pat Halcox: Trumpet; Ian Wheeler: Alto Saxophone; John Slaughter: Guitar; Stu Morrison: Banjo; Jackie Flavelle: Bass; Graham Burbidge: Drums; Brian Auger: Catcalls & Organ; Barry Jenkins: Catcalls; Vic Briggs: Catcalls; Viv Prince: Cymbal dropping & Catcalls; Jane Asher: Catcalls; Madeleine Hirsiger: Catcalls; Ottilie Patterson: Catcalls; John Ryan: Catcalls; Gustav Karl Lovenz Schneeweiss-Moody Catcalls & B. Vocals; Giorgio Gomelsky: Voice
Chappell Studios, London, UK 07/20/67

Cat Call [a.k.a. Catswalk] (P. McCartney) 3:03 (2/10) (10/20/67)

Donald Christopher Barber was born on April 17, 1930 in Welwyn, England. His Chris Barber Jazz Band has been a British institution since 1954. He teamed up with Lonnie Donegan* and played on his ground-breaking international skiffle hit *Rock Island Line*. Barber's biggest hit was *Petite Fleur* in 1959 which was a Top 10.

Chris had known The Beatles since their days at the Cavern when it was still a jazz club. Shortly after Paul McCartney bought his home in the St. John's Wood section of London in the mid-1960s from a friend of Barber's, the two stopped by for a visit. Chris asked McCartney if he had any songs he'd written that he never used. Paul offered him *Catswalk* from early in The Beatles' career, which McCartney told him was never used because it was an instrumental. A Beatles' recording of *Catswalk*, probably made at a Cavern rehearsal, has turned up on numerous unauthorized records.

Chris says he first recorded *Catswalk* as a straightforward jazz number, with McCartney in attendance, in a studio at his Marquee Club in London. Barber recalls, "McCartney thought the song should be a more lighthearted, big production number with catcalls — a sort of joke song or put-on." So a second (released) version was recorded at Chappell Studios according to McCartney's specifications. Brian Auger, who plays organ on what was re-titled *Cat Call*, and Chris confirm that McCartney was heavily involved in the production of the recording. Chris also recalls Paul playing one-handed organ on it, but Auger remembers McCartney playing piano. Chris continues to record and tour. For more information go to www.chrisbarber.net

Count Basie

Basie On The Beatles
Happy Tiger-HT 1007 (album 12") (09/xx/70)
Ringo Starr: Liner Notes

Legendary jazz bandleader and pianist Count Basie was born William James Basie on August 21, 1904 in Red Bank, New Jersey. His mother taught him to play piano but he also loved to play drums. He gained notice during the Harlem renaissance in the 1920s. By the mid-1930s he'd formed the Count Basie Orchestra and played with, among other jazz legends, Benny Goodman and Duke Ellington. His hits include *One O'clock Jump*, *L'il Darlin'* and *April In Paris.* Basie released the albums *Basie's Beatle Bag* in 1966 and *Basie On The Beatles* in 1970, which include cover versions of their songs. According to the liner notes of the 1970 album written by Ringo Starr, on October 1, 1969 Ringo asked Basie if he would do an arrangement of *Night And Day* for his *Sentimental Journey* album (the album credits bandleader Chico O'Farrill as the arranger). Five days later a complete score arrived, so Ringo gave thanks by writing the liner notes. The album was issued on CD-ROM in 2002. Count Basie died on April 26, 1984.

Mike Batt

Mike Batt's The Hunting Of The Snark [Various Artists]
Epic/Adventure-CD SNARK 1 (CDEPC 57023) (UK) (11/24/86)
Producer: Mike Batt
George Harrison: Guitar†; Mike Batt: Lead Vocals, Piano, Arrangement & Conductor; Tom Nicholl: Drums; Frank McDonald: Bass; Chris Spedding: Guitar; Alan Parker: Guitar; Ray Cooper: Percussion; John Gielgud: Narration; John Hurt: Narration; The London Symphony Orchestra: Orchestrations
CTS, London & FPSHOT†, UK 01/26/85†

Children Of The Sky (M. Batt-[Spoken Verse by L. Carroll]) 5:30 (2)

Mike Batt, born on February 6, 1949 in Southampton, England, is primarily a producer, arranger, composer and conductor. He has also held executive positions with a number of prestigious, music related organizations. At the age of 18 he was a producer for Liberty Records where in 1969 he released a cover version of The Beatles' song *Your Mother Should Know.* Batt made some recordings around 1971 at The Beatles' Apple Studios but none of them participated. In the mid-1970s Batt had a string of hits with The Wombles, and has since worked successfully with a number of artists including Steeleye Span, Andrew Lloyd Webber, Cliff Richard and David Essex. He had a hit with the song *Summertime City* in 1975. His late 1970's albums *Schizophonia* and *Tarot Suite* produced several hits in Europe. Batt attended recording sessions for Paul McCartney's *Tug Of War* album in Montserrat in early 1981 but made no musical contributions.

Batt composed and scored the musical *The Hunting of The Snark* that was based on Lewis Carroll's 1874 poem *Snark.* The recordings contain musical contributions from many artists including Julian Lennon*. Batt told his and George Harrison's close friend, percussionist Ray Cooper, that he wanted Harrison to overdub some guitar on his song *Children Of The Sky* for the project. Cooper took the tapes to Harrison, who in turn invited Batt to FPSHOT studio for the overdub session. Batt recalls, "As he was doing the overdub I'd be pointing to the next fret as if to say, 'Move your finger up to there.' I said to myself, 'I don't even play guitar and here I am pointing to George Harrison's frets during a live overdub!' That was crazy, and yet he was very tolerant of my presence. George suggested I come over to do some jamming and writing together, which we later did, but nothing ever came of it. Later I said, 'When are we going to get together and write this masterpiece?' He said, 'Well actually something crap would do to start with.' He had such a dry sense of humor. It was a lovely experience working with him." Batt said Harrison didn't sing backing vocals on *Children Of The Sky* as has been reported. For more information go to www.mikebatt.com

The Beach Boys
Caribou/Brother-ZK 39946 (09/27/85)
Producer: Steve Levine
Ringo Starr: Drums & Timpani; Alan Jardine: Lead Vocals, B. Vocals & Electric Guitars; Mike Love: Lead Vocals; Brian Wilson: Piano, DX1 & Vocal Arrangement; Simon Humphrey: Bass; Julian Lindsay: Organ; John Alder: Electric Guitars; Steve Levine: Fairlight Programming; The Beach Boys: Vocal Arrangement; Jeff Foskett: B. Vocals; Carl Wilson: B. Vocals; Bruce Johnston: B. Vocals
Red Bus Studios, London, UK probably 08/xx/84

California Calling (A. Jardine-B. Wilson) 2:46 (6) (06/10/85)

Fourth Of July. A Rockin' Celebration Of America [Various Artists]
Love Foundation For American Music Entertainment And Art-[matrix #] PLAT 86 (album 12") (12/xx/86)
Producer: Ted Mather
Ringo Starr: Drums; Jeff Foskett: Lead Vocals & Guitar; Mike Love: Lead Vocals; Alan Jardine: Guitar & B. Vocals; Carl Wilson: Guitar & B. Vocals; Ed Carter: Bass & B. Vocals; Bruce Johnston: Handclaps & B. Vocals; Mike Kowalski: Percussion & B. Vocals; John Lodge: Acoustic Guitar & B. Vocals; Justin Hayward: Acoustic Guitar & B. Vocals; Mike Meros: Synthesizer & Keyboards; Billy Hinsche: Electric Piano; Brian Wilson: Piano & B. Vocals
The Mall, Washington DC 07/04/84

Back In The U.S.S.R. [live] (J. Lennon-P. McCartney) 3:00 (1/1)

Good Vibrations (Thirty Years Of The Beach Boys)
Capitol-C2 0777 7 81294 2 4 (CDP 0777 7 81296 2 2) (06/29/93)
Producer: Brian Wilson
Paul McCartney: (possible) Munching Sounds; Brian Wilson: Lead Vocals, Keyboards & (probable) Bass; Al Jardine: B. Vocals; Mike Love: B. Vocals; Carl Wilson: B. Vocals; Dennis Wilson: B. Vocals; Bruce Johnston: B. Vocals
Columbia Studios, Los Angeles, CA 04/12/67

Vegetables (B. Wilson-V.D. Parks) 3:28 (2-26)

Hawthorne, CA (Birthplace Of A Musical Legacy)
Capitol-72435-31583-2-3 (05/22/01)
Producer: The Beach Boys
Paul McCartney: (possible) Munching Sounds; Al Jardine: B. Vocals; Mike Love: B. Vocals; Carl Wilson: B. Vocals; Dennis Wilson: B. Vocals; Bruce Johnston: B. Vocals; Brian Wilson: Lead Vocals & (probable) Bass
Columbia Studios, Los Angeles, CA probably 03/03/67, 04/10-11/67 & 06/xx/67

Vegetables (B. Wilson-V.D. Parks) 2:59 (2-7)

I Gotta Blues [Ringo Starr]
Pebbles P-02005 [unauthorized release] (xx/xx/02)
Ringo Starr: Drums; Jeff Foskett: B. Vocals & Guitar; Ed Carter: Bass & B. Vocals; Bruce Johnston: Handclaps & B. Vocals; Mike Kowalski: Percussion & B. Vocals; John Lodge: Acoustic Guitar & B. Vocals; Justin Hayward: Acoustic Guitar & B. Vocals; Mike Meros: Synthesizer & Keyboards; Billy Hinsche: Electric Piano; Brian Wilson: Piano & B. Vocals
The Mall, Washington DC 07/04/84

Fun, Fun, Fun (B. Wilson-M. Love) 3:32 (11)
Additionally: **Ringo Starr: Dialogue**; Mike Love: Lead Vocals; Carl Wilson: Guitar & B. Vocals; Alan Jardine: Guitar & B. Vocals

Good Vibrations (B. Wilson-M. Love) 4:51 (9)
Additionally: Carl Wilson: Lead Vocals & Guitar; Alan Jardine: Guitar & B. Vocals; Mike Love: Vocals & Theremin

Help Me Rhonda (B. Wilson-M. Love) 3:12 (10)
Additionally: Al Jardine: Lead Vocals; Mike Love: B. Vocals; Carl Wilson: Guitar & B. Vocals

The Pet Sounds Sessions
Capitol-C2 7243 8 37662 2 2 (11/04/97)
Paul McCartney: Printed Interview

Together At The Rock And Roll Hall Of Fame
Living Legend-LLRCD 101(Italy) [unauthorized release] (xx/xx/93)
Producer: [unknown]
George Harrison: Guitar & B. Vocals; Ringo Starr: Drums; Mike Love: Vocals; Carl Wilson: Vocals & (probable) Guitar; Brian Wilson: Vocals; Alan Jardine: Vocals & (probable) Guitar; Bruce Johnston: B. Vocals; probably one or more of the following: Ben E. King: B. Vocals & Handclaps; Julian Lennon: B. Vocals & Handclaps; Paul Shaffer: Keyboards; Billy Joel: Keyboards & B. Vocals; Bruce Springsteen: B. Vocals & Percussion; Patti Scialfa: Handclaps &

Left to right: Mike Love, Alan Jardine, Bruce Johnston and Kristofer Engelhardt, Pine Knob Clarkston (Detroit), MI August 20, 1997. Photo by Gon'l, © Kristofer Engelhardt.

B. Vocals; Little Richard: Percussion; Elton John: Keyboards & B. Vocals; Anton Fig: Drums; Bob Dylan: Guitar; Dave Edmunds: Guitar; Les Paul: Guitar; Jeff Beck: Electric Guitar; Mick Jagger: Percussion; Mary Wilson: B. Vocals; Yoko Ono: Handclaps; Sean Lennon: Handclaps; Sid McGinnis: Guitar; John Fogerty: Guitar or Handclaps; Arlo Guthrie: Guitar or Handclaps; Peter Wolf: Handclaps; Johnny Moore: Handclaps; Joe Blunt: Handclaps; Clyde Brown: Handclaps; Bill Pinkney: Handclaps; Charlie Thomas: Handclaps; Max Weinberg: Percussion; Will Lee: Bass
Grand Ballroom Waldorf-Astoria Hotel, New York, NY 01/20/88

Barbara Ann [live] (F. Fassert) 3:29 (9)

The Beach Boys formed in Hawthorne (Los Angeles), California in 1961. They included guitarist Alan Jardine, born on September 3, 1942, in Lima, Ohio; brothers Brian Wilson*, drummer Dennis Wilson, born December 4, 1944, and guitarist Carl Wilson, born December 21, 1946; their front man, cousin Mike Love was born March 15, 1941. All were born in the Los Angeles area. Jardine, a school mate of Brian's, temporarily left the group between early 1962 and mid-1963 and was replaced by the Wilson's neighbor David Marks.

Brian, the group's leader, gifted songwriter and producer, modeled their sound on the harmonies of The Four Freshmen. Their early hits such as *All Summer Long*, *Surfin' USA*, *Shut Down* and *California Girls* were based on the themes of summer, surfing, cars and girls. The Beach Boys were arguably the most popular rock 'n' roll group in the early 1960s but their supremacy was tested in 1964 by the British music invasion spearheaded by The Beatles. Coincidentally, both groups were signed to Capitol and due to the close spelling of the groups' names their records were usually racked next to each others. Naturally, they envied and admired each others' work. The Beach Boys showed their appreciation in 1965 by covering The Beatles' songs, which they did throughout their career.

By this time, Brian had suffered a nervous breakdown and quit touring to concentrate on writing and producing for the group. Glen Campbell filled in for a short time before Bruce Johnston, born Benjamin Baldwin on June 27, 1942, in Peoria, Illinois, took his place. Bruce had previously produced and sung on recordings for The Beach Boys-styled group The Rip Chords along with Terry Melcher during their days as producers at Columbia Records. Johnston had also worked with Phil Spector*, who Brian greatly admired.

The Beatles' 1965 album *Rubber Soul* inspired Brian's production of *Pet Sounds*. The album, which ignored the band's pop sound and lyrical themes, is regarded as their best work. During this period, The Beach Boys hired Derek Taylor who was instrumental in helping them break into the UK market. Johnston says there was great excitement when he premiered *Pet Sounds* for John Lennon, Paul McCartney and Keith Moon* during a visit to the UK in May 1966. By the end of the year The Beach Boys had topped the US and UK charts with their mini-rock symphony song *Good Vibrations* unseating The Beatles in *NME* magazine's annual poll as the World's Best Group. McCartney has often stated that *Pet Sounds* and its song *God Only Knows* are his all-time favorites. He says the album motivated and inspired The Beatles during the recording of their album *Sgt. Pepper's Lonely Hearts Club Band*. When *Pet Sounds* was released on CD in 1990, it was to include a printed interview with McCartney. Due to production problems it wasn't included but was made available on request. The printed interview was included in *The Pet Sounds Sessions* set released in 1997. In it McCartney affectionately states, "I'm still a big fan. I figure, with what you're gonna write here, he'll know that. Just let Brian know that I love him, and that I still think he's gonna do great things. Tell him good luck, stay healthy for me and think good, positive thoughts." The box set also includes a printed interview with George Martin*.

Brian's follow-up to *Pet Sounds* was an elaborate concept album called *Smile*. Though *Pet Sounds* had received the highest acclaim from critics, it was a relative commercial failure at the time. The Beach Boys were forming Brother Records, as The Beatles did some months later with Apple. Numerous legal battles with Capitol threatened *Smile's* release. Band members expressed concern over the musical course Brian was charting, and the cost and time *Smile* was taking to complete. In the spring of 1967 Brian, who was frustrated, disillusioned and mentally fragile, abandoned *Smile*. The world was soon delighting in The Beatles' *Sgt. Pepper's Lonely Hearts Club Band* album and The Beach Boys were quickly becoming a forgotten surf band from another era. The whole episode marked the end of Brian's creative marathon. He continued to withdraw from the group as his mental and physical health deteriorated so other members assumed greater responsibilities.

In September 1967 The Beach Boys released the hurriedly recorded and minimally produced remnants of *Smile* called *Smiley Smile* on Brother Records. In the liner notes of the *Smiley Smile* CD Jardine states, "The night before a big tour, I was out in the studio recording the vocal for *Vegetables* when, to my surprise, Paul McCartney walked in and joined Brian at the console. And, briefly, the two most influential musical Gemini's in the world had a chance to work together. I remember waiting for long periods of time between takes to get to the next section or verse. Brian seemed to have lost track of the session. Paul would come on the talk-back and say something like 'good take, Al'." McCartney has never been officially credited as producer on any released versions of *Vegetables*. Johnston says, "Paul was just in the booth, more as support of Brian because he thought so highly of *Pet Sounds*. According to Brian, "Paul attended the sessions with Derek Taylor, and gave suggestions but he didn't actually produce anything. His being there was an inspiration." Brian also says Paul played *She's Leaving Home* for them on piano. The Beach Boys' tour referenced by Al began on April 13, 1967 on the East Coast, making a session in Los Angeles the night before unlikely. Most reliable sources place the session with McCartney on April 10, and his departure for London on April 11, making it likely that the sessions took place on the evening of April 10 and early morning of April 11. Brad Elliott, author of the 1982 book *Surf's Up! The Beach Boys On Record, 1961 - 1981*, states that on April 11 McCartney attended a Beach Boys' session and, along with DJ Rodney Bingenheimer and Roger McGuinn, sang background vocals on an unreleased version of *Vegetables*. Brian confirms Rodney and Roger's presence and says, "We were just warming up, they're not on the final track." Bingenheimer correctly recalls the sessions taking place late at night at Columbia Studios, "There were a lot of different people there. I think Dean Torrence [from The Beach Boys-styled duo Jan & Dean] was there. Brian had everyone name off a vegetable. McCartney named off a vegetable but I don't remember what one." Bingenheimer doesn't recall McCartney having anything to do with the production of *Vegetables*. No Beach Boys' versions have surfaced featuring different people naming off vegetables. The *Smiley Smile* CD liner notes also claim that McCartney joined The Beach Boys munching on raw vegetables for percussion. In McCartney's fan club magazine, *Club Sandwich* (winter 1994 issue No. 72), Paul responded to a fan's question: "Is it true that you can be heard munching vegetables on The Beach Boys track *Vegetables*? The CD liner notes say so." McCartney replied, "Do they? Well, I was certainly at a few Beach Boys sessions, and if someone gave me, say, an apple, I would have munched it, and if there'd been a microphone nearby I suppose it might have gone down on tape. But I don't remember doing it knowingly." Brian says, "I had brought some vegetables down there for the atmosphere. Paul was chewing on a stick of celery." Portions of the original *Smile* sessions were released in 1993 on the CD box set *Good Vibrations (Thirty Years Of The Beach Boys)*. It includes a version of *Vegetables* that is considerably longer and more complex than the version on *Smiley Smile* reportedly recorded the night McCartney was in attendance. This version also features munching sounds. It's listed as being recorded on April 12, but most accounts suggest the more complex recordings produced by Brian are from the earlier *Smile* sessions, and the more sparsely produced versions are from the *Smiley Smile* sessions that came much later. Perhaps this is the version to which Elliott is referring. Both versions of *Vegetables* released by The Beach Boys obviously contain fragments of recordings from different sessions. With all the confusion surrounding these sessions, and the large volume of bits and pieces of tape that were intended to be used in the *Smile* project, Brian is uncertain whether McCartney's munching sounds were used on any of the released versions.

Elliott's book also states that McCartney added bass to The Beach Boys' recording of *On Top Of Old Smokey* that evening. Mal Evans, who reported on McCartney's trip to Los Angeles in the July 1967 issue of *The Beatles Book Monthly* magazine, also states McCartney played guitar on *On Top Of Old Smokey*. Brian doesn't recall The Beach Boys recording that song. If the song was performed it was probably nothing more than a warm-up jam that either wasn't recorded or kept.

The Beatles threw a costume party on December 21, 1967 at the Royal Lancaster Hotel in London for the cast and crew of their *Magical Mystery Tour* film. Mike and Bruce were invited to attend. According to Bruce, The Beatles danced around the two Beach Boys and joined them onstage in a performance of *Sloop John B*.

In February 1968 Mike, along with The Beatles, was a student of Transcendental Meditation at Maharishi Mahesh Yogi's (a.k.a. Mahesh Prasad Verma) ashram in Rishikesh, India. While there, The Beatles wrote much of what would comprise *The Beatles* (white) album. McCartney came up with the song *Back In The U.S.S.R.*, which The Beatles recorded very much in the style of The Beach Boys. He reportedly auditioned the song in India for Mike who suggested he include references to Soviet girls just as The Beach Boys had done in their song *California Girls*. Bruce says Paul agreed to do a cameo as a clerk in the video for The Beach Boy's hit *Do It Again* when he was in Los Angeles in June 1968 but was unable to attend the shoot due to a scheduling conflict.

Melody Maker magazine reported in its July 10 and 17, 1971 issues that George Harrison visited The Beach Boys in New York while they were filming a TV special with Ike and Tina Turner*. It also says that Harrison recorded with The Beach Boys — possibly on the final tracks for their album [*Surf's Up*]. Bruce has no recollection of Harrison's presence at these events and disputes the report. However, Brian says, "George was there [during a session for the *Surf's Up* album] but he didn't play."

Dennis severely injured his hand in 1971 and drumming duties were filled by Ricky (a.k.a. Rikki) Fataar. [Fataar would later play the part of Harrison (Stig O'Hara) in The Rutles (see The Bonzo Dog Band, Monty Python).] Fataar had been a member of Brother Records' group Flame with Blondie Chaplin, who several months later officially replaced Bruce. [Bruce continued to record (un-credited) with the group on occasion. He won the Grammy Award for Song of the Year in 1977 for composing Barry Manilow's hit *I Write The Songs*. He rejoined The Beach Boys in 1978.] Fataar and Chaplin left the group in 1974.

In 1975 therapist Eugene Landy was hired to rehabilitate Brian and return him to his former role in the group, which resulted in his sporadic appearances and flourishes of creativity during the second half of the 1970s. McCartney is seen in the 1976 NBC TV special *The Beach Boys: It's OK* attending Brian's birthday party. [The scene with McCartney is included on the 2002 DVD *The Beach Boys An American Band* (Artisan-12584).] By the early 1980s Brian's mental and physical health had deteriorated dramatically, as had that of Dennis, and they were essentially barred from the group. Landy was again hired to help Brian, with considerable success. On December 28, 1983 Dennis drowned in the frigid waters of Marina Del Ray Harbor.

Ringo made a guest appearance with The Beach Boys at their annual Fourth of July celebration in Washington DC in 1984 playing drums on *Back In The U.S.S.R.*, *Good*

Vibrations, *Help Me Rhonda*, *Fun, Fun, Fun*, *You Can't Do That* and *Day Tripper*. That evening he joined them in Miami playing drums on *Back In The U.S.S.R*, *Dizzy, Miss Lizzy* and *Slow Down*. Portions of the Washington DC concert were televised and are available on unauthorized releases. *Back In The U.S.S.R.* was released in 1986 on the mail order album *Fourth Of July - A Rockin' Celebration Of America*, though it incorrectly lists the song as being recorded in 1985. Ringo was scheduled for the '85 show but canceled at the last minute.

Ringo played on the song *California Calling* from the 1985 album *The Beach Boys*. On January 20, 1988 The Beach Boys, along with The Beatles, were inducted into the Rock and Roll Hall of Fame at the Waldorf-Astoria Hotel in New York. The group, along with George and Ringo, took part in the all-star jam at the end of the evening's events, portions of which are available on unauthorized releases. The ceremonies were marred by Love's unflattering remarks about McCartney, The Beatles and others. The Beach Boys last chart topping song was *Kokomo* in 1988. Love, Jardine and Johnson attended the Natural Law Political Party's fund-raiser at the Royal Albert Hall in London on April 6, 1992 at George Harrison's request. The Party promotes Transcendental Meditation as a means of solving political problems. Love joined Ringo and Paul during Paul's performance of *Cosmically Conscious* at a benefit for Transcendental Meditation on April 4, 2009 at Radio City Music Hall in New York.

Brian has had little to do with The Beach Boys since the mid-1990s instead concentrating on his successful solo career. In 1997 David Marks was asked to fill in for an ailing Carl Wilson who died on February 6, 1998. Following Carl's death, Al Jardine stopped touring with The Beach Boys and tours with his Endless Summer Band. Love and Johnston, with others, continue to tour as The Beach Boys. For more information go to www.thebeachboys.com, www.aljardine.com, www.beachboysband.net

Cliff Bennett And The Rebel Rousers

Lennon & McCartney Songbook
Connoisseur Collection-VSOP CD 150 (UK/EEC) (07/02/90)
Producer: Paul McCartney & David Paramor
Paul McCartney: Piano & Arrangement; Cliff Bennett: Lead Vocals; Chas Hodges: Bass & Lead Guitar; Maurice Groves: Saxophone; Sid Phillips: Saxophone; Roy Young: Keyboards; Mike Burt: Drums
EMI-Abbey Road Studios, London, UK late 07/xx/66

Got To Get You Into My Life (J. Lennon-**P. McCartney**) 2:29 (10) (08/05/66)

Cliff Bennett was born on June 4, 1940 in Slough, England. The Beatles and Bennett likely first met when both had engagements at the Star-Club in Hamburg, Germany in December 1962. The London-based Cliff Bennett And The Rebel Rousers recorded for Parlophone a year before The Beatles did. The band's numerous members over the years included Nicky Hopkins*. In 1964 they had their first UK Top 10 hit with *One Way Love*.

Being represented by NEMS at the time, Cliff Bennett And The Rebel Rousers, who then included Roy Young (see Tony Sheridan), appeared on the bill with The Beatles during their 1966 tour of Germany. The Beatles had recently recorded *Got To Get You Into My Life* for their forthcoming album *Revolver*. Cliff recalls, "We were on tour in Germany when Paul came into the dressing room and said, 'We've written a great song and we think it would be ideal for you,' and demonstrated the song for us on acoustic guitars. Following a break in the tour, Paul came into the studio to help produce and arrange the song for us. Our producer, Dave Paramor just took a back seat. Paul was a great believer in our band and was encouraging everybody. He played the glissando on the piano on the recording. He came back the next day when we recorded the vocals with his jacket over his pajamas and wearing slippers because he lived just around the corner." Cliff says additional horn players were brought in to play on the song. He says it's the only recording of his to which any of The Beatles contributed. Bennett's version of *Got To Get You Into My Life* was a UK Top 10 but any chance for its global success was doomed when The Beatles simultaneously released their version on *Revolver*. Though it wasn't released before The Beatles' version, because of McCartney's involvement, it obviously was intended to be a composition contribution to Bennett.

Bennett had some success in Europe but was

virtually unknown in America. Roy Young replaced Cliff Bennett in The Rebel Rousers in 1968 but disbanded the group to form the Roy Young Band the following year. Cliff formed The Cliff Bennett Band who released a cover song of The Beatles' *Back In The U.S.S.R.* in 1968 before breaking up in 1969. Cliff has since worked with several other bands and reformed The Rebel Rousers with several original members.

Tony Bennett

Duets (An American Classic)
RPM/Columbia/Sony-82876 88736 2/CVD-57847 (DVD) (09/26/06)
Producer: Phil Ramone
Paul McCartney: Duet Vocals†; Tony Bennett: Duet Vocals; Lee Musiker: Piano; Paul Langosch: Bass; Harold Jones: Drums; Gary Sargent: Guitar; Pinchas Zukerman: Violin; Chris Botti: Trumpet; Jorge Calandrelli: Orchestrations & Conductor; Torrie Zito: Brass Arrangements & Conductor
EMI-Abbey Road Studios†, London, UK 03/31/06

Tony Bennett, Pine Knob, Clarkston (Detroit), MI August 20, 2000. © and photo by Kristofer Engelhardt.

The Very Thought Of You (R. Noble) 4:01 (4)

Paul McCartney: Acoustic Together Bridge School Benefit Concert 2004
NOW-2004351 [unauthorized release] (xx/xx/04)
Paul McCartney: Duet Vocals; Tony Bennett: Duet Vocals; Lee Musiker: Piano; Clayton Cameron: Drums; Paul Langosch: Bass; Gray Sargent: Guitar
Shoreline Amphitheatre, Mountain View, CA 10/24/04

The Very Thought Of You [live] (R. Noble) 5:42 (16)

Tony Bennett was born Anthony Benedetto in New York, New York on August 3, 1926. He had an avid interest in jazz and popular singers, and graphic arts, which he pursued at the High School of Industrial Art in New York before dropping out to work as a singing waiter to help support his family. He served in the US Army in Europe toward the end of World War II. When the war ended he was assigned to entertain troops under the name Joe Bari. After the military, he began to develop his impeccable knack for vocal phrasing. In 1949 Bob Hope saw him open for Pearl Bailey and offered him a spot on his tour. Hope suggested he simplify his name to Tony Bennett. Bennett was soon signed to Columbia Records and in 1951 had two number one hits, *Because Of You* and *Cold, Cold Heart*, along with the Top 20 hit *Blue Velvet*. He was soon following in the footsteps of Frank Sinatra (who later called him "the best singer in the business") as a teen idol. His recordings of *Rags To Riches* and *Stranger In Paradise* reached the top of the charts in 1953. In the early 1960s Bennett had success with *The Best Is Yet To Come*, *I've Got The World On A String*, *The Good Life* and his signature song *I Left My Heart In San Francisco*.

With the advent of The Beatles and the British Invasion in the mid-1960s, singers of pop and jazz standards such as Bennett fell out of favor. Ironically, Tony passed the torch presenting The Beatles with *NME* magazine's Poll-Winners' Award at Empire Pool, Wembley (London) on April 11, 1965. By the end of the decade a reluctant and struggling Bennett began covering songs by rock artists, including The Beatles, but without success. By 1980 he'd fallen on hard times. His son Danny came to his rescue in the form of manager and producer, with engineering assistance from his other son Daegal. They set in motion their father's comeback in the mid-1980s, when aging baby boomers were giving a second listen to their parent's music. Bennett appeared on a number of contemporary TV, shows including MTV, purveying his musical roots while embracing his new audience, and musicians such as Elvis Costello* and Diana Krall.

On October 23 and 24, 2004 Paul McCartney and Tony Bennett sang *The Very Thought Of You* together at Neil Young's* Bridge School Benefit Concert. Tony introduced Paul saying, "The nicest human being I ever met; the greatest musician who ever lived." Paul remarked, "This song is a surprise for my wife Heather [Mills]* who's in the audience. This is our song and Tony did us the honor of recording it for the first dance at our wedding, so Tony's OK by me!" The performance is available on a number of unauthorized releases. In 2006 Tony released his most successful album, *Duets (An American Classic)*, which included duets with, among other Elton John*, George Michael*, James Taylor*, Stevie Wonder* and Paul McCartney who Bennett says requested they do *The Very Thought Of You*. McCartney also makes a brief appearance in the album's bonus DVD and a much longer appearance in the 2007 DVD *Duets: The Making of an American Classic* (Sony-707 864). With millions in record sales and over a dozen Grammy Awards behind him, Tony continues to record and tour tirelessly to large and enthusiastic audiences. He has also received acclaim from critics for his paintings, and numerous honors for his charitable work and support of arts education. For more information go to www.exploringthearts.org www.tonybennett.net, www.benedettoarts.com

George Benson & Al Jarreau

Givin' It Up
Concord/Monster Music Group CCD-2316-2 (10/24/06)
Producer: John Burk
Paul McCartney: Vocals; George Benson: Vocals & Guitar; Al Jarreau: Vocals; Randy Waldman: Piano; Michael Broening: Organ; Patrice Rushen: Fender Rhodes Electric Piano; Dean Parks: Guitar; Abraham Laboriel: Electric Bass; Vinnie Colaiuta: Drums; Paulinho Da Costa: Percussion; Alethea Mills: B. Vocals; Chavonne Morris: B. Vocals; De'Ante Duckett: B. Vocals
Henson Studios, Hollywood, CA 04/18-22 &/or 24 &/or 25/06

Bring It On Home To Me (S. Cooke) 4:25 (13)

Jazz guitarist and vocalist George Benson was born on March 22, 1943 in Pittsburgh, Pennsylvania. He gained notice in the mid-1960s playing with such jazz legends as Miles Davis. He also had considerable success in 1969 with *The Other Side Of Abbey Road* his album of covers from The Beatles' *Abbey Road* album. Between 1976 and 1981 he had a Top Five hit with *Give Me The Night*, Top 10 hits with *This Masquerade* and *On Broadway*, a Top 20 hit with *Love Ballad*, and Top 40 hits with *The Greatest Love Of All* and *Turn Your Love Around*. His last Top 40 hit was *Lady Love Me (One More Time)* in 1983. He has won 10 Grammy Awards and is a NEA Jazz Master. He continues to record and tour. For more information go to www.georgebenson.com

Multiple Grammy Award winning jazz singer Al Jarreau was born on March 12, 1940 in Milwaukee, Wisconsin. He sang in his church choir and was in a singing group in college. He earned degrees in psychology and vocational rehabilitation. By the late 1960s he was pursuing a career in music appearing in clubs and on national TV shows. In 1975 he signed a record deal with Warner Bros. He had a Top 20 hit with *We're In This Love Together* in 1981, and just missed having a Top 20 hit with *Mornin'* in 1983 and the theme to the TV show *Moonlighting* in 1987. For more information go to www.aljarreau.com

Benson and Jarreau teamed up in 2006 to record the album *Givin' It Up* at Henson Studios in Los Angeles. Paul McCartney was also at the studio then recording his album *Memory Almost Full*. Paul dropped in on their sessions and sang on *Bring It On Home To Me*, which he recorded in two takes, included on *Givin' It Up*. Benson says, "Sir Paul and I have been casual friends for a long time and there is a great mutual respect between us for the work we do. Paul, being the most influential singers, musicians and composers in the world, makes it an honor on my part to know him. I was especially honored to have him on the *Givin' It Up* record with Al Jarreau and myself. I will never stop thanking him for being such a real person."

The Mike Douglas Show with John Lennon & Yoko Ono
Rhino R3 2438 (R3 2428/29/30/31/32) (VHS) (05/26/98)
Producer: Jay Lebow, WBS in association with Mike Douglas Entertainments Inc. & Michael Krauss
Chuck Berry: Lead Vocals & Guitar; Gary Van Scyoc: Bass; Adam Ippolito: Keyboards; Richard Frank Jr.: Drums; Stan Bronstein: Saxophone & Tambourine; Wayne Tex Gabriel: Guitar; Jerry Rubin: Percussion; Yoko Ono: Percussion
KYW TV Studios, Philadelphia, PA mid-01/xx/72 or 02/02/72; airdate: 02/16/72

Johnny B. Goode [live] (C. Berry) 2:56 (Tape 3)
Additionally: **John Lennon: B. Vocals & Guitar**

Memphis, Tennessee [live] (C. Berry) 3:09 (Tape 3)
Additionally: **John Lennon: Duet Vocals & Guitar**; Yoko Ono: B. Vocals

Chuck Berry was born on October 18, 1926 in St. Louis, Missouri. He is one of the founding fathers of rock 'n' roll. Between 1955 and 1959 he wrote and recorded such classic hits as *Maybellene*, *You Can't Catch Me*, *Roll Over Beethoven*, *School Days*, *Rock & Roll Music*, *Carol*, *Johnny B. Goode*, *Sweet Little Sixteen*, *Little Queenie* and *Memphis, Tennessee*. His string of hits ended following his arrest and incarceration in the early 1960s. While Berry was behind bars the landscape of American music was changing. The Beach Boys* rewrote the lyrics to *Sweet Little Sixteen* and re-titled it *Surfin' USA*. Following Berry's release from prison he was greeted by the sounds of The Beatles and The Rolling Stones echoing back his music from England. In 1964 Berry had hits with *Nadine (Is It You?)*, *No Particular Place To Go* (a rewrite of *School Days*) and *You Never Can Tell*. Berry continued to tour and record during the second half of the 1960s but without chart success.

Nearly every rock 'n' roll band has cut its teeth on Chuck Berry's music and The Beatles were

Chuck Berry and Kristofer Engelhardt, Soaring Eagle Casino, Mt. Pleasant, MI December 27, 1999. © Kristofer Engelhardt.

no exception. Their early repertoire included over a dozen Berry classics, many of which they would later record. Most of them were sung by John Lennon who was a huge Chuck Berry fan. Lennon and Ringo Starr attended Berry's performance at Brian Epstein's Saville Theatre in London on February 19, 1967. George Harrison considered *Roll Over Beethoven* one of his top 10 favorite songs. Paul McCartney has admitted that he copied the bass riff of his composition *I Saw Her Standing There* from Berry's *I'm Talking About You.* McCartney covered Berry's composition *Brown Eyed Handsome Man* on his 1999 album *Run Devil Run.*

When Lennon wrote The Beatles' hit *Come Together*, he borrowed a line and some of the melody from Berry's *You Can't Catch Me.* Morris Levy, who owned the publishing rights to *You Can't Catch Me*, sued Lennon for copyright infringement. As part of an out-of-court settlement, Lennon agreed to record three songs, including *You Can't Catch Me*, which Levy owned the publishing rights to, for his oldies album, *Rock 'N' Roll.* Lennon also recorded *Sweet Little Sixteen* for the album.

Berry was one of the guests Lennon wanted when he and Yoko Ono* were co-hosts of TV's *The Mike Douglas Show* for a week in early 1972. [Berry had appeared on the bill with Lennon and the Plastic Ono Band at the *Toronto Rock 'n' Roll Revival* on September 13, 1969 but the two had never met.] Lennon introduced Berry as, "My hero!" and said, "If you were to try and give rock 'n' roll another name you might call it Chuck Berry." Berry performed *Memphis, Tennessee* and *Johnny B Goode* backed by Lennon, Elephant's Memory*, Yoko and political activist Jerry Rubin. The following year Berry was backed by Elephant's Memory on his album *Bio.*

Berry's only number one hit was his sexually suggestive, audience participation recording of *My Ding-A-Ling* recorded live in 1972 with backing from The Roy Young Band (see Cliff Bennett And The Rebel Rousers). Berry was given a Lifetime Achievement Award at the 1985 Grammy Awards. The following year Berry, with his early innovative songwriting, guitar style and stage "duck walk," became the first inductee into the Rock and Roll Hall of Fame. *Hail! Hail! Rock 'n' Roll*, a 1987 documentary film about Berry, included Julian Lennon* reprising his dad's performance with Berry on *Johnny B. Goode.* The film also included archival footage of John Lennon. Berry's recording of *Johnny B. Goode* was included on a record enclosed on the Voyager space probes. Berry continues to tour well into his sixth decade in music and often uses pickup or house bands because they usually know all of his songs. For more information go to www.chuckberry.com

Cilla Black

CILLA The Best Of 1963/78
Parlophone/EMI 7243 5 84124 2 0 (EU) (05/26/03) **Paul McCartney: Liner Notes**

I'll Still Love You (When Every Song Is Sung) (G. Harrison) 3:05 (3-23)
Producer: David MacKay
Probably Morgan Studios, London, UK probably 10/xx/74 or possibly 02-04/xx/74

It's For You (J. Lennon-**P. McCartney**) intro: 0:10/2:20 (1-1) (07/31/64)
Producer: George Martin
Paul McCartney: Piano & Arrangement; **John Lennon: Arrangement & Dialogue**; Cilla Black: Lead Vocals; Johnny Person: Piano; Kenny Clarke: Drums; Judd Proctor: Guitar; George Martin: Orchestra Conductor
EMI-Abbey Road Studios, London, UK 06/29/64

Cilla 1963-1973 The Abbey Road Decade
Zonophone-7243 8 57053 2 8 (UK) (07/04/97)
Producer: George Martin

Love Of The Loved (J. Lennon-**P. McCartney**) 2:01 (1-1) (09/27/63)
Cilla Black: Lead Vocals; George Martin: Orchestra Conductor
EMI-Abbey Road Studios, London, UK 08/28/63

M'Innamoro (Step Inside Love) (Italian Version) (J. Lennon-P. McCartney-[Mogol: Translation]) 2:21 (2-23) (probably 03/xx/68)
Cilla Black: Lead Vocals; Mike Vickers: Musical Direction & Arrangement; Vicki Brown: B. Vocals; Judd Proctor: Guitar
EMI-Abbey Road Studios, London, UK 02/28/68 & probably 03/xx/68

Step Inside Love (J. Lennon-**P. McCartney**) 2:21 (2-1) (03/08/68)
Cilla Black: Lead Vocals; Mike Vickers: Musical Direction & Arrangement; Vicki Brown: B. Vocals; Judd Proctor: Guitar
EMI-Abbey Road Studios, London, UK 02/28/68

Step Inside Love (Original Demo) (J. Lennon-**P. McCartney**) 2:51 (3-12)
Paul McCartney: B. Vocals & Acoustic Guitar; Cilla Black: Lead Vocals
EMI-Abbey Road Studios, London, UK 11/21/67

Unbootlegged 19 [The Beatles]
No Tapo-NTR-0501 (CD-R) [unauthorized release] (xx/x/05)

Snowman Song [live] 0:42 (4)
Ringo Starr: B. Vocals; Cilla Black: Lead Vocals; Basil Brush: B. Vocals; Ronnie Hazelhurst Orchestra

Unbootlegged 25 [version one] [The Beatles]
No Tapo-NTR-0603 (CD-R) [unauthorized release] (xx/xx/06)
Producer: George Martin
Paul McCartney: Acoustic Guitar & B. Vocals; Cilla Black: Lead Vocals; George Martin: Piano
Chappell Studios, London 11/21/67

Step Inside Love (J. Lennon-**P. McCartney**) 23:45 (2, 3, 4, 5, 6, 7, 8, 9, 10, 11, 12 &13)

Cilla Black was born Priscilla White on May 27, 1943 in Liverpool, England. As a teenager she would informally get up on Liverpool club stages and sing with local bands such as Kingsize Taylor & The Dominoes and Rory Storm & The Hurricanes. She often sang the song *Boys* with The Hurricanes' drummer, Ringo Starr. She changed her last name as a result of an article in Liverpool's *Mersey Beat* magazine, which mistakenly referred to her as Cilla Black. John Lennon encouraged Brian Epstein to sign her to a contract with NEMS. She auditioned the song *Summertime* for Epstein in mid-1963, backed by The Beatles, at the Majestic Ballroom in Birkenhead (Liverpool area) but they hadn't rehearsed and played it in the wrong key for her. A few months later, Epstein saw her perform again and signed her. Her first major appearances were as part of *The Beatles Christmas Show* in 1963. She also appeared on the UK TV specials *Around The Beatles* in 1964 and *The Music Of Lennon And McCartney* in 1965.

Cilla exclusively recorded three songs credited to Lennon-McCartney as composers. The first, *Love Of The Loved*, was an early McCartney composition, that The Beatles performed live and auditioned for Decca Records in early 1962 (available on a number of the Decca audition releases). An acetate of McCartney's acoustic guitar demo of the song for Cilla exists. Lennon and McCartney attended Cilla's recording session for the song, which was a UK top 40 hit in 1963, but it's doubtful they made any contribution. Her recording was a UK Top 40 hit in 1963. Lennon and McCartney reportedly also attended Cilla's recording of the Bacharach-David song *Anyone Who Had A Heart*, which topped the UK charts in 1964, though there's no indication they contributed to it either. That year *You're My World*, her adaptation of an Italian song, also topped the UK charts and was her only US Top 40 hit.

It's For You was Cilla's next attempt at a McCartney song. McCartney reportedly recorded two very different demos of it for Cilla. Lennon and McCartney attended her recording session to help arrange the song. She recorded three versions. The final version, with McCartney on piano, was a UK Top 10 hit. Lennon recorded a plug for it that appeared on promotional copies (Capitol PRO-2720) of the single in the US, and years later on the 2003 album *CILLA The Best Of 1963/78*, though it doesn't contain the full plug. McCartney recalls plugging the song to DJs during The Beatles' US tour in 1964.

Lastly, McCartney wrote Black's UK Top 10 hit *Step Inside Love* as the theme song to her first TV series *Cilla*, which debuted in January 1968 on BBC. [Ringo appeared on the show on February 6, singing a duet with Cilla on the songs *Do You Like Me?* and *Nellie Dean*.] On November 21, 1967 the BBC produced a two-minute promotional film of McCartney rehearsing *Step Inside Love* with Cilla at Chappell Studios in London. Approximately 25 minutes of the rehearsal, featuring McCartney on acoustic guitar singing along with Cilla, has turned up on unauthorized records. They also recorded a demo of the song with McCartney on backing vocals and acoustic guitar. Later that day, Cilla recorded a finished version of the song though it's unlikely McCartney contributed to it. However, the version of the song that was first released was a re-recording made on February 28, 1968 at Abbey Road Studios. McCartney, who was at the Maharishi Mahesh Yogi's ashram in India at the time, wasn't present. Cilla later overdubbed her vocals, sung in Italian, to the February 28 backing, which was released in Italy. She may have also dubbed vocals sung in French and Spanish. McCartney recorded a brief version of the song during sessions for *The Beatles* (white) album in 1968 that was included on their 1996 album *Anthology 3*.

Ringo taped his second appearance on the *Cilla* TV show on October 1, 1970, which aired on February 13, 1971, singing *Act Naturally* with Cilla, backed by the BBC's Orchestra. Ringo taped another appearance in Scandinavia for *Cilla In Scandinavia* on June

24, this time singing the *Snowman Song* with Cilla and Basil Brush, the puppet fox, which aired on November 27, 1971 and has appeared on unauthorized releases.

Cilla's last major hit was *Something Tells Me (Something's Gonna Happen Tonight)*, which was a UK Top Five hit in 1971. George Harrison attempted to bolster Cilla's recording career by producing *I'll Still Love You (When Every Song Is Sung)*, which he wrote, and reportedly *You've Gotta Stay With Me*, co-written with Paul Woodall, though no song with that title has ever surfaced. The songs were recorded at Apple Studios in 1971 with an all-star lineup including Harrison on guitar, Ringo on drums, Klaus Voormann* on bass and Eric Clapton* on guitar. [Harrison had earlier offered *I'll Still Love You* to Apple artists Mary Hopkin* and Ronnie Spector*, and later to Leon Russell*. It was first released by Ringo on his 1976 album *Rotogravure*.] Apparently, Cilla was unhappy with the results due in part to painful dental work done before the session. Harrison had also written the song *The Light That Has Lighted The World* for Cilla to record but recorded it for his *Living In The Material World* album instead. Cilla re-recorded *I'll Still Love You* in 1974 with producer David MacKay; though it isn't known if any of the original backing tracks were used. It was eventually released on *CILLA The Best Of 1963/78*. Because this recording predates Ringo's recording and was intended for release first by Cilla, it is considered a Harrison contribution to Cilla. Ringo once offered Cilla *Back Off Boogaloo*, but she preferred *Photograph*. Ringo rightly felt *Photograph* would be a hit for him and was unwilling to turn it over to Cilla.

On September 7, 1993 it was reported that Cilla and Ringo were at Abbey Road Studios for a recording session, though as yet nothing has been released. That month, Ringo and McCartney contributed video material for the ITV special *Cilla-A Celebration*. In 1996 London's *Daily Mirror* made the unlikely claim that EMI had discovered 20 tracks of Cilla singing with The Beatles. According to Cilla's son Robert Willis, about 30 tracks were discovered, some of them Cilla's covers of The Beatles' songs, of which she has released many, but only one (*Step Inside Love*) features contributions from a Beatle. *Cilla 1963-1973 The Abbey Road Decade* album released in 1997 includes *Love Of The Loved, It's For You* and four versions of *Step Inside Love* including the original (first take) version recorded on November 21, 1967. Over the decades Cilla has become one of the most popular TV entertainers in the UK though she has been less active in recent years. For more information go to www.cillablack.com

John Foster And Sons Ltd. Black Dyke Mills Band

Thingumybob / Yellow Submarine
Apple-1800 (7" single) (08/26/68)
Producer: Paul McCartney

Thingumybob (J. Lennon-**P. McCartney**) 1:51 (1/1)
Paul McCartney: Conductor & Arrangement; The Black Dyke Mills Band: all instruments; Geoffrey Brand: Conductor
Victoria Hall, Bradford, Saltaire, Yorkshire, UK 06/30/68

Yellow Submarine (J. Lennon-P. McCartney) 2:56 (2/1)
Paul McCartney: Conductor & Arrangement; The Black Dyke Mills Band: all instruments; Geoffrey Brand: Conductor
The square of the Victoria Hall, Bradford, Saltaire, Yorkshire, UK 06/30/68

Paul McCartney was commissioned to write the instrumental theme for ITV's London Weekend Television comedy series *Thingumybob*. He first turned to The George Martin* Orchestra to record it. Unsatisfied with it, McCartney produced a recording of it, and *Yellow Submarine*, using The Black Dyke Mills Band, a well-known British brass band of 39 members founded in the 1940s by the Yorkshire firm of John Foster and Sons Ltd. *Yellow Submarine* was likely chosen to tie-in with the recent release of The Beatles' animated film *Yellow Submarine*. The main conductor was Geoffrey Brand, but McCartney also helped in the conducting and arrangement of the recordings.

Thingumybob, along with The Beatles' mega-hit single *Hey Jude*, was one of the first four Apple Records, which were released concurrently, overshadowing its chances on the charts. McCartney would later employ The Black Dyke Mills Band on his album *Back To The Egg*. The Black Dyke Mills Band continues to perform. For more information go to
www.blackdykeband.co.uk

Blind Faith (Rick Grech)

Blind Faith
RSO-825 094-2 (Germany) (04/xx/86)
Producer: Blind Faith
Morgan Studio, London, UK 10/07/69

Exchange And Mart (S. Winwood-E. Clapton-G. Baker-R. Grech) 4:15 (7)
George Harrison: (possible) Guitar; Eric Clapton: Guitar; Alan White: Drums; Rick Grech: Violin & Bass; Steve Winwood: Mandolin

Spending All My Days (S. Winwood-E. Clapton-G. Baker-R. Grech) 3:00 (8)
George Harrison: (possible) Guitar; Rick Grech: Lead Vocals & Bass; Eric Clapton: Guitar; Alan White: Drums; (probable) Steve Winwood: Keyboards

Blind Faith was formed in early 1969. It was rumored that George Harrison was asked to join the group. The name was chosen because of all the hype they received before their debut. Members were Eric Clapton*, vocalist and keyboardists Steve Winwood, born on May 12, 1948 in Birmingham, England, drummer Ginger Baker (see Cream), and bassist Rick Grech, born on November 1, 1946 in Bordeaux, France. Grech first gained notice in the group Family. Winwood gained fame in The Spencer Davis Group and later in the band Traffic (see Dave Mason, Jim Capaldi*). During one of Traffic's many respites, Winwood joined Blind Faith. Though there was no official announcement, Blind Faith, unable to forge an identity with a public longing to hear Cream and Traffic songs, fell apart following their US tour in August 1969.

Clapton started working with Blind Faith's opening act Delaney & Bonnie & Friends*. Baker formed the short-lived group Ginger Baker's Air Force, which included, among others, Denny Laine*, Grech and Winwood. Winwood's solo recordings turned into Traffic's album *John Barleycorn Must Die*. In October 1969 Grech began recording a solo album. Harrison, along with members of Blind Faith, was reported to have taken part in the sessions. Harrison supposedly produced several tracks for Grech in 1971. A collection of Grech's odds and ends, including his work with other groups, titled *The Last Five Years* (RSO-9 SO 876) was released in 1973. It isn't known if Harrison contributed to the album. The song *Hey Mr. Policeman* includes Harrison-styled guitar work and the song *Face In The Clouds* features a lead sitar.

Steve Winwood and Kristofer Engelhardt, Midland Center For The Arts, Midland, MI June 29, 2005. Photo by Scott Baker, © Kristofer Engelhardt.

The 1986 German CD release of the *Blind Faith* album contains the previously unreleased jams *Exchange And Mart* and *Spending All My Days* credited as being produced by Blind Faith and recorded on October 7, 1969. According to Mark Roberty's book, Eric *Clapton The Complete Recording Sessions, 1963 – 1992*, they are from Grech's solo album sessions and include Harrison on guitar. Winwood and Alan White confirmed that they play on the recordings and that they're from the Grech sessions. However, they don't recall if Harrison was involved. Roberty also lists Baker, Clapton, Trevor Burton, Capaldi, Chris Wood and Graham Bond taking part in the sessions though it's unclear if he's referring to these two tracks. Denny Laine was also reported to be involved in these sessions. It is surprising that Roberty lists White on drums but doesn't list who plays mandolin or keyboards (Winwood). This seems odd as the CD lists Winwood, Clapton, Baker and Grech as the composers. It would be logical for the composers of these two loose "jams" to play their respective instruments, and would qualify them as Blind Faith recordings.

Grech later joined Winwood in a reformed Traffic but left in late 1971. He was a member of The Crickets* for two years before joining the band KGB in 1975. On September 14, 1979 Grech, along with a host of other rock dignitaries, took part in the grand finale of Paul McCartney's annual *Buddy Holly Week* celebration at London's Hammersmith Odeon. Rick Grech died on March 17, 1990. Winwood contributed to the 1979 album *George Harrison*, and to the song *Flying Hour* available only with the 1988 limited edition book *Songs By George Harrison* (Genesis Publications). Winwood's 1986 album, *Back In The High Life*, was certified Multi-Platinum and included the number one hit *Higher Love*. For more information go to www.stevewinwood.com, www.ginger-baker.com

Colonel Doug Bogie

Cokey Cokey / Away In A Manger
Ring O'-2017 104 (7" single) (UK) (11/21/75)
Producer: Doug Bogie

Away In A Manger (trad. Arr: D. Bogie) 3:54 (2/1)
Ringo Starr: (possible) Drums; Colonel Doug Bogie: Lead Vocals; Eric Clapton: (possible) Guitar
xx/xx/75

The mysterious Colonel Doug Bogie was reported to be one of Ringo Starr's favorite performers and was signed to Ring O'Records. A variety of sources have long claimed that Ringo plays drums on *Away In A Manger*. However, there is no official credit of him playing on it or the single's A-side *Cokey Cokey*. The single also supposedly features Eric Clapton* on guitar, further bolstering the possibility of Ringo contributing to the single. Listening to this single could easily lead one to believe that Clapton and Ringo contributed to at least *Away In A Manger*. The single was also available in the US (ABC-12148). Some at ABC erroneously claimed that the Colonel was Ringo under a pseudonym.

The Bonzo Dog Band

The Bonzo Dog Band Cornology Vol. 2 - The Outro
EMI-0777 7 99597 2 2 (CZ 500) (UK) (06/22/92)
Producer: Paul McCartney & Gus Dudgeon
Paul McCartney: Ukulele; Neil Innes: Lead Vocals; probably the following: Roger Ruskin Spear: Saxophone, Kazoos, Jew's Harp & Models; Rodney Slater: Reeds & Trumpet; Vivian Stanshall: Tuba & Tube Percussion; "Leg's" Larry Smith: Drums; Vernon Dudley Bohay-Nowell: Banjo; Martin "Sam Spoons" Stafford: Tambourine; Dennis Cowan: Bass
Chappell Studios, London, UK 07/xx/68

I'm The Urban Spaceman (N. Innes) 2:22 (6) (10/11/68)

The Bonzo Dog Band (a.k.a. The Bonzo Dog Dada Band, The Bonzo Dog Doo Dah Band) was a loose consortium of British born poets, musicians and comedians that formed in the early 1960s. The members were Vivian Stanshall, born on March 21, 1943 in Shillingford; Neil Innes, born on December 9, 1944 in Danbury; Rodney Slater, born on November 8, 1941 in Lincolnshire; Roger Ruskin Spear, born on June 29, 1943 in London and "Legs" Larry Smith*. Some of the

Neil Innes and Kristofer Engelhardt, The Fest For Beatles Fans, Hotel O'Hare, Rosemont (Chicago), IL, August 16, 2008. Photo by Kim "Howard" Johnson, © Kristofer Engelhardt.

other members included Bob Kerr, Martin "Sam Spoons" Ash, born on February 8, 1942 in Bridgewater; Dennis Cowan, born on May 6, 1947 in London and Vernon Dudley Bohay-Nowell.

Larry Smith recalls, "We'd bump into The Beatles at Abbey Road Studios where The Bonzo's initially recorded. We were massive fans. Being a comedy troupe we were friends with The Scaffold*, which included Paul McCartney's brother Mike. Paul wanted to have a band backing a stripper in The Beatles' *Magical Mystery Tour* TV special and we were suggested, which is how I first met George and The Beatles. We mimed to our song *Death Cab For Cutie* in the film." They attended the film's post-production party at the Royal Lancaster Hotel on December 21, 1967 and jammed with The Beatles on such songs as *Lawdy Miss Clawdy* and *Long Tall Sally*. Smith says, "We had George, Paul and The Beach Boys* onstage jamming while John was in the audience shouting obscenities."

In 1968 Paul McCartney helped produce (under the alias Apollo C. Vermouth) and played on The Bonzo Dog Band's song *I'm The Urban Spaceman*. Smith remembers, "We were a little apprehensive at first, to say the least, but then Paul said, 'Hey guys, this is what I did last night,' and proceeded to play *Hey Jude* on the piano. He was very hands-on producing our recording in about three hours because we were more than willing to let him have his way. He wanted my drumming to be like Ringo's, and be simple because he played ukulele on it. We adored him for producing and playing on what was a great session. However our producer Gus Dudgeon took some hell the next day from Chappell Studio's somber, white-coated technicians who'd heard we put water in the euphonium for sound effects. As a result, we were banned from their studio." The song was their only UK Top 10 hit. The Bonzo's broke up in 1970, but with reshuffled membership regrouped briefly in 1972 before they drifted into other projects. Despite rumors, Innes and Smith don't think any of The Beatles contributed to any of The Bonzo Dog Band's related or solo recordings. Innes became a member of Grimms in 1973, which included Stanshall and Mike McGear*.

By the mid-1970, George Harrison had become good friends with Smith, Innes, and Eric Idle and Michael Palin of Monty Python*. Innes appears in Harrison's music video for *Crackerbox Palace* and Harrison appeared on Innes and Idle's BBC TV comedy series

Rutland Weekend Television. An outgrowth of *Rutland Weekend Television* was the band The Rutles, a parody of The Beatles. The Rutles made their US TV debut on *Saturday Night Live*, which had previously featured Harrison and members of Monty Python. The show's producer, Lorne Michaels agreed to produce the TV documentary *All You Need Is Cash* on the history of The Rutles. Harrison furnished a mid-1970s, unreleased version of *The Beatles Anthology* film tentatively titled *The Long And Winding Road* as a reference guide. The parody stars Innes as "Ron Nasty" (John Lennon), Idle as "Dirk McQuickly" (Paul McCartney), John Halsey as "Barry Wom" (Ringo Starr) and Rikki (a.k.a. Ricky) Fataar as "Stig O'Hara" (George Harrison). The parody features a cameo of Harrison interviewing Michael Palin who plays The Rutles' press officer "Eric Manchester" (Derek Taylor). It also features cameos by Bill Murray, Roger McGough*, Ron Wood*, Mick Jagger* and Paul Simon*. The documentary includes music parodies from such Rutles albums as *Meet The Rutles*, *Tragical History Tour*, *Sgt. Rutters* and *Let It Rot*. Harrison was delighted with the results as reportedly was Lennon, though Starr and especially McCartney were supposedly less amused at the time. *All You Need Is Cash* first aired on March 22, 1978 and was issued in 2001 on DVD (Rhino-R2 976641). Contrary to rumors, Innes says "George didn't contribute to any of The Rutles recordings in any way, but he was very supportive throughout the project."

Vivian Stanshall died on March 5, 1995. McCartney gave tribute to Viv in the press and in his *Club Sandwich* fan club magazine. McCartney featured the music of The Bonzo Dog Band on his 1995 radio series *Oobu Joobu*. Innes has been a frequent guest at conventions and festivals for fans of The Beatles. The Bonzo Dog Band reformed in 2006 around most of their core members. For more information go to www.bonzodog.co.uk, www.gingergeezer.net, www.neilinnes.org, www.threebonzosandapiano.co.uk

David Bowie

Fame '90
Rykodisc-RCD5 1018 (03/26/90)
Producer: David Bowie & Harry Maslin
John Lennon: Guitar & B. Vocals; David Bowie: Lead Vocals & Guitar; Earl Slick: Guitar; Carlos Alomar: Guitar; Emir Kassam: Bass; Willie Weeks: Bass; Dennis Davis: Drums; Andy Newmark: Drums; Ralph McDonald: Percussion; Pablo Rosario: Percussion; Larry Washington: Percussion; Jean Fineberg: B. Vocals; Jean Millington: B. Vocals
Electric Ladyland Studios, New York, NY 01/xx/75

Fame '90 (Absolutely Nothing Premeditated/ Epic Mix) (D. Bowie-**J. Lennon**-C. Alomar) 14:25 (2-5)
Remixed by: Dave Barratt xx/xx/90

Fame '90 (Gass Mix) (D. Bowie-**J. Lennon**-C. Alomar) 3:39 (2-3)
Remixed by: Jon Gass xx/xx/90

Fame '90 (Hip Hop Mix) (D. Bowie-**J. Lennon**-C. Alomar) 5:59 (2-4)
Remixed by: Arthur Baker xx/xx/90

Fame '90 (House Mix) (D. Bowie-**J. Lennon**-C. Alomar) 5:58 (2-2)
Remixed by: Arthur Baker xx/xx/90

Fame '90 (with Queen Latifah) (D. Bowie-**J. Lennon**-C. Alomar) 4:08 (2-1)
Remixed by: D.J. Mark The 45 King xx/xx/90

Fame '90
EMI-USA-SPRO-04547/04532 (single 12" promotional only) (xx/xx/90)
Producer: David Bowie & Harry Maslin
John Lennon: Guitar & B. Vocals; David Bowie: Lead Vocals & Guitar; Earl Slick: Guitar; Carlos Alomar: Guitar; Emir Kassam: Bass; Willie Weeks: Bass; Dennis Davis: Drums; Andy Newmark: Drums; Ralph McDonald: Percussion; Pablo Rosario: Percussion; Larry Washington: Percussion; Jean Fineberg: B. Vocals; Jean Millington: B. Vocals
Electric Ladyland Studios, New York, NY 01/xx/75

Fame '90 (Acapulco Rap) (D. Bowie-**J. Lennon**-C. Alomar) 1:04 (2-3)
Remixed by: D.J. Mark The 45 King xx/xx/90

Fame '90 (Bonus-Beats Instrumental a.k.a. Bonus Beat Mix) (D. Bowie-**J. Lennon**-C. Alomar) 4:41 (2-2)
Remixed by: D.J. Mark The 45 King xx/xx/90

Fame '90 (Queen Latifah's Rap Version) (D. Bowie-**J. Lennon**-C. Alomar) 4:24 (2-1)
Remixed by: Ron Fair xx/xx/90

Hip Hop Roots
Tommy Boy-TBAD-81625 (08/23/05)
Producer: David Bowie & Harry Maslin
John Lennon: Guitar & B. Vocals; David Bowie: Lead Vocals & Guitar; Earl Slick: Guitar; Carlos Alomar: Guitar; Emir Kassam: Bass; Willie Weeks: Bass; Dennis Davis: Drums; Andy Newmark: Drums; Ralph McDonald: Percussion; Pablo Rosario: Percussion; Larry Washington: Percussion; Jean Fineberg: B. Vocals; Jean Millington: B. Vocals
Electric Ladyland Studios, New York, NY 01/xx/75

Fame (D. Bowie-**J. Lennon**-C. Alomar) 4:49 (5)
Extended Edit by: Jazzy Jay xx/xx/95

Young Americans
Rykodisc-RCD 10140 (05/14/91) (03/10/75)
Producer: David Bowie & Harry Maslin
Electric Ladyland Studios, New York, NY 01/xx/75

Across The Universe (J. Lennon-P. McCartney) 4:30 (1-6)
John Lennon: Guitar; David Bowie: Lead Vocals & Guitar; Earl Slick: Guitar; Carlos Alomar: Guitar; Emir Kassam: Bass; Willie Weeks: Bass; Dennis Davis: Drums; Andy Newmark: Drums

Fame (D. Bowie-**J. Lennon**-C. Alomar) 4:12 (1-8) (03/10/75)
John Lennon: Guitar & B. Vocals; David Bowie: Lead Vocals & Guitar; Earl Slick: Guitar; Carlos Alomar: Guitar; Emir Kassam: Bass; Willie Weeks: Bass; Dennis Davis: Drums; Andy Newmark: Drums; Ralph McDonald: Percussion; Pablo Rosario: Percussion; Larry Washington: Percussion; Jean Fineberg: B. Vocals; Jean Millington: B. Vocals

David Bowie was born David Jones on January 8, 1947 in London, England. He later adopted the name Bowie (after the knife) so as not to be confused with actor Davy Jones (later of the group The Monkees). David started playing guitar and saxophone as a young teen. He first worked as a commercial artist before fronting a number of unsuccessful pop groups in the mid-1960s. He also pursued a career in acting, which later helped him create stage characters such as Ziggy Stardust and the Thin White Duke, establishing himself as a glitter rock star and pioneer of rock androgyny. Bowie had a great deal of difficulty getting his musical career started and reportedly was rejected by Paul McCartney for Apple.

Bowie's audience grew steadily throughout the 1970s and '80s as he continued to experiment with his personae and musical styles. His many memorable hits include *Changes*, *The Jean Genie*, *Golden Years*, *Let's Dance*, *Modern Love* and *Blue Jean*. He has also successfully written and produced songs for other artists. Bowie appeared on Broadway in the leading role of *The Elephant Man* and starred in the films *The Man Who Fell To Earth*, *The Hunger* and *Labyrinth*.

Bowie and John Lennon first met at a party in Los Angeles in February 1974. By January 1975 both were residents of New York and socialized together. Bowie told Lennon he was going to record *Across The Universe*. John was never happy with The Beatles' recording of his composition and agreed to play rhythm guitar on Bowie's recording. According to May Pang, while in the studio, Lennon and guitarist Carlos Alomar composed the music to the song *Fame* while Bowie went off and composed the lyrics. Pang said Lennon's portion of the composition was inspired by the song *Shame, Shame, Shame*, a recent hit by Shirley & Company. Bowie says Alomar borrowed his riff from The Flares' song *Foot Stompin'*. Lennon also sings backing vocals and plays guitar on *Fame*. A recording of *Let's Twist Again* on unauthorized records claiming to be Lennon and Bowie is evidently false. Bowie omitted two songs from his just completed *Young Americans* album to include the two songs to which Lennon contributed. Earl Slick and Andy Newmark (who has worked with George Harrison) who also played on the sessions worked with Lennon in 1980 for his albums *Double Fantasy* and *Milk And Honey*.

When *Fame*, Bowie's first number one hit, was initially issued in 1975, it incorrectly listed L. Andross (it's Luther Vandross), instead of Carlos Alomar, along with Bowie and Lennon as the song's composers. All issues since 1978 have corrected the mistake. In 1990 a number of remixes of *Fame*, re-titled *Fame '90*, were made to promote the re-mastering of Bowie's recordings and his tour. Since that time other remixes have been released, some only available on promotional cassettes or CD-Rs including *Fame (Humberto Gatics Sonic Mix)*, longer versions of *Fame (Gass Mix)* and *Fame '90 (Absolutely Nothing Premeditated/Epic Mix)*, *Fame (Go Home Productions Remix)* and a version with an alternate ending and overdubbed flutes included on the unauthorised release *20th Century Boy* (BOW-0198/DB20CB). All the remixed versions contain some portion of the original recording featuring

Lennon. One of the remixes was used for a video for *Fame* included on the 1991 video release *The World's Greatest Artists Sing LENNON A Tribute*. Bowie has recorded covers of several Lennon compositions.

McCartney played acoustic guitar during Bowie and Mick Jagger's* performance of their duet hit *Dancing In The Street* at *The Prince's Trust 10th Anniversary Concert* at London's Wembley Arena on June 20, 1986. Bowie was inducted into the Rock and Roll Hall of Fame in 1996. In 1997 he edged past McCartney as Britain's richest musician in *Business Age* magazine's rankings. Bowie has been less active in recent years. For more information go to www.davidbowie.com

Delaney Bramlett

Delaney & Friends-Class Reunion
Prodigal-P6-10017S1 (album 12") (xx/xx/77)
Producer: Ray Ruff & Jimmy Bowen
Ringo Starr: Drums; Delaney Bramlett: Lead Vocals; Jim Keltner: Drums; additionally, one or more of the following: Spider Taylor: Lead Guitar; Randy Sharp: Guitar; Chuck Rainey: Bass; Chris Etheridge: Bass; Rick Sutherland: Keyboards; Jim Hobson: Keyboards; Stu Perry: Drums; Sidney Sharp: Strings; Samuel Boghossian: Strings; Harry Hyams: Strings; Ronald Folsom: Strings; Murray Adler: Strings; James Getzoff: Strings; David D. Turner: Strings; Jesse Ehrlich: Strings; Raymond Kelley: Strings; William Kurasch: Strings; Chuck Findley: Horns; Ollie Mitchell: Horns; Jackie Kelso: Horns; Slyde Hyde: Horns; Quitman Dennis: Horns; Clydie King: B. Vocals; Sherlie Matthews: B. Vocals; Monalisa Young: B. Vocals; Susie Allanson: B. Vocals; Pat Erickson: B. Vocals; Patti Quatro: B. Vocals
Gold Star Recording Studio, Los Angeles, CA xx/xx/77 [unless noted otherwise]

For Old Time's Sake (R. Sharp) 3:02 (2/3)
Heritage Recording Studio, Los Angeles, CA xx/xx/77

I Think I Got It (D. Bramlett) 3:12 (2/1)

I Wish It Would Rain (N. Whitfield-B. Strong-R. Penzabene) 2:58 (1/3)

Locked Up In Alabama (D. Bramlett) 4:30 (1/1)

You Were The Light (R. Sharp) 3:17 (2/5)
Heritage Recording Studio, Los Angeles, CA xx/xx/77

We Can't Be Seen Together / We Can't Be Seen Together
Columbia-4-45781 (7" single) (probably promotional only) (xx/xx/73)
Producer: Delaney Bramlett & Doug Gilmore
Delaney Bramlett: Lead Vocals & Guitar; Tim Hedding: Keyboards; Larry Savola: Trombone; Jerry Jumonville: Saxophone; Darrell Leonard: Trumpet; Ron Grayson: Drums; Robert Wilson: Bass
United Western Studios, Los Angeles, CA probably xx/xx/73

We Can't Be Seen Together (**[G. Harrison]**-D. Bramlett-D. Gilmore) 2:27 (1/1)

Delaney Bramlett was born on July 1, 1939 in Pontotoc, Mississippi. He first tasted success in the mid-1960s as a member of the Shindogs, the house band on ABC TV's *Shindig*, on which The Beatles appeared. He married singer Bonnie O'Farrell with whom he formed the group Delaney & Bonnie & Friends*. He released several albums on Columbia Records following the breakup of his marriage and musical act with Bonnie in 1972. According to Delaney and Bonnie, his 1973 Columbia single *We Can't Be Seen Together* was written with George Harrison around the time George toured with them in 1969. Delaney says he didn't credit Harrison on it because he felt Harrison should have credited him for helping write *My Sweet Lord*.

Album liner notes of *Delaney & Friends-Class Reunion* state in part, "There comes a time in every artist's life when he wants to say 'thank you' to those who have helped on this album, past albums, jam sessions, concerts, and who have 'just been my friends.' THANK YOU. Ringo Starr, George Harrison, Paul McCartney, John Lennon." Many artists who worked with The Beatles are also thanked in the list of almost 300 people. None of The Beatles are listed in the specific musical credited of the album but according to Delaney, Ringo played drums on five songs on the album and four other songs from the sessions that remain unreleased including one titled *When This Day Ends*. Delaney died on December 27, 2008. For more information go to www.delaneybramlett.com

David Bromberg

David Bromberg
Sony-SRCS 6284 (Japan) (06/30/98) (02/16/72)
Producer: David Bromberg
George Harrison: Slide Guitar; David Bromberg: Lead Vocals & Acoustic Guitar; David Nichterne: Piano; Jody Stecher: Mandolin; David Amram: French Horn; Willow Scarlett: Harmonica; Steve Burgh: Bass; Steve Mosley: Drums
World Control Headquarters, Philadelphia, PA & Columbia Studios, New York, NY xx/xx/70 or xx/xx/71

The Holdup [live-version one] (G. Harrison-D. Bromberg) 3:00 (8)

David Bromberg was born September 19, 1945, in Philadelphia, Pennsylvania. He has dedicated much of his life to collecting, making, repairing and expertly playing violins, mandolins, banjos and guitars. He spent his formative years involved in New York's Greenwich Village folk music scene. The critically acclaimed Bromberg has worked as a producer and session player with many famous musicians including Bob Dylan*.

George Harrison was on business in the New York area in late 1970 when he and Bromberg met and wrote *The Holdup*. David says, "It was written with George in about a half-hour. It just came out of us. It was recorded live in Philadelphia, and George overdubbed the slide guitar part at a church in New York — Columbia's largest studio. George isn't credited but everyone else is." Bromberg and Harrison appeared on TV's *The David Frost Show* on December 3, 1971 performing *The Holdup*. Bromberg later recorded another version of *The Holdup*, without Harrison, for his album *Wanted Dead Or Alive*.

David contributed to Ringo Starr's album *Ringo* in 1973 and to his 1977 album *Ringo The 4th*. David Bromberg continues working with stringed instruments and still occasionally performs and records. For more information go to www.davidbromberg.net

Gary Brooker

The Best Of Ringo Starr And His All-Starr Band...So Far
Image-ID0828RO (DVD) (10/23/01)
Producer: Michael Drumm; David & Ryan Hewitt (music mixers); Peter Skorich (video); Executive Producer: Ringo Starr & David Fishof
Ringo Starr: Drums; Gary Brooker: Lead Vocals & Keyboards; Jack Bruce: Bass; Peter Frampton: Guitar; Simon Kirke: Drums; Mark Rivera: Keyboards
Pine Knob Music Theater, Clarkston (Detroit), MI 05/30/97

A Whiter Shade Of Pale [live] (G. Brooker-K. Reid-M. Fisher) 5:23 (18) (07/28/98)
[Also available on *Ringo Starr And His All Starr Band The Anthology...So Far*. Koch-KOC-CD-8312 (3-12) (07/24/01) (02/05/01)]

Lead Me To The Water
Line-LICD 9.00015 0 (Germany) (xx/xx/87) (03/01/82)
Producer: Gary Brooker
The Farm Studios, Surrey, UK xx/xx/82

The Cycle (G. Brooker) 3:20 (5)
George Harrison: B. Vocals; Gary Brooker: Lead Vocals & Keyboards; Phil Collins: Drums & B. Vocals; Tim Renwick: Guitar; Dave Markee: Bass; Phil Aaberg: Keyboards

Mineral Man (G. Brooker) 3:19 (1)
George Harrison: Guitar; Gary Brooker: Lead Vocals & Keyboards; Phil Collins: Drums; Eric Clapton: Guitar; Albert Lee: Guitar; Peter Maunu: Guitar; Tim Renwick: Guitar; Dave Markee: Bass; Mel Collins: Saxophones; Kent Middleton: Percussion

Ringo Starr And His All-Starr Band: A Stary Night In Russia
(DVD-R) [unauthorized release] (xx/xx/99)
Ringo Starr: Drums; Gary Brooker: Lead Vocals & Keyboards; Jack Bruce: Bass; Peter Frampton: Guitar; Simon Kirke: Drums; Mark Rivera: Percussion
Concert Hall, Moscow, Russia 08/25/98

Whisky Train [live] (R.Trower-K. Reid) 5:14 (3)

Ringo Starr And His Fourth All-Starr Band
MPI-MP7292 (VHS) (07/28/98)

Producer: David & Ryan Hewitt (music mixers); Peter Skorich (video); Executive Producer: Ringo Starr & David Fishof
Ringo Starr: Drums; Gary Brooker: Lead Vocals & Keyboards; Jack Bruce: Bass & B. Vocals; Peter Frampton: Guitar & B. Vocals; Simon Kirke: Drums; Mark Rivera: Percussion & B. Vocals
Pine Knob Music Theater, Clarkston (Detroit), MI 05/30/97

The Devil Came From Kansas [live] (G. Brooker-K. Reid) 4:51 (3)

Keyboardist, Gary Brooker was born on May 29, 1945 in London, England but grew up in Southend-on-Sea. Gary's first taste of success was in the early 1960's R&B band The Paramounts, which included Robin Trower. They were signed to NEMS, the same record label as The Beatles, and toured with them in December 1965.

Brooker, along with Trower, Mathew Fisher and songwriter Keith Reid, were core members of Procol Harum formed in 1967. They soon had a mega-hit with *A Whiter Shade Of Pale*, which was a favorite of The Beatles. Their only other major hit was in 1972 with an orchestrated re-recording of *Conquistador* from their debut album. In 1973 Trower pursued a successful solo career and is a noted guitarist. Procol Harum covered The Beatles' song *Eight Days A Week* in 1975 and broke up in 1977.

Gary has had a close personal and working relationship with Eric Clapton* and George Harrison. He contributed to Harrison's albums *All Things Must Pass* in 1970, *Somewhere In England* in 1981 and *Gone Troppo* in 1982. Harrison is listed as playing guitar in the general credits of Gary's 1982 album *Lead Me To The Water*. According to Gary, Harrison plays on the song *Mineral Man*, and sings backing vocals on *The Cycle*. The album also includes contributions from Steve Holly, a member of Wings when Brooker was part of the Rockestra ensemble on Wings' 1979 album *Back To The Egg* and on the 1981 album *Concerts For The People Of Kampuchea* recorded at London's Hammersmith Odeon on December 29, 1979.)

Gary contributed keyboards to Ringo's 1983 album *Old Wave*. He joined Ringo Starr's All-Starr Band tour in 1997, 1998 and 1999 performing *The Devil Came From Kansas, Conquistador*, *Whiskey Train* and *Whiter Shade Of Pale* with backing from Ringo on drums. He was a part of the Harrison tribute *Concert For George* in 2002. Gary Brooker continues to write, record and tour, sometimes under the Procol Harum and Paramounts name. He has also been involved in several projects with the London Symphony Orchestra*. For more information go to www.procolharum.com

Vicki Brown

About Love And Life
Polydor-847 266-2 (Netherlands) (09/xx/90)
Producer: Sam Brown
George Harrison: Slide Guitar†; Vicki Brown: Lead Vocals; Phil Palmer: Guitar; Ian Maidman: Bass; Tim Goldsmith: Drums; Jesse Bailey: Piano & Keyboards; Andre Hoekstra: Percussion; Joe Brown: Ukulele: Tony Palmer: Steel Drums; Chris Ballin: B. Vocals; Mario Frendo: B. Vocals; Derek Green: B. Vocals; Paul A. Lee: B. Vocals; Zetia Massiah: B. Vocals; Juliet Roberts: B. Vocals; Iris Sutherland: B. Vocals
FPSHOT†, EMI-Abbey Road Studios, London, UK & Wisseloord, Holland probably xx/xx/90

Lu Le La (N. Lancaster-C. Corbett) 4:07 (10)

Vicki Brown was born Victoria Haseman on August 23, 1940 in Liverpool, England. She was a member of the singing groups The Vernons Girls and The Breakways. The Vernons Girls were part of The Beatles' UK tour during the autumn of 1963. The group recorded the novelty song *We Love The Beatles*. Other members of the group recorded the novelty song *We Love You Beatles* under the name Carefrees. Those recordings didn't include Vicki.

Vicki married early 1960's rock guitarist Joe Brown of Joe Brown And His Bruvvers. Vicki enjoyed much success, particularly in the Netherlands where she, along with the New London Choral, had a Top Five hit with *Stay With Me 'Til The Morning* in 1986. That year she appeared as a backing vocalist in the video for Paul McCartney's song *Only Love Remains*. The following year she had a Top 20 hit in the Netherlands with *Can't Let Go*.

Joe is also no stranger to The Beatles, who opened numerous shows for him during the early '60s. The Beatles included Joe's hit *A Picture Of*

You, sung by George Harrison, in their repertoire in 1962 and performed the song during their second BBC radio appearance. Joe released a cover of *With A Little Help From My Friends* in June 1967, which was a UK Top 40 hit.

Vicki and Joe were Harrison's neighbors and contributed to his 1982 album *Gone Troppo*. Vicki sang duet vocals with Harrison on the theme song for the film *Shanghai Surprise* (see Various Artists-Shanghai Surprise). A video of the two recording it appears on the DVD included with *George Harrison The Dark Horse Years 1976-1992*. Harrison, who was greatly influenced by Joe's ukulele playing, wrote the foreword for Joe's 1986 autobiography *Brown Sauce: The Life And Times Of Joe Brown*. Joe joined Harrison and Carl Perkins* for a musical jam at HandMade Films' 10th Anniversary celebration in October 1988. Harrison contributed slide guitar to the song *Lu Le La* from Vicki's 1990 album, *About Love And Life*. The couple's daughter Sam, who produced the recording, has also had a successful recording career. Vicki died on June 16, 1991. In 1992 Harrison appeared in a musical sequence in the documentary *Mister Roadrunner* playing ukulele on the song *Between The Devil And The Deep Blue Sea*, with a backup band that included Joe Brown, Jools Holland and others (later included on Harrison's 2002 album *Brainwashed*, to which Sam also contributed). That year Harrison announced plans to work with Joe on some recordings but nothing has ever surfaced. Joe's manager John Taylor says, "Joe, George and I would play songs together at parties and such, but nothing of Joe's with George was recorded that I'm aware of." Joe and Sam took part in the Harrison tribute *Concert For George* in 2002.

Jack Bruce

The Best Of Ringo Starr And His All-Starr Band...So Far
Image-ID0828RO (DVD) (10/23/01)
Producer: Michael Drumm; David & Ryan Hewitt (music mixers); Peter Skorich (video); Executive Producer: Ringo Starr & David Fishof
Ringo Starr: Drums; Jack Bruce: Lead Vocals & Bass; Peter Frampton: Guitar & B. Vocals; Simon Kirke: Drums
Pine Knob Music Theater, Clarkston (Detroit), MI 05/30/97

Sunshine Of Your Love [live] (J. Bruce-P. Brown-E. Clapton) 7:34 (16) (07/28/98)
[Also available on *Ringo Starr And His All Starr Band The Anthology...So Far*. Koch-KOC-CD-8312 (3-3) (07/24/01) (02/05/01)]

Songs For A Tailor
Polydor-835 242-2 (06/xx/88) (08/29/69)
Producer: Felix Pappalardi
George Harrison: Guitar; Jack Bruce: Lead Vocals, Piano & Bass; Harry Beckett: Trumpet; Henry Lather: Trumpet; Dick Heckstall-Smith: Tenor & Soprano Saxophones; Art Theman: Tenor & Soprano Saxophones; Jon Hiseman: Drums
Morgan Studios, London, UK 05/11/69

Never Tell Your Mother She's Out Of Tune (J. Bruce-P. Brown) 3:39 (1)

Ringo Starr And His Fourth All-Starr Band
MPI-MP7292 (VHS) (07/28/98)
Producer: David & Ryan Hewitt (music mixers); Peter Skorich (video); Executive Producer: Ringo Starr & David Fishof
Ringo Starr: Drums; Jack Bruce: Lead Vocals & Bass; Peter Frampton: Guitar; Simon Kirke: Drums; Gary Brooker: Keyboards & B. Vocals; Mark Rivera: Percussion & B. Vocals
Pine Knob Music Theater, Clarkston (Detroit), MI 05/30/97

I Feel Free [live] (J. Bruce-P. Brown) 3:01 (17)
[Also available on *Ringo Starr And His All Starr Band The Anthology...So Far*. Koch-KOC-CD-8312 (3-9) (07/24/01) (02/05/01)]

White Room [live] (J. Bruce-P. Brown) 7:01 (21)
Additionally: Gary Brooker: Keyboards (only); Mark Rivera: Saxophone & Percussion (only)

John "Jack" Bruce was born on May 14, 1943 in Glasgow, Scotland into a musical family. He won a scholarship as a teenager to the Royal Scottish Academy of Music for cello and composition. The first bands of note that Bruce joined were Alexis Korner's Blues Inc., which included Charlie Watts (see The Rolling Stones), the Graham Bond Organization (a.k.a. Graham Bond Quartet, see Duffy Power), which included Ginger Baker (see Blind Faith), Manfred Mann (see Paul Jones) and John Mayall's Bluesbreakers (see Eric Clapton). However, Bruce will probably be remembered most as the songwriter and front man for the band Cream*, which included Clapton and Baker.

Following Cream's breakup, Bruce recorded his 1969 album *Songs For A Tailor*, and asked George Harrison to play on *Never Tell Your Mother She's Out Of Tune* from it because, "I was impressed with Harrison's guitar work on Cream's song *Badge*. George showed up an hour early and was quite nervous and careful to be in tune. It was done as a live track in the studio. The session was very good, very easy and a lot of fun." Bruce said Harrison used the pseudonym L'Angelo Misterioso (used for *Badge*) (see Jesse Ed Davis) to avoid royalty payments. Bruce revived the power trio concept in the 1970s with (Leslie) West, Bruce and (Corky) Laing; in the 1980s with Bill Lordan and Robin Trower in BLT; and finally in the 1990s with Gary Moore* and Bruce's old partner Ginger Baker in BBM.

Bruce was a member of Ringo Starr's All-Starr Band tour in 1997, 1998, 1999 and 2000 performing *Sunshine Of Your Love*, *I Feel Free* and *White Room* with Ringo backing him on drums. Jack recalls, "Ringo wanted me to be in his first All-Starr Band in 1989 but I wasn't available. The next time he asked me I was available and very happy to do it. We got to tour the US and Europe – places like Russia, which had recently opened up so that was very interesting. I had never worked with any of the musicians before and only really knew Ringo. Everyone was very professional. Peter Frampton* is a fantastic guitar player — incredibly underrated. Because Ringo's from Liverpool, and I'm from Glasgow, we have a similar dry sense of humor, so we're pretty funny together. I always felt sorry for Ringo and his wife Barbara because they never went out very much. While in Chicago once I said to him, 'Why don't we just go out for a walk?' He said, 'I couldn't do that. People would just start gathering around.' I said, 'Let's give it a try.' So we went out and started walking. I've walked with Mick Jagger* and other famous people, but as I was walking with Ringo a couple of people recognized him, and then more and more, and suddenly there was a huge crowd around him and he had to split. It's The Beatles' fame, which is a step above others' fame. I think it's hard for him. It's something I wouldn't want. I learned a lot from Ringo. I learned about dealing with an audience. I used to take myself a bit too seriously and he helped me to realize that in the end we're just entertainers. I enjoyed the tours because things always went smoothly. It was easy going — more like fun. It was nice to be a sideman for a change because there wasn't all the pressure on me. Ringo's talent is much maligned – he's a great drummer! He is one of the very few, apart from Ginger Baker, who is able to get the feel of *I Feel Free*, which is a very challenging drum part because it's somewhere between a rock and jazz feel. I asked Ginger to come to our Denver, Colorado show in 1997. I introduced him as a young member of the Denver Fire Department because he was a volunteer fireman there at the time. He played drums on *White Room* and I think *I Feel Free*." Bruce was part of *A Walk Down Abbey Road: A Tribute To The Beatles* tour in 2002. Jack Bruce continues to tour and collaborate with well-known musicians. For more information go to www.jackbruce.com

Brute Force

Extemporaneous
Rev-Ola-CR-REV 36 (UK) (04/19/04)
Producer: The Tokens (Phil Margo, Mitch Margo, Hank Medress & Jay Siegel) & [Stephen Friedland]; **[Re-produced by: George Harrison]†**
Stephen Friedland: Lead Vocals, Keyboards & Mellotron; Phil Margo: Drums; Mitch Margo: Bass; Royal Philharmonic Orchestra†; John Barham: String Arrangement†
Olmsted Studios, New York, NY probably spring/xx/68 & Trident Studios, London, UK probably 12/xx/68 & 01/xx/69†

King Of Fuh (Brute Force) 3:04 (18) (05/16/69)

Brute Force was born Stephen Friedland on September 29, 1940 in Jersey City, New Jersey. In 1964, Friedland joined The Tokens, of *The Lion Sleeps Tonight* fame, playing keyboard and guitar. He became known professionally as Brute Force. His attempt to swim the Bering Strait was chronicled in the September 20, 1968 issue of *Life* magazine. Around this time he, along with The Tokens, recorded a song he wrote about a land called Fuh and its king. Friedland recalls, "The song was inspired by a poem I had written in '67 about a furry king who went where he wanted to go and did what he wanted to do. Furry king led to 'fuh' king, which I turned around to *King Of Fuh*, and weaved those words into a song that's really about individuality and beauty — a song that explores language taboo."

Friedland was a friend Tom Dawes from the group The Cyrkle (the name and spelling adopted at the suggestion of John Lennon) who was signed to NEMS and toured America with The Beatles in 1966. Friedland gave Dawes a tape of *King Of Fuh* who in turn gave it to Nat Weiss a close friend and business associate of Epstein's and The Beatles. George Harrison heard the song at Weiss's apartment in New York in November 1968. Harrison soon went to work refining the recording. Friedland received a letter from Mal Evans explaining that Harrison had remixed *King Of Fuh* and added a string section provided by the Royal Philharmonic Orchestra. Evans also recounted how amused the orchestra members were by the song. Friedland says, "I think Harrison re-did the bass. He may have kicked up the percussion a bit too. He made it prettier by changing the melodic line of the strings; really a super mix."

Apple planned to release it as a single on February 14, 1969 but when management at EMI, who were responsible for pressing and distributing Apple, heard the lyrics to *King Of Fuh* (the story of a "Fuh King") they wanted nothing to do with it. Apple had a limited number of records pressed elsewhere and distributed it themselves primarily as a mail order item. Though promotional copies were distributed by Apple in England, the clever but profane song could never receive airplay. *King Of Fuh* was released on CD in 2004. Brute has also written the musical *The Fuh King Thing* based upon *King Of Fuh.*

Ironically, Friedland was also a staff writer for Bright Tunes Music Corp (see Delaney & Bonnie & Friends), which was owned by The Tokens. Friedland wrote The Chiffons' Top 40 hit *Nobody Knows What's Goin' On (In My Mind But Me).* His version was used for the B-side of Apple's *King Of Fuh* single but he doubts Harrison did anything to *Nobody Knows.*

Friedland is now primarily a variety entertainer incorporating his talents as comedian, musician and songwriter. He has appeared on TV and in a number of films including *Ghostbusters* and *Sea Of Love.* For more information go to www.brutesforce.com

Eric Burdon & Billy Preston

Steal This Movie (Music From The Motion Picture)
Artemis Records-751038-2 (07/25/00)
Producer: Mark Hudson
Ringo Starr: Drums & B. Vocals; Eric Burdon: Lead Vocals; Billy Preston: Lead Vocals & Keyboards; Jim Cox: Keyboards; Pat Zicari: Saxophone; Mark Hudson: Percussion & B. Vocals; Scott Gordon: Percussion; Sarah Hudson: B. Vocals; Marc Fantini: B. Vocals; Steffan Fantini: B. Vocals; Christina Rasch: B. Vocals
Shovelhole Studios, Santa Monica, CA probably 04/xx/00

Power To The People (J. Lennon) 3:22 (8)

Eric Burdon was born May 11, 1941 in Newcastle-upon-Tyne, England. Burdon is a founding member and lead vocalist of the blues-rock band The Animals who formed in 1962. They were part of the British music invasion in 1964. Between 1964 and 1966 they had a number one hit with *House Of The Rising Sun*, a Top 10 hit with *See See Rider*, and the Top 20 hits *I'm Crying, Don't Let Me Be Misunderstood, We Gotta Get Out Of This Place* and *Don't Bring Me Down.* By 1967 Burdon was the only original member and renamed the group Eric Burdon and The Animals (a.k.a. The New Animals). They adopted a more contemporary, psychedelic sound, and scored a Top 10 hit with *San Francisco Nights*, and Top 20 hits with *Monterey* and *When I Was Young.* Their last Top 20 hit was *Sky Pilot (Part 1)* in 1968. In 1970 Burdon joined forces with the band War with whom he had the Top Five hit *Spill The Wine*, which was his last chart success. He continued to record and tour as The Eric Burdon Band for a number of years and attempted a few reunions with original members of The Animals in the early '80's.

Eric and Billy Preston* sang vocals on a new recording of John Lennon's song *Power To The People* with Ringo on drums. It was included on the soundtrack album *Steal This Movie* about political activist Abbie Hoffman. Eric says, "The producers called and asked me if I'd put my voice on the track. I went to the studio in Los Angeles and did my part. The only person there was the engineer. Ringo and Billy Preston weren't there. I didn't even know they were on the track!" Ringo's contribution was almost certainly the result of his close working relationship with the recording's producer, Mark Hudson*. Burdon continues to record and tour with a new band of Animals. www.ericburdon.com

Lori Burton (and Patrick Jude*)

Beatles Undercover
C.G. Publishing-CGPINT8008 (Canada) (09/07/98)
Producer: John Lennon & Roy Cicala
Record Plant Studios, New York, NY probably 01/xx/75 [unless noted otherwise]

Answer Me, My Love (C. Sigman-G. Winkler-F. Rauch) 2:47 (3)
John Lennon: (probable) Arrangement; Lori Burton: Lead Vocals; probably one or more of the following: Patrick Jude: Percussion; Mark Rivera: Saxophone; John Corbert: Keyboards; Vinnie Appice: Drums; Daniel Elfassy: Drums; Joe Bassin: Trombone; Bob Livingood: Trumpet; Rick: Bass; Kenny Papa; Kenny Sambolin
Record Plant Studios, New York, NY 01/13/75

Let's Spend The Night Together* (M. Jagger-K. Richard) 3:14 (2)
John Lennon: (probable) Arrangement; Lori Burton: Lead Vocals; Patrick Jude: Lead Vocals & (probable) Percussion; probably one or more of the following: Mark Rivera: Saxophone; John Corbert: Keyboards; Vinnie Appice: Drums; Daniel Elfassy: Drums; Joe Bassin: Trombone; Bob Livingood: Trumpet; Rick: Bass; Kenny Papa; Kenny Sambolin

[None]
[Unreleased]
Producer: John Lennon & Roy Cicala
Lori Burton: Lead Vocals; probably one or more of the following: Patrick Jude: Percussion; Mark Rivera: Saxophone; John Corbert: Keyboards; Vinnie Appice: Drums; Daniel Elfassy: Drums; Joe Bassin: Trombone; Bob Livingood: Trumpet; Rick: Bass; Kenny Papa; Kenny Sambolin

The Big Hurt (W. Shanklin)

[None]
[Unreleased]
Producer: John Lennon & Roy Cicala
Lori Burton: Lead Vocals; probably one or more of the following: Patrick Jude: Percussion; Mark Rivera: Saxophone; John Corbert: Keyboards; Vinnie Appice: Drums; Daniel Elfassy: Drums; Joe Bassin: Trombone; Bob Livingood: Trumpet; Rick: Bass; Kenny Papa; Kenny Sambolin
Record Plant Studios, New York, NY probably 01/xx/75 or possibly (mid-to late)/xx/74

Incantation (R. Cicala-**J. Lennon**)

Lori Burton was born Dolores Squeglia on September 30, 1940 in New Haven, Connecticut. She began singing with her father's band, the Jimmy Nichols Orchestra, at an early age and within a few years was singing in nightclubs and writing songs. Lori married recording engineer Roy Cicala. She signed to Morris Levy's Roulette Records in 1964, took the stage name Lori Burton and began writing songs with Pam Sawyer. In 1965 their compositions *Ain't Gonna Eat Out My Heart Anymore* by The (Young) Rascals (see Felix Cavaliere) (later covered by Michael Jackson*) and Patti Labelle & The Blue Bells' *All Or Nothing* were on the charts. Lori and Pam also wrote the 1966 hit *Forget About Me* by Prince Harold. The two were writers for Motown Records in the mid-1960s. Lori's album *Breakout* was released by Mercury Records in 1967. In 1969 Lori and Roy produced a cover of The Box Tops' 1967 hit *The Letter* for The Arbors, which became a Top 20 hit.

By the early 1970's Roy was one of the music industry's top engineers and owner of The Record Plant Studios in New York. Well-known studio guitarist Hugh McCracken says, "He's probably the best mixer on the planet!" Under Roy's tutelage, Record Plant fostered some of today's top producers and engineers, including Jack Douglas, Jimmy Iovine, Jimmy Ienner and Shelly Yakus. In the summer of 1971 Roy helped engineer overdubs for John Lennon's album *Imagine*. It was the beginning of a long personal and professional relationship that included Roy's work on Lennon's albums *Some Time In New York City*, *Mind Games*, *Walls And Bridges*, *Rock 'N' Roll*, *Menlove Ave.*, and John & Yoko's final recordings at the Record Plant shortly before Lennon's death in 1980.

In early 1975 Lennon agreed to help Roy produce some recordings for Lori. Lori had previously sung backing vocals on Lennon's *#9 Dream* (listed as one of the 44th Street Fairies, which also included May Pang, Joey Dambra and Lennon) and (un-credited) on *Luck Of The Irish*. Lennon wanted to produce disco versions of some of the recordings. Lori was backed by a group of musicians Roy discovered called Bomf, fronted by singer and actor Patrick Jude. The group had originally been called Community Apple when they were fronted by Dambra. The group eventually became known as Dog

Left to right: Kristofer Engelhardt, May Pang, Lori Burton and husband, West Nyack, NY March 26, 1999. © Kristofer Engelhardt.

Roy Cicala and Les Paul, Iridium Club, New York, NY March 27, 2000. © and photo by Kristofer Engelhardt.

Soldier*. Information concerning Lennon's contributions to Lori's recordings is taken from existing Record Plant tape boxes and extensive interviews with many of those present. There seems to be general agreement that Lennon contributed to Lori's recordings of *The Big Hurt*, *Answer Me, My Love*, *Incantation* and a duet with Jude of *Let's Spend The Night Together.* By all accounts, Lennon didn't perform on any of these recordings. According to Pang, *Answer Me, My Love* was an old Nat King Cole number that Lennon liked and rearranged for Lori. Record Plant tape boxes list Lennon as producing *Answer Me, My Love* on January 13, 1975, which falls into the period Pang thinks most of Lennon's work on Burton's recordings took place. *The Big Hurt* was a cover of the Toni Fisher hit from 1960. Lori and May are certain that Lennon produced both songs and, to a lesser degree, *Let's Spend The Night Together.* According to Jude, Lennon also arranged this cover of The Rolling Stones'* song. According to Lori, *Incantation* was a song Roy had originally written called *Jubilation* recorded by Community Apple. Lennon rewrote the lyrics and re-titled it *Incantation.* Lennon's lyrics were inspired by a Native American he had met named Rolling Thunder. Roy then recorded Lennon's version with a group called Visitor, but wasn't happy with it, so he had Lori sing it. Dog Soldier also recorded a version with Jude singing it. Pang was not aware of Lennon producing any versions of *Incantation.* However, Lori and Patrick are certain that Lennon helped produce their respective versions. *Answer Me, My Love* and *Let's Spend The Night Together* were given an exclusive release on a CD accompanying the book *Beatles Undercover* in 1998.

Roy and Lori were divorced in 1979. The Record Plant in New York closed in 1989. Roy then helped open a new studio in the New York area called IIWII (it is what it is), a favorite saying between him and John Lennon. Roy currently lives in Brazil where he continues to work in the recording business. Lori retired from the music business years ago.

Jim Capaldi

Living On The Outside
Steamhammer/SPV-SPV 085-72512 (Germany) (10/11/01)
Producer: Jim Capaldi & Rene Tinner
George Harrison: Solo Guitar; Jim Capaldi: Vocals & Percussion; Mick Dolan: Guitar & Bass; Paul Weller: B. Vocals; Ian Paice: Drums; Helmut "Jumpy" Zerlett: Organ
Can Studio Weilerswist, Germany & Mayfair Studios, London, UK

Anna Julia (M. Camelo-J. Capaldi) 3:34 (3)

Oh Lord Why Lord? (P. Trim-M. Bouchar) 4:24 (8)

Some Come Running
Island-7 91024-2 (11/01/88)
Producer: Jim Capaldi
George Harrison: Guitar†; Jim Capaldi: Lead Vocals & Drums; Chris Parren: Keyboards; Eric Clapton: Guitar; Rosko Gee: Bass; Andy Mac Pherson: Mix
FPSHOT† & Backyard Studios, Surrey, UK 07/xx/88

Nicola Jim Capaldi was born on August 2, 1944 in Evesham, England. Jim's early interest in music was fostered by his father who was a music teacher. Jim was playing drums and forming bands as a teenager, and was signed to Pye Records as a member of the Hellions, which included Dave Mason*. The Hellions, like The Beatles, did a stint at the Star-Club in Hamburg, Germany. In 1967 Capaldi and Mason, along with Chris Wood and Steve Winwood (see Blind Faith) formed the group Traffic, one of rock's most revered bands. Jim has long been recognized for his song lyrics including those for Bob Marley's *This Is Reggae Music.*

Jim and George Harrison had known each other and associated with many of the same musicians for years, so it isn't surprising that Harrison plays guitar on *Oh Lord Why Lord?*, a song dedicated to South African activist Steve Biko, from Jim's 1988 album *Some Come Running.* George also made a cameo in the song's music video. Jim wrote the song *You Got A Hold On Me* for Harrison to record but there isn't any evidence he recorded it. Harrison also played on *Anna Julia* from Jim's 2001 album *Living On The Edge.* Some CD's also include the video for the song though Harrison doesn't appear in it. Jim took part in the Harrison tribute *Concert For George* in 2002 Jim Capaldi died on January 28, 2005. For more information go to www.jimcapaldi.com

Belinda Carlisle

Leave A Light On
Virgin-VSCDT (662719-211) (single) (UK) (09/xx/89)
Producer: Rick Nowels; Extended Mix by: Jason Corsaro
George Harrison: Slide Guitar†; Belinda Carlisle: Lead Vocals; Rick Nowels: Guitar; Charles Judge: Keyboards; Ben Schultz: 12 String Guitar; John Pierce: Bass; Rudy Richman: Drums; X.Y. Jones: Guitar; Ellen Shipley: B. Vocals; Maria Vidal: B. Vocals; Donna Delory: B. Vocals; Bekka Bramlett: B. Vocals
One on One, Los Angeles, CA & FPSHOT†, UK xx/xx/88 & xx/xx/89

Leave A Light On (Extended Mix) (R. Nowels-E. Shipley) 8:04 (3)

Runaway Horses
MCA-MCAD 6339 (10/03/89)
Producer: Rick Nowels
One on One, Los Angeles, CA & FPSHOT†, UK xx/xx/88 & xx/xx/89

Deep Deep Ocean (B. Steinberg-T. Kelly-A. Sky) 4:05 (7)
George Harrison: Six String Guitar & Twelve String Bass†; Belinda Carlisle: Lead Vocals; Charles Judge: Keyboards; Ben Schultz: Guitar; John Pierce: Bass; Kenny Aronoff: Drums; X.Y. Jones: Guitar; Ellen Shipley: B. Vocals; Maria Vidal: B. Vocals; Donna Delory: B. Vocals; Bekka Bramlett: B. Vocals

Leave A Light On (R. Nowels-E. Shipley) 4:33 (1) (09/xx/89)
George Harrison: Slide Guitar†; Belinda Carlisle: Lead Vocals; Rick Nowels: Guitar; Charles Judge: Keyboards; Ben Schultz: 12 String Guitar; John Pierce: Bass; Rudy Richman: Drums; X.Y. Jones: Guitar; Ellen Shipley: B. Vocals; Maria Vidal: B. Vocals; Donna Delory: B. Vocals; Bekka Bramlett: B. Vocals

Summer Rain (7" Edit)/Summer Rain (Justin Strauss Mix)/Leave A Light On (Kamikazee Mix)
Virgin-VSCDT-1323 (single) (UK) (01/13/90)
Producer: Rick Nowels
George Harrison: Slide Guitar†; Belinda Carlisle: Lead Vocals; Rick Nowels: Guitar; Charles Judge: Keyboards; Ben Schultz: 12 String Guitar; John Pierce: Bass; Rudy Richman: Drums; X.Y. Jones: Guitar; Ellen Shipley: B. Vocals; Maria Vidal: B. Vocals; Donna Delory: B. Vocals; Bekka Bramlett: B. Vocals
One on One, Los Angeles, CA & FPSHOT†, UK xx/xx/88 & xx/xx/89

Leave A Light On (Kamikazee Mix) (R. Nowels-E. Shipley) 4:51 (3)

Belinda Carlisle was born on August 17, 1958 in Los Angeles, California. She is the most successful member of The Go-Go's who had the Top 10 hits *We Got The Beat* and *Vacation* in 1982, and the Top 20 hits *Our Lips Are Sealed* in 1981 and *Head Over Heels* in 1984. They disbanded in 1985 but have reunited, with Carlisle, on several occasions since their initial formation in 1978.

Carlisle's solo career got off to a successful start with the Top Five hit *Mad About You* in 1986. She topped the charts in the US and UK with *Heaven Is A Place On Earth* in 1987. She had a Top Five hit with *I Get Weak* and a Top 10 hit with *Circle In The Sand* in 1988.

Rick Nowels, who produced Carlisle's 1989 album *Runaway Horses* and wrote many of the songs on it, recounts, "I met George Harrison at a party in Los Angeles in 1987, and he complimented me on *Heaven Is A Place On Earth*, which I had produced and co-written for Belinda. Later, when I was working on *Runaway Horses*, we contacted George to see if he was interested in playing on the album. He said he would be happy to play, and to send him the tapes, and tell him what we wanted and what songs to play on. I wrote him very specific notes asking him to play on *Leave A Light On* and *Deep Deep Ocean*. I arranged *Leave A Light On* with a 16-bar solo instead of an eight-bar solo to give George some room to stretch. After I got the tapes back, to my delight, George called me and asked if it was all right and said, 'You owe me a beer.' He even wrote specific notes on how to mix it. He was very friendly." *Leave A Light On* was a major international hit due in large part to Harrison's stunning slide guitar solo. An extended version and remixed version of the song was issued on singles in the UK. Carlisle is married to Morgan Mason, son of actor James Mason. She continues to record and perform. For more information go to www.belindacarlisle.tv, www.gogos.com

Ringo Starr And His All Starr Band The Anthology...So Far
Koch-KOC-CD-8312 (07/24/01) (02/05/01)
Executive Producer: Ringo Starr & David Fishof
SummerFest, Miller Oasis, Milwaukee, WI 07/01/00

All By Myself [live] (S. Rachmaninoff-E. Carmen) 7:42 (3-14)
Ringo Starr: Drums; Eric Carmen: Lead Vocals & Keyboards; Dave Edmunds: Electric Guitar; Jack Bruce: Bass; Simon Kirke: Drums; Mark Rivera: Keyboards

Hungry Eyes [live] (J. De Nicola-F. Previte) 3:50 (3-13) (02/05/01)
Ringo Starr: Drums; Eric Carmen: Lead Vocals & Keyboards; Dave Edmunds: Electric Guitar & B. Vocals; Jack Bruce: Bass & B. Vocals; Simon Kirke: Drums; Mark Rivera: Saxophone & Percussion

Eric Carmen was born August 11, 1949 in Cleveland, Ohio. As a youngster, he often sat on the stage with his aunt as she rehearsed with the Cleveland Symphony Orchestra. He was a prodigy who at two-and-a-half years of age was the youngest student ever enrolled at the Cleveland Institute of Music, and was playing violin, piano and writing songs before he was a teenager. Eric says, "I was greatly influenced by The Beatles, especially Lennon and McCartney's great songwriting. I was never shy about letting those influences show in my songwriting. I started playing in a rock band around age 15, but I couldn't very well carry my piano around, so I learned to play guitar. We played more than a few covers of Beatles' songs."

Eric was later in the band Cyrus Erie who released a single for Epic Records in 1969. In late 1970 Eric and a Cyrus Erie band member formed The Raspberries with members of another popular Cleveland band The Choir. The Raspberries had a Top Five hit with *Go All The Way* and a Top 20 hit with *I Wanna Be With You* in 1972. They had a Top 40 hit with *Let's Pretend* in 1973.

The Raspberries were recording at New York's Record Plant Studios in 1974. Eric recalls, "I've met and worked with many famous people but John Lennon was the most charismatic human I've ever met! I knocked him to the floor opening the studio's bathroom door – not exactly how I envisioned meeting a Beatle for the first time, but he was very understanding. The Beatles' Mellotron was at the studio, which I was allowed to play. I discovered a portion of *Strawberry Fields Forever* saved on it. I felt as if I'd discovered the Holy Grail. I looked across the room and saw John grinning as he watched me play. He recruited me and Michael McBride to clap to help a group of kids he'd gathered keep time on the song *Loop De Loop*, which he was producing for Harry Nilsson*. I struggled over what to say when I learned John and I were to be formally introduced, but before I could say a word he offered his hand and said, 'Love your record. Ringo and I are going to do promotion for you.' I was dumbfounded! Like an idiot I said, 'I like your records too.' He'd heard our song *Overnight Sensation (Hit Record)* in the studio and loved it." [The song's producer, Jimmy Ienner denies rumors that Lennon helped him mix it but says Lennon loved the song, which did become a hit record.] The Raspberries broke up in 1975, but reunited in 2004 and have made live appearances since that time. Their 2007 album *Live On Sunset Strip* includes a photo of Lennon wearing a Raspberries' sweatshirt.

Carmen's self-titled 1975 solo album includes *All By Myself* and *Never Gonna Fall In Love Again*, which were Top 40 hits. In 1977 he had a Top 40 hit with *She Did It* and in 1978 a Top 20 hit with *Change Of Heart.* Carmen returned to the Top 10 in 1988 with *Hungry Eyes*, from the hit movie *Dirty Dancing*, and *Make Me Lose Control.* He has also written Top 10 hits for Shaun Cassidy, and Mike Reno and Ann Wilson.

Eric says, "I knew David Fishof and worked with him as part of the *Dirty Dancing Tour* in 1988. He asked me if I might be interested in joining Ringo's All-Starr Band tour in 2000, which I was. Apparently there were a few other keyboard players in the running, but a few weeks later he called me and said, 'Ringo wants you!' I received a CD in the mail with the band's songs. I had no preconceptions because I hadn't seen any of the All-Starr Bands perform. I've played a number of instruments in bands, so I wasn't sure exactly what they wanted me to play. For example, *Yellow Submarine* didn't originally have any keyboards and the part that stood out for me to play was the big, acoustic guitar sound, so that's what I learned. I had this device that turned an electric guitar into a big, 12-string, acoustic guitar sound. Their sound man raved about it during rehearsals

Eric Carmen, circa 2008. © and photo by Gene Taylor, courtesy of Eric Carmen and Al Kaston.

but Ringo said, 'I'm really missing the keyboards.' I told him there weren't any keyboards on *Yellow Submarine*. He said, 'Well there were when Gary Brooker* played it. All those in favor of keyboards raise your hands.' A couple of hands went up so he said, 'Done!' So I switched to piano. I thought he would want it to sound exactly like the original recording but later he said to me, 'Eric, I'm sensing you're a perfectionist — like Mark Hudson*.' I told him, 'Yes, I am a perfectionist. I was one of those teenagers who saw The Beatles on *The Ed Sullivan Show*. The bands I was in learned to cover those songs exactly the way they were on the record because that's how bands were evaluated. I just want to do a great job.' He said, 'Well Eric, whatever we do here is not gonna be The Beatles and it's not gonna be The Raspberries — we're just having a bit of fun. Just go with it.' My perfectionist drive to sound exactly like the record wasn't what he wanted. He was after a much looser sound and having us do our thing. Once I understood that, things became easier and much more fun.

"When I first met Ringo, I was thinking to myself, 'wow – a Beatle!' I said, 'You're Ringo Starr,' and he said, 'And you're Eric Carmen.' He'd already been on tour with all of the other guys in the band and I was the new guy, and the only American, so I was at a distinct disadvantage, especially because of their British humor. Ringo's sense of humor, in a sweet way, is to cut the legs out from under you whenever you give him the opportunity. Ringo may not always love rehearsing but he's not above shooting one across the bow. He was a bit crotchety during a rehearsal of *Back Off Boogaloo*. I knew the words but I hadn't been told what parts to sing on the chorus, and Ringo said, 'You should know the words by now Eric.'

"Ringo initially told me, 'I've been listening to your songs and I think I'll have Simon Kirke* play drums on *Go All The Way*. There's too many fills and it's way too taxing for me.' During rehearsals the band tried to jam their way through my songs, which doesn't easily work, so I had to teach them all the parts. Dave Edmunds* remarked once, 'There's a fucking chord for every word!' We'd rehearsed The Raspberries' song *Tonight* but I realized it wasn't going to work. Ringo asked, 'Was it a hit?' I said, 'It was a Top 40 hit.' Mark Rivera suggested my song *Hungry Eyes*. Again, Ringo asked, 'Was it a hit?' I said, 'It was a Top Five hit.' He said, 'That's it! We're doing *Hungry Eyes*.'

"He also played drums on my song *All By Myself*. During an interview we were asked whose songs were the hardest to learn and all of the band members pointed at me." Kirke recalls, "Ringo wanted to hear us run through *All By Myself* before he would consider it for inclusion in the set. It was all going rather swimmingly until Eric signaled the band to drop out. With puzzled looks we did as we were asked and listened while Eric launched into an interminable neoclassical solo piece. Ringo feigned a yawn to me after about 15 seconds and after a minute more abruptly rapped a drum stick on the edge of his snare. Eric's performance ground to a halt. 'How long does this go on Eric?' growled Ringo. 'About another minute – the whole thing is two minutes long. It's on the album,' added Eric rather lamely. 'Well trim it down a bit for fuck's sake. We're all nodding off here,' replied Ringo. Never one to mince words was our Ringo. 'How long can I make it then?' Eric asked tremulously, his dreams of a Yanni-like moment evaporating rapidly. 'Twenty seconds!' Ringo replied. 'But that's impossible!' said Eric. 'Then we don't do the song…next,' Ringo said as his foot came down. Eric managed to salvage something out of it and I thought it was a vast improvement on the original."

Eric says, "Ringo encouraged me to do a solo spot on the tour even though I hadn't rehearsed anything. When I'd come off stage, he'd often say, 'Great job, great song.' I came to appreciate just how innovative and underrated Ringo's drumming is. There were times when I would get up on his drum riser and play guitar, and he would throw in some fills that I'd only previously heard on some of The Beatles' recordings because I'm such a student of their music. I would smile at him when I'd hear these, and he'd knowingly smile back at me, which was always great, and do another one. I'd like to think that I was encouraging him. I would do anything I could to make his day better.

"There was a very funny and ironic moment on the Miller Beer Stage at Milwaukee's SummerFest when I played *Roll Out The Barrel* [a.k.a. *Beer Barrel Polka*], which perfectly fit the chords of my solo on *No No Song* and Ringo shot me that 'very clever' look. However, that 'pinch yourself — as good as it gets' moment came when we did the *Late Show With David Letterman* in the Ed Sullivan Theater, and I realized I was performing on the same stage where I'd first seen Ringo and The Beatles, and dreamed of being in a band like that someday. The entire All-Starr experience was very moving for me and we all received very nice little gifts at the end." For more information go to www.ericcarmen.com, www.raspberriesonline.com

Paul Carrack

Ringo Starr & His All-Starr Band Tour 2003
Warner Music Vision-R2 970326 (DVD) (09/21/04)
Producer: (Mixer: Bruce Sugar; Re-recording: Elmo Ponsdomenech & Andre Perreault);
Executive Producer: Ringo Starr & David Fishof
Ringo Starr: Drums; Paul Carrack: Lead Vocals & Keyboards; Sheila Escovedo: Drums & B. Vocals; John Waite: Bass & B. Vocals; Colin Hay: Electric Guitar & B. Vocals; Mark Rivera: Saxophone & B. Vocals
Casino Rama, Rama, Ontario, Canada 07/24/03

How Long [live] (P. Carrack) 4:22 (4) (03/23/04)
[Also available on Koch-KOC-CD-9549 (4)]

The Living Years [live] (M. Rutherford-B. Robertson) 6:10 (4) (03/23/04)
Additionally: Mark Rivera: Keyboards & B. Vocals (only)
[Also available on Koch-KOC-CD-9549 (4)]

Paul Carrack was born on April 22, 1951 in Sheffield, England. He's a keyboardist, vocalist and successful songwriter whose career has been punctuated by session work and periodic service in several of the same bands while maintaining a solo career. He first gained notice in Warm Dust who released several albums in the early 1970s. Following their breakup he helped form the band Ace, and wrote and sang their 1975 Top Five hit *How Long* before they broke up in 1977. In the late 1970s and early '80s he backed Frankie Miller and was a member of Roxy Music before releasing his first solo album. He replaced Jools Holland* in Squeeze in 1981 singing their hit *Tempted*, but soon left (he also worked with them in 1993) to do solo and session work for such artists as B.B. King*, Eric Clapton* and Elton John*. He's also been a member of Mike + The Mechanics singing on their Top 10 hit *Silent Running (On Dangerous Ground)* in 1985 and on their number one hit *The Living Years* in 1988. He had a solo Top 10 hit with *Don't Shed A Tear* in 1987. He has also worked with Timothy B. Schmit* and wrote, with Jim Capaldi* and Peter Vale, The Eagles' 1995 hit *Love Will Keep Us Alive*.

Paul was a member of Ringo Starr's All-Starr Band tour in 2003 performing *How Long*, *The Living Years*, and *Tempted* with Ringo backing him on drums. Paul recounts, "I'd been approached by David Fishof about being in the All-Starr Band a couple of times and unfortunately had to turn him down due to other commitments. I'd seen the All-Starrs perform in London years earlier and I loved it. It looked like so much fun. I thought I'd missed my chance but fortunately they asked me a third time when I was able to accept. We rehearsed at Casino Rama in Canada for about 10 days. We were well taken care of. Everything came together pretty quickly. Mark Rivera had the job of pulling it all together. Ringo was not the most demanding band leader, he just wanted to play his drums, have fun and be Ringo. He was in great form with his razor sharp wit and didn't miss a thing. I've worked with many great and famous artists, but I'm not sure I got my head around working with a Beatle. I saw The Beatles live in Sheffield when I was a teenager and was blown away! I was a huge fan. I had their wallpaper in my bedroom. I was playing drums in bands in school, so naturally Ringo was my favorite. I dreamed of having a Ludwig drum kit just like his. He's one of the most famous people on the planet. He's had an amazing life but he talks about the same things that all bands experience. I loved it when he would come out with anecdotes of the early days." For more information go to www.carrack-uk.com

Johnny Cash

The Essential Johnny Cash
Sony/Legacy Recordings-696998629028 (02/12/02) **Paul McCartney: Liner Notes**

Water From The Wells Of Home
Mercury-834 778-2 (11/08/88)
Producer: Paul McCartney
Paul McCartney: Bass, Vocals & Guitar; Johnny Cash: Lead Vocals & (probable) Rhythm Guitar; Hamish Stuart: Guitar & B. Vocals; Chris Whitten: Drums & B. Vocals; Marty Stuart &/or Mark Howard: Mandolin; Ralph Mooney &/or Lloyd Green: Pedal Steel Guitar; Jack Clement, &/or Mark Howard &/or Emmylou Harris: Rhythm Guitar; Joey Miskulin: Accordion; Jack Clement &/or Lloyd Green: Dobro Guitar; Jack Clement: (probable) Ukulele; June Carter Cash: Autoharp & B. Vocals; Linda McCartney: B. Vocals; Tom T. Hall: B. Vocals; Cindy Cash: B. Vocals
Hog Hill Mill Studios, Sussex, UK & Nashville, TN 05/09/88

New Moon Over Jamaica (T. Hall-J. Cash-P. McCartney) 3:12 (9)

Johnny Cash was born on February 26, 1932 in Kingsland, but grew up in Dyees, Arkansas. He was legally named J.R. because his parents couldn't decide on a first name. He learned to play guitar and began writing songs prior to serving in the military were he chose the name John. In the mid-1950s he began recording for Sun Records alongside Elvis Presley, Jerry Lee Lewis* and Carl Perkins*. He had Top 20 hits for Sun with *I Walk The Line* in 1956, *Ballad Of A Teenage Queen* and *Guess Things Happen That Way* in 1958, and *Ring Of Fire* for Columbia Records in 1963, which were all number one hits on the country charts. *Ring Of Fire* was written by his friends and country artists, Merle Kilgore and June Carter. Cash and Carter became a duet act and were married in 1968. That year Cash recorded the multi-million-selling live album *At Folsom Prison*. He nearly reached the top of the charts with *A Boy Named Sue* in 1969. Cash was one of the first and most frequent country artists to have crossover success on the pop charts. He was also one of the first to work with a wide range of well-known country and rock artists over the years including Waylon Jennings, Willie Nelson, Bob Dylan*, Roy Orbison*, Tom Petty* and U2. His last Top 40 hit, also a number one hit on the country charts, was *One Piece At A Time* in 1976, though his career and popularity saw a huge resurgence in the 2000s with his American Recordings' series of albums. Cash won numerous Grammy Awards, is a member of the Country Music Hall of Fame and the Rock and Roll Hall of Fame. His daughter Rosanne Cash, from his first marriage, is a country music star. His son John Carter Cash also has a career in music.

Cash and Paul McCartney have had a long love affair with Jamaica. While on vacation there, the two met (Cash had a home on the island) and composed the song *New Moon Over Jamaica*. McCartney featured the original, reggae demo of the song on his 1995 radio series *Oobu Joobu*. A country music version was arranged and recorded with Cash at McCartney's studio in Sussex, England. The song appeared on Cash's 1988 album *Water From The Wells Of Home*. Cash also recorded a duet with Paul of McCartney's song *Man We Was Lonely*, which has yet to be released. [Cash has also recorded covers of other Beatles' songs.] Carla Lane says she, McCartney, Cash and Tom T. Hall wrote a country song about animal rights that Cash was expected to record but nothing has surfaced. McCartney contributed notes to the 2002 album *The Essential Johnny Cash*. Johnny Cash died September 12, 2003. For more information go to www.johnnycash.com

Felix Cavaliere

The Best Of Ringo Starr And His All-Starr Band...So Far
Image-ID0828RO (DVD) (10/23/01)
Producer: Michael Drumm; Greg Delancy (music mixer); Executive Producer: Ringo Starr & David Fishof
Ringo Starr: Drums; Felix Cavaliere: Lead Vocals & Keyboards; Mark Farner: Guitar & B. Vocals; Zak Starkey: Drums; John Entwistle: Bass; Randy Bachman: Guitar; Billy Preston: Keyboards & B. Vocals; Mark Rivera: Saxophone, Percussion & B. Vocals
Nippon Budakon Hall, Tokyo, Japan 06/27/95

Groovin' [live] (F. Cavaliere-E. Brigati) 4:22 (12) (02/05/01)

[Also available on *Ringo Starr And His All Starr Band The Anthology...So Far.* Koch-KOC-CD-8312 (2-7) (07/24/01)]

Ringo Starr And His All Starr Band The Anthology...So Far
Koch-KOC-CD-8312 (07/24/01) (02/05/01)
Producer: Greg Delancy (mixer); Executive Producer: Ringo Starr & David Fishof
Ringo Starr: Drums; Felix Cavaliere: Lead Vocals & Keyboards; Mark Farner: Guitar & B. Vocals; Zak Starkey: Drums; John Entwistle: Bass; Randy Bachman: Guitar; Billy Preston: Keyboards & B. Vocals; Mark Rivera: Saxophone, Percussion & B. Vocals
Nippon Budakon Hall, Tokyo, Japan 06/27/95

People Got To Be Free [live] (F. Cavaliere-E. Brigati) 4:33 (2-6) (08/12/97)

Ringo Starr And His All-Starr Band: A Starry Night In Tokyo
ASB-001 [unauthorized release] xx/xx/96
Producer: NHK TV, Japan
Ringo Starr: Drums; Felix Cavaliere: Lead Vocals & Keyboards; Mark Farner: Guitar & B. Vocals; Zak Starkey: Drums; John Entwistle: Bass; Randy Bachman: Guitar & B. Vocals; Billy Preston: Keyboards & B. Vocals; Mark Rivera: Percussion & B. Vocals
Nippon Budakon Hall, Tokyo, Japan 06/27/95

Good Lovin' [live] (R. Clark-A. Resnick) 5:36 (16)

Felix Cavaliere was born on November 29, 1942 in Pelham, New York. Felix studied piano as a youngster. He was a member of the doo-wop group The Stereos during high school and formed a band called Felix & The Escorts while a student at Syracuse University. Felix recalls, "My father wanted me to be a doctor, but he soon realized I had a band but no grades." Cavaliere joined the group Joey Dee and the Starliters, which also included David Brigati. They toured Europe, playing at the Star-Club in Hamburg, Germany and backed Tony Sheridan* on one of his recordings. They crossed paths with The Beatles who were starting to become

Kristofer Engelhardt and Felix Cavaliere, Memorial Park, Frankenmuth, MI June 3, 2000. Photo by Peter Noone, © Kristofer Engelhardt.

popular, inspiring Cavaliere to form a band. He hired drummer Dino Danelli to play in a band with him in Las Vegas before returning to New York to rejoin the Starliters, which then included guitarist Gene Cornish. Gene Cornish & The Unbeetables had recently released the novelty single *I Wanna Be A Beatle.*

In late 1964 Felix, Dino, Gene and Brigati's brother Eddie formed a group. They briefly backed comedian Soupy Sales who called them a bunch of rascals and the name stuck. After hearing their powerful, self-penned R&B at a club in New York, promoter Sid Bernstein became their manager and Ahmet Ertegun, head of Atlantic Records, signed them as the label's first white act. Bernstein, who was the promoter for The Beatles' historic appearance at Shea Stadium in 1965, had The Rascals sit in the stadium's dugout and used the occasion to flash "The Rascals Are Coming" across the stadium's scoreboard. Brian Epstein was enraged and made Bernstein remove it. Bernstein (without their knowledge) legally modified the group's name to The Young Rascals in late 1965 fearing a lawsuit from another band with a similar name. Felix recalls, "We went absolutely bananas because of the obvious reference to The Little Rascals [a child comedy act dating from the 1920s]. It was so un-cool, but the damage was done and stuck with us our whole career." [The group dropped the "Young" in 1968.] Between 1966 and 1968 they had number one hits with *Good Lovin'*, *Groovin'* and *People Got To Be Free*; Top Five hits with *How Can I Be Sure* and *A Beautiful Morning*; a Top 10 hit with *A Girl Like You*, and Top 20 hits with *You Better Run*, *(I've Been) Lonely Too Long* and *It's Wonderful.* All but *Good Lovin'* were written by Cavaliere and Brigati. By 1971 Brigati and Cornish had left the group, which broke up the following year. Felix laments, "We had a great band but I didn't realize that along with that talent were four dominant males."

Felix released a couple of albums in the mid-1970s and had a Top 40 hit in 1980 with *Only A Lonely Heart Sees.* The Rascals (minus Brigati) reunited for a US tour in 1988, but the following year Cornish and Danelli sued Felix over the rights to The Rascals' name. Felix was part of The Peace Choir, organized by John Lennon and Yoko Ono's* son Sean, who recorded a cover of Lennon's *Give Peace A Chance* in 1991.

Felix was a member of Ringo Starr's All-Starr Band tour in 1995. During his performances he wove such other artists' hits as *Love Train* and *Respect Yourself* into *People Got To Be Free*; *My Girl*, *Apples, Peaches, Pumpkin Pie* and *Just My Imagination* into *Groovin'* and *La Bamba* into *Good Lovin'*. Ringo played drums on all of Cavaliere's performances. Their performance in Tokyo was recorded and filmed, which was broadcast on Japanese TV. Unfortunately, the tour was cut short when Ringo learned that his daughter was quite ill. Felix declares, "I'm very fortunate that I'm still able to be involved in music. I've been very lucky and I had a dream come true working with Ringo." The Rascals were inducted into the Rock and Roll Hall of Fame in 1997. Cavaliere was inducted into the Songwriters Hall of Fame in 2009. Felix Cavaliere continues to tour and record. For more information go to www.felixcavaliere.com

Cheech And Chong

Cheech And Chong's Greatest Hits
Warner Bros.-3614-2 (02/05/91)
Producer: Lou Adler
George Harrison: Guitar; Cheech Marin: Lead Vocals; Tommy Chong: B. Vocals; Carole King: Electric Piano; Nicky Hopkins: Piano; Tom Scott: Saxophone; Billy Preston: Organ; Klaus Voormann: Bass; Jim Keltner: Percussion; George Bohanon: Horns; Dick Hyde: Horns; Paul Hubinon: Horns; Jimmy Karstein: Drums; Michelle Phillips: B. Vocals; Darlene Love: B. Vocals; Fanita Jones: B. Vocals; Jean King: B. Vocals; Viva Marshall: B. Vocals & Hi
A&M Studios, Los Angeles, CA probably 04/xx/73

Basketball Jones (T. Chong-C. Marin) 4:00 (4) (08/20/73)

Tommy Chong was born on May 23, 1938 in Edmonton, Alberta, Canada. Richard "Cheech" Marin was born on July 13, 1946 in Los Angeles, California. The two met after Cheech moved to Canada in 1968 to avoid being drafted during the Vietnam War. Chong had been a guitarist with Bobby Taylor & The Vancouvers. He and Cheech started a rock band but soon realized they made a great comedy team. By the early 1970s they were the kings of drug culture humor based around marijuana and had a number of hit comedy albums. Ironically, Marin's father was a 30-year veteran of the Los Angeles Police Department.

Cheech and Chong were recording at A&M Studios in Los Angeles once when Cheech says, "Our producer Lou Adler knew everybody at another session there, including George Harrison, and asked them if they'd play on our song *Basketball Jones*. George liked the chords to it and played guitar on it. I don't know if he knew about the humorous lyrics because I'm not sure we even had the lyrics finished yet." The lyrics are a parody of the Black American male's passion for basketball and the song *Love Jones* by the Brighter Side Of Darkness. It was first released on their album *Los Cochinos* in July 1973. Given the musicians involved, it was probably recorded in April 1973 when Harrison was producing the album *Shankar Family & Friends* (see Ravi Shankar). At the time, A&M Records distributed Dark Horse who had their office at A&M studios. Cheech says, "We often saw Ringo during this period. We called him granny because he was older than most of us. We would also see John Lennon at the studios and at parties at Adler's house, which John had rented. He was always full of great quips."

Between the late 1970s and mid-1980s, Cheech and Chong also made a number of successful comedy films including *Up In Smoke,* and appeared in the Monty Python* spin-off film *Yellowbeard.* In 1985 they had another hit with a parody of Bruce Springsteen's* song *Born In The USA* called *Born In East L.A.* just before they broke up. Cheech went on to appear in, or do character voices, in dozens of films, and has been a cast member of several successful TV series' including *Golden Palace* and *Nash Bridges.* Chong also continued to appear in comedy films and performed standup comedy. Cheech and Chong reunited in 2008. They continue to tour and plan to make more films together. Chong's daughters Rae Dawn and Robbi are successful actresses. For more information go to www.cheechandchong.com

The Christians, Holly Johnson, Paul McCartney, Gerry Marsden & Stock Aitken Waterman

Ferry Cross The Mersey
PWL-PWL PWCD 41 (single) (UK) (05/02/89)
Producer: Michael Stock, Matt Aitken & Pete Waterman
Paul McCartney: Vocals & Guitar; Russell Christian: Vocals; Garry Christian: Vocals; Henry Priestman: Vocals; Holly Johnson: Vocals; Gerry Marsden: Vocals; Michael Stock: Vocals & Instruments; Matt Aitken: Vocals & Instruments; Pete Waterman: Vocals & Instruments
PWL Studios, London, UK 04/20/89

Ferry Cross The Mersey (G. Marsden) 3:55 (1)

On April 15, 1989, during a football (soccer) match between Liverpool and Nottingham Forest, nearly 100 people were killed and several hundred others hospitalized after being crushed within the confines of an overcrowded section of Hillsborough Stadium in Sheffield, England. The Christians, Gerry Marsden (see Gerry & The Pacemakers), Paul McCartney, Holly Johnson, Michael Stock, Matt Aitken and Pete Waterman recorded a remake of Marsden's *Ferry Cross The Mersey* and donated the proceeds to The Hillsborough Disaster Fund to aid victims. Stock has said working with McCartney on the song was one of his biggest thrills. According to Waterman, McCartney not only sang, but also played guitar on the song and that Stock, Aitken and him furnished the balance of the instrumental backing. Waterman also considers the events surrounding the charity single to be one of the greatest times of his life.

At the time, The Christians were a Liverpool R&B group comprising Russell Christian, born on July 8, 1956 and his brother Garry, born on February 27, 1955 both in Liverpool, England, and Henry Priestman, born on July 21 1955 in Kingston-upon-Hull, England. They had a UK Top 10 hit with *Harvest For The World* in 1988, and UK Top 20 hits with *Ideal World* in 1987 and *Words* in 1989. The Christians performed The Beatles' song *Revolution* at *The John Lennon Scholarship Concert* in Liverpool on May 5, 1990. Garry is the only original member still in the group. For more information go to www.thechristianslive.com

William Holly Johnson was born on February 9, 1960 in Liverpool, England. He was a member of the Liverpool band Frankie Goes To Hollywood.

Their 1984 album, *Welcome To The Pleasure Dome* was a UK number one hit along with its songs *Relax* (a US Top 10 hit), *Two Tribes* and *The Power Of Love*. The title track was a UK Top Five hit. The group disbanded in 1987. Johnson continues to record sporadically and has become a critically acclaimed painter.

Michael Stock was born on December 3, 1951 in Margate, England. Matt Aitken was born on August 25, 1956 in Coventry, England. Pete Waterman was born on January 15, 1947 in Coventry, England. Waterman says he first met The Beatles right after they dropped the "Silver" from their name. He later worked at Apple for a brief period. During the 1980s Stock, Aitken and Waterman were one of the UK's most successful songwriting, production and record company (PWL) teams. Waterman chose the name PWL (Pete Waterman Ltd.) following McCartney's warning that using his full name was too egotistical. By the end of the 1980s the team had racked up over a dozen number one hits in the UK including Dead Or Alive's *You Spin Me Round*, Mel And Kim's *Respectable*, Rick Astley's *Never Gonna Give You Up* and Kylie Minogue's *I Should Be So Lucky*. Waterman advises anyone who wants a hit record to analyze The Beatles, and then he says, "We might start hearing music again!" Stock and Aitken have since parted company with Waterman. For more information go to www.pwl-empire.com, www.mikestockmusic.com

John Christie

4th Of July / Old Enough To Know Better Young Enough To Cry
Capitol-3928 (7" single) (07/01/74)
Producer: Dave Clark & [Mike Smith]
John Christie: Lead Vocals

4th Of July (**P. McCartney**-L. McCartney) 2:27 (1/1) (06/28/74)

The *4th Of July* was produced by Dave Clark, leader of the popular mid-1960s band The Dave Clark Five. Following their demise, Clark turned to music and TV production. Apparently, Clark, during sessions he produced for John Christie, requested a song from McCartney who sent him a home demo of *4th Of July*. A brief portion of McCartney singing the song appears on unauthorized releases. Christie contributed to Dave Clark's *Time — The Musical* in 1986, which also included contributions from Jimmy Helms* and Julian Lennon*.

Eric Clapton

Concert For George
WSM-R2 970241 (DVD) (11/18/03)
Producer: Jeff Lynne (audio); Ray Cooper, Olivia Harrison & Jon Kamen
Paul McCartney: Piano & Vocals; Ringo Starr: Drums; Eric Clapton: Electric Guitar & Lead Vocals; Jeff Lynne: B. Vocals & Acoustic Guitar; Billy Preston: Keyboards & B. Vocals; Dhani Harrison: Acoustic Guitar; Jim Keltner: Drums; Jim Horn: Alto Sax; Ray Cooper: Percussion; Jim Capaldi: Tambourine; Gary Brooker: Keyboards & B. Vocals; Andy Fairweather Low: Acoustic Guitar & B. Vocals; Tom Scott: Tenor Saxophone; Tessa Niles: B. Vocals; Katie Kissoon: B. Vocals; Dave Bronze: Bass; Albert Lee: Electric Guitar; Marc Mann: Electric Guitar; Chris Stainton: Keyboards; Henry Spinetti: Drums; Phil Capaldi: Tambourine
Royal Albert Hall, London, UK 11/29/02

While My Guitar Gently Weeps [live] (G. Harrison) 5:48 (1-23)
[Also available on WSM-R2 74546 (2-17)]

Far From The Madding Crowd [Delaney & Bonnie & Friends]
Mid Valley-308 [unauthorized release] (xx/xx/05)
Producer: Danish TV
George Harrison: Guitar; Delaney Bramlett: Lead Vocals & Rhythm Guitar; Bonnie Bramlett: Vocals & Tambourine; Eric Clapton: Lead Guitar; Billy Preston: Keyboards; Carl Radle: Bass; Jim Gordon: Drums; Bobby Whitlock: Organ & B. Vocals; Jim Price: Trumpet & Trombone; Bobby Keys: Saxophone; Tex Johnson: Congas & Bongo Drums; Rita Coolidge: B. Vocals
Falkoner Theatre, Copenhagen, Denmark 12/12/69

Eric Clapton, Saginaw Civic Center, Saginaw MI, June 5, 1979. © and photo by Kristofer Engelhardt.

Don't Know Why [live] (D. Bramlett-E. Clapton) 5:10 (2)

It's Still Much Better Being A Guitar Player [George Harrison]
Pebbles-P-02003/4 (CD-R) [unauthorized release] (xx/x/06)
George Harrison: Guitar; Eric Clapton: Guitar; Phil Palmer: Guitar; Greg Phillinganes: Keyboards; Nathan East: Bass; Steve Ferrone: Drums; Ray Cooper: Percussion
The Forum, Los Angeles, CA 05/01/90

Crossroads [live] (R. Johnson) 6:48 (2-15)
Additionally: Eric Clapton: Lead Vocals

[Instrumental blues jam]/For You Blue [live] (G. Harrison) 2:01 (2-14)

Sunshine Of Your Love/Strangers In The Night [live] (E. Clapton-J. Bruce-P. Brown/B. Kaempfert) 4:37 (2-16)
Additionally: Eric Clapton: Lead Vocals; Nathan East: B. Vocals; Greg Phillinganes: B. Vocals; Katie Kissoon: B. Vocals; Tessa Niles: B. Vocals

Journeyman
Reprise/Duck-9 26074-2 (11/07/89)
Producer: Russ Titelman
George Harrison: Guitar & Harmony Vocals; Eric Clapton: Lead Vocals & Guitar; Rob Mounsey: Synthesizer; Robbie Kondor: Synthesizer Programming; Greg Phillinganes: Synthesizer; Alan Clark: Synthesizer; Darryl Jones: Bass; Jim Keltner: Drums & Drum Programming; Jimmy Bralower: Drum Programming; Carol Steele: Percussion
Power Station Studios, New York, NY 04/xx/89 [unless noted otherwise]

Run So Far (**G. Harrison**) 4:06 (8)

Nobody's Child: Romanian Angel Appeal [Various Artists]
Warner Bros.-9 26280-2 (07/24/90)
Producer: Russ Titelman
George Harrison: Guitar & B. Vocals; Eric Clapton: Lead Vocals & Guitar; Nathan East: Bass; Rob Mounsey: Keyboards; Robbie Kondor: Keyboards; Jim Keltner: Drums
Power Station Studios, New York, NY 04-05/xx/89

That Kind Of Woman (**G. Harrison**) 3:56 (10)

Party At The Palace [Various Artists]
BBC Opus Arte-OA 0857 D (DVD) (07/09/02)
Producer: Cerrie Frost
Paul McCartney: Vocals & Piano; Eric Clapton: Lead Vocals & Lead Guitar; Paul Wickens: Keyboards; Phil Collins: Drums; Ray Cooper: Percussion; The Royal Academy of Music Symphony Orchestra
Buckingham Palace Garden, London, UK 06/03/02

While My Guitar Gently Weeps (G. Harrison) 5:14 (36)

Unbootlegged 14 [The Beatles]
No Tapo-NTR-0301 (CD-R) [unauthorized release] (xx/xx/04)
Eric Clapton: Lead Vocals & Guitar; Carl Radle: Bass; Jamie Oldaker: Drums; Dick Sims: Keyboards; George Terry: Guitar

Badge [live] (**G. Harrison**-E. Clapton-**[R. Starkey]**) 8:18 (1-19)
Additionally: **Ringo Starr: Tambourine**; Yvonne Elliman: B. Vocals; Macy Levy: B. Vocals
Le Pavilion, Paris, France 06/14/77

Further On Up The Road [live] (J. Veasey-D. Robey) 9:04 (1-20)
Additionally: **George Harrison: Guitar**; Elton John: Keyboards
Civic Hall, Guildford, UK 12/07/78

Eric Clapton was born on March 30, 1945 in Ripley, England. He was raised by his grandparents, thinking his young mother Patricia

Clapton, was his sister until he was nine. His father Edward Fryer, a soldier stationed in England during the war, returned to his native Canada after the war.

Eric's career in rock and blues began in 1963 with The Roosters, which earlier had included Brian Jones of The Rolling Stones*, and Paul Jones* and Tom McGuinness later in Manfred Mann. Clapton was briefly in Casey Jones and The Engineers, and the blues-oriented Yardbirds but he disliked their recording of the pop song *For Your Love,* which became the band's first Top 10 hit, and joined John Mayall's Bluesbreakers in 1965. The group included bassist Jack Bruce*. Bruce had been a member of the Graham Bond Organization (a.k.a. Graham Bond Quartet, see Duffy Power) with drummer Ginger Baker (see Blind Faith) who Clapton also knew. In 1966 the three formed Cream*. Following Cream's breakup in late 1968 Clapton, Baker, Rick Grech and Steve Winwood formed Blind Faith*, which lasted less than a year.

Eric's association with George Harrison began in December 1964 when the Yardbirds opened for *Another Beatles Christmas Show*, a three-week engagement at London's Hammersmith Odeon Theatre. Eric was part of The Beatles' live performance of *All You Need Is Love* for the BBC TV program *Our World*, telecast live on June 25, 1967. In December 1967 Harrison recruited Clapton to play on his first solo album, the soundtrack to the film *Wonderwall.*

Eric played guitar on Harrison's song *While My Guitar Gently Weeps* on *The Beatles* (white) album in 1968. Harrison wrote the song *Savoy Truffle* on the album about Eric's love for chocolate and the dental problems it caused him. Eric supposedly also played on *Not Guilty* from album's sessions, though none of the versions that have surfaced, including the one on The Beatles' 1996 album *Anthology 3*, seem to feature Eric. Harrison was inspired to write *Here Comes The Sun* in Eric's backyard during an unusually sunny spring day in 1969. Between 1968 and 1970 Eric contributed to recordings Harrison produced for Jackie Lomax*, Doris Troy* and Billy Preston*.

On December 11 1968, Eric, Mitch Mitchell of Jimi Hendrix Experience, Keith Richards of The Rolling Stones and John Lennon, performed *Yer Blues* for The Rolling Stones' film *Rock And Roll Circus.* Eric performed with Lennon on September 13 at *Toronto's Rock 'n' Roll Revival* released on the Plastic Ono Band album *Live Peace In Toronto 1969.* Eric also played on their studio recording of *Cold Turkey* released as a single around the same time.

In late fall of 1969, Eric and Harrison joined Delaney & Bonnie & Friends'* tour of England and Scandinavia. An album from the tour was released along with several unauthorized releases of their performances at the Falkoner Theatre in Copenhagen, Denmark, which include Clapton singing his and Delaney Bramlett's* composition *Don't Know Why*, featuring Harrison on guitar. Upon their return to the UK they backed up Lennon and Yoko Ono* at The Lyceum Ballroom in London included on the Lennons' 1972 album *Some Time in New York City.*

According to Marc Roberty's book *Eric Clapton: The Complete Recording Sessions 1963-1992, Melody Maker* magazine reported that Eric contributed to sessions for Ringo's song *It Don't Come Easy* at Apple Studios in March 1970, though it's unlikely he's on the released version. Shortly thereafter Eric, and Carl Radle, Jim Gordon and Bobby Whitlock* from Delaney & Bonnie & Friends, formed another short-lived group called Derek And The Dominos*.

Eric took part in an all-star jam session with Ringo, Bobby Keys*, Klaus Voormann*, Charlie Watts and others during a party Ringo threw at Ronnie Scott's Club in London on New Year's Eve 1970. Eric was part of Harrison's *The Concert For Bangla Desh* on August 1, 1971 at New York's Madison Square Garden. Eric took part in sessions for Lennon's 1971 album *Imagine*, though he's not credited so his playing may not have been used. Over the next few years Eric's personal problems and infatuation with Harrison's wife began to seriously interfere with his career and his relationship with Harrison.

The credits for the song *Bye Bye Love* on Harrison's 1974 album *Dark Horse* list "Rhythm Ace and Pattie + Eric Clapton." The credits also contain a religious message to Eric. The album notes that Eric appears courtesy of RSO Records. Roberty states emphatically in his book *Eric Clapton The Complete Recording Sessions 1963-1992* that Eric didn't contribute to any songs on the *Dark Horse* album. Given the bitterness and reference to Eric and Pattie's romantic involvement in the amended lyrics of this Everly Brothers'* hit, it's likely the credit is purely symbolic. There are other unsubstantiated claims of Eric collaborating with Harrison. Eric's 1976 album *No Reason To Cry* thanks Geoffrey Harrison. Patti, who was living with Eric at the time, often referred to George as Geoffrey, leading to speculation he contributed to the album, despite any evidence.

Eric contributed to Ringo's 1976 album *Rotogravure*. Ringo joined Eric and his band playing tambourine during their performance of *Badge* in Paris, France in 1977, which is included on unauthorized releases. Eric contributed to Ringo's 1983 album *Old Wave*, and was also reported to have been involved in Ringo's aborted sessions produced by Chips Moman in Memphis in 1987

Harrison and Elton John* joined Eric during his performance of *Further On Up The Road* in Guildford, England in 1978. The appearance was featured in the film *Eric Clapton And His Rolling Hotel* released in 1980. The performance is also available on unauthorized releases. Eric plays on *Love Comes To Everyone* from the 1979 album *George Harrison*. [Eric covered the song on his 2005 album *Back Home*.] Harrison referred to "slowhand" (Clapton's nick-name) in his 1982 song *Mystical One*. On May 19, 1979 Eric nearly pulled off the impossible bringing together Ringo, George and Paul McCartney in a musical jam at his post-wedding reception to Pattie. By the mid-1980s Eric's marriage to Pattie had disintegrated.

Eric was part of the 1985 TV special *Blue Suede Shoes (A Rockabilly Session with Carl Perkins and Friends Starring George Harrison, Ringo Starr, Eric Clapton, Rosanne Cash & Dave Edmunds)*. Eric performed with McCartney and many other stars at *The Prince's Trust 10th Anniversary Birthday Party* at London's Wembley Arena on June 20, 1986. On June 5 and 6, 1987 Eric performed with Harrison and Ringo at the same venue for the *Prince's Trust Rock Concert*. Both performances were released. Eric contributed to Harrison's 1987 album *Cloud Nine*. Harrison's compositions *Run So Far* and *That Kind Of Woman* were recorded for Eric's 1989 album *Journeyman*. *That Kind Of Woman* didn't make the album and was recorded by Gary Moore*. [Eric's version, with Harrison on guitar, was released on the 1990 charity album *Nobody's Child: Romanian Angel Appeal* benefiting Romanian orphans.] Harrison also offered Eric his song *Cheer Down* for *Journeyman*, which was bypassed. Harrison's version was featured on the soundtrack of the movie *Lethal Weapon 2*, which included Eric's music.

Harrison attended many of Eric's performances. In 1990 he joined Eric onstage at the Los Angeles Forum playing guitar on *Crossroads*, *Sunshine Of Your Love* and an instrumental blues jam, that includes riffs from Harrison's Beatles' song *For You Blues*, which are available on unauthorized releases. Eric and Harrison toured Japan in December 1991. Harrison was backed by Eric and his band captured on Harrison's album *Live In Japan*. Harrison didn't appear onstage during Eric's set.

Eric backed McCartney on several songs during their performance at the *Music For Montserrat* benefit concert organized by George Martin*, held on September 15, 1997 at London's Royal Albert Hall. Clapton also played with McCartney at his Rock and Roll Hall of Fame induction in 1999. Eric joined Paul at the *Concert For New York City* on October 20, 2001 at Madison Square Garden. Eric also contributed to McCartney's recording of the song *Freedom*. Eric was inducted into the Rock and Roll Hall of Fame in 2000. McCartney joined Eric on *While My Guitar Gently Weeps* at *Party At The Palace* in celebration of Queen Elizabeth's 50 years of rule in 2002 (see Various Artists Sir Paul McCartney, Rod Stewart, Joe Cocker, Ladysmith Black Mambazo). Eric was the musical director for the Harrison tribute *Concert For George* in 2002. He performed with Ringo, McCartney and Harrison's son Dhani on several songs, and they joined Eric on *While My Guitar Gently Weeps*. The song is credited to McCartney and Clapton, but Eric is the lead vocalist. Eric contributed to Ringo's 2003 album *Ringo Rama*. On December 31, 2004 Ringo was backed by Eric and his band on several songs at the Woking Leisure Centre, UK. He also performed with Eric and his band, including Gary Brooker*, Joe Walsh* and others that same date in 2008. Eric Clapton continues to write, record and tour. For more information go to www.ericclapton.com

John Cleese / Bill Oddie / Ringo Starr

The Anti-Heroin Project
It's A Live-In World [Various Artists]
EMI-AHP LP 1 11/12 (12" albums) (UK) (11/24/86)
Producer: Charlie Foskett & [Bill Oddie]
Ringo Starr: Drums & B. Vocals; Bill Oddie: Lead Vocals; Michael Palin: B. Vocals; John Cleese: Dialogue
Startling Studios, Ascot, UK 08/xx/86

Naughty Atom Bomb (K. Craddock-C. Gibson) 3:00 (2/1/2)

Ringo Starr plays drums and provides backing vocals on the song *Naughty Atom Bomb* recorded as a contribution to the Anti-Heroin Project album *It's A Live-In World* for The Phoenix House Charity. The album doesn't include detailed credits for the song, but it was reportedly recorded in August 1986 at Startling Studios. The lead vocals are sung by Bill Oddie of the comedy troupe The Goodies. Monty Python* members Michael Palin and John Cleese also contributed to the song. In a 1990 interview Cleese seemed to have no recollection of Ringo's involvement in spite of his being credited on the record. Others involved recall two recording sessions and that Ringo's contributions ended up in the final mix. Cleese also thought that Oddie had written and produced the track. He is probably correct about Oddie being involved in the production, as Charlie Foskett is credited primarily as executive producer on the album. The album also includes an anti-heroin message by Starr called *You Know It Makes Sense*, a contribution by Ringo's son Zak and McCartney's cousin Kate Robbins* to the title track, and the song *Simple As That* by Paul McCartney.

Clarence Clemons

Ringo Starr And His All-Starr Band
Pioneer Artists-PA-090-007 (LD 12") (07/xx/90)
Producer: Tim Snow (video); Joe Walsh & Jim Nipar (music); Executive Producer: Ringo Starr & David Fishof
Greek Theatre, Los Angeles, CA 09/03/89

Quarter To Three [live] (F. Guida-J. Royster-G. Anderson-E. Barge) 3:50 (2/5)
Ringo Starr: Drums; Clarence Clemons: Lead Vocals & Saxophone; Billy Preston: Keyboards & B. Vocals; Jim Keltner: Drums; Levon Helm: Drums; Nils Lofgren: Guitar & B. Vocals; Joe Walsh: Guitar & B. Vocals; Rick Danko: Bass & B. Vocals; Dr. John: Keyboards & B. Vocals
[Also available on *Ringo Starr And His All Starr Band The Anthology...So Far.* Koch-KOC-CD-8312 (1-7) (07/24/01) (02/05/01);]

You're A Friend Of Mine [live] (N. Walden-J. Cohen-C. Clemons) 5:43 (1/9)
Ringo Starr: Drums; Clarence Clemons: Lead Vocals & Saxophone; Billy Preston: Keyboards & B. Vocals; Jim Keltner: Drums; Levon Helm: Drums; Nils Lofgren: Guitar; Joe Walsh: Guitar; Rick Danko: Bass; Dr. John: Keyboards

Clarence Clemons was born on January 11, 1942 in Norfolk, Virginia. He attended Maryland State College on football and music scholarships. He played semi-pro football before injuries from a car accident steered him toward a musical career playing saxophone. In 1971 he began working with Bruce Springsteen* and has been a member of his E Street Band since the mid-1970s. He has also pursued a solo career having several successful albums, and has worked with many artists including Aretha Franklin*, Ian Hunter*, Greg Lake*, Alvin Lee* and Roy Orbison*. His duet with Jackson Browne of *You're A Friend Of Mine* was a Top 20 hit in 1986.

Clemons was a member of Ringo Starr's All-Starr Band tour in 1989 performing *You're A Friend Of Mind* and *Quarter To Three* with Ringo backing him on drums. Clemons made a guest appearance on Paul McCartney's 1995 radio series *Oobu Joobu*. Clemons currently divides his time playing with his band Temple Of Soul, the E Street Band, writing scripts and acting. For more information go to www.clarence-clemons.com

Joe Cocker

John "Joe" Cocker was born on May 20, 1944 in Sheffield, England. During the early 1960s Cocker was in the band the Cavaliers, and later fronted Vance Arnold & The Avengers. Following their successful opening for The Rolling Stones, Joe was signed to Decca Records who released his cover of *I'll Cry Instead* in 1964. It was the first of a number of songs written by members of The Beatles that Joe has covered.

In 1968 Joe teamed up with Chris Stainton and Henry McCullough (a member of Wings in 1972-73) forming what would become The Grease Band. His cover of The Beatles' song *With A Little Help From My Friends*, topped the UK charts. John Lennon and Paul McCartney were so impressed that they took out a congratulatory advertisement in Britain's *NME* magazine. Joe's performance of it at the *Woodstock Music And Art Fair* in 1969 quickly made him an international rock star.

In the spring of 1969 there was great tension within The Beatles and they were unsure of what to do with some of the recordings they had made that would later be used on their albums *Abbey Road* and *Let It Be*. George Harrison and McCartney invited Joe to pick some songs from these recordings. His first choice was reportedly *Oh Darling*, (Joe claims that it was *Golden Slumbers*) a song certainly suited to Joe's vocal style, but McCartney apparently vetoed his choice and urged him to record *She Came In Through The Bathroom Window*. Joe was also offered *Let It Be*, which was also offered to Aretha Franklin*. Joe says Harrison and McCartney helped him record rough reference demos of *Something*, which Harrison also considered giving to Frank Sinatra and Jackie Lomax*, and *She Came In Through The Bathroom Window* at Apple Studios. Photos of Harrison playing guitar, piano and singing to Joe at Apple appeared in issues of *The Beatles Book Monthly* magazine. It isn't known if Joe sang to these demos or if the tapes still exist. Mark Lewisohn states in his book *The Beatles Recording Sessions* that Harrison played guitar on Cocker's recording of *Something*. Joe maintains he took the tapes back to Los Angeles and completely re-recorded *Something* and *She Came In Through The Bathroom Window* for his album *Joe Cocker!*. Glyn Johns, one of the engineers for that album also recalls the songs being re-recorded in Los Angeles, which rules out any musical involvement by Harrison, or McCartney for that matter, on any of Cocker's released recordings. Joe's versions were released some weeks after The Beatles' released their versions on their 1969 album *Abbey Road*. *She Came In Through The Bathroom Window* was a Top 40 hit for Cocker. Joe also recorded *Let It Be* for the album but it wasn't included, likely because The Beatles hadn't released their version of it yet. Joe's version was released years later and is available on the 1999 re-mastered CD of *Joe Cocker!* (A&M-088490420-2).

In early 1970 Cocker formed the short-lived band Mad Dogs & Englishmen from the remnants of Delaney & Bonnie & Friends*. Britain's *Disc* magazine reported in early 1971 that Harrison and Leon Russell* sat in on a Cocker session, but Joe discounts this. In June 1971 *Melody Maker* magazine reported that Ringo contributed to some recording sessions with Joe, Steve Winwood and Chris Stainton at Island Studios. Joe says Ringo jammed with the band, but doubts if any tapes, if they were made, still exist and that nothing with Ringo was ever released.

Joe has had an uncanny ability throughout his career to adapt songs he covers to his unique vocal style and turn them into hits. He had a Top 10 hit with *The Letter* and Top 20 hit with *Cry Me A River* in 1970, a Top Five hit with Billy Preston's* *You Are So Beautiful* in 1975, a number one hit, with Jennifer Warnes, of *Up Where We Belong* in 1982 and a Top Five hit with *When The Night Comes* in 1989.

Joe performed two of Lennon's songs at *The John Lennon Scholarship Concert* held on May 5, 1990 in Liverpool. Another of his backing bands included former Wings' drummer Steve Holly. Joe was the opening act for some of Ringo Starr's All-Starr Band performances in Europe in 1992. Joe joined Paul McCartney on *All You Need Is Love* at *Party At The Palace* (see Various Artists Sir Paul McCartney, Rod Stewart, Joe Cocker, Ladysmith Black Mambazo). Joe Cocker continues to tour. For more information go to www.cocker.com

Alma Cogan

A Celebration
EMI-EM 1280 (12" albums) (UK) (11/02/87) **Paul McCartney: Liner Notes**

Celebration: The Ultimate Collection
EMI-0946 3 63779 2 6 (UK) (05/08/06)
Producer: George Martin
Paul McCartney: (possible) Tambourine; Alma Cogan: Lead Vocals
EMI-Abbey Road Studios, London, UK10/02 & 05/64

I Knew Right Away (A. Cogan-S. Foster) 2:00 (2-11) (10/30/64)

Alma Cogan was born Alma Cohen on May 19, 1932 in London, England. She was one of Britain's most popular and flamboyant singers from the early 1950s through the mid-1960s. She was known as "the girl with the laugh in her voice." The Beatles grew up listening to her hits such as *Bell Bottom Blues*, *Sugartime* and *Dreamboat*. The Beatles first met her on January 12, 1964 during rehearsals for the TV show *Sunday Night At The London Palladium*. They immediately hit it off and became frequent guests at her family's home. She became close friends of Brian Epstein and John Lennon. Lennon called her Sara Sequin because she wore many sequins and allegedly had an affair with her. McCartney has admitted he was somewhat infatuated with her sister Sandra who later became known as the actress Sandra Caron.

Alma, who recorded for EMI, also crossed paths with The Beatles at Abbey Road Studios, so it's not surprising that Lennon and McCartney are rumored to be involved in Cogan's recordings. In the October 23, 1964 issue of *NME* it says, "As a friendly gesture, Paul McCartney plays tambourine on the next Alma Cogan single." Numerous reliable publications have listed McCartney as playing tambourine on *I Knew Right Away*, the B-side of Cogan's October 1964 single *It's You*, including the 1975 book *All Together Now* by Harry Castleman and Walter Podrazik. In their 1985 book *The End Of The Beatles?* they concluded, after hearing no tambourine on the single, and doing further investigation, that McCartney had nothing to do with the single. Arno Guzek, a noted expert on The Beatles, checked with EMI, who confirmed that McCartney had no involvement with it. However, EMI publicity executive Brian Southall states in his book *Abbey Road* that McCartney played tambourine on *I Knew Right Away*. Mark Lewisohn's 1987 book, *25 Years In The Life* credits McCaretney playing tambourine on *It's You*. McCartney's *Club Sandwich* (spring 1988 issue Nos. 47/48) fan magazine denies his involvement possibly based on previous, published dismissals, so perhaps many sources are quoting each other's misinformation. Nevertheless, it sounds like there may be a tambourine buried in the mix at the beginning of *I Knew Right Away*; though none is apparent on *It's You*. JAEP, the company Epstein set up to handle George Harrison's compositions, published *I Knew Right Away*, while *It's You* was published by Dick James Music who handled The Beatles' publishing.

In 1965 Cogan wanted to record an entire album of songs written by The Beatles. EMI wasn't keen about the idea, but five covers of their songs did turn up on her next album *Alma* including *Yesterday* and *Eight Day's A Week*. Lennon and McCartney were reported to have attended Cogan's recording session for *Eight Day's A Week* in October 1965. Cogan's official website says, "Paul McCartney famously wrote the first draft of *Yesterday* at Alma's flat, and she became the first woman to record it." McCartney claims he only played it for her to see if she thought the melody was from another song. According to Alma's sister, John and Paul played in the orchestra on one of Alma's tracks. However David Gooch, who produced (initially un-credited) the sessions for Alma says emphatically that none of The Beatles sat in on any of his sessions with Cogan. Perhaps Cogan's sister is referring to the single *It's You / I Knew Right Away*. *Eight Day's A Week* was released as a single with a cover of The Beatles' song *Help!* Its picture sleeve has the subtitle *The Beatles Help Alma For Christmas*, which no doubt fueled speculation about their involvement. Cogan died on October 26, 1966. McCartney contributed brief liner notes to the 1987 Cogan retrospective album *A Celebration*.

Billy Connolly / Chris Tummings & The Singing Rebels Band

Filmtracks-The Best Of British Film Music [Various Artists]
London Filmtrax-MCPS 820 252-2 (820254-2) (Germany) (07/xx/85)
Producer: Mike Moran
George Harrison: Guitar & B. Vocals; **Ringo Starr: Drums**; Billy Connolly: Lead Vocals & Guitar; Eric Clapton: Guitar; Christopher Tummings: Keyboards & B. Vocals; Chris Stainton: Bass; Ray Cooper: Drums; Mike Moran: Keyboards; Jon Lord: Keyboards; Jenny Bogle: B. Vocals; Anastasia Rodriquez: B. Vocals
FPSHOT, UK xx/xx/84

Freedom (E. Clapton-I. La Frenais) 4:37 (2-10) (05/31/85)

William "Billy" Connolly was born on November 24, 1942 in Glasgow, Scotland. He's a successful actor, comedian and musician. He was a member of the late '60s group the Humblebums. His 1975 parody of Tammy Wynette's hit *D.I.V.O.R.C.E.* was a number one hit in the UK. Billy introduced Paul McCartney's Rockestra ensemble at the *Concerts For The People Of Kampuchea* at London's Hammersmith Odeon on December 29, 1979.

Billy was given a co-starring role in *Water*,

HandMade Films' comedy about colonialism, exploitation and revolution on a Caribbean island. Billy suspects he got the part because, "They couldn't imagine anyone else crazy enough to do it and because I had a musical background." George Harrison was the executive producer of *Water* and contributed to the soundtrack (see Jimmy Helms). Harrison, Ringo Starr and Eric Clapton* made a cameo in the film as members of The Singing Rebels Band performing the song *Freedom* sung by Connolly. Billy recounts, "The song was recorded at George's house. Eric turned up to hear us record and ended up playing on it." The big budget film premiered on January 18, 1985. It was issued on DVD (Anchor Bay-DV13087) in 2006.

Ringo was seen in attendance at *An Audience With Billy Connolly* on October 21, 1985, which was broadcast five days later on ITV's London Weekend Television. Billy was nominated for a BAFTA for his role in the 1997 film *Mrs. Brown*. He recorded a cover of The Beatles' song *Being For The Benefit Of Mr. Kite* for George Martin's* 1998 album *In My Life*. For more information go to www.billyconnolly.com

Elvis Costello

All This Useless Beauty
Warner Bros.-9 46198-2 (05/14/96)
Producer: Geoff Emerick & Elvis Costello
Elvis Costello: Lead Vocals, Guitars & Bass; Bruce Thomas: Bass; Steve Nieve: Keyboards; Pete Thomas: Drums
Windmill Lane Recording, Dublin, Ireland &/or Westside Studio, London, UK xx/xx/95 or xx/xx/96

Shallow Grave (**P. McCartney**-D. Mac Manus) 2:01 (7)

The Elvis Costello Hour
Warner Brothers Words & Music Series.-# 165 PRO-A-3488 (promotional only) (12" albums) (02/07/89)
Producer: Elvis Costello, Kevin Killen & T-Bone Burnett
Paul McCartney: Bass & B. Vocals; Elvis Costello: Guitars, Piano, Organ, Tambourine & Melodica; T-Bone Burnett: Guitars; Ralph Forbes: Electric Drums; Jim Keltner: Snare Drums; Michael Blair: Glockenspiel & Bells; Cait O' Riordan: Maracas; Roger McGuinn: 12 String Electric Guitar
One or more of the following studios: Ocean Way, Los Angeles, CA, Southlake, New Orleans; Windmill Land, Dublin, Ireland &/or Air, London, UK xx/xx/87 or xx/xx/88
This Town (The Bastard Mix) (D. Mac Manus) 4:26 (1/2/1)

The McCartney/Mac Manus Collaboration
Vigotone VG-174 (CD-R) [unauthorized release] (xx/xx/98)
Producer: Paul McCartney & probably one or more of the following: Elvis Costello, Neil Dorfsman, Mitchell Froom
Hog Hill Mill Studios, Sussex, UK 09-10/xx/87

Playboy To A Man (**P. McCartney**-D. Mac Manus) 2:52 (6)
Paul McCartney: Vocals, Piano & Guitar; Elvis Costello: Vocals & Guitar

So Like Candy (**P. McCartney**-D. Mac Manus) 3:28 (4)
Paul McCartney: Vocals & Guitar; Elvis Costello: Vocals & Guitar

Tommy's Coming Home (**P. McCartney**-D. Mac Manus) 4:08 (3)
Paul McCartney: Vocals & Guitar; Elvis Costello: Vocals & Guitar

Twenty-Five Fingers (**P. McCartney**-D. Mac Manus) 2:26 (2)
Paul McCartney: Vocals, Bass & Guitar; Elvis Costello: Vocals & Guitar
Mighty Like A Rose
Warner Bros.-9 26575-2 (05/14/91)
Producer: Mitchell Froom, Kevin Killen & D.P.A. Mac Manus (Elvis Costello)
Ocean Way Studio, Los Angeles, CA & possibly Westside Studio, London, UK probably 09-10/xx/90

Playboy To A Man (P. McCartney-D. Mac Manus) 3:17 (11)
Elvis Costello: Lead Vocals, Guitar & Organ; Marc Ribot: Guitar; Jerry Scheff: Bass; Jim Keltner: Drums; Larry Knechtel: Piano; Mitchell Froom: Piano & Organ; Benmont Tench: Piano

So Like Candy (**P. McCartney**-D. Mac Manus 4:36 (9)
Elvis Costello: Lead Vocals & Guitars; Marc Ribot: Guitars; Jerry Scheff: Bass; Jim Keltner: Drums; Larry Knechtel: Piano; Mitchell Froom:

Mellotron, Chamberlain & Celeste; T. Bone Wolk: Bass

Put It There
Polygram Music Video-081 649-1 (LD 12") (xx/xx/89)
Producer: Paul McCartney & probably one or more of the following: Elvis Costello, Neil Dorfsman, Mitchell Froom (music); Chip Chipperfield (video)
Probably Hog Hill Mill Studios, Sussex, UK probably xx/xx/88

My Brave Face (Part 1) (**P. McCartney**-D. Mac Manus) 0:30 (1/1)
Paul McCartney: Bass Guitar; Elvis Costello: Lead Vocals & Acoustic Guitar

My Brave Face (Part 2) (**P. McCartney**-D. Mac Manus) 0:10 (1/1)
Paul McCartney: Bass Guitar; Elvis Costello: Lead Vocals & Acoustic Guitar

My Brave Face (Part 3) (**P. McCartney**-D. Mac Manus) 0:45 (2/1)
Paul McCartney: Bass & Keyboards; Elvis Costello: Lead Vocals & Electric Guitar; Hamish Stuart: Keyboards; Chris Whitten: Drums

Spike
Warner Bros.-9 25848-2 (02/07/89)
Producer: Elvis Costello, Kevin Killen & T-Bone Burnett
One or more of the following studios: Ocean Way, Los Angeles, CA, Southlake, New Orleans; Windmill Land, Dublin, Ireland &/or Air, London, UK xx/xx/87 & xx/xx/88

Pads, Paws and Claws (**P. McCartney**-D. Mac Manus) 2:54 (10)
Elvis Costello: Lead Vocals, Guitars, Piano & Bass; Marc Ribot: Guitars; Jerry Marotta: Drums; Michael Blair: Marimba and Martian: Dog Bark; Jerry Scheff: Bass; T-Bone Burnett: Bass

This Town (D. Mac Manus) 4:26 (1)
Paul McCartney: Bass & B. Vocals; Elvis Costello: Lead Vocals, Guitars, Piano, Organ, Tambourine & Melodica; T-Bone Burnett: Guitars; Ralph Forbes: Electric Drums; Jim Keltner: Snare Drums; Michael Blair: Glockenspiel & Bells; Cait O' Riordan: Maracas; Roger McGuinn: 12 String Electric Guitar

Veronica (**P. McCartney**-D. Mac Manus) 3:10 (4)
Paul McCartney: Bass; Elvis Costello: Lead Vocals & Guitar; T-Bone Burnett: Guitar; Jerry Marotta: Drums; Michael Blair: Glockenspiel & Tympani; Benmont Tench: Piano & Spinet; Mitchell Froom: Electric Piano & Chamberlain

Elvis Costello (Elvis came from Presley and Costello was his great-grandmother's maiden name) was born Declan Mac Manus on August 25, 1954 in London, England. His father Ross sang with Joe Loss & His Orchestra (who once appeared on a bill with The Beatles). He was playing guitar and writing songs by the age of 15. By the mid-1970s he was performing part-time with the band Flip City. He also worked as a roadie for Brinsley Schwarz. His friendship with their bass player Nick Lowe led to a major record contract.

Costello, with his backing group The Attractions, gained fame as a brash, post-punk, new-wave artist in the late 1970s and early '80s. His singles were far more successful in the UK than in the US despite high praise for his songwriting and respectable US album sales. Nonetheless, his songs *(What's So Funny 'Bout) Peace, Love And Understanding*, *Pump It Up*, *Oliver's Army*, *Accidents Will Happen*, *Radio, Radio*, *Everyday I Write The Book* and others, have become rock classics. Costello contributed to the 1984 Yoko Ono tribute album *Every Man Has A Woman* (see Spirit Choir).

Costello first met Paul McCartney when they appeared on the bill at the *Concerts For The People Of Kampuchea* on December 29, 1979. The two would occasionally run into each other at AIR Studios in London during the first half of the 1980s. McCartney approached Costello in mid-1987 with the idea of writing and recording together. He accurately sensed that Costello would provide a competitive, counterpoint writing partnership similar to the one he had with John Lennon. Costello reportedly found McCartney to be quite practical and formal about songwriting. Twelve co-compositions have been released, seven by McCartney (*My Brave Face*, *You Want Her Too*, *Don't Be Careless Love*, *Back On My Feet*, *That Day Is Done*, *Mistress And Maid* and *The Lovers That Never Were*). Costello issued two co-compositions on his album *Spike*, two on *Mighty Like A Rose*, and one on *All This Useless Beauty*, which also thanks McCartney. The promotional album *The Elvis Costello Hour* contains an alternate mix of *This Town* called *The Bastard Mix* (actually *The Sweetheart Mix*). When Costello released *So Like Candy* as a single in 1991 he included a demo version of *Veronica* on the B-side but it doesn't contain any musical contribution by McCartney. *Veronica* proved to be one of Costello's highest charting singles.

McCartney's video release *Put It There*, promoting his album *Flowers In The Dirt*, includes a cameo by Costello singing *My Brave Face* with backing from McCartney. It's available on VHS, LD and DVD (PAL format only).

At least three known McCartney-Mac Manus compositions, *I Don't Want To Confess*, *Twenty-Five Fingers* and *Tommy's Coming Home*, have yet to be officially released. The latter two were included on the unauthorized release *The McCartney/Mac Manus Collaboration*, which also includes McCartney and Costello demos of some of their co-compositions. Only those demos on which McCartney plays that were later released by Costello are considered contributions. Because *Twenty-Five Fingers and Tommy's Coming Home* haven't been officially released by either artist, and are sung by both artists, they are considered a McCartney contribution to a Costello recording.

Costello and McCartney performed their co-composition *Mistress And Maid* and The Beatles' *One After 909* together on March 23, 1995 at St. James Palace in London at a benefit for the Royal College Of Music (see Anya Alexeyev). The entire performance is available on the unauthorized release *Paul McCartney, Elvis Costello & Friends-A Royal Performance* (Strawberry Records-STR 005). A portion of *One After 909* was also featured on McCartney's 1995 radio series *Oobu Joobu*, which also featured several of Costello's songs, including his demo with McCartney of *The Lovers That Never Were.*

Over the years, Costello has covered a number of Lennon and McCartney compositions live or on record. On April 10, 1999 he performed McCartney's compositions *Warm And Beautiful* and *That Day Is Done*, and joined Paul on *Let It Be* at *Here, There and Everywhere – A Concert For Linda* (see Linda McCartney) at the Royal Albert Hall in London. Elvis Costello and The Attractions were inducted into the Rock and Roll Hall of Fame in 2003. Paul appeared on the TV show *Spectacle/Elvis Costello with Paul McCartney* in 2010. Elvis Costello continues to tour, write, record and explored different musical styles with, among others, his current wife, jazz singer Diana Krall and Allen Toussaint and famed songwriter Burt Bacharach. For more information go to www.elviscostello.com

Kyoko Cox

Unbootlegged 25 [version one] [The Beatles]
No Tapo-NTR-0603 (CD-R) [unauthorized release] (xx/xx/06)
Producer: John Lennon
John Lennon: Electric Guitar, Vocals & Drum programming; Kyoko Cox: Lead Vocals
Tittenhurst Park, Ascot, UK 05-06/xx/69

[Untitled "jam"]/Yellow Submarine (J. Lennon-K. Cox/J. Lennon-P. McCartney) 22:49 (14-24)

Kyoko Cox was born on August 8, 1963 in Tokyo, Japan. She is the daughter of Yoko Ono* by her second husband, artist, musician and avant-garde film-maker Anthony Cox. The marriage ended in early 1969 as a result of Ono's relationship with John Lennon. Kyoko spent time with John and Yoko at their Tittenhurst Park home in the UK in the spring and summer of 1969. During Kyoko's stay John made some improvisational recordings with her, some based around The Beatles' song *Yellow Submarine*, to a programmed drum track, his electric guitar, backing vocals and vocal coaching. Some of these recordings have appeared on unauthorized releases. Kyoko accompanied John and Yoko to Montreal, Canada for their "bed-in for peace," during which time *Give Peace A Chance* was recorded, and appears in documentary footage of the event. Later that year, Yoko recorded the song *Don't Worry Kyoko (Mummy's Only Looking For A Hand In The Snow).* In late December 1969, instead of attending what would prove to be The Beatles' final recording sessions some days later, John and Yoko went to Aalborg, Denmark where Anthony and Kyoko were living, and stayed nearly a month in an attempt to resolve custody issues that had developed. During the visit John made more recordings with him and Kyoko on acoustic guitars. Apparently Lennon considered releasing an album of the material. Before John left Denmark he gave Cox about 70 minutes of the recordings on cassette tapes. Several weeks later, between February 8-10, Cox documented he and Kyoko's visit with John and Yoko on nearly 10 hours of video now titled *3 Days In The Life*, the release of which has been blocked by Yoko.

Unfortunately, the custody disputes continued and Cox soon vanished with Kyoko. In April 1971

John and Yoko were taken into police custody in Majorca, Spain having been accused by Cox of abducting Kyoko. Authorities released Kyoko to her father and the two again vanished. One of the main reasons John and Yoko relocated to the US was because it was where the legal jurisdiction regarding custody was and where it was stipulated the child was to be raised. John and Yoko tried for many years to locate Kyoko but without success. Cox and Kyoko continued to move frequently and under assumed names. Kyoko sent Yoko a letter of sympathy following John's murder in 1980 but left no means of contract. In the mid-1990s, shortly after Kyoko gave birth to a daughter, she reestablished contact with her mother and the two have remained close ever since. Kyoko is reportedly married with two children and teaching in Colorado.

Cream

Crossroads
Polydor-835 261-2 (04/18/88)
Producer: Felix Pappalardi
George Harrison: Rhythm Guitar; Eric Clapton: Lead Vocals & Lead Guitar; Jack Bruce: Bass; Ginger Baker: Drums; Felix Pappalardi: Piano & Mellotron
IBC Studios, London, UK 12/xx/68

Badge (**G. Harrison**-E. Clapton-**[R. Starkey]**) 2:45 (2-4) (02/05/69)

The psychedelic rock and blues trio Cream was formed in 1966 by Eric Clapton*, Jack Bruce* and drummer Peter "Ginger" Baker, born August 19, 1939 in London, England. Bruce had worked with Clapton in John Mayall's Bluesbreakers and Baker in the Graham Bond Quartet (a.k.a. the Graham Bond Organization, see Duffy Power). The trio only lasted about two years, due to constant clashes between Bruce and Baker, but in that time they released four albums containing such timeless classics as *Crossroads*, *I Feel Free*, the Top Five hit *Sunshine Of Your Love* and the Top 10 hit *White Room*.

In 1968, soon after recordings for *The Beatles* (white) album on which Clapton played, George Harrison, with a little help from Ringo Starr, wrote some song lyrics. He approached Eric about finishing the song with him for inclusion on Cream's final album, appropriately titled *Goodbye,* released shortly after the group's breakup in late 1968. Above some of the lyrics of the untitled song, Harrison had written "bridge," the musical term. Eric thought it said "badge." Finding the misinterpretation amusing they named the song *Badge*. Due to contractual restraints, Harrison's rhythm guitar contribution to it was credited to L'Angelo Misterioso. Harrison used this alias on several occasions during this period (see Jesse Ed Davis). Harrison considered *Badge* out one of his top 10 favorite songs.

Baker later moved to Akeja, Nigeria (outside Lagos) and built ARC Studios. Paul McCartney and Wings recorded portions of their 1973 album *Band On The Run* at ARC. Baker claims he helped out on drums and assisted with the production of the album, though he is not credited. Cream performed during their induction into the Rock and Roll Hall of Fame in 1993 and reunited for some shows in 2005. For more information go to www.cream2005.com

The Crickets

T-Shirt
Epic-EK 44446 (11/04/88)
Producer: Paul McCartney
Paul McCartney: Piano & B. Vocals; Gordon Payne: Guitar & Vocals; Jerry Allison: Guitar & Drums; Joe B. Mauldin: Bass
Hog Hill Mill Studios, Sussex, UK Spring/xx/88

T-Shirt (J. Imray) 3:05 (5) (08/29/88)

The Crickets originally consisted of Buddy Holly on guitar and vocals, Sonny Curtis on guitar, Don Guess on bass and Jerry Allison, born August 31, 1939 in Hillsboro, Texas, on drums. Niki Sullivan replaced Curtis and Joe B. Mauldin, born July 8, 1940 in Lubbock, Texas, replaced Guess just as the group found success. Over the years, The Crickets have also included singer and guitarist Gordon Payne, born in Shawnee, Oklahoma on November 30, 1951, Nanci Griffiths, Rick Grech (see Blind Faith), Bobby Keys*, Tonio K., Albert Lee, Glen

Hardin, Keith Allison and others. The current lineup includes Allison, Mauldin and Curtis. The Crickets were one of the earliest rock 'n' roll bands to write their hits. In the fall of 1958, Buddy Holly left The Crickets to pursue a solo career. While on tour, his airplane crashed shortly after take-off from Clear Lake, Iowa on February 3, 1959 killing all on board. The Crickets continued to record and perform throughout the 1960s (around core members Curtis and Allison), and as solo artists and as back-up for other artists.

In February 1964 Curtis released the novelty song *A Beatle I Want To Be*, and recorded an album covering The Beatles' songs. The Crickets also recorded covers of The Beatles' songs in 1964. The jacket of The Crickets' 1970 album *Rockin' 50's Rock 'n' Roll* (Barnaby-9 Z 30268), produced by Delaney Bramlett* and featuring Eric Clapton*, included a reprinted message to The Crickets from The Beatles dated January 24, 1963. According to Allison and Bramlett, The Beatles didn't contribute to the album. The reprinted message isn't considered a contribution.

Few artists influenced the songwriting of John Lennon and Paul McCartney more than Buddy Holly. The Beatles included a number of Holly and The Crickets' compositions in their early repertoire. Their earliest known recording, known as the Quarry Men, was of The Crickets' *That'll Be The Day* in 1958, eventually included on The Beatles' 1995 album *Anthology 1*. They recorded Holly's composition *Words Of Love* in 1964. Lennon recorded *Peggy Sue* and McCartney recorded *Maybe Baby* both written by Holly. It was no accident that The Beatles' name bore a striking similarity to The Crickets. Gordon Payne recalls McCartney telling them, 'We copied you guys – the style, the name — you know – the insects. We used the double meaning of [the word] 'Beat' intentionally and as a direct influence from The Crickets. If it weren't for The Crickets, there wouldn't have been The Beatles.' "You should have seen the pride in Jerry and Joe B.'s eyes," says Payne. Allison says, "It was quite a pleasure to hear that we influenced the all-time best group, The Beatles."

McCartney purchased most of Buddy Holly and The Crickets' music publishing catalogue in the mid-1970s. Not surprisingly, George Harrison also bid to obtain the catalogue. McCartney put the catalogue to good use on Denny Laine's* 1977 album *Holly Days*, which he produced. Most of The Crickets' post-Holly success has been enjoyed in England. In September 1976 McCartney launched the annual *Buddy Holly Week* in London in celebration of Holly's birthday. McCartney is usually in attendance, and occasionally performs during the event often singing *Rave On* or *Oh Boy!* with The Crickets or other guest stars. Allison recalls, "We first met Paul and Linda McCartney* in 1978 when they flew us to London for the *Buddy Holly Week* celebrations. We did other *Holly Week* celebrations and some parties with them, which were all great fun." McCartney, in association with BBC TV, produced the 1985 documentary *The Real Buddy Holly Story* (released by White Star-D1790 on DVD in 2004) in which he narrates and performs covers of Holly's material. Buddy Holly was inducted as a charter member into the Rock and Roll Hall of Fame in 1986.

In 1988 McCartney gathered with and The Crickets, consisting of Allison, Mauldin and Payne, at his studio in Sussex to produce *T-Shirt*, the winning song from the previous year's *Buddy Holly Week* song competition. Payne recalls, "It was very exciting recording with Paul. He's very professional and the recording process is very important to him. He explained to us why he'd closed up the windows in his studio saying, 'We don't want musicians to be able to look outside and be distracted by anything. We want the focus totally on music.' We marveled at his famous Hofner bass, which still had the song list from The Beatles' last live concert taped to the top of the body. We played Paul our arrangement of *T-Shirt* telling him we had omitted the bridge because we didn't think it worked when we played it live. He asked me to sing the omitted bridge. He had me slow it down and put it at the front of the song with the short introduction we had arranged. It worked perfectly. It was magic and I began to appreciate his brilliance. Later, he asked if he could sing harmony with me on it. I thought, 'Pinch me, I'm singing with Paul McCartney!' Later, listening to the playback, Paul asked, 'Do you think it needs piano in the solo?' We all chimed in saying, 'Yes.' He asked the engineer to playback the track, and he played the perfect part on the piano in one take. He played one chord in a hole of the guitar part that floored me. I've been around some great musicians in my career, but that day I experienced firsthand just how great a musician Paul McCartney is.

"After the session Paul suggested we meet him later for dinner. We arrived at the restaurant before Paul, who called and told us to go ahead and order. Jerry and Joanie, considering the fact that the McCartneys were vegetarians, ordered accordingly, but Joe B and I, being good ol' farm boys from Texas and Oklahoma, ordered meat and potatoes. The McCartneys soon arrived and asked us if we'd ordered vegetarian. I stuttered out a, 'Well, uh, I uh...' Joe B. came back with, 'I ordered fish. That's okay isn't it?' Linda said, 'It has a heart doesn't it?''You know, I've been thinking about turning vegetarian. What's good here?' Joe B. asked, as he picked up the menu. We all had a great laugh at his comeback. Paul suggested the vegetarian ravioli, so we changed our order, and it was lovely. It was a perfect ending to a great day of music and fun. Paul made us feel like family the entire day – and every day since then. What I like most about Paul is that he is very thoughtful and has a kind and gentle heart that you don't always see with many great artists. After I returned home, my wife and I received the largest bouquet of flowers we had ever seen. It was literally three feet across with every flower imaginable. The florist in our tiny town in Tennessee didn't believe it was really from Paul McCartney. What a gentleman."

McCartney also appeared in the video for *T-Shirt*. The song was released in time for the 12th anniversary of the *Buddy Holly Week* celebrations with a T-Shirt design competition. McCartney also made an appearance in the 1990 film documentary of The Crickets, *My Love Is Bigger Than A Cadillac*. Mauldin says that contrary to reports, McCartney didn't record a version of *Rave On* with The Crickets. For more information go to www.thecrickets.com

Crowbar

KE32746
Epic-KE 32746 (album 12") (probably 01/xx/74)
Producer: Jack Douglas
John Lennon: (possible) B. Vocals; Yoko Ono (possible) B. Vocals; Kelly Jay: Lead Vocals & (probable) Keyboards; Sonnie Bernardi: Drums; Jozef Chirowski: Keyboards & B. Vocals; John Gibbard: Guitars & B. Vocals; Roland Greenway: Bass & B. Vocals; Rheal Lanthier: Guitars & B. Vocals; Sneaky Pete: (probable) Pedal Steel Guitar
Record Plant Studios, New York, NY 07-08/xx/73

Rocky Mountain Tragedy (K. Jay-R. Greenway) 5:30 (2/2)

Crowbar was a Canadian band led by Kelly Jay, born Henry Blake Fordham in Toronto, Ontario on December 1, 1941. The core of what was to become Crowbar formed in the Toronto area in 1965 around Jay, Roland Greenway and Rheal Lanthier. Some years later, with the addition of Richard "King Biscuit Boy" Newell, John Gibbard, Larry Atamanuik, Johnny Rutter and Richard Bell, they backed Ronnie Hawkins* in a band known as And Many Others. They met John Lennon and Yoko Ono* at the *Toronto Rock 'n' Roll Revival* on September 13, 1969 and again a few months later when the Lennons stayed at Hawkins' house outside Toronto. Kelly says he tried, without success, to get Lennon to jam with them at the time. In early 1970 Hawkins fired the band reportedly saying, "They could fuck up a crowbar." The name stuck but Rutter left the band, as did Atamanuik who joined the band Seatrain and was replaced by Sonnie Bernardi. Bell left to become part of the Full Tilt Boogie Band backing Janis Joplin and was replaced by Jozef Chirowski. Bell would later become a member of The Band. Newel soon left as well. Crowbar had a hit in Canada in 1971 with *Oh What A Feeling*, which received considerable airplay in the US.

In the summer of 1973 Crowbar was at Record Plant Studios in New York to record an album for Epic Records. Yoko Ono was also there recording her album *Feeling The Space*. Jay says she befriended the band paying a few bar tabs along the way. A short time later, John Lennon showed up to record his album *Mind Games*. Jay says Lennon recruited members of Crowbar to sing background vocals and do handclaps for his *Mind Games* album (probably on the song *Only People*).

Jay says, "Our producer, Jack Douglas, didn't feel my storytelling at the beginning of our song *Rocky Mountain Tragedy* was very convincing. He asked me, 'What do you drink?' I told him, 'Canadian Club.' He said, 'All we've got is Southern Comfort.' I quickly downed much of the bottle. The re-take of the track went down very well, but the whiskey didn't. I'd eaten a lot of Waldorf salad earlier and was soon on my knees in the studio's heavily mirrored bathroom relieving myself of the whiskey and the Waldorf. I felt some hands on my back, and a voice with a heavy Liverpool accent saying, 'Go ahead Kelly, puke it up man, I know how you feel. That feels better doesn't it?' I turned my head slightly and saw some boots as I slobbered on them,saying, 'Oh God, sorry Mr. Lennon!'"

Kelly clearly recalls Douglas later saying that after they left that night, that he grabbed John and Yoko as they were leaving, and put them, along with others around, in the hallway and had them sing on the chorus of *Rocky Mountain Tragedy*. Douglas admitted in the mid-1990s, "It's been more than 20 years and I really can't remember whether I used John and Yoko on any of the Crowbar sessions, but it's possible." Dennis Ferrante, a recording engineer at Record Plant, says that when they needed echo on a song they recorded in the hallway. Yoko recorded a promotional radio spot for Crowbar's Epic album *KE32746* (the catalogue number was used for the title). John, Yoko and May Pang are thanked in the album's credits. Crowbar broke up shortly after the album's release though some of the original members have reformed on occasion since that time.

The Crowd

You'll Never Walk Alone / Messages
Spartan-BRAD 1 (7" single) (UK) (06/07/85)
Producer: Graham Gouldman & Ray Levy
Paul McCartney: Message; Tim Healy: Message; Gary Holton: Message; Phil Lynott: Message; Rolf Harris: Message; Rose Marie: Message; Chris Norman: Message; Ann Nolans: Message; Ian "Lemmy" Kilmister: Message; Kiki Dee: Message; Keith Chegwin: Message; John Conteh: Message; Graham

Gouldman: Keyboards
CTS &/or Livingstone Studios, London, UK
05/20/85

Messages (G. Gouldman-**P. McCartney**-T. Healy-G. Holton-P. Lynott-R. Harris-R. Marie-C. Norman-A. Nolans-I. Kilmister-K. Dee-K. Chegwin-J. Conteh) 3:17 (2/1)

On May 11, 1985 over 50 people were killed and hundreds hospitalized after a fire broke out at Valley Parade Stadium in Bradford, England during a soccer match between Bradford City and Lincoln City. Gerry Marsden of Gerry & The Pacemakers* gathered a crowd of musicians to record a new version of their hit *You'll Never Walk Alone* to raise money for the Bradford City Disaster Fund set up to aid victims. The Crowd included among others, Denny Laine*, Kenny Lynch*, John Entwistle* and Ringo Starr's son Zak Starkey, with backing and production by Graham Gouldman (see 10cc). Paul McCartney and others unable to attend the sessions, telephoned in a "Message" of sympathy and support that was included on the record's B-side. McCartney's "Message" is also included on the 12" single release.

Burton Cummings

Ringo Starr And His All Starr Band Volume 2- Live From Montreux
Videoarts Music-VALJ-3369 (LD 12") (Japan) (probably 11/xx/93)
Producer: Ringo Starr (music); Jim Beach & Louise Velazquez (film); Executive Producer: Ringo Starr, David Fishof & Hilary Gerrard
Montreux Jazz Festival, Montreux, Switzerland
07/13/92

American Woman [live] (R. Bachman-B. Cummings-G. Peterson-M. Cale) 5:50 (2/8) (09/14/93)
Ringo Starr: Drums; Burton Cummings: Lead Vocals & Harmonica; Joe Walsh: Acoustic & Electric Guitar; Todd Rundgren: Guitar; Nils Lofgren: Acoustic & Electric Guitar; Dave Edmunds: Guitar; Timothy B. Schmit: Bass; Tim Cappello: Percussion; Zak Starkey: Drums
[Also available on *Ringo Starr And His All Starr Band The Anthology...So Far.* Koch-KOC-CD-8312 (2-14) (07/24/01) (02/05/01);]

No Time [live] (R. Bachman-B. Cummings) 4:31 (1/4)
Ringo Starr: Drums; Burton Cummings: Lead Vocals & Electric Guitar; Joe Walsh: Electric Guitar & B. Vocals; Todd Rundgren: Electric Guitar & B. Vocals; Nils Lofgren: Electric Guitar & B. Vocals; Dave Edmunds: Electric Guitar & B. Vocals; Timothy B. Schmit: Bass & B. Vocals; Tim Cappello: Percussion; Zak Starkey: Drums

Burton Cummings was born on December 31, 1947 in Winnipeg, Manitoba, Canada. He joined The Guess Who in 1966 who had formed in Winnipeg several years earlier, and originally consisted of Randy Bachman*, Chad Allan, Bob Ashley, Jim Kale and Garry Peterson. Cummings' keyboards, lead vocals and songwriting had a major impact on the band's sound. Their songs *These Eyes* and *Laughing* reached the Top 10 in 1969. In 1970 *American Woman* and *No Sugar Tonight* topped the charts, and *No Time* was a Top Five hit. That year Bachman, at odds with Cummings and the rock 'n' roll lifestyle of the band, left at the height of their success. Cummings continued to turn out hits such as *Share The Land, Albert Flasher* and their final Top 10 hit *Clap For The Wolfman,* in 1974, but personnel changes had eroded the band into little more than a back-up for Cummings who disbanded the group in 1975 and went solo. He had a Top 10 hit with *Stand Tall* in 1976. His 1979 album *Dream Of A Child* was the first Canadian album to be certified Multi-Platinum. His 1991 album *Plus Signs* was also certified Platinum. The Guess Who has regrouped a number of times since 1977 with, and without, Bachman and Cummings. They have recorded sporadically, including a cover of a The Beatles' song, and continue to make appearances along with personnel changes. Cummings and Bachman have been performing together since 2003.

Cummings was a part of Ringo Starr's All-Starr Band tour in 1992 performing *American Woman* and *No Time* with Ringo backing him on drums. Randy Bachman joined Ringo's All-Starr Band tour in 1995. For more information go to www.officialburtoncummings.com, www.bachmancummings.com, www.theguesswho.com

Roger Daltrey

One Of The Boys
Repertoire-REP 4643-WY (Germany) (01/28/98) (05/13/77)
Producer: David Courtney & Tony Meehan
Roger Daltrey: Lead Vocals; Rod Argent: Keyboards; Brian Odgers or John Entwistle: Bass; Stuart Tosh: Drums; Jimmy McCulloch: Guitar &/or Paul Keogh: Guitar; Phil Kenzie: Saxophone; Jimmy Jewell: Saxophone; Tony Rivers: B. Vocals; John Perry: B. Vocals; Stuart Calver: B. Vocals; Tony Meehan: Arrangements
Ramport Studios, London, UK xx/xx/76 &/or xx/xx/77

Giddy (**P. McCartney**) 4:46 (7)

Roger Daltrey was born on March 1, 1944 in London, England. He is known primarily as the lead vocalist of The Who (see John Entwistle, Keith Moon) singing on such classics of theirs as *My Generation*, *I Can See For Miles*, *Magic Bus*, *See Me, Feel Me*, *Won't Get Fooled Again*, *Behind Blue Eyes* and *Who Are You*. In their formative years The Who often covered The Beatles' songs in performance. During the mid-60s The Who were managed by Allen Klein.

In 1973 Daltrey had the UK Top Five hit *Giving It All Away* from his first of many solo albums. His song *Without Your Love* was a Top 20 hit in 1980. He has appeared in a number of stage productions, such as Mike Batt's* *Hunting Of The Snark*, and over 30 films including 1975's *Lisztomania* (Warner Home Video Laserdisc 11117) in which Ringo Starr plays The Pope.

Daltrey's 1977 album *One Of The Boys* includes the song *Giddy* written by Paul McCartney. Rod Argent, who plays keyboards on the song, say McCartney came in with all kinds of ideas for *Giddy* but didn't play on it. Jimmy McCulloch, who was probably a member of Wings at the time, is credited as one of the guitarists on the album. Additionally given special thanks are Hank B. Marvin, Alvin Lee*, Eric Clapton*, Andy Fairweather Low and Mick Ronson. McCartney's version of *Giddy* remains unreleased, though the "Rode All Night" portion of the song, recorded by McCartney during sessions for his album *Ram*, is available on unauthorized releases.

The Who's Pete Townshend was part of the Rockestra ensemble on Wings' 1979 album *Back To The Egg* and on the 1981 album *Concerts For The People Of Kampuchea* recorded at London's Hammersmith Odeon on December 29, 1979. The Who was inducted into the Rock and Roll Hall of Fame in 1990. Daltrey and Townshend sang with McCartney at the *Concert For New York City* on October 20, 2001 at Madison Square Garden. For more information go to www.thewho.com

Left to right: Gon'l, Roger Daltrey and Kristofer Engelhardt, Meadow Brook Music Festival, Rochester Hills (Detroit), MI July 8, 1998. Photo by Susan Long, © Kristofer Engelhardt.

Rick Danko

Ringo Starr And His All-Starr Band
Pioneer Artists-PA-090-007 (LD 12") (07/xx/90)

Producer: Tim Snow (video); Joe Walsh & Jim Nipar (music); Executive Producer: Ringo Starr & David Fishof
Ringo Starr: Drums; Rick Danko: Lead Vocals & Bass; Billy Preston: Keyboards; Jim Keltner: Drums; Levon Helm: Drums; Nils Lofgren: Accordion; Garth Hudson: Accordion; Joe Walsh: Guitar; Clarence Clemons: Saxophone; Dr. John: Keyboards
Greek Theatre, Los Angeles, CA 09/03/89

Shape I'm In [live] (R. Robertson) 4:19 (1/10)

Rick Danko was born on December 29, 1942 in Simcoe, Ontario, Canada. Danko was a member of the group The Band*. Rick also released several solo albums and did extensive session work. He contributed to Ringo Starr's 1973 album *Ringo*. Danko, and fellow member of The Band, Levon Helm*, was a member of Ringo Starr's All-Starr Band tour in 1989 performing *Shape I'm In* with Ringo backing him on drums. He was in a trio with Eric Andersen and Jonas Fjeld. Their 1992 album *Danko / Fjeld / Anderson*, received praise from critics and was awarded album of the year in the sparsely populated Norway where it sold over 100,000 copies. Danko died on December 10, 1999.

Jesse Ed Davis

Jesse Ed Davis/Ululu
Wounded Bird-WOU-346 (11/02/04)
Producer: (possibly) **George Harrison**, Jesse Ed Davis & Albhy Galuten
George Harrison: (possible) Guitar; Jesse Ed Davis: Lead Vocals & Guitar; Dr. John: Keyboards; Billy Rich: Bass; Jim Keltner: Drums; Merry Clayton: B. Vocals; Vanetta Fields: B. Vocals; Clydie King: B. Vocals; The Charles Chalmers Singers: B. Vocals
Criteria Sound, Miami, FL &/or Record Plant Studios &/or Village Recorder, Los Angeles, CA xx/xx/71 &/or xx/xx/72

Sue Me, Sue You Blues (G. Harrison) 2:45 (12) (01/25/72)

Keep Me Comin'
Wounded Bird-WOU 2133 (04/08/08) (01/01/73)
Producer: Jesse Ed Davis
George Harrison: (possible) involvement; Jesse Ed Davis: Lead Vocals & Guitar; one or more of the following: James Gordon: Keyboards; Bob Glaub &/or Bill Plummer: Bass; Jim Keltner: Drums; Bobby Torres: Congas; Felix Falcon: Percussion; John Angelos: Harmonica; Bobby Bruce: Violin; Gary Barone: Trumpet & Flugelhorn; Jerry Jumonville: Alto Saxophone; Clifford Scott &/or John Smith: Tenor Saxophone; George Bohannon &/or Jacques Ellis: Trombone; Howard Johnson: Baritone Saxophone; Oma Drake &/or Julie Tillman &/or Carolyn Willis &/or Patti Daley &/or Chris O'Dell &/or Russell Saunkeah &/or Billy Davis &/or Johnny Angel: B. Vocals
Paramount Recorders, Los Angeles, CA xx/12/72

Live! The Silver Wilburys [Various Artists]
[none]-SWP 87-2 (Korea) [unauthorized release] (xx/xx/88)
Producer: Palomino Club
George Harrison: Guitar; Jesse Ed Davis: Lead Vocal & Guitar; Taj Mahal: Harmonica & B. Vocals; Jim Ehinger: Keyboards; Bobby Tsukamoto: Bass; Mark Shark: Guitar; Gary Ray: Drums
Palomino Club, Los Angeles, CA 02/19/87

Farther On Down The Road (You Will Accompany Me) [live] T. Mahal- J. Davis 3:53 (1)

Jesse Ed Davis was born on September 21, 1944 in Norman, Oklahoma. He started playing in bands in high school and later toured with Conway Twitty. He met John Lennon on December 10, 1968 on the set of The Rolling Stones'* *Rock And Roll Circus* TV special as a member of the band Taj Mahal*. He came to George Harrison's attention through their mutual association with members of Delaney & Bonnie & Friends*. Davis was known primarily as a session guitarist who worked for a wide range of artists including Eric Clapton*, B.B. King*, Steve Miller*, Keith Moon*, Harry Nilsson* and Rod Stewart*.

There's been speculation, though no solid evidence, that Harrison contributed to Davis' first album *Jesse Davis* released in 1970 in part because it includes contributions from Clapton, Leon Russell* and Jackie Lomax* who'd also recently worked with Harrison. Lomax thinks Harrison may have contributed to the sessions for the album, portions of which were recorded in London in April 1970.

Davis' 1972 album *Ululu* contains Harrison's composition *Sue Me, Sue You Blues.* His recording was issued well over a year before Harrison's version. Harrison probably felt at the time that it wasn't a good idea to release his song about The Beatles suing each other. Davis said Harrison offered him the song when he was in Los Angeles in mid-1971 recording his song *Bangla Desh*, which ultimately led to Jesse's participation in *The Concert For Bangla Desh.* An article in the January 1993 issue of *Beatles Book Monthly* magazine mentions Harrison took part in sessions for a Jesse Ed Davis album in late 1971. This would almost certainly be for *Ululu.* If true, in addition to contributing *Sue Me, Sue You Blues*, Harrison may have also helped arrange, produce or play guitar on it, or other songs on *Ululu* but it's difficult to tell because the two guitarists' styles are similar. Jim Keltner, who drummed on *Ululu*, doesn't recall Harrison being present at any of the sessions, including *Sue Me, Sue You Blues.*

The liner notes for Davis' 1973 album *Keep Me Comin'* list a cameo by Bette Y El Mysterioso. Harrison had previously used the pseudonym of L'Angelo Misterioso (see Jack Bruce, Cream, Delaney & Bonnie & Friends). The cameos also list a Leon, Bonnie and Billy, no doubt referring to Russell*, Bramlett* and Preston*. A Merry (probably Clayton), Mick, Nino and Rod are also mentioned. Peter Waddington, Steve Delaney, Rusty Pelican and Marshall Brevitz are given honorable mention. It isn't known what songs, if any, Harrison may have contributed to on the album. Bob Glaub and Keltner, who were at most of the album's sessions, don't recall Harrison being present but say it's possible he could have overdubbed some guitar work when they weren't present. The record includes an interview in which Davis talks about *The Concert For Bangla Desh, Sue Me, Sue You Blues* and having a cassette recording of himself and Harrison jamming on The Beatles' songs. However, he makes no mention of Harrison playing on any of his studio recordings. Songs on the album include *Big Dipper/She's A Pain/Where Am I Now (When I Need Me)/Natural Anthem/Who Pulled The Plug?/Ching, Ching, China Boy/Bacon Fat/No Diga Mas/6:00 Bugalu/Keep Me Comin'.*

Davis was a constant companion of Lennon and Ringo Starr during their stays in Los Angeles between 1973 and 1974. He played on Lennon's 1974 album *Walls And Bridges*, his 1975 album *Rock 'N' Roll* and his posthumous album *Menlove Avenue* released in 1986. Davis performed the Lennon composition *Mucho Mungo* on the Westwood One radio series *The Lost Lennon Tapes*, claiming he was Lennon's inspiration for the song but May Pang disputes this. Davis contributed to Ringo's 1974 album *Goodnight Vienna*, his 1976 album *Rotogravure* and Harrison's 1975 album *Extra Texture (Read All About It).*

Harrison, John Fogerty* and Bob Dylan* played with Taj Mahal* and the Graffiti Band featuring Jesse Ed Davis at the Palomino Club in Hollywood on February 19, 1987. The performance is available on the unauthorized release *Live! The Silver Wilburys*, which features lead vocals by Davis on *Farther On Down The Road (You Will Accompany Me).* It may never be known if any of The Beatles played on any of his studio recordings as Jesse Ed Davis died on June 22, 1988.

Kiki Dee

With A Little Help To My Friends [Ringo Starr]
No Label Records-NLR 9904 (CD-R) [unauthorized release] (xx/xx/99)
Ringo Starr: Drums; Kiki Dee: Lead Vocals; Doug Kershaw: Fiddle; Todd Rundgren: Guitar; Bill Wyman: Bass; Dave Mason: Guitar & Vocals; Kasim Sultan: Bass & B. Vocals; Roger Powell: Keyboards; John Wilcox: Drums
Las Vegas, NV 09/03/79

Jumpin' Jack Flash [live] (M. Jagger-K. Richards) 3:24 (2)

Kiki Dee was born Pauline Matthews in Bradford, England on March 6, 1947. She began her musical career in the mid-1960s singing with local bands before becoming a backing vocalist on recordings for artists such as Dusty Springfield. Though she released several recordings, which received considerable airplay, and was later signed to Motown Records, her solo career didn't ignite until she teamed up with mentor Elton John* and signed to his Rocket Records label in 1973. That year she has a UK Top 20 hit with *Amoureuse*. Her recording of *I've Got The Music In Me* was a Top 20 hit in 1974. Her duet with Elton of his and Bernie Taupin's* song *Don't Go Breaking My Heart* topped the US and UK charts in 1976. Kiki was part of an all-star band that included Ringo Starr, which was formed to perform on the *Jerry Lewis Muscular Dystrophy Telethon* in 1979. In 1981 she had a UK Top 20 hit with *Star*. She and Elton's duet cover of *True Love* was a UK Top Five hit in 1993. More recently she has worked in theater, while continuing to record with a wide range of artists including Dave Stewart (see Platinumweird) and Carmelo Luggeri. For more information go to www.kikiandcarmelo.com

Deep Purple

The Bible III
Crystal Sound-CS 17 [unauthorized release]
George Harrison: Guitar; Ritchie Blackmore: Guitar; Jon Lord: Keyboards; Ian Paice: Drums; Ian Gillan: Vocals; Roger Glover: Bass
Entertainment Centre, Sydney, Australia
12/13/84

Lucille [live] (A. Collins-R. Penniman) 6:55 (8)

Deep Purple formed in 1968, taking their name from that popular song. The band has experienced a number of personnel changes over the years, but during their heyday consisted of the Brits, Richard "Ritchie" Blackmore, born April 14, 1945 in Weston-super-Mare; Jon Lord, born June 9, 1941 in Leicester; Ian Paice, born June 29, 1948 in Nottingham; Ian Gillan, born August 19, 1945 in London, and Roger Glover, born November 30, 1945 in Brecon, Wales. Though covering several Beatles' songs, they are considered pioneers of heavy metal rock. Their song *Hush* was a Top Five hit in 1968. Their 1972 album *Machine Head* yielded the hits *Space Truckin'*, *Highway Star* and their Top Five hit *Smoke On The Water*. They had a hit with *Woman From Tokyo* in 1973, the year that Glover and Gillan departed. The group disbanded shortly after Blackmore's departure in 1975. Members joined other popular groups or formed spin-off bands.

Paice and Lord, who was a neighbor of George Harrison's, were all good friends. Lord, Paice, Mick Ralphs, Boz Burrell and Simon Kirke* performed together in the nearby village of Pishill in December 1978 dubbing themselves the Pisshole Artists. Kirke recalls, "Mick Ralphs and I spent some time with George at his house helping him record a few tracks. George expressed a desire to play live again – but definitely 'low key,' so we went to a local pub. We were announced as 'a local, up-and-coming band.' The patrons were in a state of shock as we marched to the stage, as was my brother when George apologized profusely for trampling on his foot, which made his night! We played Deep Purple's *Hush*, Bad Company's *Feel Like Making Love* and rock 'n' roll standards before the night became a bit of a drunken haze. Everyone loved the gig. A few locals asked us if we'd come back and George said, 'We would but I don't think the landlord can afford us!'" Lord contributed to Harrison's 1982 album *Gone Troppo* and his 2002 album *Brainwashed*. He played with Billy Connolly / Chris Tummings & The Singing Rebels Band*, which included Harrison. There's no evidence that Harrison contributed to any of Lord's recordings.

Deep Purple reformed in 1984 with their heyday lineup. During a performance in Sydney, Australia on December 13, 1984 Harrison joined Deep Purple onstage introducing himself as "Arnold from Liverpool" (probably in reference to Arnold Grove, the street in Liverpool where he lived as a child), playing guitar during their encore of *Lucille*. Harrison, who had a home in Australia, was there at the time promoting Derek Taylor's book *Fifty Years Adrift*.

Paice was Paul McCartney's drummer on his 1999 album *Run Devil Run* and for his live performances in support of it. Deep Purple, with members Gillan, Glover and Paice, continue to record and tour. For more information go to www.deeppurple.com

Artifacts III (Not Fade Away: 1969-1971)
Big Music / BIGBX 009.4 (BIG 4033) (Italy) [unauthorized release] (probably 02/xx/95)
Producer: Danish TV
George Harrison: Guitar; Delaney Bramlett: Lead Vocals & Rhythm Guitar; Bonnie Bramlett: Lead Vocals & Tambourine; Eric Clapton: Lead Guitar; Billy Preston: Keyboards; Guitar; Carl Radle: Bass; Jim Gordon: Drums; Bobby Whitlock: Organ & B. Vocals; Jim Price: on Horns; Bobby Keys: Saxophone; Tex Johnson: Congas & Bongo Drums; Rita Coolidge: B. Vocals
Falkoner Theatre, Copenhagen, Denmark 12/12/69

Only You Know And I Know [live] (D. Mason) (1-3) 4:34

Delaney & Bonnie & Friends-On Tour With Eric Clapton
Atco-33326-2 (05/18/89) (04/07/70)
Producer: Jimmy Miller & Delaney Bramlett
George Harrison: Guitar; Delaney Bramlett: Lead Vocals & Rhythm Guitar; Bonnie Bramlett: Vocals & Tambourine; Eric Clapton: Lead Guitar; Dave Mason: Guitar; Carl Radle: Bass; Jim Gordon: Drums; Bobby Whitlock: Organ & B. Vocals; Jim Price: Trumpet & Trombone; Bobby Keys: Saxophone; Tex Johnson: Congas & Bongo Drums; Rita Coolidge: B. Vocals
Probably Fairfield Hall, Croydon, or possibly Colston Hall, Bristol or Empire Theatre, Liverpool, UK probably 12/07/69 or possibly 12/02 or 05/69 [unless noted otherwise]

Coming Home [live] (B. Bramlett-E. Clapton) 5:30 (7)
Fairfield Hall, Croydon, UK 12/07/69

I Don't Want To Discuss It [live] (B. Beatty-D. Cooper-E. Shelby) 4:55 (4)
Additionally: Bonnie Bramlett: Lead Vocals

Little Richard Medley: Tutti-Frutti/The Girl Can't Help It/Long Tall Sally/Jenny Jenny [live] (R. Penniman-D. LaBostrie/B. Troup/E. Johnson-R. Blackwell-R. Penniman/ E. Johnson-R. Penniman) 5:45 (8)

Only You Know And I Know [live] (D. Mason) 4:10 (3)
Additionally: Bonnie Bramlett: Lead Vocals
Fairfield Hall, Croydon, UK 12/07/69

Poor Elijah - Tribute To Johnson (Medley) [live] (D. Bramlett-J. Ford-L. Russell) 5:00 (2)
Additionally: Bonnie Bramlett: Lead Vocals

That's What My Man Is For [live] (B. Griffin) 4:30 (5)
Additionally: Bonnie Bramlett: Lead Vocals; Delaney Bramlett: Rhythm Guitar & Vocals (only)

Things Get Better [live] (E. Floyd-S. Cropper-W. Jackson) 4:20 (1)
Additionally: Bonnie Bramlett: Lead Vocals

Where There's A Will, There's A Way [live] (B. Bramlett-B. Whitlock) 4:57 (6)
Additionally: Delaney Bramlett: Vocals & Rhythm Guitar (only)

Far From The Madding Crowd
Mid Valley-308 [unauthorized release] (xx/xx/05)
Producer: Danish TV
George Harrison: Guitar; Delaney Bramlett: Lead Vocals & Rhythm Guitar; Bonnie Bramlett: Vocals & Tambourine; Eric Clapton: Lead Guitar; Billy Preston: Keyboards; Carl Radle: Bass; Jim Gordon: Drums; Bobby Whitlock: Organ & B. Vocals; Jim Price: on Horns; Bobby Keys: Saxophone; Tex Johnson: Congas & Bongo Drums; Rita Coolidge: B. Vocals
Falkoner Theatre, Copenhagen, Denmark 12/12/69

Coming Home [live] (B. Bramlett-E. Clapton) (7) 7:19

I Don't Want To Discuss It [live] (B. Beatty-D. Cooper-E. Shelby) 5:41 (5)
Additionally: Bonnie Bramlett: Lead Vocals

Little Richard Medley: Tutti-Frutti/The Girl Can't Help It/Long Tall Sally/Jenny Jenny [live] (R. Penniman-D. LaBostrie/B. Troup/E. Johnson-R. Blackwell-R. Penniman/ E. Johnson-R. Penniman) 7:14 (8)

My Baby Specializes [live] (D. Porter-I. Hayes) 4:21 (4)

Poor Elijah-Tribute To Johnson (Medley) [live] (D. Bramlett-J. Ford-L. Russell) 5:12 (1)
Additionally: Bonnie Bramlett: Lead Vocals

That's What My Man Is For [live] **(**B. Griffin) 5:06 (6)
Additionally: Bonnie Bramlett: Lead Vocals; Delaney Bramlett: Rhythm Guitar & Vocals (only)

Where There's A Will, There's A Way [live] **(**B. Bramlett-B. Whitlock) 5:18 (3)
Additionally: Delaney Bramlett: Vocals & Rhythm Guitar (only)

Delaney & Bonnie & Friends were formed by Delaney Bramlett* and Bonnie Lynn O'Farrell who was born on November 8, 1944 in Acton, Illinois. Bonnie knew she wanted to be a professional singer when she was five years old and singing in her church choir. She got her first brief taste of the big time as one of Ike and Tina Turner's* Ikettes. Being their first white singer Bonnie says, "There was an attempt made on our lives because of the integration thing. I was a 15-year-old virgin, white chick with black dudes, but Ike and all the guys were gentlemen. I wore a black wig and artificial tanning lotion, which turned me bright orange and streaked, but I was having a great time." Later she moved to California, met Delaney in 1967 and married him a week later.

Delaney & Bonnie put together some of the best studio musicians in rock to form their band known as Friends including Leon Russell*, Jim Price (see All Occasion Brass Band), Bobby Whitlock*, Bobby Keys*, Jim Keltner (see Attitudes), Carl Radle (see Derek and the Dominos) and others. George Harrison saw them perform at a private party in Los Angeles in the fall of 1968. Bonnie says George took tapes of the group back to England. Alan Pariser, an associate of The Beatles, attempted to sign them away from their contract with Elektra Records to Apple. Their album *The Original Delaney & Bonnie - Accept No Substitute* was scheduled for release in May 1969 on Apple (SAPCOR-7 in the UK), but was withdrawn (copies exist) and instead issued on Elektra.

Eric Clapton* reportedly first saw Delaney & Bonnie during a US tour with Cream*. Harrison apparently renewed Eric's interest in them. They were hired as the opening act for Eric's band Blind Faith* for their US tour in the summer of 1969 and Eric began joining them onstage. They went to the UK that fall to help Eric record his first solo album and they toured Europe together. Harrison and Ringo Starr were in attendance at their UK tour opener at the Royal Albert Hall in London on December 1, 1969. Harrison went backstage after the show and his offer to join the tour was accepted. From December 2-7 they played Colston Hall in Bristol, Town Hall in Birmingham, City Hall in Sheffield, City Hall in Newcastle-upon-Tyne, Empire Theatre in Liverpool and Fairfield Hall in Croydon. A live album was released titled *Delaney & Bonnie & Friends - On Tour With Eric Clapton*. Harrison wasn't credited except for the "Special Thanks to: Mysterioso" (see: Jack Bruce, Jesse Ed Davis). According to Delaney, the entire tour was recorded. He and Bonnie thought the album was compiled primarily from their performances in Croydon and Bristol, and possibly Liverpool. Bonnie said, "These were our best shows." Delaney also thought that maybe some of the London show was used but Bonnie doubts it because, "It was opening night and we were still getting all the bugs out." Marc Roberty claims in his book *Eric Clapton - The Complete Recording Sessions, 1963-1992* that only the London and Croydon shows were recorded and that the Croydon shows were used for the album. Any songs recorded in London wouldn't include Harrison. Based on the introductions *Coming Home* and *Only You Know And I Know* were recorded at Croydon. The album only contains a portion of their performances at each show. The group also performed a number of other songs such as *My Baby Specializes*, *Tell Me*, *Mississippi's Burning*, *Come On In My Kitchen*, *Howling For My Baby*, and a few other Howlin' Wolf* and Robert Johnson songs. Eric was featured singing *Don't Know Why*, which he wrote with Delaney. Delaney and Bonnie also said that a shy Harrison was finally goaded into singing some oldies during the tour, mostly Carl Perkins* numbers such as *Everybody's Trying To Be My Baby*, *Blue Suede Shoes* and the Rosie and the Originals ballad *Angel Baby*. Delaney suspects that Atlantic probably still has the out-takes, including Harrison's brief set.

Harrison also accompanied the group to Copenhagen, Denmark for shows at the Falkoner Theatre on December 10, 11 and 12, and to Sweden playing in Stockholm and Gothenburg on December 13 and 14. Some of the Falkoner Theatre performances are available on the unauthorized releases *Artifacts III*, and *Far From The Madding Crowd* that also includes a DVD with a portion of the December 12 performance shown on Danish TV. Billy Preston* joined them in Scandinavia but Dave Mason* did not. Delaney says he helped Harrison learn Mason's slide guitar parts setting in motion Harrison's familiar trademark guitar style. Delaney revealed that George's behavior on tour was more reminiscent of his Hamburg days than one might expect from the "spiritual" Beatle, which included getting caught breaking into a friend's pub after hours to help themselves, and stealing Delaney's pants on the bus just before they arrived at their hotel, forcing Delaney to enter the hotel wrapped in a newspaper.

Delaney said, "During the tour George asked me how to write a gospel song. I used the chord patterns of the Chiffons' 1963 hit *He's So Fine* as a demo. [The Chiffons were on the bill with The Beatles at their first American concert on February 11, 1964.] George and the rest of us worked on a gospel anthem based around my demo, which developed into his song *My Sweet Lord*." When Harrison released the song about a year later, Delaney asked George why he wasn't given credit for helping to develop the smash hit. Bonnie questions Delaney's recollections saying *My Sweet Lord* was probably born out of an ad-lib medley of gospel songs including *Oh Happy Day* that the band jammed on one night in a hotel room. Bobby Keys recalls *My Sweet Lord* being sung on the tour bus. Delaney says that when Harrison was sued for plagiarism by Bright Tunes, the owners of *He's So Fine*, he was asked to testify but he was advised by his attorneys not to get involved. Harrison maintained in court that *My Sweet Lord* was primarily inspired by the Edwin Hawkins Singers' arrangement of the traditional gospel song *Oh Happy Day*, which was a hit at the time. [Harrison employed the services of the Edwin Hawkins Singers to back Billy Preston on his version of *My Sweet Lord*.] The court found Harrison guilty of plagiarism. Harrison was then double-dealt by Allen Klein, who bought the rights to *He's So Fine* and sued for damages. The two eventually settled with Harrison being able to own the rights to *My Sweet Lord* in main regions.

Following the tour the group, including Harrison, backed up John Lennon and Yoko Ono* on December 15 at London's Lyceum Ballroom for the UNICEF *Peace For Christmas* benefit performance later included on the Lennons' 1972 album *Some Time In New York City*. Most of the Friends soon split from Delaney & Bonnie to join Joe Cocker's* Mad Dogs & Englishmen tour, which also included Leon Russell. Following the tour, in the summer of 1970, Radle, Whitlock and Jim Gordon teamed up with Clapton to form the short-lived group Derek And The Dominos*. Many of the Friends would later work on numerous solo Beatles' recordings and side projects.

Delaney & Bonnie and a new set of Friends recorded several more albums. 1971 was their most successful year on the charts with the Top 20 hits *Never Ending Song Of Love* and *Only You Know And I Know*. Their song *Groupie*, retitled *Superstar*, was a Top Five hit for the Carpenters that year. The 1972 Atco Records single *Where There's A Will, There's A Way* is edited from the version on *Delaney & Bonnie & Friends - On Tour With Eric Clapton*. Delaney & Bonnie recorded one more album, ironically titled *D&B Together*, before their marriage, and musical act, ended in 1972. They released several solo albums following their breakup.

In early 1975 Bonnie was rehearsing for a tour with drummer Joe English when Joe got the call from Paul McCartney to join his band Wings. In 1988 Bonnie married Danny Sheridan from the Eli Radish Band. Danny encouraged her to take up acting. She appeared in the films *Fame* and *The Doors*, and was a regular for several seasons on ABC TV's popular sitcom *Roseanne*. In May 1992 Bonnie, Danny, Jimmy Crespo and Dallas Taylor were rehearsing their new band Bandaloo Doctors in a Hollywood studio. Down the hall, Ringo Starr And His All-Starr Band were rehearsing for their tour. After only three days of rehearsing, Ringo dropped in and asked if they'd open for his tour. Danny said that Ringo was very generous, helpful and enthusiastic about Bandaloo Doctors during the tour.

Separately, Delaney and Bonnie continued to write, do session work and record (including covers of The Beatles' songs). Their daughter Bekka has had a successful singing career working with Fleetwood Mac (see Mick Fleetwood), Faith Hill and many others. For more information go to www.delaneybramlett.com, www.bonniebramlett.com

The Karl Denver Trio

The Beatles At The Beeb/The Fab Four-Radio Active Vol. 1
Pyramid- RFT CD 005 [unauthorized release] (xx/xx/88)
Producer: Bryant Marriott
George Harrison: Guitar & B. Vocals; **John Lennon: Guitar & B. Vocals**; **Paul McCartney: Bass**; **Ringo Starr: Drums**; Karl Denver: Lead Vocals & Guitar; Kevin Neill: Guitar; Gerry Cottrell: Guitar
BBC Piccadilly Studios, London, UK 04/01/63

Side By Side (H. Wood) 0:50 (7)

Karl Denver was born Angus McKenzie in Glasgow, Scotland on December 16, 1931. He took up guitar while recovering from wounds suffered during the Korean War. Later he made his way to Nashville, Tennessee to pursue a career in country and folk music. He used the stage name Karl (the name of his deceased son) Denver (having lived in Colorado), before having to return to the UK in 1959. There he formed The Karl Denver Trio with Manchester natives Gerard "Gerry" Cottrell born on December 18, 1933 and Kevin Neill born on July 25, 1931. Noted TV and record producer Jack Good secured them a contract with Decca Records and produced their recordings featuring Karl's distinctive falsetto yodeling. Between 1961 and 1963 in the UK they had a Top Five hit with *Wimoweh* (a.k.a. *The Lion Sleeps Tonight*), Top 10 hits with *Marcheta*, *Mexicali Rose* and *Never Goodbye*, and Top 20 hits with *A Little Love, A Little Kiss* and *Still*.

On April 1, 1963 The Beatles taped two appearances on BBC radio's Light Programme series *Side By Side* and backed the show's host, The Karl Denver Trio, on the show's theme song *Side By Side*. The shows aired on April 22 and May 13. On April 4 The Beatles recorded their final appearance on the show, which aired on June 24, 1963. The Beatles joined the Karl Denver Tro during their finale of *Swanee River* on ABC TV's *Shindig* on October 3, 1964, and broadcast on the 7th.

The Karl Denver Trio managed Top 40 hits with *My World Of Blue* and *Love Me With All Your Heart* in 1964, but groups like The Beatles hurt the popularity of folk groups such as The Karl Denver Trio. Cottrell left in 1979 and was replaced by Keith Elliott. In 1989 the revised trio stumbled into the lower half of the UK charts when the popular Manchester group Happy Mondays had them guest on their song *Lazyitis* (a reworking of The Beatles' song *Ticket To Ride*) and an updated recording of *Wimoweh*. They continued to record and perform until the death of Karl Denver on December 21, 1998. Gerry Cottrell died on November 24, 2006. Kevin Neill continues to perform in clubs in the UK.

Derek And The Dominos

Crossroads
Polydor-835 261-2 (04/18/88)
Producer: Phil Spector

Roll It Over (E. Clapton-B. Whitlock) 4:29 (2-13) (09/14/70)
George Harrison: Guitar & B. Vocals; Eric Clapton: Lead Vocals & Guitar; Dave Mason: Guitar & B. Vocals; Bobby Whitlock: Lead Vocals & Piano; Carl Radle: Bass; Jim Gordon: Drums
Probably Apple Studios or EMI-Abbey Road Studios, London or possibly FPSHOT, UK probably 06/18/70

Tell The Truth (E. Clapton-B. Whitlock) 3:23 (2-12) (09/14/70)
George Harrison: Guitar; Eric Clapton: Lead Vocals & Guitar; Bobby Whitlock: Guitar; Carl Radle: Bass; Jim Gordon: Drums
Probably Apple or EMI-Abbey Road Studios, possibly Trident Studios, London, UK probably 06/18/70 possibly 08/05/70

Derek And The Dominos formed around Eric Clapton*, Carl Radle who was born on June 18, 1942 in Tulsa, Oklahoma, Jim Gordon who was born on July 14, 1945 in Los Angeles, California and Bobby Whitlock*. All had been members of Delaney & Bonnie & Friends*. Dave Mason,* and guitarist Duane Allman of The Allman Brothers Band who was born on November 20, 1946 in Nashville, Tennessee, also held brief membership in the short-lived group. The band began working as backing musicians on George Harrison's album *All Things Must Pass* in late spring and summer of 1970.

Their first single *Tell The Truth / Roll It Over*,

produced by Phil Spector*, was born out of their work on Harrison's album. The single was quickly withdrawn at the band's request because they preferred their newly recorded (album) version of *Tell The Truth* produced by Tom Dowd. [Had Atco Records analyzed the sexually suggestive lyrics of *Roll It Over* they surely wouldn't have released it.] Several reliable publications, including Mark Roberty's book *Eric Clapton: The Complete Recording Sessions 1963-1992*, credit Harrison playing guitar on the single version of *Tell The Truth* and *Roll It Over*. The credits on Eric's retrospective CD set *Crossroads* don't list Harrison playing on the single version of *Tell The Truth*, but credit him playing on *Roll It Over*. Harrison's other contributions on *Crossroads* are fully noted, so it's unlikely other contributions by him would be omitted except by oversight. In *Clapton: The Autobiography* Eric recalls Harrison being present for the recording of both songs. In the notes accompanying the re-mixed *All Things Must Pass* album released in 2001, Harrison states, "We even recorded two of the Dominoes' songs, *Roll It Over* and *Tell The Truth*, during the *All Things Must Pass* sessions, which they re-recorded later." Given Spector's liberal use of musicians to create his trademark "wall of sound" it's very likely that Harrison's guitar is buried in the mix on both sides of the single. There is also considerable confusion regarding where and when these songs were recorded. Eric's autobiography says both songs were recorded at Abbey Road Studios. *Crossroads* says *Roll It Over* was recorded at FPSHOT (Harrison's home studio) in the summer of 1970 during sessions for the *All Things Must Pass*, and *Tell The Truth* was recorded at Trident Studios on August 5, 1970. Roberty's book says the songs were recorded at Apple Studios on June 18, 1970, as do other sources. Harrison, who'd only acquired the home a few months earlier, probably didn't have a functional studio there yet. *Crossroads* lists *Roll It Over* as being mixed at Trident Studios on August 5, 1970, the same day *Tell The Truth* was recorded, so perhaps this contributed to the confusion regarding when they were recorded. Whitlock says that *Tell The Truth* and *Roll It Over* were recorded at Abbey Road Studios and that Harrison didn't contribute to either song. However, he recalls recording at Harrison's home during this period. *Crossroads* also lists Dave Mason (who played guitar on *All Things Must Pass*) as playing guitar and singing on *Roll It Over*. Whitlock says Mason wasn't around when *Tell The Truth* and *Roll It Over* were recorded. Whitlock correctly points out that he and Clapton played guitar and sang lead vocals on both songs. If Whitlock is mistaken, then it would seem more likely that the two songs were recorded at different times, and possibly at different studios.

The mega-hit *Layla*, from their critically acclaimed *Layla And Other Assorted Love Songs*, their only studio album release, was a thinly veiled reference to the portrait of the woman on the album's front jacket and the object of Eric's affections, George's wife, Pattie Boyd Harrison. Eric was romantically involved with Pattie's younger sister Paula at the time. Derek And The Dominos broke up in the spring of 1971. Thereafter Clapton would bill himself as a solo act. Duane Allman was killed on October 29, 1971. Jim Gordon has been imprisoned or confined to a mental hospital since murdering his mother in 1983. Carl Radle died on May 30, 1980.

Johnny Devlin & The Devils

25 Rare Recycled RCA Rock Relics [Various Artists]
RCA-VPL 1 0240 (album 12") (Australia) (xx/xx/79)
Producer: Johnny Devlin
Johnny Devlin: Lead Vocals
AWA Studios, Sydney, Australia probably 01/xx/65

Won't You Be My Baby? ([P. McCartney] J. Devlin) 2:38 (1/7) (xx/xx/65)

Johnny Devlin was born on May 11, 1938 in Raetihi, New Zealand but grew up in Wanganui, New Zealand. Devlin's late 1950's cover of *Lawdy Miss Clawdy* was the first record to be certified Gold in New Zealand. It made the Elvis-styled Devlin a teen idol there, and in Australia where he's lived most of his life. His composition *Surfside*, recorded by The Denvermen in 1962, was the first chart topping instrumental in Australia.

Devlin and his group The Devils were a supporting act on The Beatles' tour of Australia and New Zealand in June 1964. Devlin says, "Touring with The Beatles was probably the highlight of my career. They were fabulous. They invited me to all of their parties. I had written a song called *Won't You Be My Baby?* and played it backstage at Sydney Stadium for Paul McCartney, but he didn't like it. He took the guitar and fiddled around with it a bit and said, 'Why don't you do this?' He put a couple of chords in here, there and everywhere and it sounded better. I recorded it in early 1965 and it was a minor hit single in Australia." Devlin cannot recall if he used studio musicians or The Devils (probably Bob Taylor, Kevin McKeefry, Colin Luck and Barry Coupland) to back him on it. The recording was included on the 1979 album *25 Rare Recycled RCA Rock Relics* and is also available on Devlin's LP *Stag-O-Lee* (Canetoad Records-CTLP-006 Australia). None of these records lists McCartney as co-composer but Devlin says, "I thought in all fairness that I should mention Paul as contributing to it. I'm quite sure the song is registered in our names." Devlin has sporadically recorded, performed, made TV appearances, rock documentaries and managed other artists.

Dr. John

The Best Of Ringo Starr And His All-Starr Band...So Far
Image-ID0828RO (DVD) (10/23/01)
Producer: Michael Drumm; Tim Snow (video); Joe Walsh & Jim Nipar (music); Executive Producer: Ringo Starr & David Fishof
Ringo Starr: Drums; Dr. John: Lead Vocals & Keyboards; Billy Preston: Keyboards; Jim Keltner: Drums; Levon Helm: Drums; Nils Lofgren: Guitar; Joe Walsh: Guitar; Rick Danko: Bass; Clarence Clemons: Saxophone
Greek Theatre, Los Angeles, CA 09/03/89

Iko Iko [live] (R.L. Hawkins-B. Hawkins-J. Johnson-J. Crawford) 6:05 (2) (07/xx/90)
[Also available on *Ringo Starr and his All Starr Band The Anthology...So Far.* Koch-KOC-CD-8312 (1-3) (07/24/01) (02/05/01)]

Dr. John, Sully's, Dearborn (Detroit), MI 1993.
© and photo by Kristofer Engelhardt.

Ringo Starr And His All-Starr Band
Pioneer Artists-PA-090-007 (LD 12") (07/xx/90)
Producer: Tim Snow (video); Joe Walsh & Jim Nipar (music); Executive Producer: Ringo Starr & David Fishof
Greek Theatre, Los Angeles, CA 09/03/89

Right Place Wrong Time [live] (M. Rebennack) 3:52 (2/4)
Ringo Starr: Drums; Dr. John: Lead Vocals & Keyboards; Billy Preston: Keyboards; Jim Keltner: Drums; Levon Helm: Drums; Nils Lofgren: Guitar; Joe Walsh: Guitar; Rick Danko: Bass; Clarence Clemons: Saxophone
Greek Theatre, Los Angeles, CA 09/03/89

Malcolm John Rebennack Jr. a.k.a. Dr. John (The Night Tripper) or Dr. John Creaux was born on November 21, 1940 in New Orleans, Louisiana. He is regarded as one of the finest purveyors of the New Orleans sound, mixing jazz, funk, gospel, R&B and Creole music, into a style that's been called swamp rock. His hits include *Right Place, Wrong Time* and *Such A Night*, but for over 40 years he's been a successful songwriter and session player for artists such as Eric Clapton*, Taj Mahal*, Harry Nilsson*, The Rolling Stones*, Chris Barber*, Phil Spector* and many others. John started out as a guitar player but switched to the keyboards in the 1960s. He sometimes performs in wild Mardi Gras-styled costumes.

In early December 1973 John Lennon, Cher, Bobby Womack, Elton John* and Bonnie Bramlett (see Delaney & Bonnie & Friends) joined Dr. John onstage while he performed *Cold, Cold, Cold* and *Mama Don't Want No* at Hollywood's Troubadour Club. Lennon's contributions were limited to repetitive discordant sounds on keyboards. The performance probably took place following one of the recording sessions for Lennon's album *Rock 'N' Roll*, to which Dr. John had contributed. Dr. John contributed to Ringo Starr's 1974 album *Goodnight Vienna*, his 1976 album *Rotogravure* and his 1978 album *Bad Boy*.

Dr. John's 1975 album *Hollywood Be Thy Name* includes a cover of The Beatles' song *Yesterday* and credits Ringo as Master Of Ceremonies. According to Dr. John, Ringo played the part of Master Of Ceremonies in an unused film to promote *Hollywood Be Thy Name* but didn't contribute to the album. The footage was shot in August 1975 at Cherokee Studios in Los Angeles, which was decorated and renamed Willie Purple's Nightclub for the occasion.

Dr. John was a member of Ringo Starr's All-Starr Band tour in 1989 performing *Iko Iko* and *Right Place, Wrong Time* with Ringo backing him on drums. John joined Ringo's All-Starr Band at the Mohegan Sun Arena in Uncasville, Connecticut on June 22, 2008 for *With A Little Help From My Friends*. Dr. John is still in high demand as a session player and continues to play the club circuit. For more information go to www.drjohn.org

Dog Soldier

April Rainbow
Cutting Room (10" acetate single) [unreleased]
Producer: John Lennon & Roy Cicala
Patrick Jude: Lead Vocals; probably one or more of the following: Mark Rivera: Saxophone; John Corbert: Keyboards; Vinnie Appice: Drums; Joe Bassin: Trombone; Bob Livingood: Trumpet; Rick: Bass; Joe Crupi: Guitar; Angelo Arcuri: Bass; Kenny Papa; Kenny Sambolin
Record Plant Studios, New York, NY 01/22/75

April Rainbow (J. Corbert) 3:05 (1/1)

Beatles Undercover
C.G. Publishing-CGPINT8008 (Canada) (09/07/98)
Producer: John Lennon & Roy Cicala
Patrick Jude: Lead Vocals & (possible) Percussion; probably one or more of the following: Mark Rivera: Saxophone; John Corbert: Keyboards; Vinnie Appice: Drums; Joe Bassin: Trombone; Bob Livingood: Trumpet; Rick: Bass; Joe Crupi: Guitar; Angelo Arcuri: Bass; Kenny Papa; Kenny Sambolin
Record Plant Studios, New York, NY xx/xx/74 or xx/xx/75

Incantation (R. Cicala-J. Lennon) 3:55 (1)

[None]
[Unreleased]
Producer: John Lennon & Roy Cicala
Patrick Jude: Lead Vocals; probably one or more of the following: Mark Rivera: Saxophone; John Corbert: Keyboards; Vinnie Appice: Drums; Joe Bassin: Trombone; Bob Livingood: Trumpet; Rick: Bass; Kenny Papa; Kenny Sambolin; Joe Crupi: Guitar; Angelo Arcuri: Bass
Record Plant Studios, New York, NY probably 01/xx/75

Everyday Living (P. Jude-M. Rivera-J. Corbert-V. Appice) 3:01

You Can't Do That (J. Lennon-P. McCartney)
Additionally: Patrick Jude: (possible) Percussion

Dog Soldier (not the mid-1970s UK band) was first known as Community Apple when fronted by singer Joey Dambra (who contributed backing vocals to John Lennon's song *#9* Dream), then Bomf, an acronym for Band Of Mother Fuckers (see Lori Burton). According to May Pang, Lennon suggested the name Dog Soldier, from his lyrics to the song *Incantation*. The band was dubbed John Lennon etc. when they backed him at the Waldorf Astoria Hotel for *A Salute To Sir Lew Grade* on April 18, 1975, which proved to be his last live show.

Dog Soldier's lead singer was Patrick Jude, born Patrick Jude Petrullo on February 25, 1951 in Hoboken, New Jersey. In 1974 Jude, a singer, dancer and actor most of his life, wanted to return to fronting a rock band after playing the role of Judas in *Jesus Christ Superstar* on Broadway. He answered an ad in the *Village Voice* looking for a dynamic front man, which led to an audition at Record Plant Studios in New York. The studio's owner Roy Cicala took him to meet the lyricist of the song they wanted him to sing. Jude entered a studio control room and was greeted by John Lennon listening to a playback of his audition saying, "Great voice man!" Jude recalls, "I was speechless and couldn't sleep for days." Jude says he later did handclaps on Lennon's recording of *Whatever Gets You Thru The Night*.

Another member of Dog Soldier was Mark Rivera. Rivera has since played saxophone for many musicians including Hall & Oates*, Simon and Garfunkel (see Paul Simon), Elton John* and Billy Joel*. The musically versatile Rivera

Left to right: Patrick Jude, John Hanti, Kristofer Engelhardt and Brute Force, Barnes & Noble, New York, NY, March 25, 1999. Photo by Coward, © Kristofer Engelhardt.

filled a variety of roles as musical director of Ringo Starr's All-Starr Band tours in 1995, 1997, 1998, 2000, 2001 and 2003. The drummer in Dog Soldier was Vinnie Appice who has since worked with Rick Derringer, DIO and Black Sabbath.

According to Jude, Lennon was involved in four of Dog Soldier's recordings at Record Plant Studios in late 1974 or early 1975. Two of the songs, *Everyday Living* and *April Rainbow*, were Dog Soldier compositions that John produced. Another song, *Incantation*, was originally written by Cicala with new lyrics written by Lennon. John also produced Dog Soldier's version of his Beatles' song *You Can't Do That*. Jude said almost an album's worth of Dog Soldier material was recorded and was probably going to come out on Apple. He thinks the album was going to be titled *Incantation*. Cicala says, "Because Dog Soldier had mostly original songs, John and Capitol wanted them to record a cover version of *You Can't Do That*. When we were ready to mix the whole album, John got back together with Yoko and disappeared."

Fats Domino

They Call Me The Fat Man-The Legendary Imperial Recordings
Capitol-9678426 (12/01/91) **Paul McCartney: Liner Notes**

Antoine "Fats" Domino was born on February 26, 1928 in New Orleans. Signed to Imperial Records, the singer, songwriter and pianist's song *The Fat Man* reached number two on the R&B charts in 1949. It was one of the first songs to contain elements of what would later be termed rock 'n' roll. During the first half of the 1950s he had nearly a dozen Top 10 hits on the R&B charts. In 1955 he had his first Top 10 hit with *Ain't That A Shame* and three number one hits on the R&B charts. During the second half of the 1950's he had Top Five hits with *Blueberry Hill*, *Blue Monday* and *I'm Walkin'*, and Top 10 hits with *Valley Of Tears*, *It's You I Love*, *Whole Lotta Loving*, *I Want To Walk You Home* and *Be My Guest*. He also had Top 20 hits in the early 1960s with *Three Nights A Week*, *Walking To New Orleans*, *My Girl Josephine* and *Let The Four Winds Blow*.

Despite dwindling chart success since then he has continued to perform, though less so in recent years due to failing health. Domino was a charter inductee into the Rock and Roll Hall of Fame in 1986. He had to be rescued from the balcony of his home in New Orleans following Hurricane Katrina in 2005.

The Beatles were fans of Domino, particularly Paul McCartney. The Beatles met with Domino in New Orleans on September 16, 1964 during their US tour. McCartney emulated his songwriting, especially on his Beatles' song *Lady Madonna*. Ironically, Domino's last song to enter the charts was his cover of the song in 1968. The booklet included with the 1991 CD set *They Call Me The Fat Man-The Legendary Imperial Recordings* contains the following: "Fats was one of the most exciting performers to come out of the '50s, and was an enormous influence upon my early career. I still perform, with great joy, his classic *Ain't That A Shame*. Later I met him in New Orleans, and I vividly remember his magnificent diamond wristwatch!"- Paul McCartney, July 1991. McCartney has recorded covers of Domino's songs *I'm In Love Again*, *I'm Gonna Be A Wheel Someday*, *Coquette*, *Ain't That A Shame*, and *I Want To Walk You Home* included on the 2007 album *Goin' Home A Tribute To Fats Domino*, which also includes John Lennon's cover of *Ain't That A Shame*.

Lonnie Donegan

Puttin' On The Style
United Artists-UA-LA 827-H (album 12") (01/09/78)
Producer: Adam Faith
Larrabee Studios, Los Angeles, CA 07 &/or 08/xx/77

Ham 'n' Eggs (trad. Arr: L. Donegan) 3:10 (1/3)
Ringo Starr: Drums; Lonnie Donegan: Lead Vocals & 12-String Guitar; Dave Wyntor: Bass; Peter Jameson: Acoustic & Slide Guitar; Peter Banks: Guitar; Peter Wingfield: Piano; Leo Sayer: Harp

Have A Drink On Me (Take A Whiff On Me) (H. Ledbetter-J. Lomax-A. Lomax-L. Donegan-P. Buchanan) 3:00 (1/2)
Ringo Starr: Drums; Lonnie Donegan: Lead Vocals & Banjo; Dave Wyntor: Bass; Peter Jameson: Acoustic & Slide Guitar; Peter Wingfield: Piano; Albert Lee: Lead Guitar; Southern California Community Choir-Arr. Rev. James Cleveland: B. Vocals

[None]
[Unreleased]
Producer: Lonnie Donegan
George Harrison: Guitar; Lonnie Donegan: Lead Vocals & Banjo; Dave Peacock: Bass; Chas Hodges: Guitar; Mick Burt: Drums
Essex Studios, London & FPSHOT, UK xx/xx/79

Everybody's Making It Big But Me (C. Hodges-D. Peacock)

Massage Parlour (C. Hodges-D. Peacock)

Punchy And The Willer Warbler (C. Hodges-D. Peacock)

Lonnie Donegan was born Anthony Donegan on April 29, 1931 in Glasgow, Scotland but was raised in London, England. His father was a violinist in the National Scottish Orchestra. Lonnie began playing drums at age 13 but later switched to guitar and banjo. The name Lonnie was borrowed from the blues artist Lonnie Johnson. Donegan's early career included membership in a variety of jazz bands including a stint with Chris Barber's Jazz Band (see Chris Barber & His Band).

While in Barber's band, Donegan was dubbed the "king of skiffle" following his global mega-hit *Rock Island Line* in 1956. Between 1957 and 1960 he had eight UK Top Five hits, including *Cumberland Gap* and *Gamblin' Man*, which topped the UK charts. *Does Your Chewing Gum Lose Its Flavor (On The Bedpost Overnight)* was a Top Five hit in 1959. He inspired many youngsters in the UK to take up music, including John Lennon, Paul McCartney and George Harrison, laying the foundation for a generation of British rock stars. The first bands Ringo Starr was in were called The Eddie Clayton Skiffle Group and Darktown Skiffle Group. Harrison and McCartney attended Donegan's performances at Liverpool's Empire Theatre as teenagers. One of the songs that survives on tape from Lennon and The Quarry Men's performance at the Woolton Parish Fete at St. Peter's Church (the day John met Paul) was Donegan's current hit *Puttin' On The Style*. [The Westwood One radio series *The Lost Lennon Tapes* features home demos by Lennon during the '70s singing several Donegan classics.] Donegan established a folk music society, which also acted as his fan club, whose membership included Harrison. Donegan thought The Beatles played at one of the fan club's meetings at the Cavern Club in Liverpool. Ironically, Donegan's success waned in the mid-1960s following the British music invasion he helped inspire. He continued to perform until heart problems slowed his pace in the mid-1970s.

On June 24, 1976 McCartney threw a party in Los Angeles to celebrate the successful completion of Wings' US tour. Guests Leo Sayer, Adam Faith*, Elton John* and Ringo started singing Donegan's songs together. At McCartney's suggestion, Faith got the assembled to commit to helping him record a new album for Donegan featuring some of his hits. Ringo contributed to the album along with other Donegan admirers including Klaus Voormann*, Ron Wood*, Zoot Money*, Jim Keltner (see Attitudes) and Nicky Hopkins*. Donegan said Ringo's contributions were recorded at Larrabee Studios in Los Angeles. He said he also made some recordings with Harrison and Chas & Dave in 1979. Donegan was featured in the 1982 film documentary *The Complete Beatles*. He became active in music publishing and acting, and played the leading role in the British musical comedy *Mr. Cincers* in 1984. Lonnie Donegan was scheduled to appear at the *Concert For George* but died on November 4, 2002 just weeks before the event. For more information go to www.lonniedoneganinc.com

Donovan

No. 3 Abbey Road N.W.8
Vigotone-VT-116 [unauthorized release] (xx/xx/93)
Producer: Paul McCartney
Paul McCartney's home studio, St. John's Wood, London, UK probably 11/xx/68-01/xx/69

Good Morning Mr. Wind (D. Leitch) 1:31 (6)
Paul McCartney: Guitar & Dialogue; Donovan Leitch: Lead Vocals & Guitar

Lalena (D. Leitch) 3:26 (4)
Paul McCartney: Guitar & B. Vocals; Donovan Leitch: Lead Vocals & Guitar

Land Of Gisch (D. Leitch) 0:48 (8)
Paul McCartney: Dialogue; Donovan Leitch: Lead Vocals & Guitar

Unicorn (D. Leitch) 1:04 (3)
Donovan Leitch: Lead Vocals & Guitar

The Walrus And The Carpenter (D. Leitch-L. Carroll) 1:07 (7)
Paul McCartney: Dialogue; Donovan Leitch: Lead Vocals & Guitar

Rising
Permanent-PERM CD 2 (UK) (11/11/90)
Producer: Patrick Hehir
Donovan Leitch: Lead Vocals & Guitar
Carnegie Hall, New York, NY probably xx/xx/71

Hurdy Gurdy Man [live] ([**G. Harrison**] D. Leitch) 6:04 (3)

Troubadour The Definitive Collection/1964-1976
Epic/Legacy-E2K 46986 (EK 48691) (08/xx/92)
Producer: Mickie Most
Trident Studios, London, UK 10/xx/66

Mellow Yellow (D. Leitch) 3:40 (1-13) (10/24/66)
Paul McCartney: Dialogue; Donovan Leitch: Lead Vocals & Acoustic Guitar; John Paul Jones: Bass; Bobby Orr: Drums; Danny Moss: Horns; Ronnie Ross: Horns

Donovan Leitch was born in Glasgow, Scotland on May 10, 1946. He has spent most of his musical career as a folk singer. His self-penned *Catch The Wind* and *Colours* reached the UK Top 10 in 1965. However, most of his commercial success, especially in the US, was achieved with his more rock-oriented material in the latter half of the 1960s.

Bob Dylan* introduced Donovan to The Beatles during his 1965 UK tour. Donovan's only number one hit *Sunshine Superman* in 1966, was originally subtitled *For John and Paul* as a tribute to Lennon and McCartney. It likely set in motion a rumor mill, for few artists have been the subject of more false rumors regarding musical involvement with The Beatles than Donovan. Donovan has repeatedly stated he did not contribute to The Beatles' recording of *Yellow Submarine*, except for suggesting the lyrics "Sky of blue, sea of green." He did not help write their songs *Eleanor Rigby* or *Rocky Raccoon*. McCartney's only contribution to Donovan's 1966 Top 10 hit *Mellow Yellow* was as one of the revelers in the party portion of the song. [In McCartney's *1989 World Tour Program* he lists under session work,

"Donovan (bass on a few tracks around *Mellow Yellow*)."] However, Donovan doesn't recall McCartney making bass contributions to any of his recordings. He did rehearse with McCartney for Mary Hopkin's* 1969 album *Post Card*, portions of which appear on the unauthorized album *No. 3 Abbey Road N.W.8*. McCartney did not contribute to Donovan's 1968 Top 10 hit *Atlantis*. Though songs from Donovan's 1973 album *Cosmic Wheels* were published by Apple Music, when he was managed by Allen Klein, (and Apple acetates of his demos exist), he says The Beatles had nothing to do with them. Donovan says he didn't contribute to George Harrison's 1987 album *Cloud* Nine, though he wrote a song for Harrison called *Dear Heart*, but he doesn't know if Harrison recorded it.

Donovan appears in a film documentary The Beatles made during their recording of *A Day In The Life*, a portion of which appeared in *The Beatles Anthology* film. His personal and musical relationship with The Beatles grew during their stay together at the Maharishi Mahesh Yogi's ashram in Rishikesh, India in early 1968. There he taught Lennon and McCartney the claw hammer style of guitar picking that they used on a number of songs such as *Julia* and *Blackbird* featured on *The Beatles* (white) album in 1968. [Lennon and McCartney also incorporated the style on many of their solo recordings.] He helped Harrison write the (unreleased) song *Dhera Dun* in India, which Harrison briefly performed in *The Beatles Anthology* film. At the ashram Donovan wrote his 1968 hits *Jennifer Juniper*, about Harrison's sister-in-law Jenny Boyd, and *Hurdy Gurdy Man*, which was a Top Five hit.

Harrison contributed a verse to *Hurdy Gurdy Man* there but it was omitted when Donovan first recorded it due to the long guitar solo. Later, during live performances of the song, he would recount Harrison's involvement, and include George's verse. A version recorded at Carnegie Hall in New York, probably in 1971, is included on his1990 UK album *Rising*. The album's notes include a quotation from Lennon from 1968, which reads "Donovan is as important and influential as Bob Dylan and we are...listen the man's a poet." Its posthumous inclusion isn't considered a Lennon contribution to the album's liner notes and wasn't included on the US release re-titled *The Classics Live* (Great Northern Arts-GNA-61007-2). Another performance of *Hurdy Gurdy Man*, with the Harrison lyrics, is included on Donovan's obscure 1973 album *Live In Japan-Spring Tour 1973* (Epic-ECPM-25). The live performance, probably recorded in 1971, is the preferred version as it is longer, more complete and recorded earlier than the 1973 version.

McCartney featured Donovan's music on his 1995 radio series *Oobu Joobu*. Donovan joined Ringo and Paul during Paul's performance of *Cosmically Conscious* at a benefit for Transcendental Meditation on April 4, 2009 at Radio City Music Hall in New York. Donovan maintains a loyal following, and his career and music are currently enjoying a revival as he continues to compose, record and tour. His children Donovan Jr. and Ione Skye have successful acting careers. For more information go to www.donovan.ie

DONOVAN

Drew & Dy

Dedicated To Love / Taurus The Bull
Fontana-6007014 (7" single) (UK) (05/xx/70)
Producer: Roger Greenaway & Chris Thomas
Paul McCartney: Bass Arranger; Keith Drewett: Vocals; Peter Dymond: Vocals; Alan Parker: Bass; Jim Sullivan: Guitars
Regent Sound Studios, London 10/03 & 08/69

Dedicated To Love (K. Drewett-P. Dymond) 2:27 (1/1)

[None]
Apple Corps Ltd. (12" acetate) (UK) [unreleased]
Producer: Paul McCartney
Paul McCartney: Piano & B. Vocals; Keith Drewett: Guitar & Vocals; Peter Dymond: Guitar & Vocals; Farnham Haines: Guitar; Steve: Drums
Trident Studios, London 08/10/68

Dedicated To Love (K. Drewett-P. Dymond) 2:25 (1/3)

Tales Of Frankie Rabbit (K. Drewett-P. Dymond) 3:12 (1/1)

Taurus The Bull (K. Drewett-P. Dymond) 4:02 (1/2)

The British duo Drew & Dy were Keith Drewett, born on May 19, 1947 in Bristol, England and Peter Dymond, born on August 2, 1947 in Glasgow, Scotland. They began playing music and writing songs together as schoolmates. By 1965 they were performing professionally and released their first single in 1967.

Drew & Dy were in London to audition for producer Tony Hiller (see Jungle Juice) on May 22,

Drew & Dy circa 1968.
Photo © and courtesy of Peter Diamond.

1968. Peter, who kept a diary during this period, recalls, "While in a taxi, we saw Paul McCartney outside the Apple Boutique in Baker Street. We ran up to him, and asked him to listen to our songs and tell us if they were any good. He took us inside and we played some songs for him. He had someone get a ReVox tape recorder and we recorded about eight songs." McCartney later wrote the duo telling them he liked their songs, especially *Taurus The Bull* and *Tales Of Frankie Rabbit*. [McCartney did a brief rendition of *Tales Of Frankie Rabbit* during The Beatles' *Let It Be* rehearsals in early 1969.] The duo was soon offered a contract with Apple and met again with McCartney at Apple in Savile Row to shape up their songs.

Peter says, "One of the best days of our lives was the 13 hour recording session at Trident Studios on August 10, 1968 when Paul produced three of our songs. He also played piano on them and sang harmony vocals. He rearranged the bass line on our song *Dedicated To Love* and taught it to the bass player, a Hawaiian whose name I forget. He didn't change the structure of the song but it was a big contribution. It was about the catchiest thing on the song. Our manager, Farnham Haines played guitar on the sessions and Steve, whose last name I forget, was the drummer. Mal Evans was there as was Paul's girlfriend, Francie Schwartz. Paul had amazing energy working straight through without food and wasn't tired at the end, though we were. He did a little performance of *Lady Madonna* and played us The Beatles' *Hey Jude* and Mary Hopkin's *Those Were The Days*, which hadn't been released yet. Our recordings really weren't acceptable for release. Paul said it wasn't our fault because Apple's assistant Peter Brown had forgotten to book session musicians and that we would record them again later. Nothing happened for about a year, and because of our involvement with The Beatles, other record companies were interested in us. Being young and impatient we asked to be released from our contract and went with A.I.R.

"I got a copy of *Dedicated To Love* with McCartney playing piano and singing harmonies. Later I got copies of *Tales Of Frankie Rabbit* and *Taurus The Bull*, which Paul also played on but his vocals are pretty much mixed out." Dymond also has a version of *Dedicated To Love*, with McCartney's vocals mostly mixed out, that is a minute longer. An Apple acetate of these recordings also includes *The Flying Machine* and *Tale Of Two Cities*, but Peter says these two songs were from their initial recordings at the Apple Boutique and don't include any contributions from Paul.

Dedicated To Love backed with *Taurus The Bull* was released as a single on Fontana Records in the UK in 1970. The label states both songs were produced for A.I.R. London by Chris Thomas. Peter says these were re-recordings done at Regent Studios with studio musicians and that most of the production was done by Roger Greenaway because Thomas was still in training. Peter says that McCartney's basic bass arrangement was used on the A.I.R. version.

Drew & Dy later had a number of their compositions recorded by other artists including David Essex and the Swedish group Stardust. Peter still has a career in music and occasionally gets together with Keith to develop musical ideas.

Bob Dylan

Bobfest Rehearsals October 1992
Yellow Cat-YC 036/37 [unauthorized release] (02/xx/97)
Producer: Jeff Rosen & Don DeVito
George Harrison: Guitar & Vocals; Bob Dylan: Guitar & Vocals; Eric Clapton Guitar & Vocals; Neil Young: Guitar & B. Vocals; G. E. Smith: Guitar; Anton Fig: Drums; Tom Petty: Guitar & B. Vocals; Roger McGuinn: Guitar & Vocals; Jim Keltner: Drums; Donald Dunn: Bass; Steve Cropper: Guitar; Al Kooper: Organ; Stan Lynch: Percussion
Madison Square Garden, New York, NY probably 10/16/92

My Back Pages [rehearsal - 4 takes] (B. Dylan) combined time 26:49 (1-11, 12, 13, 14 &15)

The Bootleg Series Volumes 1-3 [rare & unreleased] 1961-1991
Columbia-C3K 47382 (CK 47400) (03/25/91)
Producer: Bob Johnson
George Harrison: Electric Guitar; Bob Dylan: Lead Vocals, Guitar & Harmonica; Charlie Daniels: Bass; Russ Kunkel: Drums
Columbia Studio B, New York, NY 05/01/70

If Not For You (B. Dylan) 3:32 (2-15)

The Concert For Bangla Desh
Apple/Capitol-0946335880 28 (10/25/05) (12/20/71)

Producer: George Harrison & Phil Spector
George Harrison: Electric Guitar; **Ringo Starr: Tambourine**; Bob Dylan: Lead Vocals, Harmonica & Acoustic Guitar; Leon Russell: Bass
Madison Square Garden, New York, NY 12/01/71 [evening]

Mr. Tambourine Man [live] (B. Dylan) 4:06 (2-6)

The Concert For Bangla Desh
Apple/Rhino-R2 970481 (DVD) (10/25/05) (10/xx/83)
Producer: George Harrison & Allen Klein (film); **George Harrison** & Phil Spector (music)
George Harrison: Electric Guitar; **Ringo Starr: Tambourine**; Bob Dylan: Lead Vocals, Harmonica & Acoustic Guitar; Leon Russell: Bass
Madison Square Garden, New York, NY 12/01/71 [afternoon or evening unless noted otherwise]

A Hard Rain's Gonna Fall [live] (B. Dylan) 5:04 (1-13)
[Also available on Apple/Capitol-0946335880 28 (2-3) (10/25/05) (12/20/71)]

Blowin' In The Wind [live] (B. Dylan) 3:34 (1-15)
[Also available on Apple/Capitol-0946335880 28 (2-5) (10/25/05) (12/20/71)]

If Not For You [rehearsal] (B. Dylan) 2:50 (2-2) (10/25/05)
George Harrison: Acoustic Guitar & B. Vocals; Bob Dylan: Lead Vocals & Acoustic Guitar

It Takes A Lot To Laugh, It Takes A Train To Cry [live] (B. Dylan) 2:54
(1-14) (10/xx/83)
[Also available on Apple/Capitol-0946335880 28 (2-4) (10/25/05) (12/20/71)]

Just Like A Woman [live] (B. Dylan) 4:14 (1-16)
Additionally: **George Harrison: B. Vocals**; Leon Russell: B. Vocals
[Also available on Apple/Capitol-0946335880 28 (2-7) (10/25/05) (12/20/71)]

Love Minus Zero/No Limit [live] (B. Dylan) 4:00 (2-4) (10/25/05)
Madison Square Garden, New York, NY 12/01/71 (afternoon)
[Also available on Apple/Capitol-0946335880 28 (2-10) (10/25/05) (12/20/71)]

New Morning
Columbia-CK 30290 (07/25/89) (10/21/70)
Producer: Bob Johnson
George Harrison: (probable) Electric Guitar; Bob Dylan: Lead Vocals & (possible) Piano; probably the following: Bob Johnson: Piano; Charlie Daniels: Bass; Al Kooper: Keyboards; Russ Kunkel: Drums
Columbia Studios, New York, NY probably 05/01/70 &/or 06/05/70

Went To See The Gypsy (B. Dylan) 2:48 (4)

Odds & Ends (Unsurpassed Maestro Vol. 1)
Sick Cat-006 [unauthorized release] (xx/xx/93)
Producer: Bob Johnson
George Harrison: Electric Guitar; Bob Dylan: Lead Vocals & Acoustic Guitar; Russ Kunkel: Drums; Charlie Daniels: Bass
Columbia Studio B, New York, NY 05/01/70

Working On A Guru (B. Dylan) 3:38 (8)

Shot Of Love
Columbia-CK 37496 (06/18/90) (08/12/81)
Producer: Chuck Plotkin & Bob Dylan
Ringo Starr: Drums (Tom Tom); Bob Dylan: Lead Vocals & Piano; Jim Keltner: Drums; Chuck Plotkin: Drums; Donald "Duck" Dunn: Bass; Wm "Smitty" Smith: Organ; Ron Wood: Guitar; Clydie King: B. Vocals
Clover Recorders, Los Angeles, CA 05/xx/80

Heart Of Mine (B. Dylan) 4:32 (2)

The 30th Anniversary Concert Celebration
Columbia Music Video-ML2 49165 (LD 12") (08/xx/93)
Producer: Jeff Rosen & Don DeVito
Madison Square Garden, New York, NY 10/16/92

Knockin' On Heaven's Door [live] (B. Dylan) 5:38 (2/4/3)
George Harrison: Guitar & B. Vocals; Bob Dylan: Lead Vocals & Guitar; Neil Young: Guitar & B. Vocals; Eric Clapton Guitar & B. Vocals; Ron Wood: Guitar & B. Vocals; G. E. Smith: Guitar; Tom Petty: Guitar & B. Vocals; Roger McGuinn: Guitar & B. Vocals; George Thorogood: Guitar & B. Vocals; Jim Keltner: Drums; Booker T. Jones: Keyboards; Anton Fig: Drums; Al Kooper: Keyboards; Donald Dunn: Bass; Steve Cropper: Guitar; Tracy Chapman: B. Vocals; June Carter: B. Vocals; Johnny Cash: B. Vocals; Kris Kristofferson: B. Vocals; Paddy Clancy: B. Vocals & Guitar; Bobby Clancy: B. Vocals; Liam Clancy: B. Vocals; Robbie O'Connell: B. Vocals; Tommy Makem: B. Vocals; Rosanne Cash: B. Vocals; Mary-Chapin Carpenter: B. Vocals; Shawn Colvin: B. Vocals; Chrissie Hynde: B. Vocals; Richie Havens: B.

Vocals; Lou Reed: B. Vocals; Stan Lynch: Percussion & B. Vocals; Sinead O'Connor: B. Vocals; Sylvia Hawkins: B. Vocals; Willie Nelson: B. Vocals
[Also available on Columbia-C2K 53230 (2-13) (08/24/93)]

My Back Pages [live] (B. Dylan) 4:39 (2/4/2)
George Harrison: Guitar & Vocals; Bob Dylan: Guitar & Vocals; Eric Clapton Guitar & Vocals; Neil Young: Guitar & Vocals; G. E. Smith: Guitar; Anton Fig: Drums; Tom Petty: Guitar & Vocals; Roger McGuinn: Guitar & Vocals; Jim Keltner: Drums; Donald Dunn: Bass; Steve Cropper: Guitar; Al Kooper: Organ; Stan Lynch: Percussion
[Also available on Columbia-C2K 53230 (2-12) (08/24/93)]

Together At The Rock And Roll Hall Of Fame [Various Artists]
Living Legend-LLRCD 101(Italy) [unauthorized release] (xx/xx/93)
Producer: [unknown]
Grand Ballroom Waldorf-Astoria Hotel, New York, NY 01/20/88

All Along The Watchtower [live] (B. Dylan) 8:08 (4)
George Harrison: Guitar & Vocals; Ringo Starr: Drums; Paul Shaffer: Keyboards; Mike Love: Handclaps; Bruce Johnston: Handclaps; Billy Joel: Keyboards; Bruce Springsteen: Tambourine; Little Richard: Handclaps; Elton John: Keyboards; Anton Fig: Drums; Bob Dylan: Guitar & Vocals; Dave Edmunds: Guitar; Les Paul: Guitar; Jeff Beck: Electric Guitar; Mick Jagger: Handclaps, B. Vocals & Tambourine; Mary Wilson: B. Vocals; Carl Wilson: Handclaps; Brian Wilson: Handclaps; Yoko Ono: Handclaps; Sean Lennon: Handclaps; Sid McGinnis: Guitar; Ben E. King: Handclaps; John Fogerty: Handclaps; Arlo Guthrie: Handclaps; Peter Wolf: Handclaps; Johnny Moore: Handclaps; Joe Blunt: Handclaps; Clyde Brown: Handclaps; Julian Lennon: Handclaps; Bill Pinkney: Handclaps; Charlie Thomas: Handclaps; Max Weinberg: Handclaps; Will Lee: Bass; Patti Scialfa: Handclaps & B. Vocals

Like A Rolling Stone [live] (B. Dylan) 8:00 (11)
George Harrison: Guitar; Ringo Starr: (possible) Drums; Bob Dylan: Lead Vocals; Mick Jagger: B. Vocals; Bruce Springsteen: Vocals; Jeff Beck: Guitar; probably one or more of the following: Paul Shaffer: Keyboards; Jeff Beck: Electric Guitar; Jeff Lynne: Electric Guitar; Bruce Johnston: B. Vocals; Billy Joel: B. Vocals & Keyboards; John Fogerty: Electric Guitar & B. Vocals; Bob Dylan: Electric Guitar; Little Steven Van Zandt: Tambourine; Patti Scialfa: Handclaps & B. Vocals; Mary Wilson: B. Vocals & Handclaps; Al Jardine: Guitar & Percussion; Mike Love: B. Vocals & Tambourine; Dave Edmunds: Electric Guitar; Max Weinberg: Drums; Arlo Guthrie: Guitar; Ben E. King: Handclaps & B. Vocals; Sid McGinnis: Guitar; Will Lee: Bass; Nile Rodgers: Guitar; Johnny Moore: Handclaps; Joe Blunt: Handclaps; Clyde Brown: Handclaps; Bill Pinkney: Handclaps; Charlie Thomas: Handclaps

Unbootlegged 11 (Rolling Ringo Review)
No Tapo-NTR-0202 (CD-R) [unauthorized release] (xx/xx/05)
Ringo Starr: Drums; Bob Dylan: Guitar & Vocals; Bob Neuwirth: Guitar; T-Bone Burnett: Guitar; Roger McGuinn: Guitar; Mick Ronson: Guitar; Rob Stoner: Bass; Steven Soles: Guitar; Joe Vitale: Drums; Howie Wyeth: Drums; Additionally, one or more of the following: David Mansfield: Steel Guitar, Mandolin, Violin or Dobro, Scarlet Rivera: Violin
Houston Astrodome, Houston, TX 01/25/76

Hurricane [live] (B. Dylan-J. Levy) 8:27 (16)

Isis [live] (B. Dylan-J. Levy) 5:35 (8)

I Threw It All Away [live] (B. Dylan) 4:23 (7)

Just Like A Woman [live] (B. Dylan) 5:44 (15)

Lay, Lady, Lay [live] (B. Dylan) 3:52 (14)

Oh Sister [live] (B. Dylan-J. Levy) 2:51 (11)

One More Cup Of Coffee (Valley Below) [live] (B. Dylan) 3:42 (12)

Positively 4th Street [live] (B. Dylan) 4:08 (9)

Ride 'em Jew Boy [live] (K. Friedman) 4:19 (17)
Additionally: Kinky Friedman: Vocals; Bob Dylan: Guitar (only)

Sara (B. Dylan) [live] 4:19 (13)

Unbootlegged 14 [The Beatles]
No Tapo-NTR-0301 (CD-R) [unauthorized release] (xx/xx/04)
George Harrison: Slide Guitar & Vocals; Bob Dylan: Guitar & Vocals; Tom Petty: Guitar & B. Vocals; Mike Campbell: Guitar; Benmont Tench: Keyboards; Howie Epstein: Bass; Stan Lynch: Drums; Roger McGuinn: Guitar;

Left to right: George Harrison, Duane Eddy and Bob Dylan, Hollywood Palace, Los Angeles, CA, February 27, 1987. © and photo by Tom Bert.

Madelyn Quebec: B. Vocals; Carol Dennis: B. Vocals; Queen Esther Marrow: B. Vocals
Wembley Arena, London, UK 10/17/87

Rainy Day Women Nos. 12 & 35 [live] (B. Dylan) 3:26 (26)

Under The Red Sky
Columbia-CK 46794 (09/11/90)
Producer: Don & Dave Was & Bob Dylan
George Harrison: Slide Guitar†; Bob Dylan: Lead Vocals, Accordion & Acoustic Guitar; Waddy Wachtel: Guitar; Al Kooper: Keyboards; Don Was: Bass; Kenny Aronoff: Drums
Probably Ocean Way Studios, The Record Plant Studios† & possibly The Complex, Los Angeles, CA 01 & 03-04†/xx/90

Under The Red Sky (B. Dylan) 4:03 (2)

With A Little Help To My Friends [Ringo Starr]
No Label Records-NLR 9904 (CD-R) [unauthorized release] (xx/xx/99)
Ringo Starr: Drums; Bob Dylan: Lead Vocals & Guitar; Tony Garnier: Bass; G. E. Smith: Guitar
Les Arenes in Frejus, France 06/13/89

Highway 61 Revisited [live] (B. Dylan) 4:14 (4)

Like A Rolling Stone [live] (B. Dylan) 6:34 (5)

Yesterday
Winged Wheel-WW 9420 (Italy) [unauthorized release] (probably 02/xx/95)
Producer: Bob Johnston
Columbia Studio B, New York, NY 05/01/70
George Harrison: Electric Guitar & B. Vocals; Bob Dylan: Lead Vocals & Acoustic Guitar; Charlie Daniels: Bass; Russ Kunkel: Drums

All I Have To Do Is Dream (B. Bryant) 2:44 (3)

Cupid (S. Cooke) 3:45 (2)

Da Doo Ron Ron (P. Spector-J. Barry-E. Greenwich) 2:06 (17)
Additionally: Bob Dylan: Harmonica

Medley: Don't Think Twice, It's All Right/Corrina Corrina (B. Dylan/J. Williams-B. Chatmon-M. Parish-Arr: B. Dylan) 1:46 (14)
Additionally: Bob Johnston: Piano

Fishin' Blues (H. Thomas) 1:50 (9)

Gates Of Eden (B. Dylan) 4:19 (4)

(Ghost) Riders In The Sky (S. Jones) 3:41 (1)
Honey, Just Allow Me One More Chance (H. Thomas-B. Dylan) 2:36 (10)
Additionally: **George Harrison: Electric Guitar** (only)

I Don't Believe You (She Acts Like We Never Have Met) (B. Dylan) 3:14 (6)
Additionally: **George Harrison: Electric Guitar** (only)

I Threw It All Away (B. Dylan) 2:30 (5)

Just Like Tom Thumb's Blues (B. Dylan) 3:56 (16)
Additionally: **George Harrison: Guitar & B. Vocals**; Bob Dylan: Harmonica; Bob Johnston: Piano

Mama, You've Been On My Mind (B. Dylan) 3:09 (13)
Additionally: Bob Johnston: Piano

Matchbox [a.k.a. **Matchbox Blues**] (C. Perkins-trad. L. Jefferson) 3:35 (7)

One Too Many Mornings [take one] (B. Dylan) 2:16 (18)
Additionally: Bob Johnston: Piano

One Too Many Mornings [take two] (B. Dylan) 3:46 (19)
Additionally: Bob Johnston: Piano

Rainy Day Women Nos. 12 & 35 (B. Dylan) 1:07 (11)
Additionally: **George Harrison: Electric Guitar** (only)

Song To Woody (B. Dylan) 4:26 (12)
Additionally: **George Harrison: Electric Guitar** (only); Bob Dylan: Harmonica

Yesterday (J. Lennon-P. McCartney) 3:15 (15)

Your True Love (C. Perkins) 1:36 (8)

Bob Dylan was born Robert Zimmerman in Duluth, Minnesota on May 24, 1941 but raised in the small town of Hibbing in northern Minnesota. It was an unlikely setting for a Jewish person who would evolve into a protest singer. Zimmerman formed several rock bands in high school, but began emulating traditional American blues and folk singers such as Woody Guthrie, and changed his last name to Dylan. He moved to Greenwich Village in 1961 and was soon signed to Columbia Records. His esoteric and politically and socially conscious lyrics were an inspiration to the counterculture revolution of the 1960s. Due to his quirky vocals he was initially more successful as a songwriter to more commercial folk acts such as girlfriend Joan Baez, and Peter, Paul & Mary who reached the Top 10 with his songs *Blowin' In The Wind* and *Don't Think Twice, It's Alright* in 1963.

The Beatles gave their first serious listen to Dylan's music in early 1964 and, as John Lennon later remarked, "Fell in love." They first met Dylan in New York during their US tour in August 1964. Bob, who had apparently misinterpreted the lyrics ("I can't hide" as "I get high") to The Beatles' hit *I Want To Hold Your Hand* brought along some marijuana and by most accounts was the first person to introduce them to it.

Dylan has reinvented himself musically throughout his career. He was heckled during his performance at the prestigious *Newport Folk Festival* in July 1965 for playing an electric guitar to music that soon became known as folk-rock. Bands such as The Byrds [*Mr. Tambourine Man*], The Turtles [*It Ain't Me Babe*] and singer Cher [*All I Really Want To Do*] had folk-rock hits with these Dylan songs. In 1965 Bob scored a Top Five hit with *Like A Rolling Stone* and a Top 10 hit with *Positively 4th Street*. He began to back himself with The Hawks, later known simply as The Band* (see Levon Helm, Rick Danko, Ronnie Hawkins).

The Beatles also embarked on the folk-rock voyage recording "Dylanesque" songs, mostly written by Lennon, including *Norwegian Wood*, on which Bob reportedly based his song *Fourth Time Around*. The notes in the Dylan box set *Biograph* mention, "It's an interesting footnote to music history that along an early English tour [probably 1965 or 1966], Dylan would visit the home of John Lennon and the two would pen a song together. 'I don't remember what it was, though,' said Dylan. 'We played some stuff into a tape recorder but I don't know what happened to it. I can remember playing it and the recorder was on. I don't remember anything about the song.' Lennon would later comment on their relationship. 'I've grown up enough to communicate with him...Both of us were always uptight, you know, and of course I wouldn't know whether he was uptight because I was so uptight, and then when he wasn't uptight, I was — all that bit. But we just sat it out because we just liked being together.'" The documentary film *Eat The Document* of Dylan's 1966 UK tour includes a segment with Lennon that was later edited out.

Dylan had a Top Five hit with *Rainy Day Women Nos. 12 & 35* and a Top 20 hit with *I Want You* in 1966 before a motorcycle accident sidelined him and signaled his retreat from the limelight for a number of years. The Beatles included a photo of Dylan on the cover of their *Sgt. Pepper's Lonely Hearts Club Band* album in 1967. In 1968 Manfred Mann (see Paul Jones) had a Top 10 hit with Bob's song *The Mighty Quinn* (*Quinn The Eskimo*). The Beatles' *Rubber Soul* album photographs appear to be hidden in the tree on the front of Dylan's 1968 album *John Wesley Harding*. The album includes *All Along The Watchtower*, which Jimi Hendrix later turned into a Top 10 hit. Dylan worked with Johnny Cash* on his 1969 country-flavored album *Nashville Skyline*, which includes his Top 10 hit *Lay Lady Lay*.

George Harrison visited Bob at his home in Woodstock, NY in November 1968. While there the two wrote *I'd Have You Anytime* (Bob contributed the bridge). Harrison reportedly also wrote *All Things Must Pass* there. On August 31, 1969 Harrison, Starr and Lennon attended a then-rare Dylan performance on the Isle Of Wight, and met with him and The Band prior to the show. Lennon later tried, without success, to get Bob to contribute to his recording of *Cold Turkey*.

On May 1, 1970 at Columbia Studios in New York, Harrison took part in sessions for Dylan's *New Morning* album, which began essentially as a warm-up consisting of Dylan numbers and oldies, including a swipe at The Beatles' song *Yesterday*, but progressed to more finished recordings. Clinton Heylin's comprehensive book *Bob Dylan: The Recording Sessions 1960-1994* documents distinct afternoon and evening sessions with Dylan on guitar, piano, harmonica and vocals, Harrison and Ron Cornelius on guitar, Alvin Rogers (afternoon only) and Russ Kunkel (evening only) on drums, Charlie Daniels on bass and Al Kooper on guitar, piano and vocals. However, Kooper says he didn't attend any sessions including Harrison and never sang on any recordings for *New Morning*. Daniels says Kunkel was the only drummer and that Cornelius wasn't present. It's apparent from listening to the recordings that most, if not all, of the piano was played by producer Bob Johnston. This casts doubt on the reliability of Heylan's information. Daniels also thinks he plays acoustic guitar on a couple of tracks. Daniels says that Harrison played electric guitar throughout the session, and that his involvement was supposed to be kept secret for legal reasons. Daniels didn't think any recordings from the session ended up on *New Morning*. However, *If Not For You* (different from the version on Dylan's *New Morning* album) from the May 1st session was officially released some 20 years later on Dylan album *The Bootleg Series*. [Harrison covered the song on his 1970 album *All Things Must Pass*.] Kooper, who plays on and produced some of the *New Morning* sessions, is certain that Harrison plays guitar on the version of *Went To See The Gypsy* on *New Morning*. It's the one song on the album that sounds like it was taken from the May 1st sessions. However, Heylin's book doesn't list any of the tracks from the session with Harrison as being used on *New Morning*. Another 20 of the 25 songs known to have been recorded at the May 1st sessions have turned up on a number of unauthorized releases. Three tracks, alternate versions of *Sign On The Window*, *Time Passes Slowly* and *It Ain't Me Babe*, have yet to surface on any release.

Two Harrison songs, *Every Time Somebody Comes To Town* and *I'd Have You Anytime*, featuring Dylan also appear on unauthorized releases and were probably recorded during Harrison's time with Bob in New York in 1968 or 1970. Harrison's song *Behind That Locked Door* was written about Bob's reclusive period. Harrison is rumored to have helped Leon Russell* produce *Watching The River Flow* and *When I Paint My Masterpiece* from a Dylan session in March 1971. But Jim Keltner (see Attitudes), who drummed on the sessions, refutes this.

The reclusive Dylan reluctantly accepted Harrison's invitation to appear at *The Concert For Bangla Desh* on August 1, 1971. Dylan's *Love Minus Zero / No Limit*, performed only during the afternoon show and included in the 2005 DVD release, was replaced by *Mr. Tambourine Man* during the evening show. It was included on the album but omitted from the film, which premiered in March 1972.

Lennon sang, "I don't believe in Zimmerman" on *God* from his 1970 album *John Lennon / Plastic Ono Band*. [Brief clips of Dylan appear in the posthumous video for *God* released on *The John Lennon Video Collection* in 1992.] However, in 1972 Lennon sought Dylan's support for a never realized political tour he was planning, which was to culminate in San Diego at the Republican National Convention's nomination of Richard Nixon. Bob and Allen Ginsberg* co-wrote and recorded the song *Going To San Diego*, which Lennon almost had released on Apple.

The March 10, 1973 issue of *Melody Maker* magazine says Lennon was "in Los Angeles with Dylan to help remix their tapes he had cut down in Mexico City in January." Dylan resumed work on those tapes in Los Angeles in February. There's no supporting evidence that Lennon was involved in these recordings, or in Los Angeles before March because the Lennons were moving into their Dakota apartment in New York. Lennon also wouldn't have traveled outside the US during this period because of a deportation order, which would have prevented his reentry, making his involvement with these recordings highly unlikely.

Dylan's Rolling Thunder Revue tour featured guest appearances by numerous acts such as The Alpha Band*, Kinky Friedman*, and Ringo Starr on January 25, 1976 at the Houston Astrodome. This performance is available on unauthorized releases. Dylan's song *Abandoned Love*, recorded during this period but not released until 1985, was also recorded by Harrison, whose version remains unreleased.

In 1979 Bob converted to Christianity and proclaimed it in the lyrics of his gospel single *Gotta Serve Somebody*. Lennon reacted cynically to Bob's religious convictions composing several parodies of Dylan's song with posthumous titles such as *Serve Yourself* [*Gotta Serve Somebody*], *Lord Take This Makeup Off Of Me* [*Knockin' On Heaven's Door*] and *Ballad Of Reuter's News Of The World*.

Dylan's single *Heart Of Mine* features Ringo on drums on it and the B-side *Groom's Still Waiting At The Altar* were included on Dylan's album *Shot Of Love*. There's considerable confusion regarding who plays on the B-side. In his *Biograph* release, Dylan says that "maybe" Ringo plays on it, but that he "can't remember." In the April 1993 issue of *DISCoveries* magazine Ringo is quoted as saying, "We had a discussion — Bob and I. I said to him, 'Thanks a lot. I come all the way down for the session and you wipe me off.' Bob replied, 'You're not listening!'" Perhaps Ringo is referring to the A-side of the single. Jim Keltner, the credited drummer on the B-side, is certain that Ringo wasn't present at the sessions for *Groom's Still Waiting At The Altar*. Keltner correctly recalls that it was an entirely different session and group of musicians to those on *Heart Of Mine*.

In 1985 Harrison recorded and released Dylan's composition *I Don't Want To Do It*, produced by Dave Edmunds*, which Harrison initially considered including on his album *All Things Must Pass*. Harrison reportedly talked Ringo into recording it for his 1976 album *Rotogravure* but it wasn't included and, along with Bob's version, remains unreleased. Dylan's 1986 album *Knocked Out Loaded* thanks a "George," though given the recording dates, musicians and studios used there's no indication of any involvement by Harrison, though it's possible he could have contributed to out-takes. Dylan, Harrison and John Fogerty* performed with Taj Mahal* and the Graffiti Band featuring Jesse Ed Davis* at Hollywood's Palomino Club on February 19, 1987. Harrison played his distinctive slide guitar and sang with Bob during his performance of *Rainy Day Women Nos. 12 & 35* on October 17, 1987 in London, which is available on unauthorized releases. Dylan contributed to Ringo's unreleased recording of *Wish I Know Now (What I Knew Then)* from his aborted sessions produced by Chips Moman in Memphis in 1987. On June 13, 1989 Ringo joined Bob onstage at Les Arenes in Frejus, France drumming on *Highway 61 Revisited* and *Like A Rolling Stone*, which are available on unauthorized releases.

On January 20, 1988 Dylan, along with The Beatles, was inducted into the Rock and Roll Hall of Fame at the Waldorf-Astoria Hotel in New York. Bob, along with George and Ringo, took part in the all-star jam at the end of the evening's events, portions of which are available on unauthorized releases. That year also saw the beginning of Harrison and Dylan's greatest collaboration. Harrison, attempting to record a B-side for a single, recruited Tom Petty* to help. Petty was working with Dylan and suggested they rehearse the number at Bob's home studio. Roy Orbison* was performing in the area and was asked to drop by and help as were Jeff Lynne* and Keltner. They hit it off so well that they decided to record an album and called themselves the Traveling Wilburys. The album was a huge success prompting a second album two years later.

Harrison contributed slide guitar to the title track of Dylan's *Under The Red Sky* album in 1990. The album's credits list Sorcerer Sound in New York, and Ocean Way, The Complex and The Record Plant Studios in Los Angeles. Several books on Dylan list the title song as being recorded at The Complex, and at Record Plant, which is probably where Harrison's guitar was overdubbed, but according to Al Kooper the basic tracks were recorded at Ocean Way. Pat Schneider, a recording engineer working at

Ocean Way then, also recalls it being done there. That year on tour Bob performed The Beatles' song *Nowhere Man*.

On October 16, 1992 some of music's biggest names, including The Band, Johnny Cash, Eric Clapton*, Tom Petty, Ron Wood*, Roger McGuinn and Harrison, gathered at Madison Square Garden to celebrate the 30th anniversary of Dylan's recording career. Harrison performed *Absolutely Sweet Marie* and joined in the finale of *My Back Pages* and *Knockin' On Heaven's Door*, which are included on *The 30th Anniversary Concert Celebration* album and video release, though his performance of *If Not For You* wasn't included. Portions of Harrison's rehearsal for the performance are available on the unauthorized release *Bobfest Rehearsals October 1992*. Bob Dylan continues to write, record and tour. For more information go to www.bobdylan.com

Duane Eddy

Duane Eddy
Capitol-CDP 7 46897 2 (06/19/87)
Producer: [George Harrison] & Jeff Lynne [unless noted otherwise]
George Harrison: Slide Guitar; Duane Eddy: Guitar; Jeff Lynne: Keyboards & Synthesizers; Jim Horn: Saxophone; Jim Keltner: Drums; Jeff Lynne: Bass [unless noted otherwise]
FPSHOT, UK late 01 & 02/10-11/87 [unless noted otherwise]

Rockestra Theme (P. McCartney) 4:00 (2)
Producer: Paul McCartney
Paul McCartney: Bass & B. Vocals; Duane Eddy: Guitar; Phil Pickett: Piano & B. Vocals; Nick Glennie-Smith: Keyboards, Fairlight & B. Vocals; Jim Horn: Tenor Saxophone; Charlie Morgan: Drums & B. Vocals
Hog Hill Mill Studios, Sussex, UK 02/04/87

Theme For Something Really Important (J. Lynne) 4:09 (3)

The Trembler (R. Shankar-D. Eddy) 3:30 (6)

Duane Eddy
Capitol-12CL 463 (12" single) (UK) (10/21/87)
Producer: Paul McCartney & remixed by Bert Bevan
Paul McCartney: Bass & B. Vocals; Duane Eddy: Guitar; Phil Pickett: Piano & B. Vocals; Nick Glennie-Smith: Keyboards, Fairlight & B. Vocals; Jim Horn: Tenor Saxophone; Charlie Morgan: Drums & B. Vocals
Hog Hill Mill Studios, Sussex, UK 02/04/87

Rockestra Theme [extended version] (P. McCartney) 6:26 (1/1)

Duane Eddy was born in Corning, New York on April 26, 1938. He began playing guitar at the age of five. Eddy's family moved to Arizona where, in 1955, he began playing professionally. Eddy teamed up with producer Lee Hazlewood creating his signature twang-sounding guitar style that eventually earned him the title of biggest selling rock instrumentalist.

Eddy's trademark Gretsch guitar, and his Top 10 hit *Rebel Rouser*, featuring his backup band The Rebels, caught the attention of George Harrison in 1958. George and his brother Peter soon formed a group named The Rebels. The Beatles often performed *Ramrod* and other songs made popular by Eddy in their early '60's live sets. Eddy had more than a dozen Top 40 hits between 1958 and 1962 including the Top 20 hits *Cannonball*, *Forty Miles Of Bad Road*, *Because They're Young*, *Pepe* and *Dance With The Guitar Man*. Eddy appeared on TV and in several films in the early 1960s.

In 1963 when *NME* magazine asked Harrison who his favorite band was he replied, "The Duane Eddy Group." [Rebels' members Jim Horn*, Steve Douglas and Larry Knechtel (a member of the '70's group Bread) became members of Phil Spector's* famous "wrecking crew" of session players.] Eddy nearly vanished from the charts after the British music invasion of 1964. During the 1970s he covered Harrison's Beatles' song *Something,* and contributed to, or produced recordings for other artists including Phil Everly (see The Everly Brothers). Eddy's *Play Me Like You Play Your Guitar* was a major international hit (except the US) in 1975. In 1986 his remake of *Peter Gunn* with the group The Art Of Noise earned him a Grammy Award.

In 1987 Eddy had no problem enlisting Paul McCartney and Harrison to contribute to his album *Duane Eddy*. McCartney produced Eddy's cover of Wings' song *Rochestra Theme* at his Hog Hill Mill Studios. An extended and remixed version of the song was released on a UK 12" single. *Rockestra* was a suggested title for the album. McCartney featured Eddy's *Rockestra Theme* on an episode of his 1995 radio series *Oobu Joobu*. The series was produced by Duane's longtime friend Eddy Pumer, who had initially put Duane in touch with McCartney. The episode, which commemorated the 30th anniversary of the release of *Yesterday*, also included Eddy's brief rendition of *Yesterday* recorded for the occasion along with a message of congratulations.

Harrison's contributions to the *Duane Eddy* album took place at FPSHOT just prior to and after McCartney's contributions. According to Eddy and Jeff Lynne, Harrison (though not credited) helped Lynne produce *Theme For Something Really Important* and *The Trembler*. In an interview in the November 1987 issue of *Guitar Player* magazine, Harrison said that Ravi Shankar* had made a tape of the basic melody of *The Trembler* years earlier. Harrison played the tape for Lynne and the two decided to simplify the song before Eddy wrote the bridge. Eddy says that collaboration pleased Harrison immensely. According to Eddy, Harrison also came up with the title for the album track *Rockabilly Holiday* (a play on rockabilly and singer Billie Holiday), though he didn't contribute to that recording. At the time, Eddy played guitar on some songs for Harrison's album *Cloud Nine*, but Eddy say, "It just didn't sound right for the songs and wasn't used." Lynne and Eddy recall having some great jams with George, Jim Horn and James Burton during the recordings at FPSHOT. Duane Eddy was inducted into the Rock and Roll Hall in 1994 along with John Lennon. His many recordings, which continue to grace soundtracks and advertisements, have easily exceeded 100 million in sales.

Dave Edmunds

Ringo Starr And His All Starr Band The Anthology…So Far
Koch-KOC-CD-8312 (07/24/01) (02/05/01)
Producer: Jim Sanders (mixer); Executive Producer: Ringo Starr & David Fishof
Ringo Starr: Drums; Dave Edmunds: Lead Vocals & Guitar; Jack Bruce: Keyboards; Eric Carmen: Bass & B. Vocals; Simon Kirke: Drums; Mark Rivera: Percussion
SummerFest, Miller Oasis, Milwaukee, WI 07/01/00

I Hear You Knocking [live] (D. Bartholomew-P. King) 2:58 (3-4)

Ringo Starr And His All-Starr Band Volume 2-Live From Montreux
Videoarts-VALJ-3369 (LD 12") (Japan) (probably 11/xx/93)
Producer: Ringo Starr (music); Jim Beach & Louise Velazquez (film); Executive Producer: Ringo Starr, David Fishof & Hilary Gerrard
Montreux Jazz Festival, Montreux, Switzerland 07/13/92

Girls Talk [live] (E. Costello) 3:25 (1/5)
Ringo Starr: Drums; Dave Edmunds: Lead Vocals & Electric Guitar; Joe Walsh: Acoustic Guitar & B. Vocals; Todd Rundgren: Tambourine, Electric Guitar & B. Vocals; Burton Cummings: Keyboards & B. Vocals; Nils Lofgren: Acoustic Guitar & B. Vocals; Timothy B. Schmit: Bass & B. Vocals; Tim Cappello: Percussion; Zak Starkey: Drums
[Also available on *Ringo Starr And His All Starr Band The Anthology…So Far*. Koch-KOC-CD-8312 (2-5) (07/24/01) (02/05/01)]

I Hear You Knocking [live] (Bartholomew-King) 3:48 (2/7)
Ringo Starr: Drums; Dave Edmunds: Lead Vocals & Electric Guitar; Joe Walsh: Electric Guitar; Todd Rundgren: Electric Guitar & B. Vocals; Burton Cummings: Keyboards & B. Vocals; Nils Lofgren: Electric Guitar & B. Vocals; Timothy B. Schmit: Bass & B. Vocals; Tim Cappello: Percussion; Zak Starkey: Drums

Dave Edmunds was born April 15, 1944 in Cardiff, Wales. He has been a highly respected guitarist since the mid-1960s when he was in such groups as Image, Human Beans and Love Sculpture. He is most often identified with the revival of rockabilly music in England. He has also been a successful producer for many artists including The Everly Brothers*, K. D. Lang, Status Quo, Del Shannon* and The Stray Cats. Dave's remake of the Smiley Lewis hit *I Hear You Knocking* was a Top Five hit in 1970, and his cover of Elvis Costello's* *Girls Talk* was a UK Top Five hit in 1979.

Dave was also a member of Rockpile in the '70s and when they were part of Paul McCartney's Rockestra ensemble on the album *Concerts For The People Of Kampuchea* recorded at London's Hammersmith Odeon on December 29, 1979. In 1983 Dave was part of McCartney's short-term band for his 1984 film and soundtrack *Give My Regards To Broadstreet*. On September 4, 1990 he backed McCartney onstage at the Lone Star Roadhouse in New York during the annual Buddy Holly Week celebrations.

Edmunds, who was producing the soundtrack for the 1985 film *Porky's Revenge*, produced his neighbor and friend George Harrison's recording of Bob Dylan's* song *I Don't Want To Do It* for it. Edmunds persuaded Harrison to perform before a live audience for *Blue Suede Shoes-(A Rockabilly Session with Carl Perkins and Friends Starring George Harrison, Ringo Starr, Eric Clapton, Rosanne Cash & Dave Edmunds*) (see Carl Perkins) TV special on October 21, 1985. Dave was the person Harrison put in charge of contacting Jeff Lynne* when he first sought his services as a producer.

Dave was reported to have been involved in Ringo's aborted sessions produced by Chips Moman in Memphis in 1987. Edmunds joined Ringo Starr's All-Starr Band tour in 1992 performing *Girls Talk* and *I Hear You Knocking*, and in 2000 performing *I Hear You Knocking* and *I Knew The Bride (When She Used To Rock And Roll)* with Ringo on drums. He also performed The Beatles' song *Lady Madonna* but without Ringo. Edmunds also performed three Beatles' songs at *The John Lennon Scholarship Concert* held on May 5, 1990 in Liverpool, for which he was the musical director. Edmunds has been less active in recent years. For more information go to
www.daveedmundsmusic.com

Electric Light Orchestra

Zoom
Epic-EK85336 (06/12/01)
Producer: Jeff Lynne
Ringo Starr: Drums; Jeff Lynne: Vocals, Guitars, Keyboards & Bass
Jeff Lynne's home studio, Los Angeles, CA xx/xx/99-01

A Long Time Gone (J. Lynne) 3:15 (10)
Additionally: **George Harrison: Slide Guitar**; Jeff Lynne: Drums; Dave Boruff: Saxophone

All She Wanted (J. Lynne) 3:14 (12)
Additionally: **George Harrison: Slide Guitar**; Jeff Lynne: Drums; Rosie Vela: B. Vocals; Laura Lynne: B. Vocals; Suzie Katayama: Cello

Easy Money (J. Lynne) 2:51 (7)

Moment In Paradise (J. Lynne) 3:36 (2)
Additionally: Marc Mann: Rhythm Guitar

Electric Light Orchestra (a.k.a. ELO) formed in 1972 around Birmingham, England natives Jeff Lynne*; singer and guitarist Roy Wood, born on November 8, 1946 (who soon left the band); Richard Tandy, born on March 26, 1948 (who joined the band shortly after its inception) on guitar and keyboards, and drummer Beverley "Bev" Bevan, born on November 24, 1946. All had been members of the group The Move, and Lynne and Wood had previously been in the band Idle Race. Despite numerous solo projects, and a dozen personnel changes over the years, Lynne, Tandy and Bevan remained the core of the band.

ELO is often compared to The Beatles because they continued to evolve a style of orchestral rock The Beatles used on their 1967 album *Sgt. Pepper's Lonely Hearts Club Band.* Individually and collectively they have recorded covers of The Beatles' songs. Between 1974 and 1979 they had Top 20 hits with *Strange Magic* and *Livin' Thing*, Top 10 hits with *Can't Get It Out Of My Head*, *Evil Woman*, *Telephone Line*, *Shine A Little Love* and a Top Five hit with *Don't Bring Me Down.* ELO's last Top 10 hit was *Hold On Tight* in 1981, by which time their music had lost favor to the minimalist sound and production styles of punk and new wave music. Their last group effort was the album *Balance Of Power* released around the time of Lynne, Bevan and Tandy's March 15, 1986 appearance at the charity concert *Heartbeat '86* in Birmingham, England. George Harrison and Denny Laine* also made guest appearances at the concert. Bevan went on to form Electric Light Orchestra II.

An ELO album, in name only, titled *Zoom* was released in 2001. With the exception of Richard Tandy playing on one song, it was essentially a Jeff Lynne (who owns the ELO name) album featuring a number of special guests including Harrison and Ringo Starr. For more information go to www.elomusic.com

Elephant's Memory

Elephant's Memory
Apple-SMAS 3389 (album 12") (09/18/72)
Producer: John Lennon & Yoko Ono
Stan Bronstein: Lead Vocals & Saxophone; Wayne Tex Gabriel: Guitar & B. Vocals; Rick Frank: Drums; Adam Ippolito: Keyboards & B. Vocals; Gary Van Scyoc: Bass & B. Vocals
Record Plant Studios, New York, NY 04-05/xx/72

Baddest Of The Mean (S. Bronstein-R. Frank-G. Van Scyoc-A. Ippolito-W. Gabriel-[C. Meyer]) 8:46 (1/2)
Additionally: **John Lennon B. Vocals & Handclaps**; Yoko Ono: B. Vocals; Rick Frank: Percussion; Adam Ippolito: Trumpet; Chris Robison: B. Vocals & Handclaps; Suzy Puntz: B. Vocals

Chuck 'N Bo (S. Bronstein-R. Frank-W. Gabriel) 4:33 (1/4)
Additionally: **John Lennon: Percussion & B. Vocals**; Rick Frank: B. Vocals; Yoko Ono: B. Vocals

Cryin' Blacksheep Blues (R. Frank-S. Bronstein-D. Price) 4:27 (1/3)
Additionally: **John Lennon: Guitar & B. Vocals**; Wayne Tex Gabriel: Guitar (only); Adam Ippolito: Keyboards & Trumpet (only)

Gypsy Wolf (S. Bronstein-R. Frank) 3:58 (2/1)
Additionally: **John Lennon: B. Vocals**; Rick Frank: Cherokee Indian Drum, B. Vocals & Percussion; Yoko Ono: B. Vocals

Liberation Special (R. Frank-S. Bronstein) 5:28 (1/1)
Additionally: Stan Bronstein: Percussion; Rick Frank: B. Vocals; Adam Ippolito: Keyboards (only); Martha Velez: B. Vocals; Toni Wine: B. Vocals; Hilda Harris: B. Vocals; Linda November: B. Vocals

Life (W. Gabriel) 3:42 (2/3)
Additionally: Wayne Tex Gabriel: Lead Vocals & Guitar (only); Rick Frank: Percussion; Adam Ippolito: Keyboards (only); Stan Bronstein: Saxophone (only); Keith Johnson: Trumpet; Martha Velez: B. Vocals; Toni Wine: B. Vocals; Hilda Harris: B. Vocals; Linda November: B. Vocals

Local Plastic Ono Band (R. Frank) 2:00 (2/6)
Additionally: **John Lennon: B. Vocals**; Rick Frank: Lead Vocals & Percussion; Wayne Tex Gabriel: B. Vocals (only); Adam Ippolito: B. Vocals (only); Stan Bronstein: Saxophone, Sea Green Alto Saxophone, B. Vocals & Percussion (only); Yoko Ono: Breath Rhythms & B. Vocals

Madness (A. Ippolito-R. Frank-S. Bronstein) 3:10 (2/2)
Additionally: Rick Frank: Percussion; Adam Ippolito: Keyboards (only); Martha Velez: B. Vocals; Toni Wine: B. Vocals; Hilda Harris: B. Vocals; Linda November: B. Vocals

Power Boogie (S. Bronstein-R. Frank-C. Meyer) 3:50 (2/5)
Additionally: **John Lennon: Guitar & B. Vocals**; Stan Bronstein: Lead Vocals (only); Rick Frank: B. Vocals & Percussion; Yoko Ono: B. Vocals; David Peel: B. Vocals; Myron Yules: B. Vocals

Wind Ridge (**[J. Lennon]**-G. Van Scyoc) 3:20 (2/4)
Additionally: **John Lennon: Electric Piano**; Gary Van Scyoc: Lead Vocals, Bass & Acoustic Guitar (only); Wayne Tex Gabriel: Guitar (only)

Elephant's Memory formed in 1969 and quickly gained notice for their contributions to the *Midnight Cowboy* soundtrack. Between 1969 and 1974 the band went through numerous personnel changes and briefly included Carly Simon*, Martha Velez, Chris Robison (a.k.a. Chris Meyer) and Myron Yules. They had only one minor hit, the song *Mongoose* in 1969. In 1972 the band consisted of drummer Rick Frank, born February 12, 1942 in New York, New York; saxophonist Stan Bronstein, born July 17, 1938 in Brooklyn, New York; bassist Gary Van Scyoc, born November 21, 1946 in Waynesburg, Pennsylvania; Wayne Tex Gabriel, born December 24, 1955 in Houston, Texas and keyboardist Adam Ippolito, born in Bergenfield, New Jersey in 1946.

Near the dawn of 1972 John Lennon, who'd started performing for political causes, found himself in need of a backing band. Political activist and friend Jerry Rubin suggested he go see the New York-based band Elephant's Memory. Lennon was impressed by their raw brand of rock 'n' roll. They were first assigned to back up John, Yoko Ono* and Chuck Berry* during the Lennons' weeklong appearance on TV's *The Mike Douglas Show* in February 1972. Van Scyoc says, "I was standing next to John backstage when Douglas opened the first show singing McCartney's Beatles' song *Michelle*. John said, 'Fucking hell!' He was not pleased. I guess Douglas' staff didn't do much research into The Beatles' catalog." They also backed up the Lennons on their album *Some Time In New York City* in March and on ABC TV's *The Dick Cavett Show* in May 1972.

In return for their work, the Lennons assisted on, and produced their album *Elephant's Memory* in the spring of 1972 and had it released on Apple. According to Frank, Lennon was very appreciative of them, great to work with in the studio and very committed to producing their album. According to Van Scyoc, John wrote a major piano line for the song *Wind Ridge* but refused to take credit for it. John wanted the song to be the single. Lennon mentioned he'd written a song about Chuck Berry and Bo Diddley in the November 6, 1971 issue of *Melody Maker* magazine leading to speculation that Elephant's Memory's song *Chuck 'N Bo* was written or inspired by John, but Gabriel and Van Scyoc deny this. According to Van Scyoc, Lennon hated his song *Forty-Two Down The Line*, and said it was the only song that wasn't released, though Frank said there were other unreleased songs from the sessions. Chris Robison says he helped write, and that he and Lennon sing backing vocals and do handclaps on *Baddest Of The Mean*, and that his girlfriend Suzy Puntz and Yoko also sings backing vocals on it. [Elephant's Memory later recorded the song *Everglade Woman*, without assistance from Lennon, but the scheduled release of it on Apple was cancelled.] The album received little promotion from Apple and didn't do well on the charts.

Elephant's Memory backed the Lennons at the *One To One* benefit concert's afternoon and evening shows on August 30, 1972 at New York's Madison Square Garden. Van Scyoc recalls, "We rehearsed for about two weeks. John was a real hard worker, running us through the set for the performance two times a day." Several days later they also appeared together on the *Jerry Lewis Muscular Dystrophy Telethon*. According to Van Scyoc, Lennon bought the band $100,000 worth of musical equipment and rehearsed with them in preparation for a tour that would also serve as a forum for the Lennons' political message. However the Lennons, urged by their attorneys to keep a low political profile until John's deportation case could be resolved, abandon the idea of touring, leaving little use for a backup band. The group's last official assignment with the Lennons was backing up Yoko on her *Approximately Infinite Universe* album in the fall of 1972. Elephant's Memory split amicably with the Lennons after less than a year as their backup band.

Elephant's Memory went on to back Chuck Berry on his 1973 album *Bio*, and recorded several more albums but fell apart in 1978. In 1986 band members were part of a lawsuit against Yoko. Van Scyoc says, "The lawsuit was initiated by Adam who was cut from the movie *Live In New York City* by Yoko and shots were inserted of her playing Adam's keyboard parts. The suit was settled seven long years later." Gabriel, who formed the band Limozine in the early 1980s, was asked to be a member of Ringo's 1995 All-Starr Band but arrangements were not able to be made in time for him to join the tour. Rick Frank died some years ago.

Bill Elliott And Elastic Oz Band

God Save Us / Do The Oz
Apple-1835 (7" single) (07/07/71)
Producer: John Lennon, Yoko Ono, Mal Evans & Phil Spector
John Lennon: Guitar & B. Vocals; **Ringo Starr: Drums**; Bill Elliott: Lead Vocals; Bobby Keys: (probable) Saxophone; Klaus Voormann: Bass; Diane: Keyboards
Ascot Sound Studios, Ascot 05/xx/71 & 06/01/71 & probably Apple or possibly EMI-Abbey Road Studio, London, UK 06/xx/71

God Save Us (**J. Lennon**-Y. Ono) 3:10 (1/1)

The Elastic Oz Band, and their recordings, was organized by John Lennon to help pay the legal expenses for an appeal by several editors of the UK magazine *OZ* who were sentenced to 15 months in prison for violating the UK's Obscene Publications Act, because of sexually oriented drawings, sent in by students, in issue 28 in May 1970 called *School Kids Issue*. Lennon subscribed to *OZ* (noted in the editors' defense) and was outraged by the sentence and censorship of the press. Musician and writer Charles Shaar Murray recounted events surrounding the recording of *God Save Us* in the May 1997 issue of *Mojo* magazine. Murray said the session took place at Ascot Studios [probably in May 1971] and included himself and Lennon on acoustic guitar, Ringo on drums, Klaus Voormann* on bass, *Oz* editors Felix Dennis (who later founded *Maxim* magazine), Richard Neville and Jim Anderson on percussion, a Diane on piano and acoustic guitar, a "Magic" Michael handling the lead vocals and assorted backing vocalists. Murray recalls Phil Spector producing the session and that Yoko Ono and Evans were also in attendance. Apparently a Michelle also played acoustic guitar. Murray noted that when the song was released the acoustic guitars had been replaced by electric guitars and the lead vocals were now sung by Bill Elliott. Apparently, Lennon didn't want to give the impression that the record was to be his latest single, which could have diverted royalties away from to the cause, so he omitted his vocal track. [*God Save Us* with Lennon's lead vocal guide was officially released in 1998 on the posthumous album *John Lennon Anthology*.] The lyrics, and song title was originally *God Save Oz* but Lennon changed it because the US market knew little about *Oz*. The released version contains a horn section, but doesn't contain any noticeable number of backing vocalists or percussion. All of this seems to indicate that only a portion of the backing from the session Murray attended survived, or that the backing was completely re-recorded. Though not present, Bob Purvis, Elliott's musical partner in Splinter*, says that his vocal overdubs were recorded at Apple Studios to a finished backing track, and that none of The Beatles were present. Other reports claim it was recorded, at least in part, at Abbey Road Studios. The A-side was credited to Bill Elliott And Elastic Oz Band (a la Plastic Ono Band), while the B-side, *Do The Oz*, sung by Lennon and thus a Lennon song, was simply credited to Elastic Oz Band. The Lennons were among the many who demonstrated on August 11, 1971 supporting the *OZ* defendants and protesting the UK government's policy in Northern Ireland. An interview with the Lennons, along with their rendition of *Keep Right On To The End Of The Road*, was featured on a flexi-disc included in an issue of *OZ* later that summer.

John Entwistle

Ringo Starr And His All Starr Band The Anthology...So Far
Koch-KOC-CD-8312 (07/24/01) (02/05/01)
Producer: Greg Delancy (mixer); Executive Producer: Ringo Starr & David Fishof
Ringo Starr: Drums; John Entwistle: Lead Vocals & Bass; Mark Farner: Guitar & B. Vocals; Zak Starkey: Drums; Randy Bachman: Guitar; Felix Cavaliere: Keyboards; Billy Preston: Keyboards & B. Vocals; Mark Rivera: Percussion
Nippon Budakon Hall, Tokyo, Japan 06/27/95

Boris The Spider [live] (J. Entwistle) 2:34 (1-14) (08/12/97)

John Entwistle was born on October 9, 1944 in London, England. He and school mate Pete Townshend shared membership in several bands in the late 1950s. Entwistle went on to play bass in a band call The Detours that included Roger Daltrey*, and before long Townshend. With the addition of Keith Moon* they soon became known as The Who. Entwistle wrote a number of songs for The Who, most notably *Boris The Spider*, *My Wife* and *Fiddle About*. [Ringo Starr recorded a cover of *Fiddle About* released in 1972.] He was the first member of The Who to release a solo album, *Smash Your Head Against The Wall*, in 1971 and would go on to release another half-a-dozen albums.

Entwistle contributed to Ringo's 1983 album *Old Wave*. He produced recordings for the band Nightfly, which included Ringo's son Zak. Entwistle was a member of Ringo Starr's All-Starr in 1995 performing *Boris The Spider* with Ringo backing him on drums. Entwistle was part of *A Walk Down Abbey Road: A Tribute To The Beatles* tour in 2001. John Entwistle died on June 27, 2002 on the eve of The Who's US tour. His cover of *Here Comes The Sun* was included on the 2003 album *Songs From The Material World: A Tribute To George Harrison*. For more information go to www.johnentwistle.com

The Escorts

From The Blue Angel
Edsel-EDCD 422 (UK) (06/xx/95)
John Kinrade: Guitar & Vocals; Mike Gregory: Bass & Vocals; Paddy Chambers: Guitar & Vocals; Tommy Kelly: Drums
Maximum Sound Studios, London, UK 11/xx/66

From Head To Toe (W. Robinson) 2:28 (11) (11/18/66)
Producer: probably **Paul McCartney**
Additionally: **Paul McCartney: Tambourine;** Chris Finlay: Piano & B. Vocals

Night Time ([probably **P. McCartney]** P. Chambers) 2:50 (12) (11/18/66)
Producer: possibly **Paul McCartney**

The Escorts were a popular Liverpool band in the early 1960s originally consisting of UK natives Terry Sylvester on rhythm guitar; lead guitarist John Kinrade, born in 1946; bassist Mike Gregory, born November 7, 1946 in Liverpool; singer Ray Walker and John Foster on drums. Ringo Starr, who was Foster's cousin, helped The Escorts get bookings. The Escorts appeared on the bill with The Beatles when they gave their last performance at the Cavern on August 3, 1963. Foster left the group and was replaced by Pete Clark, then Kenny Goodlass and eventually by Tommy Kelly. Sylvester left for the Swinging Blue Jeans and later joined The Hollies. He was eventually replaced by Patrick "Paddy" Chambers, born April 30, 1944 in Liverpool, of the trio Paddy, Klaus and Gibson. [Klaus is Klaus Voormann*. Gibson is Gibson Kemp who replaced Ringo in Rory Storm & The Hurricanes* when he left to join The Beatles. Kemp later married Astrid Kirchherr former fiancée of Stu Sutcliffe of The Beatles. Paddy, Klaus and Gibson were signed to NEMS for a time.] Gregory and Goodlass joined the Swinging Blue Jeans after The Escorts broke up in 1967. Clark worked as a session drummer for Apple. Paddy Chambers died on September 18, 2000.

The Escorts' final single was a cover of The Miracles' *From Head To Toe* backed with *Night Time* (Columbia-DB 8061), released in the UK in late 1966. For years it was reported that Paul McCartney had produced *From Head To Toe*. Later reports claimed he only played tambourine on the song. Chambers confirms in the liner notes of *From The Blue Angel* album that McCartney plays tambourine but makes no mention of any other involvement by him. The book *The Beatles London*, co-written by Mark Lewisohn, claims McCartney plays tambourine and co-produced it, reopening the debate regarding McCartney's role. Other reports claim McCartney also helped compose *Night Time* adding to the possibility of greater involvement by him than just playing tambourine on the single.

Sheila E. (Escovedo)

Ringo Starr & His All Starr Band Live 2006
Koch KOC-DV-4543 (DVD) (07/08/08)
Producer: Brent Carpenter; Executive Producer: Ringo Starr
Ringo Starr: Drums; Sheila Escovedo: Lead Vocals & Drums; Richard Marx: E. Guitar; Billy Squier: Electric Guitar; Hamish Stuart: Bass & B. Vocals; Rod Argent: Keyboards; Edgar Winter: Saxophone
Mohegan Sun, Uncasville, CT 07/16/06

A Love Bizarre [live] (Prince-S. Escovedo) 6:09 (7)
[Also available on Koch-KOC-CD-4542-2 (4:25) (6) (07/08/08)]

The Glamorous Life [live] (Prince) 4:50 (21)
Additionally: Richard Marx: B. Vocals; Edgar Winter: Keyboards (only)
[Also available on Koch-KOC-CD-4542-2 (3:03) (13) (07/08/08)]

Ringo Starr & His All-Starr Band Tour 2003
Warner Music Vision-R2 970326 (DVD) (09/21/04)
Producer: (Mixer: Bruce Sugar; Re-recording: Elmo Ponsdomenech & Andre Perreault);
Executive Producer: Ringo Starr & David Fishof
Ringo Starr: Drums; Sheila Escovedo: Lead Vocals & Drums; John Waite: Bass; Colin Hay: Electric Guitar & B. Vocals; Paul Carrack: Keyboards & B. Vocals; Mark Rivera: Saxophone
Casino Rama, Rama, Ontario, Canada 07/24/03

A Love Bizarre [live] (Prince-S. Escovedo) 5:01 (7)
Additionally: John Waite: B. Vocals
[Also available on Koch-KOC-CD-9549 (4:05) (7) (03/23/04)]

The Glamorous Life [live] (Prince) 8:28 (13)
[Also available on Koch-KOC-CD-9549 (4:49) (13) (03/23/04)]

Ringo Starr & His New All-Starr Band
Pioneer/Win Media-11907 (DVD) (10/01/02)
Producer: (recorded, mixed and mastered by: Glen Robinson); Executive Producer: Ringo Starr & David Fishof
Ringo Starr: Drums; Sheila Escovedo: Lead Vocals & Drums; Howard Jones: Keyboards; Roger Hodgson: Electric Guitar; Greg Lake: Bass & B. Vocals; Mark Rivera: Saxophone; Ian Hunter: Acoustic Guitar
Rosemont Theater, Rosemont (Chicago), IL 08/22/01

The Glamorous Life [live] (Prince) 8:15 (15)
[Also available on King Biscuit Flower Hour/Razor & Tie-7930188003-2 (8:59) (10) (08/06/02)]

Sheila E. was born Sheila Escovedo on December 12, 1957 in Oakland, California. She hails from a highly musical family. Her father Pete, a percussionist, was instrumental in his daughter's early interest in drumming, violin and guitar, as were his four musician brothers. Sheila was performing professionally by age 15. Her music is rooted in Latin rhythms, jazz and R&B, but she has worked with a broad range of musicians including Prince, Herbie Hancock, Stevie Wonder*, Gloria Estefan, Luciano Pavarotti, Carl Perkins*, Stevie Nicks and many others. While working with Prince in 1984 she had a Top 10 hit with her recording of his composition *The Glamorous Life* and a Top 20 hit in 1985 with *A Love Bizarre*, which she co-wrote with him.

Sheila E. was a member of Ringo Starr's All-Starr Band in 2001, 2003 and 2006 performing *The Glamorous Life* and *A Love Bizarre* with Ringo joining her on drums. She joined Ringo on *With A Little Help From My Friends* in 2008 in California at Humphrey's in San Diego on July 27 and the Pala Casino's Starlight Theater in Pala on July 29. Members of her family have also performed with her and Ringo on several of his All-Starr Band dates. The times of her songs with Ringo vary considerably between the CDs and DVDs and are noted. Sheila E. continues to write, record, do session work and tour. For more information go to www.sheilae.com

Ringo Starr All-Starr Band VIP pass, courtesy of David Fishof.

EB 84
Mercury-822 431-2 (Germany/US) (11/16/88) (10/05/84)
Producer: Dave Edmunds
Paul McCartney: Guitar & (possible) Keyboards; Don Everly: Vocals; Phil Everly: Vocals; Dave Edmunds: Guitar; Pete Wingfield: Keyboards; Albert Lee: Guitar; John Giblin: Bass; Terry Williams: Drums; Gerry Conway: Drums; Phil Donnelly: Guitar
Maison Rouge Studios, London, UK probably 07/xx/84

On The Wings Of A Nightingale (**P. McCartney**) 2:34 (1)

Heartaches & Harmonies
Rhino-R2 71779 (10/18/94) (08/24/84) **Paul McCartney: Liner Notes**
Producer: Dave Edmunds; **Remixed by: Paul McCartney**
Paul McCartney: Guitar & (possible) Keyboards; Don Everly: Vocals; Phil Everly: Vocals; Dave Edmunds: Guitar; Pete Wingfield: Keyboards; Albert Lee: Guitar; John Giblin: Bass; Terry Williams: Drums; Gerry Conway: Drums; Phil Donnelly: Guitar
Maison Rouge Studios, London, UK probably 07/xx/84

On The Wings Of A Nightingale [single version] (**P. McCartney**) 2:34 (4-19)

Isaac Donald Everly was born on February 1, 1937 in Brownie, Kentucky. His brother Phillip was born on January 19, 1939 in Chicago, Illinois. Their parents, who were country music artists, moved the family several times in search of work before settling in Shenandoah, Iowa where their live *Everly Family Show* found success on local radio stations. The boys performed on the show and over time developed a more rock 'n' roll sound based around their harmony vocals. Their career was given a boost by Chet Atkins*, and the songwriting talents of Felice and Boudleaux Bryant. Between 1957 to 1962 they had number one hits with *Wake Up Little Susie*, *All I Have To Do Is Dream* and *Cathy's Clown*; Top Five hits with *Bye Bye Love*, *Bird Dog*, *Problems* and *('Til) I Kissed You*, and

Left to right: Phil Everly, Kristofer Engelhardt and Don Everly, Leelanau Sands Casino, Suttons Bay (Traverse City), MI April 6, 2000. © Kristofer Engelhardt.

Top 10 hits with *Devoted To You*, *When Will I Be Loved*, *So Sad (To Watch Good Love Go Bad)*, *Walk Right Back*, *Crying In The Rain* and *That's Old Fashioned (That's The Way Love Should Be)*.

The Beatles' 1963 recording of *One After 909* is a perfect example of the tremendous influence The Everly Brothers had on them. [George Harrison released a cover of *Bye Bye Love* in 1974. Paul McCartney apparently paid a little tribute by mentioning Phil and Don in the lyrics of his 1976 Wings' hit *Let 'Em In*.] Success eluded The Everly Brothers following the British music invasion of 1964, though they continued to record and tour throughout the 1960s. By 1973 a myriad of personal problems came to a head during a performance and the duo split up. On September 14, 1979 Don performed with McCartney at the annual Buddy Holly Week celebrations at the Hammersmith Odeon in London, UK. The brothers worked separately for nearly 10 years before straightening out their personal lives and patching up their differences. They reunited onstage at The Royal Albert Hall in London on September 22 and 23, 1983, the video of which shows McCartney in the audience. Ringo was also in attendance.

McCartney gladly contributed his composition *On The Wings Of A Nightingale* to The Everly Brothers' album *EB 84*. He attended the sessions, adding guitar, and remixed the recording for the single version of the song, which was a UK Top Five hit. Don thinks McCartney may have also contributed keyboards to the song. The single version is available on their box set *Heartaches & Harmonies*. The booklet of which includes an introduction by McCartney. McCartney's version of the song has yet to be released, though his demo version appears on unauthorized releases. The duo has covered two of McCartney's Beatles' songs. The Everly Brothers were charter inductees into the Rock and Roll Hall of Fame in 1986. The Everly Brothers have been less active in recent years.

Adam Faith

Adam Faith
Parlophone-PCS 3025 (album 12") (UK) (probably 11/xx/61) or possibly (early/xx/62)
Producer: probably John Burgess
Adam Faith: Lead Vocals; John Barry: Conductor & Arranger and His Orchestra
Probably EMI-Abbey Road Studios, London, UK probably (late/xx/61) or or possibly (early/xx/62)

I've Just Fallen For Someone ([J. Lennon]-J. Askew) 2:32 (1/2)

Free As A Bird
FAB-FAB 1 [unauthorized release] (probably 01/xx/96)
Producer: probably Francis Hitching
John Lennon: B. Vocals; George Harrison: B. Vocals; Adam Faith: Lead Vocals; Doris Troy: B. Vocals; probably one or more of the following: Ray Davies: Guitar & B. Vocals; Dave Davies: Guitar & B. Vocals; Pete Quaife: Bass; Mike Avory: Drums; Jeff Beck: Guitar; Chris Dreja: Guitar; Jim McCarty: Drums; Keith Relf: B. Vocals & Harmonica; Paul Samwell-Smith: Bass; Peter Noone: B. Vocals; Derek Leckenby: Guitar; Keith Hopwood: Guitar; Karl Green: Bass; Barry Whitwam: Drums; Brian Parker: Guitar; John Rogan: Bass; Peter Thorpe: Guitar; Bob Henrit: Drums; Russ Ballard: Guitar
Wembley Studios, Studio One, London, UK 04/16/65

I Need Your Lovin' [live] (B. Robinson-D. Gardner-J. McDouglas-C. Lewis) 2:13 (11)

I Survive
Angel Air-SJPCD 314 (UK) (02/09/10) (09/02/74)
Producer: Adam Faith & David Courtney
Paul McCartney: Synthesizer; Adam Faith: Lead Vocals; Bob Henritt: Drums; Russ Ballard: Guitar; Dave Wintour: Bass; Dave Courtney: Piano
Kingsway Recorders, London, UK xx/xx/74

Change (A. Faith-D. Courtney) 4:00 (5)
Additionally: Del Newman: String Arrangement

Goodbye (A. Faith-D. Courtney) 4:01 (8)
Additionally: Russ Ballard: Piano Solo

Never Say Goodbye (A. Faith-D. Courtney) 4:04 (7)

Star Song (A. Faith-D. Courtney) 5:58 (10)
Additionally: Paul McCartney: B. Vocals (only); Andrew Powell: String Arrangement; Linda McCartney: B. Vocals

Adam Faith was born Terry Nelhams-Wright on June 23, 1940 in London, England. He was greatly influenced by Lonnie Donegan* and the Skiffle craze. Faith was a huge teen idol in Britain during the late 1950s and early '60s. He topped the UK charts with the songs *What Do You Want* and *Poor Me*. Like many teen idols, he also pursued a career in acting.

In either 1961 or early 1962 Parlophone released the album *Adam Faith*, which contains the song *I've Just Fallen For Someone* written by John Askew a.k.a. Darren Young*, who maintains that John Lennon, though not credited, helped him write the song. Though Faith's version was released first, both versions utilized the same conductor and arranger, and were probably recorded at the same studio using the same producer, making it likely that at least some recording of Young's version was used by Faith as a guide.

On April 16, 1965 Faith appeared on the UK TV show *Ready Steady Goes Live!* Other musical guests included Doris Troy*, The Kinks, The Yardbirds and Herman's Hermits. John Lennon and George Harrison dropped by to promote The Beatles' new single *Ticket To Ride*. The show's finale was Don Gardner & Dee Dee Ford's 1962 hit *I Need Your Lovin'* sung by Faith and backed by nearly all of the show's guests, including prominent backing vocals by Lennon, Harrison and Troy. Faith recorded a cover of The Beatles' song *I Wanna Be Your Man* released later that year.

Faith was familiar to Americans as a regular on Jack Good's mid-1960's TV rock music show *Shindig*, though his only US Top 40 hit was *It's Alright*. Later he starred in the UK TV series *Budgie* and *Love Hurts*, and hosted *Dosh,* a financial advice show. Faith also found success as a manager and producer for such artists as Leo Sayer, Roger Daltrey* and Lonnie Donegan.

Faith took over the role of Mike in *Stardust*, the 1975 sequel to the 1973 film *That'll Be The Day* in which Ringo played the role. Both films starred David Essex. [Paul and Linda McCartney*, and Denny Laine* mimed to Essex's performance of *Gonna Make You A Star* on *Top Of The Pops* on November 21, 1974 (taped on the previous day).]

Following a serious auto accident, Faith attempted to revive his musical career with his 1974 album *I Survive*. Paul and Linda McCartney contributed to the album as a personal favor to their old friend. In 1977 Faith took part in the *Scouse The Mouse* project along with Ringo Starr. Adam Faith died on March 8, 2003. For more information go to www.adamfaith.org.uk

Marianne Faithfull

Lennon & McCartney Song Book
Connoisseur Collection-VSOP CD 150 (UK/EEC) (07/02/90) (10/22/65)
Producer: [**Paul McCartney** & Mike Leander] Tony Calder
Marianne Faithfull: Lead Vocals; Singers from the Royal College of Music
Decca Studios, London, UK 10/09/65 or 10/11/65

Yesterday (J. Lennon-P. McCartney) 2:15 (23)

Marianne (Marian) Faithfull was born on December 29, 1946 in London, England. She is the daughter of Baroness Erisso Sacher-Masoch, and Major Glynn Faithfull, a psychologist and university lecturer. Americans remember her most for her trance-like rendition of the Mick Jagger* and Keith Richards' (see The Rolling Stones) composition *As Tears Go By*, which was a Top 40 hit in 1964. She also had Top 40 hits with *Come And Stay With Me*, *This Little Bird* and *Summer Nights* in 1965.

On October 9, 1965 (some sources list October 11th) Paul McCartney visited Faithfull in the studios during her cover recording of his composition *Yesterday*. Marianne says, "Paul and I had a very close and unique friendship. He helped me on much of my work. I was very young and he's quite a patriarchal guy. I looked up to him. He was very obsessed with his craft. He helped me a lot with *Yesterday*. He started to teach me, and this went on for a long time. It was a serious lesson and I knew that one day it would be useful to me. What he was suggesting was everything that was done on *Yesterday*. I guess co-producer is as good a word as any, but it doesn't quite cover it – it was more than that." In Barry Miles' 1997 authorized biography *McCartney Many Years From Now*, McCartney recalls attending Faithfull's session for *Yesterday* at Decca Studios, but doesn't remember if he contributed anything to it. Faithfull admits, and McCartney confirms, that she wasn't the sort of person who easily welcomed suggestions. During the session McCartney got to know the musical director, Mike Leander. [In 1967 McCartney had

Leander arrange the score of his Beatles' song *She's Leaving Home*, and the Lennon and McCartney instrumental *Shirley's Wild Accordion* for The Beatles' *Magical Mystery Tour* soundtrack, though it wasn't used.] McCartney stressed to Marianne the importance of releasing her version of *Yesterday* before Matt Monro's* cover version. Monroe's version, released two weeks before Faithfull's, was a UK Top 10 hit, while Faithfull's version was only a UK Top 40 hit. A 22-second film clip of McCartney performing *Yesterday* was used as an introduction to Faithfull's rendition of the song on *The Music Of Lennon & McCartney*, which aired December 17, 1965 on UK TV.

Faithfull married art dealer John Dunbar in 1965. [On November 9, 1966 Dunbar introduced John Lennon to avant-garde artist Yoko Ono* at a private preview of her exhibit *Unfinished Paintings and Objects* at his Indica Gallery. Dunbar was also involved in making avant-garde films with McCartney.] Faithfull sang in the chorus of The Beatles' 1966 song *Yellow Submarine*. By the end of 1966 she had separated from Dunbar and become Mick Jagger's steady girlfriend.

Marianne appeared in a film documentary of The Beatles' recording *A Day In The Life*. A picture of McCartney, Glyn Johns and Mick Jagger at a Faithfull recording session appears in McCartney's fan club magazine *Club Sandwich* (summer 1996 issue No. 78). In it, readers are asked to help identify when the picture was taken and what song was being recorded. The photo shows McCartney wearing the identical outfit he wore at a pre-release press party for The Beatles' *Sgt. Pepper's Lonely Hearts Club Band* album held at Brian Epstein's home in London on May 19, 1967. Documents indicated that Faithfull recorded The Beatles' song *With A Little Help From My Friends* at Decca Studios on May 20, 1967. McCartney therefore must have attended the session on the night of the 19th and early morning of the 20th. He had to be instrumental in making it possible for Faithfull to record his composition of the still unreleased Beatles' song. Mike Leander is listed as the producer for the sessions. It isn't known if McCartney directly contributed to the recording. Marianne has little recollection of her recording of *With A Little Help From My Friends*, which remains unreleased.

Marianne was part of The Beatles' live performance of *All You Need Is Love* for the BBC TV program *Our World*, telecast live on June 25, 1967. Faithfull, along with Jagger and The Beatles, attended a seminar in August 1967 in Bangor, Wales on Transcendental Meditation given by Maharishi Mahesh Yogi. During the visit The Beatles learned of Epstein's death.

In *Club Sandwich* (winter 1994 issue No. 72) McCartney says he offered her a song he had written called *Etcetera*. "I offered it to Marianne Faithfull and Mick Jagger, who were looking for a song for Marianne to record, but it wasn't what she wanted. I think she was looking for an *Eleanor Rigby* and instead I offered her an *Etcetera*." [McCartney recalls in Miles' biography that *Etcetera* was a poor attempt to come up with a song for Faithfull, and that maybe she was looking for something more baroque like *Yesterday*.] McCartney recorded a demo of *Etcetera* during sessions for *The Beatles* (white) album in 1968. Marianne doesn't recall McCartney offering her a song called *Etcetera*.

Faithfull turned to acting in the late 1960s. By 1970 her relationship with Jagger had ended as her personal problems mounted. She wouldn't appear on the charts until 1979 when *The Ballad Of Lucy Jordan*, from her critically acclaimed album *Broken English*, which includes a cover of Lennon's song *Working Class Hero*, broke the top half of the UK charts. Her voice, void of its youthful innocence, served as a reminder of the personal difficulties she had overcome. She denies reports that she recorded any songs with George Harrison. She has covered Beatles' songs, and songs from their solo career. Faithfull performed at *Here, There and Everywhere – A Concert For Linda* (see Linda McCartney) at the Royal Albert Hall in London on April 10, 1999. She continues to record, perform and make appearances in films and on TV. For more information go to www.mariannefaithfull.org.uk

Mark Farner

Ringo Starr And His All Starr Band The Anthology…So Far
Koch-KOC-CD-8312 (07/24/01)
Producer: Greg Delancy (mixer); Executive Producer: Ringo Starr & David Fishof
Ringo Starr: Drums; Mark Farner: Lead Vocals & Electric Guitar; Zak Starkey: Drums; John Entwistle: Bass; Randy Bachman: Electric Guitar & B. Vocals; Felix Cavaliere: Keyboards & B. Vocals; Billy Preston: Keyboards & B. Vocals; Mark Rivera: Percussion & B. Vocals
Nippon Budakon Hall, Tokyo, Japan 06/27/95

Some Kind Of Wonderful [live] (J. Ellison) 4:54 (1-15)

Ringo Starr And His Third All-Starr Band Volume 1
Blockbuster Exclusive-[matrix #]
0ERE4<5297>RINGOSTARR ADFL (08/12/97)
Producer: Greg Delancy (mixer); Executive Producer: Ringo Starr & David Fishof
Ringo Starr: Drums; Mark Farner: Lead Vocals & Lead Guitar; Zak Starkey: Drums; John Entwistle: Bass; Randy Bachman: Guitar & B. Vocals; Felix Cavaliere: Keyboards & B. Vocals; Billy Preston: Keyboards & B. Vocals; Mark Rivera: Percussion & B. Vocals
Nippon Budakon Hall, Tokyo, Japan 06/27/95

The Loco-Motion [live] (G. Goffin-C. King) 3:07 (4)

Singer, songwriter and guitarist Mark Farner was born on September 29, 1948 in Flint, Michigan. Farner played in a couple of well-known local bands including The Bossmen, and Terry Knight & The Pack (a.k.a. The Fabulous Pack, that included drummer Don Brewer. The group had a Top 50 hit with the song *I (Who Have Nothing)* in 1966. In 1969 Farner and Brewer recruited bassist Mel Schacher, a latter-day member of ? [Question Mark] and the Mysterians, a Michigan band who had a num-

Kristofer Engelhardt and Mark Farner with the book "From Grand Funk to Grace" by Kristofer Engelhardt, Mark Farner's home, Petoskey, MI December 18, 2000. Photo by Lesia Farner, © Kristofer Engelhardt.

ber one hit with the song *96 Tears* in 1966. They appointed Knight to be their manager and producer. Knight dubbed them Grand Funk Railroad after the Grand Trunk Railroad line. Over the next six years they were one of the biggest selling American rock groups. In 1970 their song *I'm Your Captain* (a.k.a. *Closer To Home*) was a Top 40 hit. In 1971 they sold out New York's Shea Stadium, breaking the attendance record previously held by The Beatles. The group fired Knight in 1972, retaining attorney John Eastman (see Linda McCartney), setting in motion bitter and lengthy legal disputes with Knight. Grand Funk's anthem *We're An American Band*, produced by Todd Rundgren*, topped the charts in 1973. In 1974 their cover of *The Loco-Motion* was also a number one hit. Their singles *Some Kind Of Wonderful* and *Bad Time* reached the Top 10 in 1975. The group broke up after the release of their 1976 album *Good Singin' Good Playin'* produced by Frank Zappa*. Farner released two solo albums, and from 1981 to 1983 he, Brewer and bassist Dennis Bellinger reformed Grand Funk but without much chart success. Farner released several Christian-rock oriented albums in the late '80s and early '90s. His song *Isn't It Amazing* was a number two on the Inspirational charts.

Ringo Starr's All-Starr Band tour producer David Fishof, who'd previously worked with Farner, recommended him for their 1995 tour. Mark performed *The Loco-Motion* and *Some Kind Of Wonderful* with Ringo backing him on drums. Mark says, "I love Ringo. He's a good man and has a good heart. I know that with the success of The Beatles you could have a jaded perspective if you didn't keep your feet on the ground. During a press conference I was asked what it was like to work with a Beatle. When I said he puts his pants on one leg at a time just like me, Ringo patted me on the back and said, 'Thank you brother.' He wasn't offended. He was elated that I saw him as just a man. Working with Ringo and the others in the band was a musical stretch for me. The only thing I had done professionally was my stuff. It was a very good and necessary experience for me. I needed to do that from a songwriter's standpoint to give me a different perspective, which it did. It was also humbling because I would have to ask the other guys how they played their stuff. Billy Preston was a virtuoso. Randy Bachman was takin' care of business – he's a businessman. Felix Cavaliere is a brother and I love him. John Entwistle was a heartfelt individual. I loved playing with him but because of his hearing loss he played loud as hell! Mark Rivera is the solid, unsung hero of the band." Farner joined Ringo Starr's All-Starr Band during their performance of *With A Little Help From My Friends* at the Universal Amphitheatre in Los Angeles on May 3, 1997. Grand Funk reformed with all three original members in 1997, but Farner hasn't worked with the group since 1998. Farner was part of *A Walk Down Abbey Road: A Tribute To The Beatles* tour in 2002. Mark Farner continues to write, record and tour. For more information go to www.markfarner.com

Fred & Horst Fascher

The Beatles Live/At The Star Club in Hamburg, Germany; 1962
Overseas-38 CP-44 (Japan) (10/xx/85)
Producer: Adrian Barber & Ted Taylor; (re-produced by: Larry Grossberg)
George Harrison: Lead Guitar; **John Lennon: Rhythm Guitar**; **Paul McCartney: Bass**; **Ringo Starr: Drums**
Star-Club, Hamburg, Germany 12/25/62

Be-Bop-A-Lula (G. Vincent-T. Davis) 2:29 (23) (04/08/77)
Additionally: Fred Fascher: Lead Vocals

Hallelujah, I Love Her So (R. Charles) 2:10 (24) (04/08/77)
Additionally: Horst Fascher: Lead Vocals

Fred Fascher was born April 23, 1945 and his brother Horst was born on February 5, 1936 in Hamburg, Germany. In 1960 Horst, a former German boxing champion, was a bouncer at Bruno Koschmider's Kaiserkeller Club in the St. Pauli district of Hamburg. St. Pauli was known for its legalized prostitution, strip clubs and pick-up bars headlining American rock 'n' roll acts, making it a magnet for off duty seamen and foreign troops stationed in Germany after the war. Supplementing these artists were a number of lesser-known and more affordable English artists such as Tony Sheridan*, Roy Young, Derry And The Seniors (see Freddie Starr), The Undertakers (see Jackie Lomax), Billy J. Kramer with The Dakotas*, The Strangers*, Gerry & The Pacemakers* and Rory Storm & The Hurricanes*. Allan Williams, a Liverpool club owner and booking agent, arranged The Beatles' engagement at Koschmider's Indra Club on the infamous Reeperbahn in St. Pauli in August 1960. In October, Koschmider moved The

Beatles to his more up-scale Kaiserkeller Club where they met Horst Fascher. Fascher befriended them acting as their bodyguard in the risky and risqué St. Pauli. St. Pauli was the epitome of sex, drugs and rock 'n' roll, and served as a proving ground and playground for the young and inexperienced Beatles.

Fascher soon went to work at Peter Eckhorn's Top Ten Club on the Reeperbahn, featuring Tony Sheridan. [Fascher later managed Sheridan and Roy Young.] During their off-hours, The Beatles would perform with Sheridan, a violation of their contract with Koschmider, which in part led to their expulsion from Germany for a time. Eckhorn arranged with The Beatles for them to play at his Top Ten Club from late March to July 1961. Because The Beatles negotiated directly with Eckhorn, they didn't give Williams a percentage, so he severed ties with them.

In January 1962 Manfred Weissleder sent Roy Young and Horst to Liverpool where they signed a contract with Epstein to have The Beatles help open Weissleder's plush new Star-Club in St. Pauli in April 1962. Horst had been hired to help manage the Star-Club. His brother Fred was the club's headwaiter. The Beatles made a return engagement at the Star-Club during the first half of November, before their final engagement from December 18-31, 1962. At the Star-Club The Beatles shared the bill with their musical heroes Gene Vincent and Little Richard*. Well-known producer Adrian Barber, who had been a member of the popular Liverpool group Cass And The Cassanovas, later renamed The Big Three, was the sound and stage manager of the Star-Club in 1962. Barber says he and Ted Taylor of Kingsize Taylor & The Dominoes, put Taylor's tape recorder on a table with a single microphone pointed towards the stage to record performances as an ambiance test. Taylor kept the tapes that had captured his group, Cliff Bennett And The Rebel Rousers* and The Beatles during their performances.

Nearly a decade later Taylor and Allan Williams tried to interest a number of record companies, including Polydor and Apple, to buy the recordings on the condition that they receive a percentage of the sales. Any release by Apple had to be approved by The Beatles, who reportedly were opposed to releasing the recordings. George Harrison and Ringo met with Williams in 1975 but refused to deal with him for the tapes. In 1976 Williams and Taylor sold the tapes to Paul Murphy of Lingasong Records in England. Murphy (a.k.a. Paul Rogers) had been a Polydor Record's A&R Manager and Producer who had worked with Sheridan, and was a part-time member of one of Rory Storm's early bands. Lingasong, after first trying to market the tapes to Apple, EMI and other record companies, sold the worldwide distribution rights to Double H Licensing Co. Double H invested considerable time and money trying to improve the tapes' crude sound quality. At the time, EMI was preparing to release the live album *The Beatles At The Hollywood Bowl*. When the Star-Club recordings were about to be released, EMI rightfully claimed ownership as The Beatles were under contract to them when they were taped. Double H (falsely) implied that they were recorded prior to The Beatles' contract with EMI. The British High Court ruled that because The Beatles had turned down purchasing the tapes, and because EMI had done little to claim ownership in the past, they didn't have a case. Though EMI appealed the ruling, they probably felt the inferior Star-Club recordings weren't worth the fight and wouldn't seriously affect sales of *The Beatles At The Hollywood Bowl*. [Years later The Beatles and Apple returned to the courts successfully halting the release of the Star-Club recordings on CD.]

The Star-Club recordings were issued first in Germany by Bellaphon Records in April 1977. In response EMI expedited the release of *The Beatles At The Hollywood Bowl*, the first previously unreleased recordings issued by EMI since The Beatles' breakup in 1970. The Star-Club recordings were subsequently released on a number of different record labels throughout the world, often incorrectly identifying or including numbers not performed by The Beatles. Initially, there was some confusion regarding the songs *Be-Bop-A-Lula* and *Hallelujah, I Love Her So*. The initial releases identified them as being by The Beatles with lead vocals by Star-Club waiter Horst Obber. The word "ober" is often used in German for waiter. Given the Fascher brothers' positions at the club this would be a logical reference, which likely led to the confusion concerning the surname. According to Horst, his brother Fred sings *Be-Bop-A-Lula* and he sings *Hallelujah, I Love Her So*. Horst says, "When I had a few beers, I was a little more confident and I would get up and sing sometimes! I would only sing the songs I knew the words to because my English was not so good then." Hans

Gottfridsson concludes in his book *The Beatles From Cavern To Star-Club* concludes that the recordings with the Faschers were made on Christmas Day.

On December 15, 1978 Sheridan was the headline act for the opening night at a new Star-Club in Hamburg in which Horst was involved. Ringo and Harrison were in attendance. Horst says that Paul McCartney has remained a close friend over the years, especially during troubled times. Horst works as a rock promoter, and is an occasional guest at conventions and festivals for fans of The Beatles. For more information go to www.star-club-entertainment.de

First Mistake

Gotta Sing, Gotta Dance / Gotta Sing, Gotta Dance (Party Mix)
Monopol-L4949 (7" single) (probably Sweden) [probably unauthorized release] (probably xx/xx/86)

Gotta Sing, Gotta Dance (**P. McCartney**) (1/1)

Gotta Sing, Gotta Dance (Party Mix) (**P. McCartney**) (2/1)

In 1973 it was reported that Paul McCartney would write songs for a musical film titled *Gotta Sing, Gotta Dance*. The film was to star McCartney's friend, singer, actress and model Twiggy Lawson (Lesley Hornby), but the film wasn't made. McCartney reportedly wrote the song in 1968. He performed the song, with full choreography, on his *James Paul McCartney* TV special in 1973 but never released the song.

Over a decade later an obscure band called *First Mistake* (the name possibly borrowed from those lyrics in McCartney's song *Too Many People*) issued an odd and scarce single with two versions of *Gotta Sing, Gotta Dance*. The label doesn't carry an MPL copyright and the catalogue number is identical to The Beatles' first single, *Love Me Do*, for Parlophone. If this is not accidental it may indicate that it is not an authorized release. Curiously, Twiggy released an album titled *Gotta Sing, Gotta Dance* in 2009, though it didn't contain that song.

Mick Fleetwood

The Visitor
Great Expectations-PIPCD 020 (France) (11/09/90) (06/30/81)
Producer: Richard Dashut & Mick Fleetwood
George Harrison: 12 String Guitar, Slide Guitar & B. Vocals†; George Hawkins: Lead Vocals, Bass, Piano & Guitar; Mick Fleetwood: Drums & Percussion; Adjo Group: B. Vocals; Sara Recor: B. Vocals
Ghana Film Industries Studios, Accra, Ghana 01-02/xx/81; Jimmy Page's Sol Studios (The Mill), Cookham, Berkshire, UK 04/xx/81†

Walk A Thin Line (L. Buckingham) 3:19 (6)

Michael "Mick" Fleetwood was born on June 24, 1947 in Redruth, England. He began playing drums in his teens in bands such as The Cheynes, Peter B's Looners, and Shotgun Express that included Rod Stewart*. Fleetwood, bassist John McVie and guitarist Peter Green, who had been early members of John Mayall's Bluesbreakers, and Jeremy Spencer formed the blues-oriented band Fleetwood Mac in 1967.

Fleetwood Mac nearly signed to Apple in 1969 but got a better offer from Warner Bros. Records. Numerous personnel and musical changes have become the band's hallmark. In 1970 Green was replaced by Danny Kirwan. Also joining the band was Christine Perfect, who became Christine McVie after marrying John. In 1971 Spencer was replaced by Bob Welch and Kirwan was replaced by Bob Weston and Dave Walker. By 1975 only Fleetwood and the McVies remained before the most famous and longest lasting lineup was formed with the addition of Lindsey Buckingham and Stevie Nicks. During the next five years they would release three of rock's biggest selling albums, *Fleetwood Mac*, *Rumors* and *Tusk*. Of their many hits *Rhiannon (Will You Ever Win)*, *Say You Love Me*, *Go Your Own Way*, *Don't Stop*, *You Make Loving Fun*, *Sara*, *Hold Me* and *Gypsy* have become rock classics. The band was plagued by personal problems but managed to stay together while pursuing solo projects.

Mick Fleetwood traveled to Ghana, West Africa in 1981 to record an African-flavored album titled *The Visitor*. The album included *Walk A Thin Line*, which featured a guest appearance by George Harrison that was recorded in England. Fleetwood had been married to Harrison's sister-in-law, Jenny Boyd. [A video of Harrison performing *Go Your Own Way* on acoustic guitar was shown at a Warner Bros. luncheon in 1976.]

Lindsey Buckingham left Fleetwood Mac in 1987. Rick Vito and Billy Burnette (son of the rockabilly star Johnny Burnette) helped out on tours. Vito left the group in 1991 and Stevie Nicks departed in 1993.

In 1992 Nicks joined Ringo Starr's All-Starr Band during their performance of *With A Little Help From My Friends* at the Greek Theatre in Los Angeles. In 1995 she sang a duet with Ringo on *Lay Down Your Arms* from the album *For The Love Of Harry: Everybody Sings Nilsson* (see Harry Nilsson). Nicks is the only member of Fleetwood Mac who has had significant chart success on her own.

In the mid-1990s Fleetwood Mac included Dave Mason* and Bekka Bramlett (daughter of Bonnie and Delaney Bramlett*). In 1997 Fleetwood, Buckingham, Nicks and the McVies reunited, though Christine has since dropped out. Fleetwood Mac was inducted into the Rock and Roll Hall of Fame in 1998. Mick continues to record and tour with and without Fleetwood Mac. For more information go to www.fleetwoodmac.com, www.mickfleetwood.com

John Fogerty

Live! The Silver Wilburys [Various Artists]
[none]-SWP 87-2 (Korea) [unauthorized release] (xx/xx/88)
Producer: Palomino Club
George Harrison: Guitar; John Fogerty: Vocals & Guitar; Jesse Ed Davis: Guitar; Bobby Tsukamoto: Bass; Mark Shark: Guitar; Gary Ray: Drums; Jim Ehinger: Keyboards; Bob Dylan: Guitar; Taj Mahal: B. Vocals
Palomino Club, Los Angeles, CA 02/19/87

Blue Suede Shoes [live] C. Perkins 2:50 (7)
Additionally: **George Harrison: Vocals**; Taj Mahal: Harmonica

In The Midnight Hour [live] (S. Cropper-W. Pickett) 3:20 (5)

Knock On Wood [live] (S. Cropper-E. Floyd) 3:55 (4)
Additionally: Taj Mahal: Harmonica

Proud Mary [live] (J. Fogerty) 4:23 (9)

Together At The Rock And Roll Hall Of Fame [Various Artists]
Living Legend-LLRCD 101(Italy) [unauthorized release] (xx/xx/93)
Producer: [unknown]
George Harrison: (probable) Guitar; Ringo Starr: (possible) Drums; John Fogerty: Lead Vocals & Guitar; probably one or more of the following: Bruce Springsteen: Percussion; Paul Shaffer: Keyboards; Billy Joel: Keyboards; Mike Love: Percussion; Bruce Johnston: Handclaps; Little Richard: Handclaps; Elton John: Keyboards; Anton Fig: Drums; Bob Dylan: Guitar; Dave Edmunds: Guitar; Les Paul: Guitar; Jeff Beck: Electric Guitar; Mick Jagger: Percussion; Mary Wilson: Percussion; Carl Wilson: Percussion; Brian Wilson: Handclaps; Yoko Ono: Handclaps; Sean Lennon: Handclaps; Sid McGinnis: Guitar; Ben E. King: Handclaps; Arlo Guthrie: Handclaps or Guitar; Peter Wolf: Handclaps; Johnny Moore: Handclaps; Joe Blunt: Handclaps; Clyde Brown: Handclaps; Julian Lennon: Percussion; Bill Pinkney: Handclaps; Charlie Thomas: Handclaps; Max Weinberg: Handclaps; Will Lee: Bass; Patti Scialfa: Handclaps & B. Vocals
Grand Ballroom Waldorf-Astoria Hotel, New York, NY 01/20/88

Born On The Bayou [live] (J. Fogerty) 5:23 (10)

Multi-instrumentalist John Fogerty, born on May 28, 1945 in Berkeley, California, was the primary creative force in the band Creedence Clearwater Revival that included Stu Cook, Doug Clifford, and John's older brother Tom. John's songwriting, production, distinctive vocals, and the group's unique sound, often described as a cross between rockabilly and what is called swamp rock, were the keys to their lasting popularity. The band formed around 1959 under various names but without much success. Things improved considerably soon after they changed their name to Creedence Clearwater Revival in 1967. In 1968 they a Top 20 hit with a remake of Dale Hawkins' (see Ronnie Hawkins) *Suzie Q*. Between 1969 and 1971 they were America's most popular rock band with nine million-selling singles and five million-selling albums. Among their Top 10 hits are *Proud Mary, Bad Moon Rising, Green River, Fortunate Son, Down On The Corner, Travelin' Band, Who'll Stop The Rain, Up Around The Bend* and *Have You Ever Seen The Rain.* However, John's prominence, and the departure of Tom, led to the group's rapid disintegration in 1972. Tom and John's solo careers were unsuccessful and by the late 1970s they had all but dropped out of the music business. Cook and Clifford continued on in several other groups. John restarted his career with his 1985 Top 10 hit *The Old Man Down The Road.*

On February 19, 1987 John joined Taj Mahal* and the Graffiti Band, featuring Jesse Ed Davis*, and George Harrison and Bob Dylan* onstage at Hollywood's Palomino Club. The performance is available on the unauthorized release *Live! The Silver Wilburys* and on copies of the club's house video. John was part of the all-star jam with George and Ringo Starr when The Beatles were inducted into the Rock and Roll Hall of Fame on January 20, 1988 at New York's Waldorf Astoria Hotel, portions of which are available on unauthorized releases.

Tom Fogerty died in 1990. Creedence Clearwater Revival was inducted into the Rock and Roll Hall of Fame in 1993. Stu Cook and Doug Clifford have been touring as Creedence Clearwater Revisited since 1995. John Fogerty continues to write, record and tour. For more information go to www.johnfogerty.com

The Fourmost

The Best Of The Fourmost
EMI Gold-0946 3 31318 2 8 (UK) (07/11/05)
Producer: George Martin
Billy Hatton: Vocals & Bass; Brian O'Hara: Vocals & Lead Guitar; Mike Millward: Vocals & Rhythm Guitar; Dave Lovelady; Drums

Hello Little Girl (**J. Lennon**-P. McCartney) 1:50 (1) (08/30/63)
EMI-Abbey Road Studios, London, UK 07/03/63

I'm In Love (**J. Lennon**-P. McCartney) 2:07 (3) (11/15/63)
EMI-Abbey Road Studios, London, UK 10-11/xx/63

Rosetta / Just Like Before
CBS-4041 (7" single) (UK) (02/21/69)
Producer: Paul McCartney
Brian O'Hara: Lead Vocals & Guitar; Dave Lovelady: Drums & B. Vocals; Billy Hatton: Bass & B. Vocals; Joey Bowers: Guitar & B. Vocals
01/xx/69

Just Like Before (A. Benny [a.k.a. B. O'Hara]) 2:30 (1/2)

Rosetta (E. Hines-H. Woode) 2:11 (1/1)
Additionally: **Paul McCartney: Piano & Arrangement**

The Fourmost, whose members were born and grew up in the Liverpool, England area, originally were called The Four Jays and then The Four Mosts before revising their name. They were often on bills with The Beatles with whom they became good friend. They were known as much for their unique brand of humor onstage as their music. The group consisted of Brian Redman, Joey Bowers, Billy Hatton, born June 9, 1941 on bass and vocals and Brian O'Hara, born March 12, 1942 on lead guitar and vocals. In 1962 Dave Lovelady, born October 16, 1942 replaced Redman on drums and Mike Millward, born May 9, 1942 (Bromborough) replaced Bowers on rhythm guitar. Bowers replaced Millward following his death in March 1966. George Peckham, another brief member of the group, later worked for Apple.

Hello Little Girl is one of the first songs John Lennon ever wrote. The Beatles recorded it at their failed Decca Records audition in early 1962. [It was officially released on *The Beatles Anthology 1* album in 1995.] Instead, it was offered to the NEMS' groups The Fourmost and Gerry & The Pacemakers*. Brian O'Hara recalled, "We were given a demo of Lennon and Harrison playing acoustic guitars and singing the song. We had about two days to learn it and we rehearsed it on the way down to the studio on our bus. Lennon was reading his poetry on the other side of the tape, but I think we sent it back to Brian Epstein after we were done with it." Gerry & The Pacemakers decided against releasing their version. [It wasn't released until 1991.] The Fourmost's release was a UK Top 10 hit in 1963. [An alternate version of The Fourmost's *Hello Little Girl* appears on the unauthorized release *Maybe You Can Drive My Car* (Yellow Dog/Orange-019).]

I'm in Love, also written by Lennon, was also offered to The Fourmost and the NEMS' group Billy J. Kramer with The Dakotas*. [Kramer's version wasn't released until 1991.] The Fourmost's version was issued as their second single in November 1963 and was a UK Top 20 hit. Lennon's demo of the song was featured on the Westwood One radio series *The Lost Lennon Tapes*. The Fourmost were also offered the Lennon and McCartney composition *One And One Is Two* (see The Strangers with Mike Shannon). According to O'Hara, "McCartney came into the studio, and played bass on *One And One Is Two*, but there just wasn't any meat in the song and we couldn't get anywhere with it."

The Fourmost, being more of a cabaret and comedy act, were perfect for the bill on *The Beatles Christmas Show* in 1963. They had four additional hits in the UK, including *A Little Loving* in 1964, but none of their songs found success in the US. They appeared in Gerry & The Pacemakers' 1965 film *Ferry Cross The Mersey*, and their song *I Love You Too* was included on the soundtrack. That song also appeared on the unauthorized release *Indian Rope Trick* credited as Paul McCartney with The Fourmost, but O'Hara said McCartney had absolutely nothing to do with the song. The Fourmost also recorded covers of The Beatles' songs, one under the pseudonym The Format.

In 1969 McCartney suggested to O'Hara that The Fourmost record the old jazz standard *Rosetta*, and volunteered to arrange and produce it for them. McCartney also produced the single's B-side *Just Like Before*. O'Hara wrote the song under the pseudonym A. Benny and said it was assigned to Apple Music Publishing in thanks for McCartney's help. According to O'Hara and Lovelady, McCartney liked the way the group could mimic ('a pinch off The Mills Brothers') instruments with their voices, which The Beatles had done on *Lady Madonna*. So on *Rosetta*, O'Hara made trumpet sounds and the rest of the group made trombone sounds. Lovelady was playing piano during the session, but O'Hara suggested he play it badly, correctly predicting that McCartney would take over playing piano on it.

The Fourmost carried on for about another decade until Hatton, Lovelady and Bower formed the group Clouds. Brian O'Hara died on June 27, 1999. The Fourmost, without any original members, still perform in the UK. For more information go to www.thefourmost.co.uk

Peter Frampton

Ringo Starr And His Fourth All-Starr Band
MPI-MP7292 (VHS) (07/28/98)
Producer: David & Ryan Hewitt (music mixers); Peter Skorich (video); Executive Producer: Ringo Starr & David Fishof
Ringo Starr: Drums; Peter Frampton: Lead Vocals & Guitar; Gary Brooker: Keyboards; Jack Bruce: Bass; Simon Kirke: Drums; Mark Rivera: Percussion
Pine Knob Music Theater, Clarkston (Detroit), MI 05/30/97

Baby, I Love Your Way [live] (P. Frampton) 4:32 (8) Additionally: Gary Brooker: B. Vocals; Mark Rivera: B. Vocals
[Also available on *Ringo Starr And His All Starr Band The Anthology...So Far*. Koch-KOC-CD-8312 (3-7) (07/24/01) (02/05/01)]

Do You Feel Like We Do [live] (P. Frampton) 18:50 (20)
Additionally: Gary Brooker: B. Vocals; Jack Bruce: B. Vocals; Mark Rivera: B. Vocals
Show Me The Way [live] (P. Frampton) 4:35 (4)
Additionally: Peter Frampton: Talk Box; Gary Brooker: B. Vocals; Mark Rivera: Acoustic Guitar & B. Vocals; Jack Bruce: B. Vocals
[Also available on *Ringo Starr And His All Starr Band The Anthology...So Far*. Koch-KOC-CD-8312 (3-2) (07/24/01) (02/05/01)]

Wind Of Change
A&M-PCCY-10231 (Japan) (10/xx/91) (07/10/72)
Producer: Peter Frampton
Olympic Studios, London, UK 11/xx/71-02/xx/72

Alright (P. Frampton) 4:21 (10)
Ringo Starr: Drums; Peter Frampton: Lead Vocals, Guitars & Percussion; Klaus Voormann: Bass; Billy Preston: Piano & Organ; Frank Carillo: Rhythm Guitar, Percussion & B. Vocals; Andrew Bown: Percussion & B. Vocals

The Lodger (P. Frampton) 5:40 (8)
Ringo Starr: Drums; Peter Frampton: Lead Vocals, Guitars & Door Percussion; Frank Carillo: Guitars; Andrew Bown: Bass; Jim Price: Brass

Peter Frampton was born on April 22, 1950 in Beckenham (London), England. He quickly became known as a guitar whiz kid and formed his first band at the age of 10. He appeared on the UK TV show *Ready Steady Go!* when he was 14, joined the band The Herd at 16 and by the age of 19 found fame with the band Humble Pie.

Peter was soon in demand as a session player. He contributed to Doris Troy's* 1970 album for Apple meeting and working with George Harrison and Ringo Starr. This led to his playing (un-credited) acoustic guitar on Harrison's 1970 album *All Things Must Pass.* Peter lived around the corner from Ringo at the time and would hang out at his place. Frampton, Starr and Harrison played on Harry Nilsson's* 1972 album *Son Of Schmilsson*, and he made an appearance in a musical scene in Nilsson and Ringo's film *Son Of Dracula*. He now says nostalgically "I was just a whore then – I would play for anybody!"

Ringo played drums on *Alright* and *The Lodger* from Frampton's 1972 debut album *Wind Of Change*. Peter recalls that the only time he ever had to audition for anyone was when he asked Ringo to play on his recordings; "He liked everything!" According to Peter an early backing track of *Lady Lieright* with Ringo on drums was recorded, but a more "unplugged" version without Ringo ended up on the album. Peter returned the favor by playing guitar on Ringo's 1976 album *Rotogravure*.

Peter's constant touring paid off in 1976 with the release of *Frampton Comes Alive.* It yielded the hits *Show Me The Way*, *Baby, I Love Your Way* and *Do You Feel Like We Do* and became one of the biggest selling albums ever. The title track of his follow-up album *I'm In You* in 1977 was also a huge hit. In the mid-1970s Frampton was reportedly considered as a replacement for Mick Taylor in The Rolling Stones* and was voted one of the top 10 rock guitarists in a *New York Times* poll. In 1978 Frampton starred in Robert Stigwood's musical film *Sgt. Pepper's Lonely Hearts Club Band*, which fully elevated him to the status of teeny bopper heart throb. He prefers to forget the film, which detracted from his more serious musical side then, though ironically it has become a cult classic. Peter was a member of his grammar school mate, David Bowie's touring band in 1987.

Kristofer Engelhardt and Peter Frampton, Pine Knob, Clarkston (Detroit), MI August 12, 2000. © Kristofer Engelhardt

Frampton joined Ringo Starr's All-Starr Band tours in 1997 and 1998 performing *Show Me The Way*, *Baby, I Love Your Way* and *Do You Feel Like We Do* with backing from Ringo on drums. He also performed *Norwegian Wood* in tribute to John Lennon. Peter says he had a ball and found Ringo to be very laid back, humorous and a great bandleader. Peter has recorded over a dozen albums including covers of Beatles' songs. Peter Frampton continues to record, do session work and perform to large, enthusiastic crowds. For more information go to www.frampton.com

Aretha Franklin

Lennon & McCartney Songbook
Connoisseur Collection-VSOP CD 150 (UK/EEC) (07/02/90) (02/21/70)
Producer: Jerry Wexler, Tom Dowd & Arif Mardin
Aretha Franklin: Lead Vocals & Piano; Jimmy Johnson: Guitar; David Hood: Bass; Barry Beckett: Keyboards; Roger Hawkins: Drums; King Curtis: (probable) Saxophone; Cissy Houston: (probable) B. Vocals; Sylvia Shemwell: (probable) B. Vocals; Estelle Brown: (probable) B. Vocals; Myrna Smith: (probable) B. Vocals
Atlantic Recording Studios, New York, NY probably 05/26-30/69 or possibly 10/xx/69 or 12/xx/69

Let It Be (J. Lennon-**P. McCartney**) 3:28 (2)

Aretha Franklin was born on March 25, 1942 in Memphis, Tennessee but has spent most of her life in Detroit, Michigan. Her father was a well-known gospel preacher and singer. Her mother, who died when Aretha was six, was also a gospel singer. Aretha's path to musical stardom was fostered at an early age by gospel singers Mahalia Jackson, James Cleveland and the Ward Sisters, who were friends of her family. She began recording in her father's church in Detroit for Checker Records when she was 14. Between 1960 and 1966 she was recording light jazz and R&B for Columbia Records, but with limited success.

By 1967 Aretha had switched to Atlantic Records. With producer Jerry Wexler, she became one of the world's most successful female singers by covering other artists' minor hits, and rearranging them to suit her dynamic soul and gospel voice. By 1968 she had topped the charts with *Respect*; had Top Five hits with *Baby I Love You*, *Chain Of Fools*, *(Sweet Sweet Baby) Since You've Been Gone*; had Top 10 hit with *I Never Loved A Man (The Way I Love You)*, *(You Make Me Feel Like A) Natural Woman*, *Think*, *The House That Jack Built* and *I Say A Little Prayer*. Between 1971 and 1973 she had Top Five hits with *Spanish Harlem*, *Day Dreaming*, *Until You Come Back To Me (That's What I'm Gonna Do)*, and Top 10 hits with *Bridge Over Troubled Water* and *Rock Steady*. In 1985 she had a Top Five hit with *Freeway of Love*. She has won 18 Grammy Awards. Aretha Franklin's only other number one hit was a duet with George Michael* of *I Knew You Were Waiting (For Me)* in 1987, the year she was inducted into the Rock and Roll Hall of Fame.

Aretha Franklin and The Beatles have long admired each other's music, and she has covered several of their songs during her career. In 1969 there was great tension within The Beatles and they were unsure of what to do with some of the recordings they had made for what would later become the album and the motion picture *Let It Be*. By mid-1969 these recordings were appearing on unauthorized records. Apparently, Paul McCartney felt his song *Let It Be* was suited for Franklin's gospel voice. [McCartney offered *Let It Be* to Joe Cocker* in 1969.] According to Jerry Wexler, "They sent me an acetate. I don't remember if it was Paul or The Beatles organization, with the suggestion that I do the song with Aretha. I loved it. I played it for Aretha but she didn't like it! Later she decided that she did like it, so we cut it and had it in the can. I got a legal stop order from them [The Beatles] mandating that I could not put out the record. Once their record was out, I could legally put it out. I could have legally put it out before The Beatles' version if I would have acted in time." The Beatles' version of *Let It Be* was officially presented to the world on *The Ed Sullivan Show* on March 1, 1970. But the *Billboard* magazine has reported that Aretha's album *This Girl's In Love With You*, containing *Let It Be*, was released on January 15, 1970 (they have also listed February 21). If either date is correct, Aretha's version did precede The Beatles' official release. If the release was delayed, as Wexler maintains it legally had to be, then *Billboard's* dates are erroneous. However, because the song was originally intended for Franklin to release first, and because it may or could have been released first, it is considered a composition contribution. The song was probably recorded in May 1969 according to David Hood and Jimmy Johnson, who played on the session. Some sources list it as being recorded in October or December 1969. Wexler also revealed that Franklin began recording a cover of McCartney's Beatles' song *The Fool On The Hill* but it was never completed. Aretha Franklin continues to tour and record.

Kinky Friedman

Lasso From El Paso
Varese Sarabande/Sony-VSD-5994 (03/23/99) (11/05/76)
Producer: Huey P. Meaux
Ringo Starr "The Voice Of Jesus†;" Kinky Friedman: Lead Vocals; one or more of the following: Jim Atkinson: Guitar & B. Vocals; T-Bone Burnett: Guitar & Keyboards; Tom Culpepper: Guitar; Kinky Friedman: Guitar; Bill Ham: Guitar; Mick Ronson: Guitar; Steve Soles: Guitar; Ron Wood: Guitar; Brian Clarke: Bass; Rick Danko: Bass & B. Vocals; Terry Danko: Bass & B. Vocals; Rob Stoner: Bass; Ira Wilkes: Bass; Major Boles: Drums & Percussion; Gary Burke: Drums & Percussion; Teddy Jack Eddy: B. Vocals, Drums & Percussion; Levon Helm: Guitar, B. Vocals, Drums & Percussion; Richard Manuel: Keyboards, Drums & Percussion; Dahrell Norris: Drums & Percussion; Howie Wyeth: Drums & Percussion; Ken Lauber: Keyboards; Jewford Shelby: Keyboards; Red Young: Keyboards; Snakebite Jacobs: Horns; Tracey Balin: B. Vocals; Roscoe West: B. Vocals; The Rolling Thunder Revue: B. Vocals; Van Dyke Parks: Keyboards; Lowell George: Guitar
Cherokee Studios†, &/or probably Shangri-La Studios, &/or Haji Sound Studio, Los Angeles, CA &/or Sugar Hill, Houston, TX probably 04/xx/76

Men's Room, L.A. (B. Fowler) 2:10 (8)

Richard "Kinky" Friedman was born on November 1, 1944 in Chicago, Illinois but has spent most of his life in Texas. Friedman first recorded with the surf music band King Arthur and The Carrots in 1966. Since that time he has been a country singer, songwriter and leader of The Texas Jewboys. His political, humorous and vulgar lyrics, combined with outrageous stage outfits, have not always endeared him to the mainstream country music crowd, especially with songs such as *They Ain't Makin' Jews Like Jesus Anymore, Get Your Biscuits In The Oven And Your Buns In Bed* and *Ride 'em Jewboy.* He has all but given up his music career stating, "When the horse dies, get off!" He has also written a number of successful books. In 2006 he was an independent candidate for Governor of Texas.

Ringo Starr's contribution to the album *Lasso From El Paso* was the result of his involvement in Bob Dylan's* Rolling Thunder Revue tour, which included Friedman and The Alpha Band*. Kinky recalls Ringo's "Voice Of Jesus" portion of the song *Men's Room, L.A.* as being recorded at Cherokee Studios in Los Angeles. According to Kinky, Ringo was "flying by Jewish radar and improvised it on the spot." For more information go to www.kinkyfriedman.com

Gerry & The Pacemakers

The Best of Gerry & The Pacemakers, The Definitive Collection
United Artists-CDP-7-96093-2 (10/08/91)
Producer: George Martin
Gerry Marsden: Lead Vocals & Lead Guitar; Leslie Chadwick: Bass; Freddie Marsden: Drums; Leslie Maguire: B. Vocals

Hello Little Girl (**J. Lennon**-P. McCartney) 1:51 (6)
Additionally: Les Chadwick: B. Vocals
EMI-Abbey Road Studios, London, UK 07/17/63

How Do You Do It? (M. Murray) 1:53 (1) (03/xx/63)
Additionally: **John Lennon: Arrangement**; **Paul McCartney: Arrangement**; Les Maguire: Piano (only)
EMI-Abbey Road Studios, London, UK 01/22/63

Lennon / McCartney Songbook [Gerry Marsden]
K-Tel-ONE 1274 (album 12") (xx/xx/85) **Paul McCartney: Liner Notes**

Liverpool, England natives, guitarist Gerard "Gerry" Marsden, born on September 24, 1942 and his brother Freddie, born on October 23, 1940 on drums, were the core of what became Gerry & The Pacemakers. Early members of the group included Brian O'Hara of The Fourmost* and Arthur McMahon. Heyday members included John Leslie Chadwick, born on May 11, 1943 on bass and Leslie Maguire, born on December 27, 1941 (Wallasey), England on keyboards. Maguire had been a member of The Undertakers (see Jackie Lomax). They were one of the Liverpool area natives most popular groups in Liverpool during the early 1960s. They were often on bills with The Beatles in Liverpool, and in Hamburg, Germany, where the two groups developed a close and competitive relationship. They were signed to NEMS, and like most NEMS' artists were signed to EMI and produced by George Martin*.

During the summer of 1962 Martin mailed a demo to The Beatles of Mitch Murray's song *How Do You Do It?* performed with backing by The Dave Clark Five. [Murray reportedly intended to have Adam Faith* record the song.] Martin wanted the song to be The Beatles' first single for EMI. The Beatles, who wanted one of their compositions to be their first single, disliked the song and re-arranged it considerably before halfheartedly recording it in early September at their second session for EMI. They persuaded Martin to release their composition *Love Me Do* as their first single. When the song failed to reach the UK Top 10, Martin urged them to reconsider *How Do You Do It?* Martin felt sure the song could be a number one hit and challenged Lennon and McCartney to write a number one hit, which they did in the UK with a rearranged version of *Please Please Me*. Martin was still convinced *How Do You Do It?* was a potential number one hit. In 1963 he produced The Beatles' arrangement of the song for Gerry & The Pacemakers, which became their first UK number one hit, followed by another Murray composition, *I Like It*.

Epstein took advantage of Lennon and McCartney's songwriting recognition, assigning their leftovers to other NEMS' artists. Around the same time in mid-1963, George Martin produced Gerry & The Pacemakers' and The Fourmost's* recordings of *Hello Little Girl*. The song is an early Lennon composition The Beatles frequently performed, and auditioned for Decca Records in early 1962 but never recorded for EMI. Marsden didn't want it issued then. [It was eventually released in 1991 on *The Best of Gerry & The Pacemakers, The Definitive Collection*.] The Fourmost's version became a UK Top 10 hit some weeks later. The Pacemakers' version is considered a composition contribution because it was also given to them with the idea of possibly having them release it first.

Gerry & The Pacemakers' had their third and final UK number one hit was *You'll Never Walk Along* in the fall of 1963. In 1964 the group had three UK Top 10 hits with *I'm The One, Don't Let The Sun Catch You Crying* and *Ferry Cross The Mersey*. They only had one UK Top 20 hit in 1965 with *I'll Be There* and broke up the following year. Three of their UK hits reached the Top 10 in the US.

Gerry Marsden has since played a variety of roles onstage and on TV. He appeared in the *James Paul McCartney* TV special in 1973, and has performed over the years with a new group of Pacemakers. In 1985 Marsden recorded a benefit single for the Bradford City Football Club Disaster Fund (see The Crowd) to which McCartney contributed. That year McCartney provided the liner notes to Gerry's album *Lennon / McCartney Songbook*, containing covers of their classic compositions. In 1989 Marsden and McCartney again came to the aid of families hit by disaster by donating proceeds of a re-recording of *Ferry Cross The Mersey* to The Hillsborough Football Disaster Fund (see The Christians, Holly Johnson, Paul McCartney, Gerry Marsden & Stock Aitken Waterman). The Beatles' recordings of *How Do You Do It?* and *Hello Little Girl* were officially released on their album *Anthology 1* in 1995. Freddie Marsden died on December 9, 2006. For more information go to www.gerrymarsden.co.uk

GetBack!

GetBack! is a tribute and impersonation band of The Beatles that came together as a result of their being a part of the stage show *Beatlemania*, which first opened on Broadway in 1976. When the show closed in 1988 four of its members got together and formed the touring band GetBack! They have been performing ever since. They focus on all stages of The Beatles' musical career in their performance and dress. Jack Patrilla, who plays Paul McCartney in the band, saw The Beatles perform on *The Ed Sullivan Show* and, like countless others of his generation, was inspired to pursue a career in music. Patrilla says, "I think the longevity of our band is due to the fact that when we aren't playing The Beatles, we're just us. My Paul character goes away when the costume comes off. If it doesn't then I need medication! However, there was no way The Beatles could get out of being The Beatles. They were always captive to their fame. Fortunately, we don't have to deal with that kind of pressure. We know we're not The Beatles. We just try to recapture their magic. As long as we have an audience who enjoy our shows, there will hopefully be another show. What makes it worthwhile are the good vibes that pour from the audience. The music is fun and means something to them. We just soak up the reflected adoration."

Patrilla recalls one very special moment, "We were doing a show in Canada and Ringo was in town, heard about us, and came by. He must have liked what he heard or he wouldn't have gotten up onstage behind the drums. I think he did it on a dare. We were sweating bullets! We wanted to be the audience that night. I'm not sure the audience knew that the Beatle impersonator who looked like Ringo really was Ringo. He drummed on *A Hard Day's Night* and *I Saw Her Standing There*, and he played them exactly like on their records but after all he created those drum parts. Just when we thought of asking him to join the band, he was off, saying, 'Thanks lads, it was fun!'" For more information go to www.getbackbeatlemania.com

Allen Ginsberg

The Ballad Of The Skeletons
Mouth Almighty/Mercury-697 120 101-2 (single) (10/15/96)
Producer: Lenny Kaye
Paul McCartney: Guitar, Maracas, Hammond Organ & Drums†; Allen Ginsberg: Dialogue; Mark Ribot: Guitar; Lenny Kaye: Bass; David Mansfield: Guitar; Philip Glass: Keyboards
Hog Hill Mill Studios, Sussex, UK† & Kampo Culture Center, New York, NY probably 10/xx/95† & 05-06/xx/96

The Ballad Of The Skeletons (A. Ginsberg-P. Glass-**P. McCartney**) 7:46 (1)

The Ballad Of The Skeletons (Clean) (A. Ginsberg-P. Glass-**P. McCartney**) 7:46 (4)

The Ballad Of The Skeletons (Edit) (A. Ginsberg-P. Glass-**P. McCartney**) 4:07 (2)

No More To Say & Nothing To Weep For – An Elegy For Allen Ginsberg
Warner Vision International/NVC Arts/Kultur-D4141 (DVD) (07/17/07)
Producer: Colin Still
Paul McCartney: Guitar; Allen Ginsberg: Dialogue
Royal Albert Hall, London, UK 10/16/95

The Ballad of The Skeletons [edit] (A. Ginsberg-**P. McCartney**) 0:41 (1)

Unbootlegged 08 – Get That Fly [John Lennon]
No Label Records-NLR-0402 (CD-R) [unauthorized release] (xx/xx/04)
Producer: probably **John Lennon** & Phil Spector
John Lennon: B. Vocals & Guitar; **Ringo Starr: B. Vocals & (probable) Percussion**; Allen Ginsberg: Lead Vocals & Harmonium; Phil Spector: Guitar; Elliot Mintz: B. Vocals; Nicky Hopkins: B. Vocals; Klaus Voormann: B. Vocals; Jim Keltner: B. Vocals & (probable) Percussion; Eric Clapton: Guitar & B. Vocals; Mal Evans: B. Vocals; Neil Aspinall: B. Vocals; May Pang: B. Vocals; Maureen Starkey: B. Vocals; Yoko Ono: B. Vocals; (and others)
[Hotel Syracuse, Syracuse, NY 10/09/71

Nurse's Song (W. Blake-A. Ginsberg) 4:07 (34)

Unbootlegged 27 [The Beatles]
No Tapo-NTR 0801 (CD-R) [unauthorized release] (xx/xx/08)
Paul McCartney: Guitar; Allen Ginsberg: Dialogue
Royal Albert Hall, London, UK 10/16/95

The Ballad Of The Skeletons (A. Ginsberg-**P. McCartney**) 6:46 (1-3)

Irwin Allen Ginsberg was born on June 3, 1926 in Newark, New Jersey. His father was a poet and teacher. Allen was surrounded by controversy throughout most of his career, starting with the publication of his book *Howl and Other Poems* in 1956. That book set the tone for his politically and sexually abrasive, stream-of-consciousness literary style, which helped define the "Beat Generation" of writers and poets in the 1950s. As a political activist in the turbulent 1960s he became a spokesperson of pacifism and is credited with coining the phrase "flower power."

On May 9, 1965 Bob Dylan* invited Ginsberg to his room at the Savoy Hotel in London to meet The Beatles. Ginsberg and Barry Miles made occasional visits to Paul McCartney's home in London in the mid-1960s. [Miles co-owned the Indica Gallery where John Lennon met Yoko Ono. He would later write biographies on McCartney and Ginsberg.] Ginsberg was in the studio when Lennon and McCartney sang backing vocals on The Rolling Stones'* single *We Love You*. In 1969 Zapple Records, a spoken-word and avant-garde division of Apple, that Miles helped run, apparently considered releasing an album of Ginsberg's music set to

William Blake's poems.

Lennon phoned Ginsberg in New York during his Montreal "bed-in for peace" in mid-1969. Ginsberg made a cameo in Yoko Ono's 1970 *Film No. 12 (Up Your Legs Forever).* He spent time with the Lennons shortly after their move to New York's Greenwich Village in 1971. He was one of the invited guests at Yoko's one woman art show *This Is Not Here*, which opened on John's 31st birthday in Syracuse, New York on October 9, 1971. Following the opening, Ginsberg joined Lennon, Ringo, Phil Spector* and others for a jam session that is available on the unauthorized releases *John Lennon-Let's Have A Party* and *John Lennon: Unbootlegged 08 – Get That Fly.* Ginsberg began the jam with a series of mantras and did his rendition of Blake's *Nurse's Song* before the jam turned to rock and blues standards.

Lennon and Allen Klein indicated to Ginsberg that they were interested in releasing recordings of his on Apple. On November 17 and 20, 1971 Ginsberg, with help from Dylan, recorded an album's worth of material at Record Plant Studios in New York. The album was tentatively titled *Holy Soul & Jelly Roll* and reported to include such songs as *Going To San Diego*, *Nurse's Song* and *September On Jessore Road.* [Some of these recordings were released by Rhino Records in 1994.] According to Ginsberg, Lennon told him the album would not be released on Apple because he was secretly trying to break off his business ties with Klein (which he later did). *Going To San Diego* was featured on *The Lost Lennon Tapes* radio series giving further rise to speculation that Lennon may have contributed to these recordings. According to Ginsberg, Lennon didn't contribute directly to any of his studio recordings, though he and John did jam at the Lennons' Greenwich Village apartment. Ginsberg said Lennon suggested that he use a string quartet arrangement on *September On Jessore Road*, similar to what The Beatles used on *Eleanor Rigby*, after hearing Ginsberg perform it at the *John Sinclair Freedom Rally.* Ginsberg appeared onstage with the Lennons at the *One To One* benefit concerts on August 30, 1972 at Madison Square Garden for the encore of *Give Peace A Chance.*

Ginsberg gave a poetry reading billed as *Return Of The Reforgotten* at the Royal Albert Hall in London on October 16, 1995. He was accompanied by McCartney on electric guitar during the reading of *The Ballad Of The Skeletons*, which is available on unauthorized releases. A brief portion of the nearly seven minute performance is available on the DVD *No More To Say & Nothing To Weep For – An Elegy For Allen Ginsberg.* The collaboration was the result of a visit Ginsberg had made to McCartney's home during which he asked Paul to recommend some guitarists. *The Ballad Of The Skeletons* is a political song that Ginsberg later recorded, with help from McCartney, and released as a single in time for the 1996 US elections. The single also contains a "clean" version of the song, which omits profanities, and an alternate edited version. McCartney took Ginsberg's advice and collaborated with poet Tom Pickard on his *Standing Stone* poem (see The London Symphony Orchestra & Chorus). Just before Ginsberg's death on April 5, 1997, *Billboard* magazine reported plans were underway for McCartney, Dylan, Beck and Ginsberg to team up for a music and spoken word performance on MTV's *Unplugged.* For more information go to www.allenginsberg.org

Godley & Creme

Freeze Frame
Polydor-831 555-2 (xx/xx/88) (11/30/79)
Producer: Kevin Godley & Lol Creme
Paul McCartney: B. Vocals; Kevin Godley: Lead Vocals, Cowbell & Percussion; Lol Creme: Lead Guitar, Bass, Keyboards, Harmonica & B. Vocals
Surrey Sound Studios, Surrey, UK xx/xx/79

Get Well Soon (K. Godley-L.Creme) 4:35 (8)

Kevin Godley, born on October 7, 1945 and Lol Creme, born on September 19, 1947, both in Prestwich (Manchester), England gained notice in the group 10cc*, which also included Eric Stewart and Graham Gouldman. Paul McCartney's involvement with Godley and Creme began during work on his brother Mike McGear's* 1974 album *McGear.* Godley and Creme left 10cc to concentrate on inventing new musical devices, and produce music videos, including several for McCartney. One of their more famous videos was for George Harrison's 1987 song *When We Was Fab*, which includes a cameo by Ringo Starr, but not McCartney as has been rumored. McCartney contributed to Godley & Creme's 1979 album *Freeze Frame.* Godley and Creme had a Top 20 hit with *Cry* in 1985. They briefly reunited with Stewart and Gouldman for 10cc's album *Meanwhile* in 1992 to which McCartney contributed. In 1995 Godley directed the music video for The Beatles' single *Real Love.* Creme joined the group Art Of Noise in 1998.

Around Grapefruit
Repertoire-REP 5044 (Germany) (08/23/05) (12/xx/68)
George Alexander: Bass & B. Vocals; Geoff Swettenham: Drums & B. Vocals; Pete Swettenham: Acoustic Guitar & B. Vocals; John Perry: Lead Vocals & Acoustic Guitar
Probably Advision Studios, possibly Trident, Regent Sound, IBC, De Lane Lea or EMI's Abbey Road Studios; London, UK probably 04-06/xx/68 or possibly 01/xx/68 [unless noted otherwise]

C'mon Marianne (L.R. Brown-R. Bloodworth) 2:36 (5) (07/xx/68)
Producer: Grapefruit & Terry Melcher
Additionally: **John Lennon: Horn Arrangement**; John Perry: Lead Vocals & Electric Guitar (only)
Probably Trident Studios, London, UK 04-06/xx/68

Lullaby (G. Alexander) 3:29 (6)
Producer (portion of backing track only): Paul McCartney & John Lennon
Additionally: George Alexander: Lead Vocals & Bass (only); John Perry: Acoustic Guitar (only)
Advision Studios, London, UK probably 01/xx/68

Yes (J. Perry) 2:20 (4) (04/xx/68)
Producer: [**Paul McCartney**] Grapefruit
Additionally: Pete Swettenham: Keyboards

94 Baker Street (The Pop-Psych Sounds of the Apple Era 1967-1969) [Various Artists]
RPM-RPM 270 (UK) (1/04/03)
Producer: Paul McCartney & John Lennon
George Alexander: Lead Vocals & Bass; John Perry: Acoustic Guitar; Pete Swettenham: Acoustic Guitar & B. Vocals; Geoff Swettenham: Drums & B. Vocals
Advision Studios, London, UK probably 01/xx/68

Lullaby (G. Alexander) 3:12 (6)

The group Grapefruit consisted of London, England natives Geoff Swettenham, born on March 8, 1948, his brother Pete, born on April 24, 1949 and John Perry, born on July 16, 1949. Its other member was George Alexander, born Alexander Young on December 28, 1946 in Glasgow, Scotland. All but Alexander were in a band called the Sugarbeats before becoming members of the group Tony Rivers & The Castaways who'd covered a Beatles' song in 1966 and were singed to NEMS. Paul McCartney attended their performance at Brian Epstein's Saville Theatre on November 19, 1967.

Terry Doran, a Liverpool friend and associate of Epstein and The Beatles, who was in charge of Apple Music Publishing, signed Alexander on as a songwriter. [Alexander's brother George, whose first name Alexander borrowed, was in the mid-'60s group The Easybeats and his brothers Angus and Malcolm are members of the group AC/DC.] John Perry says, "I met Doran who told me he worked for a company called Apple, which I later learned was The Beatles' company. We had this idea of forming a four piece group that would replace The Beatles' pop image because they were sort of psychedelic at the time. Apple liked the idea. We met with Alexander, whose songs we liked." On December 11, 1967 they became one of the earliest acts signed to Apple Music Publishing and were managed by Doran. John Lennon suggested the name Grapefruit, the title of a book by Yoko Ono*, which he had been reading.

The Swettenhams and Perry recall Lennon and McCartney attending one of their first recording sessions, and Pete remembers McCartney hanging around playing tambourine but doesn't think anything resulted from those sessions. They, and their producer Terry Melcher, say none of The Beatles attended any sessions for their first single *Dear Delilah*. [Melcher, the son of actress Doris Day, was a songwriter and producer known for his work with The Byrds and Bruce Johnston of The Beach Boys*. Melcher was probably suggested by Derek Taylor who had been a publicist for both groups.] The Beatles (minus George Harrison) attended an RCA Records' press reception, and another at the Hanover Grand in London on January 17, 1968 to help promote the release of *Dear Delilah*, which just missed being a UK Top 20 hit. It was released on RCA in the UK, and Melcher's Equinox label in the US because Apple didn't yet have a record label.

According to Perry and the Swettenhams, McCartney and Lennon produced and engineered the backing track of their song *Lullaby* at Advision Studio. [This probably explains why a demo acetate of *Lullaby* was discovered many years later among Lennon's personal belongings, mistaken by some to be an unreleased Beatles' demo.] Spencer Davis, who also attended the session, said McCartney handled most of the duties and thinks Paul sang in the background as well. Perry and the Swettenhams don't recall McCartney or Lennon performing on *Lullaby*, or any other recordings of theirs. Geoff say, "I think I would remember if Paul had played something on one of our tracks." Perry recalls, "Lennon and McCartney wanted to put *Lullaby* out as a single. We didn't like their version. Can you believe it? How bloody stupid can you get?" Grapefruit later decided to add an orchestra to *Lullaby*, which appears on their first album *Around Grapefruit*. The un-orchestrated version is included on the album *94 Baker Street (The Pop-Psych Sounds of the Apple Era 1967-1969)*. Alexander's wife says she has several more versions of *Lullaby* including one with Harrison playing zither.

The Swettenhams and Perry say they, not Melcher, produced their second single *Yes / Elevator*. They recall McCartney being present to give advice and help (padding drums etc.) with the recording of *Yes*. McCartney directed a promotional video for *Elevator* at the Albert Memorial Statue in London on May 26, 1968. Perry and Pete say Lennon basically arranged the brass part of *C'mon Marianne*, which was the group's third single and Perry thinks Melcher produced it. Mike Vickers, formerly of the group Manfred Mann (see Paul Jones), scored Lennon's ideas for the arrangement. [Vickers had conducted the orchestra for The Beatles' live performance of *All You Need Is Love* for the BBC TV program *Our World*, telecast live on June 25, 1967.]

Around Grapefruit was released in late 1968 on EMI's Stateside label in the UK and Dunhill in the US. The album's liner notes were written by Derek Taylor. Melcher is listed as the sole producer. Though he did produce some of Grapefruit's first recordings he had to return to the US, so the group says they took over most of the production, though the final mixing was done by Melcher. According to Mark Lewisohn, Lennon and McCartney acted as un-credited executive producers of *Around Grapefruit*. Perry recalls, "McCartney, Harrison and Lennon stopped by during a couple of other sessions. I remember Lennon trying to get me to play something on the guitar to sound like an airplane landing. We were tied up with them quite deeply."

Perry recalls one historic moment, "I was in Trident Studios and Paul ushered me over to the microphone to sing on the chorus of *Hey Jude*. When I put on the headphones they were very loud and I shouted an obscenity." [Perry's remark can faintly be heard at about 2:58 into the recording.] Grapefruit's association with Apple ended in November 1968. During The Beatles' recording sessions for the album *Let It Be* in January 1969, Lennon suggested their then unreleased song *Two Of Us* might be suitable for Grapefruit, though they never recorded it. [Several months later the Apple group Mortimer* recorded *Two Of Us*.]

Grapefruit had a second album, *Deep Water*, released by RCA in 1969 and a single on the Deram label in 1971 before disbanding. Geoff briefly worked with, and almost joined, Badfinger* but is now an accountant. Pete assisted Geoff Emerick with the engineering of McCartney's 1973 album *Band On The Run*, and on a Linda McCartney* recording but has since left the music business. Perry sings on Cliff Richard's 1976 hit *Devil Woman*, and now concentrates on Christian and gospel recordings. George Alexander died on August 4, 1997.

Sylvia Griffin

Love's A State Of Mind
Rocket/Phonogram-870 377-2/BLACD 7 (single) (Germany/UK) (05/27/88)
Producer: Chris Thomas
George Harrison: Slide Guitar†; Sylvia Griffin: Lead Vocals; David Paton: Bass; Charlie Morgan: Drums; Robbie McIntosh: Guitar; Rod Bowkett: Keyboards
Air Studio, London & FPSHOT†, UK 01/16/88 & 03/05/88†

Love's A State Of Mind (S. Griffin-R. Bowkett) 3:14 (1)

Sylvia Griffin studied at the Royal College of Music and was trained as an opera singer. She has branched out into stage musicals, performing on the cabaret circuit, doing session work and writing songs. She has toured with the Natural Theatre Company in *Henry VIII - Diary Of A Serial Killer*, a comedy about Henry VIII returning from the dead to advise Prince Charles on how to handle women.

She was a member of the "synthpop" group Kissing The Pink in the 1980s. Griffin met George Harrison at a party given by Elton John*. Harrison liked her song *Love's A State Of Mind* and agreed to play on it. The other guitarist on the song, Robbie McIntosh became a member of Paul McCartney's band in 1988.

Daryl Hall And John Oates

Along The Red Ledge
Friday Music-P2 211978 (07/29/08) (08/21/78)
Producer: David Foster
George Harrison: Guitar; Daryl Hall: Lead Vocals; John Oates: B. Vocals; probably one or more of the following: Kenny Passarelli: Bass; Caleb Quaye: Guitar; Roger Pope: Drums; David Kent: Synthesizer
Davlen, &/or Sunset Studios, Los Angeles, CA &/or Hit Factory, New York, NY probably xx/xx/78

The Last Time (D. Hall) 2:47 (3)

Daryl Hall was born Daryl Hohl on October 11, 1949 in Pottstown, Pennsylvania. John Oates was born on April 7, 1949, in New York, New York but grew up in Philadelphia. Both took an avid interest in music at an early age and met in 1967 during a battle of the bands competition in Philadelphia. They soon teamed up playing in various doo-wop and R&B bands. By 1972 they were signed to Atlantic Records but lacking success with the label signed with RCA in 1975. The following year *Sara Smile* became their first of many Top Five hits for the label. Atlantic wisely reissued their 1974 single *She's Gone*, which quickly became a Top 10 hit. Their first number one hit for RCA was *Rich Girl* in 1977. In 1978 George Harrison contributed to their album *Along The Red Ledge*. Between 1981 and 1985 they topped the charts with the songs *Kiss On My List*, *Private Eyes*, *I Can't Go For That*, *Maneater* and *Out Of Touch*; had Top Five hits with *You Make My Dreams*, *Say It Isn't So* and *Method Of Modern Love*, and Top 10 hits with *Did It In A Minute*, *One On One*, *Family Man* and *Adult Education*. In 1986 the dynamic duo took a break to pursue solo projects but had a Top Five hit for Arista Records in 1988 with *Everything Your Heart Desires*. Their last Top 20 hit was *So Close* in 1990. Hall and Oates performed two of Lennon's Beatles' compositions at *The John Lennon Scholarship Concert* held on May 5, 1990. Although Hall and Oates have been less active on the charts in recent years, they continue to delight large audiences wherever they perform their seemingly endless list of hits. For more information go to www.hallandoates.com

Left to right: Daryl Hall, Kristofer Engelhardt and John Oates, Soaring Eagle Casino, Mt. Pleasant, MI August 29, 2002. © Kristofer Engelhardt

Roy Harper

An Introduction To Roy Harper [Various Artists]
Chrysalis-PRO 620 (album 12" promotional only) (02/xx/76)
Producer: Bob Harris
Paul McCartney: Promotional interview
EMI-Abbey Road Studios, London, UK xx/xx/76

Conversation with Paul McCartney (**P. McCartney**) 1:34-in total (2/1)

One Of Those Days In England (Bullinamingvase)
Science Friction-HUCD021 (Austria) (11/xx/96) (02/11/77)
Paul McCartney: B. Vocals; Roy Harper: Lead Vocals & Guitar; Andy Roberts: Guitar & B. Vocals; Henry McCullough: Guitar; David Lawson: Keyboards; Dave C. Drill: Bass; John Halsey: Drums; Linda McCartney: B. Vocals; Alvin Lee: Guitar
EMI-Abbey Road Studios, London, UK probably fall & probably winter 76†

One Of Those Days In England (Part 1) (R. Harper) 3:25 (1)
Producer: Roy Harper & Peter Jenner
Additionally: B.J. Cole: Steel Guitar

One Of Those Days In England (Parts 2-10) [Part 10 reprise] (R. Harper) 1:58 (6-part 10†)
Producer: Roy Harper & John Leckie

Roy Harper's mother died within weeks of his being born on June 12, 1941 in Manchester, England. Harper, a poet, actor and musician is little known in the US but is highly respected by his musical peers in the UK. He has worked with Led Zeppelin and Pink Floyd among many others.

Paul McCartney contributed a brief interview to *An Introduction To Roy Harper*, an album promoting Roy's 1976 album *When An Old Cricketer Leaves The Crease*. The interview is also available on the rare 1996 triple CD set *Song Of The Ages*. According to Roy, Paul and Linda McCartney* sang backing vocals on *One Of Those Days In England (Part 1)*, which is the single version of the song that opens his 1977 album *One Of Those Days In England (Bullinamingvase)*. The album closes with a continuous suite titled *One Of Those Days In England (Parts 2-10)*. Roy said that Paul and Linda also sang backing vocals on the reprise *One Of Those Days In England (Part 10)*. *Part 1* was recorded after *Parts 2-10* at the suggestion of producer Peter Jenner, who thought an edited version had hit potential. Roy says Henry McCullough (then a former member of Wings) plays guitar on *One Of Those Days In England (Part 1)*. Jimmy McCulloch, who was Henry's replacement in Wings at the time, contributed to other portions of the album. Roy Harper, who has released nearly two dozen studio albums over the last five decades, continues to write, record and perform. For more information go to www.royharper.co.uk

Rolf Harris

The Lost Lennon Tapes
Westwood One Radio Network-[Matrix #] LT 91-18 (12" albums promotional only) (04/29/91)
Producer: Bryant Marriott
John Lennon: B. Vocals; **George Harrison: B. Vocals & Electric Guitar**; **Paul McCartney: Bass & B. Vocals**; Rolf Harris: Lead Vocals & Wobbleboard
BBC Paris Studios, London, UK 12/18/63

Tie Me Kangaroo Down, Sport (R. Harris) 2:47 (1/1/2)

Rolf Harris was born on March 30, 1930 in Perth, Australia. He learned to play the piano as a youngster, and became an accomplished painter and cartoonist. With horn-rims (and later a goatee) he looked the part of the teaching job he gave up before moving to the UK to seek a career in art and show business. He found success in 1960, in part from a sheet of Masonite dubbed the "Wobble-board," on his international hit novelty song *Tie Me Kangaroo Down, Sport*. His second hit, *Sun Arise* in 1962, was based on an Australian aboriginal chant.

Rolf first met The Beatles when he interviewed them for the BBC. On April 18, 1963 he appeared on the bill with them at their first Royal Albert Hall performance in London on *Swinging Sound '63*, broadcast live on BBC radio. Harris was The Beatles' guest host on the first in a series of BBC radio shows titled *From Us To You* taped on December 18, 1963 and broadcast on the 26th. During the show, The Beatles backed Harris on a version of *Tie Me Kangaroo Down, Sport* that featured revised lyrics referring to the group.

Rolf was on the bill of *The Beatles Christmas Show* in 1963. Rolf recalled in his autobiography *Can You Tell What It Is Yet?* that during one performance John Lennon grabbed a microphone backstage and broke into his act with some embarrassing remarks. He angrily confronted them about it after the show, but says that they were so humorously disarming, that they brought him to laughter, and that he never suffered at their hands again. Harris' cartoon drawing of the show was sent to members of The Beatles' Fan Club as a souvenir. Rolf recorded a song called *Ringo For President* released in 1964. Over the years he became a successful entertainer and presenter on UK TV, incorporating his talents in comedy, music, drawing and painting. He was awarded the MBE in 1968, the OBE in 1977 and the CBE in 2006. Rolf Harris still records, performs and makes regular appearances on UK TV and radio. For more information go to www.rolfharris.com

Bobby Hatfield

Oo Wee Baby, I Love You/ Rock 'N' Roll Woman
Warner Bros.-WB 7566 (7" single) (03/01/72)
Producer: Richard Perry
Ringo Starr: Drums; Bobby Hatfield: Lead Vocals; Chris Stainton: Keyboards; Klaus Voormann: Bass; Bobby Keys: (probable) Saxophone
Apple Studios, London, UK 12/xx/71

Oo Wee Baby, I Love You So (R. Parker) 3:35 (1/1)

Bobby Hatfield was born August 10, 1940 in Beaver Dam, Wisconsin but his family relocated to Anaheim, California when he was a youngster. Bobby began singing professionally while in college where he met and teamed up with Bill Medley to form the R&B duo The Righteous Brothers. They were one of the supporting acts on The Beatles' tour of the US in 1964. Their greatest success came at the hands of Phil Spector*, who in 1964 and 1965 produced their number one hit *You've Lost That Lovin' Feelin'*, their Top Five hits *Unchained Melody* and *Ebb Tide* and their Top 10 hit *Just Once In My Life*. Their contract with Spector's Philles Records was bought out by Verve (MGM) Records with whom they had the Top 10 hit *(You're My) Soul And Inspiration* in 1966. By 1968 Medley had left The Righteous Brothers and the two worked as solo artists, though Bobby also worked under The Righteous Brothers name with Jimmy Walker.

Bobby was working with producer Richard Perry in December 1971 when Perry was called away to London to work with the group Fanny at Apple Studios. [The Beatles had been impressed with Perry's production of Tiny Tim and in late 1969 Ringo asked Perry to arrange the title track for his first solo album *Sentimental Journey*.] Perry flew Bobby to London to continue work on his recordings at Apple. Perry says, "Ringo sat in on Hatfield's sessions as a favor to me. He's great, he never turned me down."

The Righteous Brothers reformed on numerous occasions. They had a Top Five hit in 1974 with *Rock And Roll Heaven*, a tribute to some of rock's late, great stars, and performed a reworked version of it on an *American Bandstand* anniversary special on ABC TV in 1981 as a tribute to John Lennon. *Unchained Melody* reentered the Top 20 in the charts in 1990 following the inclusion of it on the soundtrack to the film *Ghost*. The Righteous Brothers performed frequently from the 1990s until Hatfield's sudden death just before a show on November 5, 2003. They were inducted into the Rock and Roll Hall of Fame earlier that year. For more information go to
www.righteousbrothers.com

The Righteous Brothers

MAR 24, 2000

DEAR CHRISTOFER,

THE WAY I LOOK AT IT IS.... YOU OWE ME ABOUT $50,000. THAT'S WHAT I "PLANNED" TO WIN IN THE CASINO. INSTEAD, I STARTED PERUSING YOUR BOOK AND NEVER LEFT MY ROOM!

DAMN! SO MUCH STUFF! SPECTOR "TALES" THAT EVEN I HADN'T HEARD BEFORE.

DIDN'T KNOW YOKO RECORDED THAT MANY THINGS. OR FOR THAT MATTER, WHY?

SO MANY FAMILIAR NAMES.... SO MANY GREAT TIMES! BILL AND I ALWAYS HAD A SECRET PONY BEER KEG IN OUR 'SHINDIG' DRESSING ROOM. (JACK GOODE WOULDN'T HAVE APPROVED.) NATURALLY, THAT'S WHERE THE "IN CROWD" WOULD HANG. ONE NIGHT THE PARTY STARTED EARLY AND WE GOT JIMMY O'NEIL SO SHIT-FACED HE COULDN'T READ THE CUE CARDS. BY THE TIME WE FINALLY FINISHED TAPING, MOST OF THE KIDS IN THE AUDIENCE HAD GONE HOME AND THE REST WERE HALF ASLEEP.

ANYHOW, CONGRATULATIONS ON A MONUMENTAL ACHIEVEMENT! WISHING YOU ALL THE BEST —

RIGHTEOUSLY,

Bobby Hatfield

P.S. FORGET ABOUT THE '50K'.... IT WAS WORTH IT!

9841 Hot Springs Drive • Huntington Beach, CA 92646

Ronnie Hawkins

John Lennon On Ronnie Hawkins The Short Rap / John Lennon On
Ronnie Hawkins The Long Rap
Cotillion-PR-104-PL/PR-105-PL (single 7" promotional only) (xx/xx/70)
Producer: probably Ritchie Yorke
John Lennon: Promotional Interview
Ronnie Hawkins' home, Mississauga (Toronto), Ontario, Canada
12/18-20/69

John Lennon on Ronnie Hawkins The Short Rap (J. Lennon) 0:06 (1/1)

John Lennon on Ronnie Hawkins The Long Rap (J. Lennon) 1:24 (1/2)

Ronnie "The Hawk" Hawkins was born on January 10, 1935 in Huntsville, Arkansas. From childhood he knew that he wanted to be a music star like his uncle Delmar "Skipper" Hawkins and cousin Dale Hawkins (of Suzie Q fame). He formed bands in high school and later played the club circuit rubbing shoulders with most of rock's founding fathers. He later backed Carl Perkins*, and Conway Twitty, who told him that Canada was the land of endless gigs. In 1958 Hawkins, along with his band, which included Levon Helm*, headed to Toronto where Hawkins says he could be a big fish in a small pond. Hawkins signed to Roulette Records in 1959 and had hits with the songs *Forty Days* and *Mary Lou*. His band The Hawks included Helm and four Canadians. Following their split with Hawkins several years later they became known simply as The Band*.

John Lennon and Yoko Ono* were in Toronto in mid-December 1969 to promote their Plastic Ono Band album *Live Peace In Toronto 1969*, recorded there that September, and to make plans for a rock 'n' roll peace festival to be held there the following summer (it never happened). Hawkins invited the Lennons to stay at his farmhouse on the outskirts of Toronto. While there, Lennon signed his limited edition erotic lithographs, and heard Ronnie's latest recording *Down In The Alley*, featuring Duane Allman on guitar. He was so impressed that he offered to record a radio spot to promote the song. Hawkins says the promotion came at a price as the Lennons had left him with a large amount of unpaid transatlantic telephone bills. Hawkins also accompanied the Lennons to Ottawa to meet with Canadian Prime Minister Trudeau. Later, he traveled the world at the Lennons' request as an emissary for their *War Is Over (If You Want It)* peace campaign.

It was reported that Ringo Starr performed at a benefit concert organized by Hawkins in Peterborough, Ontario on June 30, 1996. Later reports confirmed that the person identified as Ringo was a well-known Ringo impersonator. Though Hawkins maintains legendary status in his adopted homeland of Canada, because he was never a major draw in the US he says he's "a legend in my spare time." He has recorded numerous albums, had some acting roles and hosted the TV series *Honky Tonk*. Hawkins has been less active in recent years. For more information go to www.ronniehawkins.com

Screamin' Jay Hawkins

Screamin' The Blues
Red Lightnin'-RLCD0075 (UK) (01/01/96) (xx/xx/73)
Producer: possibly **Paul McCartney**
Paul McCartney: (possible) Drums & (possible) B. Vocals; Screamin' Jay Hawkins: Lead Vocals & Piano; Linda McCartney: (possible) B. Vocals
Possibly Houston, TX or A&R Studios, New York, NY possibly 11-12/xx/70 or 01-03/xx/71

Monkberry Moon Delight (P. McCartney-L. McCartney) 3:18 (15)

Screamin' Jay Hawkins was born Jalacy Hawkins in Cleveland, Ohio on July 18, 1929. Hawkins started out on piano and saxophone as a youngster, but turned to boxing for a time. By the early 1950s Hawkins had begun a musical career that would span several decades. He toured with The Fats Domino* Revue and as part of Alan Freed's package tours in the mid-1950s. Hawkins is best remembered as the "drunken screamer" of the 1956 hit *I Put A Spell On You*, and his flamboyant and macabre performances, which no doubt influenced artists such as Screaming Lord Sutch, Arthur Brown and Alice Cooper. Hawkins also appeared in several films.

One of the pre-show concert songs played over the public-address system on Paul McCartney's 1993 tour was Hawkins' version of McCartney's song *Monkberry Moon Delight*, which was apparently first issued as a single (Queen Bee-1313) in 1973. Hawkins' version is also available on his compilation album *Screamin' The Blues* and is credited as probably being recorded in Houston in 1970. If that's correct then McCartney must have given it to Hawkins, probably with the intention that he release it before McCartney's version was released in 1971, qualifying it as a composition contribution. Hawkins' arrangement is virtually identical to the version McCartney released, but with slightly different (original, misinterpreted or revised) lyrics. The drumming introduction sounds identical to McCartney's drumming on *My Dark Hour* by The Steve Miller Band*, and the background vocals sound like they might possibly be sung by Paul and Linda McCartney*. However, there's no evidence McCartney was in Houston during this period. Perhaps Hawkins recorded the song after McCartney's screaming version was released, feeling the vocal style suited him, and faithfully reproduced the background vocals. If McCartney performs on Hawkins' version it was probably recorded at A&R Studios in New York in January 1971 during sessions for McCartney's album *Ram*. McCartney didn't have a band when he arrived in New York, and began auditioning musicians and looking for a permanent drummer. Hawkins lived and performed in New York during much of the 1970s, so it's possible he and McCartney could have spent time in a studio there recording *Monkberry Moon Delight*. The track following it on the compilation (the B-side to the single) lists the credits as "same as above," but it doesn't sound at all like it's from the same sessions. Screamin' Jay Hawkins died on February 12, 2000.

Colin Hay

Ringo Starr & His All-Starr Band Tour 2003
Warner Music Vision-R2 970326 (DVD) (09/21/04)
Producer: (Mixer: Bruce Sugar; Re-recording: Elmo Ponsdomenech & Andre Perreault); Executive Producer: Ringo Starr & David Fishof
Ringo Starr: Drums; Colin Hay: Lead Vocals & Electric Guitar; Paul Carrack: Keyboards & B. Vocals; Sheila Escovedo: Drums & B. Vocals; John Waite: Bass & B. Vocals; Mark Rivera: Flute & B. Vocals
Casino Rama, Rama, Ontario, Canada 07/24/03

Down Under [live] (R. Strykert-C. Hay) 4:09 (5)
[Also available on Koch-KOC-CD-9549 (5) (03/23/04)]

Who Can It Be Now? [live] (C. Hay) 3:46 (15)
Additionally: John Waite: Bass (only); Mark Rivera: Saxophone & B. Vocals (only)
[Also available on Koch-KOC-CD-9549 (15) (03/23/04)]

Sound Stage Ringo Starr And The Roundheads
E1 Entertainment-E1E-DV-6696 (DVD) (09/15/09)
Producer: Ringo Starr & Mark Hudson (music); Joe Thomas (video)
Ringo Starr: Drums; Colin Hay: Lead Vocals & Electric Guitar; Greg Bissonette: Drums; Mark Hudson: Acoustic Guitar & B. Vocals; Steve Dundas: Electric Guitar; Gary Burr: Electric Guitar & B. Vocals; Mark Hart: Keyboards & B. Vocals; Mark Bissonette: Bass & B. Vocals; James Perkins: Saxophone
Genesee Theater, Waukegan, IL 06/24/09

Who Can It Be Now? [live] (C. Hay) 3:34 (5)

Colin Hay was born on June 29, 1953 in Saltcoats, Scotland but he and his family relocated to Australia when he was a teenager. In 1979 he was singing and playing guitar in what would become the internationally famous band, Men At Work who had the number one hits *Down Under* and *Who Can It Be Now?*, and the Top Five hit *Overkill* in the early 1980s. When the group broke up several years later, Hay pursued a solo recording and acting career. Men At Work, with varying members including Hay, have reformed on occasion. In 2005, with assistance from Heather Mills McCartney*, Hay rereleased his song *My Brilliant Feet*, in tribute to UK soccer legend George Best, for charity.

Hay was a member of Ringo Starr's All-Starr Band in 2003 and 2008 performing *Down Under*, *Who Can It Be Now?*, and *Overkill* with Ringo backing him on drums. Hay recalls, "My booking agent called me saying Ringo's people were interested in me for his 2003 All-Starr Band tour. What an exciting day that was! There were The Beatles – and then there was everyone else, so of course I said, 'Yes.' During the rehearsals it was a combination of accurately learning the songs and getting to know the other band members – quickly! The song selection isn't complicated. Obviously you play your best known songs and Ringo usually plays his best known songs, plus a few newer songs from current albums. The idea is to sound as much like a real band as possible. Ringo is a great bandleader, very natural and a fabulous drummer to play with. What's most impressive is that Ringo and these bands are able to sound like they've been together for years. This is mainly due to Ringo as a connecting entity, and Mark Rivera, Ringo's long-standing musical director who whips these bands into shape in about 10 days. Obviously, each band sounded better and better as the tour progressed. It's difficult to contrast the 2003 and 2008 bands because they were essentially different, but there was great musical chemistry in both. The 2003 band was sparser. I was the only guitarist and Paul Carrack was the main keyboardist. I really looked forward to playing Carrack's and John Waite's songs because they have two of the best voices in the world! In 2008 we had Billy Squier on guitar, and Gary Wright and Edgar Winter on keyboards, and I loved playing with Hamish Stuart*. We had Sheila E in 2003 and Gregg Bissonette 2008, both great drummers, not to mention Ringo! It's hard to convey Ringo's humor or spontaneity unless you are there. We would often jam during the sound checks, which was great because Ringo was always interested in messing around with new musical ideas, which is one of my favorite things to do. The reason the tours work so consistently, with so many different musicians, from so many different backgrounds, is that we all love Ringo and we all want to be in The Beatles." Hay was a guest at Ringo and his band The Roundheads' performance at the Genesee Theater in Waukegan, Illinois on June 24 for broadcast on PBS TV on August 25, 2005. Ringo backed Hay on *Who Can It Be Now?* and Hay joined Ringo on *With A Little Help From My Friends* during the show. Hay continues to write, record and tour. For more information go to www.colinhay.com

The Jeff Healey Band

Hell To Pay
Arista-ARCD 8632 (05/25/90)
Producer: Ed Stasium
George Harrison: Acoustic Guitar & B. Vocals; Jeff Healey: Lead Vocals & Guitar; Joe Rockman: Bass; Tom Stephen: Drums; Jeff Lynne: B. Vocals & Acoustic Guitar; Paul Shaffer: Keyboards
Le Studio, Morin Heights, Quebec, Canada & Rumbo Recorders, Los Angeles, CA 02/xx/90

While My Guitar Gently Weeps (G. Harrison) 5:13 (7)

Norman Jeffery Healey was born on March 25, 1966 in Toronto, Ontario, Canada. As an infant he developed cancer in both eyes, which had to be removed. He received his first guitar at age three. His father, who played steel guitar, taught Jeff to play on his lap. By age 14, Jeff was playing bars and clubs in Toronto. In 1985 he formed The Jeff Healey Band with Joe Rockman and Tom Stephen. Their 1988 debut album *See The Light*, sold over a million copies and included the Top Five hit *Angel Eyes*. Most Americans got their first glimpse of Healey in the 1989 film *Road House*.

Healey's band regularly performed The Beatles' song *While My Guitar Gently Weeps*. They recorded it in 1990 despite objections from their record company who didn't think it should be included on their album *Hell To Pay*. They contacted its composer, George Harrison to see if he might be interested in contributing to the song. To their surprise, they received a call from Harrison instructing them to send the tape to Rumbo Recorders where he was working on Jeff Lynne's* *Armchair Theatre* album. Healey said the tape was returned within days containing guitars and backing vocals overdubbed by Harrison and Lynne.

The Jeff Healey Band was the opening act for Ringo Starr's All-Starr Band in Toronto in 1992. Healey joined them during Ringo's performance of *Yellow Submarine*, *Act Naturally* and *With A Little Help From My Friends*. The Jeff Healey Band also recorded a cover version of The Beatles' song *Yer Blues*. Healey established himself as a top blues and jazz guitarist working with many artists including Chris Barber*. He often hosted radio shows in Canada. Jeff Healey finally succumbed to cancer on March 2, 2008. For more information go to www.jeffhealey.com

Levon Helm

The Best Of Ringo Starr And His All-Starr Band...So Far
Image-ID0828RO (DVD) (10/23/01)
Producer: Michael Drumm; Tim Snow (video); Joe Walsh & Jim Nipar (music); Executive Producer: Ringo Starr & David Fishof
Ringo Starr: Drums; Levon Helm: Vocals & Drums; Billy Preston: Keyboards & B. Vocals; Jim Keltner: Drums; Nils Lofgren: Guitar; Joe Walsh: Guitar & B. Vocals; Rick Danko: Bass & Vocals; Clarence Clemons: Saxophone, B. Vocals & Tambourine; Dr. John: Keyboards & Vocals; Garth Hudson: Accordion
Greek Theatre, Los Angeles, CA 09/03/89

The Weight [live] (R. Robertson) 5:48 (3) (07/xx/90)
[Also available on *Ringo Starr And His All Starr Band The Anthology...So Far.* Koch-KOC-CD-8312 (1-3) (07/24/01) (02/05/01)]
Ringo Starr And His All-Starr Band
Pioneer Artists-PA-090-007 (LD 12") (07/xx/90)

Producer: Tim Snow (video); Joe Walsh & Jim Nipar (music); Executive Producer: Ringo Starr & David Fishof
Greek Theatre, Los Angeles, CA 09/03/89

Up On Cripple Creek [live] (R. Robertson) 5:43 (2/1)
Ringo Starr: Drums; Levon Helm: Lead Vocals & Drums; Billy Preston: Keyboards & B. Vocals; Jim Keltner: Drums; Nils Lofgren: Guitar; Joe Walsh: Guitar & B. Vocals; Rick Danko: Bass & B. Vocals; Clarence Clemons: Saxophone; Dr. John: Keyboards

Levon Helm was born Mark Lavon Helm on May 26, 1940 in Marvell, Arkansas. He began playing guitar and drums at an early age, and formed a band while still in high school. In 1958 he joined Ronnie Hawkins'* band The Hawks who headed for Toronto, Canada. The Hawks eventually consisted of four Canadians and Helm. They split from Hawkins in 1963. Helm drifted in and out of the group until 1967 when he joined them permanently and they became known simply as The Band*. Helm has also had a fairly successful career as an actor co-starring in a number of films including *Coal Miner's Daughter*, *The Right Stuff*, *End Of The Line* and *The Doll Maker*, and has been the narrator for a number TV documentaries on music.

Levon, like other members of The Band, had previously worked with Ringo Starr on his solo album *Ringo*. Starr invited Helm to drum with him during his All-Starr Band tour in 1989. Helm performed *Up On Cripple Creek* and *The Weight* along with Ringo on drums. He also drummed with Ringo Starr's All-Starr Band on *With A Little Help From My Friends* on June 24, 2008 at Radio City Music Hall in New York. Helm has released half-a-dozen solo albums since 1977 including his 2007 Grammy Award winning *Dirt Farmer*. He continues to record and perform with The Levon Helm Band, which includes his daughter. For more information go to www.levonhelm.com

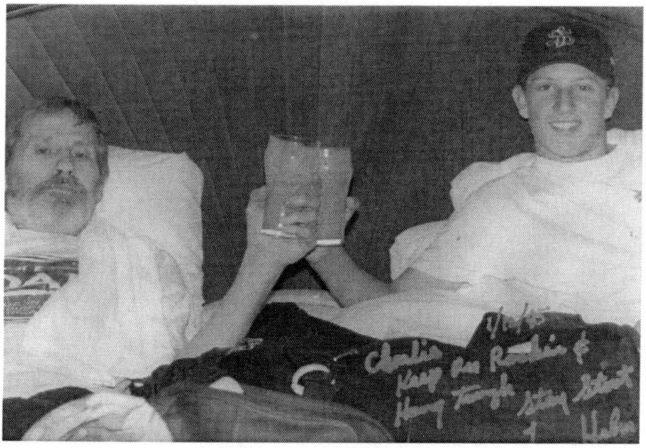

Levon Helm and Charlie Engelhardt, Kalamazoo, MI October 1, 1994. © and photo by Kristofer Engelhardt.

Jimmy Helms

Water [Various Artists]
London Filmtrax-YEAR 2 820 263-1 (album 12")
(UK) (06/28/85)
Producer: Mike Moran
xx/xx/84

Celebration (**G. Harrison**-M. Moran) 3:45 (2/4)
(05/31/85)
George Harrison: Guitar; Jimmy Helms: Lead Vocals

Focus Of Attention (M. Moran-D. Clement-**G. Harrison**) 2:06 (1/6)
Jimmy Helms: Lead Vocals

Jimmy Helms was born in Florida in 1944. He joined the Fort Jackson Army Band. After his stint in the service he moved to England in the early 1960s and signed to Pye Records. He had a Top 10 hit in the UK with *I'm Gonna Make You An Offer You Can't Refuse* in 1973. Helms has contributed to a number of other artists' projects and recordings, including those of The Scaffold*.

Helms recorded the songs *Focus Of Attention*, with George Harrison as co-composer, and *Celebration*, with Harrison as co-composer and guitarist, for the soundtrack of HandMade Films' *Water* in 1985 (see Billy Connolly/Chris Tummings and The Singing Rebels Band). Since the late 1980s, Helms has found success in the dance band Londonbeat who had an international hit with his composition *I've Been Thinking About You* in 1990.

David Hentschel

Sta*rtling Music
Ring O'Records-ST-11372 (album 12")
(02/17/75)
Producer: David Hentschel & John Gilbert
Ringo Starr: Finger Clicks; David Hentschel: Synthesizer; John Gilbert: Finger Clicks
Startling Studio, Ascot, UK 09/xx/74

Step Lightly (R. Starkey) 3:39 (1/3)

David Hentschel was born on January 30, 1952 in Sussex, England. Hentschel began his musical career as an assistant recording engineer at Trident Studios in London in 1970. One of the first projects on which he worked (un-credited) was on George Harrison's *All Things Must Past* album. David recalls, "I had only been working a few months. I was 18-years-old and a huge fan of The Beatles. During a break, engineer Ken Scott happened to mention to George that I had recorded some demos. George asked to hear them and began to play his guitar along to them. That was quite a buzz for me! Unfortunately none of this playing ever got recorded onto my demos. Later, I worked on some of the vocal overdubs, and other bits and pieces on Paul McCartney's album *Red Rose Speedway*."

When Trident bought a synthesizer in 1973,Hentschel took to the instrument with a passion. He has worked with many artists including Harry Nilsson*, Carly Simon*, Jim Webb*and Frank Zappa*, and is probably recognized most for his synthesizer work on Elton John's* song *Funeral For A Friend*.

Hentschel says, "I wanted to do more freelance work. My manager John Gilbert knew Neil Aspinall and through them I became involved in the *Sta*rling Music* album project because Ringo was looking for something for his new record label Ring O'Records. Ringo had bought a new ARP 2500 synthesizer for his home studio specifically for the album. He was around for most of the recording, so he had to appear on it. We also had one attempted songwriting session one night." Hentschel has gone on to become a successful producer and scored soundtracks for films such as *Educating Rita*. For more information go to www.thekeyboard.co.uk

Roger Hodgson

Ringo Starr & His New All-Starr Band
Pioneer/Win Media-11907 (DVD) (10/01/02)
Producer: (recorded, mixed and mastered by: Glen Robinson); Executive Producer: Ringo Starr & David Fishof
Ringo Starr: Drums; Roger Hodgson: Lead Vocals & Keyboards; Sheila Escovedo: Drums; Howard Jones: Keyboards; Greg Lake: Bass; Mark Rivera: Saxophone & Percussion; Ian Hunter: Acoustic Guitar
Rosemont Theater, Rosemont (Chicago), IL 08/22/01

Give A Little Bit [live] (R. Davis-R. Hodgson) 4:22 (11)
Additionally: **Ringo Starr: Percussion** (only); Roger Hodgson: Acoustic Guitar; Ian Hunter: B. Vocals; Howard Jones: B. Vocals; Mark Rivera: B. Vocals, Electric Guitar & Saxophone (only)
[Also available on King Biscuit Flower Hour/Razor & Tie-7930188003-2 (6) (08/06/02)]

The Logical Song [live] (R. Davis-R. Hodgson) 3:46 (3)
[Also available on King Biscuit Flower Hour/Razor & Tie-7930188003-2 (3) (08/06/02)]

Take The Long Way Home [live] (R. Davis-R. Hodgson) 4:23 (16)
Additionally: Ian Hunter: B. Vocals; Howard Jones: B. Vocals; Mark Rivera: Clarinet, Harmonica & B. Vocals (only)
[Also available on King Biscuit Flower Hour/Razor & Tie-7930188003-2 (13) (08/06/02)]

Charles Roger Hodgson was born on March 21, 1950 in Portsmouth, England. By age 12, he had taught himself to play guitar and was writing songs. Later he learned to play piano, bass, drums and cello. His first single, with backing from Elton John*, was released in 1969. That year he teamed up with songwriter Rick Davis in the formation of Supertramp. Among Supertramp's many hits, with primary songwriting and vocals from Hodgson, are 1975's *Dreamer*, 1977's *Give A Little Bit*, and 1979's *The Logical Song* and *Take The Long Way Home* from their mega-million-selling album *Breakfast In America*. Hodgson's last hit with the group was 1982's *It's Raining Again* before he departed to pursue a solo career. In 1987 Roger sustained serious injuries in a fall requiring lengthy rehabilitation and marking a retreat from the music business for about a decade. Supertramp disbanded around the same time, and for about the same period, but has since reformed on occasion but without Hodgson.

Ringo Starr and Roger Hodgson, Freedom Hill, Sterling Heights (Detroit), MI July 28, 2001.
© and photo by Kristofer Engelhardt.

Hodgson was a member of Ringo Starr's All-Starr Band in 2001 performing *Give A Little Bit*, *The Logical Song* and *Take The Long Way Home* with backing from Ringo on drums and percussion. Roger says, "David

Fishof contacted me about joining Ringo's All-Starr Band for their summer 2001 tour. I was going through a painful divorce, so it was a pleasant surprise because The Beatles had been a huge influence on me. They were like an alternate reality for me as a teenager at boarding school. They showed me what was possible musically and fanned my dreams of being in a successful rock 'n' roll band. I certainly had my doubts about the motley crew of musicians Ringo had assembled for the tour. He drew from very different musical styles, from Sheila E* and Howard Jones*, to Greg Lake*, Ian Hunter* and myself, but it worked out very well. Ringo was surprised during rehearsals at what a stickler I was for getting things right on my songs, even his drum parts! Ringo's a very large character. He has a wit that can chop you off at the knees, which I think he exhibits many times unconsciously, but he has a very good heart. I got a much more real picture of what it was like for The Beatles, and what they went through, as he told me of their exploits. I began to feel a lot of compassion for him when I realized how trapped he often was in his hotel room because he's so recognizable. It was a pleasure playing with him. He has a very special feel when he plays. The way he made *Logical Song* swing brought a smile to my face every night." Hodgson continues to write, record and tour. For more information go to www.rogerhodgson.com

Mary Hopkin

An Jenem Tag / Turn! Turn! Turn! (To Every Thing There is A Season)
Apple-0-23 910 (7" single) (Germany) (10/25/68)
Producer: Paul McCartney
Paul McCartney: Acoustic Guitar & (possible) Percussion; Mary Hopkin: Lead Vocals & Acoustic Guitar; Gilbert Webster: Cembalon
Trident Studios & EMI-Abbey Road Studios, London, UK 07/xx/68

An Jenem Tag [Those Were The Days-sung in German] (G. Raskin-[B. Fomin]) 5:06 (1/1)

Le Temps des Fleurs / Turn! Turn! Turn (To Every Thing There is A Season)
Apple-APF 503 (7" single) (France) (10/25/68)
Producer: Paul McCartney
Paul McCartney: Acoustic Guitar & (possible) Percussion; Mary Hopkin: Lead Vocals & Acoustic Guitar; Gilbert Webster: Cembalon
Trident & EMI-Abbey Road Studios, London, UK 07/xx/68

Le Temps des Fleurs [Those Were The Days-sung in French] (G. Raskin-[B. Fomin]) 5:06 (1/1)

Post Card
Apple-CDP 7975782 (Germany) (11/19/91) (02/21/69) **Modified UK-style jacket back design with notes by: Paul McCartney**
Producer: Paul McCartney
EMI-Abbey Road Studios, London, UK 11/xx/68-01/xx/69 [unless noted otherwise]

En Aquellos Dias (Those Were The Days-sung in Spanish) (G. Raskin-[B. Fomin]) 5:09 (18) (10/25/68)
Paul McCartney: Acoustic Guitar & (possible) Percussion; Mary Hopkin: Lead Vocals & Acoustic Guitar; Gilbert Webster: Cembalon
Trident & EMI-Abbey Road Studios, London, UK 07/xx/68

The Game (G. Martin) 2:40 (14)
Mary Hopkin: Lead Vocals; George Martin: Piano; Jeanne Dolmetsch: Recorder; Marguerite Dolmetsch; Recorder; Paul Blood: Recorder; Brian Blood: Recorder; Peter Blood: Recorder; Christine Blood: Recorder

Happiness Runs (Pebble And The Man) (D. Leitch) 2:03 (3)
Paul McCartney: Bass; Mary Hopkin: Lead Vocals & Guitar; Donovan Leitch: Guitar

The Honeymoon Song (M. Theodorakis) 2:07 (6)
Paul McCartney: Tambourine & (possible) Guitar; Mary Hopkin: Lead Vocals; The Mike Cotton Sound (Jim Garforth: Drums; Bernie: Bass; John Beecham: Horns; Mike Cotton: Horns; Nick: Horns; Derek Tearle: Guitar)
Trident Studio, London, UK 11/xx/68-01/xx/69

Inch Worm (F. Loesser) 2:33 (8)
Mary Hopkin: Lead Vocals
Probably EMI-Abbey Road, or Trident or possibly Apple Studios, London, UK 11/xx/68-01/xx/69

Lord Of The Reedy River (D. Leitch) 2:37 (2)
Mary Hopkin: Lead Vocals; Paul McCartney: Guitar; Donovan Leitch: Guitar & B. Vocals

Love Is The Sweetest Thing (R. Noble) 3:43 (4)
Paul McCartney: (probable) Guitar & (probable) Bass; Mary Hopkin: Lead Vocals
Probably EMI-Abbey Road, or Trident or possibly Apple Studios, London, UK 11/xx/68-01/xx/69

Lullaby Of The Leaves (J. Young-B. Petkere) 2:33 (10)
Paul McCartney: (probable) Guitar; Mary Hopkin: Lead Vocals
Probably EMI-Abbey Road, or Trident or possibly Apple Studios, London, UK 11/xx/68-01/xx/69

Prince En Avignon (J. Bourtayre) 3:20 (13)
Paul McCartney: (probable) Guitar, (probable) Drums & (probable) Bass; Mary Hopkin: Lead Vocals
Probably EMI-Abbey Road, or Trident or possibly Apple Studios, London, UK 11/xx/68-01/xx/69

The Puppy Song (H. Nilsson) 2:42 (7)
Paul McCartney: (probable) Piano & (probable) Bass; Mary Hopkin: Lead Vocals
Probably EMI-Abbey Road, or Trident or possibly Apple Studios, London, UK 11/xx/68-01/xx/69

Quelli Erano Giorni ("Those Were The Days"-sung in Italian) (G. Raskin-[B. Fomin]) 5:08 (17) (10/25/68)
Paul McCartney: Acoustic Guitar & (possibly) Percussion; Mary Hopkin: Lead Vocals & Acoustic Guitar; Gilbert Webster: Cembalon
Trident & EMI-Abbey Road Studios, London, UK 07/xx/68

Someone To Watch Over Me (I. Gershwin-G. Gershwin) 2:02 (12)
Paul McCartney: Arrangement; Mary Hopkin: Lead Vocals; The Mike Cotton Sound (Jim Garforth: Drums; Bernie: Bass; Mike Cotton: Horns; Nick: Horns; Derek Tearle: Guitar); George Martin: (probable) Piano

There's No Business Like Show Business (I. Berlin) 4:03 (15)
Paul McCartney: Conductor; Mary Hopkin: Lead Vocals; The Mike Cotton Sound (Jim Garforth: Drums; Bernie: Drums); George Martin: Piano

Those Were The Days (G. Raskin-[B. Fomin]) 5:08 (1) (08/26/68)
Paul McCartney: Acoustic Guitar & (possible) Percussion; Mary Hopkin: Lead Vocals & Acoustic Guitar; Gilbert Webster: Cembalon
Trident & EMI-Abbey Road Studios, London, UK 07/xx/68

Turn! Turn! Turn! (To Everything There Is A Season) (P. Seeger) 2:50 (16) (08/26/68)

Mary Hopkin: Lead Vocals & Acoustic Guitar
Probably Trident or possibly EMI Abbey Road Studios, London, UK 07/xx/68

Voyage Of The Moon (D. Leitch) 5:52 (9)
Paul McCartney: Guitar; Mary Hopkin: Lead Vocals; Donovan Leitch: Guitar

Y Blodyn Gwyn (E. J. Hughes-R. H. Jones) 3:08 (5)
Mary Hopkin: Lead Vocals
Probably EMI-Abbey Road, Trident or possibly Apple Studios, London, UK 11/xx/68-01/xx/69

Young Love (C. Joyner-R. Carty) 2:11 (11)
Paul McCartney: Arrangement; Mary Hopkin: Lead Vocals; The Mike Cotton Sound (Jim Garforth: Drums; Bernie: Bass; John Beecham: Horns; Mike Cotton: Horns; Nick: Horns; Derek Tearle: Guitar); The London Welsh Choir: B. Vocals

Those Were The Days
Apple-7243 8 30197 2 4 (UK) (03/27/95) (09/25/72)
Producer: Paul McCartney

The Fields Of St. Etienne (B. Gallagher-G. Lyle) 3:08 (10) (06/15/70)
Paul McCartney: Acoustic Guitar & (probable) Bass; **Ringo Starr: Drums**; Mary Hopkin: Lead Vocals & (probable) Acoustic Guitar
Probably EMI-Abbey Road, or possibly Apple or Trident Studio, London, UK 08/xx/69

Goodbye (J. Lennon-**P. McCartney**) 2:23 (2) (03/28/69)
Paul McCartney: Acoustic Guitars, Bass & Thigh-slap Percussion; Mary Hopkin: Lead Vocals & Guitar
Probably EMI-Abbey Road, Trident or Apple Studios, London, UK xx/xx/68 or xx/xx/69

Lontano Dagli Occhi (S. Endrigo-S. Bardotti) 3:22 (7) (03/07/69)
Paul McCartney: Arrangement, (probable) Bass & (probable) Piano; Mary Hopkin: Lead Vocals
Morgan Studios, London, UK 03/1-2/69

Que Sera, Sera (What Will Be, Will Be) (J. Livingston-R. Evans) 3:05 (6)
(06/15/70)

Paul McCartney: Electric Guitar, Acoustic Guitar, Bass & Arrangement; **Ringo Starr: Drums**; Mary Hopkin: Lead Vocals
EMI-Abbey Road Studios, London, UK 07-08/xx/69

Sparrow (B. Gallagher-G. Lyle) 3:09 (8) (03/28/69)
Paul McCartney: (probable) Bass; Mary Hopkin: Lead Vocals
Morgan Studios, London, UK 03/1-2/69

Mary Hopkin was born May 3, 1950 in Pontardawe, Wales. She started singing in her church choir when she was four years old. Later, she performed in local clubs and on Welsh TV. She sang primarily Welsh folk songs but was also influenced by American and UK folksingers such as Donovan*. Singer, actress and model Twiggy Lawson (Lesley Hornby) recommended Hopkin to Paul McCartney after seeing her on the UK TV talent show *Opportunity Knocks*.

McCartney signed Hopkin to Apple in May 1968. Over the next year he would invested considerable time and effort trying to make her an international star. Hopkin's debut on Apple was the single *Those Were The Days*, a Lithuanian folk song adapted by American folksingers Gene (Raskin) and Francesca. For years McCartney had urged artists, such as Denny Laine* and his band The Moody Blues, to record the song. He was convinced Mary's recording could launch her and Apple globally, so he had her record vocal overdubs in French, German, Italian and Spanish. He was proved right when the song became a huge international hit in 1968. Only The Beatles' Apple debut single *Hey Jude*, on which Mary claims she sings in the chorus, kept it from being a number one hit in many countries. Mary also claims she sang in the chorus of The Beatles' song *Let It Be*, though she isn't sure if she's featured on the released versions. [Linda McCartney* stated in the 1989 Paul McCartney World Tour booklet, "The first thing I ever did was with The Beatles. I sang harmonies on *Let It Be*. It was supposed to be me and Mary Hopkin, but she had to go home."]

McCartney produced and played on Mary's debut album *Post Card*. The track listing on the back of the album's jacket, along with some doodles, was in McCartney's handwriting. McCartney's soon to be wife Linda took the jacket's front photo. To further bolster Mary's international appeal, McCartney produced *Y Blodyn Gwyn* sung in Welsh, *Prince En Avignon* sung in French and *Lontano Dagli Occhi* sung in Italian. [*Lontano Dagli Occhi* was first issued on a single in Italy, later included on Mary's "best of" album *Those Were The Days*.] Unfortunately for Mary, *Post Card* was more of a showcase for McCartney's love affair with show tunes than for Mary's Welsh folk music. Though there are no musical credits on *Post Card*, it is well-known that McCartney contributed a significant amount of the instrumental backing, including guitars, probably piano and possibly drums. Ringo Starr may also have contributed drums or other percussion instruments. Other known contributors to the album include Donovan, George Martin*, who conducted the orchestra and played piano, and The Mike Cotton Sound. [The Mike Cotton Sound had been a part of *Another Beatles Christmas Show* in 1964.]

McCartney produced his catchy composition *Goodbye* for Mary, which became her second Top 20 hit for Apple in 1969. A promotional video was made (though never broadcast) of McCartney and Hopkin recording the song. McCartney's demo of *Goodbye* has appeared on unauthorized releases.

McCartney produced and reportedly, with Ringo, provide the entire musical backing on Hopkin's next scheduled single *Que Sera, Sera (What Will Be, Will Be) / The Fields Of St. Etienne*. Hopkin apparently wasn't thrilled with the single, and didn't want it released, which probably explains why the UK release of it was cancelled twice in favor of other singles, such as Mary's last UK Top 10 hit *Knock Knock Who's There*. There's no evidence the single was first issued in France (Apple-16) in September 1969, shortly after it was recorded, as is alleged. [Apple-16 was the catalogue number assigned to the cancelled release of *On Our Way Home)Two Of Us*) by Mortimer*.] It was apparently first released in the US in June 1970. The songs were later included on *Those Were The Days* but Mickie Most was erroneously credited as producing *Que Sera, Sera* on that album. George Harrison reportedly offered his composition *I'll Still Love You* (originally titled *When Every Song Is Sung*) to Hopkin; though there's no evidence she recorded it. Apple released several more singles by Hopkin and an album produced by her then husband, Tony Visconti. Mary, like most with the label, became disillusioned with Apple and let her contract expire.

Mary was a backing vocalist (under the name Mary Visconti) during the mid-1970s for several artists including David Bowie*. She had several releases on her husband Tony's Good Earth Records before their marriage ended in the early 1980s. [Tony was later married to May Pang for a time.] Mary became a member of the trio Sundance in 1980. In 1984 she joined a group called Oasis that also included Peter Skellern*. Mary contributed to a 1988 album project of Dylan Thomas' *Under Milk Wood* produced by George Martin. She continues to write songs and occasionally release new recordings. For more information go to www.maryhopkin.co.uk

Nicky Hopkins

The Tin Man Was A Dreamer
Sony-SRCS 6450 (Japan) (02/01/95) (04/23/73)
Producer: Nicky Hopkins & David Briggs
George Harrison: Lead Guitar; Nicky Hopkins: Vocals & Keyboards; Klaus Voormann: Bass; Bobby Keys: Saxophone; Prairie Prince: Drums; Ray Cooper: Percussion & Congas
Apple Studios, London, UK 01-04/xx73 &/or 07/xx/73

Banana Anna (N. Hopkins-J. Williams) 3:40 (7)
Additionally: Jerry Williams: Vocals

Edward (N. Hopkins) 5:20 (3)
Additionally: Nicky Hopkins: Keyboards (only)

Speed On (N. Hopkins-J. Williams) 4:01 (5)
Additionally: Jerry Williams: Vocals; Mick Taylor: Rhythm Guitar; Jim Horn: Saxophone; Jim Price: Trumpet

Waiting For The Band (N. Hopkins) 2:16 (2)
Additionally: Jerry Williams: Vocals; Ray Cooper: Percussion (only)

Nicholas "Nicky" Hopkins was born on February 24, 1944 in London, England. Hopkins was a classically trained musician who attended Britain's Royal Academy of Music. He is best remembered as a session keyboardist for Donovan*, The Rolling Stones*, The Who (see Roger Daltrey, John Entwistle, Keith Moon), The Small Faces (see Rod Stewart, Kenney Jones, Ian McLagan), The Steve Miller Band*, Ravi Shankar*, Carly Simon*, Marc Bolan (see T. Rex) and many others. Hopkins was a member of The Jeff Beck Group, Quicksilver Messenger Service and Sky (see John Williams) among other bands.

Hopkins first met The Beatles in Hamburg, Germany as a member of Cliff Bennett And The Rebel Rousers*. Nicky played keyboards on The Beatles' single version of *Revolution* in 1968. During the first half of the 1970s he contributed to John Lennon and Yoko Ono's* single *Happy Xmas* and album *Some Time In New York City*; to sessions for Lennon's albums *Imagine* and *Walls And Bridges*; George Harrison's albums *Living In The Material World*, *Dark Horse* and *Extra Texture (Read All About It)*, and Ringo Starr's albums *Ringo* and *Goodnight Vienna*. He played on Paul McCartney and Wings' songs *Jet* and *Listen To What The Man Said* for McCartney's appearance on the BBC TV show *Wogan* taped on November 19, 1987 and broadcast the following day. McCartney teamed up with Hopkins and others for the 1988 charity single *Children In Need* (see Spirit Of Play). Nicky also played on McCartney's 1989 album *Flowers In The Dirt*. Hopkins recorded a cover of The Beatles' song *Yesterday*.

Hopkins made several attempts at a solo career including the album *The Tin Man Was A Dreamer* recorded at Apple Studios, probably during the sessions for Harrison's album *Living In The Material World* using many of the same musicians including George. Nicky Hopkins died on September 6, 1994.

Jim Horn

Work It Out
Warner Bros.-9 25911-2 (03/xx/90)
Producer: Larry Knechtel & Jim Horn
George Harrison; Slide Guitar; Larry Knechtel: Keyboards & Synthesizers; Michael Rhodes: Bass; Paul Leim: Drums; Larry Byrom: Electric Guitar; Jim Horn: Soprano Saxophone
FPSHOT, UK & Nightingale Studios, Nashville, TN xx/xx/88

Take Away The Sadness (R. Tandy-J. Horn) 4:00 (2)

Jim Horn was born in Los Angeles, California. He began taking music lessons at the age of eight, and was playing trumpet and saxophone several years later. He has long been considered one of the top session horn players whose resume reads like a musical encyclopedia. He has also been a steady working partner with Duane Eddy* for years.

Leon Russell* recommended Horn to George Harrison for *The Concert For Bangla Desh* in 1971. Harrison's 1974 US tour band included Horn. During the first half of the 1970s Jim contributed to Harrison's albums *Living In The Material World*, *Dark Horse* and *Extra Texture (Read All About It)*, and *Cloud Nine* in 1987. He also contributed to the *Traveling Wilburys'* albums (see Bob Dylan, Jeff Lynne, Roy Orbison, Tom Petty) affectionately dubbed a "Sidebury." Harrison, Petty and Lynne returned the favor by contributing to Horn's 1990 album

Work It Out. Horn reminisces, "George was kind enough to add his beautiful and spiritual slide guitar fills, and a solo that only he could have played. We had some great moments together. George would talk about politics, music and the 'material world.' He had the most honest and inquisitive look in his eyes, and in the sound of his voice. I miss flying to England and working with him. God bless you George!"

Jim contributed to Ringo's albums *Ringo* in 1973 and *Time Takes Time* in 1992. He participated in (unreleased) sessions for John Lennon's 1975 album *Rock 'n' Roll.* Jim took part in the tracks Paul McCartney produced for the 1987 album *Duane Eddy.* George and Ringo appeared in a video sampler for Horn's 1988 album *Neon Nights.* In 2001 Jim released the album *A Beatles Tribute* with cover versions of their songs. He took part in the Harrison tribute *Concert For George* in 2002. Jim Horn continues to do session work. For more information go to www.jimhorn.com

Larry Hosford

Crosswords
Shelter-SRL 52003 (album 12") (08/02/76)
Producer: Dino Airali & Larry Hosford
Capitol Records Studio A & B†, Los Angeles, CA
probably 11/xx/75

Direct Me (L. Hosford) 3:30 (3)
George Harrison: Slide Guitar†; Larry Hosford: Lead Vocals & Acoustic Guitar; Pat Hubbard: B. Vocals; Ann Hughes: B. Vocals; Gary Roda: Pedal Steel Guitar & B. Vocals; Duane Sousa: Bass & B. Vocals; Jim Norris: Drums, Percussion & B. Vocals; Doug Haywood: B. Vocals; Dino Airali: B. Vocals; Frank Reckard: Acoustic Guitar; Leon Russell: Piano & Vibes

Wishing I Could (L. Hosford) 3:14 (5) (07/06/76)
George Harrison: B. Vocals†; Larry Hosford: Lead Vocals & Acoustic Guitar; Harold Bradley: Acoustic Guitar; Billy Sanford: Acoustic Guitar; Bob Moore: Bass; Buddy Harman: Drums; Leon Russell: B. Vocals; Jerry Miller: Acoustic Guitar; Tom Scribner: "The Lost Sound Of The Musical Saw;" Jeff Gylkinson: Harmonica

Larry Hosford was born on September 9, 1943 in Salinas, California. He began playing guitar with his father, who was a barn dance fiddler. In the mid-1960s Larry played in the E-Types, which he calls, "A Beatles clone band – the Salinas Beatles." They released a cover of The Beatles' song *Love Of The Loved* (see Cilla Black) in 1964. Larry next worked with the rock band Snail who released two albums. Larry's shift to country rock caught the attention of producer Dino Airali who got him signed to Shelter Records in the mid-1970s. Hosford had moderate chart success with the songs *Long Distance Kisses* and *King Takes The Queen.*

George Harrison's involvement with Larry's album *Crossroads* came through Airali who he had met through their mutual friend David Foster (see Attitudes). Airali says, "I went over and met George and we talked for a while and got along real well. He eventually had me become the General Manager of Dark Horse. During that time, I had an obligation to finish Larry's album *Crossroads.* I told George about that, and he said he would love to be able to just be looked at as a guitar player hired to do a session. I played Larry's music for him and he liked it. I asked him if he would like to play guitar on the session and he said, 'Sure.' Leon Russell*, who I had known for years, liked Larry's writing and he played keyboards." Foster and Russell had recently contributed to Harrison's 1975 album *Extra Texture (Read All About It),* which also thanks Airali. According to Hosford, "Harrison was prepared when he got to the studio because he had been given tapes of my music. He was loose and very easy to work with, which made me want to be loose too. He played slide guitar on *Direct Me.* Then he, Leon and I went to the piano and worked up the three-part harmony for *Wishing I Could* — three-part harmony, 'Like we use to do with the lads,' George said. Harrison's endorsement of my music meant a lot to me." Larry Hosford continues to write, record and perform, and sells good quality (CD-R) copies of *Crosswords* on his website www.larryhosford.com

Howlin' Wolf

The London Howlin' Wolf Sessions Deluxe Edition
MCA/Chess-088 112 985-2 (EU) (07/26/89) (07/26/71)
Producer: Norman Dayron
Ringo Starr: Drums; Howlin' Wolf: Lead Vocals; Eric Clapton: Lead Guitar; Steve Winwood: Piano; Bill Wyman: (probable) Cowbell; Charlie Watts: (possible) Percussion; Hubert Sumlin: Rhythm Guitar; Klaus Voormann: Bass; Joe Miller: Horns; Jordan Sandke: Horns; Dennis Lansing: Horns
Olympic Studios, London, UK 05/02/70

I Ain't Superstitious (W. Dixon) 3:29 (1-2) (07/26/71)

I Ain't Superstitious (Alternate Take) (W. Dixon) 4:10 (2-6)

I Ain't Superstitious (Alternate Take) (W. Dixon) 3:53 (2-10)

Howlin' Wolf was born Chester Burnett on June 10, 1910 in White Station, (West Point) Mississippi. His mother was a gospel street singer. He began playing guitar at an early age, and practiced with such blues legends as Charley Patton and Sonny Boy Williamson. He formed a band in Memphis in the late 1940s that included James Cotton, Junior Parker and Willie Johnson. In the early 1950s Wolf made some recordings for Sam Phillips of Sun Records before moving to Chicago and signing with Chess Records where he recorded such blues classics as *Spoonful*, *Smokestack Lightnin*, *Little Red Rooster* and *I Ain't Superstitious*. Wolf's style of blues had a major influence on UK artists such as The Rolling Stones*, Eric Clapton* and The Yardbirds.

It was not surprising then that such rock luminaries as Clapton, Ian Stewart, Charlie Watts, Bill Wyman, Steve Winwood (see Blind Faith) and Ringo Starr, using the pseudonym "Richie", would contribute to *The London Howlin' Wolf Sessions* released in 1971. Ringo drummed on the track *I Ain't Superstitious*. The Wolf, who ceased to howl on January 10, 1976, was inducted into the Rock and Roll Hall of Fame in 1991. For more information go to www.howlin-wolf.com

Mark Hudson

The Artist
Mark Hudson Music-[None] (CD-R) (09/14/09) (03/27/09)
Producer: Mark Hudson
Ringo Starr: Dialogue & Drums; Mark Hudson: Dialogue, Lead Vocals, B. Vocals, Guitar, Bass & Keyboards
Whatinthewhatthe? Studio, Los Angeles, CA

So You Are A Star (M. Hudson-B. Hudson-B. Hudson) 3:26 (4)

Mark Hudson was born Mario Salerno on August 23, 1951 in Portland, Oregon. Soon after seeing The Beatles perform at Portland's Coliseum on August 22, 1965 he joined his brothers Bill and Brett in a band. Mark played the drums, like his hero Ringo Starr. They recorded for several record companies during the latter half of the 1960s calling themselves the New Yorkers but without much success. Renamed The Hudson Brothers in the mid-1970s they had Top 40 hits with *So You Are A Star*, and *Rendezvous* written with Bruce Johnston of The Beach Boys* and produced by Bernie Taupin*. John Lennon reportedly referred to them as the kings of Saturday morning because of *The Hudson Brothers Razzle Dazzle Show* on CBS TV. In 1980, known simply as Hudson, they released the album *Damn Those Kids*, which thanks Lennon and includes a cover of his Beatles' song *Anytime At All*. They had already broken up when their cult-classic film *Hysterical* was released in 1983. Mark pursued work in music production, songwriting and TV. He co-starred in the TV show *Sara* and was the musical director for *The Late Show Starring Joan Rivers*. Songwriting success came his way via Aerosmith with whom he has written a dozen songs including 1993's *Livin' On The Edge*. He has also produced recordings for Aerosmith, Hanson, Ozzy Osbourne and others. His composition *It's Chico Time* was a number one hit in the UK for Chico Slimani in 2006. His daughter is singer Sarah Hudson and his niece is actress Kate Hudson.

Mark met John Lennon and Ringo Starr in Los Angeles during the mid-1970s through their mutual friendship with Harry Nilsson*. In the early 1990s Mark was working with Phil Ramone who was producing tracks for Ringo's 1992 album *Time Takes Time*, to which Mark contributed backing vocals. Between 1997 and

2006 Mark provided musical backing, and helped produce and compose most of the songs on Ringo's albums *Vertical Man*, *VH1 Storytellers*, *I Wanna Be Santa Claus*, *Ringo Rama*, *Choose Love*, *Live At Soundstage* and *Liverpool 8*, and helped produce *Ringo Starr And Friends*. He was also a member of Ringo's band The Roundheads. In an article on Mark by Matt Hurwitz, published in *Mix* magazine in July 2003, Ringo remarks, "Mark puts the fun back in recording. We always have such a great time. We sing through toys! He had found a toy in a store called a Megamouth and we used it on the record. He lets the musician know that anything is possible." That year Mark and Ringo formed Pumkinhead Records, which released an album by Liam Lynch*. Mark released his first solo album *The Artist* in 2009, which includes an earlier remake of *So You Are A Star* with backing from Ringo on drums, as the two haven't worked together in a number of years. Mark Hudson has been a frequent guest at conventions and festivals for fans of The Beatles, and David Fishof's Rock 'n' Roll Fantasy Camp. He continues to write, record and produce. For more information go to www.markhudson.com

Ian Hunter

Ringo Starr And His All Starr Band-Extended Versions
BMG-75517465252 (04/01/03)
Producer: Ringo Starr & David Fishof
Ringo Starr: Drums; Ian Hunter: Lead Vocals & Keyboards; Sheila Escovedo: Drums; Howard Jones: Keyboards; Greg Lake: Bass; Mark Rivera: Saxophone
Rosemont Theater, Rosemont (Chicago), IL 08/22/01

Irene Wilde [live] (I. Hunter) 4:34 (4)

Ringo Starr & His New All-Starr Band
Pioneer/Win Media-11907 (DVD) (10/01/02)
Producer: (recorded, mixed and mastered by: Glen Robinson); Executive Producer: Ringo Starr & David Fishof
Ringo Starr: Drums; Ian Hunter: Lead Vocals, Keyboards & Electric Guitar; Roger Hodgson: Electric Guitar & B. Vocals; Sheila Escovedo: Drums & B. Vocals; Howard Jones: Keyboards & B. Vocals; Greg Lake: Bass & B. Vocals; Mark Rivera: Electric Guitar & B. Vocals
Rosemont Theater, Rosemont (Chicago), IL 08/22/01

All The Young Dudes [live] (D. Bowie) 5:02 (17)
Additionally: Ian Hunter: Acoustic Guitar; Sheila Escovedo: Drums (only); Greg Lake: Bass (only) [Also available on King Biscuit Flower Hour/Razor & Tie-7930188003-2 (14) (08/06/02)]

Cleveland Rocks [live] (I. Hunter) 7:25 (4)

Ian Hunter was born Ian Hunter Patterson on June 3, 1939 in Oswestry, England. He was in several bands between the late 1950s and mid-1960s and, like The Beatles, played the clubs of Hamburg, Germany. Hunter also played with Billy Fury (see Various Artists - Without You – A Billy Fury Tribute). He was a member of Mott The Hoople whose 1972 international rock anthem *All The Young Dudes*, written by David Bowie*, mentions The Beatles. They had several more hits in the UK over the next two years, including *Honaloochie Boogie*, *All The Way From Memphis*, *Roll Away The Stone* and *The Golden Age Of Rock 'n' Roll*. When Mick Ralphs left the group in 1973 to form Bad Company (see Simon Kirke), and Ian left the following year, the band soon dissolved. Ian's first solo single, *Once Bitten Twice Shy*, was a UK Top 40 hit in 1975. [The song was a Top Five hit for the band Great White in 1989.] Hunter's 1979 album *You're Never Alone With A Schizophrenic* contained his compositions *Cleveland Rocks*, a cover version of which became the theme song for ABC TV's *The Drew Carey Show*, and *Ships*, which Barry Manilow turned into a Top 10 hit. Hunter has worked with a number of notables over the years including, Clarence Clemons*, Todd Rundgren* and Roy Young (see Cliff Bennett And The Rebel Rousers, Tony Sheridan).

Hunter says, "It's an eerie feeling when out of the blue you get a message on your answering machine from Ringo Starr – a Beatle! He asked me to join his All-Starr Band tour in 2000 but I had other commitments. He rang me up again in 2001 and asked me what I thought of his band. It was a very talented but odd combination of musicians, and not very 'rock 'n' roll.' We rehearsed at Casino Rama north of Toronto, Canada. It was like boot camp, until we got to the fun parts. Ringo hates rehearsing, and doesn't like playing drum solos and Sheila E.*, the other drummer, was making him do them. Sheila's very matronly, and makes you do things you don't want to do. She told me off once when I was goofing off with Howard Jones* who I liked. Mark Rivera, the musical director, is like a dad and would moan if

Ian Hunter Freedom Hill, Sterling Heights (Detroit), MI July 28, 2001. © and photo by Kristofer Engelhardt.

you did anything differently. Greg Lake* is a direct bloke, but he's also quite compassionate underneath all of his armor and I liked him. Roger Hodgson* asked, 'Who's playing lead guitar?' I said, 'I'm not!' Roger turned out to be an excellent lead guitarist. His former band Supertramp was huge in Canada, so he was stealing the show there. Ringo would always turn up his amp when he walked by but Roger would turn it way back down again. It didn't add up to rock 'n' roll but it added up to an extremely good band and show." Hunter performed *Cleveland Rocks*, *Irene Wilde*, *I Still Love Rock 'n' Roll* and *All The Young Dudes* with backing from Ringo on drums. Ian says, "There's always that deference from those around Ringo because he's a Beatles, but I found him to be very personable, enjoyable to work with and a lot of fun. He was a bit upset during the tour because of all the untrue news reports about the imminent demise of George Harrison. Ringo's very ordinary and down to earth. You never lose that working class upbringing he had living in a house that was condemned. He and I have kids the same age — and kicked them out at the same age! He's full of stories and quite outspoken about many things including The Beatles — past and present. He told me about some pretty daft "Liverpool humor" things they had done. We were looked after very well on his tour, with private jets and first class hotels, but then there are perks to being a Beatle! His crew was wonderful too. If you said you liked cheese or cigarettes there would suddenly be a lot. Tour producer David Fishof was fine by me. I think he and Ringo had a couple of run-ins but the tour was remarkably free of aggravation, though it took me a month to get my gear back! Overall it was a fabulous experience and I made a lot of money." Hunter continues to write, record and tour. For more information go to www.ianhunter.com

Indian Mosk

[None]
Apple [Unreleased]
Producer: John Lennon & Peter Bendrey
Indian Mosk: Vocals
Record Plant Studios, New York, NY 11/16/71

Bodhnath (Gellupka) I [unknown]

Bodhnath Part II [unknown]

Indian Mosk is listed as the artist on a box of unreleased recordings found in the tape library from the old Record Plant Studios in New York with John Lennon listed as producer. Jack Douglas, who would later produce John and Yoko Ono's* 1980 sessions for *Double Fantasy* and *Milk And Honey*, is listed as the engineer but he has no recollection of these sessions, who Indian Mosk was or for what use the recordings were intended. The tape box lists the client as Apple. Other tape boxes from the same source and time period suggest that these recordings may have been intended for use in an ABKCO film soundtrack. [ABKCO released soundtrack albums on Apple for the films *Come Together* and *El Topo* in 1971.] It's more likely that these recordings were intended for use in some John and Yoko project that was later abandoned. May Pang theorizes that John put his name to the project to identify him as the specific client and that the Lennons' personal assistant, Peter Bendrey probably did most, if not all, of the production (see Tibetan Chants). If true, Lennon would more rightly be considered the executive producer.

Print Out
Tusk-008 (album 12") (Barbados) (xx/xx/84)
Producer: Ivory
Maxie Taylor: Drums; Jimmy Duncan: Guitar; Andrew Bourne: Lead Guitar; Phillip Brennan: Bass; Wayne Gibbs: Keyboards
Paradise Alley Studio, Barbados xx/xx/84

Freedom Land (**P. McCartney**) 4:13 (2/4)
Additionally: Phillip Brennan: Lead Vocals

Runaway (**P. McCartney**) 3:32 (1/5)
Additionally: Wayne Gibbs: Lead Vocals
[Also available on *Nostalgia* CRS Music-CRS-CD093 (CD/DVD) (17) (11/xx/05)]

Ivory is a rock band that formed in Barbados in 1965 that was greatly influenced by The Beatles. They were signed for a time, under a different name, to NEMS. In 1984 they consisted of Barbados natives Maxie Taylor, born on August 24, 1954 on drums; Wayne Gibbs, born on August 13, 1952 on keyboards; Andrew Bourne, born on February 2, 1956 on lead guitar; Jimmy Duncan, born on February 2, 1954 on guitar and Philip Brennan on bass, who was born on October 28, 1953 in St. Andrew, Jamaica. They broke up in 1990 but have been giving annual reunion concerts since 2005.

The Barbados press reported in 1982 that Paul McCartney showed up to record at Ivory's Paradise Alley Studio. Jimmy Duncan says, "In 1979 my landlord called me saying he was renting Maddox House to Paul and Linda McCartney*. He gave me their number, and suggested I call them, though I was very hesitant at first. One of the staff answered and Paul came to the phone. I told him I was a local musician and had called to welcome him to Barbados. He thanked me and invited me over for tea, so Phillip and I went to meet him. They greeted us like old friends and were exceptionally hospitable. At the time they were working on the design for their *Back To The Egg* album jacket and explained the concept to us. We told Paul about Ivory and invited him to our Paradise Alley recording studio. He respectfully declined saying he had recently spent much time in the studio working on his latest album and just wanted to 'chill out' and vacation. Thrilled that we had met him, we thanked him and said our goodbyes.

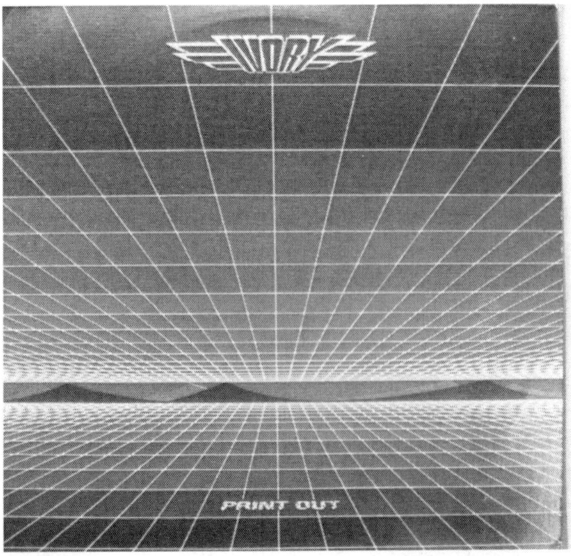

"My landlord called me in February 1982 saying that Paul was back and staying at Landmark House. Again, we were invited over for tea and treated like old friends. Linda was absolutely charming, and you could see and feel the amazing bond between her and Paul. I didn't want to go near the subject of John Lennon, who had recently been murdered, but Paul raised the subject and began telling me at length about his writing partnership with John saying, 'We felt that there was a third person there with us.' He was remorseful about losing him. Paul and Linda told us how they became vegetarians saying they were driving in England behind a lorry full of chickens on route to slaughter, looked at each other and said, 'That's it, no more meat.' I felt honored that he was comfortable sharing these things with me. He told me about the recordings he'd just finished for *Tug Of War*. I invited him to our studio again but he declined for the same reasons as before.

"We were working in the studio a few days later, took a break for lunch and padlocked the door. I got a call from Derek Fields, our lead singer then, telling me that he was locked inside the studio and that Paul McCartney was outside banging on the locked door. He assured me it was no joke! We hurried back to the studio to find Paul sitting outside on the steps with his acoustic guitar. We told him we were working on a commercial, so he told us to keep on working. He made a few suggestions and when we were finished he said, 'Let's go do something — Lets play.' We were stunned! It was enough that he came to our studio, but now we were about to jam with him? He sat at the piano and started playing *Let it Be* and we jammed through a couple of other Beatles' standards. He and I began playing *Blackbird* on acoustic guitars, which is one of my favorite songs. He forgot the bridge and asked me to show it to him. I was beside myself showing Paul McCartney his song! Then he said, 'Let's create something,' and got Maxie to play a reggae groove; then Paul started singing and playing a song [*Freedom Land*]. He was making up lyrics about his experience at our studio. We all followed and created our own thing. We recorded this track basically live, and then added some percussion and background vocals. Paul's enthusiasm and energy was amazing. He was hooting and hollering as if he were live onstage. He was having a blast and we were feeding off his amazing vibe. Word that Paul was in our studio spread like a wildfire. The press started calling and asked if they could come over and do an interview, but Paul declined. After about six hours we stopped and said our goodbyes. We were at the studio very early the next day and stayed late hoping Paul might return. We did the same thing the next day but to no avail. When I got home I rang Paul up. Linda answered and said, 'He's on his way to your studio.' We hurried back to the studio to find Paul waiting for us again on the steps playing his acoustic guitar. He had a song he wrote called *Runaway* that he wanted to record in a few different styles. It was a beautiful ballad, which was how we first laid it down. Then we did a more up tempo version. Finally he did it with a fast Caribbean-style rhythm and sang it with his imitation of a Barbadian dialect, which had us in hysterics. We spent about six hours that night recording and doing some rough mixes for Paul. We asked him if we could rework these songs for Ivory's next album. He said we could but couldn't use his vocals. So we had in our possession two McCartney songs; a six minute reggae song called *Freedom Land* and a beautiful ballad in three styles called *Runaway*. Ivory re-recorded these songs in 1984 for our album *Print Out*, which was only released in Barbados on our Tusk label.

"Paul was staying at Porters Great House in Barbados in 1984. The last time we called him there Linda answered and said there was something going on and that Paul would have to call us later, but we never heard from him again. We learned a short time later that he and Linda were being busted at the house for possession of marijuana. To my knowledge Paul has never returned to Barbados."

Michael Jackson (with Paul McCartney)

Thriller
Epic-EK 38112 (11/29/82) (10/25/82)
Producer: Quincy Jones
Paul McCartney: Vocals; Michael Jackson: Vocals & Vocal Arrangement; Greg Phillinganes: Rhodes; David Paich: Piano & Rhythm Arrangement; David Foster: Synthesizer & Synthesizer Arrangement; Steve Porcaro: Synthesizer Programming; Dean Parks: Guitar; Steve Lukather: Guitar; Louis Johnson: Bass; Jeff Porcaro: Drums; Quincy Jones: Vocal Arrangement & Rhythm Arrangement; Jerry Hey: String Arrangement & Conductor; Jerry Vinci: Concertmaster
Westlake Audio Studios, Los Angeles, CA 04/14-15/82

The Girl Is Mine (M. Jackson) 3:42 (3)

Michael Jackson was born August 29, 1958 in Gary, Indiana. He and older brothers Tito, Jermaine, Jackie and Marlon began performing in the Gary area in the mid-1960s becoming known as The Jackson Five. A string of number one hits followed their signing with Motown Records in 1969 including *I Want You Back*, *ABC*, *The Love You Save* and *I'll Be There*, along with nearly a dozen Top 20 hits. The band left Motown in 1975 and became known as The Jacksons. Their sisters Janet and La Toya later had successful musical careers. Michael launched his solo career in the early 1970s having a number one hit with *Ben*, and Top Five hits with *Got To Be There* and *Rockin' Robin*. Jackson's 1979 album *Off The Wall*, produced by Quincy Jones, restarted his solo career with the number one hits *Don't Stop 'Til You Get Enough* and *Rock With You*, and the Top 10 hits *She's Out Of My Life* and *Off The Wall*.

Off The Wall also included a cover of Paul McCartney's song *Girlfriend.* In his autobiography *Moonwalk,* Jackson recounted being invited by Linda McCartney's* daughter Heather to a party on March 24, 1975, celebrating the completion of Wings' album *Venus And Mars*, aboard the ocean liner Queen Mary docked in Long Beach, California and meeting Paul McCartney. Other guests included George Harrison. [Jackson and Harrison appeared together on the BBC Radio One program *Roundtable* on February 9, 1979 judging new record releases.] According to *Moonwalk*, shortly after the party, McCartney invited Jackson to another party and sang his song *Girlfriend* for Jackson, saying he had written it for him to record. McCartney and Jackson never worked on the song together. McCartney ended up recording the song for his 1978 album *London Town.* During sessions for *Off The Wall*, Jones suggested that Michael record a McCartney song he had recently heard called *Girlfriend.* Considering the unusual coincidence, Jackson decided to record the song. However, according to McCartney, as quoted in Ray Coleman's book *Yesterday & Today*, *Girlfriend* wasn't composed with Jackson in mind.

Jackson phoned McCartney on Christmas Day 1980 with an offer to collaborate. Jackson went to the UK in May 1981 where he and McCartney co-wrote and recorded *The Man* and the number one hit *Say Say Say.* McCartney essentially wrote the music and Jackson the lyrics. The recordings were finished off in Los Angeles in April 1982 and in the UK in February 1983. They were featured on McCartney's 1983 album *Pipes Of Peace*. Jackson also appeared in McCartney's music video for *Say Say Say*. Jackson asked McCartney for some business advice. He told him to get a manager he could trust, make and own music videos and invest in music publishing (as McCartney had successfully done). McCartney thought Jackson was joking when he suggested that he was going to buy his (the Lennon-McCartney publishing catalogue, Northern Songs) songs.

In April 1982 McCartney recorded a vocal duet in Los Angeles with Jackson on *The Girl Is Mine*, the first Top Five hit off Jackson's album *Thriller*, which also includes the number one hits *Beat It* and *Billie Jean*, the Top Five hits *Thriller* and *Wanna Be Startin' Somethin'* and the Top 10 hits *Human Nature* and *P.Y.T. (Pretty Young Thing).* Jackson's videos for those songs were also highly successful, particularly because of their special effects and Jackson's self-choreographed dance scenes. *Thriller*, also produced by Jones, thanks McCartney in the credits, and has become one of the biggest selling albums of all time.

In March 1985 Jackson, wealthy from the sales of *Thriller*, visited McCartney and once again hinted that he might buy his songs. The Beatles had lost controlling interest in their Northern Songs Publishing Company in March 1969 and sold off their minority shares to the controlling interest ATV (Associated Television) in October 1969. This came about as a result of their financial difficulties at Apple, disputes over being managed by Allen Klein and the legacy of Brian Epstein's mismanagement. After John Lennon's death, McCartney and Yoko Ono* joined forces to try to buy back the catalogue priced at around $20 million. McCartney reportedly bristled at having to pay $20 million to buy back songs he had written and originally owned. Apparently Ono convinced him that if they held out a little longer she could get it for less. On August 10, 1985 Jackson bought, for a reported $47,500,000, the publishing rights to a catalogue, which included the vast majority of the Lennon-McCartney compositions, compositions by George Harrison and Ringo Starr (Starkey), and some songs written separately by Lennon and McCartney after the breakup of The Beatles. Following Jackson's purchase, The Beatles were unsuccessful in stopping him from allowing the songs to be used in commercials. McCartney and Jackson's friendship ended as a result of his purchase and commercial use of the songs. In November 1995 a merger creating Sony/ATV Music Publishing was formed between Jackson and Sony, which include the Lennon-McCartney catalogue. Jackson reportedly received close to $100 million for the merger, while retaining half an interest that is currently estimated to be worth a minimum of $500 million.

Lennon and Ono's son Sean was a guest at Jackson's home, and made a cameo in Jackson's film *Moonwalker* in which Jackson performed Lennon's Beatles' song *Come Together*, included on the 1991 video release *The World's Greatest Artists Sing LENNON A Tribute.* Jackson married Elvis Presley's daughter Lisa Marie in 1994. They were divorced in 1996. Jackson was inducted into the Rock and Roll Hall of Fame in 2001. He died on June 25, 2009. For more information go to www.michaeljackson.com

From Then To Now (As Times Goes By)
Blue Moon-BMCD28 [unauthorized release] (xx/xx//94)
Producer: Anthony Eaton
Wembley Arena, London, UK 06/20/86

Dancing In The Street (W. Stevenson-M. Gaye) 3:06 (16)
Paul McCartney: Spoken intro, B. Vocals & Acoustic Guitar; Mick Jagger: Duet Vocals; David Bowie: Duet Vocals; Eric Clapton: Guitar; Mark Knopfler: Electric Guitar; John Illsley: Bass; Rick Parfitt: Guitar; Francis Rossi: Guitar; Elton John: Piano; Phil Collins: Drums; Howard Jones: Keyboards; Midge Ure: Guitar; Brian Adams: Guitar

Leon Russell
DCC/Shelter-GZS-1049 (Japan/Canada) (11/18/93)
Producer: Denny Cordell & Leon Russell
Ringo Starr: Drums; Mick Jagger: Lead Vocals; Chris Stainton: Guitar; Bill Wyman: Bass; Leon Russell: Piano
Olympic Sound Studios, London, UK 09-10/xx/69

(Can't Seem To) Get A Line On You [A.K.A. Shine A Light] (L. Russell [M. Jagger-K. Richards]) 4:16 (17)

The Very Best Of Mick Jagger
Atlantic/Rhino-R2 328636 (+ DVD) (10/02/07)
Producer: John Lennon
John Lennon: (possible Guitar); Mick Jagger: Lead Vocals; Jim Keltner: Drums; Harry Nilsson: B. Vocals & (possible) Keyboards; Jesse Ed Davis: Guitar; Danny Kortchmar: Guitar; Jack Bruce: Bass; Bobby Keys: Horns; Trevor Lawrence: Horns; Al Kooper: Keyboards. Additionally, possibly one or more of the following: Bruce Gary: Drums; Joe De Aguero: Percussion; Rocky Djubano: Percussion; Mike Finnegan: Keyboards; Wolfgang Metz: Bass; Paul Stallworth: Bass; Steve Madaio: Trumpet; Jim Price: Horns; Billy Preston: Keyboards
Record Plant Studios, Los Angeles, CA probably 12/xx/73 or 01-03/xx/74

Too Many Cooks (Spoil The Soup) (A. Bond-R. Dumbar-E. Wayne) 3:22 (9) (01/14/91)

Michael "Mick" Jagger was born on July 26, 1943 in Dartford, England. Jagger, like other members of The Rolling Stones*, has long maintained a solo career and contributed to a number of other artists' recordings including Yoko Ono's* *Approximately Infinite Universe* album. Jagger sings lead vocals on the song *(Can't Seem To) Get A Line On You* on the 1993 reissue of the album *Leon Russell**. Ringo plays drums on the song, which is actually an early working version of *Shine A Light*, which The Rolling Stones* released in 1972.

The star-studded Mick Jagger recording of *Too Many Cooks Spoil The Soup* was produced by John Lennon, probably in December 1973, at Record Plant Studios in Los Angeles, during a break in sessions for Lennon's *Rock 'N' Roll* album to which Jagger and fellow Rolling Stones' member Charlie Watts contributed. It was the result of a weekly jam session of top Los Angeles studio musicians affectionately known as The Jim Keltner Fan Club, which centered on drummer Jim Keltner (see Attitudes). There isn't agreement concerning the dates and musicians listed for the recording of it on *The Very Best Of Mick Jagger*. According to Keltner, and Lee Kiefer who says he arranged for and engineered the sessions, Ringo was present but didn't participate. Keltner thought producer Richard Perry helped Lennon with the editing, but Kiefer, May Pang and Al Kooper deny Perry's presence. Kiefer and Pang insist *Too Many Cooks Spoil The Soup* was recorded in late December 1973. Jack Bruce* said the session had to take place between January and March 1974 when he was at Record Plant recording his album *Out Of The Storm*. According to Bruce, "The session began with Lennon doing *Stand By Me* for hours before it evolved into the recordings for *Too Many Cooks*." Other reports say they also jammed on *Hey Paula*. Drummer Bruce Gary (later a member of the group The Knack) says Keltner walked out of the studio, and that he ended up drumming on the track. Gary concurs with Jack's recollections as to the recording dates, but is certain they only jammed on *Bring It On Home To Me*, not *Stand By Me*, and that it was after the takes for *Too Many Cooks*. [Lennon would end up recording both songs for his *Rock 'N' Roll* album.] Gary doesn't recall Ringo or Al Kooper being present, and says Billy Preston* played keyboards. Kiefer says, "Many people participated in the session, including studio employees on backing vocals, and others playing acoustic guitar that I don't remember." He says he, Danny Kortchmar, Kooper, Jagger and Lennon were involved in the production. He recalls Preston and Kooper playing keyboards, thinks Harry Nilsson* and Mike Finnegan also played keyboards, Paul Stallworth and Wolfgang Metz played bass, Steve Madaio and Jim Price played horns, and Joe De Aguero and Rocky Djubano played percussion. Kiefer says they only recorded one backing track, and that Keltner and Gary drummed on it, but that there were three takes of the song (the album's liner notes say it was recorded in one take). Also present was former Apple employee Chris O'Dell, who says in her 2009 book *Miss O'Dell: My Hard Days And Long Nights With The Beatles, The Stones, Bob Dylan, Eric Clapton And The Women They Loved*, that the sessions took place in early April 1974. Pang thinks two versions of *Too Many Cooks* were recorded, so perhaps this is the source of the confusion regarding dates and musicians. She says the song was never considered for release on Apple, as had been reported, and that it wasn't initially released because Jagger wasn't happy with the results. The song was officially debuted in 1991 on the Westwood One radio series *The Lost Lennon Tapes* but wasn't commercially released until 2007. Lennon reportedly produced Jagger recording a cover of *Please Don't Ever Change* at New York's Record Plant Studios on April 29, 1974 but the recording has never surfaced. Perhaps it's confused with *Too Many Cooks Spoil The Soup*, which has "don't change" in the lyrics and was recorded at Record Plant in Los Angeles.

Paul McCartney played acoustic guitar while Mick Jagger and David Bowie* sang their duet hit *Dancing In The Street* at *The Prince's Trust 10th Anniversary Concert* on June 20, 1986, which is available on unauthorized releases. For more information go to www.mickjagger.com

Jay-Z & Linkin Park

24 Carat Unbootlegged [The Beatles]
No Tapo-NTR-0602 (CD-R) [unauthorized release] (xx/xx/06)
Producer: Walter Miller
Paul McCartney: Vocals; Jay-Z: Vocals; Chester Bennington: Vocals; Joe Hahn: Programming; Dave Farrell: Bass; Mike Shinoda: Guitar; Bradford Delson: Keyboards; Robert Bourdon: Drums
Staples Center, Los Angeles, CA 02/08/06

Medley: Numb/Encore/Yesterday (C. Bennington-R. Bourdon-B. Delson-D. Farrell-J. Hahn-M. Shinoda/S. Carter-K. West/J. Lennon-P. McCartney) 3:37 (41)

Rap singer Jay-Z was born Shawn Carter on December 4, 1969 in New York, New York. He attended high school with rappers AZ, The Notorious B.I.G. and Busta Rhymes. He is one of rap and hip hop's most successful artists. Since 1996, when he formed Roc-A-Fella Records, he has racked up 10 Platinum certified albums. He's had Top Five hits with *03 Bonnie & Clyde* in 2002, *Dirt Off Your Shoulder* in 2004 and *Swagga Like Us* in 2008. He's had Top 10 hits with *Izzo (H.O.V.A.)* and *Girls, Girls, Girls* in 2001, *Excuse Me Miss* and *Change Clothes* in 2003 and *Show Me What You Got* in 2006. An a cappella version of Jay-Z's *The Black Album* was paired with samples from *The Beatles* (white) album for Danger Mouse's *The Grey Album* in 2004, which created a legal battle with The Beatles' record label EMI. Jay-Z is married to R&B singer Beyoncé Knowles. He has fostered and worked with some of rap, hip hop and rock's biggest artists including Linkin Park. For more information go to www.rocafella.com

The "nu-metal," rap-rock group Linkin Park formed in 1996 in Los Angeles, California first under the name Xero and then Hybrid Theory. The band includes Los Angeles natives Bradford Delson, born on December 1, 1977, Robert Bourdon, born on January 20, 1979 and Mike Shinoda, born on February 11, 1977. The other members include Chester Bennington, born on March 20, 1976 in Phoenix, Arizona, Joe Hahn, born on March 15, 1977 in Dallas, Texas and Dave "Phoenix" Farrell, born on February 8, 1977 in Plymouth, Massachusetts. Success arrived in 2000 with the release of their first album *Hybrid Theory*, which was eventually certified Diamond. It included the Top Five hit *In The End*. Their follow up album *Meteora* topped the charts in 2003 and included the Top 20 hits *Numb* and *Breaking The Habit*. In 2004 they teamed up with rapper Jay-Z on the number one hit album *Collision Course*. It included the Grammy award winning mash up of their hit *Numb* and Jay-Z's song *Encore*. Back by an orchestra, Linkin Park and Jay-Z performed *Numb/Encore* at the Grammy Awards in 2006. Two thirds of the way through their performance they mashed in the song *Yesterday* with Paul McCartney joining in on vocals. Linkin Park's 2007 album *Minutes To Midnight* also topped the chart and included the Top 10 hit *What I've Done* and the Top 20 hit *Shadow Of The Day*. For more information go to www.linkinpark.com

Billy Joel

Rock And Roll Hall Of Fame & Museum
Time Life-24943-X (Whole Lotta Shakin' Live) (24633-X) (DVD) (10/20/09)
Producer: Bob Sarles & Christina Keating
Paul McCartney: Vocals; Billy Joel: Lead Vocals & Keyboards; Eric Clapton: Guitar; Robbie Robertson: Guitar; Dion: Vocals & Maracas; Chris Isaak: Vocals & Maracas; Bonnie Raitt: B. Vocals; probably one or more of the following: Anton Fig: Drums; Sid McGinnis: Guitar; Will Lee: Bass
Grand Ballroom Waldorf-Astoria Hotel, New York, NY 03/15/99

What'd I Say (R. Charles) 4:53 (5-2)

William "Billy" Joel was born in New York, New York on May 9, 1949 but has spent most of his life in the Long Island region of New York. His father was an accomplished classical pianist and his half-brother Alexander is a noted conductor. Billy began taking classical piano lessons as a youngster but took an interest in rock 'n' roll, especially after seeing The Beatles on *The Ed Sullivan Show*. He was in a number of local rock bands who released a few records and had a regional following during the latter half of the 1960s. He left high school before graduating stating he wasn't going to Columbia University, but Columbia Records. His songwriting on his first solo album, *Cold Spring Harbor*, released by Family Productions in 1971, showed promise of great things to come. He signed with Columbia Records and had his first Top 40 hit with *Piano Man* in 1973. Between 1977 and 1993 Joel had Top Ten hits with his songs *You May Be Right*, *An Innocent Man*, *You're Only Human (Second Wind)*, *Modern Woman*, *A Matter Of Trust* and *I Go To Extremes*; Top Five hits with *Just The Way You Are*, *My Life*, *Uptown Girl* and *The River Of Dreams*, and number one hits with *It's Still Rock And Roll To Me*, *Tell Her About It* and *We Didn't Start The Fire*. A dozen of Joel's albums have been certified Multi-Platinum.

One of his live albums includes a cover of McCartney's Beatles' song *Back In The USSR*. Joel's longtime band member Mark Rivera (see Dog Soldier) has worked extensively with Ringo Starr's All-Starr Band. Billy was inducted into the Rock and Roll Hall of Fame in 1999 along with Paul McCartney. At the induction ceremonies McCartney joined Joel in his performance of Ray Charles' song *What'd I Say* included on the Time Life DVD series *Rock And Roll Hall Of Fame & Museum* issued in several configurations in 2009. Paul joined Billy, who backed him on *I Saw Her Standing There* and *Let It Be*, during Joel's concert on July 18, 2008 at Shea Stadium just before it was demolished. On July 17, 2009 Joel returned the favor joining McCartney on *I Saw Her Standing There* at the opening of Citi Field, Shea's replacement, included on McCartney's 2009 CD and DVD *Good Evening New York City*. Billy Joel has recorded less in recent years turning more to classical music and touring, often with Elton John*. For more information go to www.billyjoel.com

Elton John (Elton John Band Featuring John Lennon and The Muscle Shoals Horns)

The Beatles: Artifacts III (Sue Me Sue You: 1972-1975) [Various Artists]
Big Music-BIGBX 009.4 (BIG 4034) (Italy) [unauthorized release] (probably 02/xx/95)
Producer: Gus Dudgeon
John Lennon: Vocals & Guitar; Elton John: Vocals & Piano; Ray Cooper: Percussion; Davey Johnstone: Guitar; Dee Murray: Bass; Nigel Olsson: Drums; Muscle Shoals Horns (Harvey Thompson: Saxophone; Ronnie Eades: Baritone Saxophone; Harrison Calloway: Trumpet; Charles Rose: Trombone)
Record Plant Studios, New York, NY 11/24/74

I Saw Her Standing There [rehearsal] (J. Lennon-P. McCartney) 2:54 (2-19)

Here And There
Rocket-314-528164-2 (05/14/96)(06/19/89)
Producer: Gus Dudgeon (remixed by Gus Dudgeon†)
John Lennon: Vocals & Guitar; Elton John: Vocals & Piano; Ray Cooper: Percussion; Davey Johnstone: Guitar & B. Vocals; Dee Murray: Bass & B. Vocals; Nigel Olsson: Drums; Muscle Shoals Horns (Harvey Thompson: Saxophone; Ronnie Eades: Baritone Saxophone; Harrison Calloway: Trumpet; Charles Rose: Trombone)

Madison Square Garden, New York, NY 11/28/74 & Metropolis Studios, London, UK† (remixed: 03/xx/95†)

The Bitch Is Back [live] (E. John-B. Taupin) 4:23 (2-13)
Additionally: **John Lennon: Tambourine** (only); Bernie Taupin: Tambourine

I Saw Her Standing There [live] (J. Lennon-P. McCartney) 3:17 (2-10) (02/24/75)

Lucy In The Sky With Diamonds [live] (J. Lennon-P. McCartney) 6:15 (2-9) (03/13/81)

Additionally: **John Lennon: Arrangement**

Whatever Gets You Thru The Night [live] (J. Lennon) 4:40 (2-8) (03/13/81)

To Be Continued...
MCA-MCAD4 10110 (11/12/90)
Producer: Gus Dudgeon
Caribou Ranch Studios, Nederland, CO probably 08/xx/74

Lucy In The Sky With Diamonds (J. Lennon-P. McCartney) 6:15 (3-3) (11/15/74)
John Lennon: Guitars, B. Vocals & Arrangement; Elton John: Lead Vocals, Mellotron Harpsichord & Keyboards; Dee Murray: Bass & B. Vocals; Nigel Olsson: Drums & B. Vocals; Davey Johnstone: Guitar, Sitar, B. Vocals; Ray Cooper: Tambourine & Gong

Together At The Rock And Roll Hall Of Fame [Various Artists]
Living Legend-LLRCD 101(Italy) [unauthorized release] (xx/xx/93)
Producer: [unknown]
George Harrison: (probable) Guitar & Vocals; Ringo Starr: (possible) Drums; Elton John: Lead Vocals & Keyboards; probably one or more of the following: Mary Wilson: B. Vocals; Yoko Ono: B. Vocals & Percussion; Paul Shaffer: Keyboards; Billy Joel: Keyboards & B. Vocals; Al Jardine: Guitar &/or Percussion; Mike Love: B. Vocals & Percussion; Bruce Johnston: B. Vocals & Percussion; Bruce Springsteen: B. Vocals & Percussion; Little Richard: Handclaps; Anton Fig: Drums; Bob Dylan: Guitar & B. Vocals; Dave Edmunds: Guitar; Les Paul: Guitar; Jeff Beck: Electric Guitar; Mick Jagger: B. Vocals & Percussion; Carl Wilson: Handclaps; Brian Wilson: Handclaps; Sean Lennon: Handclaps; Sid McGinnis: Guitar; Ben E. King: Handclaps; John Fogerty: Handclaps; Arlo Guthrie: Handclaps &/or Guitar; Peter Wolf: Handclaps; Johnny Moore: Handclaps; Joe Blunt: Handclaps; Clyde Brown: Handclaps; Julian Lennon: Handclaps; Bill Pinkney: Handclaps; Charlie Thomas: Handclaps; Max Weinberg: Handclaps; Will Lee: Bass; Patti Scialfa: Handclaps & B. Vocals
Grand Ballroom Waldorf-Astoria Hotel, New York, NY 01/20/88

Whole Lotta Shakin' Goin' On/Hound Dog/Honey Hush [live] (J. Hall-D. Williams/J. Leiber-M. Stoller/J. Turner) 4:46 (8)

Elton John was born Reginald Dwight on March 25, 1947 in Pinner (London), England. He was playing the piano at the age of three. He received a scholarship to study at London's Royal Academy of Music when he was 11. He joined the group Bluesology in the early 1960s. Bluesology also included Elton Dean and Long John Baldry in 1967, the year he left to pursue songwriting and adopted the name Elton John from Dean and Baldry's names. With the help of Liberty Records, he was paired with lyricist Bernie Taupin*. John and Taupin were signed on as staff writers for Dick James Music Publishing (DJM), who also handled The Beatles. John's melodies were often anonymously paired with Taupin's lyrics. By 1969 Elton was doing session work and releasing his recordings on the DJM label.

Elton's rise to stardom started in the US following his critically acclaimed performance at The Troubadour club in Los Angeles in August 1970. Within months he'd leaped from the club circuit to arena rock superstardom. He became the Liberace of glitter rock, wearing outrageous glasses and sporting outlandish costumes, which included duck suits and sequined baseball uniforms. Among his many hits are *Your Song, Rocket Man, Daniel, Bennie And The Jets, Funeral For A Friend / Love Lies Bleeding, Don't Let The Sun Go Down On Me, Philadelphia Freedom, Crocodile Rock, Island Girl* and *I'm Still Standing*. John was inducted into the Rock and Roll Hall of Fame in 1994. That year he received a Grammy and an Oscar for *Can You Feel The Love Tonight* from the soundtrack to the film *The Lion King*. He has been active in various causes, particularly the fight against AIDS. George Martin* produced Elton's 1997 re-recording of *Candle In The Wind*, a tribute single to raise money for the Diana, Princess of Wales Memorial Fund, which became the biggest selling single recording in history. The following year he was knighted.

Elton has worked with all of The Beatles. They first became aware of him during their visits to Dick James' offices in the late 1960s. He first worked with Ringo Starr in the T. Rex* film *Born To Boogie*. In 1974, Elton played piano on his composition *Snookeroo* for Ringo's *Goodnight Vienna* album. He met John Lennon in Los Angeles in October 1973 when Lennon was recording his album *Rock 'N' Roll* there. The two quickly became good friends.

Elton John VIP pass, courtesy of Elton John.

The following summer, Elton performed on Lennon's *Walls And Bridges* album. According to Lennon, Elton was certain *Whatever Gets You Thru The Night* was going to be John's first number one hit, and made a disbelieving Lennon promise that if it was, he would have to perform it live at Madison Square Garden with Elton later in the year. In the retrospective box set *To Be Continued...* Elton claims he said the album *Walls And Bridges* would become a number one hit. Lennon's version makes more sense because Elton's major contribution to *Walls And Bridges* was on *Whatever Get You Thru The Night*, and Lennon already had a number one hit album with *Imagine*.

A few weeks later, Lennon visited Elton at the Caribou Ranch Recording Studios in Colorado. While there, Elton recorded the Lennon compositions *Lucy In The Sky With Diamonds* and *One Day At A Time*. Most reliable publications list Lennon as contributing guitar and background vocals to *Lucy In The Sky With Diamonds*, but the detailed credit sheet in *To Be Continued...* only lists Lennon on guitar. However, Lennon can clearly be heard singing in the background. Lennon also stated on numerous occasions that he came up with the new reggae bridge for the song. *Lucy In The Sky With Diamonds* was the first single issued by Elton, which he didn't write that was a number one hit. Most reliable publications also list Lennon playing guitar on *One Day At A Time*, but the credits for *To Be Continued...* only lists him on background vocals, which are not readily detectable. Gus Dudgeon, who produced both songs, said, "John only performed on *Lucy In The Sky With Diamonds*. Half the time he couldn't remember the chords and had to get Davey Johnstone to show them to him. He was so unimpressed with his playing, other than the reggae bit, which was his idea, that we wiped all but that section of it. He also sang backing vocals on it. He made no contribution to *One Day At A Time*." [The credits also fail to mention that Lennon plays guitar on the Madison Square Garden performance of *I Saw Her Standing There*.] Gus lamented, "No one asked me for information for the credits and booklet, which are inaccurate. This happens often and pisses me off."

Whatever Get You Thru The Night and the album *Walls And Bridges* were number one hits and Elton held Lennon to his promise. Lennon strolled onstage in front of an audience that included Yoko Ono*, who he was estranged from at the time, and confidently sang *Whatever Gets You Through The Night*, *Lucy In The Sky With Diamonds* and *I Saw Her Standing There* with Elton. Lennon also played tambourine on the encore of *The Bitch Is Back*. Elton has stated that the band was brought to tears by the nearly 10 minutes of applause Lennon received. These live recordings, except *The Bitch Is Back*, are difficult to categorize as they appear on John Lennon and Elton John records, and are Lennon or Beatles' songs, with Lennon and Elton singing duet vocals. However, these songs are generally categorized as John Lennon contributions to an Elton John performance. They are officially credited as the Elton John Band Featuring John Lennon And The Muscle Shoals Horns, and controlled by Dick James Music (Elton) and not EMI (Lennon). Elton's *Here And There* is the only album that contains Lennon's entire performance. Over the years Elton has performed several Beatles' songs in public.

Elton remained one of Lennon's few close friends during his nearly five year retreat from music and the public, and was named godfather of John and Yoko's son, Sean. Following Lennon's murder, Elton and Taupin wrote a tribute, *Empty Garden (Hey Hey Johnny)*, which Elton performed to a very full Madison Square Garden in August 1982, joined onstage by Yoko and Sean. George Harrison joined Elton onstage for *Empty Garden (Hey Hey Johnny)* on March 19, 1982 in Sydney, Australia, which reportedly was recorded. Elton released another tribute to Lennon, *The Man Who Never Died*, in 1985. A film clip of Elton singing *Imagine* from his Central Park concert was included on the 1991 video release *The World's Greatest Artists Sing LENNON A Tribute.*

Elton played with Paul McCartney at *The Prince's Trust 10th Anniversary Concert* on June 20, 1986, and for *The Prince's Trust Rock Concert* on June 5 and 6, 1987 with Harrison and Starr, at London's Wembley Arena. Elton also appeared in the music video for *When We Was Fab* from Harrison's 1987 album *Cloud Nine* on which he also played. That year he was reportedly going to produce recordings for Ringo, which never took place. Elton was part of the all-star jam with George and Ringo when The Beatles were inducted into the Rock and Roll Hall of Fame on January 20, 1988 at New York's Waldorf Astoria Hotel, portions of which are available on unauthorized releases. Elton backed McCartney on several songs and sang a verse of *Hey Jude* during their performance at the *Music For Montserrat* benefit concert on September 15, 1997 at London's Royal Albert Hall. On May 21, 1998 Elton performed *Great Balls Of Fire* and *Twist And Shout* backed by Ringo on drums at the *Cinema Against AIDS* benefit at the *Cannes Film Festival.* Elton John continues to write, record and perform, taking his place as one of the most successful songwriters and entertainers in pop music history. For more information go to www.eltonjohn.com

Elton John, Coliseum, Fort Wayne, IN June 8, 1999.
© and photo by Kristofer Engelhardt.

Howard Jones

Ringo Starr And His All Starr Band-Extended Versions
BMG-75517465252 (04/01/03)
Producer: Ringo Starr & David Fishof
Ringo Starr: Drums; Howard Jones: Lead Vocals & Keyboards; Ian Hunter: Guitar; Roger Hodgson: Guitar & B. Vocals; Sheila Escovedo: Drums & B. Vocals; Greg Lake: Bass; Mark Rivera: Keyboards & B. Vocals
Rosemont Theater, Rosemont (Chicago), IL 08/22/01

Everlasting Love [live] (H. Jones) 5:11 (9)

Ringo Starr & His New All-Starr Band
Pioneer/Win Media-11907 (DVD) (10/01/02)

Howard Jones, Freedom Hill, Sterling Heights (Detroit), MI July 28, 2001. © and photo by Kristofer Engelhardt.

Producer: (recorded, mixed and mastered by: Glen Robinson); Executive Producer: Ringo Starr & David Fishof
Ringo Starr: Drums; Howard Jones: Lead Vocals & Keyboards; Ian Hunter: Acoustic Guitar & B. Vocals; Roger Hodgson: Electric Guitar & B. Vocals; Sheila Escovedo: Drums; Greg Lake: Bass; Mark Rivera: Percussion
Rosemont Theater, Rosemont (Chicago), IL 08/22/01

No One Is To Blame [live] (H. Jones) 5:38 (12)
[Also available on King Biscuit Flower Hour/Razor & Tie-7930188003-2 (4) (08/06/02)]

Things Can Only Get Better [live] (H. Jones) 6:33 (9)
Additionally: Ian Hunter: Acoustic Guitar (only); Sheila Escovedo: B. Vocals; Mark Rivera: Saxophone & B. Vocals (only)

Howard, born John Howard Jones on February 23, 1955 in Southampton, England, began taking piano lessons at age seven and by 15 joined his first band. His proficiency on keyboards and synthesizer earned him billing with a number of emerging UK artists in the early 1980s whose music would be termed New Wave. In 1983 he was signed to WEA Records and released the album *Human's Lib*, which was a number one hit in the UK. The album produced the Top 40 hits *New Song* and *What Is Love?* His 1985 album *Dream Into Action* was a Top 10 hit and included the Top Five hits *Things Can Only Get Better* and *No One Is To Blame*, and the Top 20 hit *Life In One Day*. He had a Top 20 hit with *You Know I Love You...Don't You?* in 1986. His last Top 20 hit was *Everlasting Love* in 1989. Jones was a member of Ringo Starr's All-Starr Band in 2001 performing *No One Is To Blame*, *Things Can Only Get Better* and *Everlasting Love* with backing from Ringo on drums. For more information go to www.howardjones.com

Kenney Jones

[None]
[Unreleased]
Producer: Mentor Williams
Paul McCartney: Bass & (possible) B. Vocals; Kenney Jones: Lead Vocals & Drums; Al Kooper: Keyboards; Mentor Williams: Guitar; Denny Laine: Guitar & B. Vocals; Danny Kortchmar: Guitar; Linda McCartney: Keyboards
Probably Record Plant or possibly Wally Heider Studios, Los Angeles, CA 03-04/xx/75

Baby Blue Eyes (M. Williams)

So High (Rock Me Baby, Roll Me Away) (M. Williams)

Kenney Jones was born September 16, 1948 in London, England. He first gained notice as the drummer and founding member of The Small Faces and later Faces (see Ian McLagan, Rod Stewart). The May 10, 1975 issue of *Melody Maker* magazine reported that Jones had cut a single in Los Angeles, produced by Mentor Williams, with contributions from Paul and Linda McCartney*. According to Jones, Paul played bass on the songs *So High (Rock Me Baby, Roll Me Away)* and *Baby Blue Eyes*, and might have sung backing vocals. Jones could not remember the studio where the songs were recorded, but thinks it might have been The Record Plant or possibly Wally Heider Studios in Los Angeles. These recordings have yet to be released.

Jones was part of the Rockestra ensemble on Wings' 1979 album *Back To The Egg* and on the 1981 album *Concerts For The People Of Kampuchea* recorded at London's Hammersmith Odeon on December 29, 1979. Jones replaced Keith Moon* in The Who (see Roger Daltrey, John Entwistle) from 1979 to 1988. Jones was in a band called The Law with Paul Rodgers (see: Simon Kirke). In 2001 he formed The Jones Gang. They had a number one hit with *Angel* in 2005. For more information go to www.thesmallfaces.com

Paul Jones

The Paul Jones Collection-Vol. 3-Come Into My Music Box
RPM-183 (UK) (xx/xx/98)
Producer: Peter Asher
Paul McCartney: Drums; Paul Jones: Lead Vocals; Jeff Beck: Guitar; Paul Samwell-Smith: Bass
EMI-Abbey Road Studios, London, UK 02/xx/68

And The Sun Will Shine (R. Gibb-B. Gibb-M. Gibb) 3:00 (15) (03/08/68)
Additionally: Nicky Hopkins: Keyboards; Clair Asher: B. Vocals; Dr. Richard Asher: B. Vocals; Mike Vickers: Arrangement & Conductor

The Dog Presides (P. Jones) 2:45 (16) (03/08/68)

Paul Jones was born Paul Pond on February 24, 1942 in Portsmouth, England. He was an original member and the lead vocalist of the band Manfred Mann, which also included Mann, Mike Hugg, Dave Richmond and Mike Vickers. Later members included Tom McGuinness, Jack Bruce* and Klaus Voormann*. Jones left Manfred Mann in 1966 to concentrate on his solo music and acting career, and was replaced by Mike D'Abo. Paul soon had hits with *High Time* and *I've Been A Bad, Bad Boy*, and formed several short-lived bands.

In 1968 Peter Asher (see Peter & Gordon) was to produce Paul's cover of The Bee Gees' song *And The Sun Will Shine*. Asher mentioned to Jones that Paul McCartney, then engaged to his sister Jane, was looking to do some session work as a drummer and wondered if Jones would be interested in having him play on his sessions. Jones, who accepted McCartney's offer, says Asher also brought along his sister Clair to play keyboards and their mother Margaret to sing backing vocals. Peter says, "Nicky Hopkins played keyboards, and Clair and my father sang backing vocals on *And The Sun Will Shine*." Jones says, "McCartney also played drums on *The Dog Presides*," the single's B-side.

Jones starred in the 1967 film *Privilege*, and has landed acting roles in the stage productions of *Cats*, *Guys And Dolls*, *Joseph And The Amazing Technicolor Dream Coat* and other productions. He and his wife have hosted a UK version of Pat Robertson's *The 700 Club* TV show. He also hosts a BBC radio show. In 1979 Jones formed The Blues Band with McGuinness. Since 1991 Jones, McGuinness, Hugg and D'Abo also tour as The Manfreds. Jones released a solo album in 2009 but has never found success in the US. For more information go to www.pauljones.eu, www.themanfreds.com, www.thebluesband.com

Jotta Herre

All You Need Is Lisboa
EMI-724359339122 (Portugal) (01/26/04)
Producer: Jose Martin
Probably Lisbon, Portugal 01-02/xx/69

Penina (P. McCartney) 3:04 (9) (probably 03/xx/69)
Anibal Cunha, Carlos Pinto, Rui Pereira: Keyboards; Giuseppe Carlo: Drums

In Paul McCartney's *Club Sandwich* fan club magazine (winter 1994 issue No. 72) Paul says, "I went to Portugal on holiday and returned to the hotel one night slightly the worse for a few drinks. There was a band playing and I ended up on the drums. The hotel was called *Penina*, I made up a song with that name, someone made inquiries about it and I gave it to them. And, no, I shouldn't think I'd ever record it myself!" Apparently, at the time McCartney didn't inform his publishing company about the composition, who reportedly were quite upset when they learned about it in the press. Contrary to previous reports, it was a Portuguese (not Dutch) band, Jotta Herre that

McCartney sat in with around mid-December 1968. Giuseppe Flamino was the group's drummer the night Paul showed up, but he was replaced some weeks later by Giuseppe Carlo. Flamino recalls that McCartney put on a great show playing drums, guitar, piano and bass with the band. He says Paul wrote the melody and lyrics around four in the morning naming the song after the hotel and offered it to the band. By most accounts they were the first to issue it on the Philips EP (431923PE) in Portugal, probably in June or July 1969. The song never charted. Jotta Herre broke up in 1975.

Around the same time Carlos Mendes, a popular Portuguese singer from the pop group Sheiks, who recorded for EMI, released a version of *Penina*. *Club Sandwich* (summer 1995 issue No. 74) lists the Mendes' single as being issued in March 1969, while other sources list the date more specifically as July 18, 1969. It would seem more likely that the earlier date is when Jotta Herre's version was released and the later date when Mendes' version was release. Though there's no confirmation that Jotta Herre's version was issued first, it is certain that McCartney intended it for them. In all likelihood, Mendes heard Jotta Herre's version, and quickly covered it to try and cash in on the obscure song written by McCartney. Both versions were included on the 2004 Portuguese CD *All You Need Is Lisboa*. Contrary to McCartney's statement, it has been reported that he recorded the song, though the only version by him known to exist is his brief piano rendition of it from rehearsals in January 1969 for The Beatles' *Let It Be* project, which is available on unauthorized releases.

The Joyful Company Of Singers

a Garland *for* Linda
EMI Classics-7243 5 56961 2 0 (04/25/00) (02/07/00) **Paul McCartney: Liner Notes**
Producer: John Fraser
The Joyful Company of Singers (Peter Broadbent: Conductor & Chorus Master; Patricia Bentley: Soprano Vocals; Hilary Brennan: Soprano Vocals; Polly Carnegie: Soprano Vocals; Cathryn Caunt: Soprano Vocals; Bridget Corderoy: Soprano Vocals; Sally Donegani: Soprano Vocals; Harriet Fraser: Soprano Vocals; Amanda Gibbs: Soprano Vocals; Claire Hills: Soprano Vocals; Victoria Kendall: Soprano Vocals; Rachel King: Soprano Vocals; Felice Kuin: Soprano Vocals; Helen Morton: Soprano Vocals; Clare Porter: Soprano Vocals; Katherine Willis: Soprano Vocals; Debbie Bright: Alto Vocals; Kathryn Cook: Alto Vocals; Rosemary Day: Alto Vocals; Denise Fabb: Alto Vocals; Henrietta Hillman: Alto Vocals; Yvette Miller: Alto Vocals; Rachel Reeves: Alto Vocals; Fiona Robinson: Alto Vocals; Lorna Youngs: Alto Vocals; Simon Colston: Tenor Vocals; Colin Fleming: Tenor Vocals; Alex Hayes: Tenor Vocals; Andrew Shepstone: Tenor Vocals; Paul Zimmerman: Tenor Vocals; Tim Bull: Bass Vocals; Tim Colborn: Bass Vocals; Peter Da Costa: Bass Vocals; Michael King: Bass Vocals; Andy Mackinder: Bass Vocals; Greg Masters: Bass Vocals; David Rees-Jones: Bass Vocals; Garrod Stephen: Bass Vocals; Chris Williams: Bass Vocals); John Harle: Arrangement
All Saints Church, London, UK 08/30/99

Nova (**P. McCartney**) 6:27 (6)

A Garland for Linda was the result of a collaboration between Paul McCartney, whose wife Linda McCartney* had recently died of cancer, and Stephen Connock a cancer survivor launching The Garland Appeal, a UK charity whose aim is to raise money and fight cancer through music. McCartney contributed his composition *Nova* to the project performed by the chamber choir The Joyful Company Of Singers. The choir was formed in 1988 and has performed throughout Europe and the US. The album features contributions from some of the UK's finest classical composers including John Rutter, John Tavener*, and Richard Rodney Bennett and David Mathews, who worked with McCartney on *Standing Stone* (see The London Symphony Orchestra & Chorus). Conductor and chorus master Peter Broadbent recalls, "I was changing in the restroom before our first rehearsal and turned around to see Sir Paul McCartney – the man who had provided the soundtrack for much of my youth. He turned up unannounced chatting to the singers, and making enthusiastic and encouraging comments during much of our rehearsal." The works were premiered on July 18, 1999 at the chapel of Charterhouse School in Surrey, UK and conducted by Richard Hickox. They were recorded and produced later that summer in London by John Fraser, who has produced nearly all of McCartney's classical works. Broadbent says, "Sir Paul wanted the CD to be recorded by EMI, and Hickox was exclusively contracted to Chandos Records, so I took over the conducting duties at that point." For more information go to www.jcos.co.uk

Laurence Juber

Standard Time
Breaking Records-BREAK 1 (album 12") (07/09/82)
Producer: Paul McCartney & Chris Thomas, & Laurence Juber & Richard Niles
Paul McCartney: Bass; Laurence Juber: Guitars; Denny Laine: Harmonica; Steve Holly: Drums
Spirit of Ranachan, Kintyre, Scotland† & Air Studios London, UK 06/xx/78† & xx/xx/79

Maisie (L. Juber) 3:10 (1/3)

Laurence Juber was born on November 12, 1952 in London, England. He began playing guitar when he was 11. He attended Goldsmith's College and the University of London and earned a bachelor's degree in music in 1975. Juber joined the National Youth Jazz Orchestra, and did session work for Cleo Laine, Shirley Bassey, John Williams*, Jimmy Rafferty and others. He was the backup guitarist during Denny Laine's* appearance on BBC TV's *David Essex Show*.

Laurence Juber, White's Bar, Saginaw, MI September 27, 2007. © and photo by Kristofer Engelhardt.

Through Laine's recommendation, Juber became the third and final lead guitarist for Wings in the summer of 1978 as recordings began for what proved to be Wings' last studio album *Back To The Egg*. Juber remembers, "I was surprised at the freedom I had to develop my guitar part with Paul. He rarely dictated to me, but instead encouraged me. He has such a clear vision that he made it easy for me to find my 'voice' within the band texture. He was also quite free with many useful tricks and tips. For example, he once suggested that I play a strummed rhythm guitar part without accenting the up and down strokes, a technique I've since used on many sessions. During the demo for the song *Love Awake* Paul and Denny played acoustic guitar, so I played bass. Paul graciously told me he liked my bass part and wanted me to do it on the master. Then he kneeled on the floor next to me and gave me a lesson in right-handed bass picking – how cool!"

In late 1979 Wings toured the UK. In January 1980, upon arrival in Japan for a tour, McCartney was arrested and jailed for possession of marijuana, and deported, forcing the tour's cancellation. Following his return to the UK, McCartney pursued solo projects, leaving Wings hanging in midair, but still utilized their talents. Juber says, "In mid-1980 Paul invited me to go to France for about 10 days of work on Ringo's 1981 album *Stop And Smell The Roses*. Laying down the first track, with Paul on piano and Ringo on drums, I was immediately struck by the amazing, potent synergy between them. I was thinking, 'Wow, I'm playing with half of The Beatles!'

Juber went to work on an instrumental solo album of old standards titled *Standard Time*. All the songs were part of McCartney's publishing catalogue that he wanted Juber to record. The album was originally intended to be more of a demonstration record of Juber's talents than a commercial release. McCartney set Wings free in 1981. In 1982 Juber released five of the standards on his Breaking Records label. The limited edition album (1,000 copies) kept the original title. It also included Juber's composition *Maisie*, recorded during sessions for *Back To The Egg*, featuring McCartney on bass. According to Juber, McCartney was also involved in the production of *Maisie*.

Juber worked with George Harrison on the *Shanghai Surprise* (see Various Artists-Shanghai Surprise) soundtrack version of Harrison's song *Breath Away From Heaven.* Juber recalls, "I became involved with George in April 1986 through producer Rob Rose who I'd worked with on a Donovan* project. My wife Hope was about to give birth to our daughter Ilsey and, as it turned out, I went straight from her delivery to the studio to work with George. Hope really wanted to meet George, who later called her and was quite charming. A few days later we took Ilsey to Village Recorders and George gave her an Indian blessing of the gift of music (which has worked really well, I might add) and some lovely toys. I played acoustic guitar on *Breath Away From Heaven* with George borrowing one of my guitars and my gear for some overdubs. George and I shared a microphone doing backing vocals while he told me stories of him and Paul recording backing vocals on the *Sgt. Pepper's Lonely Hearts Club Band* album. George and Ringo were very comfortable to work with."

Laurence has released over a dozen albums, including covers of The Beatles' songs, and has won two Grammy Awards. He has done music for CBS TV's *As The World Turns*, and scores for his father-in-law Sherwood Schwartz, producer of such well-known TV series as *Gilligan's Island* and *The Brady Bunch*. Juber, a frequent guest at conventions and festivals for fans of The Beatles, performed with fellow Wings' members Denny Laine and Steve Holly at one in the New York area in 1997. For more information go to www.laurencejuber.com

Jungle Juice

The Zoo Gang / Monkey Business
Bradleys-BRAD 7407-A (7" single) (UK) (05/24/74)
Producer: Tony Hiller
Colin Frechter: Keyboards
Pye Studios, London, UK 03/xx/74

The Zoo Gang (**P. McCartney**-L. McCartney) 2:00 (1/1)

On June 28, 1974 Paul McCartney and Wings' single *Band On The Run* was released in the UK. On the flip side was *Zoo Gang*, an instrumental written by Paul and Linda McCartney*. Few noticed that a version featured several weeks earlier as the theme song for the UK TV mini-series *The Zoo Gang* sounded slightly different. In McCartney's fan club magazine *Club Sandwich* (summer 1996 issue No. 78) it states that Sir Lew Grade, whose ATV network produced *The Zoo Gang*, and who had a publishing connection with McCartney, asked him to compose the instrumental theme music for the show. Paul and Linda wrote and recorded it but wanted to release it as the B-side of the *Band On The Run* single, which was scheduled for release several weeks after the TV series was to end. Therefore, Grade quickly ordered that some studio musicians be gathered to record the song to use for the show. It was also issued as a single by Jungle Juice, produced by Tony Hiller, on Grade's Bradleys Records on May 24, 1974, making them the first to release the McCartney composition by nearly five weeks. Hiller recalls, "I was producing for ATV music. It was a quick request to cover a song, written by Paul and Linda McCartney, by ATV who held the publishing rights. We booked various session musicians at Pye Studios in London but I don't recall any of them except Colin Frechter who played keyboards. I named the group Jungle Juice because of the song titles." For more information go to www.tonyhiller.com

Bobby Keys

Bobby Keys
Warner Bros.-K 46141 (album 12") (UK) (07/07/72)
Producer: Bobby Keys, Andy Johns & Jim Gordon
George Harrison (probable) Guitar; **Ringo Starr: (probable) Drums**. Additionally, one or more of the following: Dave Mason: Guitar; Eric Clapton: Guitar; Klaus Voormann: Bass; Jim Price: Horns; Jim Gordon: Drums; Bobby Keys: Horns; Nicky Hopkins: Keyboards; Leslie West: Guitar; Felix Pappalardi: Keyboards; Corky Laing: Drums &/or Percussion; Jack Bruce: Bass; The Dixie Flyers (probably one or more of the following: Jim Dickenson: Guitar; Charlie Freeman: Saxophone; Tommy McClure: Bass;

Sammy Creason: Drums)
One or more of the following studios: Command, Island or Olympic, London, UK 01/xx/72

Bootleg (C. Axton-D. Dunn-W. Jackson-I. Hayes) 3:42 (1/3)

Bobby Keys was born on December 18, 1943 in Slaton, Texas. By age 14 he was playing saxophone on tour with Buddy Holly and The Crickets*. During the first half of the 1970s Keys contributed to album sessions for George Harrison's *All Things Must Pass*, John Lennon's *Rock 'N' Roll*, *Some Time In New York City* and *Walls And Bridges*, and Ringo Starr's *Ringo* and *Goodnight Vienna*. He came to their attention through his membership in Delaney & Bonnie & Friends*, and was later a member of Joe Cocker's* Mad Dogs & Englishmen, who were remnants of that band. Keys has done session work for countless other artists and worked extensively with The Rolling Stones* for decades.

The reputable book *All Together Now* lists Ringo playing drums and Harrison playing guitar on the 1972 album *Bobby Keys*. Its co-author Wally Podrazik says the two were listed in the general credit on a sticker of a promotional copy of the album. It's difficult to determine what songs they may play on because their style of playing is similar to some of the other artists who play on the album, which also includes Jack Bruce*, Dave Mason*, Jim Price (see All Occasion Brass Band), Jim Gordon (see Derek And The Dominos), Nicky Hopkins*, Klaus Voormann* and Eric Clapton*, all of whom worked with George or Ringo during this period. Clapton is known to play on *Bootleg*, *Command Performance*, *Steal From A King* and *Crispy Duck*. Keys says Harrison and Ringo contributed to his album, but he doesn't recall on which tracks. However, Andy Johns (who admitted he wasn't present for all of the sessions), Jack Bruce and Jim Price don't recall any Beatles at the sessions they attended. After a more recent listen to the album, Johns and Price seriously doubt that Ringo or George play on it. If they did contribute to the album, it's likely on the song *Bootleg*. The album's remaining tracks are *Sand & Foam*, *Smokefoot*, *Alter Rock* and *Key West*.

In 1972 Keys appeared in a musical scene in Harry Nilsson* and Ringo's film *Son Of Dracula*. In 1975 Ring O'Records released Key's single *Gimmie The Key / Honky Tonk (Parts 1 & 2)*. Keys, and the record's producer Trevor Lawrence, are quite certain Ringo didn't contribute to this single. Keys still does some session work but has been less active in recent years.

Aashish Khan

[None]
[Unreleased]
George Harrison: Guitar; **Ringo Starr: Drums**; Eric Clapton: Guitar
Trident Studios, London, UK xx/xx/69 or xx/xx/70

In Praise Of Lord (We Are All Children Of God) (A. Khan)

Young Master Of The Sarod
World Pacific-WPS-21444 (album 12") (probably 10/xx/67) **George Harrison: Liner Notes**

Aashish Khan was born on December 5, 1939 in Maihar, India. He is the eldest son of Ali Akbar Khan. Aashish, like his famous father and grandfather Ustad Allauddin Khan, is a master of the sarod. He began performing with his father and grandfather when he was 12. He often fuses his North Indian classical music with Western classical, jazz and pop music. He has composed music for many Indian and Western films including *The Man Who Would Be King*, *Gandhi* and *Passage To India*. Khan has been a music faculty member of a number of universities, including the University Of Calgary in Alberta, Canada where he and his brother Pranesh founded the Allauddin School Of Performing Arts. Khan is currently serving on the faculty of the California Institute Of The Arts. He is a recipient of the Sangeet Natak Akademi, India's highest award for performing arts.

Khan has worked with Ravi Shankar* (an uncle by marriage) and George Harrison. He is featured on the album *Shankar Family & Friends,* produced by Harrison, and worked with Harrison on the soundtrack for the film *Wonderwall.* Harrison wrote the liner notes for Khan's album *Young Master Of The Sarod* during a visit in August 1967 to Ravi Shankar's Kinnara School of Indian Music in Los Angeles where Aashish taught.

Aashish said Harrison, Ringo Starr, Eric Clapton* and a keyboard player helped him record a song tentatively titled *In Praise Of Lord (We Are All Children Of God)* that was a fusion of rock and Indian music sung in the Hindi language. Khan said the song was recorded at Trident Studios in London in 1969 or 1970, and was intended for a film soundtrack [probably Raga] but was never used.

B.B. King

In London
Beat Goes On-BGOCD42 (France/UK) (01/xx/91) (10/11/71)
Producer: Ed Michel & Joe Zagarino
Ringo Starr: Drums; B.B. King: Lead Vocals & Guitar; Klaus Voormann: Bass; Gary Wright: Keyboards
Olympic Studios, London, UK 06/09-16/71

Ghetto Woman (B.B. King-D. Clark) 5:13 (5)
Additionally: Jim Price: Electric Piano; Dr. John: Guitar; Jim Gordon: Drums; Jimmie Haskell: String Arrangement & Conductor

Part-Time Love (C. Hammond) 3:17 (7)
Additionally: Jim Price: Trumpet; Bobby Keys: Tenor Saxophone

Wet Hayshark (G. Wright) 2:31 (6)
Additionally: Jim Price: Trumpet; Bobby Keys: Tenor Saxophone; Jim Gordon: Drums

B.B. King was born Riley B. King on September 16, 1925 in Itta Bene, Mississippi, in the heart of delta blues country. His formative years, like most of America's great delta blues artists, were spent working in cotton fields, singing in the church choir and as a busker. While a DJ and performer on a Memphis R&B radio station in the late 1940s, he earned the title "Beale Street Blues Boy," which was later shortened to "B.B." Topping the R&B charts with the song *Three O'Clock Blues* in 1951 soon had King playing the blues circuit. By the 1960s, he'd gained a cult following and finally international recognition with his R&B hits *Paying The Cost To Be The Boss* and *Why I Sing The Blues.* King also had a Top 20 hit with *The Thrill Is Gone* in 1970.

In June 1971 King was in London to record his album *In London* with many of the UK's rock and blues elite contributing, including Ringo Starr. *Melody Maker* magazine reported that John Lennon was also scheduled to attend the sessions, but didn't make it back from the US in time. Portions of the sessions were filmed. B.B. King was inducted into the Blues Foundation Hall of Fame in 1984 and the Rock and Roll Hall of Fame in 1987. He continues to tour extensively, record and work with blues and rock artists. For more information go to www.bbking.com

Kristofer Engelhardt and B. B. King, Interlochen Center For The Arts, Interlochen (Traverse City) MI June 17, 1999. © Kristofer Engelhardt.

Ben E. King

Rock And Roll Hall Of Fame & Museum
Time Life-24943-X (Whole Lotta Shakin' Live) (24633-X) (DVD) (10/20/09)
Producer: Bob Sarles & Christina Keating
George Harrison: Electric Guitar & (probable) B. Vocals; Ringo Starr: (possible) Drums; Ben E. King: Vocals; Julian Lennon: Vocals & Guitar; Paul Shaffer: Keyboards; Billy Joel: Keyboards & B. Vocals; Dave Edmunds: Electric Guitar; Bob Dylan: Electric Guitar; Les Paul: Electric Guitar; Jeff Beck: Electric Guitar; Mick Jagger: B. Vocals; John Fogerty: Electric Guitar; Bruce Springsteen: B. Vocals & Tambourine; Mary Wilson: B. Vocals; Mike Love: Handclaps; Alan Jardine: Handclaps; probably one or more of the following: Bruce Johnston: B. Vocals & Percussion; Little Richard: Percussion; Elton John: Keyboards; Anton Fig: Drums; Sid McGinnis: Guitar; Arlo Guthrie: Guitar or Percussion; Peter Wolf: Percussion & B. Vocals; Johnny Moore: B. Vocals & Percussion; Joe Blunt: Percussion; Clyde Brown: B. Vocals & Percussion; Bill Pinkney: B. Vocals & Percussion; Charlie Thomas: B. Vocals & Percussion; Max Weinberg: Percussion; Will Lee: Bass; Roy Bittan: Keyboards; Nile Rodgers: Guitar; Patti Scialfa: Handclaps & B. Vocals
Grand Ballroom Waldorf-Astoria Hotel, New York, NY 01/20/88

Stand By Me [live] (B. King-J. Leiber-M. Stoller) 4:30 (5-6)

Unbootlegged 5 [The Beatles]
No Label Records-NLR 0105 (CD-R) [unauthorized release] (xx/xx/01)
Producer: Midge Ure
George Harrison: Guitar & B. Vocals; Ringo Starr: Tambourine & B. Vocals; Ben E. King: Lead Vocals; Eric Clapton: Guitar & B. Vocals; Phil Collins: Drums & B. Vocals; Ray Cooper: Percussion; Midge Ure: Guitar & B. Vocals; Mark King: Bass; Jools Holland: Keyboards; Mark Brzezicki: Drums; Mike Lindup: Keyboards; Jimmy Chambers: B. Vocals; Jimmy Helms: B. Vocals; George Chandler : B. Vocals; Spook Dexter: B. Vocals; Duke Dexter B. Vocals; Frankie Dexter: B. Vocals; Brian Adams; Guitar & B. Vocals; Dave Edmunds: Guitar & B. Vocals; Jeff Lynne: Guitar & B. Vocals; Elton John: B. Vocals; Paul Young: B. Vocals; Ben Volpeliere-Pierrot: B. Vocals
Wembley Arena, London, UK 06/05/87

Stand By Me [live] (B. King-J. Leiber-M. Stoller) 7:10 (14)

Ben E. King was born Benjamin Earl Nelson on September 28, 1938 in Henderson, North Carolina but grew up in the Harlem District of New York. By 1958 Nelson was a member of the doo-wop group The Five Crowns who were soon drafted by The Drifter's management to replace the original members in the R&B group. Nelson began writing songs for The Drifters including their 1959 Top Five hit *There Goes My Baby*, which he sang. He also sang The Drifters' Top 20 hit *This Magic Moment* and their only number one hit *Save The Last Dance For Me.* He left The Drifters in 1960 and pursued a solo career under the name Ben E. King. In 1961 he had a Top 10 hit with *Spanish Harlem*, a Top Five hit with *Stand By Me*, which he co-wrote, and a Top 20 hit with *Amor* making him an international star. He had a Top 20 hit with *Don't Play That Song (You Lied)* in 1962. Like many American acts, he suffered in the charts following the British music invasion in 1964. He continued to record and finally had a Top Five hit in 1975 with *Supernatural Thing, Part 1.* During the mid-1970s King worked with the Average White Band (see Hamish Stuart). In 1986 *Stand By Me*, included on the soundtrack of the film *Stand By Me*, became a Top 10 hit for the second time.

The Beatles were huge fans of The Drifters and Ben E. King. They often performed *Save The Last Dance For Me* in their early 1960's live set. The Beatles originally intended to use a portion of their recording of the song on their *Let It Be* album. King says, "I first met The Beatles before they ever came to the US because I toured the UK often and Brian Epstein would bring them to my shows. I learned later that they were huge fans of mine. They were great kids – full of excitement about the business and very positive."

John Lennon and Paul McCartney jammed on *Stand By Me* in 1973 during their only get together in the studio after the breakup of The Beatles. Lennon was recording a cover of the song at the time, which he had a Top 20 hit with in 1975. "I loved John's cover of it. He made it belong to him. It's at the top of my list of covers of one of my songs. One of the greatest compliments a songwriter can get is to have another great songwriter cover one of your songs. It's the compliment of all complements," admits King.

George Harrison and Ringo Starr remained onstage playing as King did an encore of *Stand By Me* the first night of *The Prince's Trust Concert* in 1987. King recalls, "They didn't rehearse it with me. They just stayed on and played with me because everybody knows that song. George was one of the nicest people I ever met. We had some great conversations, not about show business but about life. He was greatly underrated as a songwriter. I've also chatted with Paul at numerous award ceremonies over the years." King and The Drifters were inducted into the Rock and Roll Hall of Fame along with The Beatles on January 20, 1988 at New York's Waldorf Astoria Hotel, and took part in the all-star jam with Harrison and Starr. On June 15, 2000 McCartney, James Taylor* and others joined King singing *Stand By Me* and *Kansas City* at ceremonies for the Songwriters Hall of Fame at the Sheraton New York Hotel & Towers. King continues to record and tour. For more information go to www.benekingstandbyme.org

Solomon King

The Best Of Solomon King
One-Up/EMI-OU 2098 (album 12") (UK)
Producer: Peter Sullivan
EMI-Abbey Road Studios, London, UK probably 07/09/68

Hava Nagila (trad. Arr: S. King) 3:10 (1/3) (08/03/68)
Ringo Starr: (probable) Handclaps & (possible) B. Vocals & (possible) Tambourine; Solomon King: Lead Vocals; Charles Blackwell: Orchestra Conductor & Arranger

Somewhere In The Crowd (L. Reed-Rae) 2:40 (2/7) (08/03/68)
Ringo Starr: (possible) B. Vocals; Solomon King: Lead Vocals; Les Reed: Orchestra Conductor & Arranger

A Hundred Years Or More / Cry Softly
Capitol-2622 (7" single)
Producer: Peter Sullivan
Ringo Starr: (possible) Tambourine; Solomon King: Lead Vocals; Johnny Harris: Arranger & Conductor
EMI-Abbey Road Studios, London, UK 07/09/68

A Hundred Years Or More (C. Tobias) 2:55 (1/1) (probably 08/xx/69)

Solomon King (a.k.a. Randy Leeds and Levi Jackson) was born Allen Levy in Lexington, Kentucky in 1932. He attended the Cincinnati Conservatory of Music as a teenager and later became a backing singer for Elvis Presley. He moved to the UK in 1965. Known as Solomon King, after signing with manager Gordon Mills, who also managed Tom Jones and Engelbert Humperdinck, he adopted a somewhat similar style. King had the UK Top Five hit *She Wears My Ring* in 1967 and a UK Top 40 hit with *When We Were Young* in 1968 before fading from the charts.

There is much confusion surrounding possible contributions by Ringo Starr to several of King's recordings. Publications of varying reliability have reported Ringo as possibly contributing background vocals, drums, tambourine and, or handclaps to King's recordings of *A Hundred Years Or More*, *Hava Nagila* and *Somewhere In The Crowd*. The September 1968 issue of *The Beatles Book Monthly* magazine reported that Ringo attended a Solomon King recording session on July 9 at Abbey Road Studios, to add a bit of handclaps while waiting for the other Beatles to arrive. Mark Lewisohn checked Abbey Road Studios' files and found that King recorded the song *A Hundred Years Or More* on that date. There are no audible handclaps but there is a prominent tambourine throughout the recording, which may be what Ringo contributed. King's recording of *Hava Nagila* does contain handclaps, and may also include Ringo playing tambourine and, or singing in the background. That single's A-side, *Somewhere In The Crowd*, is also rumored to feature Ringo on background vocals, though this may just be the result of confusion with the B-side. It's also possible that Ringo drummed on these recordings, though it sounds unlikely. Considering the evidence and the recordings, it seems likely that Ringo did the handclaps and possibly background vocals, or tambourine on *Hava Nagila*, and possibly tambourine on *A Hundred Years Or More*. *A Hundred Years Or More* was originally issued in the UK as the B-side of King's single *Goodbye My Old Gal* (Columbia-DB 8505). King returned to the US in 1980 and performed until a few years before his death on January 20, 2005.

Simon Kirke

The Best Of Ringo Starr And His All-Starr Band...So Far
Image-ID0828RO (DVD) (10/23/01)
Producer: Michael Drumm; David & Ryan Hewitt (music mixers); Peter Skorich (video); Executive Producer: Ringo Starr & David Fishof
Ringo Starr: Drums; Simon Kirke: Lead Vocals & Drums; Gary Brooker: Keyboards & B. Vocals; Jack Bruce: Bass & B. Vocals; Peter Frampton: Guitar & B. Vocals; Mark Rivera: Percussion & B. Vocals
Pine Knob Music Theater, Clarkston (Detroit), MI 05/30/97

All Right Now [live] (P. Rodgers) 4:17 (19)
[Also available on *Ringo Starr And His All Starr Band The Anthology...So Far*. Koch-KOC-CD-8312 (3-10) (07/24/01) (02/05/01)]

Ringo Starr And His Fourth All-Starr Band
MPI-MP7292 (VHS) (07/28/98)
Producer: David & Ryan Hewitt (music mixers); Peter Skorich (video); Executive Producer: Ringo Starr & David Fishof
Ringo Starr: Drums; Simon Kirke: Lead Vocals & Drums; Gary Brooker: Keyboards & B. Vocals; Jack Bruce: Bass & B. Vocals; Peter Frampton: Guitar & B. Vocals; Mark Rivera: Percussion & B. Vocals
Pine Knob Music Theater, Clarkston (Detroit), MI 05/30/97

Shooting Star [live] (P. Rodgers) 5:50 (6)
[Also available on *Ringo Starr And His All Starr Band The Anthology...So Far*. Koch-KOC-CD-8312 (3-5) (07/24/01) (02/05/01)]

Simon Kirke was born on July 28, 1949 in London, England. By the age of 14 he was singing and playing drums semi-professionally. Several years later he joined The Black Cat Bones, which included Paul Kossoff. In 1968 he and Kossoff teamed up with Paul Rodgers and Andy Fraser forming the band Free. Free had the Top Five hit *All Right Now* in 1970 before breaking up in 1973. Kirke, Rodgers, King Crimson (see: Greg Lake) member Boz Burrell and Mott The Hoople (see Ian Hunter) member Mick Ralphs (who has worked with George Harrison) formed Bad Company. Between 1974 and 1979 they had a Top Five hit with *Can't Get Enough*, a Top 10 hit with *Feel Like Making Love*, and Top 20 hits with *Movin' On*, *Young Blood* and *Rock And Roll Fantasy*. The lyrics of their hit song *Shooting Star* makes reference to The Beatles and their hit *Love Me Do*. The band broke up in 1982 but reformed in 1986 around Kirke, Ralphs, Brian Howe and others. In the early 1990s they had hits with *If You Needed Someone* and *How About That*. Howe left the band in 1994 and was replaced by Robert Hart. In 1998 Rodgers rejoined Bad Company, who with Kirke and Ralphs continues to perform while members pur-

Simon Kirke, Pine Knob Clarkston (Detroit), MI June 11, 2000. © and photo by Kristofer Engelhardt.

sue other musical projects, such as Rogers' work with Queen.

Simon Kirke was a member of Ringo Starr's All-Starr Band tours in 1997, 1998, 1999 and 2000 drumming alongside Ringo performing *All Right Now* and *Shooting Star*. Simon says, "Ringo was a great guy to work for. We got along well, in part because our drumming styles meshed so well. He had his prickly moments though. On the tour bus from Seattle to Portland we drove through the beautiful, giant redwood forests. Ringo wanted to stop so we could all stretch our legs. Todd Rundgren*, Jack Bruce*, Gary Brooker*, Tim Cappello and I wandered through the forest, taking in the clean air and marveling at the giant trees. Ringo was in a distant mood and wandered away from us. He'd found the number seven tacked onto a post somewhere in the undergrowth, which was his lucky number. He was amazed that it was in such a remote spot, which was kind of spooky. It was chilly so we wanted to head back to the bus, but Ringo wanted to stay for a while, sitting on a rock gazing at his lucky number seven. Just then a middle-aged lady was hiking up the trail. There was no way she and Ringo could avoid each other. She drew alongside him and paused for a moment. Ringo was very shy and didn't acknowledge her. She walked past him down the trail gently shaking her head, clearly flustered and not quite believing who she had just seen. I can imagine her later telling disbelieving people, 'I saw Ringo Starr in the woods today.'" Kirke contributed to Ringo's 1998 album *VH1Storytellers* as a member of Ringo's band The Roundheads. For more information go to www.freewebs.com/simonkirke, www.badcompany.com

Peter Kirtley Band

Little Children
Jubilee Action JUB 001 (single) (UK) (12/08/98)
Producer: Peter Kirtley Band
Paul McCartney: Message & Vocals†; Peter Kirtley: Guitar & Vocals; Colin Gibson: Bass & Percussion; Liam Genockey: Drums & Percussion; Kenny Craddock: Hammond, Accordion & Mandolin; Liane Carroll: Vocals & Piano; Nana Tsiboe: Cabasa
Park Gates Studios, Catsfield probably 11/02/98 & Hog Hill Mill Studios†, Sussex, UK 11/18-19/98†

Little Children (P. Kirtley) 4:57 (2)

Peter Kirtley was born on September 26, 1945 in Hebburn-upon-Tyne, England. He was in a band that played at the Star-Club in Hamburg, Germany in the mid-1960s where The Beatles had often played. By 1966 he was playing with the Alan Price Set. Later he played with Griffin (which included Plastic Ono Band member Alan White), Riff Raff, Kevin Coyne, Bert Jansch and a new incarnation of Pentangle, among other bands and artists. He released the albums *Peter Kirtley* in 1992 and *Bush Telegraph* in 1996.

In 1998 the Peter Kirtley Band released a single for Jubilee Action, a UK charity dedicated to the protection of children throughout the world. For years, law enforcement agencies in Brazil were engaged in secretly killing gangs of street children. Kirtley recalls, "I'd written *Little Children* for my album *Peter Kirtley*. There was an article in the Daily Mirror about what was happening to street kids in Brazil. I got in touch with them and they put me in touch with Jubilee Action. I told them I wanted to donate my song *Little Children* to the charity. Tom Pickard, a poet friend of mine, had recently worked with Paul McCartney on *Standing Stone* [see The London Symphony Orchestra & Chorus]. Tom and I had written some stuff together and Paul said we could use his studio, so I finished the song off there for the charity. Paul came into the studio to see us. He was really nice but he had to leave for London. I left Paul a note inviting him to contribute to the recording, and later he did!"

Jubilee Action's press release says *Little Children* includes dialogue from Sir Paul McCartney who tells the story of Anna, a young street girl, and that he can be heard throughout improvising melody and lyrics on track one. McCartney says in the press release, "I would like to do something on the track to help the street children of Brazil. I hope that it will give it a boost." The press release, and the CD label and booklet say McCartney guests on version one but he only guests on version two of *Little Children*. For more information go to www.kirtleyj.freeserve.co.uk

Billy J. Kramer with The Dakotas

The Best Of Billy J. Kramer & The Dakotas
Imperial-CDP-7-96055-2 (10/08/91)
Producer: George Martin [unless noted otherwise]
Billy J. Kramer: Lead Vocals; Tony Mansfield: Drums; Mike Maxfield: Lead Guitar; Robin MacDonald: Rhythm Guitar; Ray Jones: Bass

Bad To Me (**J. Lennon**-P. McCartney) 2:18 (3) (07/26/63)
EMI-Abbey Road Studios, London, UK 06/27/63

Do You Want To Know A Secret? (**J. Lennon**-P. McCartney) 1:59 (1) (04/26/63)
Additionally: George Martin: Piano
EMI-Abbey Road Studios, London, UK 03/21/63

From A Window (J. Lennon-**P. McCartney**) 1:53 (12) (07/17/64)
Additionally: **Paul McCartney: B. Vocals**
EMI-Abbey Road Studios, London, UK 05/29/64

I Call Your Name (**J. Lennon**-P. McCartney) 2:21 (4) (07/26/63)
EMI-Abbey Road Studios, London, UK 06/27/63

I'll Be On My Way (J. Lennon-**P. McCartney**) 1:37 (2) (04/26/63)
EMI-Abbey Road Studios, London, UK 03/21/63

I'll Keep You Satisfied (**J. Lennon-P. McCartney**) 2:05 (8) (11/01/63)
EMI-Abbey Road Studios, London, UK 10/14/63

I'm In Love (**J. Lennon**-P. McCartney) 3:40 (9)
Producer: [John Lennon] & George Martin
Additionally: **John Lennon: Dialogue**
EMI-Abbey Road Studios, London, UK 10/14/63

Singer, Billy J. Kramer was born William Ashton on August 19, 1943 in Liverpool, England. His stage name was Billy J. Kramer ("J" for Julian, at the suggestion of John Lennon; see Julian Lennon). He began his musical career in 1960 in the Liverpool band The Sandstorers who became known as Billy Forde & The Phantoms and then The Coasters, but in early 1963 when they refused to turn professional, his manager Brian Epstein recruited the popular band The Dakotas to back Kramer. The Dakotas were Manchester, England area natives Mike Maxfield, born on February 23, 1944; Ray Jones, born on October 22, 1939; Tony Mansfield, born Anthony Bookbinder on May 28, 1943, and Robin MacDonald, born on July 18, 1943 in Nairn, Scotland. Though usually called Billy J. Kramer & The Dakotas the official name was Billy J. Kramer with The Dakotas because they maintained a career separate from Kramer. The Dakotas had a UK Top 20 hit with the instrumental *The Cruel Sea* in 1963.

Billy's success was directly linked to The Beatles. He had the same manager, the same producer, the same record company, and used the same studio but, most importantly, four of his five UK Top 10 hits were composed by John Lennon and Paul McCartney. Billy recorded no less than seven of their compositions – four of which, the Top 10 hit *Bad To Me, I'll Keep You Satisfied, From A Window* and *I'm In Love,* haven't been officially released by The Beatles. The others are *Do You Want To Know A Secret?, I Call Your Name* and *I'll Be On My Way. I Call Your Name* was recorded and released by The Beatles nearly a year after Kramer's version. *I'll Be On My Way* was officially released on The Beatles' *Live At The BBC* album in 1994. Acetate demos of John and Paul performing *Bad To Me* and *I'll Be On My Way* exist.

In the notes of *The Best Of Billy J. Kramer & The Dakotas,* Billy recounts listening to the demo Lennon made for him of *Do You Want To Know A Secret?,* "I had this tape given to me, and it was John Lennon singing it with an acoustic guitar. On the tape he said, 'I'm sorry for the sound quality, but it's the quietest room I could find in the whole building.' Then he flushed the toilet." *Do You Want To Know A Secret?* is considered a Beatles' composition contribution to Kramer, even though it was recorded and released after The Beatles' version, because there is little dispute that it was specifically intended for Kramer. [Epstein reportedly offered Shane Fenton (a.k.a. Alvin Stardust) a chance to record the song first if he signed with him, but Fenton, already with other management, turned him down.] Billy recorded the song on March 14, 1963, but had to return to the studio a week later to re-record the song because his voice cracked on the only usable version they had, which likely delayed the single's release. The take with the crack in Kramer's voice was mistakenly released in Holland in the late 1960s on the album *The Mersey And The Beat,* part of EMI's *History Of British Pop Series, Volume One.* It is also noticeable by the absence of George Martin's* piano overdub. Billy's version was a UK Top Five hit.

On October 14, 1963 Lennon joined Martin in the control room to help Billy on *I'll Keep You*

Billy J. Kramer and Kristofer Engelhardt, The Fest For Beatles Fans, Hyatt Regency, Rosemont (Chicago), IL, August 16, 2008. Photo by Roni Kramer, © Kristofer Engelhardt.

Satisfied, which would become a Top 40 hit, and especially on *I'm In Love*. Lennon can be heard talking during the false take intro of *I'm In Love*, and Martin commenting on how Kramer can shout at Lennon on the upcoming Beatles' recording session. Billy liked *I'm In Love* but struggled recording it. His version wasn't released until 1991. [*I'm In Love* was first released by The Fourmost*.]

Billy J. Kramer with The Dakotas were on the bill of *The Beatles Christmas Show* in 1963. Lennon and McCartney recorded several demo versions of the song *One And One Is Two* in their George V Hotel room during The Beatles' engagement in Paris, France in January 1964 for submission to Dick James Music for Billy to record, which apparently he did. A demo of the song with McCartney on vocals and guitar is available on unauthorized releases. The song is primarily a McCartney composition. [In Lennon's 1980 *Playboy* magazine interview he said of the song, "That's another of Paul's bad attempts at writing a song."] Lennon was reported to have said that if Billy released it his career would be finished! Kramer never released the song. [It was also recorded by The Fourmost* but their version wasn't released. It was then offered to The Silkie* who rejected it. The Strangers with Mike Shannon's* release of it proved to be one of the few chart failures of a Lennon-McCartney composition proving Lennon's warning justified.] Kramer instead chose *Little Children* as his first single release in 1964. Though not a Lennon-McCartney composition it became a Top 10 hit.

Billy's last Lennon-McCartney composition contribution, and his last Top 40 hit, was *From A Window* in mid-1964. Unfortunately for Billy, by this time John and Paul were contributing much less music to Epstein's other artists. Kramer says McCartney offered him his song *Yesterday* but he turned it down. In the notes of *The Best Of Billy J. Kramer & The Dakotas*, Billy is quoted as saying that Lennon and McCartney contributed backing vocals at the end of *From A Window* but according to Billy (and Paul) only McCartney sings because he was unable to reach the high note at the end. Billy says none of The Beatles sang or played on any other of his recordings. Jones left The Dakotas a short time later and was replaced by MacDonald on bass and Mick Green, from the group Johnny Kidd & The Pirates, joining on guitar. [Green worked with McCartney on his 1988 album *Choba B CCCP*.] Billy recorded with The Dakotas until 1967 but without much success. Later, he worked with The Remo Four*. Billy has made guest appearances at festivals for fans of The Beatles, and performed as a solo artist and with original members of The Dakotas. Ray Jones died January 20, 2000. For more information go to www.billyjkramer.com

Holly Days
Magic-3930035 (France) (11/15/00) (05/06/77)
Producer: Paul McCartney
Paul McCartney: (all) Instruments & B. Vocals; Denny Laine: Lead Vocals
Rude Studios, Kintyre, Scotland, UK xx/xx/76

Fool's Paradise (N. Petty-S. LeGlaire-H. Linsley) 2:46 (5)
Additionally: Linda McCartney: B. Vocals

Heartbeat (B. Montgomery-N. Petty) 2:35 (1) (04/15/77)

I'm Gonna Love You Too (J. Mauldin-N. Petty-N. Sullivan) 2:17 (4)

I'm Looking For Someone To Love (N. Petty-B. Holly) 3:58 (10) (09/03/76)
Additionally: **Paul McCartney: (all) Instruments** (only)

[Medley] It's So Easy/Listen To Me (B. Holly-N. Petty/N. Petty-C. Hardin) 3:46 (7) (09/03/76)
Additionally: Linda McCartney: B. Vocals

Lonesome Tears (B. Holly) 3:02 (6)
Paul McCartney: (all) Instruments (only)

Look At Me (J.Allison-B. Holly-N. Petty) 3:10 (8)

Moondreams (N. Petty) 2:41 (2) (04/15/77)

Rave On (N. Petty-B. Tilghman-S. West) 1:54 (3)
Additionally: Linda McCartney: Vocals

Take Your Time (N. Petty-B. Holly) 3:49 (9)

Japanese Tears
Intertape-B-80077/500.001
(Japan/Switzerland) (xx/xx/86) (12/05/80)

I Would Only Smile (D. Laine) 3:17 (12)
Producer: probably **Paul McCartney** & Denny Laine
Paul McCartney: Bass & B. Vocals; Denny Laine: Lead Vocals & Guitar; Henry McCullough: Guitar; Denny Seiwell: Drums; Linda McCartney: B. Vocals & (probable) Keyboards
Probably Morgan Studios, London, UK probably 03/xx/72-10/xx/72 or possibly xx/xx/73

Send Me The Heart (**P. McCartney**-D. Laine) 3:36 (4)
Producer: probably **Paul McCartney** & Denny Laine
Paul McCartney: Bass & Vocals; Denny Laine: Vocals; Linda McCartney: B. Vocals; Buddy Emmens: Steel Guitar & Acoustic Guitar; Floyd Cramer: Piano; Geoff Britton: (possible) Drums
Soundshop Studios, Nashville, TN 06 or 07/xx/74

Weep For Love (D. Laine) 4:29 (13)
Producer: Paul McCartney, Denny Laine & probably Chris Thomas
Paul McCartney: B. Vocals & Bass; Denny Laine: Lead Vocals & Guitar; Laurence Juber: Guitar; Steve Holly: Drums & B. Vocals; Linda McCartney: B. Vocals
Lympne Castle, Kent, UK 09/11-29/78

Somewhere In England [George Harrison]
Pegboy-1005 (Australia) [unauthorized release] (07/xx/96)
Producer: [unknown-audience recording]
George Harrison: Vocals & Guitar; Denny Laine: Vocals & Guitar; Noddy Holder: Vocals; Robert Plant: Vocals; Jeff Lynne: Guitar & Vocals; Dave Edmunds: Guitar; Bev Bevan: Drums; Justin Hayward, Ray Thomas, Roy Wood, Steve Gibbons, Patrick Moraz, Graeme Edge, Members of UB40 (Astro, James Brown, Ali Campbell, Robin Campbell, Earl Falconer, Norman Hassan, Brian Travers, Mickey Virtue), Jasper Carrott, Jimmy Tarbuck & Richard Tandy
National Exhibition Centre in Birmingham, UK 03/15/86

Johnny B. Goode (C. Berry) 3:49 (25)

Denny Laine was born Brian Hines on October 29, 1944 on a boat off Jersey in the Channel Islands, but was raised in Birmingham, England. He was nicknamed Denny because he often played in his family's garden den. His surname was chosen in tribute to singer Cleo Laine. Buddy Holly's music inspired Laine to take up guitar as a teenager and soon he was singing in a group as Johnny Dean & The Dominators. Laine formed Denny & The Diplomats in 1962. They were on the bill with The Beatles at the Plaza Ballroom, Old Hill, UK on July 5, 1963. The Diplomats included future Electric Light Orchestra* drummer Bev Bevan before they disbanded in 1964.

Laine was an original member of The Moody Blues and sang their 1965 Top 10 hit *Go Now*. [Laine later performed this song, along with

Left to right: Laine Hines, David Peel, Denny Laine and Jo Jo Laine, Beatlefest, Crowne Plaza Meadowlands Hotel, Secaucus, New Jersey March 22, 1997. © and photo by Kristofer Engelhardt.

Richard Corey, during Wings' 1975-76 world tour.] The group was briefly signed to NEMS and was part of The Beatles' UK tour in December 1965. He left the group in October 1966. Laine helped form The Electric String Band, which only lasted a few months. Laine had little success with his song *Say You Don't Mind* released in 1967. [The song became a UK Top 20 for Colin Blunstone in 1972. Laine occasionally performed the song in concert with Wings.] In 1969 Laine joined the band Balls, which also included future Electric Light Orchestra member Richard Tandy, Plastic Ono Band (see Yoko Ono) member Alan White and Jackie Lomax*. He was also a brief member of Ginger Baker's Air Force (see Blind Faith, Cream).

In July 1971, shortly after Balls broke up, Laine received a call from Paul McCartney asking him if he would be interested in joining his new band Wings. Laine was instrumental in recruiting fellow Wings' members Henry McCullough, and later Laurence Juber* and Steve Holly. Laine played guitar on most of Wings' recordings, including those under a variety of pseudonyms. He also played a variety of other instruments, composed or co-composed, and sang lead or duet vocals on many of Wings' songs. However, only those Wings recordings featuring Laine on lead vocals that were initially released by Laine are considered contributions by McCartney. With McCartney, Laine contributed to recordings for other artists including Linda McCartney*, Mike McGear*, Scaffold* and George Harrison's 1981 song *All Those Years Ago* in tribute to John Lennon. Laine says McCartney didn't contribute to his first solo album *Ahh...Laine!* released in 1973.

In the mid-1970s McCartney purchased the publishing catalogue of Buddy Holly and The Crickets' songs, which led to Laine's 1977 album *Holly Days*. According to Laine, Ray Stevens, best known for his novelty songs, was originally scheduled to produce the album in Nashville, Tennessee with local musicians. "Stevens couldn't do the session at the time we wanted, and I think Paul was just bored up in Scotland one day and had a go at the tracks," admits Laine. He says Paul produced and played all the instruments on the album, which was recorded at McCartney's home studio in Kintyre, Scotland. Laine sang the lead vocals, and Paul and Linda supplied the backing vocals. The unauthorized release *2 Buddies On Holly Days* (Library-2323) contains slightly different (unfinished) versions of the *Holly Days* album.

There are a number of unauthorized records containing unreleased McCartney and Wings' songs featuring Laine on lead vocals, including *Takin' On A Woman*, *Old Man Loving'*, the Moody Blues' cover *I've Got A Dream*, *Find A Way Somehow* from *Ahh...Laine!* and *Luxi*, an ode to Radio Luxembourg. These songs likely represent only a small portion of the recordings that probably exist in the McCartney tape archives that prominently feature Laine. It's difficult to say whether any of these recordings were ever considered for a solo release by Laine.

Laine reportedly harbored some resentment towards McCartney feeling he was underpaid, especially for his writing contribution to Wings' 1977 mega-hit *Mull Of Kintyre.* A major blow to Wings occurred when McCartney was arrested and briefly imprisoned for possession of marijuana in Japan in January 1980 this forced the cancellation of Wings' world tour and a considerable loss of work for band members. A few months later, Paul released *McCartney II,* his second full-fledged solo album recorded the previous year. McCartney, who became reluctant to tour after the murder of Lennon in December 1980, also had difficulties securing visas as a result of his previous drug arrests, leaving little use for a band.

Laine wrote and recorded the song *Japanese Tears* triggered by the recent events in Japan, and released an album by that title in late 1980. [The album has since been reissued under other titles, including *In Flight.*] It includes the previously unreleased Wings' leftovers *I Would Only Smile* (from the *Red Rose Speedway* album sessions), *Send Me The Heart* (from sessions in Nashville in 1974) and *Weep For Love* (from the *Back To The Egg* album sessions) written, sung by and first issued under Laine's name. Wings' drummer Steve Holly played on other tracks on the album. Some tracks were recorded at Startling Studios. Though the album credits Laine as the sole producer, McCartney had a hand in the original production of the numbers involving Wings. Chris Thomas, who helped produce *The Beatles* (white) album, was probably also involved in the production of *Weep For Love.*

In early 1981 McCartney decided to use a vast array of famous musicians on recordings for his next album. Although Laine participated in some of the recordings (contained on McCartney's albums *Tug Of War* in 1982 and *Pipes Of Peace* in 1983) tensions mounted and Laine, the only original member of Wings, severed his uncertain association with McCartney. Wings' demise was announced on April 27, 1981.

Chances for a Laine and McCartney reunion were probably dashed forever when negative remarks about McCartney attributed to Laine turned up in the tabloids in 1983 and 1984. Denny says, "I have never said anything publicly that would imply that there were disagreements over money, or that I didn't have the greatest respect and love for the McCartneys. We were very close friends, and I blame certain so-called friends in the media for turning us into enemies."

On March 15, 1986 Harrison joined Laine, The Moody Blues and Robert Plant onstage for renditions of *Johnny B. Goode* and *Money (That's What I Want)* at the National Exhibition Centre in Birmingham, UK for the charity concert *Heartbeat '86.* The concert was organized by Bev Bevan. The performance was first broadcast on August 2 on BBC TV. *Johnny B. Goode* has appeared on a number of unauthorized records.

In recent years McCartney, who certainly must appreciate how the tabloids can greatly distort and exploit, has sent out invitations to Laine to attend his performances and the two have met up socially on occasion. For years Laine has been promising an autobiography to explain the full story of why Wings broke up, and says there are many more reasons than those usually mentioned.

In the late 1980s Laine employed Ringo's son, drummer Zak Starkey on one of his recordings. In 1997 he released the album *Wings At The Speed Of Denny Laine*, which consists mostly of covers of Wings' songs with which he is associated. He has also been a guest at conventions and festivals for fans of The Beatles. Laine continues to write, record, and release recordings but has yet to enjoy the level of success he did during his years with Paul McCartney.

Ringo Starr And His All Starr Band-Live In Atlantic City
(DVD-R) [unauthorized release] (xx/xx/02)
Ringo Starr: Drums; Greg Lake: Lead Vocals & Bass; Ian Hunter: Guitar & B. Vocals; Sheila Escovedo: Drums; Howard Jones: Keyboards & B. Vocals; Mark Rivera: Flute; Roger Hodgson: Guitar & B. Vocals
Trump Taj Mahal, Atlantic City, NJ 08/10/01

The Court Of The Crimson King [live] (I. McDonald-P. Sinfield) 6:22 (3)

Ringo Starr & His New All-Starr Band
Pioneer/Win Media-11907 (DVD) (10/01/02)
Producer: (recorded, mixed and mastered by: Glen Robinson); Executive Producer: Ringo Starr & David Fishof
Ringo Starr: Drums; Greg Lake: Lead Vocals & Acoustic Guitar; Howard Jones: Keyboards & B. Vocals; Ian Hunter: Acoustic Guitar & B. Vocals; Roger Hodgson: Electric Guitar & B. Vocals; Sheila Escovedo: Drums; Mark Rivera: Bass & B. Vocals
Rosemont Theater, Rosemont (Chicago), IL 08/22/01

Lucky Man [live] (G. Lake) 4:47 (10)
[Also available on King Biscuit Flower Hour/Razor & Tie-7930188003-2 (12) (08/06/02)]

Greg Lake was born on November 10, 1947 in Poole, England. Lake was a member of several bands in the middle and late 1960s. In 1968 he was asked by former schoolmate Robert Fripp to join his band, which became known as King Crimson. Lake sang, played bass, wrote songs and helped produce the band's recordings. Their song *In The Court Of The Crimson King* is considered a classic of the progressive rock genre. Lake left the group after about a year, and then served the same duties with keyboardist Keith Emerson and drummer Carl Palmer to form the band Emerson, Lake & Palmer (a.k.a. ELP). Their first hit was Lake's composition *Lucky Man* in 1971. Their only other hits were *From The Beginning* in 1972 and a rock version of Aaron Copland's *Fanfare For The Common Man* in 1977. However, most all of their albums in the 1970s were certified Platinum. Lake's solo song *I Believe In Father Christmas* was a UK Top Five hit in 1975. By 1979 ELP's progressive rock was out of style and the group disbanded. Lake recorded two solo albums during the early 1980s. In 1986 Emerson and Lake teamed up with Cozy Powell forming another ELP but that lineup only lasted a year. In 1992 the original ELP reformed, but never recaptured their former success and broke up again in 1998. Lake returned to working as a solo artist.

Lake was a member of Ringo Starr's All-Starr Band tour in 2001 performing *In The Court Of The Crimson King* and *Lucky Man* with backing from Ringo on drums. Greg recalls, "When Ringo asked me to tour with him and told me who was in the band, I told him it sounded like a very strange mix of people. He said, 'Trust me, it will work.' Ringo is one of my musical heroes, so I told him I'd love to do it. People think Ringo's a happy-go-lucky character, and he does have a great sense of humor, but he's very musically disciplined and dedicated. He's fascinated by all kinds of musical equipment and loves his drum kit. There were no creative issues playing with Ringo. He isn't a dictator. It was an open group situation, so we were pretty much free to play what we wanted. It wasn't all about Ringo. He would go over and over my songs to get them right because he cared, which really impressed me. He's an underrated drummer because he's simplistic, but no one has a feel for the drums like Ringo. You know his off-beat when you hear it. He has a lovely, acoustic drum sound.

"Ringo has the best people working for him, so things go very smoothly. I'd never worked with a woman drummer before. Sheila E* is very sweet, so I thought she'd play in a dainty way but she frightened me to death with her incredible power. It's lovely when you're in a situation where every single member is really talented and has a tremendous contribution to make. All of the musicians learned their parts very well and without exception gave it 100 percent every night to put on a great show. There was hardly a flaw during the entire tour. We always walked off stage very happy. Although we all came from different styles of music, there was a spiritual connection among all the members of the band. There was a lot of goodwill in the band because everyone tried very hard to faithfully perform everyone's material.

"Ringo's a tremendous catalyst, diplomat, problem solver and realist. He brings things down to earth. His contribution to the chemistry of The Beatles is greatly underrated. He was definitely the right person to drum in The Beatles.

Greg Lake, Freedom Hill, Sterling Heights (Detroit), MI July 28, 2001. © and photo by Kristofer Engelhardt.

Ironically, he never saw what everyone else saw because he was inside that bubble, so sometimes when you talk to him about The Beatles, you get the sense that he doesn't quite understand it all. One thing I admire about Ringo is how rationally he manages to adjust himself to the strange life that swirls around him because he's a Beatle. He's a very wise and philosophical person with great humility. He would sit by us on the plane at night after the show and tell stories, like he was telling kids a bedtime story, which was lovely. You'd have to look very hard to find someone who's done more, seen more and experienced more than Ringo. He was born into poverty, blasted into the stratosphere of fame, crashed into the pitfalls of the rock 'n' roll lifestyle and managed to right himself to normality. These are the things that are so impressive about him. It was a great experience working with Richie." Lake continues to write, record and tour. For more information go to www.greglake.com

Billy Lawrie

Ship Imagination
RCA-SF 8395 (album 12") (UK) (10/29/73)
Producer: Gary Osborne & Billy Lawrie
Morgan Studios, London UK probably 05/xx/73

Freedom (B. Lawrie-M. Gibb-L. Harvey) 4:06 (2/3)
Ringo Starr: (probable) Drums; Billy Lawrie: Lead Vocals; Leslie Harvey: Acoustic Guitar; Johnny Coleman: Piano; Roger Ball: Horns; Malcolm Duncan: Horns; Jimmy McCulloch: Guitar; Maggie Bell: B. Vocals; Lulu: B. Vocals

Rock & Roller (B. Lawrie-**R. Starkey**) 3:35 (1/2)
Billy Lawrie: Lead Vocals; Ronnie Leahy: Keyboards; Jimmy McCulloch: Guitar; Colin Allen: Drums; Steve Thompson: Bass; Roger Ball: Horns; Malcolm Duncan: Horns; Ray Cooper: Percussion: Maggie Bell: B. Vocals; Lulu: B. Vocals; Liza Strike: B. Vocals

Billy Lawrie was born on August 9, 1951 in Glasgow, Scotland. Billy says, "My older sister Marie and I loved to sing as youngsters, and were fans of The Beatles, especially Marie. She had photos of them covering the walls of her bedroom from floor to ceiling, mainly Paul McCartney. She thought Paul was God and I wasn't far behind. Marie, who was known as Lulu*, had a hit when she was just 15-years-old, so I became involved in the music world.

"My sister Lulu later married Maurice Gibb of the Bee Gees, and I was living with them in the early 1970s. Maurice and I formed a production company called Moby. We had a deal with Atlantic Records, so we were constantly writing songs, producing and working on many projects. We worked with the band Tin Tin who had a hit. We were producing tracks for Richard Harris and 12 tracks for a film he was in called *Bloomfield* (a.k.a. *The Hero*). Plus we were doing songs for my album and Maurice's never released solo album. We would exchange different bits for different projects, so it's difficult to know or remember who played on what, but Jack Bruce*, Peter Frampton*, John Bonham and Ringo played drums on some of the tracks. There were at least two or three but no more than half-a-dozen. Ringo did play on tracks for the *Bloomfield* soundtrack. Ringo and his wife Maureen lived nearby so we regularly went over to their place, or they came to our place and we jammed. Ringo could play the odd chord on the guitar or piano and once played me something that he'd written. I had another piece of a song I'd written and we put them together. That became the song *Rock & Roller*. He said he was recording soon, and wanted to use it, but I told him I wanted to cut it for what became my album *Ship Imagination*. Now that I've headed some publishing companies and managed some stars, if someone relatively unknown came to me and said, 'I've just written a song with a huge star, but I want to cut it for my unknown album, which might come out and die,' I'd say, 'Are you mad?' I think Ringo also plays drums on one or two tracks on my album such as *Freedom*, which we didn't list any drummer for in the credits. Guitarist Jimmy McCulloch, who later played with Wings, is listed in the credits as Jimmy McAnonymous." *Ship Imagination* also includes a cover of a Beatles' song. According to the book *The Beatles After The Break-Up 1970-2000* by Keith Badman, a copyright was registered on June 19, 1974 for the unreleased song *Where Are You Going?*" co-written by Ringo and Billy Lawrie. Harry Castleman and Walter Podrazik also mention this co-composition in their 1977 book *The Beatles Again?* Lawrie says, "There were many jam sessions with Ringo but I don't remember writing another songs with him, and I think I'd remember any song I wrote with a Beatle."

Gibb reportedly recorded an album's worth of synthesizer music around 1969 with Ringo, including a song called *Modulating Maurice*. None of these recordings have ever surfaced except on unauthorized releases, and Lawrie doubts that Maurice and Ringo recorded an album's worth of material together. Ringo also seems to indicate that an album wasn't recorded. Gibb did contribute to Ringo's 1970 album *Sentimental Journey*. Lawrie was probably involved in Maurice and Tin Tin's recording of the song *Have You Heard The Word* credited to The Fut, which has appeared on unauthorized releases claiming to be John Lennon and The Beatles. Lawrie has written songs for many artists including Three Dog Night, Tina Turner and Lionel Richie.

Alvin Lee (& Mylon Le Fevre*)

Detroit Diesel
Bellaphon-290.07.093 (Germany) (xx/xx/87) (xx/xx/86)
Producer: Alvin Lee
George Harrison: Slide Guitar; Alvin Lee: Lead Vocals, Guitar, Drums & Bass; Tim Hinkley: Hammond Organ
Space Studios, Buckinghamshire, UK

Free Fall
Repertoire-REP-4705-DG (Germany) (xx/xx/xx) (01/11/99)
Producer: Alvin Lee
Space Studios, Buckinghamshire, UK probably xx/xx/91 or xx/xx/92

Real Life Blues (alternate version) (A. Lee) 4:33 (11)
George Harrison: Slide Guitar; Alvin Lee: Lead Vocals & Guitar; Jon Lord: Hammond Organ; Steve Grant: Bass, Keyboards & B. Vocals; Alan Young: drums

Talk Don't Bother Me (A. Lee) 3:36 (4)

Nineteenninetyfour
Thunderbolt/Magnum Music Group-CDTB 150 (UK) (12/xx/93)
Executive Producer: Nigel Molden
George Harrison: Slide Guitar; Alvin Lee: Lead Vocals & Guitar; Steve Gould: Bass; Alan Young: Drums; Steve Grant: Keyboards
Probably Space Studios, Buckinghamshire, UK probably xx/xx/93

The Bluest Blues (A Lee) 7:27 (5)
Additionally: Tim Hinkley: Keyboards

I Want You (She's So Heavy) (J. Lennon-P. McCartney) 9:52 (12)
Additionally: Steve Gould: B. Vocals; Steve Grant: B. Vocals

On The Road To Freedom [Alvin Lee & Mylon Le Fevre*]
Repertoire/REP-4780 (Germany) (04/07/03) (11/02/73)
Producer: Alvin Lee
George Harrison: Slide Guitar, Guitar, Bass & B. Vocals; Mylon Le Fevre: Vocals; Alvin Lee: Guitar, B. Vocals; Ron Wood: 12 String Guitar; Mick Fleetwood: Drums
Possibly Space Studios, Buckinghamshire, UK 08/xx/73

So Sad (No Love Of His Own) (**G. Harrison**) 4:34 (3)

So Sad (No Love Of His Own) (Single Version) (G. Harrison) 3:00 (13) (12/17/73)

Zoom
Domino-8003-2 (Singapore) 08/25/92
Producer: Alvin Lee
Space Studios, Buckinghamshire, UK probably xx/xx/91 or xx/xx/92

Real Life Blues (A. Lee) 4:33 (2)
George Harrison: Slide Guitar; Alvin Lee: Lead Vocals & Guitar; Jon Lord: Hammond Organ; Steve Grant: Bass, Keyboards & B. Vocals

Alvin Lee was born Graham Barnes on December 19, 1944 in Nottingham, England. He played the clarinet as an adolescent but switched to guitar. By age 13 he was playing in local groups. He served in several blues and rock bands and, like The Beatles and many others developed his skills in the clubs of Hamburg, Germany as a member of The Jaymen (a.k.a. The Jaybirds).

Lee first gained notice as the leader of Ten Years After, who became internationally recognized after their appearance at the *Woodstock Music And Art Fair* in 1969. Their name had been chosen in honor of the group being formed about ten years after Elvis Presley's rise to stardom. Their only Top 40 hit was *I'd Love To Change The World* in 1971, though they had a number of successful albums, including *Cricklewood Green* and *A Space In Time.* Band members drifted into solo projects but have occasionally reformed. Lee formed a band in the late 1970s called Ten Years Later.

Alvin Lee and George Harrison were friends and neighbors, and they often worked with other musicians in their neighborhood including Gary Moore* and Joe Brown (see Vicki Brown). Lee played guitar on Harrison's song *Ding Dong; Ding Dong.* Harrison contributed his composition *So Sad (No Love Of His Own),* along with guitars, bass and backing vocals, to Lee and Mylon LeFevre's 1973 album *On The Road To Freedom.* A slightly different version was released as a single. Harrison released his version on his album *Dark Horse* a year later. Harrison and Lee wrote a song called *Shelter In Your Love,* which Harrison recorded in March 1985 that is only available on unauthorized releases. Harrison played slide guitar on *Talk Don't Bother Me* on Lee's 1986 album *Detroit Diesel.* Harrison's guitar was also featured on *Real Life Blues* on Lee's 1992 album *Zoom.* Lee released the album *Nineteenninetyfour* (a.k.a. *I Hear You Rockin'*) just before the dawn of that year, which included Harrison playing slide guitar on *The Bluest Blues* and on Lee's cover of The Beatles' *I Want You (She's So Heavy).* For more information go to www.alvinlee.com

Peggy Lee

Let's Love
Atlantic/Rhino Handmade-RHM2 7853 (02/17/04) (10/01/74)
Producer: Paul McCartney
Paul McCartney: Piano, Conductor & (probable) Bass; Peggy Lee: Lead Vocals; additionally, one or more of the following: Harvey Mason: Drums & Percussion; Gene Cipriano: Oboe; Peter Christlieb: Flute; Chuck Rainey: (possible) Bass; Erno Neufeld: Concert Master
EMI-Abbey Road Studios, London, UK 05/18/74 & Record Plant Studios, Los Angeles, CA early-06/xx/74

Let's Love (**P. McCartney**) 2:58 (1)

Rare Gems And Hidden Treasures
Capitol-72435-27564-2-1 (07/18/00) **Paul McCartney: Liner Notes**

Peggy Lee was born Norma Egstrom on May 26, 1920 in Jamestown, North Dakota. She worked with Benny Goodman's Orchestra and became one of America's foremost female pop vocalists. Between 1941and 1958 Lee had 12 Top 10 hits including *Fever,* and the number one songs *Somebody Else Is Taking My Place* and *Mañana.* She also had much success writing lyrics to her husband David Barbour's melodies. Lee is remembered for her work in the Disney film *Lady And The Tramp.*

Peggy Lee was one of the first of her generation of musicians to acknowledge the talents of The Beatles, who regularly performed and recorded her 1961 version of *Till There Was You.* Lee covered several of The Beatles' songs and co-starred in a Beatles tribute on *The Ed Sullivan Show.* John Lennon jokingly referred to her as "Peggy Leg." She has long been a favorite of Paul McCartney, who wrote and produced *Let's Love* as a gift to her in 1974. McCartney recorded the backing track at Abbey Road Studios with engineering assistance from Alan Parsons and probably played bass on it. Lee's vocals were added in Los Angeles. Lee has stated that Paul and Linda McCartney* came to the studio in Los Angeles to help her record it, and that Paul played on it and conducted it. DJ Rodney Bingenheimer, who attended the session, recalls McCartney conducting the orchestra and playing piano on *Let's Love,* but the credits don't mention McCartney conducting the orchestra. The album also contains a brief reprise of *Let's Love,* which is an edit of the full-length version. The CD release also contains an alternate version (without McCartney's involvement) of *Let's Love* that was produced by Dave Grusin. McCartney contributed liner notes to Lee's 2000 album *Rare Gems And Hidden Treasures.* Peggy Lee died on January 21, 2002. For more information go to www.peggylee.com

Julian Lennon

Help Yourself
Atlantic-82280-2 (08/20/91)
Producer: Bob Ezrin
George Harrison: Slide Guitar Arrangement; Julian Lennon: Lead & B. Vocals, & (possible) Keyboards; Steve Hunter: Slide Guitar; Matt Bissonette: Bass; (probably) Louis Molino or (possibly) Allan Schwartzberg: Drums; Scott Humphrey: Keyboards, Computer & Synthesizer Programming, & (possible) B. Vocals; (probably) Bob Ezrin: B. Vocals, Keyboards & Programming; probably one or more of the following: Paul Winger: B. Vocals; Peter Fletcher: B. Vocals; Carmen Twillie: B. Vocals; Clydene Jackson-Edwards: B. Vocals; Maxine Anderson: B. Vocals; Bobette Jamison-Harrison: B. Vocals; Clarise Wilkins: B. Vocals; Kim Edwards-Brown: B. Vocals; Olivia D'Abo: B. Vocals; Mark Spiro: B. Vocals
Amigo & The Enterprise Studios, CA probably xx/xx/91

Saltwater (Julian Lennon-M. Spiro-L. Spiro) 4:07 (2)

Saltwater
Virgin-VSCDT 1361 (single) (UK) (08/05/91)
Producer: Bob Ezrin
George Harrison: Slide Guitar Arrangement; Julian Lennon: Lead & B. Vocals, & (possible) Keyboards; Steve Hunter: Slide Guitar; Matt Bissonette: Bass; Louis Molino or Allan Schwartzberg: Drums; Scott Humphrey: Keyboards, Computer & Synthesizer Programming, & (possible) B. Vocals; (probably) Bob Ezrin: B. Vocals, Keyboards & Programming; probably one or more of the following: Paul Winger: B. Vocals; Peter Fletcher: B. Vocals; Carmen Twillie: B. Vocals; Clydene Jackson-Edwards: B. Vocals; Maxine Anderson: B. Vocals; Bobette Jamison-Harrison: B. Vocals; Clarise Wilkins: B. Vocals; Kim Edwards-Brown: B. Vocals; Olivia D'Abo: B. Vocals; Mark Spiro: B. Vocals
Amigo & The Enterprise Studios, CA probably xx/xx/91

Creo Que Voy A Llorar (Saltwater) (Julian Lennon-M. Spiro-L. Spiro) 4:07 (3)

John Charles Julian Lennon was born April 8, 1963 in Liverpool, England. He is the first son of John Lennon and his first wife Cynthia (Powell) Lennon. His name was derived from John's mother Julia, and would be the inspiration for the "J" in Billy J. Kramer with The Dakotas*. His birth and John's marriage was kept secret for a time fearing it would damage John's popularity with female fans. A childhood drawing by Julian inspired John to write *Lucy In The Sky With Diamonds*. Another of Julian's drawings was featured on *The Beatles 1968 Christmas Record*, an annual gift to members of The Beatles' Fan Club. John also wrote The Beatles' song *Goodnight* for Julian.

John and Cynthia divorced in late 1968. John married Yoko Ono* some months later and in 1971 they moved to New York. Julian was to stay in the UK to be raised by his mother. John wouldn't leave the US between 1972 and 1976 for fear of not being re-admitted due to a deportation order against him, so Julian only saw his father on occasional visits to the US.

John encouraged Julian's interest in music, and featured him playing drums on a brief rendition of *Ya Ya* included on John's *Walls And Bridges* album in 1974. After John's death many expected Julian to fill his father's musical shoes. He recorded some of his father's unreleased compositions, but apparently Yoko, who held the rights, vetoed them being released. The relationship between Julian and Yoko has often been strained, but he and his half-brother Sean (John and Yoko's son), and Yoko have appeared together on numerous occasions over the years. Julian's 1984 debut album *Valotte* was certified Platinum, and the title track and the song *Too Late For Goodbyes* were Top 10 hits. Julian's vocals were hauntingly similar to those of his dad and his grandfather Freddie Lennon. His 1986 album *The Secret Value Of Daydreaming* was certified Gold. Julian made his stage debut in Mike Batt's* 1987 musical *The Hunting of The Snark*. In 1989 he released the album *Mr. Jordon*.

It seemed inevitable that Julian and the other Beatles' musical paths would cross. Early in Julian's career Paul McCartney (who had written *Hey Jude* about Julian) and George Harrison publicly acknowledged his talents. Julian's 1991 album *Help Yourself* includes the UK Top 10 hit *Saltwater*. Julian also recorded the song in Spanish. The album gives special thanks to Mum [Cynthia] and George Harrison, among others. According to Julian, and his producer Bob Ezrin, Harrison was sent the tapes of *Saltwater* and recorded several slide guitar solos, but they decided not to use them. Instead, they combined Julian and George's slide guitar styles, and had guitarist Steve

Hunter play it on the released version. Hunter recalls, "I learned George's first half of the solo and Julian's second half. It was an honor to play anything by George. The combination of the two really worked. I played that solo on my father's old lap steel guitar." Harrison can rightly be credited for helping arrange the slide guitar solo for *Saltwater*.

Julian made his acting debut in the 1995 film *Leaving Las Vegas*. He wrote and performed, with Michael Kamen, the closing theme to the 1995 film *Mr. Holland's Opus*, which featured several of his father's songs. He released the album *Photography Smile* in 1998. He covered The Beatles' song *When I'm Sixty-Four* in 2002. Julian Lennon continues to write and record. For more information go to www.julianlennon.com

Jerry Lee Lewis

Last Man Standing
Shangri-la Entertainment/Alternative Distribution Alliance-AFT 20001-2 (09/26/06)
Producer: Jimmy Rip & James Saez
Ringo Starr: Duet Vocals & Drums; Jerry Lee Lewis: Duet Vocals & Piano; Ken Lovelace: Guitar; Jimmy Rip: Guitar; Keith Allison: Guitar; Nils Lofgren: Pedal Steel Guitar; Jim Keltner: Drums; Hutch Hutchinson: Bass; Ivan Neville: Organ
Record Plant Studios, Los Angeles, CA probably xx/xx/06

Sweet Little Sixteen (C. Berry) 3:04 (9)

Jerry Lee Lewis & Ringo Starr-The London Brasserie Grand Opening Atlanta
Rh Records [unauthorized release] (xx/xx/87)
Ringo Starr: Drums; Jerry Lee Lewis: Piano & Vocals (unless noted otherwise)
London Brasserie, Peachtree Center, Atlanta, Georgia 09/26/87

Blue Yodel #6 (Blues Like Midnight) [live] (J. Rodgers) 6:26 (4)

Get Back [live] (J. Lennon-P. McCartney) 0:23 (6)

Johnny B. Goode [live] (C. Berry) 0:36 (2)

Mony Mony [live] (B. Bloom-R. Cordell-B. Gentry-T. James) 5:47 (5)
Jermaine Jackson: Lead Vocals Note: Jerry Lee Lewis doesn't sing on this song.

Whole Lotta Shakin' Goin' On [live] (J. Hall-D. Williams) 3:11 (1)

Jerry Lee Lewis was born on September 29, 1935 in Ferriday, Louisiana. He began playing piano at an early age alongside his cousins Mickey Gilley (who later became a successful club owner) and Jimmy Swaggart (who later become a popular TV evangelist). Jerry developed a wild style of boogie-woogie playing influenced by his gospel, country and R&B roots. Like Little Richard*, Lewis was often torn between religious and secular music. He followed Elvis' lead and headed to Sun Record in Memphis in 1956 playing with Presley, Roy Orbison*, Johnny Cash* and Carl Perkins*. With Sun he had the Top Five hits *Whole Lotta Shakin' Goin' On* and *Great Balls Of Fire* in 1957, and the Top 10 hit *Breathless* in 1958. Controversy surrounding Jerry's marriages forced the cancellation of his 1958 UK tour and hindered his commercial success for years to come. However, it didn't dampen the Killer's (his nickname) unbridled performances and popularity on the club circuit. This included stints at the Star-Club in Hamburg, Germany. His only Top 40 hit in the 1960s was a cover of *What'd I Say* in 1961. By the late 1960s he'd regained acceptability and recognition as one of rock music's originators, though he had turned increasingly to country music. He had three number one hits on the country charts in 1968. His early 1970's singles *Me And Bobby McGee*, *Chantilly Lace* and *Drinkin' Wine Spo-Dee-O-Dee* were certified Gold. He continued to enjoy success on the country charts well into the 1980s. He was a charter inductee into the Rock and Roll Hall of Fame in 1986.

The Beatles were huge fans of Jerry's music and faithfully covered the arrangements of many of his hits during the early 1960s. Lewis first met John Lennon when they were on the bill at a rock 'n' roll revival in Toronto, Canada on September 13, 1969. "Lennon came into my dressing room, knelt down and kissed my boots! I was taken aback by that, but honored at the same time," says Jerry. The Beatles were an amazing and talented bunch of guys. You can't deny great talent! I'm not much on funerals because I've been to so many, but I did go to Carl Perkins' funeral and saw George Harrison again, and got to spend some time with him, though under sad circumstances. George was a good man."
During Ringo Starr's appearance on Michael

Parkinson's (see: Michael Parkinson, Jimmy Tarbuck, Tim Rice & Ringo Starr) talk show in 1981 Ringo said that he would present his compositions to the other Beatles for consideration but that they would fall on the floor laughing because he'd usually re-written a Jerry Lee Lewis' B-side. Lewis was an invited guest of Ringo's at the grand opening of Willie Nelson, Bill Wyman* and Ringo's London Brasserie in Atlanta's Peachtree Center on September 26, 1987. Lewis performed during the event. He was backed by the local band Starshower and joined onstage by Isaac Hayes, Jermaine Jackson and Ringo on drums. They jammed on a handful of songs, which are available on unauthorized releases. Ringo contributed to Jerry's 2006 best-selling album, *Last Man Standing,* singing a duet with him on *Sweet Little Sixteen.* Lewis says, "Ringo is a great guy and a great friend and we had a great time in the studio recording." Ringo and Lewis also recorded *Roll Over Beethoven*, which remains unreleased. Though un-credited, Lewis says Ringo also drummed on both songs. For more information go to www.jerryleelewis.com

Little Richard

Good Golly Miss Molly [Various Artists]
Polydor-CDP 399 (promotional single) (probably 02/xx/91)
Producer: Jeff Lynne
Ringo Starr: Drums; Little Richard: Lead Vocals & Piano; Jeff Lynne: Guitars & Bass; Jim Horn: Saxophone
Rumbo Recorders, Los Angeles, CA xx/xx/90

Good Golly, Miss Molly (R. Blackwell-J. Marascalco) 2:10 (1)

Little Richard was born Richard Penniman in Macon, Georgia on December 5, 1932. His grandfather was a preacher and Richard sang in church with his family's group the Penniman Singers. Richard's music, and heavy use of makeup and outlandish outfits, was greatly influenced by jump blues singer Billy Wright and the traveling medicine shows he'd seen. He was a pioneer of what years later would be called "glitter rock." Richard boasts that he is "the architect of rock 'n' roll" and there's ample evidence to support his claim. He began recording for RCA and Peacock Records in the early 1950s. Lloyd Price suggested he contact Specialty Records where between 1955 and 1958 Richard had Top 10 hits with *Long Tall Sally*, *Jenny Jenny*, *Keep-A-Knockin'*, *Good Golly, Miss Molly*, Top 20 hits with *Tutti Frutti* and *Rip It Up*, and Top 40 hits with *Slippin' And Slidin'*, *Lucille* and *Ooh! My Soul.* Many of these and other recordings by Richard were regulars in The Beatles' early stage repertoire. Richard renounced rock 'n' roll at the height of his career to study for the ministry. He dedicated several years to preaching and recording gospel music.

Richard returned to performing rock music in 1962 touring Europe with a band that included Billy Preston*. Brian Epstein booked Richard to top the bill along with The Beatles at the Liverpool area Tower Ballroom on October 12 and the Empire Theatre on October 28, 1962. Several days later The Beatles returned to Hamburg, Germany for their second engagement at the Star-Club where they were also on the bill with Richard. These were memorable occasions for them and they became friends with Richard, especially Paul McCartney, who idolized and copied much of Richard's vocal style, particularly on songs of his such as *I'm Down.* McCartney closed many of The Beatles' live performances with *Long Tall Sally* or *I'm Down.* Richard would typically brag that he taught The Beatles everything they knew and was responsible for their success. The Beatles considered signing Richard to Apple. Richard continued to tour during the latter half of the 1960s and on September 13, 1969, he appeared on the bill with John Lennon and the Plastic Ono Band (see Yoko Ono, Eric Clapton) at a rock 'n' roll revival in Toronto. Richard paid tribute to McCartney and The Beatles by covering their song *I Saw Her Standing There* in 1969. By the mid-1970s Richard renounced his wild rock 'n' roll lifestyle and re-embraced Christianity and his gospel career. McCartney wrote the forward to the first edition of the 1984 authorized biography *The Life And Times Of Little Richard.* Richard was a charter inductee into the Rock and Roll Hall of Fame in 1986.

In 1990 Richard re-recorded *Good Golly Miss Molly* with Ringo Starr on drums. According to its producer Jeff Lynne* the recording originally featured Benmont Tench on piano, who was replaced by Richard. The song was featured on the soundtrack of the film *King Ralph* starring John Goodman, but the recording's release was limited to an obscure cassette single (Polydor-879 678), a comparatively more available promotional CD single and the Dutch CD single (Polydor-879 678-2)

In 1991 Richard was part of The Peace Choir, organized by John and Yoko's son Sean, who made a recording of Lennon's *Give Peace A Chance*. He made a guest appearance, and his music was featured, on McCartney's 1995 radio series *Oobu Joobu*. Little Richard continues to perform, and play the role as the undisputed greatest and prettiest rock 'n' roll star of all time!

The Royal Liverpool Philharmonic Orchestra & Choir & Choristers Of Liverpool Cathedral

Liverpool Oratorio
EMI Classics-7243 5 99742 9 3 (DVD) (EU) (xx/xx/04) (02/22/91)
Producer: John Fraser (music) & Chips Chipperfield (film); Paul McCartney: Executive Producer (music)
Paul McCartney: Introduction; Kiri Te Kanawa: Soprano Vocals; Sally Burgess: Mezzo-Soprano Vocals; Jerry Hadley: Tenor Vocals; Willard White: Bass Vocals; Jeremy Budd: Boy Soloist Vocals; Carl Davis: Conductor of Royal Liverpool Philharmonic Orchestra & Choir & Choristers; Nic Raine: Assistant to Carl Davis; The Royal Liverpool Philharmonic Orchestra includes: Malcolm Stewart: Leader-First Solo Violin; Nicholas Wood: Associate Leader-First Violin; Irene Pearce: Principal-First Violin; Nicolette Brown: First Violin; Lesley Gwyther: First Violin; Clifford Bibby: First Violin; Alexander Marks: First Violin; Donald Turnbull: First Violin; Ian Bone: First Violin; John Hebbron: First Violin; Duncan Atherton: First Violin; Sonia Nash: First Violin; Johathan Pigott: First Violin; Valerie Leary: First Violin; Susan Henderson: Principal-Second Violin; Gerald Adamson: Associate Principal-Second Violin; James Hutton: Second-Violin; Justin Evans: Second Violin; Kenneth Johnson: Second Violin; Martin Burrage: Second Violin; Wynford Andrews: Second Violin; Richard Gordon-Smith: Second Violin; Helen Cookson: Second Violin; Peter Leach: Second Violin; Celia Goodwin: Second Violin; Ian Flower: Second Violin; Wendy Cochran: Second Violin; Roger Benedict: Principal-Viola; Robert Shepley: Viola; Andrea Creech: Viola; David Ruby: Viola; Richard Wallace: Viola; Alexander Ferguson: Viola; Anne Forshaw: Viola; Juliet Brien: Viola; Angela Berreen: Viola; Audrey Henning: Viola; Christopher Balmer: Viola; Avril Schepens: Viola; Timothy Walden: Principal-Flute; Anthony Ovenell: Flute; Myra Bennett: Piccolo; Jonathan Small: Principal-Oboe; Nigel Roberts: Oboe; Anna Cooper: Cor Anglais; Christopher Swann: Clarinet; Andrew Roberts: Clarinet; Colin Pownall: Bass Clarinet; Alan Pendlebury: Principal-Bassoon; Alison Lee-Browne: Bassoon; Nicholas Lander: Contra Bassoon; David Pigott: Associate Principal-Horn; Martin Taggart: Horn; Michael Ogonovsky: Horn; John Thornton: Horn; Chris Morley: Horn; Ian Blamain: Principal-Trumpet; Alan Stringer: (MBE) Principal Emeritus-Trumpet; Desmond Worthington: Trumpet; Blyth Lindsay: Tenor Trombone; Philip Goodwin: Tenor Trombone; John Langford: Bass Trombone; George Smith: Tuba; Ian Wright: Timpani; Graham Johns: Principal-Percussion; Jean Webster: Percussion; Dawn Mace: Percussion; Mair Jones: Harp; Stephen Disley: Organ; The Royal Liverpool Philharmonic Choir includes: Ian Tracey: Chorusmaster & Master Of The Choristers; Jennifer Allcock: Soprano; Kate Banbury: Soprano; Sylvia Bawden: Soprano; Ruth Bennett: Soprano; Ann Bone: Soprano; Angela Brodbelt: Soprano; Nicola Brooks: Soprano; Ruth Brown: Soprano; Jill Carlson: Soprano; Maria Casstles: Soprano; Shelagh Crosbie: Soprano; Mary Daley: Soprano; Janet Eastwood: Soprano; Carolyn Eddowes: Soprano; Ruth Greening-Jackson: Soprano; Sarah Gregory: Soprano; Janet Hare: Soprano; Joyce Hill: Soprano; Jean Hocknell: Soprano; Patricia Howley: Soprano; Anne Hughes: Soprano; Gillian Jones: Soprano; Louise Jones: Soprano; Alfreda Kennedy: Soprano; Margaret Kershaw: Soprano; Lindsey McDonald: Soprano; Margaret Marks: Soprano; Carey Marsden: Soprano; Helen McClorry: Soprano; Claudia McConnell: Soprano; Geraldine McGinity: Soprano; Elizabeth McIlwaine: Soprano; Maura McWatt: Soprano; Frankie Moor: Soprano; Margaret Morton: Soprano; Anne-Marie Obaje: Soprano; Alison Parker: Soprano; Ann Paver: Soprano; Anne Pigott: Soprano; Jane Pitts: Soprano; Margaretta Price: Soprano; Evelyn Randles: Soprano; Brenda Redmond: Soprano; Sian Roberts: Soprano; Carol Ryan: Soprano; Margaret Satterthwaite: Soprano; Kate Sharp: Soprano; Jillian Simms: Soprano; Margaret Smith: Soprano; Deborah Tate: Soprano; Eunice Theobald: Soprano; Diana Walkden: Soprano; Barbara Wall: Soprano; Janet Wareing: Soprano; Brenda Waterson: Soprano; Gillian Winstanley: Soprano; Eleanor Wright: Soprano; Kathleen Zimak: Soprano; Carolyn Allcock: Alto; Heather Barrett: Alto; Yvonne Bieniek: Alto; Andrina Boyle: Alto; Anne Broe: Alto; Susan Carver: Alto; Joan

Childe-Harmer: Alto; Sylvia Church: Alto; Maureen Clarke: Alto; Sally Daunt: Alto; Dorthy Davis: Alto; Helen Dingle: Alto; Alma Bootson: Alto; Catherine Duke: Alto; Patrica Feeney: Alto; Hilary Flett: Alto; Anne Garden: Alto; Florence Gersten: Alto; Wendy Hadfield: Alto; Pamela Hankin: Alto; Jackie Hine: Alto; Patricia Hulme: Alto; Barbara Jackson: Alto; Mavis Jenkins: Alto; Joyce Jones: Alto; Margaret Kay: Alto; Marion Kilshaw: Alto; Judith Laity: Alto; Joyce Lowdon: Alto; Veronica Maguire: Alto; Valerie McGraw: Alto; Janice Perkins: Alto; Rowena Preston: Alto; Margaret Smith: Alto; Rona Smith: Alto; Susan Smith: Alto; Olga South: Alto; Carol Stone-Williams: Alto; Norma Taylor: Alto; Mary Tew: Alto; Olive Walker: Alto; Aileen Ward: Alto; Jules Waring: Alto; Dorthy Watt: Alto; Anne Wheaton: Alto; Patrica Wheeler: Alto; Alison White: Alto; Daphne Wigmore: Alto; Eryl Williams: Alto; Lorna Winstanley: Alto; Ann Woodward: Alto; Peter Bates: Tenor; Barry Butcher: Tenor; Ian Crinyion: Tenor; John Davies: Tenor; Stephen Davies: Tenor; Fred Gilliver: Tenor; John Gilmore: Tenor; Niel Heritage: Tenor; Jim Hetherington: Tenor; Harry Holmes: Tenor; Christopher Hull: Tenor; Gwyn Jenkins: Tenor; Brian Jones: Tenor; Brian H. Jones: Tenor; Stuart Keen: Tenor; Norman Kidd: Tenor; Richard Marks: Tenor; Bruce Marsden: Tenor; John Martin: Tenor; Christopher McCurry: Tenor; Francis Morris: Tenor; Ian Naylor: Tenor; Hugh Peate: Tenor; Gordon Wilkinson: Tenor; Robert Williams: Tenor; Kenneth Wynn: Tenor: Peter Zacharias: Tenor; Noel Andrews: Bass; Timothy Atkinson: Bass; Stuart Christie: Bass; Jim Cooke: Bass; Howard Cox: Bass; Kevin Dennett: Bass; John Dingle: Bass; Alistair Doxat-Pratt: Bass; Peter Drury: Bass; Clive Eames: Bass; David Eddowes: Bass; William Gould: Bass; Gary Jones: Bass; Keith Jones: Bass; Robert Jones: Bass; David Kruger: Bass; Dennis Lavelle: Bass; Michael Lind: Bass; Robert Lowdon: Bass; Alec Mackinnon: Bass; Andrew McGowan: Bass; Robin Moor: Bass; Michael Olver: Bass; Michael Pitts: Bass; Richard Rushworth: Bass; David Scott: Bass; Toby Screech: Bass; Frank Seddon: Bass; Colin Smith: Bass; Phil Snelling: Bass; John Spielgelbert: Bass; Miles Tew: Bass; Tony Twemlow: Bass; Geoff Wells: Bass; David Wetherell: Bass; John White: Bass; Paul Whitefoot: Bass; Colin Yates: Bass; The Liverpool Cathedral Choristers include: Christopher Ambler: Chorister; Benjamin Appleton: Chorister; Andrew Berkeley: Chorister; Benjamin Bridson: Chorister; Stuart Christie: Chorister; Geoffrey Coombe: Chorister; Mark Crotty: Chorister; Michael Evans: Chorister; Stuart Gilbert: Chorister; Martin Gratton: Chorister; Austin Hewitt: Chorister; Alexander Hornby: Chorister; Michael Horton: Chorister; Benjamin Humphries: Chorister; Paul Jones: Chorister; Stuart Jones: Chorister; Andrew Kay: Chorister; Paul Kelly: Chorister; Joseph Lalgee: Chorister; David Leahey: Chorister; Neil Leahey: Chorister; Cliff Jenkinson: Chorister; Jonathan McDonald: Chorister; Ian Middlehurst: Chorister; Jeffrey Moore: Chorister; Robin Panter: Chorister; Julian Pigott: Chorister; Matthew Polglase: Chorister; Stephen Quirk: Chorister; Peter Rimmer: Chorister; Peter Shephard: Chorister; Paul Taylor: Chorister; Nicholas Thomas: Chorister; Ian Upton: Chorister; Philip White-Jones: Chorister
Liverpool Cathedral, Liverpool, UK 06/28-29/91

Paul McCartney's Liverpool Oratorio: (Movement: I. War / II. School / III. Crypt/ / IV. Father / V. Wedding / VI. Work/ VII. Crisis / VIII. Peace) [live] (**P. McCartney**-C. Davis) (1: I-VIII) **(approx. 1 hr. 41 min.)**
[Also available on EMI Classics-CDC 7 54372 2 (1: I-IV / 2: V-VIII) (approx. 1 hr. 37 min.)]

In the late 1830s Mr. William Sudlow, an amateur organist, and a group of friends regularly met at Liverpool's St. Martin's Church to perform choral music. On January 10, 1840 they formed the Liverpool Philharmonic Society. In 1988 Carl Davis was conducting the Royal Liverpool Philharmonic Orchestra's performance of his and Carla Lane's *Pigeon's Progress* (see Linda McCartney). Paul McCartney, impressed with the composer and conductor who had moved to the UK some 30 years earlier from his native New York, sent Davis a good luck message via the Philharmonic's General Manager, Brian Pidgeon. Shortly thereafter, Davis approached McCartney with the idea of contributing something for the culmination of the Philharmonic's year-long celebration of their 150th anniversary. The two composed an oratorio loosely based on McCartney's life. [Davis had previously composed and conducted the original score for Dick Clark's TV movie *Birth Of The Beatles*. He later contributed to McCartney's 1993 album *Off The Ground*.]

McCartney auditioned for the Choristers of Liverpool Cathedral when he was 11 years old but was turned down, much to his, and ultimately their embarrassment. Thirty-eight years later on June 28, 1991 the hometown boy made his triumphant return to the cathedral as the classical composer of the *Liverpool Oratorio*. The Oratorio's solo vocalists Sally Burgess and Willard White, and producer John Fraser have worked with McCartney on other classical music projects of his (see Anya Alexeyev). The *Liverpool Oratorio* has since been performed in cities around the world, where McCartney has generally received favorable reviews for his first major classical work. For more information go to www.liverpoolphil.com www.carl-davis.com

Nils Lofgren

Silver Lining
Rykodisc-RCD 10170
Producer: Kevin McCormick & Nils Lofgren
Ocean Way Studios, Los Angeles, CA xx/xx/90

Bein' Angry (N. Lofgren) 5:52 (8) (03/06/91)

Ringo Starr: B. Vocal; Nils Lofgren: Lead Vocals & Guitar; Kevin McCormick: Fretless Bass; Andy Newmark: Drums; Billy Preston: Organ

Walkin' Nerve (N. Lofgren) 3:53 (3)
Ringo Starr: Drums; Nils Lofgren: Lead Vocals & Guitar; Kevin McCormick: Bass

Ringo Starr And His All-Starr Band
Pioneer Artists-PA-090-007 (LD 12") (07/xx/90)
Tim Snow (video); Joe Walsh & Jim Nipar (music); Executive Producer: Ringo Starr & David Fishof
Ringo Starr: Drums; Nils Lofgren: Lead Vocals & Guitar; Billy Preston: Keyboards & B. Vocals; Jim Keltner: Drums; Levon Helm: Drums & B. Vocals; Joe Walsh: Guitar & B. Vocals; Rick Danko: Bass; Clarence Clemons: Saxophone; Dr. John: Keyboards
Greek Theatre, Los Angeles, CA 09/03/89

Bein Angry [live] (N. Lofgren) 4:34 (2/3)

Ringo Starr And His All-Starr Band
Rykodisc-RCD 90190 (RCD-10190 & RCD5-1019) (10/12/90)
Producer: Joe Walsh & Jim Nipar (music)
Ringo Starr: Drums; Nils Lofgren: Lead Vocals & Guitar; Billy Preston: Keyboards; Jim Keltner: Drums; Levon Helm: Drums; Joe Walsh: Guitar; Rick Danko: Bass; Clarence Clemons: Tambourine; Dr. John: Keyboards
Greek Theatre, Los Angeles, CA 09/03/89

Shine Silently [live] (N. Lofgren-D. Wagner) 6:39 (1-5)
[Also available on *Ringo Starr And His All Starr Band The Anthology...So Far.* Koch-KOC-CD-8312 (1-5) (07/24/01) (02/05/01); Executive Producer: Ringo Starr & David Fishof]

Ringo Starr And His All-Starr Band Volume 2-Live From Montreux
Videoarts-VALJ-3369 (LD 12") (Japan) (probably 11/xx/93)
Producer: Ringo Starr (music); Jim Beach & Louise Velazquez (film); Executive Producer: Ringo Starr, David Fishof & Hilary Gerrard
Montreux Jazz Festival, Montreux, Switzerland 07/13/92

Shine Silently [live] (N. Lofgren-D. Wagner) 6:29 (1/8)
Ringo Starr: Drums; Nils Lofgren: Lead Vocals & Electric Guitar; Joe Walsh: Acoustic Guitar & B. Vocals; Todd Rundgren: Acoustic Guitar & B. Vocals; Burton Cummings: Keyboards; Dave Edmunds: Electric Guitar & B. Vocals; Timothy B. Schmit: Bass & B. Vocals; Tim Cappello: Percussion; Zak Starkey: Drums

Walkin' Nerve [live] (N. Lofgren) 4:00 (2/6)
Ringo Starr: Drums; Nils Lofgren: Lead Vocals & Electric Guitar; Joe Walsh: Electric Guitar; Todd Rundgren: Electric Guitar; Burton Cummings: Keyboards & Percussion; Dave Edmunds: Electric Guitar; Timothy B. Schmit: Bass; Tim Cappello: Percussion; Zak Starkey: Drums
[Also available on *Ringo Starr And His All Starr Band The Anthology...So Far.* Koch-KOC-CD-8312 (1-13) (07/24/01) (02/05/01); Executive Producer: Ringo Starr & David Fishof]

Nils Lofgren was born on June 21, 1951 in Chicago, Illinois but spent his formative years in the Washington D.C. area where he learned to play accordion, keyboards and guitar. He was the leader of the band Grin in the early 1970s. He first gained notice playing on Neil Young's* *After The Gold Rush* album and joined his backing band Crazy Horse shortly thereafter. He was soon in demand as a top backup and session player, and had mild success as a solo artist. Lofgren became internationally famous in the mid-1980s as a member of Bruce Springsteen's E Street Band. He released a cover of The Beatles' song *Anytime At All* in 1981.

Lofgren was a member of Ringo Starr's All-Starr Band tour in 1989, performing *Bein' Angry* and *Shine Silently* with Ringo backing him on drums. Ringo contributed to the songs *Bein' Angry* and *Walkin' Nerve* on Lofgren's 1991 album *Silver Lining.* Ringo also made a cameo in the video for the album's single *Valentine*, even though he didn't contribute to the song. On May 31, 1991 Ringo joined Lofgren onstage at the Roxy in Los Angeles to play drums on *Walkin' Nerve* and about a year later played drums on the song during Lofgren's performance in London. Lofgren was also a member of

Ringo's All-Starr Band tour in 1992 performing *Shine Silently*, *Walkin' Nerve*, and The Beau Brummels' *Just A Little* that hasn't been officially released, with Ringo backing him on drums. Lofgren says Ringo didn't contribute to his 1992 album *Crooked Line* but was thanked in the credits for his general support. That fall Lofgren, as a member of the house band on the Arsenio Hall Show, backed Ringo during his performance on the show. Lofgren was unable to join Ringo's All-Starr Band tour in 1995 due to previous commitments, but did fill in for several dates as the opening act and joined the band for the encores. He also appeared on a PBS tribute to The Beatles in 1995. Lofgren opened for Ringo's All-Starr Band's performance at Wolf Trap outside Washington D.C. on May 21, 1997. He also joined Ringo's All-Starr Band for their encore at the PNC Bank Arts Center in Holmdel, New Jersey on August 3, 2003. Lofgren continues to write, record and tour with and without the E Street Band. For more information go to www.nilslofgren.com

Loma Mar Quartet

Working Classical (Orchestral And Chamber Music By Paul McCartney)
EMI Classics CDQ 7243 5 56897 2 6 (10/19/99)
Producer: John Fraser; Executive Producer: Paul McCartney
Krista Bennion Feeney: Violin; Anca Nicolau: Violin; Joanna Hood: Viola; Myron Lutzke: Cello
EMI-Abbey Road Studios, London, UK probably mid/xx/99

Haymakers (P. McCartney) 3:33 (3)

Midwife (P. McCartney) 3:33 (4)

The Loma Mar Quartet was formed in 1997. They performed at a memorial service for Linda McCartney on June 22, 1998 at Riverside Church in New York. Their first appearance on record is on *Working Classical*, an album of orchestral and chamber music interpretations of Paul McCartney compositions. McCartney chose the title as a word play on "working class." The Loma Mar Quartet performs many of the songs on the album including *Haymakers* and *Midwife*, which McCartney wrote exclusively for the album. The album also includes performances by The London Symphony Orchestra*. *Working Classical* had its premiere at the Liverpool Philharmonic Hall on October 16, 1999. The performance was also issued on VHS by PBS (794054824735).

Jackie Lomax

Is This What You Want?
Apple-CDP 7975812 (Germany) (11/19/91) (03/21/69)
Producer: George Harrison [unless noted otherwise]
Sound Recorders, Los Angeles, CA 10-11/xx/68 [unless noted otherwise]

Baby You're A Lover (J. Lomax) 3:02 (10)
George Harrison: Guitar; Jackie Lomax: Lead Vocals & Guitar; Hal Blaine: Drums; Larry Knechtel: Keyboards; Joe Osborne: Bass; Paul Beaver: Synthesizers; Bernie Krause: Synthesizers

(I) Fall Inside Your Eyes (J. Lomax) 3:08 (6)
Jackie Lomax: Lead Vocals & Guitar; Joe Osborn: Bass; Hal Blaine: Drums; Larry Knechtel: Keyboards; Paul Beaver: Synthesizer; Bernie Krause: Synthesizer

Going Back To Liverpool (J. Lomax) 3:07 (15) (11/19/91)
Producer: Paul McCartney & probably **George Harrison**
George Harrison: Guitar & B. Vocals; Jackie Lomax: Lead Vocals; Billy Preston: Keyboards & B. Vocals; Pete Clark: Drums; Billy Kinsley: Bass; Tim Renick: Guitar
Apple Studios, London, UK 03/11/69 & probably 03/12/69

How Can You Say Goodbye (J. Lomax) 4:11 (3)
George Harrison: Guitar; Jackie Lomax: Lead Vocals & Guitar; Hal Blaine: Drums; Joe Osborn: Bass; Larry Knechtel: Keyboards

How The Web Was Woven (C. Westlake-D. Most) 3:50 (17) (02/06/70)
Jackie Lomax: Lead Vocals; Leon Russell: Keyboards, Bass, Drums & Guitar
Trident Studios, London, UK 11/xx/69

I Just Don't Know (J. Lomax) 2:52 (12)
Jackie Lomax: Lead Vocals & Guitar; Hal Blaine: Drums; Joe Osborn: Bass; Larry Knechtel: Piano

Is This What You Want? (J. Lomax) 2:44 (7)
George Harrison: Guitar; Jackie Lomax: Lead Vocals & Guitar; Hal Blaine: Drums; Larry Knechtel: Piano; Joe Osborn: Bass; John Barham: String Arrangements
Sound Recorders, Los Angeles, CA & EMI-Abbey Road Studios, London, UK 10-11/xx/68

Little Yellow Pills (J. Lomax) 4:02 (7)
Jackie Lomax: Lead Vocals & Guitar; Hal Blaine: Drums; Larry Knechtel: Keyboards; Joe Osborne: Bass; Paul Beaver: Synthesizer; Bernie Krause: Synthesizer

New Day [CD version] (J. Lomax) 3:15 (13) (11/19/91)
Producer: Jackie Lomax & Mal Evans
George Harrison: Guitar; Jackie Lomax: Lead Vocals & Guitar; Billy Kinsley: Bass; Tim Renick: Guitar, Chris Hatfield: Keyboards; Pete Clark: Drums
Olympic Studios, London, UK 03-04/xx/69

Sour Milk Sea (**G. Harrison**) 3:52 (5) (08/26/68)
George Harrison: Rhythm Guitar; **Paul McCartney: Bass**; **Ringo Starr: Drums**; Jackie Lomax: Lead Vocals & Rhythm Guitar; Eric Clapton: Lead Guitar; Nicky Hopkins: Piano; Eddie Clayton: Congas
EMI-Abbey Road† & Trident Studios, London, UK 06/24†-26/68

Speak To Me (J. Lomax) 3:08 (1)
George Harrison: Guitar; Jackie Lomax: Lead Vocals & Guitar; Hal Blaine: Drums; Joe Osborn: Bass; Larry Knechtel: Keyboards; John Barham: String Arrangements
Sound Recorders, Los Angeles, CA & probably EMI-Abbey Road Studios, London, UK 10-11/xx/68

Sunset (J. Lomax) 3:54 (4)
Jackie Lomax: Lead Vocals & Guitar; Spike Heatley: Bass; Alan Branscombe: Piano; John Barham: String Arrangement
EMI-Abbey Road Studios, London, UK probably 07/xx/68

Take My Word (J. Lomax) 3:55 (8)
George Harrison: Guitar; Jackie Lomax: Lead Vocals & Guitar; Hal Blaine: Drums; Joe Osborn: Bass; John Barham: String Arrangements; Paul Beaver: Synthesizers; Bernie Krause: Synthesizers
Sound Recorders, Los Angeles, CA & probably Trident &/or EMI-Abbey Road Studios, London, UK 10-11/xx/68

The Eagle Laughs At You (J. Lomax) 2:24 (9) (08/26/68)
George Harrison: Guitar; Jackie Lomax: Lead Vocals, Bass & Guitar; Eric Clapton: Lead Guitar; Tony Newman: Drums; John Barham: Flugelhorn
Trident Studios, London, UK 06/24-26/68

Thumbin' A Ride (J. Leiber-M. Stoller) 3:56 (16) (06/02/69)
Producer: Paul McCartney
George Harrison: Guitar & B. Vocals; Jackie Lomax: Lead Vocals & Guitar; Pete Clark: Drums; Billy Kinsley: Bass; Tim Renick: Guitar; Chris Hatfield: Keyboards; Pattie (Boyd) Harrison: B. Vocals
Apple Studios, London, UK 03/11/69 & probably 03/12/69

Won't You Come Back (J. Lomax) 4:10 (14) (11/19/91)
George Harrison: Guitar; Jackie Lomax: Lead Vocals & (probable) Guitar; probably one or more of the following: Alan Branscombe, Chris Hatfield, John Barham or Nicky Hopkins: Keyboards; Spike Heatley, Billy Kinsley or Klaus Voormann: Bass; Pete Clark, Joel "Bishop" O'Brien or Tony Newman: Drums; Tim Renick: Guitar
EMI-Abbey Road Studios, London, UK xx/xx/68

You've Got Me Thinking (J. Lomax) 2:53 (11)
Jackie Lomax: Lead Vocals & Guitar; Klaus Voormann: Bass; Eric Clapton: Guitar
EMI-Abbey Road Studios, London, UK probably 06 or 09/xx/68

New Day / Thumbin' A Ride
Apple-1807 (7" single) (05/09/69)
Producer: Jackie Lomax & Mal Evans
George Harrison: Guitar; Jackie Lomax: Lead Vocals & Guitar; Billy Kinsley: Bass; Tim Renick: Guitar, Chris Hatfield: Keyboards; Pete Clark: Drums
Olympic Studios, London, UK 03-04/xx/69

New Day [single version] (J. Lomax) 2:50 (1/1)

Kristofer Engelhardt and Jackie Lomax, Beatlefest, Hilton Hotel Airport, Los Angeles, CA November 27, 1998. © Kristofer Engelhardt.

John "Jackie" Lomax was born on May 10, 1944 in Wallasey (Liverpool), England. Between 1962 and 1965 he was the bassist and lead singer of the popular Liverpool band The Undertakers, who were often on bills with The Beatles in Liverpool and Hamburg, Germany. His next group, Lomax Alliance, was signed to NEMS in the mid-1960s.

Lomax was signed to Apple Records and Music Publishing who released his first single, *Sour Milk Sea*, in 1968. Harrison wrote the song in India and recorded a home demo of it with The Beatles, which appears on unauthorized releases. Though The Beatles never properly recorded it, all of them, except John Lennon, play on Lomax's recording produced by Harrison. Even with additional backing from Eric Clapton* and Nicky Hopkins* this excellent song was eclipsed by the success of Apple's other debut singles, *Hey Jude* by The Beatles, on which Jackie sings, and *Those Were The Days* by Mary Hopkin*, and failed to chart. Three days after its release Lomax contributed backing vocals and handclaps to *Dear Prudence* for *The Beatles* (white) album.

Harrison also produced the recordings for Lomax's first and only Apple album *Is This What You Want?* released in 1969. Lomax says eight basic tracks were recorded in Los Angeles, though the less than accurate notes with the CD issue say only six tracks were recorded there, with Phil Spector's* legendary "wrecking crew" session players Hal Blaine, Larry Knechtel and Joe Osborn. Beaver & Krause also contributed to those sessions on a then revolutionary new instrument known as the Moog synthesizer. [Bernie Krause would later claim that side two of Harrison's album *Electronic Sounds* was one of Krause's recordings. Krause's name was painted over, but faintly visible, on the front of the album's jacket, lending support to his claim.] The CD notes credit *Little Yellow Pills* and the bonus track *Won't You Come Back* as being produced by Harrison, and recorded in March 1968, but Harrison was in India that entire month. [Paul Tennant of Apple's group Focal Point claims they supplied backing vocals on *Little Yellow Pills*, but the (un-credited) backing vocals on this, and most of the songs on the album, sound like female vocalists.] These notes also seem to indicate (as do many other sources) that *The Eagle Laughs At You* (the B-side to *Sour Milk Sea*) also includes McCartney and Starr, but Lomax denies their involvement. Lomax recalls most of the details for each of his recordings for Apple, but didn't attend many sessions when the backing vocals, strings and horns were overdubbed, and doesn't know who was involved, except for singer Madeline Bell, and string and horn arranger John Barham. He says Harrison played guitar on most of his Apple recordings. He is uncertain whether Harrison plays guitar on *You've Got Me Thinking* and doesn't recall who plays on *Won't You Come Back*. Lomax's album is regarded as one of Apple's best, but it too failed in the charts leaving Lomax and Harrison somewhat disillusioned.

Lomax produced his second Apple single, *New Day*, with Mal Evans. Marc Roberty's reference books on Clapton are at odds with several reliable publications regarding his involvement with Lomax. He claims that Starr and Clapton play on *New Day*, while others say only Harrison was involved. Lomax says that of those three, only Harrison played on *New Day*. The B-side was a cover of The Coasters' song *Thumbin' A Ride*, which Lomax says was McCartney's idea to record and produce because Harrison wasn't available, but says Harrison did contribute to some of the sessions. All evidence indicates that *Thumbin' A Ride* and the song *Going Back To Liverpool*, were recorded on March 11, 1969 and, or possibly on March 12. Harrison was at Apple on March 12, but was called to his home when police raided it for drugs. McCartney was married on March 12 (see Linda McCartney), though that wouldn't necessarily preclude the workaholic McCartney from being in a studio on his wedding night. The March 15 issue of *NME* magazine states, "Hours after announcing that he was to marry the following day, he [Paul] spent the evening in Apple's basement studios playing drums for two hours with George Harrison." The CD booklet with Lomax's album features a photo of Lomax on guitar, McCartney on drums and another guitarist (obscured) that is probably Harrison, in Apple Studios. Lomax says McCartney didn't end up playing drums on any of his released recordings, but other sources claim McCartney plays drums on *Thumbin' A Ride*. Harrison is clearly heard singing backing vocals on *Going Back To Liverpool*, which most likely was recorded at the same sessions as it credits McCartney as producer. Other reliable sources, including an article in *NME* on March 22, 1969, indicate that Harrison was also involved in the production of *Going Back To Liverpool*. Lomax also thinks George produced the song.

Lomax's third and final single (except for reissues) for Apple was *How The Web Was Woven* released in early 1970. It was produced by Harrison, with Leon Russell* playing all the instruments. Lomax says Harrison nearly gave him his song *Something* to record, and that he turned down Lennon's offer to record his song *Across The Universe*. An Apple acetate titled *The Millionaire* credited to Lomax reportedly exists but he doesn't recall any song of his by that title. Perhaps it is only a working title or was incorrectly identified as Lomax and might be The Iveys' (see Badfinger) song *And Her Daddy's A Millionaire*. If the acetate is an unreleased Lomax recording, Harrison likely contributed to it.

With poor record sales, the arrival of Allen Klein, and the anarchy at Apple, Lomax moved to the US and Warner Bros. Records who released two albums of his in the early 1970s. He returned to the UK briefly in 1974 joining the band Badger (see Ashton, Gardner & Dyke) but was soon back in the US where he next recorded two albums for Capitol, which like his Apple and Warner Bros. albums, failed in the charts. Lomax says none of The Beatles contributed to any of his recordings after he left Apple. In the mid-1990s he toured with an updated version of The Drifters (see Ben E. King), The Coasters and The Box Tops, playing bass and guitar. Lomax continues to write, record and perform. For more information go to
www.jackielomax.com

The London Symphony Orchestra & Chorus

Paul McCartney's Standing Stone
EMI Classics-7243 5 56484 2 6 (09/25/97)
Producer: John Fraser; **Mixed by: Paul McCartney**
The London Symphony Chorus: Vocals; The London Symphony Orchestra; Lawrence Foster: Conductor; Janice Graham: Leader; Stephen Westrop: Chorus Master
EMI-Abbey Road Studios, London, UK 03/03-04/97, 04/30/97- 05/02/97 & 07/02/97

Movement I After Heavy Light Years (1 Fire/rain. Allegro energico) (2 Cell growth. Semplice) (3 `Human' theme. Maestoso) (**P. McCartney**) 16:33 (1: 1-3)

Movement II He Awoke Startled (4 Meditation. Contemplativo) (5 Crystal ship. Con noto

scherzando) (6 Sea voyage. Pulsating, with cool jazz feel) (7 Lost at sea. Sognando) (8 Release. Allegro con spirito) (P. McCartney) 16:14 (1: 4-8)

Movement III Subtle Colours Merged Soft contours (9 Safe haven/standing stone. Pastorale con moto) (10 Peaceful moment. Andante tranquillo) (11 Messenger. Energico) (12 Lament. Lamentoso) (13 Trance. Misterioso) (14 Eclipse. Eroico) (P. McCartney) 22:56 (1: 9-14)

Movement IV Strings pluck, horns blow, drums beat (15 Glory tales. Trionfale) (16 Fugal celebration. L'istesso tempo. Fresco) (17 Rustic dance. Rustico) (18 Love duet. Andante intimo) (19 Celebration. Andante) (P. McCartney) 19:08 (1: 15-19)

Working Classical (Orchestral And Chamber Music By Paul McCartney)
EMI Classics-CDQ 7243 5 56897 2 6 (10/19/99)
Producer: John Fraser; Executive Producer: Paul McCartney
London Symphony Orchestra: Orchestral Instruments
EMI-Abbey Road Studios, London, UK mid/xx/99

Spiral (P. McCartney) 10:02 (5)
Additionally: Lawrence Foster: Conductor

Tuesday (P. McCartney) 12:26 (12)
Additionally: Andrea Quinn: Conductor

The London Symphony Orchestra was founded in London, England in 1904. It has attracted some of the world's most prestigious conductors including Hans Richter, Artur Nikisch, Andre Previn and Claudio Abbado. In 1993 Paul McCartney was commissioned by Richard Lyttelton, President of EMI Classics, to contribute a work to help celebrate EMI's 100th Anniversary in 1997. [In 1991 the label released the *Liverpool Oratorio* (see The Royal Liverpool Philharmonic Orchestra & Choir & Choristers Of Liverpool Cathedral), McCartney's first major venture into the world of classical music.]

McCartney dedicated much time over the next few years to the creation of *Standing Stone*, a symphonic poem in four movements performed and recorded by over 300 members of The London Symphony Orchestra & Chorus. He first wrote the music, and then the story as a poem, to help structure the four movements. He used an Apple PowerMac computer, programmed with QBase software, to aid him in composing and annotating the music. He also employed the help of several musicians and composers, including Steve Lodder, Richard Rodney Bennett, John Harle and David Matthews, who are credited as musical associates. They helped McCartney translate his composition and ideas into a symphony by assisting with the structuring, arrangement, orchestration and notation of *Standing Stone*. John Fraser produced the recordings, with McCartney in attendance and acting as executive producer. Lawrence Foster conducted the Orchestra & Chorus. Final mixing and editing by McCartney and Fraser took place at Hog Hill Mill Studio several weeks later.

Standing Stone is an allegory of the development of life on earth in all of its manifestations from the big bang to the present. The title and initial ideas for *Standing Stone* were taken from two of McCartney's paintings about the dawn of time, and prehistoric Celtic spiral-designs and megaliths. McCartney also felt a need to express in poetry his feelings following the death of Ivan Vaughan, a lifelong friend who had introduced him to John Lennon. McCartney took the advice of Allen Ginsberg* and sought the help of poet Tom Pickard, who edited the poem.

Standing Stone premiered at the Royal Albert Hall in London on October 14, 1997 again performed by The London Symphony Orchestra & Chorus. This date was chosen as it closely marked the 35th Anniversary of EMI's release of *Love Me Do* [released on October 5], The Beatles first record for the label. The premiere also included a symphonic rendering of *A Leaf* (see Anya Alexeyev), *The Spiral*, and other classical compositions by McCartney, including *Inebriation* performed by The Brodsky Quartet and *Stately Horn* featuring the Mike Thompson Horn Quartet. The record was a major success on the US and UK classical charts. Portions of the making and performance of *Standing Stone* were also filmed, and available in 1999 on DVD (EMI-Classics-724349224391).

In 1999 The London Symphony Orchestra performed *A Leaf*, *Spiral* and *Tuesday* composed by McCartney, on the album *Working Classical*; the latter two seeing their premier on record. *Tuesday* was the theme of an animated short film made by McCartney in 2000. The album also includes performances by the Loma Mar Quartet*. *Working Classical's* premiere at the Liverpool Royal Philharmonic Hall on October 16, 1999 was filmed and made available on VHS (PBS Home Video-B8247) in 2001. The London Symphony Orchestra released their version of McCartney's composition *Nova* in 2001 (see Joyful Company Of Singers). For more information go to www.lso.co.uk

Lyle Lovett

With A Little Help To My Friends [Ringo Starr]
No Label Records-NLR 9904 (CD-R) [unauthorized release] (xx/xx/99)
Producer: The Nashville Network
Ringo Starr: Drums; Lyle Lovett: Guitar & Lead Vocals; Don Was: Bass; Benmont Tench: Keyboards; Mark Goldenberg: Guitar; Willie Nelson: Guitar; Mickey Raphael: Harmonica
Cyclone Stadium, Ames, Iowa 04/24/93

Further Down The Line [live] (L. Lovett) 3:21 (14)
Additionally: Willie Nelson: Vocals; Jonell Mosser: B. Vocals

If I Had A Boat [live] (L. Lovett) 3:26 (13)

She Makes Me Feel Good [live] (L. Lovett) 3:26 (12)
Additionally: Jonell Mosser: B. Vocals

Lyle Lovett was born on November 1, 1957 in Klein, Texas, a town named after his great-great-grandfather, and where Lyle still resides. He pursued a career in music following his graduation from Texas A&M University. Since the mid-1980s he has become one of the most successful crossover country and western artists, in part by incorporating swing, blues, folk and jazz into his songwriting. Six of his albums have reached the Top 10 on the country charts and been certified Gold. Between 1986 and 1988 his songs *Cowboy Man*, *God Will*, *Why I Don't Know*, *Give Back My Heart* and *She's No Lady* were Top 20 hits on the country charts. He has won four Grammy Awards. Lyle has also found success acting in a number of films and on TV.

Lyle performed at the *Farm Aid VI* benefit concert on April 24, 1993 singing three of his songs backed by The New Maroons*, which included Ringo Starr and Willie Nelson. The concert was broadcast on The Nashville Network. Farm Aid was inspired by Bob Dylan* but the nearly annual concerts since 1985 have been organized by Willie Nelson, Neil Young*, John Mellencamp and Dave Matthews to raise money for struggling family farmers. For more information go to www.lylelovett.com

Lulu

Together
Mercury-4400630802 (Canada) (05/21/02)
Producer: Billy Lawrie, Lulu, Lukas Burton & Gal Asher
Paul McCartney: Vocals, Bass† & Piano†; Lulu: Lead Vocals; Sacha Skarbek: Piano; John Fortis: Bass
EMI-Abbey Road Studios 01-02/xx/76†; & Sony Music Studios, London probably 04/xx/01

Inside Thing (Let 'Em In) (P. McCartney-L. McCartney-B. Lawrie-Lulu-L. Burton) 4:47 (3)

Lulu (a.k.a. Lulu Kennedy-Cairns) was born Marie Lawrie on November 3, 1948 in Lennonxtown but she grew up in nearby Glasgow, Scotland. Between 1964 and 1967 she had UK Top 10 hits with *Shout*, *Leave A Little Love* and *The Boat That I Row*. She took the title song of the 1967 film *To Sir, With Love*, in which she appeared, to the top of the charts. She had UK Top 10 hits with *Me, The Peaceful Heart* and *I'm A Tiger* in 1968, and *Boom Bang-A-Bang* in 1969. That year she married Maurice Gibb of The Bee Gees. She also had a Top 40 hit with *Oh Me, Oh My (I'm A Fool For You Baby)* in 1969. Lulu and Gibb divorced in 1973. In 1974 she had a UK Top Five hit with *The Man Who Sold The World*. Her last Top 40 hit was *I Could Never Miss You (More Than I Do)* in 1981. In 1993 she had a UK Top 20 hit with *Independence*. Since the late 1960s Lulu has appeared in films, stage shows, and hosted a number of successful UK TV and radio shows.

Paul McCartney and Lulu have been friends for many years. Paul sang *Brown Eyed Handsome Man* and *Party* with Lulu on her BBC TV show *Red Alert* on November 13, 1999. Her duets album *Together*, a UK Top Five in 2002, includes *Inside Thing (Let 'em In)*, which incorporates a cover of *Let 'em In* with Paul supplying vocals, and samples of his original recording of *Let 'em In* with Wings. Lulu's brother Billy Lawrie*, who helped write *Inside Thing*, recalls, "Lulu and I had written *I Don't Want To Fight*, a big hit for Tina Turner (see Ike & Tina Turner) in 1993. Sony signed us as writers and we were writing for many different people. They brought us this piece that included a sample of McCartney and Wing's song *Let 'em In* by Lukas Burton and wanted us to write something around it, which ended up being the rap song *Inside Thing*. Lulu called Paul to see if he liked it and to get his permission to release it. He loved it and said something to the effect that we'd made him sound hip again. We got him to sing on the chorus with the new lyrics at Sony Music Studios on Whitfield Street in London, which Lulu and I produced. Paul thought we should release it as a single at once, and offered us some old footage for use in a promotional video, but the record company wanted us to wait until the album was completed. By the time the album finally came out musical styles had changed somewhat and the buzz was gone, so Paul wasn't that keen to give us the old footage. The album was huge but it would have been much bigger had they led it with that single first." The album also includes *We've Got Tonight* with Ronan Keating, Lulu's last UK Top Five hit. Lulu continues to record and make public appearances. For more information go to www.luluofficial.com

Kenny Lynch

Nothing But The Real Thing (The Best Of 1960-1969)
RPM-286 (UK) (11/09/04)
Producer:Wally Ridley & Peter Sullivan
Kenny Lynch: Lead Vocals; Burt Weedon: Guitar; Harry Robinson: Conductor
02 or 03/xx/63

Misery (J. Lennon-P. McCartney) 2:04 (16) (03/22/63)

Kenny Lynch was born on March 18, 1938 in London, England. He began appearing onstage when he was 12 years old singing with his sister, Jazz singer Maxine Daniels. Lynch had his first UK Top 40 hit with a cover of *Mountain Of Love* in 1960. He had UK Top 10 hits with covers of *Up On The Roof* and *You Can Never Stop Me Loving You* in 1963. He made his acting debut in the 1965 film *Dr. Terror's House Of Horrors*. He co-wrote *Sha-La-La-La-Lee*, a Top Five hit for the Small Faces (see Kenney Jones, Ian McLagan, Rod Stewart, Ron Wood) in 1966. He has also written songs recorded by Cilla Black*, Billy J. Kramer with The Dakotas*, The Everly Brothers* and others. In 1983 he returned to the charts with the song *Half The Day's Gone And We Haven't Earned A Penny*. He has been a popular entertainer and TV personality in the UK for over three decades.

Kenny first met The Beatles when they were on the bill at Liverpool's Empire Theatre on October 28, 1962. Lynch and The Beatles were on the Helen Shapiro tour in February 1963. Just before the tour, John Lennon and Paul McCartney wrote the song *Misery* with the intention of giving it to Shapiro to record. Her producer, Norrie Paramor, turned it down before Shapiro ever had a chance to hear it. While on the tour bus Lynch, who was a budding songwriter, tried to write songs with Lennon and McCartney, but gave up in frustration declaring they knew nothing about songwriting. However, Lynch liked *Misery*, performed it on the tour, and became the first artist, other than The Beatles, to record and release a Lennon and McCartney composition. Most reliable sources list it as being released on the same date as The Beatles' version but the notes of the Lynch CD *Nothing But The Real Thing (The Best Of 1960-1969)* claim it was released a week prior to their release. However, The Beatles specifically gave it to Lynch to record and release as a single, and it was given much press and airplay before its release. Unfortunately, Lynch's version failed to chart. Lynch says Lennon later berated him for using session guitarist Bert Weedon on his version. He continued to appear with The Beatles on a number of occasions over the next year. Lynch was featured on the cover of Paul McCartney and Wings' 1973 album *Band On The Run*. For more information go to www.kennylynch.co.uk

Liam Lynch

Fake Songs
S Curve/Pumkinhead-72435-83743-0-8 (+DVD) 7243490606-9-2 (04/01/03)
Producer: Liam Lynch & Mark Hudson
Ringo Starr: Drums; Liam Lynch: Lead Vocals & Guitar
Liam Lynch's home studio, Nashville, TN xx/xx/99 & Whatinthewhatthe? Studio, Los Angeles, CA early/xx/03

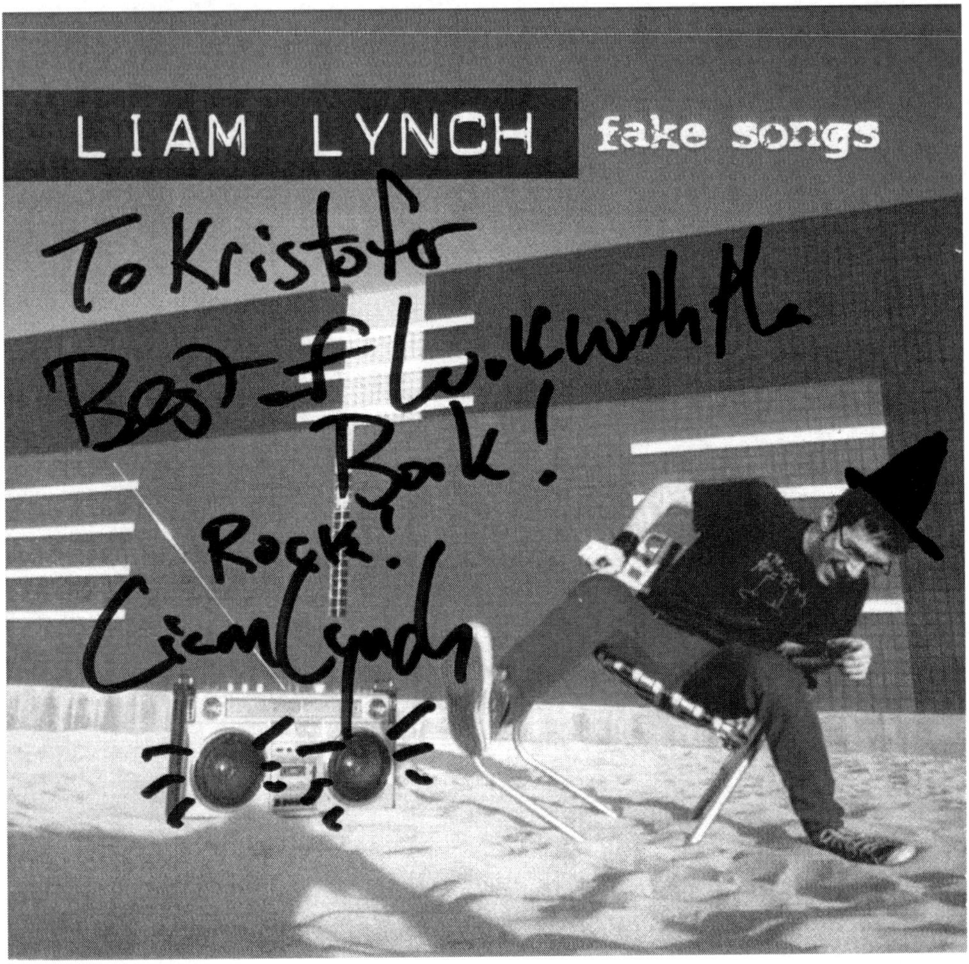

Cuz You Do (L. Lynch) 2:19 (1-5)
Additionally: Liam Lynch: Bass & Percussion

Cuz You Do [video] (L. Lynch) 9:45 (2-5)

Try Me (L. Lynch) 2:07 (1-16)
Additionally: Liam Lynch: Bass, Keyboards & Percussion

Try Me [video] (L. Lynch) 6:57 (2-5)
Additionally: **Ringo Starr: B. Vocals**

Liam Lynch was born William Niederst on September 5, 1970 in Akron, Ohio. By the age of 17 the multi-talented Lynch had recorded two albums by himself. In the mid-1990s he was one of a select few first admitted to, and graduated from, the Liverpool Institute For Performing Arts (LIPA) founded by Paul McCartney. Lynch recalls, "There were only about 40 musicians in the whole school at first. Each of us had to submit an original song on tape and McCartney then picked a small number of students to work with, on a one-on-one basis, and I was one of the lucky few chosen. I had several sessions with Paul, as well as a group project we worked on with him. I'd show him my ideas, and talk with him about lyrics and harmonies, but the first thing he told me was, 'No one can tell you how to write a song.' He helped me to realize a spirit to have when venturing into finding a song. He also said that he never knew which of his, or the other Beatles', songs people would gravitate towards, and turn into huge hits or the ones that would become classics. He just did what he was feeling at the time. Hearing him sing in the room with me – the real instrument — unfiltered without a microphone, a speaker or touched up in a studio, and how great he sounded, was mind-blowing. I was also impressed by his guitar playing — but then it was Paul McCartney! He has a great sense of humor. He didn't even hit me when I asked him if he'd be interested in playing Ringo in a Beatles cover band with me.

"At the time, Paul's wife Linda McCartney* was dying of cancer, as his mother was years earlier when he was a student in the same building, so I think being in that building was an emotional time warp for him. He seemed like his own ghost — emotional regardless because the woman of his life was dying. It must have been very strange and meaningful for him. I'm still impressed by his courage to be with his students during such a difficult time in his life. I also had a chance to work with George Martin* at LIPA. He taught me that there are no rules, to experiment, and that not following the norm produces new and surprising results."

Shortly after Lynch returned to the US he began recording what would become his album *Fake Songs*, which in 2002 was only available on his website. Lynch recalls receiving a phone call out of the blue from Ringo Starr. "He'd heard my short, funny song *United States Of Whatever* on the radio in the UK and loved it. [The song was a Top 10 hit in the UK in 2002.] He and Mark Hudson* wanted to get together with me. It was bizarre given that they didn't know I'd studied with Paul. They wanted to form a record label [Pumkinhead] so that *Fake Songs* could be properly released. We went into Mark's studio, and Ringo replaced my awful drumming on *Try Me* and *Cuz You Do*. [*Fake Songs*' bonus DVD includes video of Ringo recording the songs.] He wrote notes on his drum heads to help learn the tracks and has tape on his cymbals to mark the 'sweet spots' put there by George Martin.

"Ringo's one of the greatest drummers. He's had extreme highs and lows in his life, but he's amazingly down-to-earth, has a kind heart and is a beautiful person. His humor and sarcasm is a big part of who he is, and what seems to keep his head on his shoulders. He's a bottomless well of 'Ringo-isms' and funny stories. Who else could tell stories about being on a yacht with Salvador Dali and an astronaut? Working with him was great fun and a total honor. I have so much love for him and his spirit, and all he has done for music." Liam's podcast *Lynchland* features Ringo and George Harrison's son Dhani among the guests. Liam says, "Ringo wanted Dhani and I to meet, and invited us to his birthday party. Dhani and I hit it off, and have become great friends. We've worked together and plan to more in the future. He's a great musician and his band Thenewno2 is very cool."

Lynch has written a song called *Fake Beatles Song* in tribute to them. He says, "The Beatles were the greatest band of our times, not only in recording and songwriting, but social impact and marketing. They were also the most influential band – it's inescapable. Many musicians started making music because they were either inspired by The Beatles, or by other musicians and bands who were inspired by The Beatles."

Lynch is also an accomplished puppeteer and was the creative force behind MTV's *Sifl And Olly Show* in the late 1990s. He has directed music videos for the Foo Fighters and No Doubt, and directed and co-wrote the script and music for the films *Tenacious D In The Pick Of Destiny* and *Sarah Silverman: Jesus Is Magic*. Liam Lynch continues to write, record and produce material for other artists. For more information go to www.liamlynch.net

Vera Lynn

Singles Collection (The EMI Recordings 1960-1977)
EMI-0946 3 87328 2 2 (3 87330 2 7) (EU) (03/12/07)
Producer: Lynsey de Paul
Ringo Starr: Tambourine; Vera Lynn: Lead Vocals; Lynsey de Paul: B. Vocals; Tony Hymas: Arrangement
Marquee Studios, London, UK probably (late)/xx/75

Don't You Remember When (L. de Paul-B. Blue) 5:00 (2-12) (02/20/76)

Vera Lynn (Lynn was her grandmother's maiden name) was born Vera Welch on March 20, 1917 in East Ham (London), England. She was performing as a singer by the age of eight and by 15 she had a dance troupe. Three years later she made her debut on the radio with Joe Loss & His Orchestra. During World War II she hosted a series of weekly radio broadcasts called *Sincerely Yours*. She quickly became known as the "Forces' Sweetheart," regularly entertaining allied troops with her hits *(There'll Be Bluebirds Over) The White Cliffs Of Dover* and *We'll Meet Again* (a Top 40 hit in 1954). Following the war she maintained a successful worldwide career on stage, screen and TV. She was the first UK artist to have a number one hit in the US with the song *Auf Wiederseh'n Sweetheart*. Lynn, like The Beatles, was a regular visitor to Abbey Road Studios. She was a fan of The Beatles and recorded cover versions of their songs. Her music was featured in *The Beatles Anthology* film in 1995.

Lynn's 1976 single *Don't You Remember* was produced by successful actress, singer and songwriter Lynsey de Paul. Lynsey, who was dating Ringo Starr at the time, recalls, "Ringo turned up to collect me from the studio, we put a tambourine in his hand for a photo shoot and he ended up playing on the track." She also recalls, "Ringo had a recording studio in his house, but he was not technologically minded at the time and couldn't turn on the equipment. As we couldn't record on the proper desk, Ringo had placed a little battery operated cassette recorder on a chair in the middle of us. George Harrison was playing guitar, Ringo was playing drums and I was playing piano. We jammed from midnight to three o'clock in the morning. Unfortunately, the batteries were running low and the tape was slowing down as it recorded us. When we played it back [with new batteries] it sounded as if we were all getting faster and faster, and higher and higher in pitch, which was very funny." Lynsey says that her 1976 single, *If I Don't Get You The Next One Will* was inspired by Ringo. "We had arranged to go to dinner but he slept through the evening in his offices, so the song relates to revenge."

Jeff Lynne

Armchair Theatre
Reprise-9 26184-2 (06/11/90)
Producer: Jeff Lynne
Posh Studios, Warwickshire, UK probably 12/xx/89 &/or 01/xx/90

Every Little Thing (J. Lynne) 3:41 (1)
George Harrison: Acoustic Guitar & B. Vocals; Jeff Lynne: Lead Vocals, Electric & Acoustic Guitars; Jim Horn: Saxophones; Mette Mathiesen: Drums & Percussion; Richard Tandy: Acoustic Guitar; Phil Hatton: B. Vocals; Hema Desai: Operatic Voice; Michael Kamen: Strings

Lift Me Up (J. Lynne) 3:36 (3)
George Harrison: Slide & Acoustic Guitar, Harmony & B. Vocals; Jeff Lynne: Lead Vocals, Keyboards, Electric & Acoustic Guitars, Piano, Bass & Chair; Mette Mathiesen: Drums; Vikram A. Patil: Percussion; Nellai D. Kanan: Percussion; Fateh Singh Gangani: Percussion; Sureesh K. Lalwani: Percussion; Dave Morgan: B. Vocals; Phil Hatton: B. Vocals; Richard Tandy: Acoustic Guitar

September Song (M. Anderson-K. Weill) 2:57 (5)
George Harrison: Slide & Acoustic Guitar; Jeff Lynne: Lead Vocals, Electric Guitars, Drums, Keyboards, Bass, Choir & B. Vocals; Richard Tandy: Piano & Choir; Rita: Saw; Mette Mathiesen: Choir; Sheila Tandy: Choir; Jake Commander: Choir; Phil Hatton: Choir; Dave Morgan: Choir

Stormy Weather (T. Koehler-H. Arlen) 3:42 (9)
George Harrison: Slide & Acoustic Guitar; Jeff Lynne: Lead Vocals, Footsteps, Bass & Keyboards; Mette Mathiesen: Drums; Richard Tandy: Piano & Choir; Michael Kamen: String Arrangement & Conductor; Phil Hatton: Choir; Jake Commander: Choir; Sheila Tandy: Choir; Dave Morgan: Choir

Concert For George
WSM-R2 970241 (DVD) (11/18/03)
Producer: Jeff Lynne (audio); Ray Cooper, Olivia Harrison & Jon Kamen
Paul McCartney: Piano & B. Vocals; Ringo Starr: Drums; Jeff Lynne: Lead Vocals & Acoustic Guitar; Eric Clapton: Electric Guitar & Vocals; Klaus Voormann: Bass; Billy Preston: Keyboards; Dhani Harrison: Electric Guitar & B. Vocals; Jim Keltner: Drums; Jim Horn: Alto Saxophone; Ray Cooper: Percussion; Jim Capaldi: Percussion; Gary Brooker: Keyboards & Vocals; Andy Fairweather Low: Electric Guitar & B. Vocals; Tom Scott: Tenor Saxophone; Tessa Niles: B. Vocals; Katie Kissoon: B. Vocals; Dave Bronze: Bass; Albert Lee: Guitar; Marc Mann: Electric Guitar; Chris Stainton: Keyboards; Henry Spinetti: Drums; Tom Petty: Electric Guitar; London Metropolitan Orchestra (Andrew Brown, Roger Chase, Chris Fish, Helen Hathorn, Lynda Houghton, Ian Humphries, Zoe Martlew, Stella Page & Debbie Widdup); Michael Kamen: String Arranger & Conductor
Royal Albert Hall, London, UK 11/29/02

Wah Wah [live] (G. Harrison) 5:15 (1-25) [Also available on WSM-R2 74546 (2-19)]

Every Little Thing
Reprise-W 9799 (7599-21584-2) (Extended Play) (Germany) (06/xx/90)
Producer: Jeff Lynne
George Harrison: Acoustic Guitar & B. Vocals; Jeff Lynne: Lead Vocals, Electric & Acoustic Guitars; Jim Horn: Saxophones; Mette Mathiesen: Drums & Percussion; Richard Tandy: Acoustic Guitar; Phil Hatton: B. Vocals; Hema Desai: Operatic Voice; Michael Kamen: Strings
Posh Studios, Warwickshire, UK probably 12/xx/89 &/or 01/xx/90

Every Little Thing (Remix 12") (J. Lynne) 7:46 (1)

Singer, songwriter, producer and multi-instrumentalist Jeff Lynne was born on December 30, 1947 in Birmingham, England. He began his rise to musical stardom in the band Idle Race and later joined forces with Idle Race member Roy Wood in the band The Move, which separately evolved into Electric Light Orchestra* (a.k.a. ELO) in 1972.

By the mid-1980s ELO had stopped recording

and Jeff began producing mainstream pop artists such as Dave Edmunds*. George Harrison contacted Lynne through their mutual friend Edmunds about working together and the two quickly became friends. Jeff helped Harrison write and produce the song *Zig Zag* for the soundtrack for HandMade Films' production of *Shanghai Surprise* (see Various Artists-Shanghai Surprise). He also produced and played on Harrison's 1987 album *Cloud Nine*, and appeared in the music video for *When We Was Fab* from the album. On June 5 and 6, 1987 Jeff appeared with Harrison and Ringo Starr at London's Wembley Arena for *The Prince's Trust Rock Concert*. Lynne and Harrison also worked together on the album *Duane Eddy* (see Duane Eddy). On February 10, 1988 George and Jeff were at KLOS FM Studios in Los Angeles for the live phone-in radio show *Rockline* and performed on acoustic guitars impromptu versions of *Here Comes The Sun*, *Bells Of Rhymney*, *Mr. Tambourine Man*, *Take Me As I Am*, *That's All Right*, *Let It Be Me*, *Something* and *Every Grain Of Sand*.

Jeff has produced recordings for many artists including Brian Wilson*, Del Shannon*, Roy Orbison* and Tom Petty*. His association with Orbison and Petty led to the formation of the Traveling Wilburys, which also included Harrison and Bob Dylan*. Jeff's 1990 album *Armchair Theatre* included contributions from Harrison. Jeff says there are no unreleased recordings of him and George, only some unfinished jams. Jeff backed Ringo singing *I Call Your Name* as a contribution to *The John Lennon Scholarship Concert* held on May 5, 1990 in Liverpool and included on the 1991 video release *The World's Greatest Artists Sing LENNON A Tribute*. He also contributed to Ringo's 1992 album *Time Takes Time*.

The chance of all four Beatles reuniting for new recordings was thought impossible after the death of John Lennon in 1980, but with the help of Yoko Ono* and modern technology that changed. Ono told author Philip Norman in an interview in the UK's *Daily Mail* in November 1995 that Harrison and Neil Aspinall first approached her about the idea of the three surviving Beatles adding to John's unreleased demo recordings for use in *The Beatles Anthology*. Paul McCartney isn't certain but thinks he first approached Ono about the idea. On January 19, 1994 Ono and McCartney took part in ceremonies in New York to induct Lennon into the Rock and Roll Hall of Fame. Following the ceremonies, Yoko turned over some of John's unreleased demos to Paul. George Martin*, who had produced nearly all The Beatles' recordings, was busy reproducing recordings to be included in *The Beatles Anthology* project. Harrison recommended Lynn and McCartney eventually agreed. These historic sessions would be the closest The Beatles could ever come to a true reunion. Though three of The Beatles had recorded together on previous occasions since their breakup in 1970, they were never intended for, or considered as, Beatles' recording sessions or reunions. Several weeks after McCartney received the tapes, Ringo and Harrison gathered at McCartney's Hog Mill Studios to produce with Jeff a rough demo of Lennon's song *Free As A Bird* into a highly polished new Beatles' single. Lynne was invited back to McCartney's studio in February 1995 to help produce The Beatles' follow-up single *Real Love*.

Nearly a year later Lynne was helping produce some of McCartney's recordings for his 1997 album *Flaming Pie*. He also helped produce McCartney's 1999 cover of Buddy Holly and The Crickets'* hit *Maybe Baby*. Lynne was a major part of the Harrison tribute *Concert For George* in 2002. Jeff helped induct George Harrison into the Rock and Roll Hall of Fame in 2004. He joined Ringo Starr's All-Starr Band during their performance of *With A Little Help From My Friends* at Mandalay Bay in Las Vegas on July 1, 2006. Lynne has also recorded songs written by The Beatles. For more information go to www.elo.biz

Taj Mahal & The Graffiti Band

Live! The Silver Wilburys [Various Artists]
[none]-SWP 87-2 (Korea) [unauthorized release] (xx/xx/88)
Producer: probably Palomino Club
Palomino Club, Los Angeles, CA 02/19/87

George Harrison: Guitar; Taj Mahal: Lead Vocals; Jesse Ed Davis: Guitar; Bob Dylan: Guitar; John Fogerty: Guitar; Jim Ehinger: Keyboards; Bobby Tsukamoto: Bass; Mark Shark: Guitar; Gary Ray: Drums

Johnny B. Goode [live] (C. Berry) 4:33 (10)

Lucille [live] (A. Collins-R. Penniman) 5:54 (14)

George Harrison: Guitar; Taj Mahal: Lead Vocals & Harmonica; Jesse Ed Davis: Guitar; Bob Dylan: Guitar; John Fogerty: Guitar; Jim Ehinger: Keyboards; Bobby Tsukamoto: Bass; Mark Shark: Guitar; Gary Ray: Drums

Medley: Matchbox [a.k.a. **Matchbox Blues]/Gone Gone Gone (Gone All Down The Line)** [live] (C. Perkins-trad. L. Jefferson/C. Perkins) 7:11 (2 &3)
George Harrison: Vocals & Guitar; Taj Mahal: Vocals & Harmonica; Jesse Ed Davis: Guitar; Bob Dylan: Guitar; Jim Ehinger: Keyboards; Bobby Tsukamoto: Bass; Mark Shark: Guitar; Gary Ray: Drums

Medley: Twist And Shout [live] (P. Medley-B. Russell) 3:19 (15)
George Harrison: Guitar & B. Vocals; Taj Mahal: Vocals; John Fogerty: Vocals & Guitar; Jesse Ed Davis: Guitar & B. Vocals; Bob Dylan: Guitar & B. Vocals; Jim Ehinger: Keyboards; Bobby Tsukamoto: Bass; Mark Shark: Guitar; Gary Ray: Drums

Willie And The Hand Jive [live] (J. Otis) 5:38 (11)
George Harrison: Guitar & B. Vocals; Taj Mahal: Lead Vocals; Jesse Ed Davis: Guitar; Bob Dylan: Guitar & B. Vocals; John Fogerty: Guitar & B. Vocals; Jim Ehinger: Keyboards; Bobby Tsukamoto: Bass; Mark Shark: Guitar; Gary Ray: Drums

Taj Mahal was born Henry Fredericks on May 17, 1942 in New York, New York. His father was a well-known "be-bop" jazz musician. Henry was playing guitar by the age of five. He has been a major purveyor of world music, and has had much praise from the critics and some commercial success, primarily with blues-rock bands, including one with Jesse Ed Davis*.

On February 19, 1987 Taj, along with the Graffiti Band featuring Davis, were performing at Hollywood's Palomino Club when George Harrison, John Fogerty* and Bob Dylan* joined them onstage for well over an hour. Copies of the house video were soon circulating among collectors. The unauthorized CD *Live! The Silver Wilburys* includes most of the performance. Songs omitted from the CD that include Harrison on guitar are *Checkin' Up On My Baby, She Caught The Katy, You're Going To Need Somebody On Your Bond, Bacon Fat* and *Crosscut Saw*, all sung by Taj. Songs sung primarily by Harrison are *Honey Don't, Dizzy, Miss Lizzy, Peggy Sue* (all favorite oldies of The Beatles) and Dylan's *Watching The River Flow*, and are not considered contributions by Harrison to another artist's recordings.

Reports circulated at the time of Ringo Starr's signing with the *Private Music Records* label in 1990 that he had participated in recordings for Taj Mahal's album *Like Never Before* (Private Music-2081-2-P) at Los Angeles' Studio 55. According to Taj, Ringo attended sessions for the album but didn't contribute to any of Taj's recordings. Taj continues to record and perform. For more information go to www.tajblues.com

The Manhattan Transfer

Coming Out
Atlantic-18183-2 (08/27/90) (08/30/76)
Producer: Richard Perry
Ringo Starr: Drums; Tim Hauser: Vocals & Vocal Arrangement; Laurel Masse: Vocals; Alan Paul: Vocals; Janis Siegel: Vocals & Vocal Arrangement; Jim Keltner: Drums; Andy Muson: Bass; Ira Newbom: Guitar
Studio 55, Los Angeles, CA probably xx/xx/75

S.O.S. (G. Shury-P. Swern) 3:10 (8)
Additionally: Clarence MacDonald: Piano; Jackie Kelso: Tenor Saxophone

Zindy Lou (J. Moore-E. Smith) 2:50 (2)
Additionally: Dr. John: Piano; Doug Throngren: Percussion

The Manhattan Transfer was formed in 1969 in New York, originally performing jug band music, but broke up a short time later. Tim Hauser (the only original member) was born on December 12, 1941 in Troy, New York. He reformed the group in 1972 with Laurel Masse, born on December 29, 1951 in Holland, Michigan, Alan Paul, born Alan Paul Wichinsky on November 23, 1949 in Newark, New Jersey and Janis Siegel, born on July 23, 1952 in Brooklyn, New York. They initially enjoyed success as a New York cabaret act that specialized in doo-wop, swing, jazz, scat and ballads, and had a Top 40 hit with *Operator* in 1975. Masse left the group in 1979 following a serious car accident and was replaced by Cheryl Bentyne. In 1980 they had a Top 40 hit with *Twilight Zone/Twilight Tone* and a Top 10 hit with a cover of The Ad Libs' classic *The Boy From New York City* the following year. Their last Top 40 hit was *Spice Of Life* in 1983. They have earned 10 Grammy Awards and their 1986 album *Vocalese* received 12 Grammy nominations. They recorded a cover of The Beatles' song *Goodnight* in 1992.

Ringo became involved in The Manhattan Transfer's recording sessions for *Coming Out* as a result of his friendship with the album's producer, Richard Perry. Perry says, "I asked Ringo if he would play and he never turned me down."

Tim Hauser recalls, "Ringo and Jim Keltner produced a particular sound that was very unusual. Ringo played straight time, and Jim played time and fills. They produced a flaming sound with their simultaneous snares, coupled with their ability to get into the same groove, which I loved. That was the only time we played with Ringo." The Manhattan Transfer continues to record and perform, and remains one of the world's most popular jazz vocal groups. For more information go to www.manhattantransfer.org

George Martin

The Family Way (Original Soundtrack)
Decca-SKLA-4847 (album 12") (Australia) (xx/xx/67) (01/06/67)
Producer: George Martin
Neville Marriner: Leader of String Quartet (a.k.a. Tudor Minstrels)
CTS Studios, London, UK 11-12/xx/66

The Family Way ("Love In The Open Air") (P. McCartney) 24:19 (1/1-6 & 2/1-7)

Love In The Open Air / Theme From "The Family Way"
United Artists-UP 1165 (7" single) (UK) (12/23/66)
Producer: George Martin A.I.R. (London)
The George Martin Orchestra
EMI-Abbey Road Studios, London, UK 12/10/66

Theme from "The Family Way" (P. McCartney) 2:12 (2/1)

Love In The Open Air / Bahama Sound
United Artists-UA 50,148 (7" single) (04/24/67)
Producer: A.I.R. (London) (probably: George Martin)
The George Martin Orchestra
Probably EMI-Abbey Road Studios, London, UK probably 12/10/66

Love In The Open Air [alternate version] (P. McCartney-G. Martin) 2:18

Off The Beatle Track
One Way Records-2117793 (05/17/94) (07/10/64) **The Beatles: Liner Notes**

Produced By George Martin (50 Years In Recording)
Parlophone/EMI-07243 532631 2 6 (UK) (07/17/01)
Producer: George Martin
The George Martin Orchestra
EMI-Abbey Road Studios, London, UK 12/10/66 [unless noted otherwise]

Love In The Open Air (P. McCartney) 3:09 (4/1/22) (12/23/66)

Thingumybob (P. McCartney) 2:00 (4/1/23)
Probably EMI-Abbey Road Studios, London, UK xx/xx/68

George Martin was born January 3, 1926 in London, England. He began playing the piano as a youngster and by age 16 had formed a school dance band. Following military service during World War II he entered the Guildhall School of Music studying piano and taking oboe lessons from Margaret Asher (see Peter & Gordon.) Soon after graduation he was hired by Parlophone, where he later became a producer and A&R person. Martin seemed attracted to the off-beat and found success producing comedy records for Spike Milligan and Peter Sellers (see Peter Sellers, Terry Southern & Ringo Starr).

Some of EMI's labels had already turned down The Beatles so their manager Brian Epstein didn't hesitate to use his leverage as the owner of several major record shops in trying to persuade EMI to sign them. Epstein presented some of The Beatles' previous recordings to Martin, who wasn't overly impressed but was intrigued enough to arrange for a recording session for them on June 6, 1962. He suggested the use of a session drummer and two months later The Beatles replaced their drummer Pete Best with Ringo Starr. The sophisticated Martin took an immediate liking to the scruffy but talented musicians, and their keen sense of humor, and signed the group. Martin gained their respect when they learned he'd produced recordings for members of their favorite comedy group, The Goons.

Martin cultivated The Beatles musically in much the same way as Epstein had done with their appearance. In essence, Martin took a bar band and helped develop them into credible recording artists and songwriters. He selected many of their songs, played keyboards on some of their recordings, and arranged many of their ideas into written music. He exposed The Beatles to classical music and in doing so greatly contributed to its fusion with rock music. Martin was flexible and open to experimentation allowing The Beatles more freedom in the studio than most of his contemporaries would have tolerated. The Beatles and Martin were a musical team from 1962 until they broke up in 1970.

In 1964 Martin and his orchestra contributed the instrumental music for the soundtrack of The Beatles' first film *A Hard Day's Night*. That year he also released *Off The Beatle Track*, an album of instrumental arrangements of their songs, which includes liner notes by The Beatles. Martin seemed the obvious choice for also doing the instrumental soundtrack music to The Beatles' second film *Help!* However, the film's director Richard Lester, who didn't get on well with Martin, had his friend Ken Thorne do the film's instrumental music. [Thorne also scored the soundtrack for Lester's 1967 film *How I Won The War* co-starring John Lennon, and *The Magic Christian*.] He released instrumental cover versions of The Beatles' song *I Feel Fine* and their album *Help!* in 1965, which on the US release uses the original working titles *Auntie Gin's Theme* for *I've Just Seen A Face, That's A Nice Hat* for *It's Only Love* and *Scrambled Egg* for *Yesterday*. In August 1965 Martin, also a successful composer, conductor, arranger, musician and producer for artists such as Alma Cogan*, Billy J. Kramer with The Dakotas*, The Fourmost*, Gerry & The Pacemakers*, Cilla Black*, The Scaffold* and Rolf Harris*, left EMI and formed the production company AIR (Associated Independent Recording). However, he continued to produce and record The Beatles at EMI.

In 1966 Martin released *The Beatle Girls* album of covers of The Beatles' songs. Late that year, he worked extensively on Paul McCartney's basic compositions, *The Theme From The Family Way* and *Love In The Open Air*, for the film *The Family Way*. The Decca Records soundtrack album contains 13 instrumental variations of these songs. All credits read, "supervised and orchestrations arranged by George Martin," and don't list a producer but according to McCartney's fan club magazine *Club Sandwich* (spring 1996 issue No. 77), Martin produced the soundtrack album. The music is often assumed to have been performed by The George Martin Orchestra but Martin used a string quartet led by Neville Marriner, and a small brass section, who were later dubbed the Tudor Minstrels when Decca released the single *Love In The Open Air / Theme From The Family Way*. *Love In The Open Air* was given a brighter mix for the single and *Theme From The Family Way* consisted of two separate edits from the soundtrack album. George Martin and His Orchestra recorded a more up-tempo single version of *Love In The Open Air / Theme From The Family Way* for United Artists Records, with whom Martin was contracted, just prior to the soundtrack album's release. Martin's US single *Love In The Open Air*, released several months later, is completely different from any other version. [In 1967 a cover version of *Love In The Open Air* was released by Sounds Sensational, with The Mike Sammes Singers, who later sang backing vocals on The Beatles' recordings of *I Am The Walrus*, *Good Night* and on their album *Let It Be*. Canadian guitarist Carl Aubut released the album *Paul McCartney: The Family Way* (Philips-314 528 922-2) in 1995 with McCartney's blessing. McCartney didn't write any of the liner notes as was initially reported.]

Following 1967's *Sgt. Pepper's Lonely Hearts Club Band*, The Beatles most collaborative album with Martin, they were more skilled in production and relied less on Martin, who had grown tired of working with the bickering Beatles. [Martin wrote the 1994 companion book to the 1992 TV special *The Making Of Sgt. Pepper* in which he appeared.] Martin continued to produce them but was often absent or delegating duties to subordinates during many of the final weeks of recordings for *The Beatles* (white) album in 1968. Martin was no longer necessary to their success, or they to his success.

In 1968 McCartney had The George Martin Orchestra recorded his title song for ITV's London Weekend Television comedy series *Thingumybob*. Unsatisfied with Martin's version, McCartney turned to John Foster And Sons Ltd. Black Dyke Mills Band* to record it. [Martin's version was finally issued on the 2001 retrospective CD set *Produced By George Martin*.] That year Martin did the inspired instrumental soundtrack for The Beatles' full-length animated film *Yellow Submarine*. The film's making had previously been arranged by the late Brian Epstein. The Beatles weren't enthusiastic about the film and distanced themselves from it until they realized it was no ordinary cartoon. Martin's *London, By George!*, his last album of covers of songs by The Beatles, was also released later that year.

In January 1969 Martin began producing what was to become The Beatles *Let It Be* soundtrack album, but production duties were handed over to Glyn Johns before the sessions were aborted amid further tension within the group. [A year later the recordings were re-produced by Phil Spector*.] Following the sessions, McCartney pleaded with Martin to produce sessions for what became The Beatles' album *Abbey Road*, which proved to be their final recordings together. Martin agreed on the condition that he had greater control, and that order and civility be maintained. In December 1969 Ringo prerecorded his performance (without The Beatles) of *Octopus's Garden* for a BBC TV special on George Martin titled *With A Little Help From My Friends*. At the time, Martin was producing sessions for Ringo's first solo album *Sentimental Journey* released in 1970. It was essentially the last time any of The Beatles, except McCartney, would ever again employ the services of Martin as producer. There is no real evidence that there has ever been any personal animosity between Martin and any of The Beatles, though John Lennon typically made some rather disparaging remarks about him on occasion.

McCartney was the closest of The Beatles to Martin and had the most in common with him musically. McCartney employed Martin (uncredited) to do some of the orchestrations for his 1971 album *Ram*. Martin produced McCartney's title song to the 1973 James Bond film *Live And Let Die*. Between 1981 and 1984 McCartney recorded at Martin's AIR Studios in London, or on the Caribbean island of Montserrat, with Martin producing the albums *Tug Of War*, *Pipes Of Peace* and the soundtrack to McCartney's film *Give My Regards To Broad Street* in which Martin appears. He also appears in McCartney's 1982 music video for *Take It Away*. He made a guest appearance on McCartney's 1995 radio series *Oobu Joobu*, which featured music from *The Family Way*. McCartney has used Martin occasionally since that time, primarily for conducting and string arrangements as on his 1997 album *Flaming Pie*. He organized the 1997 benefit concert *Music For Montserrat*, which featured artists, including McCartney, who had recorded at Martin's studio on the volcano-ravaged island.

Martin has acted as The Beatles' official producer re-mastering many of their unreleased and rereleased recordings over the years. However, he didn't produce The Beatles' recordings of *Free As A Bird* or *Real Love* in the mid-1990s reportedly, in part, because his hearing was beginning to fail. Ringo used Martin for string arrangements on his 1998 album *Vertical Man*. Martin produced the demo recording of *Grow Old With Me* released in 1998 on the posthumous album *John Lennon Anthology*. He produced the 1998 album *In My Life*, which featured various artists covering The Beatles' recordings. Martin's last work on a Beatles' project was the 2006 Cirque de Soleil soundtrack album *Love*. In 2007 he contributed to a documentary on Ringo that has yet to be released.

Martin has served as an officer of the Chrysalis Records group that now controls AIR. Over the years he has produced a number of other successful recording artists including America, Jeff Beck, Gary Brooker*, Celine Dion, Elton John*, Kenny Rogers, Billy Preston*, Cheap Trick, John Williams*, Jimmy Webb* and Ultravox. He has won numerous Grammy Awards and was inducted into the Rock and Roll Hall of Fame in 1999. Though retired, Martin continues to lend his talents to a number of projects. For more information go to www.georgemartinmusic.com

Richard Marx

Ringo Starr & His All Starr Band Live 2006
Koch KOC-DV-4543 (DVD) (07/08/08)
Producer: Brent Carpenter; Executive Producer: Ringo Starr
Ringo Starr: Drums; Richard Marx: Electric Guitar & Lead Vocals; Billy Squier Electric Guitar; Sheila Escovedo: Drums; Hamish Stuart: Bass; Rod Argent: Keyboards; Edgar Winter: Keyboards & B. Vocals
Mohegan Sun, Uncasville, CT 07/16/06

Don't Mean Nothing [live] (B. Gaitsch-R. Marx) 5:09 (9)
[Also available on Koch-KOC-CD-4542-2 (7) (07/08/08)]

Should've Known Better [live] (R. Marx) 4:37 (20)
Additionally: Billy Squier: B. Vocals; Edgar Winter: Keyboards (only)

[Also available on Koch-KOC-CD-4542-2 (12) (07/08/08)]

Richard Marx was born September 16, 1963 in Chicago, Illinois. His parents were musicians who had Richard singing commercials by the age of five written by his father for his company, which produced jingles. He moved to Los Angeles following high school after receiving an offer from Lionel Richie, and ended up singing backing vocals on several of his hits and later those of Whitney Houston, Madonna (see Various Artists-Shanghai Surprise) and Kenny Rogers. Marx began writing songs for Rogers, the group Chicago and others. Between 1987 and 1994 Marx had number one hits with *Hold On To The Nights*, *Satisfied* and *Right Here Waiting*; Top Five hits with *Don't Mean Nothing*, *Should've Known Better*, *Endless Summer Nights* and *Angelia*; Top 10 hits with *Hazard* and *Now And Forever*, and Top 20 hits with *Too Late To Say Goodbye*, *Children Of The Night*, *Keep Coming Back*, *Take This Heart* and *The Way She Loves Me*. In late 1989 Marx performed The Beatles' song *Help!* at the Berlin Wall. Marx has produced recordings for a wide range of artists including Barbra Streisand, NSYNC and The Tubes.

Marx was a member of Ringo Starr's All-Starr Band in 2006 performing *Don't Mean Nothing* and *Should've Known Better* with backing from Ringo on drums. Marx recalls, "I first met Ringo on the Arsenio Hall show years earlier. He knew a couple of my songs and wanted to meet my band, which impressed me. In 2006 my manager told me Ringo wanted me in his band. I thought he had me confused with someone else. I fit the qualifications in terms of hits, but I didn't feel I fit in Ringo's band because on paper it didn't look right. Sheila E.*, who I adore, and is a fantastic drummer, was the only person with whom I'd worked. I was a huge Average White Band fan, so working with Hamish Stuart* excited me. Ringo probably knew I was musically versatile and could be a utility player, but I was frightened – almost to the point of turning him down, but how can you turn down playing with a Beatle? Billy Squier* almost quit when he heard I was going to be in the band. I told Billy, 'I'm not blowing smoke up your ass; I'm a big fan of yours!' I signed on after Billy told me he was going to play lead guitar, so I wouldn't have to be ripping solos, and could be a rhythm guitarist and vocalist.

"I don't think we had as much rehearsal time as most of Ringo's bands. Intrinsically, we all walked into rehearsals with the attitude that it wasn't about individuals, but about everybody in that band wanting to serve Ringo's music and vision. I'd heard stories about some past band members who didn't get that, and were there for their own egos and agendas. My agenda was to be a team player and Ringo often complimented me on that. I knew that if it was going to be a great experience I had to be able to say, 'I served my boss.' I'm pretty lucky to say the only boss I ever had was Ringo Starr! We gave it our all because there was a sense of gratitude to have been invited, and Ringo sensed that. It was because of that attitude that we became such a great band. I've always viewed Edgar Winter* as somewhat of a savant, and he didn't disappoint me. He's a one man band. I didn't know much about Rod Argent* other than a few hits. I wasn't prepared for the depth of his musicianship. He's an amazing keyboardist and string arranger – a genius!

"Ringo has that classic Liverpool wit. Once when no one could hear, he said to me, 'Remember Richard, you're my favorite, but don't tell the others.' Later, when I would come off stage after my solo spot he was always there to give me high fives and, with the entire band always there to hear, would say to me, 'Remember Richard, you're my favorite, but don't tell the others.' I learned that the more abuse he gives you the more he likes you. However, there are times when he'll be verbally cutting to someone and you know he means every word of it. He doesn't suffer fools gladly. You can feel like you know Ringo, but as sweet as he is, he's not easy to know. He is understandably guarded until he feels a sense of trust with you.

"As famous and talented as he is, Ringo wants another drummer with him onstage. It's his security blanket. Toward the end of an extremely hot outdoor show in Boca Raton, Florida, Sheila fainted from heatstroke! Ringo had a look of complete panic wondering if we should continue the show, but we gave him a look to continue and he resumed playing. With no disrespect for Sheila's talents, it was clear that this was going to be Ringo's best performance. People don't get the depth of his musicianship, because he's Ringo, with the 'Peace and Love' bit, but Ringo's sense of meter is incredible. I ran to the front of his drums and started screaming, 'You're a fuckin' bad ass! You fuckin' rock!' He started smiling, sat up a little higher and knew it was groovin'. Then Billy ran over. It was joyous, in spite of our concerns for Sheila, because the boss stepped up to the plate and hit a home run! I was never more proud to be in that band then at that moment. We all congratulated him. Throughout his incredible career, that moment, and how much it meant to his band, deeply moved him. Those joyous moments lasted long after that show.

"There wasn't one negative moment during the five weeks of that tour, but what I came away with most was new and lasting friendships. There isn't a more charming gentleman in the business than Rod Argent. Billy Squier and I really bonded on the tour. Billy pulled me aside once and told me what a huge surprise I turned out to be, and how much he thought of my talents. That showed humility and meant a lot. Ringo doesn't have any baggage. He really means it when he says, 'I just want to play my drums.' Ringo won't retire until he physically has to. God knows he doesn't need the money. He loves to put on a show. It's always been a major part of who he is. There's no better reason to do what he does than just loving it the way he does. He inspires me tremendously. I adore Ringo and appreciate the time I've spent with him since the tour even more. He asked me to be on the 2008 tour but I had other commitments. He and I have since gotten together to write some songs — like I was gonna turn that down!" He contributed to Ringo's 2010 album *Y Not*. Richard Marx continues to write, record and perform. For more information go to www.richardmarx.com

Dave Mason

It's Like You Never Left
One Way-A 26077 (07/18/95) (10/29/73)
Producer: Dave Mason
Record Plant &/or Sunset Sound Studios, Los Angeles, CA 05/xx/73

If You've Got Love (D. Mason) 3:25 (3)
George Harrison: Guitar; Dave Mason: Lead Vocals & Guitar; Mark Jordan: Piano; Jim Keltner: Drums; Carl Radle: Bass; Maxine Willard: B. Vocals; Clydie King: B. Vocals; Julia Tillman: B. Vocals; Kathleen Saroyan: B. Vocals

Dave Mason was born May 10, 1946 in Worcester, England. He rose to prominence in the band Traffic in 1967, which included Steve Winwood (see Blind Faith), Jim Capaldi* and Chris Wood. At the time, Mason was fairly friendly with Paul McCartney and his brother Mike McGear*. Mason recalls attending several of The Beatles' recording sessions, and said he sang backing vocals on *Across The Universe*, though it isn't known if his contribution survived the final mix of any of the released versions. Traffic's performance in The Beatles' film *Magical Mystery Tour* didn't make the final edit. Later members of Traffic included, among others, Rick Grech (see Blind Faith) and Jim Gordon (see Derek And The Dominos). Mason departed and rejoined Traffic several times before he briefly joined forces with Delaney & Bonnie & Friends. Mason is probably best remembered for writing Traffic's hit *Feelin' Alright?* and Delaney & Bonnie's hit *Only You Know And I Know*. He has worked with countless artists, including Mama Cass Elliot, Jimi Hendrix, Mike McGear*, The Rolling Stones*, The Scaffold* and Joe Walsh*. He had a Top 20 hit with *We Just Disagree* in 1977. He was a member of Fleetwood Mac (see Mick Fleetwood) between 1993 and 1995.

Mason's brief membership in Derek And The Dominos in 1970 led to work on George Harrison's album *All Things Must Pass*. In May 1973 Harrison was in Los Angeles to promote his album *Living In The Material World*. While there, he played on Mason's album *It's Like You Never Left* under the alias "Son Of Harry." To the best of Dave's recollection, this is the only contribution by any of The Beatles to one of his recordings.

While appearing in New Orleans in January 1975 Mason was visited backstage by Wings' guitarist Jimmy McCulloch. McCulloch invited Mason to Wings' recording sessions for their *Venus And Mars* album later that evening. Upon arrival, Mason was recruited to play guitar on *Listen To What The Man Said*, and the as-yet-unreleased song *The Crawl Of The Wild*, though Mason has no recollection of playing on a song by that title. That title was reportedly considered for release on Wings' 1979 album *Back To The Egg*.

Mason* joined Ringo Starr, Bill Wyman*, Todd Rundgren* and others in a band performing on the *Jerry Lewis Muscular Dystrophy Telethon* airing on September 3, 1979. Mason was selected as a member of Ringo Starr's All-Starr Band tour in 1997, and was to perform *Only You Know And I Know*, *Feelin' Alright* and *We Just Disagree*, but was dismissed following rehearsals. Mason recalls, "I was having to learn other musicians' songs, which I hadn't done in years, so I asked for a few things such as simple chord charts for their songs, which I didn't get. It wasn't like I was asking for a separate dressing room or to have

Kristofer Engelhardt and Dave Mason, The Ark, Ann Arbor, MI November 16, 2006. © and photo by Scott Baker.

them take all of the green jelly beans out of the bowl, but just simple things. There were things going on with the travel arrangements, which changed. The last day of rehearsals I had to leave early because I had a flight to Philadelphia for a concert there the next day, which I'd told Ringo's people about in advance and had given them my schedule. Evidently somebody forgot to tell Ringo. He went ballistic on the phone. I didn't need that, so I hung up! It was crazy – typical rock 'n' roll bullshit." Mason continues to perform and record to very favorable reviews. For more information go to www.dave-mason.com

Linda McCartney

Animal Magnetism [Various Artists-Suzy & The Red Stripes]
Kingsnake-KS2024 (01/09/95)
Producer: Paul McCartney & Suzy And The Red Stripes
Paul McCartney: Bass, Emulator Strings, Drums & Electric Guitar; Linda McCartney: Lead Vocals & Casio Keyboards; Robbie McIntosh: Electric Guitar; Steve Johnson: Synthesizer Strings, Trumpet & Bass Kurzweil; Carla Lane: Spoken Verse
Hog Hill Mill Studios, Sussex, UK 03/21/88 & Can Am Recorders, Los Angeles, CA 07/18/89

The White Coated Man [version 1] (**P. McCartney**-L. McCartney-C. Lane) 2:18 (3)

Appaloosa Love [Paul McCartney]
Yellow Cat-YC-065 (Holland) [unauthorized release] (06/xx/98)
Producer: Paul McCartney & John Fraser [unless noted otherwise]
Paul McCartney: Conductor; Carl Davis Conductor: London Symphony Orchestra [unless noted otherwise]
EMI-Abbey Road Studios, London, UK 01/29/92

Appaloosa Jam (L. McCartney) 2:42 (22)
Paul McCartney: Producer
Only: Linda McCartney: Keyboards; Blair Cunningham: Drums

Appaloosa Movement 1 (**P. McCartney**-L. McCartney) 1:44 (1)

Appaloosa Movement 2 (**P. McCartney**-L. McCartney) 1:14 (2)

Appaloosa Movement 3 (**P. McCartney**-L. McCartney) 0:53 (3)

Cold Cuts Vol. 2
Orange-Five (Mexico) [unauthorized release] (xx/xx/94)
Producer: Tony Visconti
Good Earth Studios, London, UK probably 12/xx/82 or 01/xx/83

Love's Full Glory (L. McCartney) 3:59 (14)
Paul McCartney (probable) involvement; Linda McCartney: Lead Vocals

Hot Hits-Cold Cuts
Condor-1963 (Korea/Australia) [unauthorized release] (xx/xx/89)
Producer: Paul McCartney
Paul McCartney: Bass, Piano, Rhodes Piano, Electric Organ & B. Vocals†; Linda McCartney: Lead Vocals, B. Vocals & Mellotron†; Davey Lutton: Drums†; Jimmy McCulloch: Electric Guitar†; Denny Laine: Acoustic Guitar†; Vasser Clements: Fiddle; Johnny Gimble: Fiddle; Thaddeus Richard: Alto Saxophone; Hewlett Quillen: Trombone; William Puett: Tenor Saxophone; George Tidwell: Trumpet; Darry McDonald: Trumpet; Normann Ray: Baritone Saxophone
EMI Pathé-Marconi Studios, Paris, France 11/20/73† & Soundshop Studios, Nashville, TN 06/xx/74

Wide Prairie (L. McCartney) 11:30 (10)

Paul McCartney's Rupert And The Frog Song also Linda McCartney's Seaside Woman / The Oriental Nightfish [Suzy & The Red Stripes]
Pioneer Artists-PA-86-MO37 (8" LD) (11/14/85)
Producer: Paul McCartney

Oriental Nightfish (L. McCartney) 2:39 (2/2)
Paul McCartney: Bass, Drums, Guitar & Mellotron; Linda McCartney: Lead Vocals, Moog & Electric Piano; Denny Laine: Flute
Air Studios, London 10/15/73
[Also available on *Wide Prairie* Capitol/MPL-CDP 7243 4 97910 2 2. (2:49) (9) (10/27/98)]

Seaside Woman (L. McCartney) 3:36 (2/1) (05/31/77)
Paul McCartney: Bass & B. Vocals; Linda McCartney: Lead Vocals, Electric Piano & B. Vocals; Denny Lane: Piano, Guitar & B. Vocals; Denny Seiwell: Drums
Air Studios, London, UK 11/27/72 (music) & Dragon Productions, London, UK probably xx/xx/79 or xx/xx/80 (video)
[Also available on *Wide Prairie* Capitol/MPL-CDP 7243 4 97910 2 2. (3:54) (8) (10/27/98)]

Oobu Joobu-Ecology
Best Buy/Mastertone/MPL-[matrix #] SA0200 878-02 (promotional only) (05/17/97)
Producer: Paul McCartney
Paul McCartney: Bass, Drums, Electric Guitar & B. Vocals; Linda McCartney: Lead Vocals, Casio Keyboards & B. Vocals; Carla Lane: Spoken Verse
Hog Hill Mill Studios, Sussex, UK 04/29/88

Cow [version 1] (**P. McCartney**-L. McCartney-C. Lane) 3:52 (7) (06/19/95)

Oobu Joobu With Paul McCartney [Various Artists-Suzy & The Red Stripes]
Westwood One Entertainment-Shows #95 22-36 (promotional only) (05/27/95-09/02/95)

Peacocks (L. McCartney) 3:25 (#95-29/3-3) (07/10/95)
Producer: probably **Paul McCartney**
Paul McCartney: B. Vocals & (probable) Instruments; Linda McCartney: Lead Vocals; Hamish Stuart: Instruments

The White Coated Man [version 2] (**P. McCartney**-L. McCartney-C. Lane) 2:36 (#95-24/3-3) (06/05/95)
Producer: Paul McCartney & Suzy And The Red Stripes
Paul McCartney: Bass, Emulator Strings, Drums & Electric Guitar; Linda McCartney: Lead Vocals & Casio Keyboards; Robbie McIntosh: Electric Guitar; Steve Johnson: Synthesizer Strings, Trumpet & Bass Kurzweil; Carla Lane: Spoken Verse
Hog Hill Mill Studios, Sussex, UK 03/21/88 & Can Am Recorders, Los Angeles, CA 07/18/89

Seaside Woman / B-Side To Seaside [Various Artists-Suzy & The Red Stripes]
Capitol-V-15244 (12" single) (08/13/86)
Producer: Paul McCartney a.k.a. Super Weed

B-Side To Seaside (Remixed by Alvin Clark) (**P. McCartney**-L. McCartney) 4:38 (2/1)
Paul McCartney: Drums, Mellotron, Electric Guitars, Moog Synthesizer, Piano, Congas, Banjo & B. Vocals; Linda McCartney: Lead Vocals & B. Vocals
EMI Abbey Road Studios, London, UK 03/16/77 & remixed probably xx/xx/86

Seaside Woman (Remixed by: Alvin Clark) (L. McCartney) 5:18 (1/1)
Paul McCartney: Bass & B. Vocals; Linda McCartney: Lead Vocals, Electric Piano & B. Vocals; Denny Lane: Piano, Guitar & B. Vocals; Denny Seiwell: Drums
Air Studios, London, UK 11/27/72 & remixed probably xx/xx/86

Unsurpassed Masters Vol. 1 [Paul McCartney & Wings]
Strawberry-STR-002 (Israel) [unauthorized release] (xx/xx/94)
Producer: [unknown-audience recording]
Paul McCartney: Bass & B. Vocals; Linda McCartney: Lead Vocals & Electric Piano; Denny Lane: Guitar & B. Vocals; Denny Seiwell: Drums; Henry McCullough: Guitar
Odeon or City Hall, Newcastle-upon-Tyne, UK 05/22/73 or 07/10/73

Seaside Woman [live] 4:27 (L. McCartney)

Wide Prairie
Capitol/MPL-CDP 7243 4 97910 2 2 (10/27/98)
Producer: Paul McCartney [unless noted otherwise]

Appaloosa (**P. McCartney**-L. McCartney) 4:44 (16)
Paul McCartney: Drums, Bass, Clarinet, Wurlitzer, Acoustic & Electric Guitar; Linda McCartney: Lead Vocals
Hog Hill Mill Studios, Sussex, UK 03/07/98

B-Side To Seaside (**P. McCartney**-L. McCartney) 2:38 (13) (05/31/77)
Paul McCartney: Drums, Mellotron, Electric Guitars, Moog Synthesizer, Piano, Congas, Banjo & B. Vocals; Linda McCartney: Lead Vocals & B. Vocals
EMI Abbey Road Studios, London, UK 03/16/77

Cow [version 2] (**P. McCartney**-L. McCartney-C. Lane) 4:24 (12)
Paul McCartney: Bass, Drums, Electric Guitar & B. Vocals; Linda McCartney: Lead Vocals, Casio Keyboards & B. Vocals; Carla Lane: Spoken Verse
Hog Hill Mill Studios, Sussex, UK 04/29/88

I Got Up (**P. McCartney**-L. McCartney) 3:19 (5)
Paul McCartney: Bass, Organ, Piano & B. Vocals; Linda McCartney: Lead Vocals & B. Vocals; Jimmy McCulloch: Guitar; Denny Laine: B. Vocals; Davey Lutton: Drums
EMI Pathé-Marconi Studios, Paris, France 11/20/73 & Hog Hill Mill Studios, Sussex, UK probably 07/09/98

The Light Comes From Within (**P. McCartney**-L. McCartney) 2:57 (6)
Paul McCartney: Bass, Electric Guitar, Piano, Wurlitzer Electric Piano & B. Vocals; Linda McCartney: Lead Vocals & Electric Piano; James McCartney: Electric & Acoustic Guitar
Hog Hill Mill Studios, Sussex, UK 03/18/98

Love's Full Glory (L. McCartney) 3:46 (4)
Producer: Paul & Linda McCartney
Paul McCartney: Bass & Drums; Linda McCartney: Lead Vocals, Piano & B. Vocals; Lloyd Green: Pedal Steel Guitar; Laurence Juber: Acoustic Guitar
Super Bear Studios, Bear-Les-Alpes, France 07/16/80 & Park Gate Studios, Sussex UK 10/xx/80

Mister Sandman (P. Ballard) 2:50 (7)
Producer: Paul McCartney & Lee Perry
Paul McCartney: Electric Guitar & B. Vocals; Linda McCartney: Lead Vocals; Billy Gardner: Rhythm Guitar; Baris Gardner: Bass; Miky Boo: Drums; Winston Write: Keyboards
Black Art Studios, Kingston, Jamaica 06/20/77 & Rude Studios, Kintyre, Scotland, UK 08/xx/77

New Orleans (L. McCartney) 3:13 (2)
Paul McCartney: Bass, Piano & B. Vocals; Linda McCartney: Lead Vocals & Piano; Denny

Laine: Acoustic & Electric Guitar; Joe English: Drums
SeaSaint Studios, New Orleans, LA 02/xx/75 & RAK Mobile 05/24/79

Sugartime (C. Phillips-O. Echols) 2:06 (14)
Producer: Paul McCartney & Lee Perry
Paul McCartney: Wurlitzer & B. Vocals; Linda McCartney: Lead Vocals; Billy Gardner: Rhythm Guitar; Baris Gardner: Bass; Miky Boo: Drums; Winston Write: Keyboards
Black Ark Studios, Kingston, Jamaica 06/20/77; Rude Studios, Kintyre, Scotland, probably xx/xx/80 & Hog Hill Mill Studios, Sussex, UK 07/07/98

The White Coated Man [version 3] (**P. McCartney**-L. McCartney-C. Lane) 2:13 (3)
Paul McCartney: Bass, Emulator Strings, Drums & Electric Guitar; Linda McCartney: Lead Vocals & Casio Keyboards; Robbie McIntosh: Electric Guitar; Steve Johnson: Synthesizer Strings, Trumpet & Bass Kurzweil; Carla Lane: Spoken Verse
Hog Hill Mill Studios, Sussex, UK 03/21/88 & Can Am Recorders, Los Angeles, CA 07/18/89

Wide Prairie (L. McCartney) 4:33 (1)
Paul McCartney: **Bass**, **Piano**, **Rhodes Piano**, **Electric Organ** & **B. Vocals**†; Linda McCartney: Lead Vocals, B. Vocals & Mellotron†; Davey Luton: Drums†; Jimmy McCulloch: Electric Guitar†; Denny Laine: Acoustic Guitar†; Vasser Clements: Fiddle; Johnny Gimble: Fiddle; Thaddeus Richard: Alto Saxophone; Hewlett Quillen: Trombone; William Puett: Tenor Saxophone; George Tidwell: Trumpet; Darry McDonald: Trumpet; Normann Ray: Baritone Saxophone
EMI Pathé-Marconi Studios, Paris, France 11/20/73† & Soundshop Studios, Nashville, TN 06/xx/74

Linda McCartney was born Linda Eastman on September 24, 1941 in Scarsdale, New York. Her father, whose family name was originally Epstein, was a prominent New York attorney who specialized in copyright law pertaining to the entertainment industry. Her mother's family founded the Lindner department store in Cleveland, Ohio. One of Lee's many clients was Jack Lawrence who wrote the song *Linda*, which was inspired by his daughter. [*Linda* was first recorded by Ray Noble with Buddy Clark in 1947, and was a hit for Jan & Dean in 1963.]

During the early 1960s Linda studied history and art in college, lost her mother in a plane crash, and married fellow student Joseph Melville See Jr. The couple had a daughter named Heather before divorcing in 1965. Linda enrolled in a photography class at the Tucson Art Center taught by Hazel Archer. She went to work for *Town & Country* magazine in New York where her photos of The Rolling Stones* in 1966 provided her with a resume as a rock photographer, which led to a photo assignment of The Beatles at Shea Stadium a short time later. Linda admits she was initially taken by John Lennon but after the photo assignment she took a greater interest in Paul McCartney. She was formally introduced to Paul at the Bag O'Nails nightclub in London on May 15, 1967 and invited to attend a press reception for The Beatles' *Sgt. Pepper's Lonely Hearts Club Band* album several days later at Brian Epstein's home. Linda had also become the unofficial resident photographer at the Fillmore East Theater in New York. When Paul was in New York and Los Angeles in May and June of 1968 for business regarding Apple, he and Linda spent more time together. That July Paul's fiancée, actress Jane Asher (see Peter & Gordon) publically announced the end their five-year relationship. By the fall of 1968 Linda had moved into Paul's house in London.

Soon Linda was attending recording sessions for *The Beatles* (white) album. The album included a poster with some photos taken by Linda. [Linda also took the photos used for the US sleeve of The Beatles' mid-1969 single *The Ballad Of John And Yoko*.] She also attended sessions in early 1969 for what became The Beatles' album *Let It Be* and sang backing vocals on the title track. Around this time Linda learned she was pregnant with the first of the couple's three children. They married on March 12, 1969. Paul distrusted Allen Klein, who had recently become involved in The Beatles' financial affairs, and instead was represented by the firm of Eastman and Eastman (Linda's father Lee and brother John).

In April 1970 Paul released his first bona fide solo album *McCartney*, which featured Linda on backing vocals, and announced that he had left The Beatles. On December 31, 1970 Paul filed a lawsuit in the London High Court seeking legal dissolution of The Beatles & Co. partnership and the appointment of a receiver to handle the group's financial affairs. [A receiver was appointed several months later but the partnership wasn't legally dissolved until 1975.] Linda's first songwriting credit came on Paul's first solo single *Another Day* released in early 1971. She sang on, and was credited as co-writing half the songs on the album *Ram*, released several months later, as being by Paul and Linda McCartney. Linda would receive composing credits with Paul on many songs. As with Yoko Ono*, when she was listed as co-composer on Lennon's releases, questions were raised by the songwriting publishers for Lennon and McCartney (Yoko and Linda weren't signed to them) as to whether Linda had helped compose the songs. Paul was accused by some of trying to compete with John artistically, personally, and in regards to their legal and financial disputes. On August 3, 1971 Paul announced the formation of the band Wings featuring Linda on keyboards and backing vocals. Fans and musicians, including those in McCartney's bands, were skeptical about Linda's inclusion in her husband's band. However, unlike the avant-garde sounds of Yoko, Linda, with her pop-rock music background, complemented many of the recordings by Paul and Wings.

Linda also sang backing vocals on a number of Ringo Starr's recordings, including *Six O'Clock*, which she co-wrote with Paul, and on George Harrison's song *All Those Years Ago* in tribute to Lennon. Her backing vocals can also be heard on recordings by Johnny Cash*, Adam Faith*, Roy Harper*, Kenney Jones*, Denny Laine*, Yoko Ono, Carly Simon* and James Taylor*. She also sang backing vocals and played keyboards on Mike McGear's* recordings, and keyboards on The Scaffold's* recordings. She was a member of all of Paul's bands until she became ill.

Linda's reggae-flavored song *Seaside Woman*, backed with the cleverly titled *B-Side To Seaside*, was released as a single on Epic Records in 1977 and reached the Top 60 in the charts. At the time, McCartney was negotiating a contract with Epic's parent company Columbia Records. [Columbia began releasing McCartney's recordings in the US and Canada in 1979]. The record was issued under the name Suzy And The Red Stripes, likely based on Rikki And The Red Streaks, an early 1960's Liverpool group, the Jamaican nickname Suzy and Jamaican Red Stripe beer. [The McCartneys were frequent visitors to Jamaica and admired its reggae music, and Linda recorded the songs *Mister Sandman* and *Sugartime* there with legendary producer Lee "Scratch" Perry. Paul made a cameo in the posthumous 1984 video for reggae star Bob Marley's song *One Love* available on the 2003 DVD *Legend* (Universal Music & Video-602498081082)]. *Seaside Woman* was recorded in 1972 and considered for Wings' 1973 album *Red Rose Speedway* before it was pared down from a double to a single record. Alternate versions of it and *B-Side To Seaside* were reportedly recorded in Paris, France in 1972 and again in 1973. A number of unauthorized releases include Linda's performance of the song during Wings' tours in 1972 and 1973. The McCartneys commissioned Oscar Grillo to animate and direct a film for *Seaside Woman*, which took first place as the official UK entry for the short film category at the 1980 *Cannes Film Festival*. The film was included, along with two other animated films set to the McCartneys' music, on the LD *Paul McCartney's Rupert And The Frog Song also Linda McCartney's Seaside Woman / The Oriental Nightfish* issued in 1985. [*Oriental Nightfish*, Linda's third released recording, was also animated by Grillo and entered in the 1978 *Cannes Film Festival*. Alternate versions of it were also reportedly recorded in Paris, France in 1972 and 1973.] A 12" single with extended remixes of *Seaside Woman* and *B-Side To Seaside* was issued in 1986.

Linda was the photographer for many of Paul's records and projects. Her photographs, including those of The Beatles, have been featured in a number of calendars, books and exhibits. She and Paul became life-long vegetarians in the early 1970s and advocates for animal rights. She started a line of vegetarian frozen foods and wrote several vegetarian cook books. Linda McCartney was diagnosed with breast cancer in late 1995, which took her life on April 17, 1998. [Paul's mother Mary also died of breast cancer.] Harrison, Ringo and George Martin* attended memorial services for her at Saint Martin-In-The-Fields Church in London on June 8, 1998.

Paul had been helping Linda write and record songs for a solo album since the early 1970s. Shortly before her death, she and Paul pulled together 16 recordings she had made since that time for an album titled *Wide Prairie* released shortly after her death. [An 11:28 version of the title track is available on unauthorized releases. Other versions were also reportedly recorded in Paris, France in 1972 and 1973.] Many of the songs on *Wide Prairie* were recorded during the 10 year period Wings were together and include backing from member's Denny Laine, Denny Seiwell, Jimmy McCulloch, Joe English and Laurence Juber*, and from later McCartney band member's Hamish Stuart*, Robbie McIntosh and Blair Cunningham.

Linda's song *Cook Of The House* on *Wide Prairie*, initially released on the 1976 album *Wings At The Speed Of Sound*, is considered a Wings' song. Linda performed the song during Wings' 1979 UK tour, and it was used as the theme song for Linda's vegetarian cooking segment on Paul's 1995, 15-week, Westwood One radio series *Oobu Joobu*. The show also featured a number of Linda's other songs, including alternate versions and the song *Peacocks* that has yet to be commercially released. [*Oobu Joobu* also featured the song *S.M.A.* by Linda's daughter Heather, which likely included some assistance from Paul and, or Linda.]

Over the years, a number of Linda's recordings have appeared on unauthorized releases, and in the McCartneys' films. Linda provided the repetitive dialogue to *Mr. H Atom*, an out-take from the 1980 *McCartney II* album. At least four versions of her song *Love's Full Glory* have surfaced. Portions of two versions were used in the 1992 film *Appaloosa* that the McCartneys made about Linda's horse Blankit. One version includes assistance from Mick Bolton and Ian Maidman, and may not include any contributions from Paul. The other version was recorded during sessions Paul produced for Ringo's album *Stop And Smell The Roses* at Super Bear Studios in France in 1980. The *Wide Prairie* album list Paul as the drummer. The notes with the *Stop And Smell The Roses* CD mention that a 7:46 demo of the song was recorded, listing the same musical lineup as *Wide Prairie*, except Ringo is credited as playing drums. Tony Visconti says he also produced a version of *Love's Full Glory* for Linda at his Good Earth Studios in London in the early 1980s. This more lush orchestrated version is available on unauthorized releases.

The centerpiece of the *Appaloosa* film was the title track written by Paul and Linda. The song was divided into two movements between which Paul added his composition subtitled *Meditation*. The entire suite was recorded in January 1992 with the London Symphony Orchestra. Paul produced the recording with John Fraser, and conducted the orchestra with Carl Davis (see London Symphony Orchestra & Chorus, The Royal Liverpool Philharmonic Orchestra & Choir and Choristers of Liverpool Cathedral, Anya Alexeyev). The film also features *Appaloosa Jam* composed by Linda. The Boston Pops Orchestra, conducted by Carl Davis, premiered *Appaloosa* at Symphony Hall in Boston on May 12, 1992 during *A Tribute To Paul McCartney*. The performance was aired on PBS TV that August. The versions of *Appaloosa* from the film appear on unauthorized releases.

In early 1995 the third and final Suzy And The Red Stripes song, *The White Coated Man*, was released on the album *Animal Magnetism* proceeds of which benefit animal rights organizations. A second version of the song was featured that summer on the *Oobu Joobu* radio series and a third version was included on *Wide Prairie. The White Coated Man* and the song *Cow* began as animal rights poems written in 1988 by Linda's close friend, and UK TV comedy writer, Carla Lane. *Cow* was featured on the *Oobu Joobu* radio series, and included on the promotional album *Oobu Joobu-Ecology* issued by the Best Buy chain with McCartney's 1997 album *Flaming Pie* and promoting Paul's *Town Hall Meeting* on VH1 TV. It is different from the version on *Wide Prairie*. For more information go to www.linda-mccartney.com

Mike McGear (and Roger McGough*)

Dance The Do / Norton
Warner Bros.-K 16573 (7" single) (UK) (07/04/75)
Producer: Paul McCartney
Strawberry Studios, Stockport, UK 01-05/xx/74

Dance The Do [single version] (**P. McCartney**-M. McGear) 2:59 (1/1)
Paul McCartney: Synthesizer, Bass & B. Vocals; Mike McGear: Lead Vocals; Denny Laine: Guitar & (probable) B. Vocals; Jimmy McCulloch: Guitar; Linda McCartney: B. Vocals & (possible) Percussion; Gerry Conway: Drums; Brian Jones: Saxophone; (probable) Gysmorchestra (invented by: Lol Cream & Kevin Godley, 10cc); Kate Robbins: B. Vocals; Viv Stanshall: B. Vocals

McGear
See For Miles-SEECD 339 (UK) (04/06/92) (09/27/74)
Producer: Paul McCartney
Strawberry Studios, Stockport, UK 01-05/xx/74 [unless noted otherwise]

The Casket (**P. McCartney**-R. McGough) 4:18 (7)
Paul McCartney: Piano; (possible) Guitar & (probable) Keyboards; Mike McGear: Lead Vocals; Paddy Moloney: Aeolian Pipes; Linda McCartney: (possible) Keyboards; Denny Laine: (possible) Guitar; Jimmy McCulloch: (possible) Guitar; Eric Stewart: (possible) Guitar; (possible) Gysmorchestra (invented by: Lol Cream & Kevin Godley of 10cc)

Dance The Do [alternate CD version] (**P. McCartney**-M. McGear) 3:53 (6)
Paul McCartney: Synthesizer, Bass & B. Vocals; Mike McGear: Lead Vocals; Denny Laine: Guitar & (probable) B. Vocals; Jimmy McCulloch: Guitar; Linda McCartney: B. Vocals & (possible) Percussion; Gerry Conway: Drums; Brian Jones: Saxophone; (probable) Gysmorchestra (invented by: Lol Cream & Kevin Godley of 10cc)

Givin' Grease A Ride (**P. McCartney**-M. McGear) 5:33 (11)
Paul McCartney: Guitar, B. Vocals, Piano, (probable) Bass & (possibly) Synthesizer; Mike McGear: Lead Vocals; Eric Stewart: Guitar;

Jimmy McCulloch: Guitar; Linda McCartney: (possible) Keyboards; Denny Laine: Guitar; Gerry Conway: Drums; (probable) Gysmorchestra (invented by: Lol Cream & Kevin Godley of 10cc)

Have You Got Problems? (**P. McCartney**-M. McGear) 6:15 (5)
Paul McCartney B. Vocals, Piano, Bass & (probable) Guitar; Mike McGear: Lead Vocals; Jimmy McCulloch: (possible) Guitar; Gerry Conway: Drums; Brian Jones: Saxophone; Linda McCartney: B. Vocals; Denny Laine: B. Vocals & (probable) Guitar

Leave It (**P. McCartney**) 3:41 (4) (09/06/74)
Paul McCartney: B. Vocals, Bass, Piano & (probable) Acoustic Guitar; Mike McGear: Lead Vocals; Denny Laine: Guitar & B. Vocals; Tony Coe: Saxophone; Denny Seiwell: Drums; Linda McCartney: B. Vocals & (possible) Keyboards
EMI-Abbey Road Studios UK 10/xx/72 or 03-04/xx/73 & possibly 01-05/xx/74

The Man Who Found God On The Moon (**P. McCartney**-M. McGear) 6:32 (12)
Paul McCartney: Piano, B. Vocals & (possible) Acoustic Guitar, (probable) Bass & (probable) Brass Arrangement; Mike McGear: Lead Vocals; Linda McCartney: B. Vocals & (possible) Keyboards; Denny Laine: (probable) Guitar & B. Vocals; Jimmy McCulloch: (possible) Guitar; Gerry Conway: Drums; Brian Jones: Saxophone; Gerry Allison: (possible) Brass Arrangement; (probably) The Halte Orchestra and Oboe Lady; (probable) Gysmorchestra (invented by: Lol Cream & Kevin Godley of 10cc); Eric Stewart: Guitar; Benna McCartney and Theran McCartney: B. Vocals; Buzz Aldrin & Mission Control on Moon: Dialogue

Norton (**P. McCartney**-M. McGear) 2:35 (3)
Paul McCartney: B. Vocals, Piano, (possible) Bass, (possible) Keyboards & (possible) Guitar; Mike McGear: Lead Vocals; Denny Laine: (probable) Guitar & (probable) B. Vocals; Gerry Conway: Drums; Eric Stewart: (possible) Guitar; Brian Jones: Saxophone; Derek Taylor: Dialogue; Jimmy McCulloch: Lead Guitar; Linda McCartney: B. Vocals & (possible) Keyboards

Rainbow Lady (**P. McCartney**-M. McGear) 3:26 (9)
Paul McCartney: Bass, B. Vocals, (probable) Acoustic Guitar, (probable) Synthesizer & (probable) Piano; Mike McGear: Lead Vocals; Denny Laine: (probable) Guitar & (possible) B. Vocals; Jimmy McCulloch: (probable) Guitar; Gerry Conway: Drums; Eric Stewart: (possible) Guitar; (probable) Gysmorchestra (invented by: Lol Cream & Kevin Godley of 10cc); Linda McCartney B. Vocals & (probable) Keyboards

Sea Breezes (B. Ferry) 4:50 (1)
Paul McCartney: Bass, Keyboards; Strings and Brass Arrangements (probable) Guitar; Mike McGear: Lead Vocals; Linda McCartney: (possible) Keyboards & (possible) Percussion; Denny Laine: (probable) Guitar; Jimmy McCulloch: (probable) Guitar; Gerry Conway: Drums; Eric Stewart: (possible) Guitar; Brian Jones: Saxophone; Gerry Allison: Strings And Brass Arrangement; The Halte Orchestra and Oboe Lady; Gysmorchestra (invented by: Lol Cream & Kevin Godley of 10cc)

Simply Love You (**P. McCartney**-M. McGear) 2:47 (10)
Paul McCartney: B. Vocals, Keyboards, Piano, (probable) Bass & (possible) Guitar; Mike McGear: Lead Vocals; Linda McCartney: B. Vocals & (probable) Keyboards; Denny Laine: B. Vocals & (probable) Guitar; Jimmy McCulloch: (possible) Guitar; Gerry Conway: Drums; Eric Stewart: (possible) Guitar; (probable) Gysmorchestra (invented by: Lol Cream & Kevin Godley of 10cc)

Sweet Baby (**P. McCartney**-M. McGear) 3:49 (8) (09/06/74)
Paul McCartney: Acoustic Guitar, B. Vocals, Keyboards & (probable) Bass; Mike McGear: Lead Vocals; Denny Laine: (probable) Guitar & (probable) B. Vocals; Jimmy McCulloch: (possible) Guitar; Gerry Conway: Drums; Eric Stewart: (possible) Guitar; Linda McCartney: Piano & B. Vocals
Mike McCartney's home & probably Strawberry Studios, Stockport, UK 01-05/xx/74

What Do We Really Know? (**P. McCartney**) 3:26 (2)
Paul McCartney: Keyboards, B. Vocals, Bass & (probable) Guitar; Mike McGear: Lead Vocals; Denny Laine: (possible) Guitar & B. Vocals; Gerry Conway: Drums; Brian Jones: Saxophone; Jimmy McCulloch: Lead Guitar; Linda McCartney: B. Vocals, (possible) Percussion & (possible) Keyboards

McGough & McGear [Roger McGough* & Mike McGear]
EMI-CDP 7 91877 2 (UK) (04/10/89) (05/17/68)
Producer: Paul McCartney
Probably De Lane Lea Studios, London, UK 06/xx/67–04/xx/68 [unless noted otherwise]

Basement Flat (R. McGough-M. McGear) 2:42 (3)
Paul McCartney: (probable) B. Vocals; Mike McGear: Lead Vocals; Mitch Mitchell: Drums; Barry Fantoni: Saxophone; Stanislas Klossowski de Rola: Percussion; probably one or more of the following: Dave Mason: B.

Vocals; John Mayall: Harpsichord; Roger McGough: B. Vocals; Jane Asher: B. Vocals; Margaret Asher: B. Vocals; Zoot Money: Keyboards; Mike Hart: B. Vocals; Vera Kantrovitch: Percussion; Carol Mason: Percussion; Martin Wilkinson: Percussion; Rosie: Percussion
Probably De Lane Lea Studios, London, UK probably 06/xx/ 67

Come Close And Sleep Now (R. McGough) 2:20 (6)
Paul McCartney: Piano & Effects; Roger McGough: Lead Vocals; Andy Roberts: Guitar

Do You Remember? ([(possibly) **P. McCartney**] R. McGough-M. McGear) 3:17 (11)
Paul McCartney: B. Vocals, Piano & Mellotron; Mike McGear: Lead Vocals; Andy Roberts: Guitar; Paul Samwell Smith: Bass; Gary Leeds: Drums; Stanislas Klossowski de Rola: Percussion; possibly one or more of the following: Graham Nash: B. Vocals; Mike Hart: B. Vocals; Vera Kantrovitch: Percussion; Carol Mason: Percussion; Martin Wilkinson: Percussion; Rosie: Percussion
Probably De Lane Lea Studios, London, UK probably 06/xx/ 67

Ex Art Student (R. McGough) 6:29 (13)
Paul McCartney: (possible) B. Vocals; Mike McGear: Vocals; Jane Asher: Vocals; Roger McGough: Vocals; William Bennet: Flute; Graham Nash: Vocals & Guitar; Jimi Hendrix: Guitar; Dave Mason: Sitar; Andy Roberts: Guitar; Mitch Mitchell: Drums; Noel Redding: Bass; John Mayall: Harpsichord; possibly one or more of the following: Mike Hart: B. Vocals; Vera Kantrovitch: Percussion; Carol Mason: Percussion; Martin Wilkinson: Percussion; Rosie: Percussion
De Lane Lea Studios, London, UK 06/20/67

From: "Frink, A Life In The Day Of" And "Summer With Monika"-Prologue Introducing a) Moanin' b) Anji (R. McGough-A. Roberts-Timmons-Graham) 9:00 (4)
Paul McCartney: Dialogue & Mellotron; Roger McGough: Dialogue; Barry Fantoni: Saxophone; Zoot Money: Keyboards; Andy Roberts: Guitar; Gary Leeds: Drums; probably one or more of the following: Noel Redding: Bass; Paul Samwell Smith: Bass; Mike Hart: B. Vocals; Vera Kantrovitch: Percussion; Carol Mason: Percussion; Martin Wilkinson: Percussion; Rosie: Percussion

From: "Frink, A Life In The Day Of" And "Summer With Monika" – Epilogue (R. McGough-A. Roberts) 1:55 (5)
Roger McGough: Dialogue; Andy Roberts: Guitar

House In My Head (R. McGough-M. McGear) 3:34 (8)
Paul McCartney: (possible) B. Vocals & (possible) Percussion, (possible) Piano; Mike McGear: Lead Vocals; Roger McGough: B. Vocals; Gary Leeds: Drums; probably one or more of the following: Dave Mason: B. Vocals; Jane Asher: B. Vocals; Margaret Asher: B. Vocals; Zoot Money: Keyboards; Paul Samwell Smith: Bass; Noel Redding: Bass; Mike Hart: B. Vocals; Vera Kantrovitch: Percussion; Carol Mason: Percussion; Martin Wilkinson: Percussion; Rosie: Percussion; Stanislas Klossowski de Rola: Percussion

Little Bit Of Heaven (R. McGough) 1:46 (2)
Paul McCartney: (possible) Keyboards; Mike McGear: Vocals; Roger McGough: Vocals; Andy Roberts: Tin Whistle

Living Room (M. McGear) 2:44 (10)
Paul McCartney: Dialogue, B. Vocals, (probable) Bass & (possible) Percussion; Mike McGear: Lead Vocals; Zoot Money: Keyboards; Andy Roberts: Guitar; Roger McGough: (probable) B. Vocals; possibly one or more of the following: Gary Leeds: Percussion; Jane Asher: B. Vocals; Margaret Asher: B. Vocals; Paul Samwell Smith: Bass; Viv Prince: Percussion; Mike Hart: B. Vocals; Vera Kantrovitch: Percussion; Carol Mason: Percussion; Martin Wilkinson: Percussion; Rosie: Percussion; Stanislas Klossowski de Rola: Percussion

Mr. Tickle (M. McGear) 3:20 (9)
Paul McCartney: (possible) Piano; Mike McGear: Dialogue; John Mayall: (probable) Piano; Zoot Money: (possible) Piano

Please Don't Run Too Fast (M. McGear) 1:33 (12)
Paul McCartney: (possible) Keyboards & (possible) Guitar; Mike McGear: Lead Vocals; possibly one or more of the following: Spencer Davis: Guitar; Dave Mason: Guitar; John Mayall: Keyboards; Zoot Money: Keyboards

So Much (R. McGough-M. McGear) 3:58 (1)
Mike McGear: Lead Vocals; Jimi Hendrix: Guitar; Graham Nash: B. Vocals;
Mitch Mitchell: Drums; Noel Redding: Bass; Andy Roberts: Guitar; Jane Asher: B. Vocals; Barry Fantoni: (probable) Saxophone; possibly one or more of the following: Spencer Davis: Guitar; Dave Mason: Guitar & B. Vocals; Spencer Davis: Guitar; Roger McGough: B. Vocals; Margaret Asher: B. Vocals; Mike Hart: B. Vocals; Vera Kantrovitch: Percussion; Carol Mason: Percussion; Martin Wilkinson: Percussion; Rosie: Percussion; Stanislas Klossowski de Rola: Percussion
De Lane Lea Studios, London, UK 06/20/67

Yellow Book (R. McGough-M. McGear) 2:15 (7)
Paul McCartney: Piano; Mike McGear: Lead Vocals; Graham Nash: B. Vocals; Gary Leeds: Drums; Stanislas Klossowski de Rola (possible) Percussion

Woman
Edsel/Island-EDCD 507 (Germany) (02/xx/97) (04/21/72)
Producer: Mike McGear
Mike McGear: Lead Vocals; John Megginson: Keyboards; Gerry Conway: Drums; Dave Richards: Bass
Strawberry Studios, Stockport &/or EMI-Abbey Road Studios, London, UK
Late/xx/71 &/or early/xx/72

Bored As Butterscotch (R. McGough-M. McGear & Friend **[P. McCartney]**) 2:52 (9)

Mike McGear was born Peter Michael McCartney on January 7, 1944 in Liverpool, England. He is the younger brother of Paul McCartney. Their mother Mary, of *Let It Be* fame, was born Mary Mohin on Sept 29, 1909 and married James McCartney, born July 7, 1902, both in Liverpool. Mary was a Catholic nurse and midwife, and Jim was a cotton salesman who also doubled as leader of Jim Mac's Band. Mary McCartney died of complications from breast cancer on October 31, 1956. Jim raised his sons Paul and Mike alone, not remarrying until 1964. He died on March 13, 1976.

Mike first performed publically with Paul at a talent contest at Butlins, a popular holiday camp in the UK, in mid-1957. Mike took on a number of odd jobs while developing an avid interest in photography. In 1962 he was asked by Merseyside Arts Festival organizers John Gorman and poet Roger McGough to take part in a comedy sketch. Following the festival, the three teamed up and eventually became known as The Scaffold*. Mike changed his last name to McGear ("gear" was Liverpool slang for cool or great) to avoid accusations that he was trying to cash in on the McCartney name, and maintain a separate identity. However, it was inevitable that Paul would offer his influence, associations and talent to Mike's recordings throughout much of his career.

On June 18, 1967 Paul was at the London offices of The Beatles' music publisher, Dick James Music, to begin work on what would become the *McGough & McGear* album. Recordings commenced several days later at De Lane Lea Studios in London. Participant Andy Roberts recalls, "I was told the studio had been booked by Paul, and that he was setting the whole thing up as a favor to his brother to help him gain some recognition as a songwriter, with Roger, of course. The contributors on the first session were myself, Mike, Roger, Dave Mason*, Gary Leeds, Barry Fantoni, Graham Nash and Paul. The word was out that the sessions were on, and for the first couple of evenings the London glitterati homed in on De Lane Lea Studios. It was really just a bunch of friends – the London club scene crowd. I also remember Prince Stash, Viv Prince, John Mayall and Jane Asher." McGough says Vera Kantrovitch, Carol Mason, Martin Wilkinson, Margaret Asher and Rosie played jingle bells. Most of the sessions took place that summer, but it was nearly a year before the album was completed and released. It was intended for release on Apple, but was issued on Parlophone because Apple wasn't operational yet. Other well-known musicians, including members of The Jimi Hendrix Experience, Zoot Money* and Spencer Davis, contributed to the album. Though credits for each song aren't available, Andy Roberts recalls specific musicians for many of the tracks. It's known that Paul sings backing vocals and plays keyboards on the album. He probably also plays bass, percussion and acoustic guitar. Mike recalls Paul playing piano and singing on *Do You Remember?* [Paul didn't contribute to The Scaffold's 1968 version of it.]

Prince Stash (Stanislas Klossowski de Rola, Baron de Watteville), who also participated says, "Through my friendship with The Rolling Stones* I became friends with The Beatles. The trumped up bust of Brian Jones and I, left me stranded in the UK without a passport. Paul McCartney took me under his wing and put me up in his London home, which led to my involvement with Mike – an extraordinarily fine human being. All I remember from the sessions is rustling the leaves on a bouquet of roses into a microphone on the song *Do You Remember*, and probably playing some percussion and singing backing vocals on it. Paul was also present, and was his usual active self in taking charge, and also sang backing vocals as I recall. [Paul and I developed a close friendship, and from that I also became close to John Lennon and George Harrison. Plans for my recording a cover of their song *A Day In the Life* were stillborn when it was banned by the BBC, but The Beatles were very good to me and determined to do something for me. I played on some sessions with them including percussion on *Baby You're A Rich Man* and *You Know My Name (Look Up The Number)*. Most of these sessions were just instrumental jams and experimenting. I'd also written lyrics people such as Jimi Hendrix liked. Paul hoped that we could collate all of this, and a song he had penned called *Suicide*, into a record for me but nothing came of it. Paul also wanted to do something with my cover of Love's song *A*

Message To Pretty, and I gave him the master tapes but they disappeared."]

The producer for *McGough & McGear* is listed as "All of Us," but Zoot Money says the primary producer was Andy Roberts and that Paul's involvement was limited more to suggestions. Andy says, "That's sweet of Zoot, and I did have a large role playing on the songs, but I had only been in a recording studio a couple of times then, and didn't have the experience or skill to deliver a production of this standard. The truth is that it was Paul all the way! Paul called the shots from the control room, and Graham Nash was his closest ally in the box. Paul did emerge to play the Mellotron and some piano. The rest of us were mostly in the studio waiting for instructions. I played acoustic guitar on all of the tracks during the time I was around as I knew Mike and Roger's songs better than anyone else." McGough reads poetry on the album including *Summer With Monika* – also the title of one of his book of poems about his wife, Thelma Pickles, who had dated Paul and John Lennon years earlier. An unreleased song from the sessions, *Oh To Be A Child (Haydn's Toy Symphony)*, reportedly features many superstars. Hunter Davis, The Beatles' authorized biographer, wrote the album's liner notes.

Mike, and several of the musicians from the *McGough & McGear* sessions, was part of The Beatles' live performance of *All You Need Is Love* for the BBC TV program *Our World*, telecast live on June 25, 1967. Weeks later, Mike also made a cameo at the end of The Beatles' TV special *Magical Mystery Tour*. McGough contributed (un-credited) to the script for The Beatles' animated film *Yellow Submarine* in 1968.

In 1971 Mike recorded his first bona fide solo album *Woman*, with help from Paul (credited as "friend") as co-composer of the song *Bored As Butterscotch*. The album features a photo of their mother Mary in her nursing uniform. Mike appeared in the 1973 *James Paul McCartney* TV special. He recorded Paul's composition *Leave It* which Paul plays on and produced, which became a UK Top 40. Mike claims in his autobiography, *Thank U Very Much,* (as do the liner notes to the UK **McGear* CD) that the song was recorded following Paul and Wings' recordings for the album *Band On The Run* in Lagos, Nigeria in August 1973. However, Denny Seiwell, the recording's drummer, is correct in asserting that at least the basic track had to be recorded prior to the trip to Lagos because he'd left Paul's band Wings by then.

During the first half of 1974, with Wings consisting only of Denny Laine* and Paul and Linda McCartney*, Paul and Mike began collaborating on what would become Mike's showcase solo album **McGear*. It features Paul as composer, producer and arranger, with help from Linda, Laine, and lead guitarist Jimmy McCulloch who joined Wings following the sessions. Paul probably plays most of the bass, keyboards and a good bit of guitar, and even some drums. Paul, Linda and Denny's backing vocals are apparent throughout the album. Laine probably plays some acoustic and electric guitar, and possibly some bass as well. Linda's instrumental role is likely limited to keyboards and percussion. Most of the album was recorded at Strawberry Studios co-owned by Eric Stewart, with contributions from 10cc*. Stewart plays guitar, and may sing backing vocals, but his fellow members in 10cc, Kevin Godley and Lol Creme (see Godley & Creme), are probably limited to playing their unique invention called the Gysmorchestra. There are also other guest appearances including Paddy Moloney of The Chieftians, Kate Robbins*, Viv Stanshall (see The Bonzo Dog Band) and Brian Jones of the early 1960's Liverpool band The Undertakers (see Jackie Lomax). The album could fairly be considered a Paul McCartney album with Mike handling the lead vocals. Though **McGear* was praised by critics, none of its well-crafted, pop-rock tracks were significant chart successes. The single *Dance The* Do, omitted from the original vinyl release, fared no better than the other singles taken from the album.

In 1977 Mike talked Paul into opening up what remained of the long-closed Apple Studios to record a demo of a song called *Knocking Down Walls Of Ignorance* with Laine, Zoot Money, Viv Stanshall, and Paul playing drums. However, when Mike submitted it to EMI they rejected it, in part, because they didn't like the drumming! In all likelihood, it's the last song ever recorded at Apple.

Mike has only released a few recordings since the mid-1970s, apparently without any assistance from Paul. Paul found Mike's song *All The Whales In The Ocean* so infectious that he often sang it during his brief imprisonment in Japan in 1980 for possession of marijuana. When it was released on a single a few months later, the credits included "help from Paul" but according to Mike, Paul didn't contribute to the recordings.

Mike reverted to using the McCartney name in the early 1980s. In addition to the autobiography, Mike has written children's books and books of his photographs (including many of The Beatles). One of his early photos of Paul was used for the cover of McCartney's 2005 album *Chaos And Creation In The Backyard.* Mike has also been a guest at conventions and festivals for fans of The Beatles. For more information go to
www.mikemccartney.co.uk

Ian McLagan

Troublemaker
Mercury-PHCR-4152 (Japan) (12/01/93) (12/10/79)
Producer: Geoff Workman
Ringo Starr: Drums; Ian McLagan: Lead Vocals & (probable) Guitar; additionally, one or more of the following: Johnny Lee Schell: Guitar; Ron Wood: Guitar; Keith Richards: Guitar; Jim Keltner: Drums; Zigaboo Modeliste: Drums; Paul Stallworth: Bass; Stanley Clarke: Bass; Ian McLagan; Keyboards; Geoff Workman: Accordion; Bobby Keys: Horns; Ron Wood: Horns; Steve Madaio: Horns
Cherokee & Shangri La Studios, Los Angeles, CA & Paris, France 02/xx/79

Hold On (I. McLagan) 3:43 (9)

Ian McLagan was born May 12, 1945 in London, England. He is best known as a member of Small Faces, which originally included Steve Marriott, Ronnie Lane, Kenney Jones* and Jimmy Winston whom McLagan replaced in 1965. In 1969 Marriott left to form Humble Pie with Peter Frampton*, and Ron Wood* and Rod Stewart*, of the Jeff Beck Group, joined the band, which renamed itself Faces. Shortly after Stewart joined the band his solo career took off and shifted the focus of Faces. Lane's departure in 1973 left the band as little more than a backup for superstar Stewart. Meanwhile, Wood joined The Rolling Stones*, and the remnants of Faces, aided by Jesse Ed Davis*, backed Stewart for the last time in 1975. In 1976 Marriott rejoined Jones and McLagan to reform Small Faces. The following year Jimmy McCulloch, who had just quit Wings, joined Small Faces. The band dissolved again in 1978. Jones replaced Keith Moon* in The Who (see Roger Daltrey, John Entwistle) and McLagan augmented Wood on The Rolling Stones' tours. Lane was part of the Rockestra ensemble on Wings' 1979 album *Back To The Egg*, and during their performance at London's Hammersmith Odeon on December 29, 1979 released on the 1981 album *Concerts For The People Of Kampuchea*. The Faces have made occasional guest appearances over the years. Marriott died in 1991 and Ronnie Lane died in 1997.

McLagan helped write the song *Tonight* on Ringo Starr's 1978 album *Bad Boy*. In 1979 McLagan issued his first solo album *Troublemaker*, which lists Ringo in the general musical credits. According to Ian, Ringo plays drums on the song *Hold On*. For more information go to www.ianmclagan.com

George Michael

Twentyfive
Sony/BMG 88697009002 (Australia) (11/06/06)
Producer: George Michael
Paul McCartney: Duet Vocals & Bass;
George Michael: Duet Vocals & Acoustic Guitar; Danny Cummings: Percussion; Phil Palmer: Guitars
Air Studios, London, UK 11/xx/05

Heal The Pain (G. Michael) 4:42 (2/1/7)

George Michael was born Georgios-Kyriacos Panayiotou on June 25, 1963 in London, England. He began his musical career in the band The Executive, but it wasn't until he and fellow band member Andrew Ridgeley formed the duo Wham! in 1981 that he found success. Between 1982 and 1986, with Michael as primary songwriter and singer, they had many international hits including *Wake Me Up Before You Go Go*, *Freedom*, *Everything She Wants*, *I'm Your Man* and *The Edge Of Heaven* before they officially split and Michael pursued a solo career.

Careless Whisper in 1984 was Michael's first international chart-topper. He sang lead vocals on the Band Aid* charity song *Do They Know It's Christmas*. His 1987 debut album *Faith* is one of the biggest selling albums ever and includes the number one hits *Faith*, *One More Try*, *Father Figure* and *Monkey*, and the Top Five hit *I Want Your Sex*. He also had number one hits with *I Knew You Were Waiting (For Me)*, a duet with Aretha Franklin*, in 1987, *Praying For Time* in 1990 and *Don't Let The Sun Go Down On Me*, a duet with Elton John*, in 1991. Throughout the 1990s he scored a dozen Top 10 hits in the UK, including the number one hits *Somebody To Love* with Queen, *Killer/Papa Was A Rollin' Stone*, *Jesus To A Child* and *Fastlove*.

On April 10, 1999 Michael performed Paul McCartney's Beatles' song *Eleanor Rigby* and *The Long And Winding Road*, and joined Paul on *Let It Be* for *Here, There and Everywhere – A Concert For Linda* (see Linda McCartney) at the Royal Albert Hall in London. In 2000 Michael purchased John Lennon's piano used to compose *Imagine*. At the *Live 8* concert in London in 2005 he joined McCartney singing *Drive My Car*. Michael's 2006 album *Twentyfive* includes a remake of his song *Heal The Pain* with McCartney on bass and duet vocals. Over the last two decades Michael's career has been plagued by controversy and personal problems. However, he still enjoys chart success in the UK and to date has sold over 100 million records. Michael has recently turned to acting, but continues to write, record and tour. For more information go to www.georgemichael.com

The Steve Miller Band

Brave New World
Capitol-CDP 7 91246 2 (08/23/94) (06/16/69)
Producer: Glyn Johns and Steve Miller
Paul McCartney: Bass, Drums, B. Vocals & Guitar; Steve Miller: Lead Vocals & Guitar
Olympic Studio, London, UK 05/09/69

My Dark Hour ([**P. McCartney**] S. Miller)
3:05 (9)

King Biscuit Flower Hour Presents The Steve Miller Band
Koch/Razor & Tie Music-88001 (06/10/03) **Paul McCartney: Liner Notes**

Steve Miller was born on October 5, 1943 in Milwaukee, Wisconsin but spent much of his youth in Texas. His mother was a singer and his father was a physician and amateur recording engineer. Steve's godfather was the legendary guitarist, Les Paul who gave Steve a few pointers on the guitar as a youngster. By age 12 Steve had formed the band The Marksmen, which would later include Boz Scaggs, and by 14 he had backed blues legend Jimmy Reed. During college he formed The Ardells with Scaggs. He also backed a number of blues legends including Howlin' Wolf*. In 1966 he moved to San Francisco and began putting together what would become The Steve Miller Band, which over the years has included, among others, Boz Scaggs and Nicky Hopkins*. The band broke into the charts in 1968 with the song *Living In The USA*.

The Steve Miller Band's 1969 album *Brave New World* contains the song *My Dark Hour*, with special thanks to Paul Ramon. In Paul McCartney's fan club magazine *Club Sandwich* (spring 1992 issue No.61) Paul recounts what he describes as a day of painful and historic events. "That was during the tense Apple time. We had a Friday night session at Olympic Studio in Barnes, and Allen Klein showed up with all the guys. It was a big showdown. And my lawyer was Jewish, so he didn't work on Friday nights. But there was Klein – he was Jewish, and he was working – so he had a big advantage. Maybe he knew my lawyer was Jewish. Anyway, they all showed up at Olympic and there was a big row – they all accused me of stalling. In my mind I was actually trying to save our future, and I was vindicated later, but at the time I was definitely 'the dark horse, the problem.' And that was actually the night we broke The Beatles. That was the big crack in the liberty bell – it never came back together after that one. So we were stuck, the session was over, and the studio was free. I hung around a little bit and met Steve Miller, who was in one of the other studios. We got chatting and he was an 'up.' After the big downer, I needed an up, so he was my security blanket. I stayed chatting for a while and then he suggested cutting something. I asked what, and he said, 'We'll make something up!' I asked if I could play drums and just thrashed around. He called it *My Dark Hour*, and we recorded it – just the two of us. I overdubbed a bit of bass and some guitar, and we sang it all. We stayed there all night. We just had to do something. I said, 'Just put me down as Paul Ramon.'" [Paul Ramon was a stage name McCartney briefly used when The Beatles backed Johnny Gentle (see Darren Young) on his tour of Scotland in May 1960.] Steve Miller was briefly signed to Apple Music Publishing in the UK.

Near the end of 1973 Miller reached the top of the charts with *The Joker*. During the second half of the 1970s and early 1980s Miller had Top 20 hits with *Fly Like An Eagle*, *Take The Money And Run* and *Rock 'N' Me*. Miller's music was featured on McCartney's 1995 radio series *Oobu Joobu* around the same time the two began working together on a number of songs that appear on McCartney's 1997 album *Flaming Pie*. Steve Miller continues to release new recordings and remains popular on tour. For more information go to www.stevemillerband.com

Heather Mills (Featuring Paul McCartney)

Vo!ce
Coda-CODARCD 004 (single) (UK) (12/13/99)
Producer: **[Paul McCartney†]** & Nikko Patrelakis [unless noted otherwise]
Paul McCartney: B. Vocals & Guitar††; Heather Mills: Dialogue; Jonathan Elvey: Piano; Stamos Semsis: Strings
Keys Studios, Athens, Greece; Panic, Coda, Ewshot Hall†† & Hog Hill Mill Studios, Sussex† UK 10/xx/99†† & 11/xx/99†

Vo!ce [Radio Edit] (N. Patrelakis-H. Mills-**P. McCartney**) 4:35 (1)
Producer: Nikko Patrelakis; **Paul McCartney: Re-mixer††**

Vo!ce [Paul McCartney's Mello Extension] (N. Patrelakis-H. Mills-**P. McCartney**) 7:18 (2)
Additionally: Paul McCartney: B. Vocals (only)†

Vo!ce [Someone U Love Mix] (N. Patrelakis-H. Mills-F. Mills-**P. McCartney**) 7:02 (3)†

Heather Mills was born on January 12, 1968 in Aldershot, England. As a youngster she studied oboe and saxophone. She worked as a model and helped start a modeling agency in 1989 but it soon closed. In 1993 she was struck by a police motorcycle resulting in the loss of her left leg below the knee. She wrote the book *Out On A Limb* about the experience and founded the Heather Mills Health Trust, which recycles prosthetic limbs. She caught the eye of Paul McCartney at the *Pride Of Britain* charity event in the spring of 1999.

In the fall of 1999 Mills, and her sister Fiona who was living in Greece and owner of Coda Records, began writing and recording the song *Vo!ce* to raise money for Heather's trust. McCartney donated over $250,000 to the trust, and offered to supply backing vocals and guitar, recorded at Mike Batt's* home studio and remixed at McCartney's home studio. Though not credited, Mills' assistant Renata Matijasevic confirmed reports that McCartney produced the *Voice* mixes *Someone U Love Mix* and *Paul McCartney's Mello Extension*, which bear considerable resemblance to McCartney's *Fireman* work.

Soon after, it was confirmed that their relationship had developed into a personal one. They were married on June 11, 2002. It was the second marriage for both (see Linda McCartney). The marriage produced daughter Beatrice born in 2003. Mills is credited with arranging Paul's song *Freedom* but her assistant denies reports that the couple had written a song together called *Hometown Papers* in response to criticism of Mills in the press in 2005. Paul and Heather separated in 2006, and were divorced in 2008 following a bitter court battle. Heather was awarded a settlement of about $50 million.

Mills lives in the UK helping raise her and McCartney's daughter. She has been actively involved in a number of charities and organizations including Adopt-A-Minefield (see: Paul Simon, James Taylor, Brian Wilson, Neil Young), The Limbless Association, PETA (People For The Ethical Treatment Of Animals, and vegetarian causes. She was a celebrity performer on the TV show *Dancing With The Stars* in 2007. For more information go to
www.heathermills.org

Adrian Mitchell

Rehearsals For The New World Tour 1993
Music With Love-MWL 21/22 [unauthorized release] (xx/xx/93)
Producer: [unknown-audience recording]
Paul McCartney: (probable) Bass &/or Guitar &/or Keyboards; Adrian Mitchell: Dialogue; additionally, probably one or more of the following: Robbie McIntosh: Guitar; Paul Wickens: Keyboards; Hamish Stuart: Bass; Linda McCartney: Keyboards
Cliffs Pavilion, Westcliff-on-Sea, UK 07/19/91

Hot Pursuit [live] (A. Mitchell-**[probably P. McCartney**-B. Cunningham-R. McIntosh-P. Wickens-H. Stuart-L. McCartney]) 1:44 (2-20)
Additionally: (probably) Blair Cunningham: Drums

Maybe Maytime (Singalong Junk) [live] **(P. McCartney**-A. Mitchell) 1:52 (2-19)
Additionally: (probably) Blair Cunningham: Drums

Song In Space [live] (A. Mitchell-**[probably P.**

McCartney-B. Cunningham-R. McIntosh-P. Wickens-H. Stuart-L. McCartney]) 0:59 (2-17)

Adrian Mitchell (a.k.a. Volcano Jones and Apeman Mudgeon) was born on October 24, 1932 in London, England. He attended Oxford University and later worked for several London newspapers. In 1961 he won the prestigious Eric Gregory Award for his poetry. He taught at a number of universities in the US and UK during the 1960s. Mitchell was regarded as one of the UK's leading contemporary poets (*Out Loud* and *The Apeman Cometh*), novelists (*The Bodyguard*) and playwrights (*Animals Can't Laugh* and *Tyger*). He also wrote songs. His writings were often charged with social commentary.

Mitchell, who was writing a weekly pop column for the *Daily Mail* in 1963 recalls, "In February I receiving a scruffy mimeographed press handout explaining how The Beatles got their name (a man came unto us on a flaming pie, etc.) and I thought, 'I want to interview whoever wrote this.' I enjoyed interviewing them. That day I saw them play to a BBC radio audience and thought they were great. [Mitchell is probably referring to The Beatles' appearance at London's Playhouse Theatre on February 20 for BBC Radio's Light Program show *Parade Of The Pops*.] I interviewed them several times after that. Paul was always the friendliest to me; he knew I was a published poet and named me as his favorite poet in *Honey* magazine." McCartney appeared, along with Mitchell, Allen Ginsberg* and others, in the Granada TV special *It's So Far Out It's Straight Down* broadcast in the UK on March 7, 1967.

Years later, Adrian had become good friends with Paul and Linda McCartney*. Paul asked Adrian if he'd like to read his poems at their concert on July 19, 1991 in Westcliff-on-Sea. Adrian said, "I was scheduled to be on holiday in France at the time. 'Oh, we'd fly you over,' Paul said. I was thrilled, so I flew over and went for rehearsals at his private studio by his home in Sussex. Paul picked out four poems – *Hot Pursuit* (about singer James Brown), *Song In Space* (about the environment), *Maybe Maytime* (for my wife Celia) and *I Like That Stuff* (a children's riddle I nearly always perform). I enjoyed the gig tremendously. I've performed poems for anti-bomb and anti-Vietnam War rallies of 100,000, but it was a gas to be backed by that right little, tight little band and my hero Paul. I felt like I'd been covered in stardust. I had my own dressing room with a refrigerator packed with wine and veggie treats. There was a limo to fetch me...wow, a bit unlike typical poetry gigs!" *Maybe Maytime* was performed to the backing of McCartney's song *Singalong Junk*. The only backing on *I Like That Stuff* is a guitar chord at the end, probably played by McCartney or Robbie McIntosh, though Mitchell cannot recall exactly who played what on the other songs because he was facing the audience. A portion of *Song In Space* was reprinted in McCartney's *New World Tour* program in 1993.

McCartney sought Adrian's advice on lyrics for his 1993 album *Off The Ground*. He said, "Paul and I sat in his studio, and he played and sang the songs from a few feet away. It was very exciting, and I found it hard to do instant comments on the lyrics, but I did make a few that I think were incorporated." Adrian edited *Blackbird Singing*, a book of McCartney's poems and lyrics published in 2001, and participated in McCartney's promotion of the book. Mitchell, like McCartney, was an advocate for animal rights and vegetarianism. Adrian Mitchell died on December 20, 2008. For more information go to www.rippingyarns.co.uk/adrian

Zoot Money

Mr. Money
Magic Moon-LUNE 1 (album 12") (UK) (09/25/80) **Jacket designed by Paul McCartney**
Executive Producer: Paul McCartney

Zoot Money was born George Bruno on July 17, 1942 in Bournemouth England. He started out in jazz and skiffle during the 1950s, and became a popular blues musician in the UK during the 1960s. His Big Roll Band included Andy Somers (a.k.a. Summers, and later a member of the band The Police). In 1966 they had a UK Top 40 hit with *Big Time Operator* before Zoot formed Dantalian's Chariot, which broke up in 1969 when Zoot and Andy joined Eric Burdon* and The New New Animals.

Zoot had a long musical relationship with Paul McCartney's brother Mike McGear* and was a brief member of The Scaffold* before it evolved into Grimms. His 1980 album *Mr. Money* was listed as an MPL production. According to Zoot, McCartney conceived the idea of having him record songs that Paul owned the music publishing rights to after hearing Zoot's cover version of his Beatles' song *Blackbird.* The entire project, which was commissioned and financed by McCartney, was subject to McCartney's approval, making him the executive producer. He was given special thanks and listed as contributing to the album's jacket design. Zoot said, "It was a general discussion between Paul and me about the album during which we explored the different 'ages of Zoot' for the album jacket's back, which I wanted for the front." Only minor changes were made to the basic design submitted by Zoot and the photographer to MPL. Though McCartney didn't directly contribute to any of the recordings, and the role of executive producer isn't normally considered a contribution, because of the wider scope of McCartney's involvement with the record, it's considered a contribution. Zoot is now involved in acting and TV commercials. For more information go to www.zootmoney.org

Matt Monro

By Request
EMI-CDP 7482752 CZ 8 (UK) (10/19/87) (11/19/86) **Paul McCartney: Liner Notes**

Matt Monro (a.k.a. Al Jordan and Terry Fitzgerald) was born Terence Parsons on December 1, 1930 in London, England. His singing style was typical of what is termed easy listening music. Monro was signed to Parlophone and produced by George Martin*. He had a UK Top 10 hit with *Portrait Of My Love* in 1960. During the next five years he had chart success in the UK with a number of songs including *My Kind Of Girl* (his only Top 20 hit), *Why Not Now*, *Gonna Build A Mountain*, *Softly As I Leave You* and *From Russia With Love*.

Monro was signed to NEMS and usually recorded at Abbey Road Studios where he got to know Paul McCartney. He covered a number of Beatles' songs including McCartney's *Yesterday*, which was a UK Top 10 hit for him in the fall of 1965. That year, he moved to the US where he worked the nightclub circuit. Monro died on February 7, 1985. McCartney contributed liner notes to *By Request*, a 1986 retrospective album of Monro's career. For more information go to www.mattmonro.com

Monty Python

Life Of Brian
Anchor Bay-DV10674 (DVD)
Producer: Eric Idle & Graham Chapman & **Mixed by: George Harrison** & Phil MacDonald (music)
John Altman: Arrangement
Unit Hotel, Tunisia & Chappell Studios, London & mixed at FPSHOT, UK 09/08/78

Always Look On The Bright Side Of Life [reprise] (E. Idle) 0:51

Monty Python Examines "The Life Of Brian" (A Conversation With Monty Python Conducted By Dave Herman)
Warner Bros. (The Warner Bros. Music Show)-WBMS 110 (album 12" promotional only) (xx/xx/79)
Producer: Drea Besch
George Harrison: Dialogue; Dave Herman: Interviewer; Monty Python: Dialogue
Probably Los Angeles, CA xx/xx/79

Monty Python Examines "The Life Of Brian" (A Conversation With Monty Python Conducted By Dave Herman) (**G. Harrison**-M. Palin-G. Chapman-J. Cleese-E. Idle-T. Jones-T. Gilliam) 28:45 (total time of LP) (2/1)

Monty Python Sings
Virgin/Capitol-V2-86253 2 (6/29/92)

Always Look On The Bright Side Of Life (E. Idle) 3:33 (1) (10/08/79)
Producer: Eric Idle & Graham Chapman; **Mixed by: George Harrison** & Phil MacDonald
Eric Idle: Lead Vocals; John Altman: Arrangement
Unit Hotel, Tunisia; Chappell Studios, London & mixed at FPSHOTUK 09/08/78

Lumberjack Song (T. Jones-M. Palin-F. Tomlinson) 3:20 (3) (11/14/75)
Producer: George Harrison
Michael Palin: Lead Vocals; probably The Fred Tomlinson Singers: B. Vocals
One or more of the following studios: Olympic Sound, Chappell &/or Redwood, London, mixed at FPSHOT, UK probably xx/xx/74 or 75

The Monty Python comedy team consisted of Englishmen Graham Chapman, born on January 8, 1941 in Leicester; John Cleese, born on October 27, 1939 in Weston-Super-Mare; Eric Idle, born on March 29, 1943 in South Shields; Terry Jones, born on February 1, 1942 in Colwyn Bay, Wales; Michael Palin, born on May 5, 1943 in Sheffield, and one American, Terry Gilliam, born on November 22, 1940 in Medicine Lake, Minnesota. They gained fame with their TV show *Monty Python's Flying Circus*, which aired in the UK between 1969 and 1974. [Prior to the show, Chapman and Cleese had co-written and appeared in the Peter Sellers'* film *The Magic Christian*, co-starring Ringo Starr.]

The Beatles were big fans of the show. On January 28, 1972 Ringo and Lulu* appeared in a brief sketch called *It's Man Chat Show* at the very end of episode 28, which first aired on October 26, 1972. It is available on *Monty Python's Flying Circus* (A&E-AAE-700831, Set 5, Season 3, DVD 9) released in 2000. John Lennon and Yoko Ono* had also planned to appear on the show before they moved to the US. Chapman co-wrote an unused script for a proposed US TV special *Our Show For Ringo* to help promote the release of Ringo's album *Goodnight Vienna* in 1974.

George Harrison was particularly fond of Monty Python and struck up a friendship with the group, especially Michael Palin and Eric Idle. Monty Python's *Lumberjack Song* was played through the public address system at the beginning of shows during Harrison's 1974 US tour. Harrison produced a recording of the song for Monty Python credited as George "Onothimagen" Harrison, a self-deprecating nickname he used for a time after his critically panned *Dark Horse* album and tour in 1974. The liner notes on Harrison's 1975 album *Extra Texture (Read All About It)* state "Also not appearing on this record: Eric Idle." Idle claims he contributed a voice to the album, and apparently did some radio ads for the album in the UK.

On December 26, 1975 Harrison appeared on Idle and Neil Innes' (see Bonzo Dog Band) BBC TV comedy series *Rutland Weekend Television* performing *The Pirate Song*. It was a parody of Harrison's legal troubles, written by Idle and Harrison, using part of the melody of *My Sweet Lord*, which he was being sued for plagiarizing from The Chiffons' song *He's So Fine* (see Delaney & Bonnie & Friends). An album titled *The Rutland Weekend Television Song Book* was issued. The final liner note on the album is "Warning. There is to be no mention of George Harrison on this record." This is in response to part of *The Pirate Song* skit with Harrison in which he wishes not to be George Harrison. According to Innes, Harrison didn't contribute to the album.

On April 20, 1976 Harrison joined Monty Python onstage at the Civic Center in New York to sing the *Lumberjack Song*. Unfortunately the version on the album *Monty Python Live At The Civic Center* is from a different performance there without Harrison. That year, Idle sang on Harrison's *This Song* written in response to his plagiarism lawsuit. Idle directed the music videos for Harrison's songs *True Love* and *Crackerbox Palace*, which co-stars Innes.

Monty Python's 1978 film *Life Of Brian* was a biblical comedy about an ordinary person named Brian who is mistaken for a messiah-like Jesus Christ. EMI, the film's original producer, backed out at the last minute due to the controversial nature of the film. Harrison stepped in and acted as executive producer, assuring the film's financial backing. The film was a box office success and helped launch Harrison's HandMade Films Company. Harrison made a cameo in the film as Mr. Papadopoulis and helped mix the closing track, *Always Look On The Bright Side Of Life*, at FPSHOT. He also contributed dialogue to the 1979 promotional interview album *Monty Python Examines The Life Of Brian (A Conversation With Monty Python Conducted By Dave Herman)*.

In 1981 HandMade Films released Gilliam's highly successful *Time Bandits* (see Various Artists-Time Bandits). Harrison contributed his song *Dream Away* for the film's closing credits. In 1982 HandMade Films released *Monty Python – Live At The Hollywood Bowl*. HandMade Film's *The Missionary* in 1982 and *A Private Function* in 1985 starred Michael Palin. Their 1982 film *Privates On Parade* starred John Cleese and their 1990 film *Nuns On The Run* starred Eric Idle.

Monty Python's members have since drifted into successful solo projects, and haven't effectively reformed since the death of Graham Chapman on October 4, 1989. Ringo was originally considered for a role in another Monty Python spin-off film, *Yellowbeard*. Harrison was originally scheduled to write the music for Gilliam's film *Brazil*. Palin wrote the liner notes for the Traveling Wilburys' (see Bob Dylan, Jeff Lynne, Roy Orbison, Tom Petty And The Heartbreakers) first album and Idle wrote the liner notes for their second (Volume 3) album. The CD *Monty Python Sings*, which includes two Harrison contributions, gives him special thanks. Palin, Idle, Jones, Gilliam and Innes took part in the Harrison tribute *Concert For George* in 2002. For more information go to www.pythonline.com

Keith Moon

Two Sides Of The Moon
Mausoleum Classix-60038-2 (07/01/97) (03/17/75)
Producer: Mal Evans, Skip Taylor & John Stronach
Record Plant Studios, Los Angeles, CA 09-12/xx/74 thru 02/xx/75

US Radio Spot (contains portions of: Crazy Like A Fox/Solid Gold/Together/In My Life) (A. Staehely-N. Barclay-H. Nilsson-J. Lennon-P. McCartney)-[K. Moon] 1:02 (11)
Ringo Starr: Drums, Announcer & "Rap"; Keith Moon: Lead Vocals & Drums; Cam Davis: B. Vocals & Drums; Paul Stallworth: Bass; Jean Millington: B. Vocals & Bass; Nickey Barclay: B. Vocals & Piano; Patti Quatro: B. Vocals & Guitar; Joe Walsh: Guitar & Arp Synthesizer; Beau Guss; Guitar; Sherlie Matthews: B. Vocals; Lorna Willard: B. Vocals; Julia Tillman: B. Vocals; Jim Keltner: Drums; Klaus Voormann: Bass; Jesse Ed Davis: Guitar; Danny Kortchmar: Guitar; Paul Lenart: Guitar; Robert Greenridge: Steel Drums; Jimmy Haskell: Arrangement & Conductor of Strings; Curly Smith: Drums; Jimmie Randall: Bass; Spencer Davis: Acoustic Guitar; Al Staehely: Acoustic Guitar; John Staehely: Electric Guitar; Jay Ferguson: Piano; Norman Kurban: Piano; Ron Hicklin: B. Vocals; August Johnson: B. Vocals; Greg Matta: B. Vocals; Irma Routen: B. Vocals; Andra Willis: B. Vocals; Clydie King: B. Vocals; Ira Hawkins: B. Vocals; James Gilstrap: B. Vocals; Gerald Garrett: B. Vocals; Carolyn Willis: B. Vocals

Two Sides Of The Moon "Deluxe Edition"
Castle/Sanctuary-CMEDD1068 (EU) (08/15/06)
Producer: Skip Taylor & John Stronach [unless noted otherwise]
Record Plant Studios, Los Angeles, CA 09-12/xx/74 [unless noted otherwise]

Do Me Good (S. Cropper) 2:44 (1-23) (07/01/97)
Producer: Steve Cropper
Ringo Starr: Drums & (probable) B. Vocals; Keith Moon: Lead Vocals; probably one or more of the following: Steve Cropper: Guitar; Klaus Voormann: Bass; Ronnie Wood: Guitar; David Bowie: Keyboards &/or B. Vocals; Jim Horn: (probable) Saxophone; Chuck Findley: (probable) Horns
Clover Recorders, Los Angeles, CA 08/26/75

Do Me Good (O.K. Mr. Starkey) (S. Cropper) 4:57 (2-22 & 23)
Producer: Steve Cropper
Ringo Starr: Drums & B. Vocals; Keith Moon: Lead Vocals; probably one or more of the following: Steve Cropper: Guitar; Klaus Voormann: Bass; Ronnie Wood: Guitar; David Bowie: Keyboards &/or B. Vocals; Jim Horn: (probable) Saxophone; Chuck Findley: (probable) Horns
Clover Recorders, Los Angeles, CA 08/26/75

I Don't Suppose (N. Barclay) 4:02 (1-12)
Producer: additionally Mal Evans
Ringo Starr: (probable) Drums; Keith Moon: Lead Vocals; probably one or more of the following: Paul Stallworth: Bass; Jean Millington: Bass; Nickey Barclay: Piano; Patti Quatro: Guitar; Beau Guss; Guitar; Jim Keltner: Drums; Klaus Voormann: Bass; Jesse Ed Davis: Guitar; Danny Kortchmar; Guitar; Paul Lenart: Guitar; Curly Smith: Drums; Jimmie Randall: Bass; Spencer Davis: Acoustic Guitar; Al Staehely: Acoustic Guitar; John Staehely: Electric Guitar; Jay Ferguson: Piano; Norman Kurban: Piano

Keith & Ringo 'Together' (**R. Starkey**-K. Moon) 0:45 (2-1)
Ringo Starr: Dialogue; Keith Moon: Dialogue
Record Plant Studios, Los Angeles, CA 11/26/74

Keith & Ringo 'Together Rap' (**R. Starkey**-K. Moon-H. Nilsson) 1:54 (2-24) (07/01/97)
Ringo Starr: Drums and "Rap"; Keith Moon: "Rap"; Jim Keltner: Drums; Klaus Voormann: Bass; Jesse Ed Davis: Guitar; Danny Kortchmar; Paul Lenart: Guitar
Record Plant Studios, Los Angeles, CA 11/26/74

Move Over Ms. L (**J. Lennon**) 3:11 (1-6) (03/17/75)
Producer: additionally Mal Evans
Keith Moon: Lead Vocals; Paul Stallworth: Bass; Joe Walsh: Guitar; Jesse Ed Davis: Guitar; Keith Moon: Drums; Ron Grinel: Drums; David Foster: Piano; Ollie Mitchell: Horns; Steve Douglas: Horns; Mal Evans: Horn Arrangements

Move Over Ms. L [Mal Evans Mix] (**J. Lennon**) 3:11 (1-20)
Producer: additionally Mal Evans
Keith Moon: Lead Vocals; Paul Stallworth: Bass; Joe Walsh: Guitar; Jesse Ed Davis: Guitar;

Keith Moon: Drums; Ron Grinel: Drums; David Foster: Piano; Ollie Mitchell: Horns; Steve Douglas: Horns; Mal Evans: Horn Arrangements

Naked Man (R. Newman) 3:18 (1-25) (07/01/97)
Producer: Steve Cropper
Ringo Starr: (probable) Drums & (probable) B. Vocals; Keith Moon: Lead Vocals; probably one or more of the following: Steve Cropper: Guitar; Klaus Voormann: Bass; Ronnie Wood: Guitar; David Bowie: B. Vocals &/or Keyboards; Brooks Honeycut: (probable) B. Vocals; Maxine Waters: (probable) B. Vocals; Julia Waters: (probable) B. Vocals; Jim Horn: (probable) Saxophone; Chuck Findley: (probable) Horns
Clover Recorders, Los Angeles, CA 09/xx/75

Real Emotion (S. Cropper) 2:56 (1-24) (07/01/97)
Producer: Steve Cropper
Ringo Starr: (probable) Drums & (probable) B. Vocals; probably one or more of the following: Steve Cropper: Guitar; Klaus Voormann: Bass; Ronnie Wood: Guitar; David Bowie: B. Vocals &/or Keyboards; Keith Moon: Lead Vocals
Clover Recorders, Los Angeles, CA 09/xx/75

Solid Gold (N. Barclay) 2:47 (1-2) (03/17/75)
Producer: additionally Mal Evans
Ringo Starr: Announcer; Keith Moon: Lead Vocals; Cam Davis: B. Vocals & Drums; Paul Stallworth: Bass; Jean Millington: B. Vocals & Bass; Nickey Barclay: B. Vocals & Piano; Patti Quatro: B. Vocals & Guitar; Joe Walsh: Guitar & Arp Synthesizer; Beau Guss; Guitar; Sherlie Matthews: B. Vocals; Lorna Willard: B. Vocals; Julia Tillman: B. Vocals

Together (H. Nilsson) 3:01 (1-10) (03/17/75)
Ringo Starr: Drums and "Rap"; Keith Moon: Vocals; Harry Nilsson: Vocals; Jim Keltner: Drums; Klaus Voormann: Bass; Jesse Ed Davis: Guitar; Danny Kortchmar; Paul Lenart: Guitar; Robert Greenridge: Steel Drums; Jimmy Haskell: Arrangement and Conductor of Strings

Together (H. Nilsson) 0:15 (2-12)
Ringo Starr: Vocals; Keith Moon: Vocals
Record Plant Studios, Los Angeles, CA 11/26/74

Together (**R. Starkey**-K. Moon) 0:52 (2-14)
Ringo Starr: Dialogue; Keith Moon: Dialogue
Record Plant Studios, Los Angeles, CA 11/26/74

Keith Moon was born on August 23, 1946 in London, England. Moon, often referred to as "Moon The Loon" or "Moonie," justly deserved his reputation as one of rock's greatest and most outrageous drummers. He joined The Escorts prior to his joining the surf music band The Beachcombers. In 1964 he challenged The Who's (see Roger Daltrey, John Entwistle) drummer during a public performance, demolishing their drummer's kit along with his membership in the group, which Moon assumed. Destroying drum kits, in which he would often place explosives, became Moon's trademark. His hotel rooms also weren't immune from major destruction. Despite his many antics, Moon was loved and respected by his peers, including all of The Beatles. Moon was part of The Beatles' live performance of *All You Need Is Love* for the BBC TV program *Our World*, telecast live on June 25, 1967. Moon was part of John Lennon and Yoko Ono's* Plastic Ono Supergroup at a benefit concert at London's Lyceum Ballroom on December 15, 1969, which is included on the Lennons' 1972 album *Some Time In New York City*.

Moon was becoming a regular on the rock party circuit, which included Ringo Starr. Moon and Ringo, who he affectionately called Bongo, became good friends and worked on a number of projects together during the 1970s. He and Starr appeared in the films *200 Motels* (see Frank Zappa), *That'll Be The Day* (Anchor Bay-DV 11373 DVD), *Born To Boogie* (see T. Rex), *Son Of Dracula* (see Harry Nilsson) and *Sextette* (Rhino-R2 976612 DVD). Ringo appears in The Who's 1979 film *The Kids Are Alright* at Moon's invitation. Ringo also appears in the film's trailer and on radio spots (contained on a one-sided promotional single — New World Pictures-CR 3926) to promote the film.

In 1974 Moon was on hiatus in Los Angeles, as was Ringo who was there recording his *Goodnight Vienna* album, and Lennon who was spending his nearly year-long "lost weekend" there recording his *Rock 'N' Roll* album and producing Harry Nilsson's* *Pussy Cats* album. Moon moved into a rented house there with Starr and Lennon. Keith decided to record a solo album and employed a cast of well-known studio players and rock stars. Mal Evans was put in charge of producing the sessions' party madness. Ringo came up with *Two Sides Of The Moon* for the album's title, and provided some drumming and dialogue. The album's cover of The Beach Boys'* *Don't Worry Baby* was released as a single but it and the album weren't successful. [Moon, who had never lost his love for surf music, performed with The Beach Boys on a number of occasions.] The album also contained a cover of Lennon's Beatles' song *In My Life*, and *Move Over Ms. L.* [Lennon recorded *Move Over Ms. L.* (it's not really about Yoko) during sessions for, (but didn't include it on) his 1974 album *Walls And Bridges.*] The song was reportedly donated by Lennon to his pal Moon's album at Evans' request. When Lennon was forced into prematurely release his *Rock 'N' Roll* album, he used *Move Over Ms. L* for the B-side of his *Stand By Me* single, released a week before Moon's release of the song in 1975. It's not known if Moon had to hold up the release, until after Lennon's release or if it was a coincidence that it came out later. However, given the circumstances, it's considered a composition contribution. Lennon, who had returned to living in New York, wasn't present at any of the sessions for Moon's album. *Two Sides Of The Moon* was rereleased in 1997 and 2006 with out-takes, and bonus tracks from a second, aborted album also with contributions from Ringo. Moon asks at the beginning of the bonus track *Do Me Good*, "Do you think The Beatles will get back together?" It's also obvious from other dialogue in the introduction that Ringo drums on this track. Unfortunately, none of the bonus tracks' credits list the songs on which Ringo plays drums. Given that several drummers were used on the album it's unlikely that Ringo contributed much drumming. Steve Cropper, who wrote two of three bonus tracks that he produced for Moon, says Ringo played on the sessions but isn't certain if he played on all the tracks. Cropper and others at the sessions also recall a song titled *My Rubbereem*, on which Ringo and comedian Peter Cook play drums. Moon also recorded a cover of The Beatles' song *When I'm 64*.

Keith Moon's lifestyle caught up with him on September 7, 1978. Ironically, he died in a London apartment owned by Nilsson, and where Mama Cass Elliot had died four years earlier. Hours before his death, Moon attended Paul McCartney's annual *Buddy Holly Week* birthday celebration (see The Crickets). The Who quickly replaced Moon with Kenney Jones* until 1989 when Simon Phillips took his place. Ringo's son Zak Starkey has played drums for The Who's tours since 1996. Moon had been a major influence in Zak's learning to play the drums.

Gary Moore

Still Got The Blues
Charisma-86167 (06/29/92) (03/26/90)
Producer: [George Harrison] Gary Moore & Ian Taylor
George Harrison: B. Vocals, Slide & Rhythm Guitar; Gary Moore: Lead Vocals & Guitar; Nicky Hopkins: Piano; Bob Daisley: Bass; Graham Walker: Drums; Martin Drover: Trumpet; Frank Mead: Alto Saxophone; Nick Pentelow: Tenor Saxophone; Nick Payn: Baritone Saxophone
FPSHOT & probably Sarm West Studio, London, UK xx/xx/89 or xx/xx/90

That Kind Of Woman (**G. Harrison**) 4:30 (10)

Gary Moore was born Robert William Gary Moore on April 4, 1952 in Belfast, Northern Ireland. Moore joined the band Skid Row in 1969 but left by 1972. In 1974 Moore joined Thin Lizzy but left after several months to join Colosseum II. He sat in with Thin Lizzy on selected dates and rejoined them between 1977 and 1979. Since that time Moore has pursued a solo career and worked with a wide range of other artists, including Andrew Lloyd Webber, Jack Bruce*, Jimmy Nail* and B.B. King*.

George Harrison often cited Moore as one of his favorite guitarists. Moore's 1990 album *Still Got The Blues* includes Harrison's composition *That Kind Of Woman*, which was originally written for, and recorded by, Eric Clapton*. Eric shelved the song, so Harrison gave his friend and neighbor, Moore a crack at it. Harrison contributed guitar and background vocals to Moore's version, and helped (un-credited) with the production. Clapton released his version a short time later.

According to Moore's manager John Martin, Harrison and Moore also recorded an untitled jam. Moore played guitar on the Traveling Wilburys' (see Bob Dylan, Jeff Lynne, Roy Orbison, Tom Petty And The Heartbreakers) song *She's My Baby*, and joined Harrison onstage during his Royal Albert Hall performance in London for the Natural Law Political Party's fund-raiser on April 6, 1992. Harrison joined in on the encore of Moore's performance of *That Kind Of Woman* and *While My Guitar Gently Weeps* at the Royal Albert Hall on October 5, 1992. Harrison and Moore reportedly jammed at the Crooked Billet Pub near their homes on October 25, 1992. The credits of Moore's album *Blues Alive* give special thanks to Harrison (for the encore appearance at Albert Hall). Though Harrison's performance was not included on the album, it was recorded and may be released in the future. For more information go to www.gary-moore.com

Mortimer

On Our Way Home
Apple-16 (7" acetate single) (UK) [unreleased]
Producer: Peter Asher
Probably Trident Studios, London, UK
early/xx/69

On Our Way Home (J. Lennon-**P. McCartney**)

The folk-rock trio Mortimer consisted of drummer Guy Masson, guitarist Tony Van Benshoten and guitarist Tom Smith. They evolved out of the New York group The Teddy Boys who had recorded for MGM, and Cameo Parkway Records in the mid-1960s whose label head Allen Klein shelved their album. The group was signed to Philips Records under the name Pinocchio & Puppets, and then Mortimer who released one self-titled album.

The group managed to get a copy of their album to John Lennon and Paul McCartney during their brief visit to New York in May 1968 to announce the launching of their Apple Corps Ltd. Guy Masson recalls, "The only reason we got to see them is because some girls outside their hotel thought we were the group The Hollies, so security ushered us inside." In the fall of 1968 Mortimer's manager suggested they head to the UK. There they heard radio advertisements soliciting songs for Apple's artist Mary Hopkin*. They headed for Apple and discovered that Lennon liked their album and passed it on to the head of Apple Publishing. They were given an audition attended by George Harrison who offered them a contract. Masson says, "Our group was gathered one afternoon [probably January 24, 1969] in Peter Asher's office at Apple, and Paul McCartney, who also liked our group, showed up and said, 'I've got a good song for these guys,' and gave us a recording of *Two Of Us*." It was one of the songs The Beatles had recently recorded for an album that would end up being released over a year later as *Let It Be*. Asher says McCartney indicated to him at the time that he didn't think The Beatles would use it. [Asher offered the song to The Everly Brothers*.] Over the next six months Mortimer recorded, mostly at Trident Studios in London, an album produced by Asher for Apple, though according to Masson none of The Beatles showed up for any of the recordings. Among others, Asher and Spike Heatley played bass, and Richard Hewson supplied keyboards and string arrangements. Mortimer's highly produced version of *Two Of Us* was scheduled for release in September 1969 as a single (Apple-16) under its original title *On Our Way Home* (acetates exist) but Apple, managed by Allen Klein at the time, cancelled the release of Mortimer's recordings and didn't renew their contract. Masson says, "Klein wiped us out twice!" Masson feels The Beatles adopted some of Mortimer's vocal harmony arrangements for their song *Because*. Mortimer broke up a short time later. Though The Beatles were first to release *Two Of Us*, on their album *Let It Be*, it is clear that they originally intended for Mortimer to released it first.

Eddie Murphy

Love's Alright
Motown-374636354-2 (02/23/93)
Producer: Eddie Murphy, David Allen Jones & Trenten Gumbs
Paul McCartney: Vocals†; Eddie Murphy: Vocals; Audrey Wheeler: Vocals; Sandi Barber: Vocals; Babyface: Vocals; Bon Jovi: Vocals; Garth Brooks: Vocals; En Vogue: Vocals; Johnny Gill: Vocals; Amy Grant: Vocals; Aaron Hall: Vocals; Hammer: Vocals; Heavy D: Vocals; Howard Hewitt: Vocals; Julio Iglesias: Vocals; Janet Jackson: Vocals; Michael Jackson: Vocals; Elton John: Vocals; Patti LaBelle: Vocals; Emmanuel Lewis: Vocals; Teddy Pendergrass: Vocals; Richie Sambora: Vocals; Luther Vandross: Vocals; Barry White: Vocals; Stevie Wonder: Vocals & Harmonica; Herbie Hancock: Piano; Stanley Clarke: Bass; David Allen Jones: Drum Programming; Trenten Gumbs: Drum Programming
Air Studios, London & Hog Hill Mill, Sussex†, UK; Bubblehill, Can Am Recorders, Capitol, Larrabee North, One On One, Record One & Aire, Los Angeles, CA; Woodland Digital, Nashville, TN; Compass Point, Bahamas & Cajun Recorders
03/xx/92

Yeah (E. Murphy-D. Jones-T. Gumbs) 4:44 (1)

Edward "Eddie" Murphy was born on April 3, 1961 in Brooklyn, New York. Murphy rose to prominence in the early 1980s on TV's *Saturday*

Night Live, creating such comic characters as Velvet Jones and Mister Robinson, and impersonating Buckwheat and Gumby. Murphy soon outgrew *Saturday Night Live* and pursued an acting career starring in such successful films as *Trading Places*, *Beverly Hills Cop*, *Coming To America*, *The Nutty Professor*, *Shrek* and *Dreamgirls*. He has also ventured into popular music with the albums *How Could It Be*, *So Happy* and *Love's Alright*.

In early 1992 Murphy approached Paul McCartney about contributing to *Yeah*, a song he was recording with an all-star lineup, with proceeds going to an educational trust charity. McCartney said "yeah" on the condition that Murphy try going meatless for a week. Murphy said "yeah," and in March 1992 arrived at Paul's studio in Sussex, England.

Jimmy Nail

Growing Up In Public
Atlantic-7 82433-2 (09/29/92) (06/xx/92)
Producer: Danny Schogger, Guy Pratt & Jimmy Nail
George Harrison: Guitar; Jimmy Nail: Lead Vocals; Guy Pratt: Guitar & Drum Programming; Danny Schogger: Keyboards, Synthesizer, Bass & Drum Programming; Katie Kissoon: B. Vocals; Linda Taylor: B. Vocals; Andy Caine: B. Vocals; Marc Fox: Percussion; Graham Ward: Drums
Livingstone Studios, London, UK probably (early)/xx/92

Real Love (G. Pratt-D. Schogger-J. Nail) 4:33 (5)

Jimmy Nail was born James Bradford on March 16, 1954 in Newcastle-upon-Tyne, England. He had ambitions of becoming a teacher but his musical education led him to front a number of local bands in the 1970s. Motown and the UK blues-rock scene of the late 1960s were his major musical influences. Though virtually unknown in the US, Nail has become a major recording artist, composer, actor and author in the UK. In the 1980s he starred in the hit TV series *Auf Wiedersehen Pet*, and later in *Spender*, which he wrote, directed and helped produce. In 1985 Nail had his first hit with a remake of Rose Royce's song *Love Don't Live Here Anymore*. He also wrote a best-selling novel about *Spender*.

Nail performed with George Harrison at a George Formby convention on March 2, 1991. The following year his *Growing Up In Public* album gave special thanks to Harrison, no doubt for his guitar work on the album's song *Real Love*. The album also included contributions from Gary Moore* and contained the UK number one hit *Ain't No Doubt*.

In the mid-1990s Nail starred in the BBC TV miniseries *Crocodile Shoes* and had a hit with its title song, and appeared in the film *Evita*. Nail's other hits include *Cowboy Dreams* in 1994 and *Big River* in 1995 when he also released a cover of John Lennon's song *Love*. Nail has been the nominee and recipient of numerous UK entertainment awards. Nail continues to write, record and act.

Nervous

[None]
[Unreleased]
Producer: Nervous & Michael Brook
Paul McCartney: Chain Saw & B. Vocals; Justin Travis: Lead Vocals; James McCartney: Tubular Bells; Mary McCartney: Whistling; Dickie Lorraine: Acoustic Guitar & B. Vocals; Dean Watkyn: Bass & B. Vocals; Paul Codish: Jew's Harp; Oscar O'Lochlinn: Drums; William Drake: Keyboards; Keith Holden: Harmonica & B. Vocals; Bernie Holden: Clarinet; Michael Brook: B. Vocals; some firemen: B. Vocals
Hog Hill Mill Studios, East Sussex, UK 07/xx/94

The Chain Saw Song (Nervous)

Justin Travis, lead singer of the group Nervous, was born on September 26, 1965 in Portsmouth, England. He attributes his interest in music to his parents who were members of skiffle bands in the UK during the 1950s. He was also greatly influenced by artists such as Jimi Hendrix, The Doors, The Byrds, Nick Drake, Tom Waits, Bob Dylan* and The Beatles. From his early teens on, Travis played in a variety of bands such as Baby Lemonade and Flik Spatula. Later, he formed the band Nervous with Dickie Lorraine (a.k.a. Richard Cripps),

William Drake, Dean Watkyn, Melvin Duffy and Barney C. Rockford.

Travis says, "Dickie knew Ringo's son Jason, and through him we got to know Paul McCartney's daughters Stella and Mary quite well. We had been friends with the McCartney family for years. Paul asked me if we'd fancy coming to his studio to make an album. We high-tailed it there for a couple of weeks in July of 1994 and had a great time. We were given full facilities, technicians and instruments, including the Mellotron with the flute reel from *Strawberry Fields Forever* on it.

"One day Paul was clearing a path for his horses in the forest with a chain saw. We were doing a track in his studio on which everybody was going to be playing something, and he wandered in with his chain saw, so we asked him to play it! It's probably the most unusual instrument he has ever been asked to play. His technicians put a microphone on the chain saw but the exhaust fumes set off the fire alarm. Soon we had two fire engines coming up the road, so we got the firemen to sing on the recording! McCartney's son James and daughter Mary play on the recording as well. The song was originally called *The Mental Song* but we appropriately re-titled it *The Chain Saw Song*. Paul was a very, very encouraging person to us and a great person to hang out with. He's our mate and we love him!" Nervous broke up in 2002.

The New Maroons

With A Little Help To My Friends [Ringo Starr]
No Label Records-NLR 9904 (CD-R) [unauthorized release] (xx/xx/99)
Producer: The Nashville Network
Ringo Starr: Drums; Jonell Mosser: Lead Vocals; Don Was: Bass, Benmont Tench: Keyboards; Mark Goldenberg: Guitar
Cyclone Stadium, Ames, Iowa 04/24/93

Something Wild [live] (J. Hiatt) 4:45 (10)

The Dark End Of The Street [live] (C. Moman-D. Penn) 3:50 (11)

The New Maroons consisted of Don Was, born Donald Fagenson in Detroit, Michigan on September 13, 1952; Benmont Tench, born Benjamin Tench III in Gainesville, Florida on September 7, 1953; Mark Goldenberg, born in Amsterdam, Netherlands on October 2, 1952; Jonell Mosser, born in Louisville, Kentucky on January 22, 1959 and Ringo Starr. Don is a bassist and highly successful producer of many artists including Joe Cocker*, Bob Dylan*, Elton John*, Carly Simon*, The Rolling Stones*, Brian Wilson* and Willie Nelson. Don also worked on the soundtrack for the film *Backbeat* about The Beatles' early career. Mark has played guitar for many artists, such as Peter Frampton*, Linda Ronstadt, Willie Nelson and Jackson Browne. Tench is a keyboardist and a founding member of Tom Petty* And The Heartbreakers. Mosser is a soul and R&B singer who has released several critically acclaimed albums, and worked with B.B. King*, Levon Helm*, Bonnie Raitt, Waylon Jennings and Patti Smyth.

The New Maroons evolved from recordings for Ringo Starr's 1992 album *Time Takes Time*. Goldenberg recalls, "It was really fun working with Don and Benmont on Ringo's album. Don told me he had been talking with Ringo and that they were thinking of putting a group together with us. Don had Jonell Mosser join us." Mosser says, "Don was in Nashville doing some recordings. He saw me perform and asked me if I'd sing on a sessions he was producing. In 1992 I think, Don called me and said he wanted to put a band together with himself, Benmont Tench and Mark Goldenberg. I said, 'Great!' Then he said, 'Ringo Starr is going to play the drums and I want you to be the singer.' I said, 'Stop it Don — you're cruel! Don't even say stuff like that.' But he was dead serious. He had me come to Ocean Way Studios in Los Angeles where he produced the recordings. I was at the low end of the totem pole fame wise but all of the band members treated me as an equal. I love The Beatles, and they formed me musically in many ways, but I think one of the reasons Don tapped me is because I don't get star struck and Ringo wasn't there to talk about The Beatles. We were there to record. Ringo's the coolest guy alive. There was no ego or weirdness with him. He was really into it — all about the music. He just wants to be a drummer. He doesn't want to be impeded by celebrity. He's been famous for a very long time, so anybody talking about The Beatles just gets in the way of the music. We did seven songs including some John Hiatt songs because we all love him. We also did a Tom Petty song but I don't remember which one. We recorded *Something Wild*, *With This Love*, *Dark End Of The Street*, *John The Revelator*, *Too Many Memories* and *Born To Lose*, which Merle Haggard sang because at one point Don also wanted a male singer in the group. Don wanted to do some things with Lyle Lovett* too, which is why I think he joined us later at *Farm Aid VI*. None of the recordings have been released. I sure hope someday we'll finish the project because we had some good things happening there and it was a lot of fun. Mark says, "We didn't really have enough for an album, and Don and Ringo became busy with other projects, so things got shelved, but Don keeps threatening to release it."

Mosser says, "They really wanted a Beatle on *Farm Aid VI* and Ringo said he'd do it if The New Maroons would do it with him. We all said, 'We'll be there!' We actually got a sound check because there was a Beatle in our band." Their performance took place in Ames, Iowa on April 24, 1993. Their entire performance was broadcast on TNN TV. They backed Lyle Lovett, and performed *Something Wild* and *Dark End Of The Street*, which they also performed at the *Together For Our Children-M.U.S.I.C.* (Musicians Unite with Stars to Immunize Children) charity concert at Royce Hall at UCLA on June 23. Their performance there of *Dark End Of The Street* was also broadcast on TV. Was and McCartney have also reportedly worked together. Tench and Was contributed to Ringo's 2010 album Y Not. For more information go to www.jonellonline.com, www.markgoldenberg.com

Harry Nilsson

Duit On Mon Dei
RCA-BVCP-7315 (Japan) (01/21/95) (03/21/75)
Producer: Harry Nilsson & Richie Schmitt

Good For God (H. Nilsson) 3:23 (11)
Ringo Starr: B. Vocals; Harry Nilsson: Lead Vocals & B. Vocals; Jim Keltner: Drums; Robert Greenidge: Steel Drums; Jesse Ed Davis: Guitar; Danny Kortchmar: Guitar; Klaus Voormann; Bass; Trevor Lawrence: Saxophone: Bobby Keys: Saxophone; Gene Cipriano: Tenor Saxophone; Carl McKnight: Percussion; Pat Murphy: Percussion
RCA's Music Center of the World, Los Angeles, CA 10/04/74

Kojak Columbo (H. Nilsson) 3:30 (4)
Ringo Starr: Drums; Harry Nilsson: Lead Vocals; Jim Keltner: Drums; Jesse Ed Davis: Guitar; Danny Kortchmar: Guitar; Klaus Voormann; Bass; Trevor Lawrence: Saxophone: Bobby Keys: Saxophone; Gene Cipriano: Saxophone; Pat Murphy: Congas; Doug Dillard: Banjo; Dr. John: Piano; Emmett Kennedy: Percussion; Milt Holland: Percussion; Joe De Aguero: Marimba
RCA's Music Center of the World, Los Angeles, CA 09-10/xx/74

Flash Harry
Mercury-6302 022 (album 12") (UK) (09/05/80)
Producer: Steve Cropper & Bruce Robb
Cherokee Studios, Los Angeles, CA 12/xx/79-03/xx/80

How Long Can Disco On (**R. Starkey**-H. Nilsson) 2:54 (2/4)
Ringo Starr: (probable) Drums; Harry Nilsson: Lead Vocals; additionally, one or more of the following: Bobby Keys: Saxophone; Danny Kortchmar: Guitar; Donald "Duck" Dunn: Bass; Fred Tackett: Guitar; Jerome Jumonville: Horns; Jim Horn: Horns; Jim Keltner: Drums; Keith Allison: Bass; Klaus Voormann: Bass; Dr. John: Piano &/or Guitar; Paul Stallworth: Bass; Ritchie Zito: Guitar; Steve Cropper: Guitar; Van Dyke Parks: Keyboards; Lowell George: Guitar; Jim Gordon: Drums; Arthur Gerst, Den Denay, Bill Payne, Jimmy Roberts, John Jarvis, Luis Damian, Rick Shlosser, Ricky Lawson, Scott Edwards, Tony Martin Jr., Fred Staehle & Wilton Felder

I've Got It (H. Nilsson-P. Botkin Jr.) 3:42 (2/2)
Ringo Starr: (possible) Drums; Harry Nilsson: Lead Vocals; additionally, one or more of the following: Bobby Keys: Saxophone; Danny Kortchmar: Guitar; Donald "Duck" Dunn: Bass; Fred Tackett: Guitar; Jerome Jumonville: Horns; Jim Horn: Horns; Jim Keltner: Drums; Keith Allison: Bass; Klaus Voormann: Bass; Dr. John: Piano &/or Guitar; Paul Stallworth: Bass; Ritchie Zito: Guitar; Steve Cropper: Guitar; Van Dyke Parks: Keyboards; Lowell George: Guitar; Jim Gordon: Drums; Arthur Gerst, Den Denay, Bill Payne, Jimmy Roberts, John Jarvis, Luis Damian, Rick Shlosser, Ricky Lawson, Scott Edwards, Tony Martin Jr., Fred Staehle & Wilton Felder

Old Dirt Road (J. Lennon-H. Nilsson) 4:26 (1/4)
Ringo Starr: (probable) Drums; Harry Nilsson: Lead Vocals; additionally, one or more of the following: Bobby Keys: Saxophone; Danny Kortchmar: Guitar; Donald "Duck" Dunn: Bass; Fred Tackett: Guitar; Jerome Jumonville: Horns; Jim Horn: Horns; Jim Keltner: Drums; Keith Allison: Bass; Klaus Voormann: Bass; Dr. John:

Piano &/or Guitar; Paul Stallworth: Bass; Ritchie Zito: Guitar; Steve Cropper: Guitar; Van Dyke Parks: Keyboards; Lowell George: Guitar; Jim Gordon: Drums; Arthur Gerst, Den Denay, Bill Payne, Jimmy Roberts, John Jarvis, Luis Damian, Rick Shlosser, Ricky Lawson, Scott Edwards, Tony Martin Jr., Fred Staehle & Wilton Felder

I Gotta Blues [Ringo Starr]
Pebbles P-02005 [unauthorized release] (xx/xx/02)
Ringo Starr: Drums & B. Vocals; Harry Nilsson: Lead Vocals; Timothy B. Schmit: B. Vocals & Bass; Todd Rundgren: B. Vocals & Guitar; Burton Cummings: Keyboards; Nils Lofgren: Guitar; Dave Edmunds: Guitar & B. Vocals; Zak Starkey: Drums; Joe Walsh: Guitar
Caesar's Palace, Las Vegas, NV 09/04/92

Without You (P. Ham-T. Evans) 3:14 (14)

The Lost Lennon Tapes
Westwood One Radio Network-[Matrix #] LT 88-38 (12" albums promotional only) (09/12/88)
Producer: John Lennon
John Lennon: Arrangement, B. Vocals & (probable) Guitar; Harry Nilsson: Lead Vocals & (probable) Keyboards
One or more of the following studios: Record Plant, New York, NY; Burbank &/or Record Plant, Los Angeles, CA 04/xx/74

Mucho Mungo/Mt. Elga [rehearsal] (J. Lennon/Adpt: H. Nilsson) 1:54/1:11 (2/2/1)

Pussy Cats
Buddha-7446599615-2 (06/15/99) (08/19/74)
Producer: John Lennon
One or more of the following studios: Burbank &/or Record Plant, Los Angeles, CA &/or Record Plant†, New York, NY 04/04/74 & 05-06/xx/74† [unless noted otherwise]

All My Life (H. Nilsson) 3:10 (4)
John Lennon: Arrangement; **Ringo Starr: Drums**; Harry Nilsson: Lead Vocals & Arrangement; Jim Keltner: Drums; Bobby Keys: Saxophone; Ken Ascher: Piano, Orchestrations & Conducting The Masked Alberts Orchestra; Klaus Voormann: Bass; Jesse Ed Davis: Guitar; Danny Kortchmar: Guitar; Sneaky Pete Kleinow: Pedal Steel Guitar; Keith Moon: Chinese Wood Blocks

Black Sails (H. Nilsson) 3:13 (9)
Harry Nilsson: Lead Vocals & Arrangement; Ken Ascher: Orchestrations & Conducting The Masked Alberts Orchestra
Record Plant Studios, New York, NY 06/18/74

Don't Forget Me (H. Nilsson) 3:38 (3)
Harry Nilsson: Lead Vocals, Piano & Arrangement; Ken Ascher: Orchestrations & Conducting The Masked Alberts Orchestra

Down By The Sea (H. Nilsson) 5:36 (11) (06/15/99)
Ringo Starr: Percussion; Harry Nilsson: Lead Vocals, Electric Piano & Arrangement; Keith Moon: Percussion; Jim Keltner: Percussion; Jane Getz: Piano; Klaus Voormann: Bass; Danny Kortchmar: Guitar; Jesse Ed Davis: Guitar; Sneaky Pete Kleinow: Pedal Steel Guitar
Burbank Studios, Los Angeles, CA 04/05/74

The Flying Saucer Song (H. Nilsson) 6:28 (12) (06/15/99)
Ringo Starr: (probably) Dialogue; John Lennon: (possible) B. Vocals; Harry Nilsson: Lead Vocals & (probable) Keyboards
Burbank Studios, Los Angeles, CA 04/01/74

Loop De Loop (T. Vann) 2:36 (8)
John Lennon: Arrangement; **Ringo Starr: Drums**; Harry Nilsson: Lead Vocals, Electric Piano & Arrangement; Keith Moon: Drums; Jim Keltner: Drums; Jim Horn: Saxophone; Bobby Keys: Saxophone; Trevor Lawrence: Saxophone; Jane Getz: Piano; Klaus Voormann: Bass; Danny Kortchmar: Guitar; Jesse Ed Davis: Guitar; Chuck Findley: Trombone; Eric Carmen: Handclaps; Michael McBride: Handclaps; "The Masked Alberts Kids Chorale" Troy Germano: B. Vocals; Kristin Turner: B. Vocals; Erik Mueller: B. Vocals; Nathalie Altman: B. Vocals; Peri Prestopino: B. Vocals; Cantey Turner: B. Vocals; Phyllida Paterson: B. Vocals; Rachel Mueller: B. Vocals; Damon Vigiano: B. Vocals; Susie Bell: David Steinberg: B. Vocals

Many Rivers To Cross (J. Cliff) 4:54 (1)
Ringo Starr: Drums; **John Lennon: B. Vocals & Arrangement;** Harry Nilsson: Lead Vocals; Jim Keltner: Drums; Bobby Keys: Saxophone; Ken Ascher: Piano, Orchestrations & Conducting The Masked Alberts Orchestra; Klaus Voormann: Willie Smith: Organ; Jesse Ed Davis: Guitar; Danny Kortchmar: Guitar; Sneaky Pete Kleinow: Pedal Steel Guitar; Lori Burton: B. Vocals

Mucho Mungo/Mt. Elga (J. Lennon/Adpt: H. Nilsson) 3:44 (7)
Ringo Starr: Maracas; John Lennon: Arrangement; Harry Nilsson: Lead Vocals & Arrangement; Jim Keltner: Drums Bobby Keys: Saxophone; Trevor Lawrence: Saxophone; Ken Ascher: Piano, Orchestrations & Conducting

The Masked Alberts Orchestra; Klaus Voormann: Bass; Jesse Ed Davis: Guitar; Danny Kortchmar: Guitar; Keith Moon: Congas; Cynthia Webb: Maracas

Old Forgotten Soldier (H. Nilsson) 4:15 (5)
Harry Nilsson: Lead Vocals, Piano & Arrangement; Klaus Voormann: Bass; Jesse Ed Davis: Guitar

Rock Around The Clock (J. DeKnight-M. Freedman) 3:11 (10)
John Lennon: Arrangement; **Ringo Starr: Drums**; Harry Nilsson: Lead Vocals, Electric Piano & Arrangement; Keith Moon: Drums; Jim Keltner: Drums; Jim Horn: Saxophone; Bobby Keys: Saxophone; Trevor Lawrence: Saxophone; Jane Getz: Piano; Klaus Voormann: Bass; Danny Kortchmar: Guitar; Jesse Ed Davis: Guitar; Chuck Findley: Trombone

Save The Last Dance For Me (D. Pomus-M. Shuman) 4:29 (6)
John Lennon: Arrangement; **Ringo Starr: Drums**; Harry Nilsson: Lead Vocals & Arrangement; Jim Keltner: Drums; Bobby Keys: Saxophone; Trevor Lawrence: Saxophone; Gene Cipriano: Saxophone; Jane Getz: Piano; Klaus Voormann: Bass; Sneaky Pete Kleinow: Pedal Steel Guitar: Jesse Ed Davis: Guitar; Danny Kortchmar: Guitar; Ken Ascher: Piano, Orchestrations & Conducting The Masked Alberts Orchestra

Subterranean Homesick Blues (B. Dylan) 3:11 (2)
John Lennon: Arrangement; **Ringo Starr: Drum**; Harry Nilsson: Lead Vocals & Clavinet; Jim Keltner: Drums; Doug Hoefer: Snare Drum; Bobby Keys: Saxophone; Trevor Lawrence: Saxophone; Ken Ascher: Electric Piano; Jesse Ed Davis: Guitar; Danny Kortchmar: Guitar; Sneaky Pete Kleinow: Pedal Steel Guitar; Klaus Voormann: Bass
Burbank Studios, Los Angeles, CA 03/28/74 & possibly Record Plant, New York, NY 04/04/74 & 05-06/xx/74

Sandman
RCA-BVCP-7316 (Japan) (01/21/95) (01/19/76)
Probably RCA's Music Center of the World, Los Angeles, CA xx/xx/75

[unknown]
Ringo Starr: "Special Thanks" (possible) Percussion, (possible) Drums & (possible) B. Vocals; Harry Nilsson: Lead Vocals; additionally, one or more of the following: Jim Keltner: Drums; Klaus Voormann: Bass; Van Dyke Parks: Keyboards; Jane Getz: Keyboards; Leon Russell: Keyboards; Joe DeAguero: Percussion; Pat Murphy: Percussion; Gary Coleman: Percussion; Emmett Kennedy: Percussion; Robert Greenidge: Percussion; Emil Richards: Percussion; Jesse Ed Davis: Guitar; Danny Kortchmar: Guitar; Fred Tackett: Guitar; Trevor Lawrence: Horns; Bobby Keys: Horns; Gene Cipriano: Horns; Jim Horn: Horns; Johnny Rotella: Horns; Jay Migliori: Horns; Doug Dillard: Banjo; Bobby Bruce: Strings; Ilene Novog: Strings; Perry Botkin Jr.: Orchestra & Strings; Special Thanks to: Joe Cocker, J. R. Shanklin, Hillary Gerrard, Mike Berniker, & Frank Mancini

Son Of Dracula (Music From The Apple Film)
RCA/Rapple-BVCP-7315 (Japan) (01/21/95) (04/01/74)
London, UK 08-10/xx/72 [unless noted otherwise]
Producer: Ringo Starr & Harry Nilsson [unless noted otherwise]

The Abdication Of Count Down (P. Buckmaster) 1:08 (13)
Harry Nilsson: Lead Vocals; one or more of the following for incidental music by Paul Buckmaster: Morris Pert: Drums; Frank Riccotti: Percussion; Ray Cooper: Percussion; Peter Robinson: Keyboards; Ann O'Dell: Keyboards; Diana Lewis: Keyboards; Barry Guy: Bass; Chris Lawrence: Bass; Martin Ford: Electric French Horn & Orchestral Organization

Count Down Meets Merlin And Amber (P. Buckmaster) 2:00 (4)
Ringo Starr: Dialogue; Harry Nilsson: Dialogue; Suzanna Leigh: Dialogue; one or more of the following for incidental music by Paul Buckmaster: Morris Pert: Drums; Frank Riccotti: Percussion; Ray Cooper: Percussion; Peter Robinson: Keyboards; Ann O'Dell: Keyboards; Diana Lewis: Keyboards; Barry Guy: Bass; Chris Lawrence: Bass; Martin Ford: Electric French Horn & Orchestral Organization

The Count's Vulnerability (P. Buckmaster) 2:09 (9)
Ringo Starr: Dialogue; Freddie Jones: Dialogue; Suzanna Leigh: Dialogue; Dennis Price: Dialogue; one or more of the following for incidental music by Paul Buckmaster: Morris Pert: Drums; Frank Riccotti: Percussion; Ray Cooper: Percussion; Peter Robinson: Keyboards; Ann O'Dell: Keyboards; Diana Lewis: Keyboards; Barry Guy: Bass; Chris Lawrence: Bass; Martin Ford: Electric French Horn & Orchestral Organization

Daybreak (H. Nilsson) 2:42 (2)
Producer: Harry Nilsson
Ringo Starr: Drums; **George Harrison: Cow Bell**; Harry Nilsson: Lead Vocals & Piano; Jim Price: Organ; Bobby Keys: High Saxophone; Klaus Voormann: Bass; Peter Frampton: Guitar; Ray Cooper: Percussion; Chris Spedding: Bouzouki; Gene Cipriano: Horns
London, UK 09/xx/72

The End (Moonbeam) (H. Nilsson) 0:48 (14)
Producer: Ringo Starr, Harry Nilsson & Richard Perry
Ringo Starr: Dialogue; Harry Nilsson: Dialogue & Mellotron; Herbie Flowers: Bass; John Uribe: Acoustic Guitar; Klaus Voormann: Acoustic Guitar

Frankenstein, Merlin & The Operation (J. Tavener) 3:15 (11)
Ringo Starr: Dialogue; Harry Nilsson: Dialogue; Suzanna Leigh: Dialogue; one or more of the following for incidental music by Paul Buckmaster: Morris Pert: Drums; Frank Riccotti: Percussion; Ray Cooper: Percussion; Peter Robinson: Keyboards; Ann O'Dell: Keyboards; Diana Lewis: Keyboards; Barry Guy: Bass; Chris Lawrence: Bass; Martin Ford: Electric French Horn & Orchestral Organization

Intro (to "Without You") 0:20 (8)
Harry Nilsson: Dialogue; Freddie Jones: Dialogue

It Is He Who Would Be King (P. Buckmaster) 3:04 (1)
Ringo Starr: Dialogue; one or more of the following for incidental music by Paul Buckmaster: Morris Pert: Drums; Frank Riccotti: Percussion; Ray Cooper: Percussion; Peter Robinson: Keyboards; Ann O'Dell: Keyboards; Diana Lewis: Keyboards; Barry Guy: Bass; Chris Lawrence: Bass; Martin Ford: Electric French Horn & Orchestral Organization

Perhaps This Is All A Dream (P. Buckmaster) 0:45 (6)
Harry Nilsson: Dialogue; Suzanna Leigh: Dialogue; one or more of the following for incidental music by Paul Buckmaster: Morris Pert: Drums; Frank Riccotti: Percussion; Ray Cooper: Percussion; Peter Robinson: Keyboards; Ann O'Dell: Keyboards; Diana Lewis: Keyboards; Barry Guy: Bass; Chris Lawrence: Bass; Martin Ford: Electric French Horn & Orchestral Organization

Son Of Schmilsson
RCA/Legacy 82876-78249-2 (05/23/06) (07/10/72)
Producer: Richard Perry [unless noted otherwise]
Trident & possibly Apple Studios, London, UK 03-05/xx/72 [unless noted otherwise]

Ambush (H. Nilsson) 5:22 (9)
Ringo Starr: Drums; Harry Nilsson: Lead Vocals & Electric Piano; Klaus Voormann: Bass; Nicky Hopkins: Piano; Chris Spedding: Guitar; Peter Frampton: Guitar; John Uribe: Lead Guitar; Ray Cooper: Tambourine; Jim Price: Trumpets, Trombone & Horn Arrangement; Bobby Keys: Saxophone
At My Front Door (E. Abner-J. Moore) 2:40 (8)
Ringo Starr: Drums; Harry Nilsson: Lead Vocals; Klaus Voormann: Bass; Piano: Nicky Hopkins: Piano; Peter Frampton: Electric Guitar; Chris Spedding: Electric Guitar; Ray Cooper: Congas; Bobby Keys: Tenor Saxophone

Daybreak [single version] (H. Nilsson) 3:06 (15) (03/25/74)
Producer: Harry Nilsson
Ringo Starr: Drums; **George Harrison: Cow Bell**; Harry Nilsson: Lead Vocals & Piano; Jim Price: Organ; Bobby Keys: High Saxophone; Klaus Voormann: Bass; Peter Frampton: Guitar; Ray Cooper: Percussion; Chris Spedding: Bouzouki; Gene Cipriano: Horns
London, UK 09/xx/72

The Most Beautiful World In The World (H. Nilsson) 3:35 (11)
Ringo Starr: Drums; Harry Nilsson: Lead Vocals; Klaus Voormann: Bass; Nicky Hopkins: Piano; Paul Keough: Guitar; Les Thatcher: Guitar; Ray Cooper: Percussion; Richard Perry: Percussion, Arrangement & Conductor of Orchestra & Choir; Kirby Johnson: Arrangement of Orchestra & Choir; Del Newman: Additional Orchestration
CTS Studios, London, UK 04-05/xx/72

Spaceman (H. Nilsson) 3:34 (6)
Ringo Starr: Drums; Harry Nilsson: Lead Vocals & Electric Piano; Klaus Voormann: Bass; John Uribe: Acoustic Guitar; Chris Spedding: Acoustic Guitar; Peter Frampton: Acoustic Guitar: Nicky Hopkins: Piano; Richard Perry: Percussion; Paul Buckmaster: Arrangement & Conductor of Orchestra
Trident & possibly Apple Studios, London, UK 04-05/xx/72

Take 54 (H. Nilsson) 4:18 (1)
Ringo Starr: Drums; Harry Nilsson: Lead Vocals & Electric Piano; Klaus Voormann: Bass & Horns; Nicky Hopkins: Piano; Lowell George: Guitar; Jim Price: Horns; Bobby Keys: Saxophone & Horns; Milt Holland: Percussion

You're Breakin' My Heart (H. Nilsson) 3:06 (5)
George Harrison: Slide Guitar; Harry Nilsson: Lead Vocals & Electric Piano; Berry Morgan: Drums; Klaus Voormann: Bass & Horns; Nicky Hopkins: Piano; Peter Frampton: Electric Guitar; Jim Price: Horns; Bobby Keys: Horns

...That's The Way It Is
RCA-BVCP-7317 (Japan) (01/21/95) (07/19/77)
Producer: Trevor Lawrence
Harry Nilsson: Vocals; Tony La Peau: Vocals; additionally, one or more of the following: Jim Keltner: Drums; Chili Charles: Drums; Klaus Voormann: Electric Bass; Dr. John: Keyboards; Van Dyke Parks: Keyboards; Jane Getz Wilson: Keyboards; David Paich: Keyboards; James Newton Howard: Keyboards; Danny Kortchmar: Guitar; Jesse Ed Davis: Guitar; Fred Tackett: Guitar; Lon Van Eaton: Guitar; Derrek Van Eaton: Guitar; Keith Allison: Guitar; Dennis Budimir: Guitar; Peter Jameson: Guitar; John Morell: Guitar; David Wolfert: Guitar; Michael Anthony: Guitar; Bobby Keys: Saxophone; Gene Cipriano: Saxophone; James Roberts: Saxophone; Buddy Collette: Saxophone; William Green: Saxophone; Jim Horn: Saxophone; Johnny Rotella: Saxophone
One or more of the following studios: Davlen Sound, Sound Labs &/or RCA's Music Center of the World, Los Angeles, CA probably 03/xx/76 &/or possibly xx/xx/77

A Thousand Miles Away (Sheppard-Miller) 2:50 (5)
Additionally: **Ringo Starr: Announcer**; additionally, one or more of the following: Lynda Laurence: Chorus; Abigale Haness: Chorus; John Lehman: Chorus; Monalisa Harrington: Chorus; Sherlie Matthews: Chorus; Joseph Greene: Chorus; William Thedford: Chorus; Deidra Askey: Chorus; Richard Glasser: Chorus

Daylight Has Caught Me (H. Nilsson-M. Rebennack) 3:49 (8)
Additionally: **Ringo Starr: (possible) Drums &/or Percussion**; additionally, one or more of the following: Doug Hoefer: Percussion; Robert Greenidge: Steel Drum; Malcolm Cecil: Synthesizer; Steven Madaio: Trumpet; Anthony Terran: Trumpet; Lew McCreary: Trombone; Richard Nash: Trombone; Benny Powell: Trombone

Harry Nilsson III (a.k.a. Bo Pete, Johnny Niles and Buck Earle) was born on June 15, 1941 in Brooklyn, New York but spent most of his life in Southern California. By the mid-1960s Nilsson had already been signed to the Mercury, Tower and RCA Record labels, and written songs with Phil Spector*. Nilsson's critically acclaimed 1967 album, *Pandemonium Shadow Show*, containing covers of two John Lennon and Paul McCartney compositions, attracted the attention (via Derek Taylor) of John and Paul, who declared in 1968 that Nilsson was their favorite "group." The Beatles tried (unsuccessfully) to sign Nilsson away from RCA to Apple. He contributed his composition *The Puppy Song*, at McCartney's request, to Mary Hopkin's* Apple album *Post Card*. His compositions were covered by a number of artists including The Monkees, and Three Dog Night who had a Top Five hit with his song *One* in 1969.

Nilsson's recording career took off with his Top 10, Grammy Award winning recording of *Everybody's Talkin'*, the theme from the 1969 film *Midnight Cowboy*, followed up by his song *I Guess The Lord Must Be In New York City*, originally intended as the theme for *Midnight Cowboy*. Americans also heard him weekly singing the theme to the ABC TV show *The Courtship Of Eddie's Father*. In 1971 Nilsson wrote and scored the critically acclaimed animated film *The Point*. [*The Point* was later rerecorded with a new narration by Ringo Starr (Pacific Family Entertainment DVD-8 80147 75179 5).] Nilsson's 1971 album *Nilsson Schmilsson* included the Top 10 hit *Coconut* and a cover of Badfinger's* *Without You*, which was Nilsson's only chart topping song.

His 1972 album *Son Of Schmilsson* includes contributions from George Harrison and Ringo Starr under the thinly-veiled pseudonyms George Harrysong and Richie Snare. Ringo's involvement was the result of his previous work with the album's producer Richard Perry. [Perry produced Ringo's and Nilsson's most successful albums. Nilsson contributed to Ringo's albums *Ringo* in 1973 and *Goodnight Vienna* in 1974, both produced by Perry.] According to Perry, the bulk of *Son Of Schmilsson* was recorded at Trident Studios and was filmed for a (unreleased) documentary. The album's credits also list additional recording and remixing at Apple Studios.

The film *Son Of Dracula*, starring Nilsson as Count Down (or Downe) and Ringo as Merlin, was released in 1974. The film was produced by Ringo and mostly shot in London beginning in August 1972. The screenplay was written by Jay Fairbanks with much revision by Ringo. The plot centers on the Count's rejection of the netherworld, and his desire to become mortal and have the ability to love. Nilsson and Starr attended the film's premiere in Atlanta, Georgia on April 19, 1974. The soundtrack album was issued on Rapple Records (a kind of merger between RCA and Apple) – no doubt because *Son Of Dracula* was released by Apple Films and Nilsson was contracted to RCA. Ringo and Harry are listed as the overall producers of the album, which features dialogue, and music from the film including Nilsson's last Top 40 hit *Daybreak* with contributions from Starr and Harrison. The single version of *Daybreak* replaces the lyric "it's pissing me off," with "it's making me cough" and is approximately 20 seconds longer. In 1974 the pair began filming a partly animated, two minute short funded by Ringo and Michael Viner* called *Harry & Ringo's Night Out*, apparently nothing more than the title suggested, which wasn't released. Nilsson also appeared in the video for Ringo's single *Only You*.

Fortunately, there was no filming of Harry and Lennon's intoxicated night out on March 12, 1974 when the two were thrown out of the Troubadour Club in Los Angeles after heckling the Smothers Brothers' comeback performance. Lennon later sent an apology and flowers to Tom and Dick Smothers. [Lennon had met Nilsson in the UK shortly after he publicly praised him, but their professional partnership didn't begin until Ringo reconnected them in Los Angeles.] Lennon, separated from Yoko Ono*, had been in Los Angeles (during what he later called his "Sinbad's Voyage" or "lost weekend") since the fall of 1973 recording his *Rock 'N' Roll* album with producer Phil Spector*. When Spector vanished with the tapes, Lennon offered to produce an album for Nilsson and the two, along with Ringo and others, moved into a rented house in Los Angeles.

The sessions began on the evening of March 28, 1974 with Nilsson doing a cover of Dylan's *Subterranean Homesick Blues* arranged by John. The evening ended with a historic jam of *Lucille*, *Sleepwalk*, *Stand By Me*, *Cupid*, *Chain Gang*, *Take This Hammer* and *Midnight Special* that included Nilsson, Lennon, Paul and Linda McCartney*, Danny Kortchmar (see Attitudes), Jesse Ed Davis*, May Pang, Mal Evans, Stevie Wonder* and Ed Freeman. It was the first, and last time John and Paul played together in a studio after the breakup of The Beatles. Some of these recordings are available on unauthorized releases. Unfortunately, Nilsson soon ruptured a vocal cord and lost his voice. With most of the backing tracks recorded, the two fled the party madness of their Los Angeles existence for Record Plant Studios in New York to do overdubs and re-record most of Nilsson's vocals for the album they planned to title *Strange Pussies* (the less offensive *Pussy Cats* was wisely substituted). Lennon also helped persuade RCA not to back out of a $5 million contract they were negotiating with Nilsson. Meanwhile, Lennon recorded his album *Walls And* Bridges, which includes the Lennon-Nilsson composition *Old Dirt Road* with Nilsson on backing vocals. Though *Pussy Cats*' first single, a cover of Jimmy Cliff's *Many Rivers To Cross*, sounded more like Lennon than Nilsson, it failed to chart. The album also included the Lennon-penned *Mucho Mungo*. Jesse Ed Davis claimed the song was originally titled *Mucho Macho* in reference to him but this is disputed by Pang. Noted Nilsson authority, Curtis Armstrong says Nilsson wrote and recorded a song called *You Are Here*, inspired by Lennon's song with the same title, but not written with Lennon as has been reported. Despite the contributions from Ringo and Lennon, *Pussy Cats* marked the beginning of the end of Nilsson's successful recording career.

Ringo also contributed to Nilsson's next album *Duit On Mon Dei*, which was originally to be titled *God's Greatest Hits*. [The title was apparently a favorite expression of Ringo's (and later Nilsson's) for putting things off. It was also printed on the front jacket of the *Ringo* album and was part of the logo of an in-house newsletter at Apple.] The album's notes include the message "If You Care About 'You Know Who's' Immigration Status – Write Your 'You Know What,'" in obvious reference to Lennon's Immigration difficulties at the time.

Nilsson's 1976 album *Sandman* lists Ringo under "Special Thanks To" possibly for percussion or backing vocals, though they are not in evidence. Nilsson contributed to Ringo's 1976 album *Rotogravure*, and they composed a song called *Party* or *Birmingham*, which was scheduled for inclusion on the album but remains unreleased. That year Nilsson also released the album *...That's The Way It Is*, which gives "A Very Special Thanks To Ringo Starr." No specific credits are listed for Ringo but he can clearly be heard announcing Tony La Peau on *A Thousand Miles Away*. He may also play drums on *Daylight Has Caught Me*. The album also features a cover of Harrison's song *That Is All* — and that is all that would be heard from Nilsson until 1980.

His 1980 album *Flash Harry*, which only saw limited release in Europe, included the Nilsson-Starr composition *How Long Can Disco On*, and Harry's version of *Old Dirt Road*. Ringo probably plays drums on these songs, and possibly on the songs *I've Got It*, but he's only listed in the album's general musical credits. It was the last album of new material released by Nilsson before his death. Armstrong says a finished recording, done at RCA in Los Angeles, exists of a song Harry and Ringo wrote called *I Want You To Sit On My Face*. He says the two also wrote a song called *Three Ships In The Harbor*.

In 1981 Ringo recorded several radio spots for Nilsson's anti-handgun campaign following the murder of John Lennon. [They were included as bonus tracks on the 1994 CD release of Ringo's *Stop And Smell The Roses* album, to which Nilsson also contributed.] Nilsson attended Ringo's wedding to actress Barbara Bach in 1981. Several of his covers of Yoko's songs were included on the 1984 Ono tribute album *Every Man Has A Woman* (see Spirit Choir). Harry contributed to Ringo's 1992 album *Time Takes Time*. He wrote a piece for *Songs By George Harrison 2*, a limited edition book published by Genesis in 1992. Nilsson gave one of his few public performances singing *Without You* during Ringo's September 4, 1992 All-Starr Band performance at Caesar's Palace in Las Vegas, which is available on unauthorized releases. He appeared in a 1994 anti-drunk driving video along with Ringo and McCartney (see R.A.D.D.).

Harry Nilsson died on January 15, 1994. Ringo reportedly helped him financially near the end of his life. Harrison and Ringo's wife Barbara attended his funeral. Shortly after his death, the CD *For The Love Of Harry: Everybody Sings Nilsson* (MusicMasters-01612-65127-2) was released featuring well-known artists covering Nilsson's songs, including *Lay Down Your Arms* performed by Ringo with Stevie Nicks. The 2006 documentary film *Who Is Harry Nilsson...(And Why Is Everybody Talkin' About Him?)* covered Nilsson's relationship with The Beatles, and features footage of Nilsson and Ringo shot during recordings for *Son Of Schmilsson*.

Don Nix

Hobos, Heroes And Street Corner Clowns
Jasrac/Blues Interactions-PCD-5175 (Japan) (03/10/97) (10/xx/73)
Producer: Don Nix [unless noted otherwise]
Apple Studios, London, UK 02-03/xx/73

I Need You (D. Nix) 2:52 (9)
George Harrison: Guitar; Don Nix: Lead Vocals & Acoustic Guitar; probably one or more of the following: Pete Carr: Drums; Eddie Hinton: Drums; &/or Roger Hawkins: Drums, David Hood: Bass, Klaus Voormann: Bass; Wayne Perkins: Guitar; Jeanie Greene: B. Vocals; Claudia Lennear: B. Vocals

The Train Don't Stop Here No More (D. Nix) 2:26 (2)
Additionally: **Producer: [George Harrison]**
George Harrison: Dialogue; Don Nix: Lead Vocals, Acoustic Guitar & Harmonica; probably the following: Klaus Voormann: Bass; Wayne Perkins: Acoustic Guitar

Don Nix was born on September 27, 1941 in Memphis, Tennessee. Nix and classmates Donald "Duck" Dunn and Steve Cropper, along with Terry Johnson, Jerry Smith, Charlie Freeman, Charles Axton and Wayne Jackson, formed The Mar-Keys. Their song *Last Night* was a Top 10 hit in 1961. Nix left The Mar-Keys in 1963. [Dunn and Cropper later became part of Booker T. And The MG's.] Nix was a major component in the Memphis music scene and Stax Records' recordings. He became a top session guitarist, saxophonist, songwriter and producer working with John Mayall, Furry Lewis, Freddie King, Leon Russell*, Delaney & Bonnie & Friends* and many others, while pursuing a solo career.

Nix met George Harrison in Los Angeles in 1971 through his girlfriend Chris O'Dell who had worked for Apple. Harrison struck up a friendship with Nix, and asked him to help assemble and be one of the background vocalists for *The Concert For Bangla Desh*. Nix was a frequent guest at Harrison's home during the early 1970s.

Advertisements for Nix's 1973 album *Hobos, Heroes And Street Corner Clowns* noted parts of it were recorded at Apple Studios and that a close listen would reveal guest artists not mentioned on the album, leading to speculation that members of The Beatles were among them. Nix says Harrison plays guitar on *I Need You* (ironically also the title of a Harrison Beatles' song), and took over production of the song *The Train Don't Stop Here No More*. He says Harrison's comment, "That's great Bob, come and hear it," at the end of that song, was his way of teasing Don about his harmonica playing sounding like Bob Dylan's* playing. Nix thinks these were probably the only tracks recorded at Apple. He doesn't recall any other specific musical credits, or if Harrison plays on any other tracks but thinks it's possible. Nix says Ringo was also at the Apple sessions, and it was reported that he plays drums on *Black Cat Moan*, but Nix is certain that song was recorded in Memphis, ruling out any involvement by Ringo, and doubts Ringo contributed to any of his recordings. Nix thinks the rest of the album was recorded in Alabama or France, also ruling out any involvement by Harrison or Ringo in sessions there. Additional tracks on the album are *She's A Friend Of Mine*, *Rainy Night In Paris (Memphis Reject)*, *Sweet Sweet Surrender*, *We Gotta Move (Keep On Rolling)*, *When I Lay My Burden Down (Traditional)*, *Miss Eleana* and *Look What The Years Have Done*.

It has been reported that Harrison also contributed to Nix's albums *Gone Too Long* and *Skyrider*. The only credits on *Gone Too Long* read "This album was recorded in France, England, Muscle Shoals, Memphis and Dallas with spiritual guidance from George Harrison, and help from a lot of good friends." Nix says Harrison gave him spiritual guidance but didn't contribute to either album. Nix continues to produce, write and record.

Phil Ochs

The Lost Lennon Tapes
Westwood One Radio Network-[Matrix #] LT 90-47 (12" albums promotional only) (11/19/71)
Producer: probably **John Lennon**
Ann Arbor, MI 12/10/71

Chords Of Fame (P. Ochs) intro 1:44/2:25 (2/2/2)
John Lennon: Slide Guitar; Phil Ochs: Lead Vocals & Guitar

Phil Ochs was born December 19, 1940 in El Paso, Texas. He attended military school, and studied journalism at Ohio State University. In the late 1950s he was part of a folk duo known as the Singing Socialists before moving to New York's Greenwich Village where he earned a reputation as a blunt, confrontational folk singer and activist. He was a gifted songwriter, but his radical, political message limited his commercial success. He was effectively blacklisted from TV and radio. His songs were anthems for the anti-war movement, and inspirations to his contemporaries such as Bob Dylan*, and Joan Baez who had a minor hit with his song *There But For Fortune*. He is best remembered for his anti-war song *I Ain't Marching Anymore*. Other Ochs' classics include *Outside Of A Small Circle Of Friends*, *The Party* and *Here's To The State Of Richard Nixon*.

Ochs was one of many performers at the *John Sinclair Freedom Rally*, headlined by John Lennon and Yoko Ono*, in Ann Arbor, Michigan on December 10, 1971. At the hotel before the concert, Lennon joined Ochs on slide guitar on Ochs' song *Chords Of Fame*, which was taped and later featured on Westwood One's *The Lost Lennon Tapes* radio series.

During a visit to Africa in 1973 Ochs was attacked and his vocal chords were severely damaged. Following the end of the Vietnam War, Ochs was essentially a man out of time, and work. He ended his life on April 9, 1976 .

Yoko Ono

A Chance Operation (The John Cage Tribute) [Various Artists]
Koch International Classics-3-7238-2 Y6x2 (10/xx/93)
Producer: Yoko Ono
Evergreen Recording Studios New York, NY Nov 11/xx/86 & 01/xx/87

Georgia Stone (Y. Ono) 20:33 (1/1/70-98)
John Lennon: Dialogue; Yoko Ono: Lead Vocals

Approximately Infinite Universe [Yoko Ono/Plastic Ono Band with Elephants Memory, Endless Strings and Choir Boys]
Rykodisc-RCD 10417/18 (07/22/97) (01/08/73)

Yoko Ono and Kristofer Engelhardt, Cranbrook Academy of Art Museum, Bloomfield Hills (Detroit), MI September 29, 1993. Photo by Phil Lopez, © Kristofer Engelhardt.

Producer: John Lennon & Yoko Ono
Yoko Ono: Lead Vocals; Wayne Tex Gabriel: Guitar; Gary Van Scyoc: Bass; Richard Frank Jr.: Drums & Percussion; Adam Ippolito: Keyboards; Stan Bronstein: Saxophone [unless noted otherwise]
Record Plant Studios, New York, NY 10-11/xx/72 [unless noted otherwise]

Air Talk (Y. Ono) 3:21 (2-6)
Additionally: Gary Van Scyoc & Adam Ippolito: Trumpet

Approximately Infinite Universe (Y. Ono) 3:20 (1-6)
Additionally: Ron Frangipane: String Orchestrations

Death Of Samantha (Y. Ono) 6:22 (1-2)
Additionally: Gary Van Scyoc: Trumpet; Adam Ippolito: Trumpet (only)

Dogtown (Y. Ono) 2:49 (2-12) (07/22/97)
Only: **John Lennon: Acoustic Guitar & B. Vocals**; Yoko Ono: Lead Vocals;
Probably John Lennon & Yoko Ono's apartment at 105 Bank Street (Greenwich Village) New York, NY probably sometime between 11/xx/71 & 04/xx/73

I Felt Like Smashing My Face In A Clear Glass Window (Y. Ono) 4:07 (2-1)

I Have A Woman Inside My Soul (Y. Ono) 5:31 (2-7)
Additionally: **John Lennon: B. Vocals & (probable) Guitar**

I Want My Love To Rest Tonight (Y. Ono) 5:11 (1-3)
Additionally: Ron Frangipane: String Orchestrations; Dennis Ferrante: B. Vocals; Note: Wayne Tex Gabriel & Stan Bronstein don't perform on this recording

Is Winter Here To Stay? (Y. Ono) 4:20 (2-10)
Additionally: **John Lennon: Guitar**; Mick Jagger: Guitar; Note: Wayne Tex Gabriel doesn't perform on this recording

Kite Song (Y. Ono) 3:19 (2-3) (07/22/97)
Additionally: John Lennon: Dialogue†; Daria

Price: Castanets; Note: Stan Bronstein doesn't perform on this recording
[Also available on *ONOBOX/(New York Rock†)*. RCD 10224/29 (RCD 10225) 3:09 (2-12) (03/03/92) (01/08/73)]

Looking Over From My Hotel Window (Y. Ono) 3:31 (2-11)
Only: Yoko Ono: Lead Vocals & Piano.

Move On Fast (Y. Ono) 3:43 (2-8) (11/13/72)
Additionally: **John Lennon: Guitar & (probable) B. Vocals**

Now Or Never (Y. Ono) 4:57 (2-9) (11/13/72)
Additionally: **John Lennon: Guitar**; George Young: Saxophone

Shiranakatta (I Didn't Know) (Y. Ono) 3:13 (2-5)
Note: Stan Bronstein doesn't perform on this recording

Song For John (Y. Ono) 2:05 (1-8)
Note: Wayne Tex Gabriel & Stan Bronstein don't perform on this recording

Waiting For The Sunrise (Y. Ono) 2:32 (1-11)
Additionally: Stan Bronstein: Flute (only); Note: Wayne Tex Gabriel doesn't perform on this recording

What A Bastard The World Is (Y. Ono) 4:33 (1-10)
Additionally: Ron Frangipane: String Orchestrations; Note: Stan Bronstein doesn't perform on this recording

What A Mess (Y. Ono) 2:41 (2-4)
Additionally: **John Lennon: B. Vocals**; Note: Wayne Tex Gabriel & Stan Bronstein don't perform on this recording

What Did I Do! (Y. Ono) 4:10 (1-4)
Additionally: Adam Ippolito & Gary Van Scyoc: Trumpet

Winter Song (Y. Ono) 3:36 (2-2)
Butterfly Studios, New York, NY 10-11/xx/72
Additionally: **John Lennon: Guitar**; Ron Frangipane: String Orchestrations; Note: Stan Bronstein doesn't perform on this recording

Yang Yang (Y. Ono) 3:50 (1-1)
Additionally: Stan Bronstein: Clarinet (only)

Aspen 7 Magazine / (The British Box-Spring And Summer) [Various Artists]
Eva Tone-Section 11-(matrix # EV-330707AXT11) (flexi-disc single 8") (probably 05/xx/69) includes: **"The John Lennon Diary 1969"**
Producer: John Lennon & Yoko Ono
John Lennon: Guitar; Yoko Ono: Lead Vocals
Probably Queen Charlotte Hospital, Second West Ward, Room 1, London or possibly John Lennon's temporary residence at 34 Montague Square, London, UK 11/4-25/68

Song For John: Let's Go On Flying / Snow Is Falling All The Time / Mum's Only Looking For Her Hand In The Snow (Y. Ono) 4:51 (1/1)

The Dick Cavett Show (John & Yoko Collection)
Shout/Sony-D2D 35887 (DVD) (11/01/05)
Producer: Judy Englander & Jeff Palo
ABC TV Studios, New York, NY
New York, NY 05/03/71; airdate: 05/11/72

We're All Water [live] (Y. Ono) (2-1) 4:20
John Lennon: Guitar; Yoko Ono: Lead Vocals; Gary Van Scyoc: Bass; Richard Frank Jr.: Drums; Adam Ippolito: Keyboards; Stan Bronstein: Saxophone; Wayne Tex Gabriel: Guitar

The Mike Douglas Show with John Lennon & Yoko Ono
Rhino-(R3 2428/29/30/31/32) (VHS) (05/26/98)
Producer: Jay Lebow, WBS in association with Mike Douglas Entertainments Inc. & Michael Krauss

Midsummer New York [live] (Y. Ono) 2:51 (2-1)
John Lennon: Guitar; Yoko Ono: Lead Vocals; Gary Van Scyoc: Bass; Adam Ippolito: Keyboards; Richard Frank Jr.: Drums; Stan Bronstein: Saxophone; Wayne Tex Gabriel: Guitar; Jerry Rubin: African Drum; Barbara Loden: African Drum
KYW TV Studios, Philadelphia, PA mid-01/xx/72 or 02/01/72; airdate: 02/15/72

Sakura (Cherry Blossoms) [live] (Trad Arr: Y. Ono) 1:34 (5-1)
John Lennon: Guitar & Dialogue; Yoko Ono: Lead Vocals; Adam Ippolito: Keyboards
KYW TV Studios, Philadelphia, PA early 02/xx/72 or 02/07/72; airdate: 02/18/72

Sisters, O Sisters [live] (Y. Ono) 2:48 (3-1)
John Lennon: Guitar & B. Vocals; Yoko Ono: Lead Vocals
KYW TV Studios, Philadelphia, PA mid-01/xx/72 or 02/02/72; airdate: 02/16/72

Feeling The Space [Yoko Ono/Plastic Ono Band and Something Different]
Rykodisc-RCD 10419 (07/22/ 97) (09/24/73)
Producer: Yoko Ono

("I Learned To Stutter")/Coffin Car [live] (Y. Ono) 2:29/4:22 (1-13) (07/22/ 97)
John Lennon: Electric Guitar; Yoko Ono: Lead Vocals & Piano
The First International Feminist Planning Conference, Harvard University, Cambridge, MA 06/03/73

Men, Men, Men (Y. Ono) 4:05 (1-12)
John Lennon: Dialogue; Yoko Ono: Lead Vocals; David Spinozza: Guitar; Ken Ascher: Piano; Gordon Edwards: Bass; Jim Keltner: Drums; Arthur Jenkins Jr.: Percussion
Record Plant Studios, New York, NY 07/xx/73

Mildred, Mildred (Y. Ono) 3:36 (1-14) (07/22/97)
John Lennon: Acoustic Guitar & B. Vocals; Yoko Ono: Lead Vocals
John Lennon & Yoko Ono's apartment at 105 Bank Street (Greenwich Village) New York, NY probably 11/xx/71-04/xx/73

Fly [Yoko Ono/Plastic Ono Band with Joe Jones Tone Deaf Music Co.]
Rykodisc-RCD 10415/16 (07/22/97) (09/20/71)
John Lennon: Drawings
Producer: John Lennon & Yoko Ono
Ascot Sound Studios, Ascot, UK 06/23/71-07/03/71 [unless noted otherwise]

Airmale (Tone Deaf Jam) (Y. Ono) 10:43 (2-1)
John Lennon with Joe Jones Tone Deaf Music Co.; Yoko Ono: Lead Vocals & Claves
Record Plant Studios, New York, NY 07/04-05/71

Between The Takes (Y. Ono) 1:56 (2-6) (07/22/97)
John Lennon: Electric Guitar; Ringo Starr: Drums; Yoko Ono: Lead Vocals; Klaus Voormann: Bass
EMI-Abbey Road Studios, London, UK 10/xx/70

Don't Count The Waves (Y. Ono) 5:22 (2-2)
John Lennon with Joe Jones Tone Deaf Music Co.; Yoko Ono: Lead Vocals & Claves; Klaus Voormann: Percussion; Jim Keltner: Tuned Drums
Record Plant Studios, New York, NY 07/04-05/71
[Also available on *Imagine.* Pioneer Artists-PA-86-164 (LD 12") (xx/xx/86) 5:35 (1/4)]

Don't Worry Kyoko (Mummy's Only Looking For A Hand In The Snow) [single version] (Y. Ono) 4:52 (1-4) (10/20/69)
John Lennon: Guitar; **Ringo Starr: Drums**; Yoko Ono: Lead Vocals; Klaus Voormann: Bass; Eric Clapton: Guitar
Lansdowne Studios, London, UK 10/03/69

Fly (Y. Ono) 22:48 (2-4)
John Lennon: Guitar; Yoko Ono: Lead Vocals

Midsummer New York (Y. Ono) 3:50 (1-1)
John Lennon: Guitar & Piano; Yoko Ono: Lead Vocals; Klaus Voormann: Bass; Chris Osborne: Dobro Guitar; Jim Keltner: Drums & Percussion
Record Plant Studios, New York, NY 07/04-05/71

Mind Holes (Y. Ono) 2:46 (1-3)
John Lennon: Guitar; Yoko Ono: Lead Vocals; Klaus Voormann: Bass; Chris Osborne: Dobro Guitar; Jim Keltner: Drums

Mind Train (Y. Ono) 16:50 (1-2)
John Lennon: Guitar; Yoko Ono: Lead Vocals; Klaus Voormann: Bass; Chris Osborne: Dobro Guitar: Jim Keltner: Drums
Mrs. Lennon (Y. Ono) 4:10 (1-5)
John Lennon: Piano & Organ; Yoko Ono: Lead Vocals; Klaus Voormann: Guitar, Bass & Bells
[Also available on *Imagine.* Pioneer Artists-PA-86-164 (LD 12") (xx/xx/86) 4:29 (1/6)]
O' Wind (Body Is The Scar Of Your Mind) (Y. Ono) 5:22 (1-8)
John Lennon: Guitar; Yoko Ono: Lead Vocals; Jim Keltner: Drums & Tabla; Jim Gordon: Tabla; Klaus Voormann: Cymbal; Bobby Keys: Claves

Open Your Box (Hirake) (Y. Ono) 3:31 (1-6)
John Lennon: Guitar; Yoko Ono: Lead Vocals; Klaus Voormann: Bass; Jim Gordon: Drums
Ascot Sound Studios, Ascot, UK 02/xx/71

Telephone Piece (Y. Ono) 0:30 (2-5)
Yoko Ono: Dialogue
Record Plant Studios, New York, NY 07/04-05/71

Toilet Piece/Unknown (Y. Ono) 0:30 (1-7)
Record Plant Studios, New York, NY 07/04-05/71

Will You Touch Me (Y. Ono) 2:45 (2-7) (07/22/97)
John Lennon: Acoustic Guitar & Dialogue; Yoko Ono: Lead Vocals
Probably John Lennon & Yoko Ono's apartment at 105 Bank Street (Greenwich Village) New York, NY 11/xx/71

You (Y. Ono) 8:57 (2-3)
Yoko Ono: Lead Vocals; Joe Jones Tone Deaf Music Co.

Record Plant Studios, New York, NY 07/04-05/71

Free As A Bird [John Lennon]
FAB / FAB 1 [unauthorized release] (probably 01/xx/96)
Producer: John Lennon & Yoko Ono
John Lennon: Guitar; Yoko Ono: Lead Vocals; Klaus Voormann: Bass

Greenfield Morning I Pushed An Empty Baby Carriage All Over The City [alternate mix] (Y. Ono) 5:30 (13)
Additionally: **Ringo Starr: Drums**; **George Harrison: Sitar**
EMI-Abbey Road Studios, London, UK 10/xx/70

Open Your Box (Hirake) [alternate take] (Y. Ono) 3:32 (12)
Additionally: Jim Gordon: Drums
Ascot Sound Studios, Ascot, UK 02/xx/71

Hot Tracks Program Service [Various Artists]
Series 1 Issue 1-SA 92756/7 (12" extended play promtional only) 9probably xx/xx/81)
Producer: John Lennon, Yoko Ono & Jack Douglas; Craig Morey†
Hit Factory Studios, New York, NY 11/xx/80, 12/06-08/80 & xx/xx/81†

Walking On Thin Ice-For John (remixed by Craig Morey†) (Y. Ono) 7:21 (2/1)
John Lennon: Lead Guitar & Keyboards; Yoko Ono: Lead Vocals; Hugh McCracken: Rhythm Guitar; Earl Slick: Rhythm Guitar; Tony Levin: Bass; Andy Newmark: Drums; Jack Douglas: Percussion

It's Alright (I See Rainbows) An Air Play
Rykodisc-RCD 10422 (08/26/97) (11/29/82)

Never Say Goodbye (Y. Ono) 4:17 (2)
Producer: Yoko Ono
John Lennon: Voice; Yoko Ono: Lead Vocals; Sean Lennon: Dialogue; additionally, one or more of the following: Neil Jason: Bass; Pete Cannarozzi: Keyboards & Synthesizer; Paul Griffin: Synthesizer; Gordon Grody: B. Vocals; Kurt Yahijan: B. Vocals; Carlos Alomar: B. Vocals; Michael Holmes: Keyboards; Paul Shaffer: Keyboards; Yogi Horton: Drums; Alan Schwartzberg: Drums; Rubens Bassini: Percussion; David A. Friedman: Percussion; Sammy Figeroa: Percussion; Roger Squitero: Percussion
Hit Factory Studios, New York, NY xx/xx/82

You're The One [previously unreleased version] (Y. Ono) 4:50 (12) (08/26/97)
Producer: John Lennon & Yoko Ono
John Lennon: Dialogue & (probable) Guitar; Yoko Ono: Lead Vocals; additionally, one or more of the following: Hugh McCracken: Guitar; Earl Slick: Guitar; Tony Levin: Bass; George Small: Keyboards; John Tropea: Guitar; Elliott Randall: Guitar; Steve Love: Guitar; Neil Jason: Bass; Wayne Pedziwiatr: Bass; Paul Griffin: Keyboards; Jimmy Maelen: Percussion; Pete Cannarozzi: Synthesizer; Ed Walsh: Oberheim Synthesizer; Gordon Grody: B. Vocals; Kurt Yahijan: B. Vocals
One or more of the following studios: Hit Factory, Sterling Sound & A&R, New York, NY &/or Automatt, San Francisco, CA 08-09/xx/80 & probably xx/xx/83

Live In New York City [John Lennon]
Pioneer Artists-PA-86-162 (LD 12") (03/31/95)
Producer: John Lennon & Yoko Ono: Overall Original Production; Yoko Ono: Executive & Music Producer xx/xx/85; Bob Fries: Music Producer xx/xx/72; Phil Spector: Recording Supervisor xx/xx/72; Gerard Meola: Video Producer xx/xx/85; Steve Gebhardt: Video Director xx/xx/72; Carol Dysinger: Video Director xx/xx/85
John Lennon: Guitar; Yoko Ono: Lead Vocals; Gary Van Scyoc: Bass; Adam Ippolito: Keyboards; Richard Frank Jr.: Drums; Stan Bronstein: Saxophone; Wayne Tex Gabriel: Guitar; Jim Keltner: Drums; John Ward: Bass
Madison Square Garden, New York, NY 08/30/72

Born In A Prison [live] (Y. Ono) 3:54 (1/9)
Additionally: John Lennon: B. Vocals

Sisters, O Sisters [live] (Y. Ono) 2:52 (1/5)
The Lost Lennon Tapes
Westwood One Radio Network-[Matrix #] LT 90-26 (12" albums promotional only) (06/25/90)
Producer: Glyn Johns &/or George Martin
John Lennon: Guitar; Paul McCartney: Drums; Yoko Ono: Lead Vocals
Apple Studios, London, UK 01/23/69

John, John (Let's Hope For Peace) (Y. Ono) 0:50 (1/3/1)

The Lost Lennon Tapes
Westwood One Radio Network-[Matrix #] LT 91-29 (12" albums promotional only) (07/15/91)
Producer: John Lennon, Yoko Ono & Jack Douglas
John Lennon: Rhythm Guitar; Yoko Ono: Lead Vocals; Tony Levin: Bass; Andy Newmark: Drums; George Small: Keyboards; Arthur Jenkins Jr.: Percussion; Earl Slick &/or Hugh McCracken: Guitar
The Hit Factory Studios, New York, NY 08-09/xx/80

No One Sees Me Like You Do [a.k.a.: Nobody Sees Me Like You Do] (Y. Ono) 3:44 (1/3/1)

The Lost Lennon Tapes
Westwood One Radio Network-[Matrix #] LT 91-35 (12" albums promotional only) (08/26/91)

No One Sees Me Like You Do [a.k.a.: Nobody Sees Me Like You Do] [rehearsal] (Y. Ono) 2:55 (1/1/2)
Producer: John Lennon, Yoko Ono & Jack Douglas
John Lennon: Rhythm Guitar & Dialogue; Yoko Ono: Lead Vocals; Tony Levin: Bass; Andy Newmark: Drums; George Small: Keyboards; Arthur Jenkins Jr.: Percussion; Earl Slick &/or Hugh McCracken: Guitar
The Hit Factory Studios, New York, NY 08/xx/80

Oh My Love (Y. Ono) 2:08 (1/1/2)
Producer: John Lennon & Yoko Ono
John Lennon: Rhythm Guitar; Yoko Ono: Lead Vocals
UK probably xx/xx/69

Miscellaneous Tracks [John Lennon]
Yellow Dog/Orange-YD-Orange 018 (Australia) [unauthorized release] (11/xx/95)
Producer: WOR TV
John Lennon: Guitar; Yoko Ono: Lead Vocals; Gary Van Scyoc: Bass; Adam Ippolito: Organ & Harmonium; Richard Frank Jr.: Drums & Percussion; Stan Bronstein: Saxophone; Wayne Tex Gabriel: Guitar
Americana Hotel, New York, NY 09/06/72

Now Or Never (Y. Ono) 4:20 (2)

One To One Concert Part 1 (Afternoon Show) [John Lennon]
Zeus-Z904001 [unauthorized release] (mid-90s)
Producer: [unknown-audience recording] **John Lennon** & Yoko Ono: Overall Original Production; Bob Fries: Music Producer xx/xx/72; Phil Spector: Recording Supervisor xx/xx/72
John Lennon: Guitar; Yoko Ono: Lead Vocals; Gary Van Scyoc: Bass; Adam Ippolito: Keyboards; Richard Frank Jr.: Drums; Stan Bronstein: Saxophone; Wayne Tex Gabriel: Guitar; Jim Keltner: Drums; John Ward: Bass
Madison Square Garden, New York, NY 08/30/72

Don't Worry Kyoko (Mummy's Only Looking For Her Hand In The Snow) [live] (Y. Ono) 4:45 (16)

Move On Fast [live] (Y. Ono) 3:59 (4)

Open Your Box (Hirake) [live] (Y. Ono) 4:00 (14)
Note: Stan Bronstein doesn't perform on this recording

We're All Water [live] (Y. Ono) 6:41 (11)

"One To One" Rehearsals Vol. 1 [John Lennon]
Orange-16 (Mexico) [unauthorized release] (xx/xx/94)
Producer: probably **John Lennon** & Yoko Ono
John Lennon: Guitar; Yoko Ono: Lead Vocals; Gary Van Scyoc: Bass; Adam Ippolito: Keyboards; Richard Frank Jr.: Drums; Stan Bronstein: Saxophone; Wayne Tex Gabriel: Guitar; John Ward: Bass; Jim Keltner: Drums
Butterfly Studios, New York, NY 08/18 &/or 20 &/or 22/72

Born In A Prison [rehearsal] (Y. Ono) 6:19 (12)
Additionally: **John Lennon: B. Vocals**

Move On Fast [rehearsal] (Y. Ono) 3:41 (5)

Sisters, O Sisters [rehearsal] (Y. Ono) 3:55 (7)

"One To One" Rehearsals Vol. 2 [John Lennon]
Orange-17 (Mexico) [unauthorized release] (xx/xx/94)
Producer: probably **John Lennon** & Yoko Ono
John Lennon: Guitar; Yoko Ono: Lead Vocals; Gary Van Scyoc: Bass; Adam Ippolito: Keyboards; Richard Frank Jr.: Drums; Stan Bronstein: Saxophone; Wayne Tex Gabriel: Guitar; John Ward: Bass; Jim Keltner: Drums
Butterfly Studios, New York, NY 08/18 &/or 20 &/or 22/72

Don't Worry Kyoko (Mummy's Only Looking For Her Hand In The Snow) [rehearsal] (Y. Ono) 5:13 (5)

Open Your Box (Hirake) [rehearsal] (Y. Ono) 3:30 (4)
Note: Stan Bronstein doesn't perform on this recording

We're All Water [rehearsal] (Y. Ono) 6:37 (2)

Yoko Ono/Plastic Ono Band
Rykodisc-RCD 10414 (06/03/97) (12/11/70)
Producer: John Lennon & Yoko Ono
John Lennon: Guitar; **Ringo Starr: Drums**; Yoko Ono: Lead Vocals; Klaus Voormann: Bass [unless noted otherwise]
EMI-Abbey Road Studios, London, UK 09/26/70-10/27/70 [unless noted otherwise]

AOS [rehearsal] (Y. Ono) 7:06 (4)
Additionally only: Ornette Coleman: Trumpet; Edward Blackwell: Drums; David Izenzon: Bass; Charles Haden: Bass
Note: John Lennon, Ringo Starr & Klaus Voormann don't perform on this recording
Albert Hall, London, UK 02/29/68

Greenfield Morning I Pushed An Empty Baby Carriage All Over The City (Y. Ono) 5:38 (3)
Additionally: **George Harrison: Sitar**

Open Your Box [previously unreleased version] (Y. Ono) 7:35 (7) (06/03/97)
Trident Studios, London, UK probably 10/xx/70 or possibly 02/xx/71

Paper Shoes (Y. Ono) 7:26 (6)

Something More Abstract (Y. Ono) 0:44 (8) (06/03/97)

The South Wind (Y. Ono) 16:38 (9) (06/03/97)
New York, NY probably 09-12/xx/70 or 06-07xx/71
Note: Klaus Voormann & Ringo Starr don't perform on this recording

Touch Me (Y. Ono) 4:37 (5)

Why (Y. Ono) 5:37 (1)
Additionally: John Lennon: B. Vocals

Why Not (Y. Ono) 9:55 (2)

ONOBOX (London Jam/New York Rock/Run, Run, Run/Kiss, Kiss, Kiss/No, No, No/A Story) Rykodisc-RCD 10224/29 (03/03/92)

Beautiful Boys (Y. Ono) 2:54 (4-6) (11/17/80)
Producer: John Lennon, Yoko Ono & Jack Douglas
John Lennon: (possible) Guitar & (possible) Keyboards; Yoko Ono: Lead Vocals; one or more of the following: Hugh McCracken: Guitar; Earl Slick: Guitar; Tony Levin: Bass; Andy Newmark: Drums; Arthur Jenkins Jr.: Percussion; Ed Walsh: Oberheim Synthesizer; George Small: Keyboards
Hit Factory Studios, New York, NY 08/15/80

Catman (The Rosies Are Coming) (Y. Ono) 5:44 (2-6) (01/08/73)
Producer: John Lennon & Yoko Ono
Yoko Ono: Lead Vocals; Wayne Tex Gabriel: Guitar; Gary Van Scyoc: Bass; Richard Frank Jr.: Drums & Percussion; Adam Ippolito: Organ; Stan Bronstein: Saxophone
Butterfly Studios, New York, NY 10-11/xx/72

Don't Be Scared (Y. Ono) 4:35 (4-10) (01/19/84)
Producer: John Lennon & Yoko Ono
John Lennon: Dialogue & (possible) Guitar; Yoko Ono: Lead Vocals; additionally, one or more of the following: Hugh McCracken: Guitar; Earl Slick: Guitar; Tony Levin: Bass; Andy Newmark: Drums; Ed Walsh: Oberheim Synthesizer; George Small: Keyboards; Howard Johnson: Horns; Grant Hungerford: Horns; John Parran: Horns; Seldon Powell: Horns; George "Young" Opalisky: Horns; Roger Rosenberg: Horns; David Tofani: Horns; Ronald Tooley: Horns; Arthur Jenkins Jr.: Percussion; John Tropea: Guitar; Elliott Randall: Guitar; Steve Love: Guitar; Neil Jason: Bass; Wayne Pedziwiatr: Bass; Yogi Horton: Drums; Allan Schwartzberg: Drums; Paul Griffin: Keyboards; Jimmy Maelen: Percussion; Pete Cannarozzi: Synthesizer; Gordon Grody: B. Vocals; Kurt Yahijan: B. Vocals; Carlos Alomar: B. Vocals; Billy Alessi: B. Vocals; Bob Alessi: B. Vocals; Pete Thorn: B. Vocals
Hit Factory Studios, &/or A&R Studios, & probably Sterling Sound, New York, NY &/or Automatt, San Francisco, CA/ 08/09/80 & probably xx/xx/83

Every Man Has A Woman Who Loves Him (Y. Ono) 4:03 (4-8) (11/17/80)
Producer: John Lennon, Yoko Ono & Jack Douglas
John Lennon: B. Vocals, Guitar & Keyboards; Yoko Ono: Lead Vocals; Hugh McCracken: Guitar; Earl Slick: Guitar; Tony Levin: Bass; Andy Newmark: Drums; Arthur Jenkins Jr.: Percussion; Ed Walsh: Oberheim Synthesizer; George Small: Keyboards
Hit Factory Studios, New York, NY 08/20/80–09/03/80

Give Me Something (Y. Ono) 1:34 (4-3) (11/17/80)
Producer: John Lennon, Yoko Ono & Jack Douglas
Yoko Ono: Lead Vocals; one or more of the following: **John Lennon: Guitar & Keyboards**; Hugh McCracken: Guitar; Earl Slick: Guitar; Tony Levin: Bass; Andy Newmark: Drums; Ed Walsh: Oberheim Synthesizer; George Small: Keyboards; Howard Johnson: Horns; Grant Hungerford: Horns; John Parran: Horns; Seldon Powell: Horns; George "Young" Opalisky: Horns; Roger Rosenberg: Horns; David Tofani: Horns; Ronald Tooley: Horns
Hit Factory Studios, New York, NY 08-09/xx/80

Hard Times Are Over (Y. Ono) 3:20 (4-9) (11/17/80)
Producer: John Lennon, Yoko Ono & Jack

Douglas
John Lennon: Guitar & B. Vocals; Yoko Ono: Lead Vocals; Hugh McCracken: Guitar; Earl Slick: Guitar; Tony Levin: Bass; Andy Newmark: Drums; George Small: Keyboards; George "Young" Opalisky: Horns; Roger Rosenberg: Horns; David Tofani: Horns; Ronald Tooley: Horns; Benny Cummings Singers-Kings Temple Choir: Choir; Arthur Jenkins Jr.: Percussion
Hit Factory & A&R Studios, New York, NY 08/19/80 & 09/10/80

Have You Seen A Horizon Lately (Y. Ono) 2:01 (4-18) (01/08/73)
Producer: John Lennon & Yoko Ono
John Lennon: Dialogue; Yoko Ono: Lead Vocals; Wayne Tex Gabriel: Guitar; Gary Van Scyoc: Bass; Richard Frank Jr.: Drums & Percussion; Adam Ippolito: Organ; Stan Bronstein: Saxophone
Record Plant Studios, New York, NY 10-11/xx/72

I'm Moving On (Y. Ono) 2:21 (4-4) (11/17/80)
Producer: John Lennon, Yoko Ono & Jack Douglas
John Lennon: (probable) Lead Guitar & (possible) Keyboards; Yoko Ono: Lead Vocals; one or more of the following: Hugh McCracken: Rhythm Guitar; Earl Slick: Rhythm Guitar; Tony Levin: Bass; Andy Newmark: Drums; George Small: Keyboards
Hit Factory Studios, New York, NY 08-09/xx/80

Kiss, Kiss, Kiss (Y. Ono) 2:40 (4-2) (10/23/80)
Producer: John Lennon, Yoko Ono & Jack Douglas
John Lennon: (probable) Guitar & (possible) Keyboards; Yoko Ono: Lead Vocals; one or more of the following: Hugh McCracken: Guitar; Earl Slick: Guitar; Tony Levin: Bass; Andy Newmark: Drums; Arthur Jenkins Jr.: Percussion; Ed Walsh: Oberheim Synthesizer; George Small: Keyboards
Hit Factory Studios, New York, NY 08/08/80

Let Me Count The Ways (Y. Ono) 3:03 (4-14) (01/19/84)
Producer: John Lennon & Yoko Ono
Yoko Ono: Lead Vocals & Piano
John and Yoko's Dakota Apartments, New York, NY probably 06/xx/80

O' Sanity (Y. Ono) 1:04 (4-12) (01/05/84)
Producer: John Lennon & Yoko Ono
John Lennon: (possible) Guitar; Yoko Ono: Lead Vocals; one or more of the following: Hugh McCracken: Guitar; Earl Slick: Guitar; Tony Levin: Bass; Andy Newmark: Drums; George Small: Keyboards; Arthur Jenkins Jr.: Percussion; John Tropea: Guitar; Elliott Randall: Guitar; Steve Love: Guitar; Neil Jason: Bass; Wayne Pedziwiatr: Bass; Yogi Horton: Drums; Allan Schwartzberg: Drums; Paul Griffin: Keyboards; Jimmy Maelen: Percussion
One or more of the following studios: Hit Factory, Sterling Sound & A&R, New York, NY &/or Automatt, San Francisco, CA 08-09/xx/80 &/or xx/xx/83

The Path (Y. Ono) 5:43 (1-15)
Producer: John Lennon & Yoko Ono
John Lennon: Keyboards; Yoko Ono: Lead Vocals
Ascot Sound Studios, Ascot, UK xx/xx/71

Peter The Dealer (Y. Ono) 4:58 (2-9) (01/08/73)
Producer: John Lennon & Yoko Ono
Yoko Ono: Lead Vocals; Wayne Tex Gabriel: Guitar; Gary Van Scyoc: Bass; Richard Frank Jr.: Drums; Adam Ippolito: Piano; Stan Bronstein: Saxophone
Record Plant Studios, New York, NY 10-11/xx/72

She Hits Back (Y. Ono) 4:04 (3-12) (11/02/73)
Producer: Yoko Ono
John Lennon: Guitar; Something Different: Chorus; Yoko Ono: Lead Vocals; David Spinozza: Guitar; Ken Ascher: Piano; Gordon Edwards: Bass; Jim Keltner: Drums; Arthur Jenkins Jr.: Percussion (with Plastic Ono Band & Something Different)
Record Plant Studios, New York, NY 07/xx/73

Sisters, O Sisters (Y. Ono) 3:46 (6-15) (04/24/72)
Producer: John Lennon, Yoko Ono & Phil Spector
John Lennon: Dialogue & Guitar; Yoko Ono: Lead Vocals; Gary Van Scyoc: Bass; Richard Frank Jr. &/or Jim Keltner: Drums & Percussion; Adam Ippolito: Keyboards; Stan Bronstein: Saxophone; Ron Frangipane: String Orchestrations
Record Plant Studios, New York, NY 03/01-20/72

Sleepless Night (Y. Ono) 3:53 (4-11) (01/19/84)
Producer: John Lennon & Yoko Ono
John Lennon: (possible) Guitar; Yoko Ono: Lead Vocals; one or more of the following: Hugh McCracken: Guitar; Earl Slick: Guitar; Tony Levin: Bass; Andy Newmark: Drums; Ed Walsh: Oberheim Synthesizer; George Small: Keyboards; Arthur Jenkins Jr.: Percussion; John Tropea: Guitar; Elliott Randall: Guitar; Steve Love: Guitar; Neil Jason: Bass; Wayne Pedziwiatr: Bass; Yogi Horton: Drums; Allan Schwartzberg: Drums; Paul Griffin: Keyboards;

Jimmy Maelen: Percussion; Pete Cannarozzi: Synthesizer
One or more of the following studios: Hit Factory, Sterling Sound & A&R, New York, NY &/or Automatt, San Francisco, CA 08-09/xx/80 &/or xx/xx/83

Walking On Thin Ice - For John (Y. Ono) 6:02 (4-1) (02/06/81)
Producer: John Lennon, Yoko Ono & Jack Douglas
John Lennon: Dialogue, Lead Guitar & Keyboards; Yoko Ono: Lead Vocals; Hugh McCracken: Rhythm Guitar; Earl Slick: Rhythm Guitar; Tony Levin: Bass; Andy Newmark: Drums; Jack Douglas: Percussion
Hit Factory Studios, New York, NY 11/xx/80 & 12/06-08/80

Woman Power (Y. Ono) 5:37 (3-14) (09/24/73)
Producer: Yoko Ono
John Lennon: Guitar; Yoko Ono: Lead Vocals; David Spinozza: Guitar; Ken Ascher: Piano; Gordon Edwards: Bass; Jim Keltner: Drums; Arthur Jenkins Jr.: Percussion; Something Different: Chorus; Sneaky Pete Kleinow: Pedal Steel Guitar
Record Plant Studios, New York, NY 07/xx/73

Yes, I'm Your Angel (Y. Ono) 3:35 (4-5) (11/17/80)
Producer: John Lennon, Yoko Ono & Jack Douglas
John Lennon: Dialogue; Yoko Ono: Lead Vocals; additionally, one or more of the following: Tony Levin: Bass; Andy Newmark: Drums; Ed Walsh: Oberheim Synthesizer; George Small: Keyboards; Howard Johnson: Horns; Grant Hungerford: Horns; John Parran: Horns; Seldon Powell: Horns; George "Young" Opalisky: Horns; Roger Rosenberg: Horns; David Tofani: Horns; Ronald Tooley: Horns; Arthur Jenkins Jr.: Percussion; Tony Davilio: Horn Arrangement
Hit Factory Studios, New York, NY 09/05/80
You're The One (Y. Ono) 4:35 (4-16) (01/19/84)
Producer: John Lennon & Yoko Ono
John Lennon: Dialogue & (possible) Guitar; Yoko Ono: Lead Vocals; additionally, one or more of the following: Hugh McCracken: Guitar; Earl Slick: Guitar; Tony Levin: Bass; George Small: Keyboards; John Tropea: Guitar; Elliott Randall: Guitar; Steve Love: Guitar; Neil Jason: Bass; Wayne Pedziwiatr: Bass; Paul Griffin: Keyboards; Jimmy Maelen: Percussion; Pete Cannarozzi: Synthesizer; Ed Walsh: Oberheim Synthesizer; Gordon Grody: B. Vocals; Kurt Yahijan: B. Vocals
One or more of the following studios: Hit Factory, Sterling Sound & A&R, New York, NY &/or Automatt, San Francisco, CA 08-09/xx/80 &/or xx/xx/83

Your Hands (Y. Ono) 3:13 (4-13) (01/19/84)
Producer: John Lennon & Yoko Ono
John Lennon: (possible) Guitar; Yoko Ono: Lead Vocals; one or more of the following: Hugh McCracken: Guitar; Earl Slick: Guitar; Tony Levin: Bass; George Small: Keyboards; John Tropea: Guitar; Elliott Randall: Guitar; Steve Love: Guitar; Neil Jason: Bass; Wayne Pedziwiatr: Bass; Paul Griffin: Keyboards; Jimmy Maelen: Percussion; Pete Cannarozzi: Synthesizer; Ed Walsh: Oberheim Synthesizer
One or more of the following studios: Hit Factory, Sterling Sound & A&R, New York, NY &/or Automatt, San Francisco, CA 08-09/xx/80 & probably xx/xx/83

Open Your Box / Power To The People
Apple-R 5892 (7" single) (UK) (03/12/71)
Producer: John Lennon & Yoko Ono
John Lennon: Guitar; Yoko Ono: Lead Vocals; Klaus Voormann: Bass; Jim Gordon: Drums
Ascot Sound Studios, Ascot & EMI-Abbey Road Studios†, London, UK
02/xx/71 & 03/04/71†

Open Your Box (Hirake) [remixed version] (Y. Ono) 3:31 (1/1)

Rock And Roll Circus [The Rolling Stones/Various Artists]
Abkco-1003-9 (DVD) (10/12/04)
Producer: Jimmy Miller, Jody Klein & Lenne Allik
John Lennon: Rhythm Guitar & B. Vocals; Yoko Ono: Lead Vocals; Eric Clapton: Lead Guitar; Keith Richards: Bass; Mitch Mitchell: Drums; Ivry Gitlis: Violin
InterTel Studios, Stonebridge House, London, UK 12/10/68

Whole Lotta Yoko (Y. Ono) 4:48 (13)
[Also available on Abkco-1268-2 (6) (10/15/96)]

S.I.R. John Winston Ono Lennon
Moonlight-ML 9506 (Czech) [unauthorized release] (08/xx/95)
Producer: probably **John Lennon** & Yoko Ono [unless noted otherwise]
John Lennon: Guitar & Dialogue; Yoko Ono: Lead Vocals; Gary Van Scyoc: Bass; Adam Ippolito: Keyboards; Richard Frank Jr.: Drums; Stan Bronstein: Saxophone; Wayne Tex Gabriel: Guitar; Jim Keltner: Drums; John Ward: Bass
Butterfly Studios, New York, NY 08/21-22/72 [unless noted otherwise]

Mind Train [rehearsal] (Y. Ono) 6:22 (12)

[Untitled "jam"] (Y. Ono) 2:21 (6)
Producer: John Lennon, Yoko Ono & Phil Spector
John Lennon: Guitar & Dialogue; Yoko Ono: Lead Vocals; Gary Van Scyoc: Bass; Richard Frank Jr. &/or Jim Keltner: Drums & Percussion; Adam Ippolito: Keyboards; Stan Bronstein: Saxophone; Wayne Tex Gabriel: Guitar
Record Plant Studios, New York, NY 03/01-20/72

Some Time In New York City [John Lennon and Yoko Ono/Plastic Ono Band with Elephant's Memory and The Invisible Strings/Plastic Ono Supergroup/Frank Zappa and The Mothers Of Invention]
Capitol-C2 93850 (05/01/90) (06/12/72)
Producer: John Lennon, Yoko Ono & Phil Spector [unless noted otherwise]

Au [a.k.a. A Small Eternity With Yoko Ono] [live] (**J. Lennon**-Y. Ono) 6:37 (2-6)
John Lennon: Feedback Guitar & Dialogue; Yoko Ono: Lead Vocals; Frank Zappa: Feedback Guitar; Don Preston: Mini Moog
Fillmore East Theater, New York, NY 06/06/71

Born In A Prison (Y. Ono) 4:02 (1-4)
John Lennon: Guitar & B. Vocals; Yoko Ono: Lead Vocals; Gary Van Scyoc: Bass; Richard Frank Jr.; Jim Keltner: Drums & Percussion; John LaBosca: Piano; Stan Bronstein: Saxophone; Ron Frangipane: String Orchestrations
Record Plant Studios, New York, NY 03/01-20/72

Don't Worry Kyoko (Mummy's Only Looking For Her Hand In The Snow) [live] (Y. Ono) 16:00 (2-2)
Producer: John Lennon & Yoko Ono [& Geoff Emerick]
John Lennon: Guitar; Yoko Ono: Lead Vocals; Jim Gordon: Drums; George Harrison: Guitar; Eric Clapton: Guitar; Klaus Voormann: Bass; Bobby Keys: Saxophone; Keith Moon: Drums; Alan White Drums: Billy Preston: Organ; Nicky Hopkins: (overdubbed) Electric Piano; Delaney Bramlett: Guitar: Bonnie Bramlett: Percussion; Jim Price: Horns; "Legs" Larry Smith: Percussion; Chris Wood: Percussion; Neil Boland: Percussion
Lyceum Ballroom, London, UK 12/15/69

Jamrag [a.k.a. Say Please, & Aaawk] [live] (**J. Lennon**-Y. Ono-[F. Zappa]) 5:36 (2-4)
John Lennon: Dialogue, B. Vocals & Guitar; Yoko Ono: Lead Vocals; Frank Zappa: Guitar & Dialogue; Mark Volman: B. Vocals; Howard Kaylan: B. Vocals; Ian Underwood: Keyboards; Aynsley Dunbar: Drums; Jim Pons: Bass; Bob Harris: Keyboards & B. Vocals; Don Preston: Mini Moog
Fillmore East, New York, NY 06/06/71

We're All Water (Y. Ono) 7:13 (1-10)
John Lennon: Guitar; Yoko Ono: Lead Vocals; Gary Van Scyoc: Bass; Richard Frank Jr.; Jim Keltner: Drums & Percussion; Adam Ippolito: Keyboards; Stan Bronstein: Saxophone; Wayne Tex Gabriel: Guitar
Record Plant Studios, New York, NY 03/01-20/72

Sweet Toronto [John Lennon And The Plastic Ono Band]
Pioneer Artists-PA11667 (DVD) (01/29/02) (xx/xx/89)
Producer: John Lennon & Yoko Ono (music); Kenneth C. Walker, Thor Eaton & Frazer Pennebaker for Pennebaker Assoc. & Alan Douglas for Douglas Corp (video)
Varsity Stadium, Toronto, Ontario Canada 09/13/69
[Also available on *Live Peace In Toronto 1969.* Apple/Capitol-CDP 0777 7 90428 2 1 (07/18/95) (12/12/69)]

Don't Worry Kyoko (Mummy's Only Looking For Her Hand In The Snow) [live] (Y. Ono) 4:44 (11)
John Lennon: Guitar; Yoko Ono: Lead Vocals; Eric Clapton: Guitar; Alan White: Drums; Klaus Voormann: Bass

John, John (Let's Hope For Peace) [live] (Y. Ono) 12:54 (12)
John Lennon: Feedback Guitar; Yoko Ono: Lead Vocals; Eric Clapton: Feedback Guitar; Alan White: Drums; Klaus Voormann: Feedback Bass

Ten For Two (John Sinclair Freedom Rally) [Various Artists]
MCP-046 (DVD) [unauthorized release] (xx/xx/07)
Producer: [unknown-audience recording] **John Lennon** & Yoko Ono: Overall Original Production
John Lennon: Guitar; Yoko Ono: Lead Vocals; Leslie Bacon: B. Vocals; Jerry Rubin: Congas; Frank Lanci: Congas; Billy Minelli: Tambourine; Tom Doyle: 12 String Guitar; Eddie Mottau: Guitar; Chris Osborne: Guitar; David Peel: Washtub Bass; Yoko Ono: Indian Drum
Crisler Arena, Ann Arbor, MI 12/10/71

Sisters, O Sisters [live] (Y. Ono) (17)

Then & Now
Pioneer-PA-85-116 (LD 12") (12/xx/84)
Producer: Glyn Johns & George Martin; Barbara Graustark (overall video)
Twickenham Films Studios, London, UK 01/10/69

[Untitled "jam"] (Y. Ono) 0:10 (1/4)
John Lennon: Guitar; **Paul McCartney: Bass**; **Ringo Starr: Drums**; Yoko Ono: Lead Vocals

Unfinished Music No. 1. Two Virgins [John Lennon and Yoko Ono]
Rykodisc-RCD 10411 (06/03/97) (11/11/68)
John Lennon: Drawings
Producer: John Lennon & Yoko Ono
John Lennon: B. Vocals, Dialogue & Instruments; Yoko Ono: Lead Vocals & Instruments [unless noted otherwise]
John Lennon's home studio at Kenwood, Weybridge, Surrey, UK probably 05/19/68 or possibly 05/02/68 [unless noted otherwise]

Remember Love (Y. Ono) 4:05 (3) (07/04/69)
Additionally: John Lennon: Acoustic Guitar (only)
Room 1742, Hotel La Reine-Elizabeth Hotel, Montreal, Canada 06/01/69 or possibly EMI-Abbey Road Studios or Apple Studios, London, UK

Two Virgins Side One (Two Virgins No. 1/Together†/Two Virgins No. 2/Two Virgins No. 3/Two Virgins No. 4/Two Virgins No. 5) (J. Lennon-Y. Ono/De Silva-Brown-Henderson†) 14:14 (1)

Two Virgins Side Two (Two Virgins No. 6/Hushabye Hushabye/Two Virgins No. 7/Two Virgins No. 8/Two Virgins No. 9/Two Virgins No. 10) (J. Lennon-Y. Ono) 14:40 (2)

Unfinished Music No. 2: Life With The Lions [John Lennon and Yoko Ono]
Rykodisc-RCD 10412 (06/03/97) (05/09/69)
Producer: John Lennon & Yoko Ono
Yoko Ono: Lead Vocals
Probably Queen Charlotte Hospital, Second West Ward, Room 1, London or possibly John Lennon's temporary residence at 34 Montague Square, London, UK (probably 11/4-25/68 [unless noted otherwise]

Cambridge 1969 [live] **(J. Lennon**-Y. Ono) 26:28 (1)
Additionally: **John Lennon: Feedback Guitar**; John Tchikai: Saxophone; John Stevens: Percussion; Mal Evans: Watch
Lady Mitchell Hall, Cambridge, UK 03/02/69

Mulberry (Y. Ono) 8:57 (7) (06/03/97)
Additionally: **John Lennon: Acoustic Guitar**

No Bed For Beatle John (J. Lennon-Y. Ono) 4:40 (2)
Additionally: **John Lennon: B. Vocals**
Queen Charlotte Hospital, Second West Ward, Room 1, London, UK 11/4-25/68

Song For John (Y. Ono) 1:29 (6) (06/03/97)
Additionally: **John Lennon: Acoustic Guitar**

Cape Clear (Vocal Remix)/Cape Clear (Instrumental Remix)/Walking On Thin Ice-For John (Re-Edit†)
Polydor-883 872-1 (12" single) (04/xx/86)
Producer: John Lennon, Yoko Ono & Jack Douglas; Joseph Watt†
Hit Factory Studios, New York, NY 11/xx/80 & 12/06-08/80 & xx/xx/86†

Walking On Thin Ice-For John (Re-Edit†) (Y. Ono) 7:17 (2/1)
John Lennon: Lead Guitar & Keyboards; Yoko Ono: Lead Vocals; Hugh McCracken: Rhythm Guitar; Earl Slick: Rhythm Guitar; Tony Levin: Bass; Andy Newmark: Drums; Jack Douglas: Percussion

Walking On Thin Ice / It Happened [edited & remixed version]†
Geffen-GEF 49683 (7" single) (02/06/81)
Producer: John Lennon†; Yoko Ono & David Spinozza
John Lennon: Dialogue; Yoko Ono: Lead Vocals; David Spinozza: Guitar; Hugh McCracken: Guitar; Gordon Edwards: Bass; Kenny Asher: Keyboards; Arthur Jenkins Jr.: Percussion; Rick Marotta: Drums
Record Plant Studios, New York, NY xx/xx/73 & xx/xx/80†

It Happened [edited & remixed version] (Y. Ono) 5:06 (2/1)

Wedding Album
Apple-SMAX 3361 (album 12") (10/20/69) **John Lennon: Drawings**

Wedding Album [John Lennon and Yoko Ono]
Rykodisc-RCD 10413 (06/03/97) (10/20/69)
Producer: John Lennon & Yoko Ono [unless noted otherwise]
John Lennon: Guitar; Yoko Ono: Lead Vocals [unless noted otherwise]
Hilton Hotel, Amsterdam, Netherlands 03/26/69 [unless noted otherwise]

Amsterdam [John, John (Let's Hope For Peace)] (Y. Ono) 5:14 (2-at the beginning)

Additionally: **John Lennon: Dialogue (only)**

Amsterdam [Stay In Bed] (Y. Ono) 0:48 (2-at the end)
Additionally: **John Lennon: Vocals**
Hilton Hotel, Amsterdam, Netherlands 03/26/69

Don't Worry Kyoko (Mummy's Only Looking For Her Hand In The Snow) (Y. Ono) 2: 14 (5) (06/03/97) (05/xx/69)
Probably Queen Charlotte Hospital, Second West Ward, Room 1, London or possibly John Lennon's temporary residence at 34 Montague Square, London, UK probably 11/4-25/68

Listen, The Snow Is Falling (Y. Ono) 3:22 (4) (12/01/71)
Producer: John Lennon, Yoko Ono & Phil Spector
Additionally: Klaus Voormann: Guitar; Hugh McCracken: Guitar; Nicky Hopkins: Keyboards & Chimes
Record Plant Studios, New York, NY 10/29/71

Who Has Seen The Wind? (**J. Lennon**-Y. Ono) 2:03 (3) (02/06/70)
Producer: John Lennon
Additionally: John Lennon: (probable) Guitar; **George Harrison: (probable) Guitar**; Yoko Ono: Flute; John Barham: Harpsichord
Trident &/or De Lane Lea Studios, London, UK possibly 01/27/70

Yoko Ono was born on February 18, 1933 in Tokyo, Japan. She was the eldest daughter of a prominent banking family who shuttled between the US and Japan before and after World War II. She attended Sarah Lawrence College in New York in the mid-1950s studying fine arts and philosophy. Yoko had an interest in music since her childhood piano lessons. In 1956 she married Japanese musician Toshi Ichiyanagi, who helped expose her to New York's avant-garde art and music scene. The marriage lasted several years before she met artist, musician and avant-garde filmmaker Anthony Cox, by whom she had a daughter, Kyoko Cox*. Cox began promoting Ono's unique brand of conceptual art, films and participatory happenings from *Cut Piece* (allowing people to cut a piece of clothing from the artist) to *Bagism* (placing the artist inside a bag). Her most notable work was her poetry book *Grapefruit* published in 1964.

The couple moved to London in the fall of 1966. Yoko soon had an exhibit titled *Unfinished Paintings and Objects* at the Indica Art Gallery owned by John Dunbar (see Marianne Faithfull), Barry Miles and Peter Asher (see Peter & Gordon) the brother of Paul McCartney's girlfriend, Jane. McCartney was a frequent visitor to the Gallery, and the first Beatle to meet Ono. He suggested to her that John Lennon might be interested in her projects. Lennon attended a preview of the exhibit on November 9, and was pleasantly amused by the off-beat humor of Ono's conceptual art. Lennon began taking greater interest in the eccentric artist who pursued him for patronization of her art projects. In October 1967 Lennon sponsored her exhibit *Yoko Plus Me*.

John invited Yoko to his home in May 1968 while his wife was away on vacation. The two began experimenting in John's home studio. John created sound effects to Yoko's distinctive warbling vocals, resulting in the album *Unfinished Music No. 1. Two Virgins*. According to the official version, they consummated their relationship following their recordings but others claim that it took place months earlier. When John's wife Cynthia returned home to find them comfortably settled in her home, she left, effectively ending their six-year marriage. EMI refused to distribute the Apple album *Unfinished Music No. 1 Two Virgins* because John and Yoko insisted the jacket feature full frontal and rear nude photos of them. It was distributed by Tetragrammaton in the US and Track Records in the UK using a brown sleeve to conceal the photos. John and Yoko became inseparable attending Beatles-related functions, and regularly staging outlandish "happenings" and media events, quickly shattering Lennon's "mop-top" image, and drawing ridicule from fans and the press. John supported and defended his love for Yoko, and her art and music, at great expense and risk to his popularity, and that of The Beatles.

The Beatles' wives and girlfriends occasionally attended their recording sessions but weren't active participants. However, John and Yoko not only felt that the other Beatles should immediately accept Yoko as the love of his life, but as his new musical partner. McCartney was initially tolerant of her avant-garde ideas, but he and George Harrison soon resented her constant presence and influence, and felt that she was driving a wedge between John, who was naturally defensive of her, and The Beatles. Yoko began lending her ideas and vocals to the recordings for *The Beatles* (white) album on such songs as *Revolution 9*, *The Continuing Story Of Bungalow Bill*, *Birthday* and *What's The New Mary Jane*. She even enlisted The Beatles in jams of her compositions during the rehearsals for the album and film *Let It Be*. [Portions of these jams are featured in the 1984 documentary *Yoko Ono Then & Now* released on LD and VHS.]

In October 1968, though still married to their respective spouses, John and Yoko announced that they were expecting a baby in February. Yoko was admitted to Queen Charlotte's Hospital in London in November and suffered a miscarriage (not the only one during her relationship with Lennon). John moved into her hospital room, during which time the two recorded material that would later be used on their album *Unfinished Music No.2. Life With The Lions.* Also probably recorded in their hospital room was a medley of acoustic demos later featured on a flexi-disc included in *Aspen*, a magazine in a box, which included a variety of art objects. One of the songs on the flexi-disc is *Song For John: Let's Go On Flying, Snow Is Falling All The Time, Mum's Only Looking For Her Hand In The Snow*, which features an early acoustic version of *Don't Worry Kyoko (Mummy's Only Looking For A Hand In The Snow)*. These songs feature John on acoustic guitar. [*Let's Go On Flying*, under the title *Song For John*, and *Mum's Only Looking For Her Hand In The Snow*, under the correct title *Don't Worry Kyoko (Mummy's Only Looking For A Hand In The Snow)*, were issued as bonus tracks on Yoko's Rykodisc releases of *Unfinished Music No.2. Life With The Lions* and *Wedding Album* in 1997.] Yoko would later record her poem about the miscarriage titled *Oh My Love*, with John on guitar. It was later featured on *The Lost Lennon Tapes* radio series in 1991. John re-wrote the song and recorded it for his 1971 album *Imagine*.] In December 1968 John and Yoko took part in The Rolling Stones'* film *Rock And Roll Circus*, which includes a performance featuring Yoko, with John backing her on guitar, on a jam called *Whole Lotta Yoko* (a.k.a. *Her Blues*).

On March 2, 1969 John played feedback guitar behind Yoko at an avant-garde jazz concert at The Lady Mitchell Hall in Cambridge, England. The performance was recorded, and included on their second album, *Unfinished Music No2. Life With The Lions*, along with such bizarre recordings as their miscarried child's heartbeat and a track of two minutes of silence. The album's back jacket has a photo of the Lennons leaving court after their arrest for possession of hashish (marijuana). [Rather than fight what Lennon maintained was a set up, he agreed to plead guilty and pay a small fine if charges against Yoko (she could have faced deportation) were dropped. It was a decision the Lennons would regret for years to come.] Apparently the Lennons also planned a third *Unfinished Music* album that reportedly included lengthy portions of people laughing. Around this time, the Lennons reportedly recorded a song titled *Peace Song*, which may be a working title for something else as nothing by this title has ever surfaced.

On March 20, 1969 John and Yoko, now divorced from their respective spouses, were married in Gibraltar. Like most of their activities throughout their relationship, their "bed-in for peace" honeymoon, which was the beginning of their campaign for world peace, was turned into a media event that was filmed, recorded and released later that year on their *Wedding Album*. On May 26, 1969 the Lennons, unable to secure a US visa, arrived in Montreal, Canada to hold their second "bed-in for peace" from their La Reine-Elizabeth Hotel room bed where they recorded *Give Peace A Chance* under the name Plastic Ono Band, the first of many incarnations of the Lennons' loose-knit group. It was the first record release to feature John's lead vocals without The Beatles, and the first of many of Lennon's singles to feature a recording by Yoko (*Remember Love*) on the B-side. The events in Montreal were filmed and later released in documentaries and on *John & Yoko's Year Of Peace* (Image-ID1785CZ DVD) and *John & Yoko Give Peace A Song* (Hip-O Records-B0006557-09 DVD).

In mid-1969 the Lennons bought a home, Tittenhurst Park in Ascot, and spent time with John's son Julian, and Yoko's daughter Kyoko, who was caught in the middle of a custody battle. [John later had a recording studio build in the home – Ascot Sound Studios.] Following the completion of recordings for The Beatles' *Abbey Road* album, John and Yoko accepted a last minute offer to perform at a rock 'n' roll revival in Toronto, Canada on September 13, 1969. The revival featured many of Lennon's early rock heroes including Jerry Lee Lewis*, Bo Diddley, Chuck Berry* and Little Richard*. They hastily assembled Eric Clapton*, Klaus Voormann* and Alan White (later a member of the group Yes, which Lennon considered signing to Apple) for their Plastic Ono Band. Among the songs John performed was the Plastic Ono Band's new single *Cold Turkey*, which was rejected by the other Beatles as too controversial because it was about heroin withdrawal. Yoko performed *Don't Worry Kyoko (Mummy's Only Looking For A Hand In The Snow,* the single's B-side, and *John, John (Let's Hope For Peace)*. The Lennons' performance was released on the album *Live Peace In Toronto 1969*. [The film *Sweet Toronto*, which included their performance, was first released in 1989 and on DVD in 2002.]

The Beatles were breaking up over personal, musical and business differences, and Lennon had made it known to the others of his intention to leave the group – though it was decided that no official announcement should be made. Lennon planned to issue his then-unreleased Beatles' recordings *You Know My Name (Look Up The Number)* and *What's The New Mary Jane* as the Plastic Ono Band's third single (Apple-1002) on December 5, 1969. The release was canceled due to objections by some of The Beatles over the use of their group recordings being issued as Plastic Ono Band recordings. Around this time, Yoko contributed to The Beatles' 1969 Christmas message record sent to fan club members, something none of the other wives or girlfriends ever did.

On December 15, 1969 John and Yoko performed at London's Lyceum Ballroom at the *Peace For Christmas* concert for UNICEF. Backing them was what was called the Plastic Ono Supergroup (with a cast of 1000's), comprising the Delaney & Bonnie & Friends* tour group, including Harrison, the backing band the Lennons used at the rock 'n' roll revival in Toronto, and other musicians including Keith Moon*. Yoko performed a 16-minute version of *Don't Worry Kyoko (Mummy's Only Looking For A Hand In The Snow)*. The Beatles' engineer Geoff Emerick produced a recording of the event. [When the recordings were released two years later, John, Yoko and Phil Spector* were listed as the producers. Spector, who wasn't at the performance, was listed in error.]

While The Beatles were trying to salvage an album and movie titled *Let It Be*, out of the previous year's filmed recordings, with production help from Spector, the Plastic Ono Band released its third single *Instant Karma / Who Has Seen The Wind*, with Spector helping out on the production. [Spector would work with the Lennons on numerous projects over the years.] Though many reliable sources list *Who Has Seen The Wind* as being recorded the same evening as *Instant Karma*, Mark Lewisohn has been unable to find any evidence that it was recorded during those sessions. Consequently, there is little information about exactly who plays on it. John Barham recalls playing on it at De Lane Lea Studios but other reliable sources list it being recorded at Trident Studios. The single credits Yoko as the sole composer. [Rykodisc's 1997 catalogue credits it as being written by Lennon and Ono.]

When McCartney used the occasion of the release of his first solo album in April 1970 to publicly announce he was leaving The Beatles, it left Lennon distrustful and embittered towards him for years. The Lennons spent much of 1970 in the UK doing battle with McCartney, the press and the government. They underwent psychotherapy at Dr. Arthur Janov's Primal Institute in Los Angeles. Part of the therapy included screaming. One result of the therapy are the albums *John Lennon / Plastic Ono Band* and *Yoko Ono / Plastic Ono Band* recorded and released in tandem utilizing most of the same studios and personnel, including Harrison and Ringo Starr. Originally the two albums were to be titled *Primal* and *Scream* respectively. They are their first true solo albums and set the pattern for their future album releases. Despite Lennon's defense and promotion of Yoko's work, he and his record company were aware that sales of his albums could suffer if they included Yoko's less commercially appealing recordings. [In the future only the *Some Time In New York City*, *Double Fantasy* and *Milk And Honey* albums would contain John and Yoko's recordings.]

Controversy surrounded the 1971 release of John and Yoko's next single, *Power To The People / Open Your Box*. The sexually suggestive lyrics of Yoko's *Open Your Box* had to be remixed to be unrecognizable before EMI would release it in the UK. Yoko's song *Touch Me* was used for the B-side in the US. The whole green Apple label, used for the A-side of Apple's singles, was used for both songs in the UK apparently indicating it was a double A-side. Later pressings put John's *Power To The People* on the split Apple B-side label.

On June 6, 1971 the Lennons joined Frank Zappa And The Mothers Of Invention* onstage at New York's Fillmore East Theater. The performance was a combination of John and Yoko's experimental music fused with Zappa's free-form jazz and comedy. Much of the song *Jamrag* consists of bits and pieces of well-known Zappa compositions. Because it's a jam, song times for each title vary widely from release to release, and are an approximation at best. [Twenty years later Zappa released his version of the performance with alternate titles that had a substantially different mix from the release produced by the Lennons and Spector.] Yoko arranged to have their performance filmed, though it has never been released.

Yoko's 1971 album *Fly*, released in tandem with Lennon's album *Imagine*, includes most of her songs previously available only on singles and the original mix of *Open Your Box* re-titled *Hirake*. It also includes the songs *Airmale (Tone Deaf Jam)*, featured in the Lennons' film

Erection, and *Fly* from their film *Fly*. [The Lennons made a number of conceptual films together between 1968 and 1972 that included musical contributions from John including *Film No 5* (a.k.a. *Smile*) and *Yoko And Me*.] The promotional film *Imagine* includes portions of both albums. [Two of Yoko's songs were omitted from the VHS and LD of the film *Imagine* that were released in 1986, and none were included on the 2000 DVD release re-titled *Gimme Some Truth*.] John's song *Imagine* took major lyrical inspiration from Yoko's book *Grapefruit*. [The inspiration for the song's melody may be even more interesting. In late 1965 John's estranged father Freddie released the autobiographical song *That's My Life (My Love And My Home)*, which he co-wrote with his producer and manager Tony Cartwright. Parts of it sound hauntingly like *Imagine*. John was known to amuse friends by playing *That's My Life*. Perhaps Freddie based his song on something he heard John working on, or perhaps John, consciously or subconsciously, wrote *Imagine* based in part on *That's My Life My Love And My Home*.]

By the fall of 1971 the Lennons had taken up permanent residence in an apartment on Bank Street in the artist district of Greenwich Village in New York. John referred to New York as the new Rome (the center of the world) and, being a seaport, said it reminded him of Liverpool. Yoko, having lived in New York much of her life, was known and appreciated by its art community. While in the US, the Lennons could also more effectively reclaim custody of Kyoko. The Lennons were soon set upon by the vanguard of New York's leftists, artists and musical underground including Jerry Rubin, Allen Ginsberg* and David Peel*. Leftist politics had become a priority for John and Yoko, resulting in a year's worth of slogan songs that are the Lennons' only true pop music collaborations, beginning with the single *Happy Xmas (War Is Over)*.

The Lennons had been persuaded by their leftist friends to perform at the *John Sinclair Freedom Rally* benefit concert on December 10, 1971 at Crisler Arena in Ann Arbor, Michigan to help get Sinclair released from prison. Sinclair was the manager of the rock group The MC5 and organizer of Michigan's leftist White Panther Party. He'd been sentenced to 10 years in prison for selling two marijuana cigarettes to undercover officers. The Lennons sympathized with the legal injustice obviously imposed because of Sinclair's political activities, something they too would soon experience. Backed by Rubin, Peel and others, Lennon performed *John Sinclair* written for the performance, and he and Yoko sang their political songs *Luck Of The Irish* and *Attica State*. Yoko performed *Sisters, O Sisters* her newly written anthem to the women's movement. They had their performance filmed for a documentary titled *Ten For Two*, though it never received general release. The Lennons' appearance drew major media attention and Sinclair was released from prison a few days later.

Shortly after the Lennons return to New York they went into Record Plant Studios to do overdubs on the Ann Arbor recordings and to produce an album for Peel. On December 16, 1971 the Lennons, backed by Peel and his band, appeared on *The David Frost Show* (broadcast on January 13, 1972) performing the same songs they did in Ann Arbor. The following day the Lennons appeared at the Apollo Theater in New York at a benefit concert for the families of victims of the Attica State Prison riots. John performed *Imagine*, and *Attica State* with Yoko, and Yoko performed *Sisters, O Sisters*.

In January 1972 the Lennons began taping segments as week-long co-hosts of TV's *The Mike Douglas Show*, which aired the week of February 14-18. The Lennons had a major hand in choosing the shows guests and topics, which included segments on macrobiotic cooking, biofeedback, participatory art and heated political discussions. The Lennons performed their current material, including Yoko's *Midsummer New York*, *Sakura* and *Sisters, O Sisters* backed by Elephant's Memory*, and performed with their guest Chuck Berry*. [Ironically, Mike Douglas had booked the Lennons to appear on his show in Hawaii in early December 1980 but they cancelled due to commitments regarding their new album. At that time, Lennon's killer was traveling from his home in Hawaii to New York to murder John Lennon.]

On March 6, 1972 Lennon's visa extension was canceled by US Immigration, paving the way for his deportation. The official reason given was that he was an undesirable alien due to his drug conviction in the UK in 1968. However, declassified documents show it was prompted by his leftist politics, and advisors to President Nixon who feared that Lennon's plans to tour with an anti-Nixon Administration message, and his fame and influence on the youth vote, were a threat to Nixon's re-election later that year.

In May 1972 the Lennons appeared on ABC TV's *The Dick Cavett Show*, again backed by Elephant's Memory, with Yoko singing *We're All Water*. The song was included on the Lennons' 1972 album *Some Time In New York City*, which is their most collaborative and political work.

The jacket features highly controversial slogans and photos, including one with the heads of Richard Nixon and Chairman Mao superimposed on nude dancers. The album also includes their performances with Zappa in New York the previous year and for UNICEF in London in 1969. The album's release was delayed in the UK by several months due to a dispute with Lennon's music publishing company over the validity of Yoko's co-compositions with John. Unlike a similar dispute with the same publishing company regarding Linda McCartney's* co-composing contributions with Paul, Yoko's contributions were obvious. Yoko was also listed in the general credits as playing drums (congas), probably on *We're All Water*.

The Lennons, on the advice of attorneys fighting John's deportation order, began taking a less offensive political tack. They committed to performing two shows at a concert for the *One To One* foundation, fronted by TV commentator Geraldo Rivera, which was raising money to help alleviate deplorable conditions at New York's Willowbrook State School, a facility for mentally retarded children. The Lennons were backed by Elephant's Memory. According to band members, recorded rehearsals, which included Jim Keltner and John Ward, began at Butterfly Studios, and continued at the nearby Fillmore East Theater, in New York. Unauthorized releases of these rehearsals (and the concerts) include songs that are not on the official releases. The *One To One* benefit concerts took place on August 30, 1972 at Madison Square Garden. During the shows Yoko performed *Sisters, O Sisters*, *Born In A Prison*, *We're All Water*, *Open Your Box*, *Move On Fast* and *Don't Worry Kyoko (Mummy's Only Looking For A Hand In The Snow)*. The Lennons struck another charitable note several days later performing on the *Jerry Lewis Muscular Dystrophy Telethon* with Yoko singing *Now Or Never*.

Yoko pursued the less politically threatening fight for women's rights and feminism. Her album *Approximately Infinite Universe*, with backing from Elephant's Memory, drew positive reviews. John is credited playing guitar on two songs under the thinly veiled pseudonym of Joel Nohnn (the letters of his name rearranged), but he is clearly evident making additional, un-credited musical and vocal (Choir Boys) contributions. According to Wayne Tex Gabriel, Elephant's Memory (though not credited) was responsible for arranging all of the songs on the album. On June 3, 1973 Yoko and John took part in The First International Feminist Planning Conference at Harvard University. Yoko performed about half-a-dozen songs accompanied by John on guitar including *I Learned To Stutter* and *Coffin Car*. [These two songs were included on Rykodisc's 1997 issue of *Feeling The Space*.] John's immigration and other difficulties, and Yoko's increasing independence and feminist activism, were taking a toll on their marriage. In the fall of 1973 Yoko issued *Feeling The Space*, an album of frustrated and bitter feminist songs she produced without John, though he contributed to two songs under the pseudonym John O'cean. May Pang thinks John's contributions to the album were recorded during his one and only visit to the sessions. John's tandem release was the non-political album *Mind Games*, utilizing the session musicians Yoko had assembled for her album.

John and Yoko separated in mid-September 1973. John headed for Los Angeles with Pang, whom Yoko had instructed to accompany him, and began recording an album produced by Spector of covers of their favorite rock 'n' roll songs. Though Lennon describes the year-and-a-half separation as his "lost weekend" it proved to be the most productive period of his solo career. It was also a highly productive period for Yoko. She recorded the album *A Story* with the same musicians she used on *Feeling The Space*. [It wouldn't be released until 1992 as part of the set *ONOBOX*.] She assembled a band and performed in New York clubs before embarking on a tour of Japan in August 1974. In mid-1974 John returned to New York to work on Harry Nilsson's* album *Pussy Cats*, and to record his album *Walls And Bridges* with help from Elton John*, which led to Lennon performing with Elton at Madison Square Garden on November 28, 1974. Yoko was in attendance and met with Lennon backstage. According to them, the meeting rekindled their love, but the two had maintained almost daily contact during their separation, and John continued to live with Pang for another two months. Yoko's 1974 single *Yume O Moto / It Happened*, only released in Japan, was her last record of the decade. The B-side credits production to Yoko and studio musician Dave Spinozza, her companion during much of her separation from John. [The song was released for the first time elsewhere as the B-side of *Walking On Thin Ice* in 1981.]

In early 1975 John returned to the Dakota Apartments in New York to live with Yoko. Yoko became pregnant and on October 9, 1975 (John's birthday) she gave birth to Sean Ono Lennon, the couple's only child. It was a momentous time for the Lennons – two days earlier John's deportation order was permanently dropped, and nine months later he was granted US residence. These events marked the beginning of the Lennons' five-year retirement from public life and recording. John became a "house husband," while Yoko managed the Lennons' financial affairs.

In early June 1980 John was part of a small crew sailing from New York to Bermuda. The journey proved perilous, and the experience gave Lennon the confidence he seemed to be lacking to step back into the public spotlight. He phoned Yoko from Bermuda with renditions of several new songs he had written. This inspired Yoko to record, under the name "friends," over an album of her songs in late June and early July 1980 at Record Plant Studios in New York. These recordings, produced by Roy Cicala (see Lori Burton) using his studio band Visitor, were never used. In August, John and Yoko booked time at New York's Hit Factory Studios with the idea of combining the best of each artist's songs for the Lennons' album *Double Fantasy*. [The remainder of the tracks would be refined at a later date for a follow-up album eventually titled *Milk And Honey*.] Most of Yoko's songs (some re-titled) were re-recordings of her songs done at Record Plant weeks earlier, while others, such as *Hard Times Are Over*, dated back to 1973. According to Jack Douglas, John contributed guitar to all of Yoko's songs from these sessions that he helped the couple produce. By 1980 artists such as The B-52's, whose style was reminiscent of Yoko's early experimental recordings, were making a "new wave" in the musical charts, so Yoko's recordings were better received.

John felt certain the musical times had finally caught up with Yoko and that her song *Walking On Thin Ice* would be her first number one hit. On December 8, 1980 time caught up with John Lennon. As he and Yoko returned to the Dakota after working on her song he was shot and killed by a deranged man. Yoko (like McCartney) coped with the tragedy by making recordings. On February 6, 1981 *Walking On Thin Ice / It Happened* was released to sympathetic and favorable reviews, and was her biggest success, especially on the dance charts. The B-side was a remixed version of the 1974 Japanese release, but the credits (incorrectly) list John as one of the producers in 1973.

Several months later Yoko released *Season Of Glass*, an album that was a reflection of her grief and anger. She used a photo of John's blood-spattered glasses, from the night he was murdered, on the cover and included gun shots on one song. She utilized the same studio and musicians used on *Double Fantasy* (and *Milk And Honey*), and some of the songs were from those sessions, such as *No One Sees Me Like You Do* (written in 1973) originally featuring John on rhythm guitar, which was re-recorded after John's death and re-titled *Nobody Sees Me Like You Do*. [Two versions of the song featuring John were included on *The Lost Lennon Tapes* radio series in 1991]. Yoko mixed John's voice into her song *Never Say Goodbye* on her 1982 album *It's Alright*. [Rykodisc's 1997 release of the album also includes a previously unreleased version of *You're The One* with contributions from John.]

In December 1983 Yoko began portioning out the remainder of the couple's unreleased material, starting with the interview album *Heart Play-unfinished dialogue* intended to promote the Lennons' album *Milk And Honey* released the following month. Most of *Milk And Honey* was recorded during the sessions for *Double Fantasy* in 1980. However, due to a dispute with Ono, co-producer Jack Douglas wasn't credited. The 1983 tribute album *Every Man Has A Woman* includes covers of Yoko's songs by 10 artists including Harry Nilsson*, Elvis Costello*, Spirit Choir*, Klaus Voormann's* band Trio, Sean Lennon, and John singing *Every Man Has A Woman Who Loves Him* recorded during sessions for *Double Fantasy*. In late 1984 Yoko joined forces with McCartney in an attempt to buy back Northern Songs Publishing, the Lennon and McCartney songwriting catalogue, from ATV but they were out-bid by Michael Jackson* in 1985. Yoko had a top 20 hit on Billboard's Dance Chart with the song *Hell In Paradise* 1985. In 1986 she released the album *John Lennon – Live In New York City* from the *One To One* benefit concerts. The companion VHS and LD contain two of her songs from the performance. Yoko continued to release Lennon-related films, videos, books and recordings throughout the latter half of the 1980s. She contributed many of their unreleased recordings for the nearly five-year-long, Westwood One radio series *The Lost Lennon Tapes*. 1992's *ONOBOX* includes edited and unedited versions of most of Yoko's recordings. It also includes the previously unreleased John and Yoko composition *The Path*. Yoko contributed her song *Georgia Stone* to the 1993 album *A Chance Operation (The John Cage Tribute)*, which contains John's dialogue.

On January 19, 1994 Ono and McCartney embraced at the ceremony in New York to induct John Lennon into the Rock and Roll Hall of Fame. Following the ceremonies, Yoko turned over some of John's unreleased demos to

McCartney to be used for the creation of a new Beatles' recording. Yoko and Sean visited McCartney at his home in East Sussex, England on March 11, 1995. While there, Yoko recorded her song *Hiroshima, Sky is Always Blue* with Sean on guitar and chimes; Paul on bass, backing vocals and probably production; Linda on celeste; their son James on guitar, and daughters Heather, Stella and Mary on percussion and backing vocals. The five minute recording was premiered on August 6, 1995 on Japanese TV to observe the 50th Anniversary of the dropping of the atomic bomb, though it hasn't seen official release.

Rykodisc issued, under Yoko's supervision, her entire Apple album catalogue in 1997, which contains alternate versions and previously unreleased bonus tracks to which John contributed. In 1998 Yoko compiled the *John Lennon Anthology* album, which includes a number of unreleased songs and material that aired on *The Lost Lennon Tapes* radio series. Since John's death, Yoko has released a number of other albums and toured — sometimes with backing from Sean, who has also found some musical success. In 2003 Ono's maxi-single of remixes of *Walking on Thin Ice* and her 2004 reworking of *Every Man Has a Woman Who Loves Him,* topped Billboard's Dance Club Play Charts. These are essentially new recordings and only contain samples of the original recordings. She has held a number of art exhibits and re-established contact with her daughter Kyoko. Yoko still resides at the Dakota, continues to champion causes, be artistically and musically creative, manage the Lennon estate and archives, and keep John's music and message alive. For more information go to www.imaginepeace.com.

Roy Orbison

Mystery Girl
Virgin-2-91058 (02/02/89)
Producer: Jeff Lynne
George Harrison: Acoustic Guitar†; Roy Orbison: Lead Vocals & Acoustic Guitar; Jeff Lynne: Acoustic Guitar, Keyboards, B. Vocals & Bass; Ray Cooper: Drums; Louis Clark: String Conductor
A&M, Rumbo Recorders &/or Chapel Studios, Los Angeles, CA & FPSHOT†, UK xx/xx/88

A Love So Beautiful (J. Lynne-R. Orbison) 3:30 (4)

The Very Best of Roy Orbison
Virgin-7243 8 42350 2 4 **George Harrison: Liner Notes**

Roy Orbison was born April 23, 1936 in Vernon, Texas but spent his formative years in Wink, Texas. He began his musical career in 1954 with the country and western group The Wink Westerners. His next group, The Teen Kings, were encouraged by Sun Records' artist Johnny Cash* to send their 1955 recording of *Ooby Dooby* to Sun. Their re-recording of it for Sun was a hit in 1956. Elvis Presley, Jerry Lee Lewis* and Carl Perkins* were also label mates of his at Sun. After The Teen Kings disbanded, Sun issued several unsuccessful singles by Orbison. Roy left Sun in 1957, moved to Nashville, and began writing ballads and pop-rock songs suiting his wide vocal range, for the prestigious Acuff-Rose Song Publishing Co. His song *Claudette* was a hit for The Everly Brothers* in 1958. Roy signed with RCA records in 1959 where his recordings, produced by Chet Atkins*, met with little success. He signed with Monument Records and between 1960 and 1964 had Top 10 hits with the songs *Only The Lonely*, *Blue Angel*, *Running Scared*, *Crying*, *Dream Baby*, *In Dreams*, *Mean Woman Blues* and *It's Over*.

As Roy was beginning his 1963 UK tour he inquired about The Beatles, who were his supporting act, and was duly informed about them by John Lennon who was standing behind him. Roy had to relinquish his top billing to The Beatles during the tour but praised them in the UK music press. During the tour he began wearing the dark sunglasses that would become his trademark. The Beatles were also fans of Roy Orbison. [They had performed *Dream Baby* on their first BBC radio performance broadcast on March 8, 1962. When they auditioned *Please Please Me* for George Martin* he thought it sounded too much like an Orbison song. Lennon admitted it was his intent to write an Orbison-styled song. The Beatles reworked it into a more up-tempo version, which became their first number one song in the UK.] In 1964 they invited Roy to the set of their film *A Hard Day's Night*, where he goaded Lennon on during his famous bathtub scene. Roy's last number one hit, *Oh, Pretty Woman* in 1964, was one of the few songs to interrupt The Beatles' dominance in the charts at the time.

Roy's signing with MGM Records in 1965 marked a lengthy period of failures and tragedies. In 1966 his wife Claudette was hit and killed by a truck while they were riding their motorcycles. While on tour in 1968 Orbison's house caught on fire killing two of his three sons. Shortly after the tragedy, Roy married German-born Barbara Wellhonen and moved to Germany for several years. He suffered from ulcers and in 1978 he underwent heart bypass surgery. By the mid-1980s the couple was living in California and Roy resumed touring. Roy Orbison was inducted into the Rock and Roll Hall of Fame in 1987.

In 1987 Paul McCartney recounted to him how *Please Please Me* was originally rejected for sounding too much like one of his songs and was receptive to the idea of producing Roy recording the song as it was originally intended to sound. Roy also considered approaching George Harrison to help him record the song.

In 1988 Jeff Lynne*, who had just produced Harrison's album *Cloud Nine*, was recruited to produce albums for Tom Petty* and Orbison. Harrison was looking for some help recording the B-side for a single, and Lynne suggested Orbison and Petty. Bob Dylan's* home studio was suggested as the meeting place and, with help from drummer Jim Keltner (see Attitudes), they formed the Traveling Wilburys. Their huge success set the stage for Roy's nearly completed comeback album, but on December 6, 1988, while visiting his mother, he suffered a heart attack and died. Harrison, Lynne and Petty were pallbearers at his funeral. His posthumously released album *Mystery Girl* contains *A Love So Beautiful* featuring Harrison on guitar, and Roy's last Top 10 hit *You Got It*. The album credits *You Got It* as being mixed at FPSHOT, but Lynne seems certain it was mixed at Rumbo Recorders in Los Angeles. Lynne says, "We did so many sessions at that point with all the Wilburys that George may have played acoustic guitar on *You Got It*." However, Lynne thinks, based on the rest of the album's credits, which he believes to be accurate, that Harrison probably didn't contribute to *You Got It*. Lynne isn't aware of Harrison contributing to any of Roy's other recordings.

A brief clip of Roy singing The Beatles' song *Help!* was included on the 1991 video release *The World's Greatest Artists Sing LENNON A Tribute*. In 1997 Virgin Records issued (mail order only) *The Very Best Of Roy Orbison*, which contains a brief ode in the liner notes from Harrison. For more information go to www.orbison.com

Buck Owens (Duet with Ringo Starr)

Act Naturally
Capitol-CDP 7 92893 2 (10/04/89)
Producer: Jerry Crutchfield & Jim Shaw
Ringo Starr: Vocals; Buck Owens: Vocals; Terry Christoffersen: Rhythm Guitar; Reggie Young: Lead Guitar; Jim McCarty: Drums; Doyle Curtsinger: Bass; Jim Shaw: Piano
EMI-Abbey Road Studios, London, UK 03/27/89

Act Naturally (J. Russell-V. Morrison) 2:59 (5) (06/21/89)

Buck Owens was born Alvis Owens Jr. on August 12, 1929 in Sherman, Texas. When Buck, as he always preferred to be called, was eight his family moved to Mesa, Arizona. Buck developed a passionate interest in the guitar, and was playing in country bands by age 16. He soon married and moved to Bakersfield, California, a town with many southern transplants. Owens and others, such as Ferlin Husky and Merle Haggard, developed a more urban, western style of country music, making Bakersfield the capitol. He also did session work for artists such as rock singer Gene Vincent. Owens had Top Five hits on the country charts with *Under Your Spell Again* in 1959 and *Excuse Me (I Think I've Got A Heartache)* in 1960. His first of 20 number one hits on the country charts was *Act Naturally* in 1963, which created controversy in country music because it includes a pronounced drum track. Owens, and his backing band The Buckaroos, was one of country music's most popular acts the latter half of the 1960s. He was a familiar face on TV between 1969 and 1986 when he co-hosted the country music comedy show *Hee Haw*.

Owens received criticism from his peers in country music for being a professed fan of The Beatles, and The Beatles, in particular Ringo Starr, were fans of his. In 1965 they recorded *Act Naturally* as their song-per-album that featured Ringo on vocals. The song took on added significance because Ringo was considered the most natural actor of The Beatles, making it Ringo's theme. In 1989 Owens and Ringo recorded a duet of *Act Naturally*, which appears on Owens' album *Act Naturally*. Ringo also appears in the music video for the song shot on June 24, 1989 in the US. Buck Owens died on March 25, 2006 just hours after performing at the Crystal Palace, a restaurant, club and museum he owned in Bakersfield. For more information go to www.buckowens.com

Buck Owens, circa 1990s, courtesy of Buck Owens.

Lindsay Pagano

Love & Faith & Inspiration
Warner Bros.-9 47953-2 (09/25/01)
Producer: [Paul McCartney] & Jude Cole
Paul McCartney: Vocals; Lindsay Pagano: Lead Vocals; David Campbell: String Arrangement; Aaron Embry: Electric Piano; Jude Cole: Guitars
Jim Henson Studios, Hollywood, CA mid-06/xx/01

So Bad (P. McCartney) 3:37 (10)

Lindsay Pagano was born on June 22, 1986 in Philadelphia, Pennsylvania. Her parents had a band and Lindsay took an avid interest in their rehearsals. They bought her a Karaoke machine to develop her singing. Lindsay recalls, "My dad videotaped me singing at my 13th birthday party. Though a series of my parents' friends that tape found its way to producer Jude Cole who thought I was great. Before I knew it, I had a record deal with Warner Bros., so my family and I decided to move to Los Angeles.

"I'd spent a lot of time at Henson Studios recording my first album *Love & Faith & Inspiration*. There were rumors that Paul McCartney was going to be recording in studio-A, where the top acts recorded. I knew who The Beatles were but I was only about 14 at the time, so Paul wasn't a big deal to me. One day I noticed my 10-year-old sister talking to someone in the studio hallway. She had no idea who it was, but I did. I introduced myself and told him I was recording in studio-C. I jokingly asked him who he was. He said, 'Oh, my name's Paul. I'm recording [his *Driving Rain* album] in studio-A. I've got to get back to work, but it's really nice to meet you.' My sister told my producer Jude Cole she'd met a guy named Paul who was recording in studio-A. Jude looked shocked! I said, 'It was Paul McCartney.' Paul became friendly with the people working on my record and started popping into our studio. I soon realized that he was a huge deal to everyone. When he was around, and I had the headphones on, I would get very nervous, but he was very cool. After a while it wasn't that big a deal for me to see him.

"Paul was hanging around once when Jude and I were discussing doing a cover song. Paul said, 'Have you heard my song *So Bad*?' I said, 'No.' He offered to get us a copy but of course Jude already had a copy of it. Jude felt that since Paul had suggested it, that it would be rude not to try it. We laid down a basic track of it with my vocals just before I had to leave for New York. When I returned, Paul told me that he had added something to it that he thought I might like. When Jude played it for me there were backing vocals and ad-libs that Paul had put on it. Jude was so star-struck that he completed it in a few takes feeling it wasn't his place to direct Paul. He told me, 'How am I supposed to produce Paul McCartney?' My sense was that Paul pretty much directed things and helped produce it. Initially, we didn't know if we were going to put it on the album, but when Paul put his backing vocals on it we couldn't leave it off! When I thanked Paul his only suggestion was that I should keep the vocals a bit more simple, so we changed a few things vocally to make it less involved. My dad really wanted to meet Paul. Paul was so cool. He told my dad about The Beatles' time in Germany and sang him *I Want To Hold Your Hand* in German. Later, Paul stopped in and said, 'This is my last day here and I want you to know that I think you're going to be a big star.' The experience with Paul was one of the highlights of my life."

Lindsay soon became known as the AOL (America On Line) Girl because her song *Everything U R* was used in their commercials. It was also the theme song for the WB TV show *Maybe It's Me* and included in the *American Pie 2* soundtrack. Lindsay says, "I toured in support of the album, but I became disillusioned with the music business, and just wanted to go back to Philadelphia and be a kid again. My parents were totally supportive of my decision." Pagano revived her musical career in 2007. For more information go to www.lindsaypaganomusic.com

Michael Parkinson, Jimmy Tarbuck, Tim Rice & Ringo Starr

Classified Document Vol. 2 [The Beatles]
Tiger Beat-TBRLP-1 (album 12") [unauthorized release] (xx/xx/88)
Producer: Graham Lindsay & Gill Stribling-Wright
Ringo Starr: Drums & Vocals; Barbara Bach: B. Vocals; Jimmy Tarbuck: Vocals & Piano; Tim Rice: Vocals; Michael Parkinson: B. Vocals; Harry Stoneham: Piano
Studio-B, BBC Television Centre, London, UK
12/12/81

Singing The Blues (M. Endsley) 2:56 (2/13)

Michael Parkinson was born on March 28, 1935 in Cudworth, England. He began working as a journalist for several UK newspapers before switching to TV in the mid-1960s. Since that time he has hosted numerous TV and radio shows in the UK. From 1971 to 1982, and from 1998 to 2004, he hosted the popular BBC TV talk show *Parkinson*, which then aired on ITV until his retirement in 2007. All of The Beatles appeared on one or more of Parkinson's shows. Parkinson was featured on the cover of Paul McCartney and Wing's 1973 album *Band On The Run*. McCartney included a portion of his 1999 appearance on the show in his 2007 video retrospective *The McCartney Years*. He also hosted the TV show *Parkinson In Australia* from 1979 to 1984. Ringo Starr and his wife Barbara Bach appeared on the show on December 12, 1981, and joined Parkinson and guests Tim Rice and Jimmy Tarbuck on *Singing The Blues*, mostly sung by Tarbuck, to close the show. They were backed by the show's band The Harry Stoneham Five. Starr and Bach also appeared on *Parkinson In Australia* the following year with Glenn Shorrock*. For more information go to www.michaelparkinson.tv

Tim Rice was born on November 10, 1944 in Amersham, England. He briefly worked for EMI in the mid-1960s. Several years later, he was producing recordings, including some for The Scaffold*, but soon embarked on a highly successful career as a lyricist. Some of his most notable works include his musical stage productions, with Andrew Lloyd Webber, of *Joseph And The Amazing Technicolor Dreamcoat* in 1967, *Jesus Christ Superstar* in 1970 and *Evita* in 1976; and the films *Aladdin* and *Beauty And The Beast* with Alan Menken, and *The Lion King* with Elton John*. He has won Grammy, Golden Globe and Tony Awards for his work. Rice was inducted into the Songwriters Hall of Fame in 1999. He is also a successful editor, author, and radio and TV personality. For more information go to www.timrice.co.uk

Jimmy Tarbuck was born on February 6, 1940 in Liverpool, England. He attended the same school as John Lennon. He is a comedian who is best known as the host of a number of UK TV shows from the 1960s to the present including *It's Tarbuck 65!*, *Winner Takes All*, *The Jimmy Tarbuck Show*, *Tarbuck's Luck*, *Tell Tarby*, *For One Night Only* and others. His daughter is actress Liza Tarbuck.

David Peel & The Lower East Side

John Lennon For President
Orange-ORA 005 (album 12") (11/11/80)
Producer: John Lennon & Yoko Ono
David Peel: Lead Vocals & Guitar; Yoko Ono: B. Vocals & Percussion; The Lower East Side: Instruments
Record Plant Studios, New York, NY probably 06/xx/72

Amerika (D. Peel) 9:29 (1/4)

The Pope Smokes Dope
Apple-SW 3391 (album 12") (04/17/72)
Producer: John Lennon & Yoko Ono [unless noted otherwise]
David Peel: Lead Vocals & (probable) Guitar; additionally one or more of the following: Eddie Mottau: Guitar; Chris Osborne: Guitar; Eddie Ryan: Drums; The Lower East Side Friends: Chorus; Tom Doyle: Guitar & B. Vocals; Bruce Bierman: B. Vocals; John Robertson: Guitar; Billy Minelli: Bass; Frank Lanci: Drums [unless noted otherwise]
Record Plant & probably Audio Techniques Studios†, New York, NY 12/13 & 22/71 & probably 04-09/xx/71† [unless noted otherwise]

The Ballad Of Bob Dylan (D. Peel) 3:19 (2/1)
Additionally: Lenny Mars: Harp, Piano, Banjo & Mandolin; Eddie Mottau: Guitar; Chris Osborne: Guitar
Record Plant Studios, New York, NY 12/22/71

The Ballad of New York City/John Lennon-Yoko Ono (D. Peel) 3:19 (1/6)
Additionally: **John Lennon: Dialogue**; Lenny Mars: Flutes; Eddie Mottau: Guitar; Chris Osborne: Guitar; Yoko Ono: Dialogue
Record Plant Studios, New York, NY 12/13/71

The Birth Control Blues (D. Peel [E. Sanders-T. Kupferberg-K. Weaver])
4:48 (2/5)
Producer: additionally probably David Peel†

The Chicago Conspiracy (D. Peel) 3:47 (2/2)
Producer: additionally probably David Peel†
Additionally: Lenny Mars: Flute & Percussion

Everybody's Smoking Marijuana (D. Peel) 4:06 (1/2)
Producer: additionally probably David Peel†

F Is Not A Dirty Word (Trad: D. Peel) 3:12 (1/3)
Record Plant Studios, New York, NY 12/13/71

The Hip Generation (D. Peel) 1:50 (2/3)
Record Plant Studios, New York, NY 12/13 & 22/71

The Hippie From New York City (D. Peel) 3:01 (1/4)
Additionally: Lenny Mars: Harp, Flute & Banjo
Record Plant Studios, New York, NY 12/14/71

I'm A Runaway (D. Peel) 3:39 (1/1)
Additionally: Lenny Mars: Flute, Percussion & Banjo; Yoko Ono: Percussion
Record Plant Studios, New York, NY 12/13/71

I'm Gonna Start Another Riot (D. Peel) 2:37 (2/4)
Producer: additionally probably David Peel†
Additionally: Lenny Mars: Percussion & Mandolin

McDonald's Farm (D. Peel) 3:13 (1/5)
Record Plant Studios, New York, NY 12/13/71

The Pope Smokes Dope (D. Peel) 2:15 (1/6)
Additionally: **John Lennon: Dialogue & (possible) B. Vocals**; Lenny Mars: Mandolin, Flute & Percussion
Record Plant Studios, New York, NY probably 11 &/or 12/xx/71

Unbootlegged 1 [The Beatles]
No Label Records-NLR 0101 (CD-R) [unauthorized release] (xx/xx/01)
Producer: probably Peter Baker
Westinghouse Broadcasting Studios, New York, NY 12/16/71; airdate: 01/13/72

The Ballad Of New York City/John Lennon-Yoko Ono [live] 3:42 (D. Peel) (4)
John Lennon: Tea Chest Bass & B. Vocals; David Peel: Lead Vocals & Guitar; Yoko Ono: Percussion; Frank Lanci: Congas; Billy Minelli: Bongos; Tom Doyle: Guitar; Lenny Mars: Flute; (probably) Sue Weiseseaberg: Tambourine

The Hippie From New York City [live] (D. Peel) 4:19 (2)
John Lennon: Tea Chest Bass & B. Vocals; David Peel: Lead Vocals & Guitar; Yoko Ono: Percussion; Jerry Rubin: Percussion; Tom Doyle: Guitar; Lenny Mars: Flute; Frank Lanci: Congas; Billy Minelli: Bongos; (probably) Sue Weiseseaberg: Tambourine

David Peel was born David Rosario in New York, New York on August 3, 1942. He gained notice in the 1960s in New York's Greenwich Village District as one of its most outrageous and controversial street singers. He recorded the albums *Have A Marijuana* in 1968 and *The American Revolution* in 1970 for Elektra Records.

In 1971 New York's radical activists introduced Peel to John Lennon, the Village's newest resident. Lennon admired Peel's raw, street-wise political message and outrageous humor, and offered to record Peel for Apple. Peel accompanied John and Yoko Ono* to Ann Arbor, Michigan for their performance at the *John Sinclair Freedom Rally* on December 10, 1971. Many in the audience first thought Peel, who somewhat resembled Lennon with his hair and round glasses, was Lennon until the Lennons appeared, and performed with backing from Peel and members of his band The Lower East Side.

Days after their performance in Ann Arbor the Lennons began producing Peel's album *The Pope Smokes Dope*. Peel says he began recording and producing the songs *I'm Gonna Start Another Riot*, *The Chicago Conspiracy*, *Birth Control Blues*, and probably *Everybody's Smoking Marijuana* in the spring or summer of 1971 at Audio Techniques Studios in New York. These songs were finished up, or completely re-recorded and produced by the Lennons at Record Plant Studios in New York. The album's controversial title and lyrics, and the promotional single, *F* [Fuck] *Is Not A Dirty Word*, could hardly have expected to receive airplay. Several publications state that John contributed backing vocals or played Dobro guitar on several of the songs on the album. John Robertson's (not the same person who plays on Peel's album) book *The Art & Music Of John Lennon* lists Lennon as playing Dobro guitar and singing backing vocals on *The Ballad of New York City/John Lennon - Yoko Ono* and *The Pope Smokes Dope*. Perhaps he's referring to John's dialogue at the beginning of these songs. [John did sing backing vocals and play washtub bass on *The Ballad Of New York City/John Lennon - Yoko Ono* and *The Hippie From New York City* when the Lennons invited Peel to appear with them on *The David Frost Show*, taped on December 16, 1971 and available on unauthorized releases.] Lower East Side guitarist Tom Doyle, and engineer Dennis Ferrante, who were present for some of the recordings for Peel's album, think John may have contributed backing vocals to *Hippie From New York City* and possibly to *I'm A Runaway*. Peel is highly skeptical of these claims and says, "I wish I could say John sang and played on my album, but I'm not aware of it and nobody told me he did. I'd never forget something like that! I know there are books that say he did, but it's never been confirmed. With 16 tracks I wasn't in control of everything; maybe they added something when I wasn't there, I don't know." Lenny Rothbart (a.k.a. Lenny Mars) says Eddie Mottau and Chris Osborne played guitar on *The Ballad of New York City/John Lennon - Yoko Ono*. Though Peel is credited as having written all the tracks on the album, *The Birth Control Blues* contains portions of The Fugs' songs *Saran Wrap*, *Slum Goddess* and *Nothing*.

By early 1972 the Lennons had teamed up with Elephant's Memory* who were their backup band for the Lennons' album *Some Time In New York City*. It includes the song *New York City*, which chronicles Lennon's introduction to Peel, and features a photo of Peel in performance with the Lennons in Ann Arbor on the album's jacket. Peel was instrumental in helping Lennon organize the *One To One* benefit concerts on August 30, 1972 at Madison Square Garden, and joined in the *Give Peace A Chance* encore. It was during this period that Lennon, in a battle with immigration to stay in the US, was advised to avoid radicals like Peel, and adopt a lower political profile.

Peel has since released several recordings highlighting his association with Lennon. Peel's 1977 album *Bring Back The Beatles* (Orange-6001) includes *My Fat Budgie* that adds Peel's music to Lennon's *A Spaniard In The Works* poem *The Fat Budgie*. The album also includes covers of songs by John Lennon and The Beatles. Peel's 1980 album *John Lennon For President* features interviews with the Lennons from the early 1970s. The album also contains the song *Amerika* produced by Lennon following sessions for *The Pope Smokes Dope* album, and first released on the soundtrack for the motion picture *Please Stand By* in which Peel appears.

David Peel is still active in the New York music scene and plans to issue his performance with the Lennons on *The David Frost Show* on CD. He continues to promote the memory of The Beatles and his admiration for John Lennon by attending the annual song rally held on John's birthday every October 9 in a portion of New York's Central Park called Strawberry Fields, dedicated to Lennon. For more information go to www.peelnyc.tripod.com

Carl Perkins

Artifacts III (Free As A Bird: 1981-1994)
Big Music-9 BIGBX 009.4 (BIG 4036) (Italy) [unauthorized release] (probably 02/xx/95)
Producer: George Martin
Paul McCartney: Keyboards, Guitar, Drums, Bass & B. Vocals; Carl Perkins: Lead Vocals
AIR Studios, Montserrat, West Indies probably 02/24/81

My Old Friend [original version] (C. Perkins) 3:20 (4-1)

Blue Suede Shoes (A Rockabilly Session With Carl Perkins And Friends Starring George Harrison, Ringo Starr, Eric Clapton, Rosanne Cash & Dave Edmunds)
Recall/Snapper-SDVD514 (DVD) (UK) (08/29/06) (xx/xx/86)
Producer: Dave Edmunds (music); Stephanie Bennett (film)
Limehouse Television Studios, London, UK 10/21/85; airdate: 01/01/86
[Also available on Snapper-SDPCD206(UK) (06/06/06)]
Blue Moon Of Kentucky [live] (M. Monroe) 1:23 (12b)
George Harrison: Guitar & B. Vocals; **Ringo Starr: Tambourine**; Carl Perkins: Lead Vocals & Guitar; Eric Clapton: Guitar & B. Vocals; Earl Slick: Acoustic Guitar; Dave Charles: Drums; Greg Perkins: Acoustic Guitar; Lee Rocker: Bass; John David: Bass; Mickey Gee: Guitar; Dave Edmunds: Acoustic Guitar & B. Vocals; Rosanne Cash: Percussion & B. Vocals; Slim Jim Phantom: Percussion; Geraint Watkins: Piano

Blue Suede Shoes [live] (C. Perkins) 3:10 (16)
Ringo Starr: Drums; **George Harrison: Guitar & B. Vocals**; Carl Perkins: Lead Vocals & Guitar; Mickey Gee: Guitar; Earl Slick: Acoustic Guitar; Dave Edmunds: Acoustic Guitar, Vocals & B. Vocals; Eric Clapton: Guitar & B. Vocals; Dave Charles: Drums; Geraint Watkins: Piano; Slim Jim Phantom: Drums; Lee Rocker: Bass; Rosanne Cash: Percussion

Blue Suede Shoes (encore) [live] (C. Perkins) 2:20 (17)
George Harrison: Vocals & Guitar; **Ringo Starr: Drums**; Carl Perkins: Vocals & Guitar; Mickey Gee: Guitar; Earl Slick: Acoustic Guitar; Dave Edmunds: Vocals & Acoustic Guitar; Eric Clapton: Guitar & B. Vocals; Dave Charles: Drums; Geraint Watkins: Piano; Slim Jim Phantom: Drums; Lee Rocker: Bass; Rosanne Cash: Percussion

Glad All Over [live] (A. Schroeder-S. Tepper-R. Bennett) 2:03 (13)
George Harrison: Vocals & Guitar; Ringo Starr: Tambourine; Carl Perkins: Vocals & Guitar; Eric Clapton: Guitar & B. Vocals; Earl Slick: Acoustic Guitar; Dave Charles: Drums; Greg Perkins: Acoustic Guitar; Lee Rocker: Bass; John David: Bass; Mickey Gee: Guitar; Dave Edmunds: Acoustic Guitar & B. Vocals; Rosanne Cash: Percussion & B. Vocals; Slim Jim Phantom: Percussion; Geraint Watkins: Piano

Gone Gone Gone (Gone All Down The Line) [live] (C. Perkins) 2:39 (15)
Ringo Starr: Drums; George Harrison: Guitar & B. Vocals; Carl Perkins: Lead Vocals & Guitar; Mickey Gee: Guitar; Earl Slick: Acoustic Guitar; Dave Edmunds: Acoustic Guitar, Vocals & B. Vocals; Eric Clapton: Guitar & B. Vocals; Dave Charles: Drums; Geraint Watkins: Piano; Slim Jim Phantom: Drums; Lee Rocker: Bass; Rosanne Cash: Percussion

Matchbox [live] [a.k.a. Matchbox Blues] (C. Perkins-trad. L. Jefferson) 3:48 (4)
Ringo Starr: Vocals & Drums; Carl Perkins: Vocals & Guitar; Eric Clapton: Vocals & Guitar; Dave Edmunds: Acoustic Guitar; Geraint Watkins: Piano; Mickey Gee: Guitar; John David: Bass

Night Train To Memphis/Amen [live] (B. Smith-M. Hughes-O. Bradley/trad.) 2:15 (12c)
George Harrison: Guitar & B. Vocals; **Ringo Starr: Tambourine**; Carl Perkins: Lead Vocals & Guitar; Eric Clapton: Guitar & B. Vocals; Earl Slick: Acoustic Guitar; Dave Charles: Drums; Greg Perkins: Acoustic Guitar; Lee Rocker: Bass; John David: Bass; Mickey Gee: Guitar; Dave Edmunds: Acoustic Guitar & B. Vocals; Rosanne Cash: Percussion & B. Vocals; Slim Jim Phantom: Percussion; Geraint Watkins: Piano

That's All Right (Mama) [live] (A. Crudup) 2:15 (12a)
George Harrison: Guitar & B. Vocals; **Ringo Starr: Tambourine**; Carl Perkins: Lead Vocals & Guitar; Eric Clapton: Guitar & B. Vocals; Earl Slick: Acoustic Guitar; Dave Charles: Drums; Greg Perkins: Acoustic Guitar; Lee Rocker: Bass; John David: Bass; Mickey Gee: Guitar; Dave Edmunds: Acoustic Guitar & B. Vocals; Rosanne Cash: Percussion & B. Vocals; Slim Jim Phantom: Percussion; Geraint Watkins: Piano

Whole Lotta Shakin' Goin' On [live] (J. Hall-D. Williams) 3:07 (14)

George Harrison: Guitar & B. Vocals; **Ringo Starr: Tambourine**; Carl Perkins: Lead Vocals & Guitar; Eric Clapton: Guitar & B. Vocals; Earl Slick: Acoustic Guitar; Dave Charles: Drums; Greg Perkins: Acoustic Guitar; Lee Rocker: Bass; John David: Bass; Mickey Gee: Guitar; Dave Edmunds: Acoustic Guitar & B. Vocals; Rosanne Cash: Percussion & B. Vocals; Slim Jim Phantom: Percussion; Geraint Watkins: Piano

The World Is Waiting For The Sunrise [live] (E. Lockhart-E. Seitz) 2:48(11)
George Harrison: Guitar Percussion & B. Vocals; Carl Perkins: Lead Guitar

Your True Love [live] (C. Perkins) 3:22 (10)
George Harrison: Vocals & Guitar; Carl Perkins: Vocals & Guitar; John David: Bass; David Charles: Drums; Dave Edmunds: Acoustic Guitar & B. Vocals; Geraint Watkins: Piano; Mickey Gee: Guitar

Go Cat Go
Dinosaur Entertainment-76401-84508-2 (10/15/96)

Distance Makes No Difference With Love (C. Perkins) 4:12 (4)
Producer: George Harrison
George Harrison: Slide Guitar, Bass, Keyboards & B. Vocals; Carl Perkins: Lead Vocals & Lead Guitar; Jim Capaldi: Drums
FPSHOT, UK 06/18-19 & 22/96

Honey Don't (C. Perkins) 2:43 (12)
Producer: Joe Walsh & Jim Nipar
Ringo Starr: Vocals; Carl Perkins: Vocals†; Billy Preston: Keyboards & B. Vocals; Jim Keltner: Drums; Levon Helm: B. Vocals & Drums; Nils Lofgren: Guitar & B. Vocals; Joe Walsh: Guitar; Rick Danko: Bass & B. Vocals; Clarence Clemons: Saxophone; Dr. John: Keyboards
Shoreline Amphitheater, Mountain View, CA 09/01/89 & StarStruck Studios, Nashville, TN† 07/xx/96

My Old Friend [duet version†] (C. Perkins) 3:21 (16)
Producer: Paul McCartney & George Martin
Paul McCartney: Piano, Guitar, Drums & Bass; Carl Perkins: Lead Vocals & Guitar; George Martin: String Arrangement
AIR Studios, Montserrat, West Indies & probably Hog Hill Mill Studios, Sussex or AIR Studios, London, UK† probably 02/24/81 & 04/xx/96†

Go Cat Go
Unapix-UPX 70131 (VHS) (02/xx/97)
Producer: Bob Maklevitch
Paul McCartney: B. Vocals & Acoustic Guitar; Carl Perkins: Lead Vocals & Electric Guitar [unless noted otherwise]
Backstage Liberty Bowl, Memphis, TN 04/27/93

Blue Suede Shoes (C. Perkins) 1:38 (6)
Additionally: **Paul McCartney: Vocals**

Lend Me Your Comb (K. Twamey-F. Wise-B. Weisman) 1:02 (4)
Additionally: **Paul McCartney: Vocals**

Matchbox [a.k.a. Matchbox Blues] (C. Perkins-trad. L. Jefferson) 1:15 (5)
Additionally: **Paul McCartney: Vocals**

Maybellene (C. Berry) 0:46 (3)

My Old Friend (C. Perkins) 3:23 (2)

The World Is Waiting For The Sunrise (E. Lockhart-E. Seitz) 1:08 (7)
Additionally: Carl Perkins: Electric Guitar (only)

George Harrison: It's Still Much Better Being A Guitar Player
Pebbles-P-02003/4 (CD-R) [unauthorized release] (xx/x/06)
George Harrison: Guitar; Carl Perkins: Lead Vocals & Guitar
Hard Rock Café, London, UK 06/15/92

Blue Suede Shoes [live] (C. Perkins) 0:49 (17)

Oobu Joobu with Paul McCartney [Various Artists]
Westwood One Entertainment-Shows #95 22-36 (promotional only) (05/27/95-09/02/950)
Producer: Eddy Pumer (overall production)
Paul McCartney: B. Vocals & Acoustic Guitar; Carl Perkins: Lead Vocals & Electric Guitar
Backstage Liberty Bowl, Memphis, TN 04/27/93

Your True Love (C. Perkins) 2:03 (95-32/4-2) (07/31/95)

Carl Perkins was born on April 9, 1932 near Tiptonville, Tennessee. The songs he heard black cotton pickers sing in the fields he worked as a boy spawned his love for music. He began his recording career in the mid-1950s at Sun Records, along with label mates Elvis Presley, Jerry Lee Lewis* and Johnny Cash*. [Perkins backed Cash during much of the '60s and '70s.] Perkins is regarded as one of the originators of rockabilly music. His first hit for Sun was *Blue Suede Shoes* in 1956, which was the label's first million- selling record. Shortly after it was released, Perkins was seriously injured in an auto accident. While he convalesced, Elvis successfully covered *Blue Suede Shoes* further slowing much of Perkins' momentum. Perkins' last song to chart for Sun was *Your True Love* in 1957.

The Beatles included nearly a dozen of Perkins' songs in their early repertoire. George Harrison was a huge fan and fashioned much of his guitar style after Perkins. The Beatles performed Perkins' song *Sure To Fall* during their Decca Records audition in early 1962. Carl's son Stan says, "My dad's first tour of the UK was with Chuck Berry*. It was a crucial time because my dad's career and personal life had pretty much hit bottom. The Beatles wanted to throw a party in their honor. Chuck didn't go but my dad went. He said they kept him up late playing, and picking his brain about his music. They invited him to their recording session at Abbey Road [June 1, 1964]. Ringo Starr asked him if he could record some of his old songs [*Matchbox*], which he had no problem with because he was struggling at the time and the royalties from their recordings of his songs were much needed. That successful tour of the UK, and meeting The Beatles, were instrumental in restoring my dad's confidence as a musician, and was a turning point in his personal life and career." Carl stated in interviews that he and The Beatles jammed on *Your True Love* and that The Beatles also did covers that day of his songs *Sawdust Dance Floor*, *Your True Love* and *Sure To Fall*. If they were recorded, they apparently no longer exist. Several months later, The Beatles also recorded Perkins' songs *Honey Don't* and *Everybody's Trying To Be My Baby*, virtually guaranteeing Perkins a fat royalty check. [The Beatles' covers of Perkins' songs, *Sure To Fall*, *Blue Suede Shoes*, *Glad All Over* and *Lend Me Your Comb* appear on their mid-1990's albums *Live At The BBC*, *Anthology 1* and *Anthology 3*.]

Paul McCartney invited Perkins to AIR Studios in Montserrat for a week in February 1981. The two warmed up on a number of Perkins' classics, including *Honey Don't*, *Boppin' The Blues* and *Lend Me Your Comb*. Perkins played his distinctive rockabilly guitar and shared vocals with Paul on the song *Get It*, which appears on McCartney's album *Tug Of War*. The night before Perkins left Montserrat, he wrote the song *My Old Friend* in thanks to Paul. Paul was said to have been moved to tears by the song, and Perkins' gesture, and they recorded it, though it wasn't released until 1996.

Harrison's good friend Dave Edmunds* was instrumental in putting together the TV special *Blue Suede Shoes (A Rockabilly Session with Carl Perkins and Friends Starring George Harrison, Ringo Starr, Eric Clapton, Rosanne Cash and Dave Edmunds)*, which aired on January 1, 1986. Along with their backing Perkins', Harrison sang *Everybody's Trying To Be My Baby* and Ringo sang *Honey Don't*. Also performed, but not aired, were *Right String (But The Wrong Yo-Yo)* and *Sure To Fall*. Perkins had also sent out invitations to McCartney who declined, possibly fearing the spectacle of a Beatles reunion.

Stan Perkins recalls, "I first met George when he flew us all to England. He had a car take us to his Friar Park home. He greeted us at the door and showed us his garden. I think we were all a little nervous meeting each other. He looked up to my dad the way I looked up to George and The Beatles. We went into his studio and jammed a bit, though it wasn't taped. He had a jukebox with nothing but Sun's records on it, including all of my dad's records on Sun. He was a really gracious host – a down-home kind of guy, not flamboyant or pretentious. What you saw was what you got. We were all comfortable and could be ourselves. He genuinely admired my dad, not only as a musician but as a man, and they became really good friends."

Perkins was inducted into the Rock and Roll Hall of Fame in 1987. He performed *Honey Don't* and *That's All Right (Mama)* with Harrison and Joe Brown (see Vicki Brown) at HandMade Film's 10th Anniversary celebration in London on October 1, 1988. A portion of the latter song, with Harrison on lead vocals, is available on unauthorized releases. Harrison also joined Perkins during his performance of *Everybody's Trying To Be My Baby*, *Honey Don't* and *Blue Suede Shoes* at London's Hard Rock Café on June 15, 1992. A portion of *Blue Suede Shoes* from that performance is available on unauthorized releases. Harrison was scheduled to produce an album for Perkins, but Perkins became ill with throat cancer. Perkins fought off the disease and resumed his career.

McCartney covered Perkins' song *Matchbox* on his 1990 album *Tripping The Live Fantastic*. McCartney had just finished a sound check for his performance at the Liberty Bowl in Memphis, Tennessee on April 27, 1993 when he was greeted backstage by Perkins and his film crew who were working on a possible TV special. Perkins correctly predicted that Paul would be eager to jam with him for the cameras. They taped *Get It*, and *Your True Love* (featured on McCartney's 1995 radio series *Oobu Joobu*), *Blue Suede Shoes*, *Lend Me Your Comb*,

Maybellene, *Matchbox*, *My Old Friend* and *The World Is Waiting For The Sunrise* (available only on the 1997 Carl Perkins' VHS release *Go Cat Go*.) According to Stan, McCartney also jammed on *Movie Magg*, *Right String (But The Wrong Yo-Yo)* and a couple of gospel songs with Carl. Perkins performed *Rave On* with McCartney at Paul's annual Buddy Holly birthday celebration in London on September 7, 1995. Stan says, "I've met Paul a few times and was a part of one of his annual Buddy Holly celebrations. He's always been very cordial."

In June 1996 Perkins recorded his composition *Distance Makes No Difference With Love* with help from Harrison at FPSHOT. The song was included on Perkins' 1996 album *Go Cat Go*. The album also includes *My Old Friend* with newly added duet vocals by McCartney. [The original recording is available on unauthorized releases.] Ringo contributed a previously unreleased, alternate version of *Honey Don't*, from his 1989 All-Starr Band tour, to the album, with vocal overdubs by Carl. [Ringo covered *Sure To Fall* on his 1981 album *Stop And Smell The Roses*.] The album also includes Lennon's performance of *Blue Suede Shoes* from the Plastic Ono Band's album *Live Peace In Toronto 1969*.

Perkins performed at the *Music For Montserrat* benefit concert at London's Royal Albert Hall on September 15, 1997. The benefit, organized by George Martin*, also included a performance by McCartney whom Perkins backed during the encore. McCartney covered Perkins' song *Movie Magg* on his 1999 album *Run Devil Run*. Stan says, "Paul also really loved my dad and his music. We made an agreement with McCartney's publishing company [in 2003] to administer my dad's song publishing rights, which has been a good association. Paul wanted to buy the catalogue but I told him it was going to cost him a hell of a lot more than the pennies he paid for the Buddy Holly catalogue, so we still own the rights."

Perkins died on January 19, 1998. Harrison performed *Your True Love* at his funeral and McCartney sent a video tribute. Stan recalls, "Several weeks after the funeral, George invited me to meet with him in Los Angeles when we were both scheduled to be there. Before I went, I asked the Rock and Roll Hall of Fame to return the guitar my father played in the TV special with George and Ringo. When George came to my hotel room I pulled out the guitar and I told him, 'I can't think of anyone more deserving of this than you.' Tears flowed down his cheeks, and he reminisced for several hours about how much my dad had meant to him and The Beatles. He said he seriously doubted he would have ever played guitar had it not have been for my dad's music. He said The Beatles borrowed my dad's records from sailors in Liverpool who had brought them back from America, and learned to play them. He said my dad was such an inspiration that he used the stage name Carl for a time [during The Beatles' tour of Scotland in 1960]. He had just undergone massive radiation treatment for throat cancer and was very curious as to how my dad had responded to the same treatments. He was frail but I knew from his attitude that he wasn't fearful of death. He was such a spiritual man. I could see he was at peace with himself and where he was at in his life. It was the last time I saw him, though he continued to call to see how our family was doing until he became really sick, which was a huge honor. It was a privilege to know him." It was reported at the time that Stan turned over some of Carl's recordings to Harrison for possible use on a future Traveling Wilburys' album.

Peter & Gordon

The Ultimate Peter & Gordon
Collectors' Choice Music/Capitol Special Markets-CCM-189-2/72435-31063-2-4 (08/14/01)
Producer: Norman Newell [unless noted otherwise]
Peter Asher: Vocals; Gordon Waller: Vocals

A World Without Love (J. Lennon-**P. McCartney**) 2:37 (1) (02/28/64)
Additionally: Vic Flick: Guitar; Geoff Love: Arrangement
EMI-Abbey Road Studios, London, UK 01/21/64

I Don't Want To See You Again (J. Lennon-**P. McCartney**) Intro: 0:15/1:59 Outro: 0:10 (3) (09/11/64) Additionally: **Paul McCartney: Dialogue**
EMI-Abbey Road Studios, London, UK 08/11/64

Nobody I Know (J. Lennon-**P. McCartney**) 2:30 (2) (05/29/64)
Additionally: Eddie King: Guitar; Geoff Love: Arrangement

EMI-Abbey Road Studios, London, UK 01/21/64

Woman (J. Lennon-**P. McCartney**) 2:24 (11) (01/10/66)
Producer: John Burgess
Additionally: **Paul McCartney: Arrangement**; Bob Leaper: Arrangement & Conductor
EMI-Abbey Road Studios, London, UK 12/31/65

Peter & Gordon were Peter Asher, born on June 22, 1944 in London, England and Gordon Waller, born on June 4, 1945 in Braemar, Scotland. Asher's mother Margaret was an instructor at the Guildhall School of Music where one of her students was George Martin*. Asher and Waller met in school as a result of their mutual interest in music, and began to develop a style reminiscent of The Everly Brothers*.

They were signed to EMI's Columbia label in January 1964. At the time, rooming next to Peter at his family's home in London was his sister's boyfriend, Paul McCartney. McCartney offered Peter his composition *A World Without Love*. It was rejected by The Beatles and originally intended for Billy J. Kramer (see Billy J. Kramer with The Dakotas). It was the first of four Top 20 hits McCartney contributed to Peter & Gordon, and their only number one. Asher says he still possesses McCartney's demo acetate of it.

Peter & Gordon released the McCartney compositions *Nobody I Know* in May and *I Don't Want To See You Again* in September 1964. [The version of *I Don't Want To See You Again* on the 2001 CD *The Ultimate Peter & Gordon* includes an introduction by McCartney.] By the end of 1964 the Lennon and McCartney songwriting team had drastically reduced the number of compositions they handed out to other artists. Peter & Gordon's next hits were *I Go To Pieces*, given to them by Del Shannon*, and a memorable version of Buddy Holly's *True Love Ways* in 1965. They also covered The Beatles' song *If I Fell*.

McCartney, tired of criticism that the Lennon-McCartney songwriting moniker guaranteed chart success, used the pseudonyms Bernard Webb, and the less common A. Smith, as the composer of *Woman*. It was his final contribution to Peter & Gordon and was a Top 20 hit in 1966 proving his point. Asher says he and McCartney picked the name Bernard Webb. McCartney told him that if he was asked why the song was published by McCartney's publishing company Northern Songs, he was to say that Webb was an old schoolmate of Paul's and that he did it as a favor, but his cover story was soon blown. Asher says none of The Beatles contributed directly to any of their recordings but that McCartney attended an early session for *Woman*. Asher recalls, "We cut the song twice. Paul was there the first day we started cutting it. He had some arrangement ideas, some of which our producer ignored, which is why I think Paul didn't come back. He wanted the song to be much smaller, and what [producer] John Burgess did was take Paul's ideas and then have [arranger] Bob Leaper turn them into a very big orchestration, which Paul and I weren't crazy about. In retrospect Paul was right. It was a great song and we could have made a better record." [During filmed portions of The Beatles' *Let It Be* rehearsals in 1969, McCartney discussed his preference for Peter & Gordon's earlier take of *Woman*, and wondered if Asher still had The Beatles' acetate of it.] Peter & Gordon also had hits in 1966 with *Lady Godiva* and *Knight In Rusty Armour*, and were a supporting act for The Beatles' tour of Germany and the Far East that year.

Peter & Gordon's folk style floundered during the psychedelic era of 1967 and 1968, and the duo drifted apart. Gordon began recording as a solo artist and later took some bit acting parts. Peter embarked on a career as a record producer with the recording of *And The Sun Will Shine* for Paul Jones*. He then became Apple's A&R Manager. Asher says his leaving Apple had nothing to do with his sister and McCartney breaking up, and everything to do with the arrival of Allen Klein. He left the UK, and became James Taylor's* full-time producer and manager following their departure from Apple. Later, he produced Linda Ronstadt, Randy Newman, Neil Diamond, Diana Ross, Cher, Bonnie Raitt and many others. Asher has twice received a Grammy Award for Producer Of The Year. He produced a song on Ringo's 1992 album *Time Takes Time*.

Peter & Gordon have been guests at conventions and festivals for fans of The Beatles, and performed together. McCartney sent them a congratulatory message on their reunion in 2006. They were reportedly scheduled to perform at the 2006 Adopt-A-Minefield gala with McCartney that was later cancelled due to his divorce proceedings with wife Heather Mills*. Asher joined Ringo Starr's All-Starr Band during their performance of *With A Little Help From My Friends* at Mandalay Bay in Las Vegas on July 1, 2006. Jane Asher has had a successful acting career in the UK. Gordon Waller died on July 17, 2009. For more information go to www.peterandgordon.net, www.gordonwaller.com

Playback [Tom Petty And The Heartbreakers]
MCA-11367-9 (DVD) (12/12/00) (xx/xx/95)
Producer: Joanne Sellar (film); Jeff Lynne, with Tom Petty & Mike Campbell (music)
George Harrison: Acoustic Guitar & B. Vocals; Tom Petty: Lead Vocals, Acoustic & Electric Guitar; Howie Epstein: B. Vocals; Mike Campbell: Acoustic & Electric Guitar; Jeff Lynne: Keyboards, B. Vocals, Bass, Acoustic & Electric Guitar; Phil Jones: Drums
Pinewood Studios, London, UK (film), M.C. Studios, Los Angeles, CA, (music) xx/xx/88 or xx/xx/89

I Won't Back Down (T. Petty-J. Lynne) 3:07 (10)
[Also available on *Full Moon Fever.* MCA-MCAD-6253 (2) (04/24/89)]

Songs And Music From The Motion Picture SHE'S THE ONE [Tom Petty And The Heartbreakers]
Warner Bros.-9 46285-2 (08/06/96)
Producer: Rick Rubin, Tom Petty & Mike Campbell
Ringo Starr: Drums; Tom Petty: Lead Vocals & probably one or more of the following: Guitar, Bass, Harmonica, Tambourine, Harpsichord & Piano; Mike Campbell: probably one or more of the following: Marxophone, Guitar, Bass & Piano; Benmont Tench: Keyboards; Howie Epstein: Bass, B. Vocals; Carl Wilson: B. Vocals
Sound City &/or Village Recorders &/or Andora Studios, Los Angeles, CA xx/xx/96

Hung Up And Over Due (T. Petty) 5:48 (14)

Wildflowers
Warner Bros.-9 45759-2 (11/01/94)
Producer: Rick Rubin, Tom Petty & Mike Campbell
Ringo Starr: Drums; Tom Petty: Lead Vocals & Acoustic Guitars; Mike Campbell: Electric Guitar, Coral Sitar & Bass; Lenny Castro: Percussion; Benmont Tench: Tack Piano & Zenon
Ocean Way Studios &/or Sound City Studios, Los Angeles, CA mid/xx/94

To Find A Friend (T. Petty) 3:21 (11)

Tom Petty was born on October 20, 1950 in Gainesville, Florida. A chance meeting with Elvis Presley at an early age and seeing The Beatles on *The Ed Sullivan Show* set Petty on his path to rock stardom. He started playing in rock bands during high school. Several years later, his band Mudcrutch was getting much notice in the Southeastern US, so they headed to Los Angeles where they secured a contract with Shelter Records.

Petty, and Mudcrutch members Benmont Tench and Mike Campbell, joined forces with Ron Blair and Stan Lynch. Under their new name they released the self-titled album *Tom Petty And The Heartbreakers* in 1976. The band acquired a cult following by echoing the styles of Bob Dylan* and The Byrds. Their first Top 10 hit was *Don't Do Me Like That* in 1979. During the 1980s they had Top 20 hits with *Refugee, The Waiting, Jammin' Me, You Got Lucky* and *Don't Come Around Here No More.* Despite disputes with record companies, solo projects, personal problems and personnel changes, the band remains active and successful. They have received over a dozen Grammy Awards and were inducted into the Rock and Roll Hall of Fame in 2002.

In 1988 Petty teamed up with George Harrison, Jeff Lynne*, Roy Orbison*, and Bob Dylan to form the Traveling Wilburys. Petty's highly successful 1989 solo album *Full Moon Fever* includes the Top 10 hits *Free Fallin'*, and the Top 20 songs *You Don't Know How It Feels* and *I Won't Back Down.* Harrison plays on, and appears in the music video for, *I Won't Back Down.* Ringo Starr also appears in the video though he doesn't play on the recording. Petty helped Harrison write the lyrics to his 1989 song *Cheer Down.* The Traveling Wilburys released their second album in 1990, and Tom Petty and The Heartbreakers released *Into The Great Wide Open* in 1991, which thanks "the entire Wilbury family," though Harrison didn't contribute to it.

Petty backed Ringo singing *I Call Your Name* as a contribution to *The John Lennon Scholarship Concert* on May 5, 1990 in Liverpool. The song is included on the 1991 video release *The World's Greatest Artists Sing LENNON A Tribute.* In 1991 Petty was part of The Peace Choir, organized by Yoko Ono* and John Lennon's son Sean, who made a recording of Lennon's song *Give Peace A Chance.*

The Heartbreakers contributed to Ringo's 1992 album *Time Takes Time.* However, Petty only played on the track *Call Me*, which the producer Jeff Lynne claims will never be released.

Ringo plays drums on *To Find A Friend* on Petty's 1994 solo album *Wildflowers.* Ringo also plays drums on the song *Hung Up And Overdue* from Tom Petty And The Heartbreakers' soundtrack album to the film *She's The One.* Petty contributed to Ringo's 1998 album *Vertical Man.*

Petty was a part of the Harrison tribute *Concert For George* in 2002. Tom inducted George Harrison into the Rock and Roll Hall of Fame in 2004. Harrison was featured in the Tom Petty And The Heartbreakers documentary *Runnin' Down A Dream* (Warner Bros.-121916-2 DVD) in 2008. For more information go to www.tom-petty.com

Platinumweird

Make Believe
Weapons Of Mass Entertainment/Interscope-B0007839-72 (10/10/06)
Producer: Dave Stewart & John Shanks [& probably Dennis Douglas]
Probably Mayfair Studios & Basing Street Studios, London, UK probably xx/xx/05 & Whatinthewhatthe? Studio, Los Angeles, CA probably 03/18/06)
Ringo Starr: Drums; Erin Grace (Kara DioGuardi): Lead Vocals; Dave Stewart: Guitar; Mark Hudson: Bass

If You Believe In Love (K. DioGuardi-D. Stewart) 3:27 (1-6)

Make Believe (E. Grace [K. DioGuardi]-D. Stewart) 3:31 (1-4)

Platinumweird is a collaboration between Dave A. Stewart, born on September 9, 1952 in Sunderland, England and Kara DioGuardi, born on December 9, 1970 in Ossining, New York. Dave met Kara while producing an album for Anastasia in 2003. Dave is best known as the guitarist, songwriter and producer for the duo Eurythmics with Annie Lennox, who between 1983 and 1986 had a number one hit with *Sweet Dreams (Are Made Of This)*, Top Five hits with *Here Comes The Rain Again* and *Would I Lie To You*, and Top 20 hits with *Sisters Are Doin' It For Themselves* and *Missionary Man.* Stewart has worked with many artists including Mick Jagger*, Bob Dylan*, Aretha Franklin* and Tom Petty*. Kara is one of the most prolific and successful songwriters of her generation. She has also produced and sang backing vocals on many of her compositions for other artists. Some of the many artists who have benefited from her talents include Avril Lavigne, Britney Spears, Celine Dion, Ashlee and Jessica Simpson, Backstreet Boys, Christina Aguilera, Enrique Iglesias, Ricky Martin, Marc Anthony, Faith Hill, Gwen Stefani, Santana, Jewel, Kelly Clarkson, Pussycat Dolls and Pink. She has received numerous BMI awards for her songs. She is also a judge on FOX TV's *American Idol.*

Stewart had a long friendship with George Harrison. Portions of the first Traveling Wilburys' album were recorded at Dave's home. He says that in the mid-1990s Harrison asked him to produce his next album, but he turned him down feeling he would have to commit too much time and couldn't do it justice. Portions of an interview that Stewart conducted at Harrison's request appeared in the electronic press kit for the 2001 reissue of the Harrison album *All Things Must Pass.* Stewart was music producer for the New York tribute concert *Come Together: A Night For John Lennon's Words & Music* shortly after the attacks of September 11, 2001. Paul McCartney and Stewart wrote the song *Whole Life* in 1995 (though not a song reportedly titled *Cello In The Ruins*). Stewart plays acoustic guitar on McCartney's recording of *Whole Life* in 2003, which appears on the 2004 Spanish charity EP *Year One On 46664* (El Diablo!/Coca Cola-8431905008082).

The *Make Believe* album by Platinumweird couldn't be more appropriately titled, as Stewart says, "We purposely are not disclosing lots of the information." Platinumweird's lead singer Erin Grace is a fictitious name for a fictitious group. The hoax was perpetrated by Dave and Kara (a.k.a. Erin Grace) and Jimmy Iovine of Interscope Records as a marketing ploy to promote Platinumweird's album. The story goes that *Make Believe* was an unfinished album by a short-lived group of Stewart's called Platinumweird from 1974. It was actually recorded in the mid-2000s around the same time as the new *Platinumweird* album, included with some copies of *Make Believe.* Dave went so far as to use all vintage 1970s equipment to recreate the sound. Fake Internet fans sites were set up, some with several songs including an alternate recording of Harrison's *This Guitar (Can't Keep From Crying).* It was re-recorded by Harrison in 1992 at Stewart's apartment, and finished off by Dave, Harrison's son Dhani, Ringo Starr and

Kara in March 2006. In mid-2006 VH1 TV aired the (mock) documentary *Rock Legends – Platinum Weird* narrated by Dan Aykroyd about the long lost, legendary mid-1970's band featured comments from Mick Jagger, Annie Lennox, Elton John*, Stevie Nicks, Dhani, Ringo and others. Some of the events recounted in the special are loosely based on Stewart's life. Ringo is credited on *Make Believe* as drumming on *If You Believe In Love* and *Make Believe*, but are the credits also make believe? Ringo collaborator, Mark Hudson* says, "The Platinumweird stuff was Dave coming to my studio and playing the tracks to Ringo and me. We then put Ringo on drums, with me on bass, and gave it back to Dave." Dave made a guest appearance during Ringo Starr And His All-Starr Band's encore on July 1, 2006 at Mandalay Bay in Las Vegas. Stewart helped produce and performs on Ringo's 2008 album *Liverpool 8*, and performed with Ringo in support of the album and appears in the video for the title track. He also hosted *Ringo Starr: Off The Record*, which aired on HBO that year. The two are working together on a stage musical called *Hople In The Fence*. Dave contributed to Ringo's 2010 album *Y Not*. For more information go to www.platinumweird.com, www.davestewart.com, www.karadioguardi.com

Duffy Power (with the Graham Bond Quartet)

Leapers And Sleepers
RPM Records-RPM D240 (EU) (08/26/02)
Producer: Ron Richards & [Ken Jones]
Duffy Power; Vocals; Ginger Baker: Drums; Jack Bruce: Bass; Graham Bond: Keyboards

I Saw Her Standing There (original "rejected" version) (Lennon-**P. McCartney)** 2:29 (1-6)
EMI Abbey Road Studios, London, UK 02/xx/63
Additionally: John McLaughlin: Guitar

I Saw Her Standing There (remake, single version) (J. Lennon-**P. McCartney)** 2:27 (1-7) (04/26/63)
EMI Abbey Road Studios, London, UK 03/20/63
Additionally: Jim Sullivan: Guitar

Duffy Power was born Ray Howard on September 9, 1941 in London, England. His stage name (taken from actor Howard Duff and Tyrone Power) came at the suggestion of his promoter, Larry Parnes. Power says, "While on tour in 1960, George Harrison and Paul McCartney showed up at the stage door in Liverpool. I chatted with them later at the Jacaranda Coffee Bar in Liverpool for some time and was impressed." In early 1963 Power was singing R&B with the Graham Bond Quartet, which included John McLaughlin, Ginger Baker (see Blind Faith, Cream) and Jack Bruce*. In the February 1, 1963 edition of *NME* magazine, Paul McCartney talks about The Beatles writing the song *Misery* for Helen Shapiro (see: Kenny Lynch) and another song for Duffy Power, which he was going to record. Some days later, Power recorded *I Saw Her Standing There*, a McCartney composition dating back to 1961 and a staple of The Beatles' stage act by 1962. The Beatles recorded the song on February 11, 1963 for their first album *Please Please Me* released on March 22, 1963. The Beatles were fond of Power and his group, but Power wasn't a fan of pop music and wasn't crazy about *I Saw Her Standing There*, though he realized it had commercial potential. Power explains, "It was through my manager via George Martin* that I was informed that The Beatles thought my version was too jazzy. I was dismayed as I was desperate to have a record released with the Graham Bond Quartet, so I re-recorded it, but wasn't that interested in The Beatles' compositions then. My understanding is that the song was for me, and I didn't know that they would release a version themselves. I never heard what they thought of my second version." Power's re-recorded version was first issued as a single (Parlophone R 5024) on April 26, 1963. Though The Beatles' version of the song was released first, they contributed the song to Power for release. Both of his versions of *I Saw Her Standing There* were released on *Leapers And Sleepers* in 2002. Power and the Graham Bond Quartet were guests on their BBC *Pop Go The Beatles* radio show taped on July 2 and broadcast on July 16, 1963.

Power later worked with The Paramounts (see Gary Brooker) and Alexis Korner's Blues Incorporated. He released a self-titled solo album in 1972 but never found any degree of commercial success. He continues to dabble in music and write songs.

Billy Preston

The Concert For Bangla Desh
Apple/Rhino-R2 970481 (DVD) (10/25/05)
Producer: George Harrison & Allen Klein (film); **George Harrison** & Phil Spector (music)
George Harrison: Rhythm Guitar; **Ringo Starr: Drums**; Billy Preston: Lead Vocals & Keyboards; Leon Russell: Piano; Jim Keltner: Drums; Eric Clapton: Lead Guitar; Jesse Ed Davis: Rhythm Guitar; Klaus Voormann: Bass; Carl Radle: Bass; Alan Beutler: B. Vocals; Marlin Greene: B. Vocals; Jeanie Greene: B. Vocals; Joe Green: B. Vocals; Dolores Hall: B. Vocals; Jackie Kelso: B. Vocals; Claudia Lennear: B. Vocals; Lou McCreary: B. Vocals; Don Nix: B. Vocals; Don Preston: B. Vocals; Pete Ham: Acoustic Guitar; Joey Molland: Acoustic Guitar; Tom Evans: Acoustic Guitar; Mike Gibbons: Percussion
Madison Square Garden, New York, NY 08/01/71 (afternoon or evening)

That's The Way God Planned It [live] (B. Preston) 4:30 (1-6) (10/xx/83)
[Also available on Apple/Capitol-0946335880 28 (1-6) (10/25/05) (12/20/71)]

Concert For George
WSM-R2 970241 (DVD) (11/18/03)
Producer: Jeff Lynne (audio); Ray Cooper, Olivia Harrison & Jon Kamen
Paul McCartney: Piano & B. Vocals; Ringo Starr: Drums; Billy Preston: Lead Vocals & Keyboards; Eric Clapton: Acoustic Guitar & B. Vocals; Jeff Lynne: Acoustic Guitar; Dhani Harrison: Acoustic Guitar; Jim Keltner: Drums; Jim Horn: Alto Sax; Ray Cooper: Percussion; Jim Capaldi: Tambourine; Gary Brooker: Keyboards & B. Vocals; Andy Fairweather Low: Electric Guitar & B. Vocals; Tom Scott: Tenor Saxophone; Samantha Brown: B. Vocals; Tessa Niles: B. Vocals; Katie Kissoon: B. Vocals; Dave Bronze: Bass; Albert Lee: Electric Guitar; Marc Mann: Electric Guitar; Chris Stainton: Keyboards; Henry Spinetti: Drums; Phil Capaldi: Percussion; London Metropolitan Orchestra (Andrew Brown, Roger Chase, Chris Fish, Helen Hathorn, Lynda Houghton, Ian Humphries, Zoe Martlew, Stella Page & Debbie Widdup); Michael Kamen: String Arranger & Conductor
Royal Albert Hall, London, UK 11/29/02

My Sweet Lord [live] (G. Harrison) 4:55 (1-24)
[Also available on WSM-R2 74546 (2-18)]

Encouraging Words
Apple-CDP 0777 7 81279 2 5 (05/18/93) (09/11/70)
Producer: George Harrison & Billy Preston [unless noted otherwise]
One or more of the following studios: Olympic, Apple, Trident &/or EMI-Abbey Road, London, UK 04-06/xx/70 [unless noted otherwise]

All That I've Got (I'm Gonna Give It To You) (B. Preston-D. Troy) 3:35 (15) (01/30/70)
Producer: George Harrison
Ringo Starr: (probable) Drums; **George Harrison: (possible) Bass**; Billy Preston: Lead Vocals & Keyboards; possibly one or more of the following: Alan White: Drums; Jim Gordon: Drums & Percussion; Klaus Voormann: Bass; Carl Radle: Bass; Bobby Keys: Horns
One or more of the following studios: Olympic, Apple, Trident &/or EMI-Abbey Road, London, UK 11/xx/69

All Things Must Pass (**G. Harrison**) 3:41 (12)
George Harrison: (probable) Guitar; **Ringo Starr: (possible) Drums**; Billy Preston: Lead Vocals & Keyboards; probably one or more of the following: Klaus Voormann: Bass; Carl Radle: Bass; Alan White: Drums; Jim Gordon: Drums; John Barham: Orchestral Arrangements

As Long As I Got My Baby (B. Preston) 2:43 (14)
Ringo Starr: (possible) Drums &/or Percussion; Billy Preston: Lead Vocals & Keyboards; probably one or more of the following: Otis Williams: B. Vocals; Eddie Kendricks: B. Vocals; Paul Williams: B. Vocals; Melvin Franklin: B. Vocals; Dennis Edwards: B. Vocals; The Funk Brothers (probably the following: Andrew Smith, Richard Allen or Uriel Jones: Drums; Eddie Watkins, James Jamerson or Bob Babbitt: Bass; Dennis Coffey or Melvin Ragin: Guitar; possibly one or more of the following: Klaus Voormann: Bass; Carl Radle: Bass; Alan White: Drums &/or Percussion; Jim Gordon: Drums &/or Percussion
One or more of the following studios: Olympic, Apple, Trident &/or EMI-Abbey Road, London, UK probably 04-06/xx/70 &/or possibly in Stockholm or Gothenburg, Sweden† or possibly 12/08-09, 13-14/69†

Encouraging Words (B. Preston) 3:32 (11)
George Harrison: Guitar; **Ringo Starr: Drums**; Billy Preston: Lead Vocals & Keyboards; Eric Clapton: Guitar; Klaus Voormann: Bass; Doris Troy: B. Vocals
Trident &/or Apple Studios, London, UK 04/xx/70

I Don't Want To Pretend (B. Preston) 2:35 (10)
George Harrison: (probable) Guitar; **Ringo Starr: (probable) Drums**; Billy Preston: Lead

Vocals & Keyboards; probably one or more of the following: Alan White: Drums; Jim Gordon: Drums; Klaus Voormann: Bass; Carl Radle: Bass

I've Got A Feeling (J. Lennon-P. McCartney) 2:50 (7)
Ringo Starr: (possible) Drums; Billy Preston: Lead Vocals & Keyboards; probably one or more of the following: Alan White: Drums; Jim Gordon: Drums; Klaus Voormann: Bass; Carl Radle: Bass

Let The Music Play (B. Preston-J. Greene-J. Kirkland) 2:41 (5)
Ringo Starr: (possible) Drums &/or Percussion; Billy Preston: Lead Vocals & Keyboards; probably one or more of the following: Alan White: Drums &/or Percussion; Jim Gordon: Drums & Percussion

Little Girl (B. Preston) 3:25 (2)
Ringo Starr: (possible) Drums; Billy Preston: Lead Vocals & Keyboards; probably one or more of the following: Alan White: Drums; Jim Gordon Drums; Klaus Voormann: Bass; Carl Radle: Bass; John Barham: Orchestral Arrangement

My Sweet Lord (**G. Harrison**) 3:19 (4)
George Harrison: (possible) Guitar; Billy Preston: Lead Vocals & Keyboards; Alan White: Drums; Edwin Hawkins Singers: B. Vocals; probably one of the following: Klaus Voormann: Bass; Carl Radle: Bass
Olympic Studios, London, UK 04-06/xx/70

Right Now (B. Preston) 3:12 (1)
George Harrison: Guitar & B. Vocals; **Ringo Starr: Drums**; Billy Preston: Lead Vocals & Keyboards; Eric Clapton: Guitar; Klaus Voormann: Bass; Doris Troy: B. Vocals
Apple &/or Trident Studios, London, UK 04-06/xx/70

The Same Thing Again (B. Preston-Herndon) 4:30 (6)
Billy Preston: Lead Vocals & Keyboards; probably the following: Bobby Keys: Horns; Klaus Voormann: Bass; Carl Radle: Bass

Sing One For The Lord (**G. Harrison**-B. Preston) 3:46 (8)
George Harrison: (probable) Guitar & (possible) Synthesizer; **Ringo Starr: (probable) Drums**; Billy Preston: Lead Vocals & Keyboards; probably one or more of the following: Klaus Voormann: Bass; Carl Radle: Bass

Use What You Got (B. Preston) 4:18 (3)
George Harrison: (possible) B. Vocals; **Ringo Starr: (possible) Drums**; Billy Preston: Lead Vocals & Keyboards; probably one or more of the following: Alan White: Drums; Jim Gordon: Drums; Bobby Keys: Horns; Klaus Voormann: Bass; Carl Radle: Bass

When You Are Mine (B. Preston) 2:42 (9)
Ringo Starr: (possible) Drums; Billy Preston: Lead Vocals & Keyboards; probably one or more of the following: Alan White: Drums; Jim Gordon: Drums; Klaus Voormann: Bass; Carl Radle: Bass; Bobby Keys: Horns

You've Been Acting Strange (B. Preston) 3:22 (13)
Ringo Starr: (probable) Drums; Billy Preston: Lead Vocals & Keyboards; probably one or more of the following: Alan White: Drums; Jim Gordon: Drums; Klaus Voormann: Bass; Carl Radle: Bass

Fort Worth Express
Hindustani Music-Raga 001-A:B [unauthorized release] (xx/xx/96)
Producer: [unknown-audience recording]
George Harrison: Guitar; Billy Preston: Lead Vocals & Keyboards; Tom Scott: Saxophone; Chuck Findley: Trumpet; Robben Ford: Guitar; Andy Newmark: Drums; Emil Richards: Percussion; Willie Weeks: Bass; Jim Horn: Saxophone; Jim Keltner: Drums [unless noted otherwise]
Tarrant County Convention Center, Fort Worth, TX 11/22/74

Nothing From Nothing [live] (B. Preston-B. Fisher) 3:40 (2-8)

Outa-Space [live] (B. Preston-J. Greene) 4:21 (2-9)
Additionally: Billy Preston: Keyboards (only)

Will It Go 'Round In Circles [live] (B. Preston-B. Fischer) 3:50 (1-4)

It's My Pleasure
Universal Music-UICY 93460 (Japan) (05/14/08) (01/20/75)
Producer: Malcolm Cecil, Robert Margouleff & Billy Preston
George Harrison: Guitar; Billy Preston: Lead Vocals & Keyboards; Ollie Brown: Drums; Malcolm Cecil: Synthesizers; Robert Margouleff: T.O.N.T.O; Lorna Maxine: B. Vocals; Julia Waters: B. Vocals; Oren Waters; B. Vocals; Luther Waters: B. Vocals
Kendun Recorders &/or Centaur Electronic Music Center, Los Angeles, CA 09-10/xx/74

That's Life (B. Preston) 3:41 (3)

I Wrote A Simple Song
Universal Music-UICY 93455 (Japan) (05/14/08) (11/08/71)

Producer: Billy Preston; **Mixed by**: probably **George Harrison**
George Harrison: Guitar; Billy Preston: Lead Vocals & Keyboards; Rocky Peoples: Tenor Saxophone; Charles Garnette: Trumpet; King Errison: Congas; Manuel Kellough: Drums; Quincy Jones: Strings & Horn Arrangement
Los Angeles, CA 08-09/xx/71

I Wrote A Simple Song (B. Preston-J. Greene) 3:23 (2)

Ringo Starr And His All-Starr Band
Pioneer Artists-PA-090-007 (LD 12") (07/xx/90)
Tim Snow (video); Joe Walsh & Jim Nipar (music); Executive Producer: Ringo Starr & David Fishof
Ringo Starr: Drums; Billy Preston: Lead Vocals & Keyboards; Jim Keltner: Drums; Levon Helm: Drums & B. Vocals; Nils Lofgren: Guitar & B. Vocals; Joe Walsh: Guitar & B. Vocals; Rick Danko: Bass & B. Vocals; Clarence Clemons: Saxophone; Dr. John: Keyboards
Greek Theatre, Los Angeles, CA 09/03/89

Will It Go 'Round In Circles [live] (B. Preston-B. Fisher) 4:02 (1/6)
[Also available on *Ringo Starr And His All Starr Band The Anthology...So Far*. Koch-KOC-CD-8312 (1-9) (07/24/01) (02/05/01);]

Ringo Starr And His All-Starr Band: A Starry Night In Tokyo
ASB-001 [unauthorized release] (xx/xx/96)
Producer: NHK TV, Japan
Ringo Starr: Drums; Billy Preston: Lead Vocals & Keyboards; Felix Cavaliere: Keyboards; Mark Farner: Guitar & B. Vocals; Zak Starkey: Drums; John Entwistle: Bass; Randy Bachman: Guitar; Mark Rivera: Saxophones
Nippon Budakon Hall, Tokyo, Japan 06/27/95

Will It Go 'Round In Circles [live] (B. Preston-B. Fisher) 2:51 (15)

Ringo Starr And His Third All-Starr Band Volume 1
Blockbuster Exclusive-[matrix #] 0ERE4<5297>RINGOSTARR ADFL (08/12/97)
Producer: Greg Delancy (mixer); Executive Producer: Ringo Starr & David Fishof
Ringo Starr: Drums; Billy Preston: Lead Vocals & Keyboards; Mark Farner: Guitar; Zak Starkey: Drums; John Entwistle: Bass; Randy Bachman: Guitar; Felix Cavaliere: Keyboards; Mark Rivera: Saxophone
Nippon Budakon Hall, Tokyo, Japan 06/27/95

Nothing From Nothing [live] (B. Fisher-B. Preston-C. Puckett) 3:18 (5)

That's The Way God Planned It
Apple-CDP 7975802 (Germany) (11/19/91) (08/22/69)
Producer: George Harrison
Probably one or more of the following studios: Olympic, Apple, Trident or EMI-Abbey Road, London, UK 04-07/xx/69 [unless noted otherwise]

Do What You Want (B. Preston) 3:41 (1)
George Harrison: Guitar; **Ringo Starr: (possible) Percussion**; Billy Preston: Lead Vocals & Keyboards; Eric Clapton: Guitar; Keith Richards: Guitar or Bass; Klaus Voormann: (possible) Bass; Madeline Bell: (probable) B. Vocals; Doris Troy: (probable) B. Vocals
Trident Studios, London, UK 04/xx/69

Everything's All Right (B. Preston-D. Troy) 2:41 (3)
Ringo Starr: (possible) Drums; Billy Preston: Lead Vocals & Keyboards; probably one or more of the following: Doris Troy: B. Vocals; Klaus Voormann: Bass; Madeline Bell: B. Vocals

It Doesn't Matter (B. Preston) 2:39 (5)
Ringo Starr: (possible) Drums &/or Percussion; Billy Preston: Lead Vocals & Keyboards; probably one or more of the following: Doris Troy: B. Vocals; Klaus Voormann: Bass; Madeline Bell: B. Vocals

Let Us All Get Together Right Now (B. Preston-D. Troy) 4:06 (9)
Ringo Starr: (probable) Drums; **George Harrison: (probable) Sitar**; Billy Preston: Lead Vocals & (probable) Keyboards; probably one or more of the following: Madeline Bell: B. Vocals; Doris Troy: B. Vocals

Morning Star (W.C. Handy-M. David) 3:16 (6)
Billy Preston: Lead Vocals & (probable) Keyboards; John Barham: Strings; probably one or more of the following: Doris Troy: B. Vocals; Madeline Bell: B. Vocals

She Belongs To Me (B. Dylan) 4:06 (4)
George Harrison: (probable) Guitar; **Ringo Starr: (possible) Drums**; Billy Preston: Lead Vocals & Keyboards; probably one or more of the following: Klaus Voormann: Bass; Doris Troy: B. Vocals; Madeline Bell: B. Vocals

That's The Way God Planned It (Parts 1 & 2) (B. Preston) 5:32 (12) (06/27/69)
George Harrison: Guitar; Ringo Starr: (possible) Percussion; Billy Preston: Lead Vocals & Keyboards; Keith Richards: Bass or Guitar, Eric Clapton: Guitar; Klaus Voormann: (possible) Bass; Ginger Baker: Drums; Madeline Bell: (probable) B. Vocals; Doris Troy: B. Vocals
Trident Studios, London, UK 04/xx/69

That's The Way God Planned It (Alternate version) (B. Preston) 4:13 (15) (11/19/91)
George Harrison: Guitar; **Ringo Starr: (possible) Percussion**; Billy Preston: Lead Vocals & Keyboards; Keith Richards: Bass or Guitar, Eric Clapton: Guitar; Klaus Voormann: (possible) Bass; Ginger Baker: Drums
Trident Studios, London, UK 04/xx/69

This Is It (B. Preston-D. Troy) 2:42 (10)
Ringo Starr: (probable) Drums; George Harrison: (probable) Guitar; Billy Preston: Lead Vocals & Keyboards; probably one or more of the following: Klaus Voormann: Bass; Madeline Bell: B. Vocals

What About You? (B. Preston) 2:07 (8) (06/27/69)
George Harrison: (possible) Guitar; **Ringo Starr: (possible) Drums &/or Percussion**; Billy Preston: Lead Vocals & Keyboards; possibly one or more of the following: Klaus Voormann: Bass; Madeline Bell: B. Vocals

Unbootlegged Vol. 23 [The Beatles (solo)]
No Topo Records NTR-0601 (CD-R) [unauthorized release] (xx/xx/06)
Ringo Starr: Drums; Billy Preston: Keyboards & Lead Vocals; Dhani Harrison: Guitar; Jim Keltner: Drums; Klaus Voormann: Bass; Chuck Findley: Horns; Jim Horn: Horns
Warner Bros. Studios, Burbank, CA 10/19/05

Isn't It A Pity (G. Harrison) 0:28 (36)

William "Billy" Preston was born on Sept 2, 1946 in Houston, Texas but grew up in Los Angeles. Billy was a child prodigy whose roots were firmly planted in gospel music. He was backing such legends as Nat King Cole, James Cleveland and Mahalia Jackson by the age of 10. He played the part of W. C. Handy as a youngster in the 1958 film *St. Louis Blues*. In the fall of 1962 Little Richard* recruited Preston for his European tour, including Liverpool and the Star-Club in Hamburg, Germany where he got to know The Beatles. He was a member of the house band on the mid-'60's rock music TV show *Shindig*.

When Preston was in the UK backing Ray Charles in September 1968 he was invited by George Harrison to visit Apple's office. He visited on January 22, 1969 and was recruited by Harrison to play with The Beatles on recordings that would eventually be used for their 1970 album and film *Let It Be*. During those sessions, they backed Preston on two unreleased songs tentatively titled *Billy's Songs 1 & 2*. On January 30, The Beatles, with Preston, played on the roof of Apple's office for what would be their last public performance. The next day Preston signed with Apple. When *Get Back* and *Don't Let Me Down* from the sessions were released a few months later as a single they were credited as The Beatles with Billy Preston, the only time the group ever gave such a co-credit. Billy also plays on *Something* and *I Want You (She's So Heavy)* on The Beatles' 1969 album *Abbey Road* in 1969.

In the spring of 1969 Harrison began producing Billy's first Apple album *That's The Way God Planned It* with contributions from Eric Clapton*, Doris Troy*, Keith Richards (see The Rolling Stones) and Ginger Baker (see Blind Faith, Cream). Harrison plays on the title track, and he and Ringo likely play on other tracks. An edited version of the title track was a UK Top 20 hit. Several album tracks were leftovers from Preston's recording sessions for Capitol, which weren't produced by Harrison.

Billy was part of the Delaney & Bonnie & Friends* tour in December 1969, which included Harrison; and when they backed up John Lennon and Yoko Ono* at London's Lyceum Ballroom. In January 1970 Apple released the single *All That I've Got (I'm Gonna Give It To You) / As I Get Older*. Harrison produced the A-side, and supposedly plays guitar on it – possibly bass as there are no other guitars on it, and it sounds like Ringo on drums. The B-side was produced by Ray Charles, who probably also plays keyboards, and there's some fuzz guitar that could have been overdubbed by Harrison.

Harrison also produced Billy's second Apple album, *Encouraging Words*, which features Ringo and many of the musicians who play on Harrison's *All Things Must Pass* album recorded around the same time. *Encouraging Words* also features session musicians Joe Greene and Jesse Kirkland, though exactly which tracks they contribute to isn't known. The album includes the first release of Harrison's compositions *All Things Must Pass*, and *My Sweet Lord*, which was scheduled to be the first single backed with *As Long As I Got My Baby*. However, Apple didn't release it as a single until 10 days after Harrison's release of *My Sweet Lord*, undoubtedly because they felt Harrison would have a hit with it. Preston's version was totally overshadowed by Harrison's multi-million-selling version. The arrangement of Billy's version was similar to the Edwin Hawkins Singers' *Oh Happy Day*, no doubt due in part to their providing backing vocals to it. Ironically Harrison first considered the Edwin Hawkins Singers to record the song. [Years later Harrison claimed in his defense in a plagiarism suit, which he lost, that *My Sweet Lord* was based on *Oh Happy Day*, not the song *He's So Fine* as was alleged.] *As Long As I Got My Baby* was reportedly recorded in Sweden using The Temptations as background singers.

Harrison and Preston spent a few days in Sweden during the Delaney & Bonnie & Friends tour, but Bobby Keys*, who was a member of the tour band, says he would have remembered or heard of a session including The Temptations had there been one. However, it does sound like The Temptations singing backing vocals. Later reports suggest it was just The Temptations' rhythm section the Funk Brothers, who contributed to a couple of tracks on *Encouraging Words*. Given the circumstances, *As Long As I Got My Baby* was likely recorded in London with The Temptations and their rhythm section. Harrison wrote *What Is Life* for Billy, but ended up recording it exclusively for *All Things Must Pass*. *Encouraging Words* includes *Sing One For The Lord* written by Harrison and Preston. [An unreleased song titled *Time To Cry* is also registered as being composed by Harrison and Preston.] The album also includes a cover of *I've Got A Feeling*, which Billy had played on for The Beatles. It would not be Preston's last cover of a Beatles' song.

Between 1969 and 1976 Preston played on Harrison's albums *All Things Must Pass*, *The Concert For Bangla Desh*, *Dark Horse*, *Extra Texture (Read All About It)* and *Thirty-Three & 1/3*; Ringo's albums *Sentimental Journey*, *Ringo* and *Goodnight Vienna*; and on Lennon's songs *Instant Karma*, *God* and a live version of *Cold Turkey* recorded at London's Lyceum Ballroom. He also played on Harrison's 1982 album *Gone Troppo*.

Billy left Apple in 1971 and released the album *I Wrote A Simple Song*. Harrison contributed guitar, credited as George H. plays on the title track. Preston expressed in the credits "my deepest appreciation to George Harrison [among others] who played a large part in making this first album possible on A&M [Records]."

According to an article in the September 16, 1971 issue of *Rolling Stone* magazine, Harrison also helped mix the album. Harrison plays guitar to *That's Life* from Billy's 1975 album *It's My Pleasure* using his familiar pseudonym Hari Georgeson. Among his hits while signed to A&M are *Outa Space*, *Will It Go' Round In Circles* and *Nothing From Nothing*. Billy performed these songs during Harrison's 1974 US tour, which are available on unauthorized releases. Preston also worked with The Rolling Stones*, Elton John*, Bob Dylan* and Aretha Franklin among many others, and helped compose Joe Cocker's* 1975 hit *You Are So Beautiful*.

Billy was a member of Ringo Starr's All-Starr Band tour in 1989 performing *Will It Go 'Round In Circles* and *Get Back*, and in 1995 performing *Nothing From Nothing* and *Will It Go 'Round In Circles*, all with backing from Ringo on drums. He also contributed to Ringo's 2005 album *Choose Love*.

Billy took part in the New York tribute concert *Come Together: A Night For John Lennon's Words & Music* shortly after the attacks of September 11, 2001. He was a part of the Harrison tribute *Concert For George* in 2002. In late 2005, he helped promote the release of *The Concert For Bangla Desh* film on DVD by performing *Give Me Love (Give Me Peace On Earth)*, *My Sweet Lord* and *Isn't It A Pity* with Harrison's son Dhani on guitar, and Ringo playing drums on *Isn't It A Pity*, for the Bangla Desh gala. Portions of this performance are available on unauthorized releases. He was also a guest at conventions and festivals for fans of The Beatles during the first half of the 2000s. Billy Preston died on June 6, 2006. For more information go to www.billypreston.net

P. J. Proby

The Legendary P.J. Proby 'At His Very Best'
See For Miles-SEE CD 72 (France) (xx/xx/89)
Producer: Ron Richards [& George Martin]
P.J. Proby: Lead Vocals; John Paul Jones: Bass; Jimmy Page: Guitar; George Martin: Arrangement & Conductor
EMI-Abbey Road Studios, London, UK 04/07/65

That Means A Lot (J. Lennon-P. McCartney) 2:31 (9) (07/05/65)

P.J. Proby was born James Marcus Smith on November 6, 1938 in Houston, Texas. Smith began his entertainment career under the name Jett Powers after moving to Los Angeles. He took bit acting parts and formed local bands before turning to songwriting. In 1963 songwriter Sharon Sheeley (Eddie Cochran's fiancée) suggested the alias P. J. Proby and introduced him to TV producer Jack Good, who later produced the rock music TV show *Shindig*. Good invited Proby to appear on the UK TV special *Around The Beatles* in the spring of 1964, which is when Proby first met the group. Proby had a string of Top 20 hits in the UK in 1964 and 1965 including *Hold Me*, *Together*, *I Apologize*, *Let The Water Run Down*, *Somewhere* and *Maria*.

The Beatles recorded John Lennon and Paul McCartney's song *That Means A Lot* on February

20, 1965 with the intention of using it for their album and motion picture *Help!*, but instead offered it to Proby who had a UK Top 40 hit with it. Proby recalls, "I was closest to Lennon; we were drinking buddies. I ran into him in a nightclub and said, 'Write me a song!' He came to me the next week with *That Means A Lot*. I asked him if I could use George Martin* as the producer and he said, 'Damn you, what do you want — my wife, my life and my children too?' So he got me Martin, which is the only time I ever recorded with him because Ron Richard was in charge of me. George did everything, the arrangement, working the boards — everything. He had everything set up and ready to record when I got to the studio." Proby thinks the orchestra that backed him on it was either Johnny Spence or an orchestra handpicked by Martin. He says The Beatles didn't attend the session. The Beatles' recording of *That Means A Lot* was officially released on their album *Anthology 2* in 1996.

Proby had a couple more UK Top 40 hits between 1966 and 1968. His only Top 40 hit song, *Niki Hoeky* in 1967, failed to chart in the UK. He was briefly a member of Canned Heat in the late 1960s. Proby released several records during the 1970s but none of them met with success. In 1977 (and again in 1995 and 1996) he starred in the role of Elvis Presley in his later years in the UK musical *Elvis*. He played himself in *Only The Lonely*, the story of his old friend Roy Orbison*, in 1994 and 1995. In 1997 he played the part of The Godfather in The Who's (see Roger Daltrey, John Entwistle, Keith Moon) *Quadrophenia* tour. P.J. Proby still performs. For more information go to www.proby.co.uk

Tommy Quickly

Beat, Beat, Beat! Volume 1: The Mersey Sound & Other Mop Top Rarities 1962-1963
Castle Music-CMDDD 282 (UK) (08/10/02)
Producer: Les Reed
Tommy Quickly: Vocals
London, UK 07/xx/63

Tip Of My Tongue (J. Lennon-**P. McCartney**)
2:02 (1-27) (07/30/63)

No Reply / [unknown]
Pye [unreleased]
Producer: Tony Hatch
Paul McCartney: Tambourine; **John Lennon: Percussion**; Tommy Quickly: Lead Vocals; Colin Manley: Lead & Rhythm Guitar; Roy Dyke: Drums; Don Andrew: Bass
Pye Studios, London, UK 07/xx/64

No Reply (**J. Lennon**-P. McCartney)

Tommy Quickly was born Tommy Quigley in Liverpool, England on July 7, 1943. He fronted a Liverpool band under the name Johnny Quickly and The Challengers. Unlike most of NEMS' artists who were signed to EMI, Quickly was signed to the Decca/Pye/Piccadilly group of labels. Quickly underwent the familiar Epstein makeover – suit and tie, and a new stage demeanor. Epstein booked Quickly on several dates with The Beatles in mid-1963, and arranged for him to record *Tip Of My Tongue*. The Beatles had recorded this Paul McCartney composition the previous year, but rejected it as their second single in favor of *Please Please Me*, which became their first number one hit in the UK. Quickly's version confirmed The Beatles' wisdom in passing on the song as it was one of the few unqualified chart failures of a Lennon-McCartney composition. Quickly was also on the bill of *The Beatles Christmas Show* in 1963.

On June 3, 1964 Lennon, McCartney and Harrison (Ringo was ill at the time) recorded a demo of John's song *No Reply*, which is included on The Beatles' 1995 album *Anthology 1*. The liner notes suggest that it may have been recorded specifically as a reference demo for Quickly. Quickly's version was recorded in July, and set for release on Pye Records on August 7, 1964 but was never issued. Colin Manley of the Remo Four*, who Epstein recruited as Quickly's backing band in 1964, vividly remembers, "The song was recorded at Pye Studios in London and produced by Tony Hatch. In addition to us, McCartney played tambourine and Lennon banged away on Coke bottles for percussion. Epstein was also there coaching Quickly who was having trouble with the vocals. John said to his chauffeur, Alf [Bicknell], 'Go out and buy a bottle of whiskey! We've done the backing, now let Tommy sing.' We all got pretty stewed. I don't think the *Anthology 1* version is the demo we heard — it's too complete — but I wish it was. I'd back my life that the demo we used had no middle eight; it didn't have any clue as to the rhythm we should use. It contained the sound of a toilet flushing at the end, which we thought was hilarious because it was typical of John's humor. I think it was recorded in a hotel room. When we heard it on the album *Beatles For Sale* we immediately noticed that it had a middle eight." Manley suspects Quickly's difficulty with the vocals and the incompleteness of the song are why it wasn't released.

Quickly was one of the supporting acts on The Beatles' UK tour in the fall of 1964. His only UK Top 40 was a cover of Hank Williams' song *The Wild Side Of Life* in 1964. Despite Epstein's efforts, Tommy was unable to keep pace with the burgeoning UK music scene, and quickly faded into obscurity. Any hopes of restarting his career were dashed by a head injury that has left him permanently disabled.

R.A.D.D. (Recording Artists Against Drunk Driving)

Don't Let The Music Die Vol. 6 [Various Artists]
NAB Broadcasters [matrix #] C309417-4 (xx/xx/96)
Producer: Paul & Dan Rothchild
Paul McCartney: Vocals; **Ringo Starr: Vocals**; Phil Collins: Vocals; David Crosby: Vocals; Graham Nash: Vocals; Little Richard: Vocals; Harry Nilsson: Vocals; Steve Berlin: Vocals; David Hidalgo: Vocals & Guitar; Conrad Lozano: Vocals; Louie Perez: Vocals; Cesar Rosas: Vocals; Weird Al Yankovic: Vocals; Melissa Etheridge: Vocals; Brett Michaels: Vocals; Clint Black: Vocals; Trisha Yearwood: Vocals; Julian Lennon: Vocals; Lisa Hartman Black: Vocals; Travis Tritt: Vocals; Katey Sagal: Vocals; Patti Smyth: Vocals; Mike Landau: Guitar; Randy Jacobs: Guitar; Jody Cortez: Drums; Dan Rothchild: Bass; Ray Manzarek: Piano; Eddy Ray Wolffe: Guitar; Clarence Clemons: Saxophone; Taras Prodaniuk or Charles Domanico: Bass; Dean Parks: Acoustic Guitar; Pete Anderson: Electric Guitar; Jeff Donavan: Drums; Skip Edwards: Keyboards
Clear Lake Audio & Ocean Way Studios, Los Angeles, CA & Hog Hill Mill Studios, Sussex, UK 12/14/93-01/21/94

Drive My Car (J. Lennon-P. McCartney) 3:38 (11) (02/07/94)

The American Music Awards premiered the video *Drive My Car* by R.A.D.D. (Recording Artists Against Drunk Driving) on February 7, 1994 (the 30th Anniversary of The Beatles' first visit to the US). R.A.D.D. is an organization which, with the help of popular recording artists, attempts to discourage people from driving while drunk. The *Drive My Car* video features many country and rock musicians, including, Julian Lennon*, Little Richard*, Ringo Starr and the song's primary composer, Paul McCartney. The full-length music video consists of four musical sections, which include a traditional cover of The Beatles' *Drive My Car*, a country music version of it, an edited in hip hop section titled *Give Up The Keys*, and a hard rock version of *Drive My Car*. Each artist's vocal performance was filmed live and edited into the final recording and music video. McCartney appears and performs in the video for about 20 seconds, and he is also seen very briefly disguised in an Afro wig. Only a few seconds of Ringo's performance with Harry Nilsson* appears in the video. Gary Legon and Marcy Gensic were in charge of the video. [Legon had previously worked on the video *Ringo Starr And His All Star Band Volume 2-Live From Montreux*.]

The *Drive My Car* promotional video and audio cassette were available via mail order for a limited time in 1994. The cassette also contains a brief message by McCartney. McCartney made it possible for R.A.D.D. to be able to use the *Drive My Car* song as their theme. The recording was released in 1996 on the album *Don't Let The Music Die*. McCartney headlined R.A.D.D.'s 1997 holiday public service media campaign to promote designated driving with a public service announcement. He received R.A.D.D.'s 1997 Founder's Award for his efforts. For more information go to www.radd.org

The Radha Krsna [Krishna] Temple (London)

The Radha Krsna Temple (London)
Apple-CDP 0777 7 81255 2 5 (05/18/93) (05/21/71)
Producer: George Harrison [unless noted otherwise]
Trident Studios, London, UK 09/xx/69-01/xx/70 [unless noted otherwise]

Bhaja Bhakata/Arotrika [or "Arati"] (Trad. Arr: M.D. Adkikary)
8:24 (3)
Lilavati devi dasi: Vocals; Jivananda dasa: Vocals; Murari dasa: Mrdanga

Bhaja Hure Mana (Trad. Arr: M. D. Adkikary) 8:53 (6)
Yamuna devi: Lead Vocals & Harmonium
Possibly The Radha Krsna Temple, London, UK 09/xx/69-01/xx/70

Govinda (Trad. Arr: M. D. Adkikary) 4:43 (1) (03/06/70)
George Harrison: Guitar; Yamuna devi: Lead Vocals; Mukunda Goswami: Organ & Kartalas; Hari Vilas dasa: Oud; Tamal Krsna Goswami: Flute; Syamasundar dasa: Kartalas & B. Vocals; Klaus Voormann: Bass; John Barham: Orchestral Arrangements; Lilaviti devi dasi: B. Vocals; Jivananda dasa: B. Vocals; Mondakini devi dasi: B. Vocals; Jyotirmayi devi dasi: B. Vocals; Malati devi dasi: B. Vocals; Janaki devi dasi: B. Vocals; Guru dasa: B. Vocals; Radharaman dasa: B. Vocals; Purandara dasa; B. Vocals; Tirthapada dasa: B. Vocals; Digvijaya dasa: B. Vocals; Prtha devi dasi: B. Vocals; Kulasekhar dasa: B. Vocals; Pantanjili devi dasi: B. Vocals

Govinda Jai Jai [or "Govinda Jaya Jaya"] (Trad. Arr: M. D. Adkikary) 5:57 (7) (03/06/70)
Lilavati devi dasi: Vocals; Jivananda dasa: Vocals

Hare Krsna [or Krishna] Mantra (Trad. Arr: M. D. Adkikary) 3:33 (4) (08/22/69)
Producer: George Harrison & Paul McCartney
George Harrison: Guitar, Bass & Harmonium; Yamuna divi: Vocals; Syamasundar dasa: Vocals; Alan White: Drums; Mukunda Das Adhikary: Mridangam & Guitar; Malati devi dasi: Kartalas, Gong & B. Vocals; Digvijaya dasa: B. Vocals; Tirthapada dasa: B. Vocals; Janaki devi dasi: B. Vocals; Prtha devi dasi: B. Vocals; Kulasekhar dasa: B. Vocals; Pantanjili devi dasi: B. Vocals
EMI-Abbey Road Studios, London, UK 07/xx/69 or possibly 03 or 04/xx/69

Prayer To The Spiritual Masters (Trad. Arr: M. D. Adkikary) 3:59 (8) (08/22/69)
Producer: George Harrison & (probable) Paul McCartney
George Harrison: (possible) B. Vocals; Syamasundar dasa: Vocals & Esraj; Mukunda Goswami: Vocals, Mrdanga & Kulasekhar; Yamuna devi: Vocals; Malati devi dasi: Vocals; Mal Evans: Piano; Pantanjali devi dasi: B. Vocals; Prtha devi dasi: B. Vocals; Tirthapada dasa: B. Vocals; Digvijaya dasa: B. Vocals
EMI-Abbey Road Studios, London, UK 07/xx/69 or possibly 03 or 04/xx/69

Sri Guruvastak [or Gurvastakam] (Trad. Arr: M. D. Adkikary) 3:12 (2)
George Harrison: (probable) Guitar, (probable) B. Vocals & (possible) Tamboura; Jivananda dasa: Vocals & (possible) Guitar; Yogesvara dasa: Vocals
Possibly The Radha Krsna Temple, London, UK 09/xx/69-01/xx/70

Sri Isopanisad (Trad. Arr: M. D. Adkikary) 4:03 (5)
George Harrison: (probable) Guitar; Jivananda dasa: Lead Vocals & Guitar
Possibly The Radha Krsna Temple, London, UK 09/xx/69-01/xx/70

Unbootlegged 12½ [The Beatles]
No Tapo-NTR 0203 (CD-R) [unauthorized release] (xx/xx/05)
Probably Bhaktivedana Manor, UK xx/xx/93

Hare Krsna [or Krishna] Mantra (Trad. Arr: M. D. Adkikary) 9:00 (7)
George Harrison: George B. Vocals & (possible) Harmonium

The Hare Krsna [or Krishna] movement was founded by Abhay Charanaravinda Bhaktivedanta Swami Prabhupada (a.k.a. Abhay Charan De). His missionaries arrived in London to set up a temple in the spring of 1968. That fall they arranged a meeting, through Allen Ginsberg*, with Apple's A&R Manager Peter Asher (see Peter & Gordon). Not surprisingly, they soon became friends with George Harrison, and with Prabhupada they took up residence for a time at John Lennon's home in Ascot. Their members were often seen roaming the streets of London chanting the *Hare Krsna Mantra*. The chant became so familiar that The Beatles did a loose rendition of it during rehearsals in January 1969 for what became their 1970 album and film *Let It Be*. Members of the Hare Krishna movement contributed backing vocals to Lennon's song *Give Peace A Chance*, recorded on June 1, 1969 at Lal Reine-Elizabeth hotel in Montreal, during the Lennons' "bed-in for peace."

Harrison plays on, and produced with Paul McCartney, The Radha Krishna Temple's first Apple single *Hare Krsna Mantra / Prayer To The Spiritual Masters*, probably during recordings at EMI for The Beatles' 1969 album *Abbey Road*. *Hare Krsna Mantra* became a Top 20 hit in the UK. Harrison assumed the same duties for their follow-up Apple single *Govinda* and album *The Radha Krsna Temple (London)*. [The album was reissued on the Spiritual Sky label several years later in the UK re-titled *Goddess of Fortune*, and in 2004 as part of the Canadian album *George Harrison From Beatles To Self-Realization: Chant & Be Happy* (XXI-XXI-CD 2 1461), which also includes a DVD interview with Harrison and Ravi Shankar* from 1997.] Unfortunately, all of these releases are lacking in detailed credits. Judging from the photos of Harrison playing guitar and harmonium in the Apple CD booklet, it is likely he plays those instruments on the album. Though harmonium is present on much of the album, it is difficult to know if Harrison plays some or all of it. There is guitar on *Sri Guruvastak* and *Sri Isopanisad*, which may be played by Harrison. There is also the possibility that Harrison is one of the many backing vocalists. Mukunda Goswami of ISKCON (International Society for Krishna Consciousness), who was involved in the recordings, was able to recall some of the participants and their contributions.

Following the arrival of Allen Klein at Apple, novelties such as The Radha Krsna Temple were left chanting in the streets. However, Harrison supported the movement the remainder of his life. In 1973 he donated the 17-acre Bhaktivedana Manor outside London to ISKCON and gave a written endorsement for the book *Divine Nature: A Spiritual Perspective On The Environmental Crisis* by Michael A. Cremo and Mukunda Goswami published by ISKCON in 1995. A nine minute version of *Hare Krsna Mantra*, reportedly recorded at the Bhaktivedana Manor in 1993, which clearly identifies Harrison's presence, appears on unauthorized releases. Goswami and other Krishna devotees reportedly were with Harrison when he died. For more information go to www.iskcon.com

Leon Redbone

Leon Redbone and Kristofer Engelhardt, The Ark, Ann Arbor, MI January 20, 2000. © Kristofer Engelhardt.

Whistling In The Wind
Private Music-01005-82117-2 (04/12/94)
Producer: Beryl Handler & Leon Redbone
Ringo Starr: Vocals†; Leon Redbone: Vocals; Giampaolo Biagi: Drums; Cyndi Cashdollar: Dobro Guitar & B. Vocals; Vince Giordano: Bass; Frank Vignola: Guitar & Mandolin; Terry Waldo: Piano; Beryl Handler: B. Vocals; Doug Epstein: B. Vocals; Ira: B. Vocals; Mitch: B. Vocals
M&I Studios, New York, NY & Ocean Way Studios, Los Angeles, CA†, xx/xx/92 & 06/07/93†

My Little Grass Shack (J. Noble-B. Cogswell-T. Harrison) 2:41 (7)

[None]
[Unreleased]
Producer: Beryl Handler & Leon Redbone
Ringo Starr: Drums†; Leon Redbone: Lead Vocals
M&I Studios, New York, NY & Ocean Way Studios, Los Angeles, CA†, xx/xx/92 & 06/07/93†

Sing Me A Song Of Hawaii (J. Nobel)

Leon Redbone was reportedly born Dickran Gobalian on August 26, 1949 in Cyprus though there is considerable doubt about this and much of Redbone's personal life due to his obsession with privacy. He first gained notice in the mid-1970s after appearing on TV's *Saturday Night Live* and years later on *The Tonight Show*. As much humorist as musician, Redbone's baritone crooning is familiar to most Americans from the theme songs for the TV shows *Mr. Belvedere* and *Harry And The Hendersons*, and from commercials, most notably for Budweiser beer. Commercials featuring Redbone were aired during Paul McCartney's 1995 radio series *Oobu Joobu*.

Ringo Starr had met Redbone on several occasions and admired his work. While both were at Ocean Way Studios, Ringo asked Redbone if he could add his vocals to *My Little Grass Shack*, and played drums on *Sing Me A Song Of Hawaii*, which remains unreleased. Redbone has released over a dozen albums, and continues to record and tour. For more information go to www.leonredbone.com

The Remo Four

In The First Place
Pilar 01CD (single) (UK) (05/25/99)
Producer: George Harrison
George Harrison: (possible) Guitar; Colin Manley: Vocals & Acoustic Guitar; Tony Ashton: Keyboards; Philip Rogers: Bass; Roy Dyke: Drums
EMI-Abbey Road Studios, London, UK probably 12/xx/67

In The First Place [Original Abbey Road Mix] (C. Manley-T. Ashton) 3:20 (1)

In The First Place [Movie Mix] (C. Manley-T. Ashton) 2:28 (2)
[Also available on *Wonderwall*. Rhino-R2 970045 DVD (01/29/02)]

The Remo Four initially called themselves The Remo Quartet when they formed in Liverpool, England in 1958 but modified their name in 1961. George Harrison and Paul McCartney were school mates of the band's guitarist and founding member Colin Manley who was born on April 16, 1942 in Liverpool, England. The Remo Four underwent numerous personnel changes throughout their career. By 1962 they were known as Johnny Sandon & The Remo Four. They were often on bills with The Beatles around Liverpool in the early 1960s and, like The Beatles, were a resident band at the Star-Club in Hamburg, Germany. They were managed by Brian Epstein who initially tried to interest them in backing Billy J. Kramer (see Billy J. Kramer with The Dakotas) before he persuaded them to back Tommy Quickly* in 1964. The Remo Four, on their own and backing Quickly, were one of the featured acts on The Beatles' fall tour of the UK in 1964.

Harrison used The Remo Four on the non-Indian music portion of his soundtrack album for the 1968 film *Wonderwall*. The group then consisted of Manley; bassist Phil Rogers, who joined in 1962; drummer Roy Dyke, born on February 13, 1945 in Liverpool, England, who joined in 1961; and keyboardist, Edward "Tony" Ashton, born on March 1, 1946 in Blackburn, England, who joined in 1965. Harrison reportedly produced an album for The Remo Four in 1968, but according to Ashton and Manley, he only produced a recording of their composition *In The First Place* at Abbey Road Studios during the sessions for *Wonderwall*. The song was inspired, in part, by the Modern Jazz Quartet's version of *Adagio From Concerto De Aranjuez*. [Members of the Modern Jazz Quartet reportedly worked with Harrison on some unreleased jazz recordings of his around this time.] Ashton and Manley think Harrison may have played guitar on the track, but only Manley's acoustic guitar is discernible. Manley recalls Harrison telling him that McCartney offered a few suggestions concerning the song's verses. *In The First Place* wasn't released until 1999 to promote the rerelease of the film *Wonderwall*, which also includes the song and a brief film clip of The Beatles.

The Remo Four broke up in 1969. Ashton and Dyke enlisted Kim Gardner to form Ashton, Gardner & Dyke*. [Ashton, Gardner & Dyke recorded a completely new song, *As It Was In The First Place*, again inspired by *Adagio From Concerto De Aranjuez*, which they included on their self-titled album in 1969.] Dyke later joined Badger (see Jackie Lomax) for a time and still dabbles in music. Ashton worked with a number of artists including Ian Paice and Jon Lord from Deep Purple*. Portions of Ashton and Lord's album *First Of The Big Bands* were recorded at Apple Studios, but Ashton said none of The Beatles contributed to it. Ashton was part of the Rockestra ensemble on Wings' 1979 album *Back To The Egg* and on the 1981 album *Concerts For The People Of Kampuchea* recorded at London's Hammersmith Odeon on December 29, 1979. Ashton's song *The Big Freedom Dance*, in tribute to John Lennon, was released in 1996. Manley, Ashton, Dyke and a new bassist, Tony Coates reunited as The Remo Four in 1997. Colin Manley died on April 9, 1999. Tony Ashton died on May 28, 2001.

Kate Robbins

Tomorrow / Crowds Of You
Anchor-ANC 1054 (7" single) (UK) (06/30/78)
Producer: Del Newman; **[Executive Producer & Involvement: Paul McCartney]**
Kate Robbins: Lead Vocals
EMI Studios, Abbey Road, London, UK probably xx/xx/78

Tomorrow (M. Charnin-C. Strouse) 3:26 (1/1)

Kate Robbins was born on August 21, 1958 in Margate, England. She is the daughter of Mike and Elizabeth Robbins. Elizabeth was the first cousin of Paul McCartney on his father's side and helped teach Paul how to play guitar. Kate has become a successful actress, impressionist and singer. She had a UK Top Five hit with the song *More Than In Love* in 1981.

Many reliable publications claim that Paul produced Kate's 1978 recording of the song *Tomorrow*. However, both sides of the record list Del Newman as the producer, but production by MPL Communications and the songs are administrated by McCartney Music, which likely led to the confusion. Kate says Paul didn't produce *Tomorrow*, but was the executive producer and played a very active role in the record's development. McCartney chose the song, which he owned the publishing rights to, for Kate. Kate thinks there were four mixes and says that Paul chose the mix for the single. Though the role of executive producer isn't generally considered a contribution, because of the wider scope of McCartney's involvement with the record, it's included. She says that Paul has advised her throughout her career and helped her set up her publishing company. Kate has also contributed backing vocals to several of Paul's recordings. In 2007 Kate and Paul began collaborating on a stage musical based on his *Liverpool Oratorio* (see: The Royal Liverpool Philharmonic Orchestra & Choir & Choristers Of Liverpool Cathedral), but Kate says the project has been shelved due to McCartney's heavy schedule. For more information go to www.katerobbins.co.uk

Ted Robbins

Unbootlegged 5 [The Beatles]
No Label Records-NLR 0105 (CD-R) [unauthorized release] (xx/xx/01)

Paul McCartney: B. Vocals & Acoustic Guitar; Ted Robbins: Lead Vocals
Air Studios, London, UK probably 11/xx/83 or possibly 11/xx/84

My Way [live] (P. Anka-C. Francois-J. Revaux) 0:36 (3)

Edward "Ted" Robbins was born on August 11, 1955 in Liverpool, England. He is the son of Mike and Elizabeth Robbins. Elizabeth is the first cousin of Paul McCartney on his father's side. Mike was a professional entertainer who was also in a band called the Four Jones Boys who'd released some records. Their daughters Emma, Amy, Jane and Kate Robbins* have careers in show business. Ted started out, like his father, as a Butlin's Redcoat (a holiday camp entertainer). He has become a successful comedian, actor, and UK radio and TV host. Since the late 1980s Ted has appeared on a number of UK TV shows including *Richard & Judy*, *Phoenix Nights*, *The Slammer*, *Quiz Night*, *Chain Letters*, *The Kate Robbins Show* and *Kate And Ted's Show*. He currently hosts a weekday show on BBC Radio Lancashire.

Ted laments, "I have my career and Paul has his. Certainly our checks don't get mixed up, but because Paul and I work in the entertainment business, and are relatives, there's enormous pressure from people asking me for favors and interviews with him, which puts me in an awkward position. It would be easy for me to take advantage of that — but I don't. However, when important things come along, and I can help — I do. In '83 or'84 the producer of my show *Weekend* for Granada TV asked me to get an interview, so I contacted Paul who said to come to Air Studios, where I think he was doing something for *Give My Regards To Broadstreet*. We took a film crew but the interview quickly dissolved into nonsense because I started asking serious questions. He looked at me cross-eyed, then I looked at him cross-eyed and he said, 'Give us *My Way*, Ted,' because at family parties we would always end up singing songs like that.

"The Paul McCartney world is a very strange world. There's the world with him together with all the relatives, and then when you step out of that he's – Sir Paul McCartney! My greatest joy is how proud Paul was of my dad. My dad ran the Fox and Hounds pub in Reading. During their mid-teens, Paul and John Lennon performed there. My dad billed them as the Nurk Twins. He told them to play like a 'W' not an 'M' (the reverse on a graph) — meaning you always start with your best stuff, maintain that in the middle of your show, and finish on a high point. Paul says he always remembered that. He called my dad 'Mr. Showbiz,' and asked his advice on many things because nobody else in our Liverpool, working class family background had any links to professional entertainment. When Paul became famous, dad would always say to him, 'Do you need a booking son? Someday I'll get you a booking in the Fox and Hounds,' which always drew huge laughter. My dad was a great influence on him and they became very close over the years. Paul and I have had long talks about him since his recent death. There are few people that know Paul as someone who looks up to somebody the way he looked up to my dad. It was genuine and mutual – they loved each other. Paul's a great fellow and I love him, and all the family loves him."

The Rolling Stones

More Hot Rocks (big hits & fazed cookies)
Abkco-96262 (09/03/02)
Producer: Andrew Loog Oldham
John Lennon: B. Vocals & Dialogue†; Paul McCartney: B. Vocals†; Mick Jagger: B. Vocals; Keith Richards: B. Vocals; Brian Jones: Mellotron & Horns; Nicky Hopkins: Piano
Olympic Studios, London, UK 06/12-13/67 & 07/xx/67† or possibly 05/18/67†

We Love You [version two])M. Jagger-K Richards) 4:21 (1-12) (09/12/69)

Rock And Roll Circus [Various Artists]
Abkco/Blink-1003-9 (DVD) (10/12/04)
Producer: Jimmy Miller, Jody Klein & Lenne Allik
Mick Jagger: Lead Vocals; Keith Richards: Guitar; Brian Jones: Guitar; Bill Wyman: Bass; Charlie Watts: Drums; Nicky Hopkins: Keyboards; Rocky Dijon: Percussion
InterTel Studios, Stonebridge House, London, UK 12/11/68

Jumping Jack Flash (M. Jagger-K. Richards) 3:35 (7) (10/15/96)
Additionally: **John Lennon: Introduction**
[Also available on Abkco-1268-2 (14)]

Salt Of The Earth (M. Jagger-K. Richards) 4:56 (12) (10/15/96)
Additionally: **Audience (inc. John Lennon): B. Vocals**; Keith Richards: Acoustic Guitar (only)
[Also available on Abkco-1268-2 (19)]

Singles Collection)(The London Years)

Abkco 1218-2 (08/04/89)
Producer: Andrew Loog Oldham [unless noted otherwise]
Mick Jagger: Lead Vocals; Charlie Watts: Drums; Bill Wyman: Bass; Keith Richards: Guitar [unless noted otherwise]

Dandelion (M. Jagger-K. Richards) 3:32 (2-14) (08/18/67)
Additionally: **John Lennon (probable) B. Vocals**†; **Paul McCartney: (probable) B. Vocals**†; Mick Jagger: B. Vocals; Keith Richards: B. Vocals; Brian Jones: Maracas & Oboe; Nicky Hopkins: Harpsichord; Ian Stewart: Organ
Olympic Studios, London, UK 11-12/xx/66, 06/12-13/67 & 07/xx/67† or possibly 05/18/67†

I Wanna Be Your Man (J. Lennon-P. McCartney) 1:42 (1-3) (11/01/63)
Producer: Additionally: Eric Easton
Kingsway Sound Studios, London, UK 10/07/63
Additionally: Brian Jones: Guitar & B. Vocals

We Love You [version one] (M. Jagger-K. Richards) 4:34 (2-13) (08/18/67)
Additionally: **John Lennon: B. Vocals & Dialogue**†; **Paul McCartney: B. Vocals**†; Mick Jagger: B. Vocals; Keith Richards: B. Vocals; Brian Jones: Mellotron & Horns; Nicky Hopkins: Piano
Olympic Studios, London, UK 06/12-13/67 & 07/xx/67† or possibly 05/18/67†

The Rolling Stones formed in 1962 around front man and songwriter Mick Jagger*; lead guitarist and songwriter Keith Richards, born on December 18, 1943 in Dartford, England; guitarist Lewis Brian Jones born on February 28, 1942 in Cheltenham, England; keyboardist Ian Stewart, born on July 18, 1938 in Pittenweem, Scotland, and bassist Bill Wyman*. Charlie Watts, born on June 2, 1941 in London, England became the group's drummer in early 1963. Their manager and producer, Andrew Loog Oldham, who'd previously handled public relations briefly for The Beatles, felt Stewart's appearance didn't fit the naughty image he hoped to create for the group, in stark contrast to the more conventional Beatles, so Stewart was essentially restricted to studio work. The Rolling Stones, particularly Jagger, Richards and Jones, would push the boundaries of acceptability in lyrics, behavior and fashion far beyond The Beatles, and much to their envy. John Lennon would later express his frustration about Brian Epstein's insistence that The Beatles' success was dependent upon abandoning their naughty image in favor of matching suits, while The Rolling Stones were able to capitalize on it. However, The Rolling Stones' image made it easier for the public to accept the more controversial aspects of The Beatles.

The Beatles reportedly first saw The Rolling Stones at their Crawdaddy Club performance in London on April 14, 1963. Several weeks later, George Harrison recommended them to Dick Rowe of Decca Records who, mindful of his rejection of The Beatles the previous year, signed them. On September 10, 1963 Oldham invited Lennon and Paul McCartney to The Rolling Stones' rehearsal at the Ken Colyer Jazz Club in London. They were looking for a song for their second single, and asked John and Paul if they had any songs they could use. They offered them their unfinished composition *I Wanna Be Your Man*, which the two completed on the spot. They recorded and released it as their second single three weeks before The Beatles' version, and it became their first UK Top 20 hit. The press often painted a picture of fierce rivalry between The Rolling Stones and The Beatles, but their competition was always friendly and they often socialized. They even coordinated record releases to avoid competition and occasionally attended each other's recording sessions. Brian contributed to the chorus of The Beatles' 1966 song *Yellow Submarine*. During the first half of 1967 Mick and Keith appeared in The Beatles' film documenting their recording of *A Day In The Life*, Mick attended their recording sessions for *Baby You're A Rich Man* and likely contributed backing vocals to it, and Brian played saxophone on The Beatles' song *You Know My Name (Look Up The Number)*. Keith, Mick and his girlfriend Marianne Faithfull* were part of The Beatles' live performance of *All You Need Is Love* for the BBC TV program *Our World*, telecast live on June 25, 1967.

During this period Mick and Brian, and Keith during a party at his home just after George Harrison had left, were arrested on drug charges and given stiff sentences. The Beatles, who would eventually face similar difficulties, decried their treatment and the UK's harsh drug laws. John and Paul sang backing vocals on The Rolling Stones' single *We Love You* in a show of support. The Rolling Stones and The Beatles' close friend Prince Stash (Stanislas Klossowski de Rola, Baron de Watteville) was present when they added their backing vocals and remembers Paul saying, 'Let's reduce it all to one track and keep going.' Stash is certain that the lead and backing vocals for *Dandelion*, the single's B-side, were also recorded then, and that John and Paul definitely also sang backing vocals on *Dandelion* as has long been rumored. The backing vocals on both songs sound very similar. There is debate about the recording dates of these songs. In Wyman's autobiography *Stone Alone* he says that the initial tracks for *We Love You* were recorded on June 12-13, 1967, and that John and Paul added their vocals in July. The Rolling Stones' *Singles Collection (The London Years)* lists both songs as being recorded in July. Other reliable publications state their backing vocals were recorded in June, though Mark Lewisohn lists May 18. [An edited version of *We Love You*, which ends with Lennon saying what sounds like, "Your health" was first issued on The Rolling Stones' 1969 compilation album *Through The Past, Darkly (Big Hits Vol. 2).*]

If imitation is the sincerest form of flattery, The Rolling Stones could fairly be accused of flattering The Beatles on numerous occasions, particularly with their 1967 album *Their Satanic Majesties Request*, which includes small photos of The Beatles and bore considerable resemblance to the Beatles 1967 album *Sgt. Pepper's Lonely Hearts Club Band*, which mentions The Rolling Stones on the cover. *Their Satanic Majesties Request* marked the departure of Oldham. Allen Klein, who had handled The Rolling Stones' financial affairs since 1965, took greater control of the band's finances. There was even talk of The Rolling Stones and The Beatles forming a business partnership. The Beatles were forming Apple at the time, and The Rolling Stones went on to form Rolling Stone Records. The Beatles hired Klein in 1969 to manage Apple in spite of The Rolling Stones' warnings about him. Both groups would spend years exorcizing Klein's control.

The proposed cover (used years later) for The Rolling Stones' 1968 album *Beggars Banquet*, including the message "John loves Yoko," was rejected by Decca. The revised cover was mostly white and not unlike *The Beatles* (white) album, which had recently been released. To promote *Beggars Banquet* the band made the TV special *Rock And Roll Circus* to be aired around Christmas. It was directed by Michael Lindsay-Hogg who, three weeks later, began directing The Beatles' film *Let It Be*. Among the performers were Marianne Faithfull, Jethro Tull, Taj Mahal*, The Who (see Roger Daltrey, John Entwistle, Keith Moon), and John Lennon and Yoko Ono*. Lennon performed *Yer Blues* in a group dubbed The Dirty Mac, which included Eric Clapton*, Mitch Mitchell (Jimi Hendrix Experience) and Keith Richards. John also sang in the select audience on the chorus of *Salt Of The Earth*. During rehearsals, Lennon, Clapton and Jagger performed *Peggy Sue*, and John played *It's Now Or Never*. Due to The Rolling Stones' dissatisfaction with their performance, and Allen Klein's control, *Rock And Roll Circus* wasn't aired or released until 1996.

In June 1969 Mick and Keith informed the increasingly dysfunctional Jones that he was being replaced by guitarist Mick Taylor. On July 3, 1969 Brian Jones drowned in his swimming pool. In 1970 The Beatles broke up, and The Rolling Stones relocated to France for tax purposes, so there was less interaction between the groups' members. Ron Wood* replaced Mick Taylor in 1975. Billy Preston* and Bobby Keys* also worked extensively with The Rolling Stones for a number of years. Ian Stewart died on December 12, 1985.

Perhaps the most telling moment of admiration and affection between The Beatles and The Rolling Stones occurred on January 20, 1988 at New York's Waldorf Astoria Hotel when Jagger (with George, Ringo and Yoko present) inducted The Beatles into the Rock and Roll Hall of Fame. Following the induction, the assembled took part in a jam session (see Various Artists - Mick Jagger, Bruce Springsteen And The Rock Hall Jam Band). A 25-year video retrospective titled *25 x 5 The Continuing Adventures Of The Rolling Stones* was issued in 1989 on VHS and LD (Image-ID6975CB) containing newsreel footage of The Beatles. That year The Rolling Stones were inducted into the Rock and Roll Hall of Fame. In 1992 Bill Wyman retired from The Rolling Stones who, after six decades, keep on rolling as one of rock's most successful bands having reached the top of the charts with the songs *(I Can't Get No) Satisfaction*, *Get Off My Cloud*, *Paint It Black*, *Ruby Tuesday*, *Honky Tonk Women*, *Brown Sugar*, *Angie* and *Miss You*, and had Top Five hits with *19th Nervous Breakdown*, *Jumpin' Jack Flash*, *Emotional Rescue*, *Start Me Up*, *Harlem Shuffle* and *Mixed Emotions*. For more information go to www.rollingstones.com

Kate Royal (Academy of St. Martin in the Fields, Boys of Magdalen College Choir, Oxford & Boys of King's College Choir, Cambridge)

Paul McCartney-Ecce Cor Meum
Angel/EMI Classics 0946 3 70424 2 7 (09/25/06) **Paul McCartney: Liner Notes**
Producer: John Fraser; Executive Producer: Paul McCartney
Kate Royal: Soprano Vocals; Academy of St. Martin in the Fields: Orchestra; Boys of Magdalen College, Oxford: Choir; Boys of King's College, Cambridge: Choir; Gavin Greenaway: Conductor; Ben Parry: Chorus Master; Colm Carey: Organ; Mark Law: Piccolo Trumpet; Terry Edwards: Director of London Voices
EMI-Abbey Road Studios & Tower of London, London, UK 03/13-17/06

Ecce Cor Meum (**P. McCartney**) 14:49 (5)

Gratia (**P. McCartney**) 10:50 (2)

Interlude (Lament) (**P. McCartney**) 3:56 (3)
Additionally: David Theodore: Oboe

Musica (**P. McCartney**) 15:14 (4)

Spiritus (**P. McCartney**) 12:00 (1)

The title *Ecce Cor Meum*, Latin for *Behold My Heart*, was inspired by an inscription Paul McCartney saw in a church. It is a four movement oratorio that McCartney began working on for the dedication of a new concert hall at Magdalen College in Oxford, England. McCartney's work on it was interrupted by the death of his wife Linda McCartney* in 1998. With encouragement from the President of the Oxford University Music Society, the work was first performed by the full Choir of the Magdalen College in November 2001 at the Sheldonian Theatre in Oxford. A recording of the work was produced by John Fraser, who has produced most of McCartney's classical works, in March 2006. The main vocalist is Kate Royal. A deluxe edition of the album with a 56 page booklet was issued in the UK. It nearly topped the Classical Albums charts, and it received the Best Album Award at the Classical Brits in 2007. The world premiere performance at the Royal Albert Hall in London on November 3, 2006 was released on DVD (EMI Classics-5099950073399) in 2008. It has also been performed in North America.

Rubyhorse

How Far Have You Come?
Horse Trade-HT-CD-2001 (11/14/2000)
Producer: Jay Joyce
George Harrison: Slide Guitar†; Gary Tussing: Cello; Joe Philpott: Guitar; Gordon Ashe: Drums; Decky Lucey: Bass; Owen Fegan: Keyboards; Dave Farrell: Vocals
Tragedy/Tragedy, &/or New Reflections &/or East Iris, Nashville, TN & FPSHO†T, UK late/xx/98 or early/xx/99† & xx/xx/01

Punchdrunk (J. Philpott-A. Ashe-D. Lucey-O. Fegan-M. Farrell) 6:04 (7)

Rise
Island-314 586 919-2 (05/21/02)
Producer: Jay Joyce
George Harrison: Slide Guitar†; Gary Tussing: Cello; Joe Philpott: Guitar; Gordon Ashe: Drums; Decky Lucey: Bass; Owen Fegan: Keyboards; Dave Farrell: Vocals
Tragedy/Tragedy, &/or New Reflections &/or East Iris, Nashville, TN & FPSHOT†, UK late/xx/98 or early/xx/99† & xx/xx/01

Punchdrunk [revised ending] (J. Philpott-A. Ashe-D. Lucey-O. Fegan-M. Farrell) 5:44 (8)

Rubyhorse members knew one another since kindergarten in Cork, Ireland. They formed a band in 1988 and released their first album in 1995. Hoping for greater success the band moved to Boston, Massachusetts in 1997 and soon gained notice.

Their album *How Far Have You Come?*, released on Horse Trade Records in 2000, was modified, re-titled *Rise* and released on Island Record in 2002. Both albums include the song *Punchdrunk* with a slide guitar contribution from George Harrison but the 2002 release features a revised ending. Band members recall, "We felt there was

Rubyhorse, Pine Knob, Clarkston (Detroit), MI August 10, 2001. © Kristofer Engelhardt.

something missing when we recorded *Punchdrunk* – like a slide guitar part. Somebody suggested George Harrison. We didn't want to bother him but his work enamored us. We didn't think it would be an insult to ask him because we believed in the song. However, we worried that a contribution by him might overshadow us and what we'd worked so hard for, but our management said that it couldn't hurt to ask, and we didn't think he would accept. Our management approached him through mutual friends, and the tapes were sent to him in England in late 1998 or early 1999. We heard that he found himself singing the song when he went to the refrigerator late one night. We think he connected with the song's lyrics because it was in the vein of his philosophy. When our producer asked how long it would take to get the tape back to us, Harrison said he'd been busy gardening, hadn't played the guitar in ages and jokingly said, 'It depends if I FedEx it, or paddle it back across the ocean.' We got the tape back a few weeks later, along with a beautiful note with a carton caricature of our band, saying how much he enjoyed the song. When we heard his slide part, which definitely belonged and completed the song, any fears we had vanished. We were flabbergasted and honored that he took the time to listen to the song, no less play on it! He did it for a simple musician's union fee too. All the words of thanks can't compensate for what he put on that song. It's probably the biggest honor we will ever receive. We hoped to meet him but sadly he died. Later, we added the *My Sweet Lord* bit to the song as a tribute to him because the chords were the same — we didn't rip it off — it just seemed appropriate." Rubyhorse's song *Sparkle* from the album managed to do well in the charts in 2002. Their critically acclaimed album *Goodbye To All That* in 2003 lacked the sales necessary for the band to continue on beyond 2005. For more information go to www.rubyhorse.com

The Best Of Ringo Starr And His All-Starr Band...So Far
Image-ID0828RO (DVD) (10/23/01)
Producer: Ringo Starr (music); Michael Drumm; Jim Beach & Louise Velazquez (Film); Executive Producer: Ringo Starr & David Fishof
Ringo Starr: Drums; Todd Rundgren: Lead Vocals & Drums; Joe Walsh: Keyboards, B. Vocals & Drums; Burton Cummings: Tambourine, Keyboards, B. Vocals & Percussion; Nils Lofgren: Acoustic Guitar & B. Vocals; Dave Edmunds: Electric Guitar & B. Vocals; Timothy B. Schmit: Bass & B. Vocals; Tim Cappello: Percussion; Zak Starkey: Drums
Montreux Jazz Festival, Montreux, Switzerland 07/13/92

Bang The Drum All Day [live] (T. Rundgren) 3:25 (8) (09/14/93)
[Also available on *Ringo Starr And His All Starr Band The Anthology...So Far.* Koch-KOC-CD-8312 (2-12) (07/24/01) (02/05/01)]

With A Little Help To My Friends {Ringo Starr]
No Label Records-NLR 9904 (CD-R) [unauthorized release] (xx/xx/99)
Ringo Starr: Drums; Todd Rundgren: Lead Vocals & Guitar; Bill Wyman: Bass; Dave Mason: Guitar & Vocals; Kiki Dee: B. Vocals; Kasim Sultan: Keyboards & B. Vocals; Roger Powell: Horns; John Wilcox: Drums
Las Vegas, NV 09/03/79

Money (That's What I Want) [live] (J. Bradford-B. Gordy) 3:24 (2)

Todd Rundgren was born on June 22, 1948 in Philadelphia (Upper Darby), Pennsylvania. Todd, like many in the mid-1960s, was greatly influenced by The Beatles and joined a number of bands. In 1967 he formed the short-lived group Nazz, a mod-styled band reminiscent of The Beatles, who had hits with *Open My Eyes* and *Hello It's Me.* By 1970 Rundgren was essentially a solo artist. His album *Runt*, which also served as a moniker for him, produced the Top 20 hit *We Gotta Get You A Woman.* He had another Top 20 hit with *I Saw The Light* in 1972. Rundgren has also found success as a studio musician and producer for other acts such as Patti Smith, Meat Loaf, Grand Funk Railroad (see Mark Farner), Cheap Trick, XTC, Hall And Oates* and The Tubes. In 1974 Rundgren formed Utopia, a side project band with whom he frequently records. He has also become heavily involved in video arts, but continues producing, touring, and recording with and without Utopia.

Rundgren's association with The Beatles began in 1971 when he was given the task of finishing up production for Badfinger* album *Straight Up.* In 1974 Rundgren and John Lennon became involved in a brief, but bitter political and musical shouting match in the music press that ended when Rundgren retracted some of his statements. In 1976 Rundgren released covers of Lennon's Beatles' songs *Rain* and *Strawberry Fields Forever.* In 1980 Todd and Utopia released *Deface The Music*, somewhat of a musical parody of The Beatles. Their 1981 album *Swing To The Right* features a photo of people burning of The Beatles' records in the US in 1966 in protest of Lennon's statement that The Beatles were more popular than Christ.

Rundgren joined Ringo Starr, Bill Wyman* and others in a band that performed on the *Jerry Lewis Muscular Dystrophy Telethon* airing on September 3, 1979. Portions of the performance appear on unauthorized releases. Todd's longtime manager Eric Gardner recalls, "One of the artists I represented was Bill Wyman. He and I had planned a number of charity projects. His girlfriend Astrid was friends with Verna Harrah, of Harrah's Hotels, who knew Jerry Lewis. Through them Lewis inquired about Bill performing on his annual *Muscular Dystrophy Telethon.* We thought it could be a trial run for the other charity projects. We called Ringo, though he thought it was a bit kitschy having a Beatle and a Rolling Stone together. Bill knew Todd because he had stayed at Todd's house when The Rolling Stones* were rehearsing in Woodstock, New York for their 1978 tour. I called Todd who said he would normally pass but said, 'You can't say no to both a Beatle and a Rolling Stone.' We all agreed that Utopia would be the rhythm section. Then someone suggested adding Dave Mason*, who turned out to be the most heroic of the band, as his father had died the day before the show and he still showed up! Doug Kershaw and Kiki Dee* magically showed up the day of the show as I recall. It was done live from a hotel in Las Vegas and broadcast on a big screen at a different hotel where Jerry was at."

Rundgren was a member of Ringo Starr's All-Starr Band tour in 1992. During the tour he performed *Bang The Drum All Day* with Ringo backing him on drums. Rundgren also performed an acoustic rendition of Lennon's Beatles' song *You've Got To Hide Your Love Away* during the All-Starr's performance in Liverpool. Rundgren was also a member of the All-Starr Band tour in 1999 performing *I Saw The Light* and *Bang The Drum All Day* with backing from Ringo on drums. Rundgren was part of *A Walk Down Abbey Road: A Tribute To The Beatles* tour in 2001 and 2002, and contributed a cover of *While My Guitar Weeps* for the 2003 album *Songs From The Material World: A Tribute To George Harrison.* For more information go to www.tr-i.com

Leon Russell

The Concert For Bangla Desh
Apple/Rhino-R2 970481 (DVD) (10/25/05)
Producer: George Harrison & Allen Klein (film); **George Harrison** & Phil Spector (music)
Madison Square Garden, New York, NY 08/01/71 (afternoon or evening)

Come On In My Kitchen [sound check] (R. Johnson) 2:32 (2-3)
George Harrison: Electric Guitar & B. Vocals; Ringo Starr: Drums; Leon Russell: Vocals & Piano; Eric Clapton: Lead Guitar; Jim Keltner: Drums
Madison Square Garden, New York, NY 08/01/71

Medley: Jumpin' Jack Flash/ Youngblood/ Jumpin' Jack Flash [live] (M. Jagger-K. Richards/J. Leiber-M. Stoller-D. Pomus) 10:12 (1-11) (10/xx/83)
George Harrison: Rhythm Guitar & B. Vocals; Ringo Starr: Drums; Leon Russell: Vocals & Piano; Don Preston: Vocals & Lead Guitar; Billy Preston: Organ; Jim Keltner: Drums; Eric Clapton: Lead Guitar; Jesse Ed Davis: Rhythm Guitar; Klaus Voormann: Bass; Carl Radle: Bass; Alan Beutler: B. Vocals; Marlin Greene: B. Vocals; Jeanie Greene: B. Vocals; Joe Green: B. Vocals; Dolores Hall: B. Vocals; Jackie Kelso: B. Vocals; Claudia Lennear: B. Vocals; Lou McCreary: B. Vocals; Don Nix: B. Vocals; Pete Ham: Acoustic Guitar; Joey Molland: Acoustic Guitar; Tom Evans: Acoustic Guitar; Mike Gibbons: Percussion
[Also available on Apple/Capitol-0946335880 28 (2-1) (10/25/05) (12/20/71)]

Leon Russell
DCC/Shelter-GZS-1049 (Japan/Canada) (11/18/93)
Producer: Denny Cordell & Leon Russell
Olympic Sound Studios, London, UK 09-10/xx/69 [unless noted otherwise]

Delta Lady (L. Russell) 4:00 (6) (02/01/70)
George Harrison: Leslie Guitar; Ringo Starr: Drums; Leon Russell: Lead Vocals & (probable) Guitar; Eric Clapton: (possible) Guitar; Bill Wyman: Bass; Steve Winwood: Organ; Bonnie Bramlett: B. Vocals; Clydie King: B. Vocals; Merry Clayton: B. Vocals
Olympic Sound Studios, London, UK 09/02 & 05/69

I Put A Spell On You (L. Russell) 4:10 (3) (02/01/70)
George Harrison: Guitar; Leon Russell: Lead Vocals; Bill Wyman: Bass; Charlie Watts: Drums; Chris Stainton: Guitar, or Percussion or Keyboards; Steve Winwood: Guitar, or Percussion or Keyboards; Clydie King: (probable) B. Vocals; Merry Clayton: (probable) B. Vocals

Indian Girl (L. Russell) 4:08 (15)
George Harrison: Acoustic Guitar; Ringo Starr: Drums; Leon Russell: Lead Vocals & Piano; Eric Clapton: Acoustic Guitar; Klaus Voormann: Bass

(The New) Sweet Home Chicago (L. Russell-M. Benno) 3:11 (13)
George Harrison: Guitar; Leon Russell: Lead Vocals, & Piano &/or Bass; Chris Stainton: Guitar, or Bass or Keyboards; Charlie Watts: Percussion; B.J. Wilson: (probable) Percussion; Steve Winwood: Keyboards, or Bass or Guitar; Clydie King: (probable) B. Vocals; Merry Clayton: (probable) B. Vocals

Pisces Apple Lady (L. Russell) 2:50 (11) (02/01/70)
George Harrison: Guitar; Ringo Starr: Drums; Leon Russell: Lead Vocals & Piano; Bill Wyman: Bass; Merry Clayton: (probable) B. Vocals; Clydie King: (probable) B. Vocals

Prince Of Peace (L. Russell-G. Dempsey) 3:05 (7) (02/01/70)
George Harrison: (probable) Acoustic Slide Guitar; Leon Russell: Lead Vocals & Piano; Eric Clapton: Lead Guitar; Bill Wyman &/or Klaus Voormann: Bass; B.J. Wilson: (probable) Percussion or Jon Hiseman: (probable) Percussion; Merry Clayton: (probable) B. Vocals; Clydie King: (probable) B. Vocals
Olympic Sound Studios, London, UK 09 &/or 10 &/or 11/xx/69

Roll Away The Stone (L. Russell-G. Dempsey) 3:06 (12) (02/01/70)
George Harrison: Guitar; Ringo Starr:

Drums; Leon Russell: Lead Vocals & Keyboards; Bill Wyman: Bass; Steve Winwood: Keyboards; Eric Clapton: Guitar; Chris Stainton: Keyboards

Shoot Out On The Plantation (L. Russell) 3:10 (4) (02/01/70)
George Harrison: Guitar; **Ringo Starr: Drums**; Leon Russell: Lead Vocals & Piano; Klaus Voormann: Bass; Steve Winwood: Piano; Jim Horn: Horns

Leon Russell was born Claude Russell Bridges on April 2, 1942 in Lawton, Oklahoma. Russell's blend of blues, country and gospel, and his musical versatility on guitars, keyboards, horns and percussion, led to session work as a member of Phil Spector's* "wall of sound—wrecking crew." He and Delaney Bramlett* were occasional members of the Shindogs, the house band on the popular mid-1960's music TV show *Shindig*. Russell followed Delaney & Bonnie & Friends'* migration to the UK in 1969. There he teamed up with English producer Denny Cordell and the two would soon form Shelter Records. Cordell also produced and managed Joe Cocker*. Russell and Cocker, along with many members of Delaney & Bonnie & Friends, toured as Mad Dogs & Englishmen.

In the late summer and fall of 1969 George Harrison and Ringo Starr took part in sessions at Olympic Studios for Leon's debut album *Leon Russell*. John Lennon was also present at some of these sessions, but didn't make any contributions. The initial releases didn't specify musicians for each track, but *ICE* magazine provided it prior to a 1993 special edition release. However, Leon has doubts as to whether Harrison plays on *Prince Of Peace* as credited. [The 1991 *Delta Lady* album (Del Rack-DRZ 918), which contains a 13-second longer fade-out on that song, has more specific musical credits for songs on *Leon Russell*, but also contains a number of errors and omissions.] [O'Dell had also dated Leon Russell*, who wrote the song Pisces Apple Lady about her. Harrison wrote the song Miss O'Dell about her.]

In an interview in *Rolling Stone* magazine about the album *Leon Russell And The Shelter People*, Russell says, "I did one session with Ringo and George, but I didn't really have any songs, and we were more or less jamming." That album included Harrison's composition *Beware Of Darkness* released after Harrison's version but states it was recorded at Island Studios on August 24-26, 1970, before Harrison's release, which Russell has confirmed. This has led to speculation that Harrison intended for Russell to release the song first or contributed to it. Jim Price, who played on *Beware of Darkness*, and Russell don't recall Harrison contributing to the recording. Russell shares vocals with Harrison on the song at *The Concert For Bangla Desh*.

Russell had his only Top 20 hit song with *Tight Rope* in 1972. He was one of the many well-known studio musicians who contributed to sessions in Los Angeles in late 1973 for Lennon's *Rock 'N' Roll* album. Russell played with Harrison during his performance in Tulsa, Oklahoma on November 21, 1974. He contributed to Harrison's 1975 album *Extra Texture (Read All About It)*. Leon and his wife Mary McCreary recorded Harrison's composition *I'll Still Love You* (originally titled *When Every Song Is Sung;* and also recorded by Cilla Black*, Ronnie Spector* and Ringo Starr). Theirs and Spector's version haven't been released. Harrison is rumored to have contributed to the Russells' *Wedding Album*, but the music and the detailed credits don't suggest it. Most likely, Harrison contributed to the Russells' version of *When Every Song Is Sung* recorded during this period and probably intended for inclusion on the *Wedding Album*. Russell was reportedly asked to be a member of Ringo Starr's All-Starr Band in the late 1990s.

During his long career Russell has worked with many of the biggest names in music including The Beach Boys*, Eric Clapton* and The Rolling Stones*. He has also performed as Russell Bridges and as a country music artist under the name Hank Wilson. Russell continues to record and tour. For more information go to www.leonrussellrecords.com

Adam Sandler

Saturday Night Live: the Best Of Adam Sandler
TRIMARK 7215D (DVD) (12/26/99)
Producer: Lorne Michaels
Paul McCartney: B. Vocals; Linda McCartney: B. Vocals; Adam Sandler: Lead Vocals & Guitar
NBC TV Studio 8-H, 30 Rockefeller Plaza, New York, NY 02/13/93

Red Hooded Sweatshirt [live] (A. Sandler) 3:31 (21)

Adam Sandler was born on September 9, 1966 in Brooklyn, New York but grew up in Manchester, New Hampshire. By the late 1980s he was doing standup comedy and appearing on a number of TV shows including *The Cosby Show*. He went to work as a comedy writer for TV's *Saturday Night Live* in 1990. The following season he was a cast member of the show. During his performance of his comedy song *Red Hooded Sweatshirt* on the show in 1993 he was joined in the chorus by Paul and Linda McCartney, who were sitting in the audience after having just performed on the show. Sandler left *Saturday Night Live* in the mid-1990s to pursue a film career. Since that time, he has starred in many popular films including *Billy Madison, Happy Gilmore, The Wedding Singer, Anger Management, Spanglish* and *I Now Pronounce You Chuck And Larry*. He has also formed the film production company Happy Madison Productions, which has had a number of successful films, and he has released several comedy albums. For more information go to www.adamsandler.com

The Scaffold

Singles A's & B's
Charly/See For Miles-CM 114 (album 12") (UK) (10/18/82)
Producer: Paul McCartney
Paul McCartney: (probable) Instruments; Mike McGear: Vocals; Roger McGough: Vocals; John Gorman: Vocals; The Stockport Gdansk Band Co-operative; (members of) 10cc; (members of) Wings
Strawberry Studios, Stockport, UK 01-05/xx/74

Ten Years After On Strawberry Jam (P. McCartney-L. McCartney) 2:52 (2/9) (05/24/74)

The Very Best Of Scaffold
EMI 7243 5 38474 2 5 (UK) (03/25/02)

Goose (R. McGough-M. McGear) 2:34 (11) (06/27/69)
Producer: Norrie Paramor & Tim Rice
Paul McCartney: Guitar; Mike McGear: Lead Vocals; Nicky Hopkins: Piano
EMI-Abbey Road Studios, London, UK xx/xx/69

Lily The Pink (Trad. Arr: J. Gorman-M. McGear-R. McGough) 4:15 (2)
(10/18/68)
Producer: Norrie Paramor & Tim Rice **[Assistance by Paul McCartney]**
Paul McCartney: (probable) Involvement; John Gorman: Vocals; Mike McGear: Vocals; Roger McGough: Vocals; Graham Nash: B. Vocals; Jack: Bruce: Bass; Tim Rice: B. Vocals; Elton John: B. Vocals
EMI-Abbey Road Studios, London, UK xx/xx/68

Liverpool Lou [single version] (D. Behan-**trad. Arr: P. McCartney**-L. McCartney) 2:58 (22) (05/24/74)
Producer: Paul McCartney
Paul McCartney: Gysmorchestra, Bass, Arrangement & (probable) B. Vocals; Mike McGear: Lead Vocals; Denny Laine: Harmonica; Jimmy McCulloch: Guitar; Gerry Conway: Drums; Linda McCartney: Piano & Arrangement; Karen & Richard Carpenter (probable) B. Vocals
Strawberry Studios, Stockport, UK probably 05/xx/74

(Stop Blowing Those) Charity Bubbles [single version] (R. McGough-M. McGear) 2:34 (10) (06/27/69)
Producer: Norrie Paramor & Tim Rice
Paul McCartney: Guitar; Mike McGear: Lead Vocals
EMI-Abbey Road Studios, London, UK xx/xx/69

Thank U Very Much (M. McGear) 2:30 (1) (11/03/67)
Producer: Tony Palmer **[Assistance by Paul McCartney]**
Mike McGear: Lead Vocals; John Gorman: B. Vocals; Roger McGough: B. Vocals
EMI-Abbey Road Studios, London, UK 07/xx/67

The Scaffold was an English trio of musicians, actors, comedians and poets. Their members were John Gorman, born on January 4, 1936 and Roger McGough, born on November 9, 1937, both in the Liverpool area, and Michael McCartney (see Mike McGear). In 1962 Merseyside Arts Festival organizers Gorman and McGough asked Mike to take part in a comedy sketch, and help organize the festival. Following the festival, the three teamed up with several other artists to form a musical, poetry and comedy act called The Liverpool One Fat Lady All Electric Show. By late 1963 the group consisted of Mike, Roger and John who were calling themselves The Scaffold, and supplying material for the UK TV series *Gazette*. They spent the next few years touring and doing TV bits, and were briefly signed to NEMS. Being Paul McCartney's brother certainly didn't hinder Mike and The Scaffold from securing management, or a recording contract with Parlophone, who released their first single in 1966.

It was inevitable that Paul would offer his influence, associations and talents to The Scaffold's recordings, though usually anonymously. According to Mike, Paul assisted in the recording of *Thank U Very Much* by giving advice and contributing to the result. The November 1967 issue of *The Beatles Book Monthly* magazine reported that McCartney "helped operate the buttons and levers up in the studio control room." The song was inspired, in part, by Mike's thanks to Paul for giving him a Nikon camera. However, Paul didn't like the lyric line "Aintree Iron" and recommended that they omit it or the song wouldn't be a hit. Paul later admitted that he had been wrong about the lyrics, which actually generated interest in what became a UK Top 10 hit. Near the end of 1968 The Scaffold scored their only UK number one hit with *Lily The Pink*, again with a little assistance from Paul. Unfortunately, The Scaffold's unique brand of Liverpool humor served as a barrier to the US market, where they never found chart success. That year McGough contributed (un-credited) to the script of The Beatles' animated film *Yellow Submarine*. Apparently, Paul was present at Abbey Road Studios on January 12, 1969 during The Scaffold's recording of humor and poetry that made up side two of their *L The P* album, though Mike doubts Paul contributed in any way. The Scaffold recorded several more albums and singles, including *(Stop Blowing Those) Charity Bubbles*, which they re-recorded and released as a single, backed with *Goose*, which feature Paul on guitar.

The Scaffold, always a loosely knit outfit, also had numerous side and solo projects. Parlophone dropped them in 1971 and Mike recorded a solo album. In 1973 The Scaffold released an album for Island Records and Gorman, Andy Roberts, Neil Innes, McGough, McGear and Viv Stanshall (see The Bonzo Dog Band) formed Grimms (an acronym using the first letter in each member's surname) who released two albums. The group also included sidemen Zoot Money*, Gerry Conway, and Adrian Henri and Brian Patten who were considered two of the UK's finest poets.

In 1974, following Mike's frustrated tenure in Grimms, Paul produced and greatly contributed to his album **McGear*. During those sessions Paul suggested that The Scaffold record Dominic Behan's folk ballad *Liverpool Lou*, and produced their recording of it, which became their third and final UK Top 10 hit. Paul also contributed to the B-side *Ten Years After On Strawberry Jam*. The Scaffold released their final album *Sold Out* in 1975, and their final single in 1977 and retired, though they have made the occasional appearance since that time.

Michael Schenker Group

[None]
[Unreleased]
Producer: Ron Nevison
Air Studios, London, UK 03/03/81

[Unknown title]
Paul McCartney: Bass; Gary Barden: Lead Vocals; Michael Schenker: Guitar; Paul Raymond: Keyboards & Guitar; Cozy Powell: Drums

Michael Schenker was born in Sarstedt, Germany on January 10, 1955. He was a member of his brother's band Scorpions in the early 1970s when he joined the group UFO. He left UFO in 1978 and briefly rejoined Scorpions before forming the Michael Schenker Group (a.k.a. MSG and McAuley Schenker Group) in 1979. The group has experienced numerous personnel changes during which time Schenker has worked with UFO.

Paul McCartney was working on his *Tug Of War* album at George Martin's* AIR Studios in March 1981 when MSG's drummer Cozy Powell recruited him to play bass on a song for their *MSG* album because their bassist, Chris Glen, missed the session. Schenker can't recall the song McCartney contributed to but said it wasn't released. The *MSG* album credits include thanks to "Paul McCartney (cheques in the post Maca)," a friendly joke, according to Schenker. For more information go to
www.michaelschenkerhimself.com

Timothy B. Schmit

Ringo Starr And His All Starr Band Volume 2-Live From Montreux
Videoarts-VALJ-3369 (LD 12") (Japan) (probably 11/xx/93)
Producer: Ringo Starr (Music); Jim Beach & Louise Velazquez (Film); Executive Producer: Ringo Starr, David Fishof & Hilary Gerrard
Ringo Starr: Percussion; Timothy B. Schmit: Lead Vocals & Bass; Todd Rundgren: B. Vocals & Acoustic Guitar; Burton Cummings: Keyboards; Nils Lofgren: Lead Guitar; Dave Edmunds: Guitar; Zak Starkey: Drums
Montreux Jazz Festival, Montreux, Switzerland 07/13/92

I Can't Tell You Why [live] (T. Schmit-D. Henley-G. Frey) 4:51 (7) (09/14/93)
[Also available on *Ringo Starr And His All Starr Band The Anthology...So Far.* Koch-KOC-CD-8312 (2-4) (07/24/01) (02/05/01);] Executive Producer: Ringo Starr & David Fishof]

Timothy B. Schmit was born on October 30, 1947 in Oakland, California. He was playing in a variety of bands by his mid-teens. He first gained notice soon after he replaced future Eagles' member Randy Meisner on bass as a member of the country rock band Poco in 1969, which also included Richie Furay and Jim Messina, formerly of Buffalo Springfield (see Stephen Stills). During Schmit's tenure, Poco was praised by the critics and had moderate album success, and Schmit's song *Keep On Tryin'* was their biggest hit then. Schmit also sang on several albums by Steely Dan while in Poco. Ironically, he left Poco in 1977 to replace Meisner on bass in The Eagles where he gained greater recognition with such songs as *I Can't Tell You Why.* Following the breakup of The Eagles in 1980, Schmit pursued a solo career and continued to do session work for many well-known artists including Julian Lennon*, and Poco on one album. Schmit had a Top 40 hit song with *Boy's Night Out* in 1987. Schmit has been a member of The Eagles since they reunited in 1994.

Schmit was a member of Ringo Starr's All-Starr Band tour in 1992 singing *I Can't Tell You Why* with backing from Ringo on percussion. Schmit says, "Soon after being asked to join the All-Starr Band, which was a huge honor in itself, I received a call at home from Ringo. I thought to myself, 'Is this really happening?' I'd seen The Beatles on *The Ed Sullivan Show* when I was a teenager, which was incredibly exciting and inspiring to me. Every night playing with Ringo in the All-Starr Band was like reliving that experience. I'd look behind me and see Ringo playing the same song in the same band as me! It was something I could only have dreamed about early in my life. Ringo called for a band meeting before our last performance. Those are usually dreaded events in bands because it often means there's a conflict or problem that needs to be resolved. He gathered us all together and then handed each of us a small, nicely wrapped box. Inside was a beautiful gold watch with 'Love, Ringo, 1992' engraved on the back. It's something I will always treasure." Schmit contributed to Ringo's albums *Vertical Man* in 1998, *I Wanna Be Santa Claus* in 1999 and *Ringo Rama* in 2003. For more information go to www.timothybschmit.com

Tom Scott

Fort Worth Express
Hindustani Music-Raga 001-A:B [unauthorized release] (xx/xx/96)
Producer: [unknown-audience recording]
George Harrison: Guitar; Billy Preston: Keyboards; Tom Scott: Saxophone; Chuck Findley: Trumpet; Robben Ford: Guitar; Andy Newmark: Drums; Emil Richards: Percussion; Willie Weeks: Bass; Jim Horn: Saxophone; Jim Keltner: Drums
Tarrant County Convention Center, Fort Worth, TX 11/22/74

Tomcat [live] (T. Scott) 3:31 (2/1/5)

New York Connection
Ode/Epic/Legacy-EX64961 (07/16/96) (12/08/75)
Producer: Tom Scott & Hank Cicalo
George Harrison: Slide Guitar†; Tom Scott: Soprano Saxophone, Flute & Lyricon; Richard Tee: Keyboards; Bob James: Electric Piano; Gary King: Bass; Steve Gadd: Drums; Ralph McDonald: Percussion; Eric Gale &/or Hugh McCracken: Guitar
Hit Factory Studios, New York, NY & A&M

Studios, Los Angeles, CA† late-08/xx/75

Appolonia (Foxtrata) (T. Scott) 3:59 (8)

Tom Scott was born on May 19, 1948 in Los Angeles, California. His mother was a classical pianist, and his father was the composer of themes for several successful films and TV shows. By the mid-1960s Tom was playing saxophone and clarinet in jazz clubs in Los Angeles, and working as a session musician. Several years later he had also become a successful composer of film and TV theme songs. By the early 1970's Tom was signed to A&M Records, had formed the band The L.A. Express and was highly sought after for recordings and tours.

In 1973 Scott added his distinctive saxophone to the album *Ringo*. The following year George Harrison recruited Scott for his *Dark Horse* album and his US tour. One of the songs performed on the tour was Scott's instrumental *Tomcat*. Scott plays on Paul McCartney's 1975 hit *Listen To What The Man Said*. He also contributed to Harrison's albums *Extra Texture (Read All About It)* in 1975 and *Thirty-Three & 1/3* in 1976. Harrison's contribution to Scott's instrumental song *Appolonia* was probably recorded during sessions for *Extra Texture (Read All About It)*. Scott additionally contributed to artists signed to Dark Horse for Harrison. He also contributed to Ringo's 1978 album *Bad Boy* and Harrison's 1981 album *Somewhere In England*. Scott has recorded a number of covers of songs by The Beatles.

In the late 1980s and early '90s Scott was the musical director for TV's *Pat Sajak Show* and *Chevy Chase Show*, and the *Academy Awards* in 1996. Scott took part in the Harrison tribute *Concert For George* in 2002. Tom Scott continues to write, record and perform. For more information go to www.tomscottmusic.com

Peter Sellers, Terry Southern & Ringo Starr

The Magic Christian
Commonwealth United/Garrison Systems-1761 (album 12" promotional only) (12/xx/69)
Producer: Commonwealth United
Ringo Starr: Dialogue
Probably London, UK xx/xx/69

Ringo Starr Radio Spots (R. Starkey) (1/2)

Peter Sellers was born Richard Sellers on September 8, 1925 in Southsea, England. He began his career in the comedy group The Goons, which included Spike Milligan and Harry Secombe. All of The Beatles were avid listeners of their radio show, and big fans of Sellers, whose comedy records for Parlophone were produced by George Martin*. The Beatles' initial impression of Martin greatly improved knowing he worked with Sellers. Martin later produced Sellers' parodies of several Beatles' songs. They met Sellers through Martin, and became lifelong friends, especially George Harrison and Ringo Starr. The Beatles chose Richard Lester as the director of their mid-1960's films *A Hard Day's Night* and *Help!*, in part, for his work with Sellers. The screenplay for *Help!* was first offered to Sellers. In 1965 Sellers presented The Beatles with their Grammy Awards and appeared on the TV special *The Music Of Lennon and McCartney*.

In January 1969 Ringo, living in a house he bought from Sellers, co-starred in the film *The Magic Christian* starring Sellers. It was based on the novel and screenplay by Terry Southern. Southern, who appeared on the cover of The Beatles' *Sgt. Pepper's Lonely Hearts Club Band* album, was one of their favorite authors — particularly Ringo. [Starr had appeared in the 1968 film *Candy* based on Southern's book.] The role of Youngman Grand (Ringo), the adopted son of Sir Guy Grand (Sellers) the world's wealthiest man, was first offered to John Lennon. Sir Guy, intent on proving that "everyone has his price," explores the extremes to which people will go to obtain money. Sellers appeared in footage The Beatles' had shot for *Let It Be*, filmed at the same time and in the same studios as *The Magic Christian*, which was likely left on the cutting room floor due to the discussion of drug use. *The Magic Christian* was produced by Dennis O'Dell, former head of Apple Films. The movie's theme song, *Come And Get It*, performed by Badfinger* and composed by Paul McCartney, was most appropriate. The score was composed by Ken Thorne. [Thorne had scored the music for the film *Help!* and the 1967 film *How I Won The War* co-starring Lennon.] The film includes many cameos, and writing contributions from Graham Chapman and John Cleese, soon to achieve fame with Monty Python*. The film closes with the song *Something In The Air* by Thunderclap Newman, which then included 16-year-old guitarist Jimmy McCulloch. [McCulloch was a member of Wings from 1974 to 1977.] Commonwealth United Records issued the promotional album *The Magic Christian* containing open-end interview Radio Spots with Ringo, Sellers and Southern to promote the film. Two 60-second and two 30-second radio spots were also included on the single *The Magic Christian Radio Spots* (Commonwealth United 103). Sellers joined Ringo singing *Octopus's Garden* on *The David Frost Show* taped and telecast on December 6, 1969. *The Magic Christian* premiered six days later. It was issued in 2003 on DVD (Artisan-13604).

A photo (backs turned) of Sellers and Harrison appears in Harrison's *Dark Horse* album, along with a quote from the film *The Producers*, a favorite of theirs. Sellers accompanied Harrison through much of his 1974 US tour. He was influential in Harrison's involvement in the film industry, and introduced him to lawyer and accountant Denis O'Brien. Harrison and O'Brien would later form the HandMade Films Co. Harrison's 1975 album *Extra Texture (Read All About It)* specifically mentions Sellers as "not appearing" on the album.

Sellers is probably best remembered as Inspector Clouseau in his *Pink Panther* movies, and for his role in *Doctor Strangelove*. Peter Sellers died on July 24, 1980 shortly after the release of his film *Being There*, which features the song *Basketball Jones* (see Cheech And Chong). The 1995 TV special *The Peter Sellers Story* includes an interview with Harrison. For more information go to www.petersellers.com

Paul Shaffer

I Gotta Blues [Ringo Starr]
Pebbles P-02005 [unauthorized release] (xx/xx/02)
Producer: Daniel Kellison
Ringo Starr: Drums; Paul Shaffer: Keyboards; Will Lee: Bass; Sid McGinnis: Guitar
NBC Studio 6A, Rockefeller Center, New York, NY 06/20/89

[instrumental jam] 0:55 (13)

The Worlds's Most Dangerous Party
SBK/ERG/EMI-0777 7 89530 2 9 (07/13/93)
Producer: Todd Rundgren
Ringo Starr: Dialogue; additionally, one or more of the following: Paul Shaffer: Keyboards; Sid McGinnis: Guitars; Will Lee: Bass & Percussion; Anton Fig: Drums & Percussion
One or more of the following studios: Hit Factory, New York, Utopia
Sound, NY, Utopia Sound, Los Angeles, CA xx/xx/93

Mysterious Ways (A. Clayton-L. Mullen-D. Evans-P. Hewson) Intro 0:29 (5)

Paul Shaffer was born on November 28, 1949 in Thunder Bay, Ontario Canada. By the mid-1960s he was playing keyboards in a local band. The musician, composer, producer, bandleader and actor first gained notice as a member of the house band for TV's *Saturday Night Live* during the second half of the 1970s. In 1982 he became the leader of The World's Most Dangerous Band on NBC TV's *Late Night With David Letterman*, now known as the CBS Orchestra for the *Late Show With David Letterman* on CBS TV, where he still serves. Ringo appeared on Letterman's show on June 20, 1989 and sat in with Shaffer's band on some brief instrumental jams, which are available on unauthorized releases. Shaffer played keyboards with Ringo Starr's All-Starr Band during much of the second half of their performance at the Garden State Arts Center in Holmdel, New Jersey on August 5, 1989. Shaffer has also been the musical director of the Rock and Roll Hall of Fame since its inception. He has gained the respect of popular musicians, many with whom he has worked, for his innovative arrangements of their songs.

Shaffer's album *The Worlds's Most Dangerous Party* was produced by Todd Rundgren*. On it Shaffer asks Ringo at the end of the song *Burning Down The House*, "Do you want to sit in with the band?" Ringo says, "Love to!" The song that follows is *Mysterious Ways*. The album credits Ringo for "Guest Appearance," but doesn't specifically credit him as playing drums, while other guests' specific musical credits are noted. Shaffer says that Ringo's only contribution was his dialogue to add to the party atmosphere of the album. [Hamish Stuart*, Robbie McIntosh and Paul Wickens, members of Paul McCartney's band then, are also listed in the credits as additional party guests.] Shaffer sat in with Ringo Starr's All-Starr Band during their performances at Caesar's in Atlantic City, New Jersey on July 22, 1995. Shaffer joined McCartney onstage at the *Concert For New York City* on October 20, 2001 at Madison Square Garden.

Paul Shaffer, circa 2000, courtesy of Paul Shaffer.

Ravi Shankar

Chants Of India
Angel-7243 8 55948 2 3 (05/06/97)
Producer: George Harrison
One or more of the following: Kalyan: Violin & Assistant; Anoushka Shankar: Conductor & Assistant; Subramaniam: Veena; Devi: Veena; Murali: Keyboards; Seenu: Mridangam; Balasai: Flute; Kamalakar: Flute; Ronu Mazumdar: Flute; Shekar: Cello; Biswas: Cello; John: Cello; Murali: Violin; Rex: Violin; Balu: Violin; Sasi: Violin; Girijan: Violin; Narayanan: Tanpura; Rebbecca Goodsell: Tanpura; Sririam: Tanpura; Venkataraman: Tanpura; Gowri Shankar: Tanpura; Babu Parameshwaran: Indian Chorus; Natesan: Indian Chorus; Ramchandran Suresh: Indian Chorus; Sashidran: Indian Chorus; Babu: Indian Chorus; Mani: Indian Chorus; Mani Kiran: Indian Chorus; Shanta Dhananjayan: Indian Chorus; Suhasini: Indian Chorus; Latha: Indian Chorus; Rashmi: Indian Chorus; Sarada: Western Chorus; Martha: Western Chorus; Vimala: Western Chours; Pearl: Western Chorus; Adela: Western Chorus; Dr. Grub: Western Chorus; Billy: Werstern Chorus; Tony: Western Chorus; Arul: Western Chorus; Ranjith: Western Chorus [unless noted otherwise]
FPSHOT, UK 07-08/xx/96 [unless noted otherwise]

Asato Maa (Trad. Arr: R. Shankar) 7:10 (4)
Additionally: **George Harrison: B. Vocals**
Sruthilaya Media Artist Studio, Madras, India 01 & 04/xx/96

Gaayatri (Trad. Arr: R. Shankar) 3:26 (7)
Additionally: **George Harrison: Bass & Glockenspiel**
Sruthilaya Media Artist Studio, Madras, India 01 & 04/xx/96

Geetaa (Trad. Arr: R. Shankar) 2:15 (10)
One or more of the following: **George Harrison: B. Vocals, Acoustic Guitar, Bass, Autoharp, Glockenspiel & Vibraphone**; Chandrashekhar: Violin, Chorus & Assistant; Anoushka Shankar: Conductor & Assistant; Balachandar: Mridamgam/Morsing; Bikram Ghosh: Tabla; Tarun Bhatacharaya: Santoor; Ronu Mazumdar: Flute; Jane Lister: Harp; Antonia Paget: Violla; Michael Paget: Viola; Stella Page: Viola; Isabel Dunn: Cello; Terry Emery: Tuned Percussion; Deepa Singh: Chorus; Hari Sivanesan: Chorus; Sivashakti Sivanesan: Chorus; Gaurav Mazumdar: Chorus; Shyamali Basu: Chorus; Sukanya Shankar: Chorus

Hari Om (R. Shankar) 3:05 (12)
Additionally: **George Harrison: B. Vocals**
Swara Laya Studio, Madras, India 01 & 04/xx/96

Mahaa Mrityunjaya (Trad. Arr: R. Shankar) 4:41 (8)
One or more of the following: **George Harrison: B. Vocals, Acoustic Guitar, Bass, Autoharp, Glockenspiel & Vibraphone**; Chandrashekhar: Violin, Chorus & Assistant; Anoushka Shankar: Conductor & Assistant; Balachandar: Mridamgam/Morsing; Bikram Ghosh: Tabla; Tarun Bhatacharaya: Santoor; Ronu Mazumdar: Flute; Jane Lister: Harp; Antonia Paget: Violla; Michael Paget: Viola; Stella Page: Viola; Isabel Dunn: Cello; Terry Emery: Tuned Percussion; Deepa Singh: Chorus; Hari Sivanesan: Chorus; Sivashakti Sivanesan: Chorus; Gaurav Mazumdar: Chorus; Shyamali Basu: Chorus; Sukanya Shankar: Chorus

Mangalam (Tala Mantra) (R. Shankar) 4:10 (11)
One or more of the following: **George Harrison: B. Vocals, Acoustic Guitar, Bass, Autoharp, Glockenspiel & Vibraphone**; Chandrashekhar: Violin, Chorus & Assistant; Anoushka Shankar: Conductor & Assistant; Balachandar: Mridamgam/Morsing; Bikram Ghosh: Tabla; Tarun Bhatacharaya: Santoor; Ronu Mazumdar: Flute; Jane Lister: Harp; Antonia Paget: Violla; Michael Paget: Viola; Stella Page: Viola; Isabel Dunn: Cello; Terry Emery: Tuned Percussion; Deepa Singh: Chorus; Hari Sivanesan: Chorus; Sivashakti Sivanesan: Chorus; Gaurav Mazumdar: Chorus; Shyamali Basu: Chorus; Sukanya Shankar: Chorus

Omkaaraaya Namaha (Trad. Arr: R. Shankar) 1:55 (2)
One or more of the following: **George Harrison: B. Vocals, Acoustic Guitar, Bass, Autoharp, Glockenspiel & Vibraphone**; Chandrashekhar: Violin, Chorus & Assistant; Anoushka Shankar: Conductor & Assistant; Balachandar: Mridamgam/Morsing; Bikram Ghosh: Tabla; Tarun Bhatacharaya: Santoor; Ronu Mazumdar: Flute; Jane Lister: Harp; Antonia Paget: Violla; Michael Paget: Viola: Stella Page: Viola; Isabel Dunn: Cello; Terry Emery: Tuned Percussion; Deepa Singh: Chorus; Hari Sivanesan: Chorus; Sivashakti Sivanesan: Chorus; Gaurav Mazumdar: Chorus; Shyamali Basu: Chorus; Sukanya Shankar: Chorus

Poornamadah (Trad. Arr: R. Shankar) 1:23 (6)

With A Little Help From My Friends

(a guide and reference book of the Beatles' contributions to other artist's recordings)

Dear Kristofer, As I am off for a tour in Europe & to record my new album 'Prayers from India' (Tentative title) in London (which George H. is going to produce). I am having this sent to Ravi. There were some major and minor flaws which I tried to correct. Pl. try to understand that my & George's Karmic association was very spontaneous & special. It certainly enriched him in his being inspired in his whole consciousness of Indian music, tradition, Religion - philosophy etc as well as my superstardom - & cult Guruship etc from mid sixties. But neither of us wanted to exploit it then or now. In fact I had to fight for years for all the misconceptions for some... Pl. read the article of Timothy White in Billboard to clear points. pl. don't forget that through the greatness of our music I've been able to influence many musicians in one way or the other which included in the field of classical, jazz, pop... wish you all the best. Ravi 6.17.'96

by Kristofer Karl Engelhardt

Additionally, one or more of the following: **George Harrison: B. Vocals, Acoustic Guitar, Bass, Autoharp, Glockenspiel & Vibraphone**
Sruthilaya Media Artist Studio, Madras, India 01 & 04/xx/96

Prabhujee (R. Shankar) 8:10 (15)
Additionally: **George Harrison: B. Vocals, Guitar & Bass**; one or more of the following: Chandrashekhar: Violin, Chorus & Assistant; Anoushka Shankar: Conductor & Assistant; Balachandar: Mridamgam/Morsing; Bikram Ghosh: Tabla; Tarun Bhatacharaya: Santoor; Ronu Mazumdar: Flute; Jane Lister: Harp; Antonia Paget: Violla; Michael Paget: Viola: Stella Page: Viola; Isabel Dunn: Cello; Terry Emery: Tuned Percussion; Deepa Singh: Chorus; Hari Sivanesan: Chorus; Sivashakti Sivanesan: Chorus; Gaurav Mazumdar: Chorus; Shyamali Basu: Chorus; Sukanya Shankar: Chorus

Sahanaa Vavatu (Trad. Arr: R. Shankar) 4:25 (5)
One or more of the following: **George Harrison: B. Vocals, Acoustic Guitar, Bass, Autoharp, Glockenspiel & Vibraphone**; Chandrashekhar: Violin, Chorus & Assistant; Anoushka Shankar: Conductor & Assistant; Balachandar: Mridamgam/Morsing; Bikram Ghosh: Tabla; Tarun Bhatacharaya: Santoor; Ronu Mazumdar: Flute; Jane Lister: Harp; Antonia Paget: Violla; Michael Paget: Viola; Stella Page: Viola; Isabel Dunn: Cello; Terry Emery: Tuned Percussion; Deepa Singh: Chorus; Hari Sivanesan: Chorus; Sivashakti Sivanesan: Chorus; Gaurav Mazumdar: Chorus; Shyamali Basu: Chorus; Sukanya Shankar: Chorus

Sarve Shaam (Trad. Arr: R. Shankar) 5:05 (16)
George Harrison: Autoharp & Marimba; Additionally, one or more of the following: Chandrashekhar: Violin, Chorus & Assistant; Anoushka Shankar: Conductor & Assistant; Balachandar: Mridamgam/Morsing; Bikram Ghosh: Tabla; Tarun Bhatacharaya: Santoor; Ronu Mazumdar: Flute; Jane Lister: Harp; Antonia Paget: Violla; Michael Paget: Viola; Stella Page: Viola; Isabel Dunn: Cello; Terry Emery: Tuned Percussion; Deepa Singh: Chorus; Hari Sivanesan: Chorus; Sivashakti Sivanesan: Chorus; Gaurav Mazumdar: Chorus; Shyamali Basu: Chorus; Sukanya Shankar: Chorus

Svara Mantra (R. Shankar) 4:36 (13)
One or more of the following: **George Harrison: Acoustic Guitar, Bass, Autoharp, Glockenspiel & Vibraphone**; Chandrashekhar: Violin & Assistant; Anoushka Shankar: Conductor & Assistant; Balachandar: Mridamgam/Morsing; Bikram Ghosh: Tabla; Tarun Bhatacharaya: Santoor; Ronu Mazumdar: Flute; Jane Lister: Harp; Antonia Paget: Violla; Michael Paget: Viola; Stella Page: Viola; Isabel Dunn: Cello; Terry Emery: Tuned Percussion

Vandanaa Trayee (Trad. Arr: R. Shankar) 4:28 (1)
Additionally: **George Harrison: Vibraphone & Acoustic Bass**
Sruthilaya Media Artist Studio, Madras, India 01 & 04/xx/96

Vedic Chanting (One) (Trad. Arr: R. Shankar) 3:10 (3)
Swara Laya Studio, Madras, India 01 & 04/xx/96

Vedic Chanting (Two) (Trad. Arr: R. Shankar) 2:14 (14)
Additionally: Ravi Shankar: Sitar; one or more of the following: Chandrashekhar: Violin, Chorus & Assistant; Anoushka Shankar: Conductor & Assistant; Balachandar: Mridamgam/Morsing; Bikram Ghosh: Tabla; Tarun Bhatacharaya: Santoor; Ronu Mazumdar: Flute; Jane Lister: Harp; Antonia Paget: Violla; Michael Paget: Viola; Stella Page: Viola; Isabel Dunn: Cello; Terry Emery: Tuned Percussion; Deepa Singh: Chorus; Hari Sivanesan: Chorus; Sivashakti Sivanesan: Chorus; Gaurav Mazumdar: Chorus; Shyamali Basu: Chorus; Sukanya Shankar: Chorus
Swara Laya Studio, Madras, India 01 & 04/xx/96 & FPSHOT, UK 07-08/xx/96

Veenaa-Murali (Trad. Arr: R. Shankar) 3:44 (9)
One or more of the following: **George Harrison: B. Vocals, Acoustic Guitar, Bass, Autoharp, Glockenspiel & Vibraphone**; Kalyan: Violin & Assistant; Anoushka Shankar: Conductor & Assistant; Subramaniam: Veena; Devi: Veena; Murali: Keyboards; Seenu: Mridangam; Balasai: Flute; Kamalakar: Flute; Ronu Mazumdar: Flute; Shekar: Cello; Biswas: Cello; John: Cello; Murali: Violin; Rex: Violin; Balu: Violin; Sasi: Violin; Girijan: Violin; Narayanan: Tanpura; Rebbecca Goodsell: Tanpura; Sririam: Venkataraman: Tanpura; Gowri Shankar: Tanpura; Babu Parameshwaran: Indian Chorus; Natesan: Indian Chorus; Ramchandran Suresh: Indian Chorus; Sashidran: Indian Chorus; Babu: Indian Chorus; Mani: Indian Chorus; Mani Kiran: Indian Chorus; Shanta Dhananjayan: Indian Chorus; Suhasini: Indian Chorus; Latha: Indian Chorus; Rashmi: Indian Chorus; Sarada: Western Chorus; Martha: Western Chorus; Vimala: Western Chours; Pearl: Western Chorus; Adela: Western Chorus; Dr. Grub: Western Chorus; Billy: Werstern Chorus; Tony: Western Chorus; Arul: Western Chorus; Ranjith: Western Chorus

Swara Laya Studio, Madras, India 01 & 04/xx/96

The Concert For Bangla Desh
Apple/Rhino-R2 970481 (DVD) (10/25/05)
Producer: George Harrison & Allen Klein (film); **George Harrison** & Phil Spector (music)
Ravi Shankar: Sitar; Ali Akbar Khan: Sarod; Alla Rakha: Tabla; Kamala Chakravarty: Tamboura
Madison Square Garden, New York, NY 12/01/71 (afternoon or evening)

(Introduction) Bangla Dhun (Sitar & Sarod Duet, Dadra Tal-6 Beats, Teental-16 Beats) [live] (Trad.) 23:39 (1: 1-2) (10/xx/83)
[Also available on Apple/Capitol-0946335880 28 (1: 1-2) (10/25/05) (12/20/71)]

Fort Worth Express
Hindustani Music-Raga 001-A:B [unauthorized release] (xx/xx/96)
Producer: [unknown-audience recording]
Tarrant County Convention Center, Fort Worth, TX 11/22/74

Dream, Nightmare & Dawn (Music For A Ballet) Part Two: Nightmare (Dispute & Violence) [live] (R. Shankar) 5:08 (1-11)
George Harrison: Guitar; Billy Preston: Keyboards; Tom Scott: Saxophone; Chuck Findley: Trumpet; Robben Ford: Guitar; Andy Newmark: Drums; Willie Weeks: Bass; Jim Horn: Saxophone; Jim Keltner: Drums; Emil Richards: Marimbas & Percussion; Ravi Shankar: Vocals, Conductor or Sitar; Hariprasad Chaurasia: Bamboo Flute; Rijram Desad: Percussion & Strings; T.V. Gopalkrishnan: Mridangam; Gopal Krishan: Vichitra Veena; Sultan Khan: Sarangi; Kartick Kumar: Sitar; Kamalesh Maitra: Percussion; Satyadev Pawar: North India Violin; Alla Rakha: Tabla; Harihar Rao: Vocals, Sitar or Percussion; Shivkumar Sharma: Santoor; L. Subramaniam: Violin

I Am Missing You [live] (R. Shankar) 4:57 (1-10)
George Harrison: Acoustic Guitar & B. Vocals; Lakshmi Shankar: Lead Vocals; Ravi Shankar: Conductor or Sitar; Hariprasad Chaurasia: Bamboo Flute; Rijram Desad: Percussion & Strings; T.V. Gopalkrishnan: Mridangam & Vocals; Gopal Krishan: Vichitra Veena; Sultan Khan: Sarangi; Kartick Kumar: Sitar; Kamalesh Maitra: Percussion; Satyadev Pawar: North India Violin; Alla Rakha: Tabla; Harihar Rao: Sitar, B. Vocals or Percussion; Viji Shankar: B. Vocals; Shivkumar Sharma: Santoor; L. Subramaniam: Violin; Kumar Shankar: B. Vocals; Tom Scott: Saxophone; Emil Richards: Percussion; Willie Weeks: Bass

Zoom Zoom Zoom [live] (R. Shankar) 5:16 (1-6)
George Harrison: Electric Guitar; Lakshmi Shankar: Lead Vocals; Ravi Shankar: Conductor; Hariprasad Chaurasia: Bamboo Flute; Rijram Desad: Percussion & Strings; T.V. Gopalkrishnan: Mridangam & Vocals; Gopal Krishan: Vichitra Veena; Sultan Khan: Sarangi; Kartick Kumar: Sitar; Kamalesh Maitra: Percussion; Satyadev Pawar: North India Violin; Alla Rakha: Tabla; Harihar Rao: Sitar, B. Vocals or Percussion; Viji Shankar: B. Vocals; Shivkumar Sharma: Santoor; L. Subramaniam: Violin; Kumar Shankar: B. Vocals; Billy Preston: Keyboards; Robben Ford: Acoustic Guitar; Andy Newmark: Drums; Willie Weeks: Bass; Jim Horn: Saxophone; Jim Keltner: Drums; Emil Richards: Marimbas

In Celebration (Orchestral And Ensembles) (Vocal And Experimental)
Angel/Dark Horse-CDCD 7243 5 55577 2 8 (7243 5 55579 2 8) (7243 5 55581 2 8) (02/20/96) **George Harrison: Liner Notes**
Producer: George Harrison

Dream, Nightmare & Dawn (Music For A Ballet) Part Two: Nightmare (Dispute & Violence) (R. Shankar) 2:59 (4-13) (09/20/74)
Ravi Shankar: Vocals & Conductor; Harihar Rao: Vocals; Klaus Voormann: Bass; L. Subramaniam: Violin; Tom Scott: Saxophones; Jim Keltner: Percussion; Ed Shaunessey: Drums; Emil Richards: Marimbas & Percussion
A&M Studios, Los Angeles, CA 04/xx/73-early/xx/74

Friar Park (R. Shankar) 5:50 (4-7) (06/xx/87)
George Harrison: Autoharp & (supposed) Synthesizer; Ravi Shankar: Sitar & Arrangement; Markandeya Mishra: Tabla; Ray Cooper: Marimba & Percussion
FPSHOT, UK xx/xx/86

I Am Missing You (R. Shankar) 3:40 (4-9) (09/20/74)
George Harrison: Autoharp, B. Vocals, Acoustic Guitar & Arrangement; **Ringo Starr: Drums**; Lakshmi Shankar: Lead Vocals; Viji Shankar: B. Vocals; Kamala Chakravarty: B. Vocals; Ravi Shankar: B. Vocals; Kumar Shankar: B. Vocals; Klaus Voormann: Bass; Tom Scott: Soprano Saxophone; Jim Keltner: Drums; Emil Richards: Percussion & Marimbas; Billy Preston: Keyboards
A&M Studios, Los Angeles, CA probably 04/xx/73

Oh Bhagawan [Oh Bhaugowan] (R. Shankar) 3:35 (4-6) (08/09/71)
Ravi Shankar: Vocals & Sitar; Sanjukta Ghosh: Vocals; Shubho Shankar: Vocals; G. Sachdev: Flute; Harihar Rao: Ek Tara

The Record Plant Studios, Los Angeles, CA 07/xx/71

(Raga) Jait (R. Shankar) 9:42 (2-2) (02/06/76)
Lakshmi Shankar: Lead Vocals; Kartick Kumar: Sitar; Kamlesh Maitra: Sarod & Tabla Tarang; Satyadev Pawar: Violin; Harihar Rao: Manjira; Viji Shankar: Tanpura; Kamala Chakravarty: Tanpura; T.V. Gopalkrishnan: Mridangam; L. Subramaniam: Violin; Gopal Kishan Veenkar: Vichitra Veena; Anantlal: Shahnai; Rijram Desad: Madal Tarang; Alla Rakha: Tabla; Shivkumar Sharma: Santoor; Hariprasad Chaurasia: Flute; Sultan Khan: Sarangi; Ravi Shankar: Arrangement & Conductor
FPSHOT, UK xx/xx/74

Supaney Mein Aye [Supane Me Aye Preetam Sainya] (R. Shankar) 4:11 (4-4) (09/20/74)
Lakshmi Shankar: Lead Vocals; Shivkumar Sharma: Santoor; Aashish Khan: Sarod; Shubho Shankar: Sitar; Al Kasey: Mandolin; Ronald Cohen: Sarangi; L. Subramaniam: Violin; Hariprasad Chaurasia: Flute; Alla Rakha: Tabla
A&M Studios, Los Angeles, CA probably 04/xx/73

Ta Na Tom (R. Shankar) 6:42 (4-10)
Lakshmi Shankar: Vocals; Viji Shankar: Vocals; Kamala Chakravarty: Vocals; T.V. Gopalkrishnan: Vocals; Rijram Desad: Vocals; Ravi Shankar: Vocals, Conductor & Arrangement; Hariprasad Chaurasia: Flute; L. Subramaniam: Violin; Satyadev Pawar: Violin; Alla Rakha: Pakawaj
FPSHOT, UK xx/xx/74

Vandana (R. Shankar) 2:37 (4-1) (02/06/76)
Lakshmi Shankar: Lead Vocals & Swaramandal; Kamlesh Maitra: Sarod & Tabla Tarang, Duggi Tarang & Ek Tara; Satyadev Pawar: Violin; Harihar Rao: Manjira & B. Vocals; Viji Shankar: B. Vocals & Tanpura; Kamala Chakravarty: B. Vocals & Tanpura; T.V. Gopalkrishnan: B. Vocals; L. Subramaniam: Violin; Kartick Kumar: Sitar; Gopal Kishan Veenkar: B. Vocals; Anantlal: Shahnai; Rijram Desad: Pakhavaj; Alla Rakha: Tabla; Shivkumar Sharma: Santoor & B. Vocals; Hariprasad Chaurasia: Flute; Sultan Khan: Sarangi; Ravi Shankar: Arrangement & Conductor
FPSHOT, UK xx/xx/74

In Concert 1972
Apple-7243 8 53817 2 0 (UK) (12/02/96) (01/22/73)
Producer: George Harrison, Al Steckler, Zakir Hussein & Phil McDonald
Ravi Shankar: Sitar; Ali Akbar Khan: Sarod; Alla Rakha: Tabla; Ashoka: Tambouras; Susan: Tambouras
Philharmonic Hall, New York, NY 10/08/72

Raga-Hem Bihag [live] (R. Shankar-A. Khan) 25:18 (1-1)

Raga-Manj Khamaj [live] (R. Shankar-A. Khan) 50:57 (1-2)

Raga-Sindhi Bhairavi [live] (R. Shankar-A. Khan) 26:18 (2-1)

Joi Bangla/Oh Bhaugowan / Raga Mishra-Jhinjhoti
Apple-1838 (7" single) (08/09/71)
Producer: George Harrison
Probably one or more of the following: Ravi Shankar: Vocals & Sitar; Ali Akbar Khan: Sarod; G. Sachdev: Flute; Harihar Rao: Ek Tara; Alla Rakha: Tabla [unless noted otherwise]
Probably Record Plant Studios, Los Angeles, CA 07/xx/71

Joi Bangla (R. Shankar) 3:18 (1/1)

Raga Mishra-Jhinjhoti (Duet Sitar & Sarod) (trad.) 6:52 (2/1)
Ravi Shankar: Sitar; Ali Akbar Khan: Sarod; Alla Rakha: Tabla

Raga
Mystic Fire Video, Island Visual Arts, PolyGram Video & Apple Films-76239 (VHS) (09/24/91)
Re-producer: George Harrison: (soundtrack only); Producer: Howard Worth (film)
Big Sur, CA 06/10-11/68

["Sitar lessons"] [live] (R. Shankar) 4:20
George Harrison: Sitar, Finger Cymbals & B. Vocals; Ravi Shankar: Lead Vocals & Sitar

Raga (Original Sound Track Album)
Apple-SWAO-3384 (album 12") (12/07/71)
Re-producer: George Harrison; Producer: [Various Producers] 06-07/xx/71
One or more of the following musicians: Ravi Shankar: Sitar & Vocals; Lakshmi Shankar: Swaramandal & Vocals; Kamala Chakravarty: B. Vocals, Tamboura & Tanpura; Alla Rakha: Pakhavaj & Tabla [unless noted otherwise]
Various locations mostly US and India, mostly 04-07/xx/68 & 07/xx/71 [unless noted otherwise]

Baba Teaching (trad.) 1:08 (1/3)
Additionally: Ustad Allauddin Khan: Sarod & Vocals

Banaras Ghat (R. Shankar) 2:45 (2/2)
Recorded in India

Birth To Death (R. Shankar) 3:10 (1/4)

Bombay Studio (Raga Parameshwari) (R. Shankar) 2:45 (2/3)
Recorded in India

Dawn To Dusk (R. Shankar) 3:38 (1/1)

Frenzy And Distortion (R. Shankar) 1:06 (2/5)
Mr. Amin: Vocals; [a Collage by Collin Walcott]

Gurur Bramha (Trad. Arr: R. Shankar) 1:10 (1/6)

Kinnara School (R. Shankar) 1:51 (2/4)
Recorded in Los Angeles, CA

Raga Desh (R. Shankar) 8:50 (2/6)
Recorded at Lincoln Center For The Performing Arts, New York, NY fall-xx/xx/67

Raga Parameshwari/Rangeswhart (R. Shankar) 4:31 (2/1)

United Nations (Raga Piloo) (R. Shankar-Y. Menuhin-C. Walcott) 4:33 (1/7)
Additionally: Yehudi Menuhin: Violin

Vedic Hymns (trad.) 1:30 (1/2)
Recorded in Madras, India

Vinus House (R. Shankar) 2:37 (1/5)
Recorded in Vinay Bharatram's home, Delhi, India

Raga Mala (The Autobiography of Ravi Shankar)
Genesis Publications ISBN 0-904351-46-7
(Editor & Introduction: George Harrison)
GENRAVICD02 (UK) (xx/xx/97)
Producer: George Harrison
Ronu Mazumdar: Flute; Bikram Ghosh: Tabla; M. Balachandar: Jews Harp & Mridagam
Sruthilaya Media Artists, Madras, India 01&/or 04/96 & FPSHOT, UK 07-08/xx/96

Dakshini (R. Shankar) (2-5)

Shankar Family & Friends
Dark Horse-SP-22002 (album 12") (10/07/74) (09/20/74)
Producer: George Harrison
One or more of the following: **George Harrison: Autoharp, Acoustic Guitar & Electric Guitar**; **Ringo Starr: Drums**; Jitendra Abhisheki: Vocals; Kamala Chakravarty: B. Vocals; Lakshmi Shankar: Swaramandal & Vocals; Shivkumar Sharma: Santoor, Shaker & B. Vocals; Kumar Shankar: B. Vocals; Ravi Shankar: Sitar, Vocals, Synthesizer & Surbahar; Shubho Shankar: Sitar & B. Vocals; Ray Kramer: Cello; W. Webb: Esraj; Dennis Budimir: Acoustic Guitar; Klaus Voormann: Bass; Nodu Mullick: Tamboura & Kartal; Krishna Temple: Kartal; Al Kasey: Mandolin; Ronald Cohen: Sarangi; Aashish Khan: Sarod, B. Vocals & Swaramandal; George Ruckert: Sarod; Fakir Muhammad: Tamboura; L. Subramaniam: Violin; Bobby Bruce: Electric Violin; Gordon Swift: Electric Violin; Ray Pizzi: Bassoon; Hariprasad Chaurasia: Flute & Cowbells; G. Sachdev: Flute; Sharad Kumar: Flute; Tom Scott: Boehm Flute, Saxophones & Clapper; Gene Cipriano: Oboe; Jim Keltner: Drums; Ed Shaunessey: Drums; Emil Richards: Percussion & Marimbas; Palghat Raghu: Mridingam; Vini Poncia: Tambourine; Alla Rakha: Pakhavaj & Tabla; Harihar Rao: Vocals & Dholak; Pranesh Khan: Dholak; Billy Preston: Organ; Fred Teague: Organ; Nicky Hopkins: Piano; Paul Beaver: Synthesizer; Malcolm Cecil: Synthesizer; Robert Margouleff: Synthesizer [unless noted otherwise]
A&M Studios, Los Angeles, CA 04/xx/73-early/xx/74

Dream, Nightmare & Dawn (Music For A Ballet) Overture (R. Shankar) 2:28 (2/1)

Dream, Nightmare & Dawn (Music For A Ballet) Part One: Dream (Festivity & Joy) (R. Shankar) 3:52 (2/2)

Dream, Nightmare & Dawn (Music For A Ballet) Part One: Dream (Love-Dance Ecstasy) (R. Shankar) 3:10 (2/3)

Dream, Nightmare & Dawn (Music For A Ballet) Part Three: Dawn (Awakening) (R. Shankar) 3:07 (2/8)

Dream, Nightmare & Dawn (Music For A Ballet) Part Three: Dawn (Peace & Hope) (R. Shankar) 4:21 (2/9)

Dream, Nightmare & Dawn (Music For A Ballet) Part Two: Nightmare (Despair & Sorrow) (R. Shankar) 3:07 (2/7)

Dream, Nightmare & Dawn (Music For A Ballet) Part Two: Nightmare (Disillusionment & Frustration) (R. Shankar) 2:51 (2/6)

Dream, Nightmare & Dawn (Music For A Ballet) Part Two: Nightmare (Lust) (R. Shankar) 3:12 (2/4)
Additionally **George Harrison: Guitar**; **Ringo Starr: Drums**

I Am Missing You (Reprise) (R. Shankar) 3:56 (1/4)

Jaya Jagadish Hare (R. Shankar-Trad.) 4:50 (1/5)

Kahan Gayelava Shyam Salone (R. Shankar) 3:15 (1/2)

Ravi Shankar's Music Festival From India
Dark Horse-SP 22007 (album 12") (02/06/76)
Producer: George Harrison
Lakshmi Shankar: Lead Vocals; one or more of the following: Kamalesh Maitra: Sarod, Madal,

Tabla Tarang, Duggi Tarang & Ek Tara; Satyadev Pawar: Violin; Lakshmi Shankar: Swaramandal; Harihar Rao: Kartal, Manjira, Dholak, B. Vocals & Gub Gubi; Viji Shankar: B. Vocals & Tanpura; Kamala Chakravarty: B. Vocals & Tanpura; T.V. Gopalkrishnan: Mridagam, Khanjira & B. Vocals; L. Subramaniam: Violin; Kartick Kumar: Sitar; Gopal Kishan Veenkar: Vichitra Veena & B. Vocals; Anantlal: Shahnai; Rijram Desad: Pakhavaj, Nal, Nagada, Madal Tarang, Huduk & Duff; Alla Rakha: Tabla; Shivkumar Sharma: Santoor, Kanoon & B. Vocals; Hariprasad Chaurasia: Flutes; Sultan Khan: Sarangi; Ravi Shankar: Arrangement & Conductor
FPSHOT, UK xx/xx/74

Bhajan (R. Shankar) 3:50 (2/2)

Chaturang (R. Shankar) 2:00 (1/4)

Dehati (R. Shankar) 10:04 (2/4)

Dhamar (R. Shankar) 5:20 (1/2)

Kajri (R. Shankar) 4:45 (2/1)

Naderdani (R. Shankar) 4:40 (2/3)

Tarana (R. Shankar) 3:50 (1/3)

Yin & Yang with Fugelsang
Queensboro-QBR-002 [unauthorized release] (xx/xx/02)
Producer: Mary Wharton
George Harrison: Vocals & Guitar; Sukanya Shankar: Vocals; Ravi Shankar: Sitar
VH1 Studios, New York, NY 05/14/97

Prabhujee (R. Shankar) 1:42 (4)

Ravi Shankar was born Robindra Shankar on April 7, 1920 in Varanasi (Benares), India. His father was abroad most of the time practicing law, teaching and working with the League of Nations. Ravi wanted to be an actor but soon developed a love for music. His family moved to Paris when he was 10, and he began performing globally in his brother Uday Shan-Kar's Company of Hindu Dancers and Musicians. This exposed Ravi to a wide variety of musical styles, later instrumental in his bridging the gap between Eastern and Western music. Ustad Allauddin Khan, India's renowned master of the sarod, joined the dance troupe in 1935. This led to Ravi devoting nearly eight years of musical training on Indian stringed instruments (sitar) under Ustad. Ravi married Ustad's daughter Annapurna in 1941. Ustad's son, Ali Akbar Khan, also became a master of the sarod, as did his son Aashish Khan*. Ali and Aashish would work extensively with Ravi. In 1952 Ravi began two decades of collaboration with violinist Yehudi Menuhin that culminated in the Grammy Award winning album *West Meets East*.

Shankar and Indian music received major global exposure in 1965 from The Beatles. The Beatles were introduced to Indian music and the sitar on the set of their film *Help!* in April 1965. The film's plot centers on Eastern religion and features Indian music scored by Ken Thorne's *Another Hard Day's Night*, on the film's soundtrack album, contains the first known use of a sitar on a pop-rock record. When The Beatles were in Los Angeles during their tour that summer, David Crosby (see Stephen Stills) recommended Ravi's album *Portrait Of A Genius* to Harrison, who became smitten by it. Harrison purchased a sitar and played it on The Beatles' song *Norwegian Wood* released in the fall of 1965. He met Ravi some months later at a dinner hosted by friends from North London's Asian Music Circle, who had assisted Harrison on his Indian-influenced song *Love You To* on The Beatles' 1966 album *Revolver*. He played at Harrison's home with John Lennon and Ringo Starr in attendance. Ravi say, "George met me and showed interest in learning sitar. I explained how difficult and horrendous it is to learn sitar and play properly, but George said he would try!" During one lesson, Ravi admonished him for stepping over a sitar to answer the phone. Harrison quickly learned that the sitar was more than just an instrument to Ravi. At Harrison's urging, The Beatles scheduled a three day layover in India during their Far East tour in mid-1966. Harrison visited India several months later to take more lessons from Ravi and they forged a lifelong friendship. Harrison also became very interested in Indian philosophy and religion, which are inseparable from Indian music. It is unlikely that The Beatles would have attended the Maharishi Mahesh Yogi's lectures on Transcendental Meditation, or traveled to his ashram in Rishikesh, India, had it not been for Harrison's initial interest in Indian music. Though known and respected in the West for some time, Ravi's association with The Beatles, and his appearance at the Monterey Pop Festival in 1967, made him an icon of the counterculture of the late 1960s. While encouraged and flattered, Ravi also found performing between sets of loud, rock bands destroying their instruments to rowdy, drugged-out kids in smoke-filled sports arenas distressing. During the remainder of his life Harrison was an advocate and intermediary for Ravi in bridging the cultural and generational gap between Eastern and Western music.
In mid-1971 Ravi told Harrison of the recent natural disasters, starvation and political strife plaguing his homeland of Bangla Desh. Harrison quickly organized *The Concert For*

Bangla Desh, with proceeds from the concert, album and film donated to benefit its people. Apple issued the Shankar single *Joi Bangla* to tie in with the benefit. The soundtrack and the Apple film *Raga* (originally titled *Messenger Out Of The East*), which Ravi and George had worked on for over two years, were also released in late 1971. Harrison makes a cameo in the film playing sitar with Ravi. Ravi says the song *Frenzy And Distortion* on the soundtrack is a musical collage by a student of his sung by an Indian musician, and not a recording by Harrison or The Beatles as rumored. Harrison also helped produce Shankar's Apple album *In Concert 1972*.

In 1973 Harrison enlisted his Eastern and Western musical friends, and produced the critically acclaimed self-titled album *Shankar Family & Friends*. It was initially planned for release on Apple but was released in 1974 on Dark Horse. Harrison, using the pseudonym Hari Georgeson, contributes to the album, as does Ringo under the pseudonym Billy Shears. Shankar Family & Friends accompanied Harrison on his 1974 US tour. George joined in on portions of their set, which included the songs *Zoom Zoom Zoom*, *Jai Sri Kalij*, *Naderdani*, *Chatpatay*, *Anurag (Romance)*, *I Am Missing You* and *Dispute And Violence*. In 1976 Dark Horse released the album *Ravi Shankar's Music Festival From India* produced by Harrison. [Dark Horse filmed *Ravi Shankar's Music Festival From India* in performance in London just before Harrison's 1974 US tour, though it hasn't been released.]

Ravi's 1987 album *Tana Mana*, partially recorded at FPSHOT, lists Harrison in the general credits as playing autoharp and synthesizer. Ravi and Frank Serafine are also listed as playing synthesizer. Ravi and Frank think the only song recorded at FPSHOT was *Friar Park*, and that George plays autoharp on it. Frank also thinks George plays synthesizer on it. In 1988 Ravi helped George and his son Dhani Harrison on *Ride Rajbun*, a track featured on the 1992 album *The Bunbury Tails*.

In 1996 Dark Horse, with Angel (EMI) Records, released the retrospective set *In Celebration*. Harrison essentially conceived the idea and, with help from Ravi's friend Alan Kozlowski, selected the tracks and produced the retrospective compilation in celebration of Ravi's 75th birthday. The set includes eight songs Harrison directly contributed to, including the previously unreleased *Ta Na Tom*. The musical credits are more detailed than on previous releases. The credits for *Friar Park* list Harrison playing autoharp, and also producing the recording but don't credit him playing synthesizer (which isn't apparent on the recording). *I Am Missing You* lists Ringo on drums and Harrison on autoharp and guitar. The song *Tana Mana* is now correctly listed as being recorded at Serafine's Studios in Los Angeles, and sung by Ravi and Lakshmi Shankar. Harrison isn't credited contributing to the song, yet in the book *The Quiet One-A Life Of George Harrison*, the author Alan Clayson claims that "George was the slightly throaty vocal refrain – in Hindi – on the title track [*Tana Mana*]". No amount of listening adds credibility to his claim.

Harrison produced and performs on Ravi's 1997 album *Chants Of India* recorded in India, and at FPSHOT. A documentary film of the recordings includes scenes with Harrison. Ravi acted primarily as arranger of the traditional Indian chants and composer of several new pieces. He accompanied Ravi during several promotional appearances for the album. On July 24, 1997 VH1 TV aired a half-hour interview with Ravi and George titled *Ying & Yang* promoting the album. The special includes Ravi, his wife Sukanya and George performing *Prabhujee*, and George playing *All Things Must Pass* on acoustic guitar, which appear on unauthorized releases. George also performed two other songs during the appearance that weren't aired. A 30-minute interview of another of these promotional appearances is included on a DVD accompanying the 2004 Canadian album *George Harrison From Beatles To Self-Realization: Chant & Be Happy* (XXI-XXI-CD 2 1461).

Harrison helped edit, and wrote the introduction to Ravi's autobiography *Raga Mala* (Genesis Publications). The song *Dakshini*, produced by and featuring Harrison, is available only on the second CD included with the book. The credits additionally list Harrison as also singing backing vocals on *I Am Missing You*. Ravi was reportedly with George when he died and admits he loved him like a son. Ravi Shankar continues to be, as George Harrison called him, "The Godfather of World Music." For more information go to www.ravishankar.org

Del Shannon

Rock On!
Acadia-ACAM8147 (UK) (09/04/07) (10/01/91)
Producer: Del Shannon
George Harrison: B. Vocals; Del Shannon: Lead Vocals & (probable) Acoustic Guitar; Billy Coiffi: B. Vocals, Electric & Acoustic Guitar; Bob Mair: Bass; Mel Watt: Drums; Michael Clark: Keyboards; Tom Petty: B. Vocals; Jeff Lynne: B. Vocals
Weddington Studios (NRG), Los Angeles, CA 05/25/88

Hot Love (D. Shannon) 3:25 (2-18) (09/xx/91)

Del Shannon was born Charles Westover in Grand Rapids, Michigan on December 30, 1934 but lived in nearby Coopersville. Shannon played ukulele as a youngster and guitar in high school bands. He performed in the US Army while stationed in Germany. After the army, he began writing songs and playing in clubs near his home in Battle Creek, Michigan. A DJ took his recordings to a music management company in Detroit, Michigan. They suggested he adopt a stage name. He came up with Del Shannon after the Cadillac Coupe DeVille and a friend named Shannon. They offered him a contract and a recording session in New York, where he recorded his composition *Runaway* in early 1961. It became his first and only number one hit. It was soon followed by the Top 10 hit *Hats Off To Larry* and the Top 20 hit *Little Town Flirt* in 1962 that he also wrote.

Del toured the UK in September 1962 and took notice of the rising popularity of The Beatles. They shared the bill with Del at the Royal Albert Hall in London on April 18, 1963. Del was so impressed with their song *From Me To You* that he recorded a cover version of it in the UK several weeks later, making him the first US artist to cover a Lennon-McCartney composition, and their first on the US charts. It wouldn't be his last cover of one of their songs. Del visited The Beatles in Florida in February 1964 and the following year in New York. John Lennon admitted that his 1964 composition *I'll Be Back* was a rewrite of one of Del's songs. Though the British music invasion had a devastating effect on US artists in the mid-1960s, Del managed to have hits with *Handy Man*, *Keep Searchin'* and *Stranger In Town*. Peter & Gordon* turned his composition *I Go To Pieces* into a Top 10 hit in 1965. Lennon and Ringo Starr attended Shannon's performance at Brian Epstein's Saville Theatre in London on February 19, 1967.

Unfortunately, mismanagement, changing musical styles and personal problems led to Del's departure from the charts. During the late 1960s and early '70s Del produced recordings for other artists, most notably the Top Five hits *Baby It's You* by Smith and *Gypsy Woman* by Brian Hyland, and recorded a wide variety of music. He also worked with Jeff Lynne* and Dave Edmunds* with praise from the critics, but not much commercial success. In the early 1980s Del hooked up with Tom Petty*, who produced his all too appropriately titled album *Drop Down And Get Me*, which includes *Sea Of Love*, Del's last Top 40 hit.

Shannon's lifelong friend, former manager and song publisher, Dan Bourgoise of Bug Music, says that in May 1988 Petty, Lynne and George Harrison, who were in the process of forming the Traveling Wilburys (see Bob Dylan, Roy Orbison) provided backing vocals on Del's song *Hot Love*, backed by The Monte Carlos. He says it's the only recording of Del's to which any of The Beatles contributed. [It was first issued, with a slightly different mix, on a single in Europe in 1991.] Following the death of Orbison there were reports that Shannon was being considered as his replacement in the Traveling Wilburys. Lynne, and Tom Petty And The Heartbreakers provided the backing and production for Shannon's critically acclaimed album *Rock On!* On February 8, 1990, during the final phases of recording the album, Del ended his life. The Traveling Wilburys recorded a cover of Del's song *Runaway* shortly after his death and released it later that year. Del Shannon was inducted into the Rock and Roll Hall of Fame in 1999. For more information go to www.delshannon.com

Beatle Bop-Hamburg Days (Once Upon A Time In Germany) [The Beatles* With Tony Sheridan] Bear Family-BCD 16583 BH (Germany) (11/06/01)
Producer: Bert Kaempfert & [Paul Murphy†]
Paul McCartney: Bass; **George Harrison: Guitar**; **Pete Best: Drums**; Tony Sheridan: Lead Vocals & Lead Guitar [unless noted otherwise]
Friedrich-Ebert-Halle, (Harburg) Hamburg, Germany 06/22-23/61 [unless noted otherwise]

My Bonnie (Lies Over The Ocean) (Mein Herz Is Bei Dir Nur) (Rock) [German Intro] (trad. Arr: T. Sheridan-Bert Kaempfert) 2:43 (2-1) (10/23/61)
Additionally: **Paul McCartney: B. Vocals**; **John Lennon: Handclaps & B. Vocals**

My Bonnie (Lies Over The Ocean) (Twist) [English Intro] (trad. Arr: T. Sheridan) 2:41 (2-2) (01/05/62)
Additionally: **Paul McCartney: B. Vocals**; **John Lennon: Handclaps & B. Vocals**

Nobody's Child (C. Coben-M. Foree-Arr: T. Sheridan) 3:53 (2-7) (02/xx/64)
Note: George Harrison doesn't perform on this recording

The Saints (When The Saints Go Marching In) (trad. Arr: T. Sheridan) 3:19 (2-4) (10/23/61)
Additionally: **Paul McCartney: B. Vocals**; **John Lennon: Guitar**

Sweet Georgia Brown [original lyric version] B. Bernie-M. Pinkard-K. Casey) 2:03 (2-10) (10/xx/62)
Additionally: **George Harrison: B. Vocals**; **Paul McCartney: Arrangement & B. Vocals**; **John Lennon: Guitar & B. Vocals**; Roy Young: Piano; Tony Sheridan: Lead Vocals (only)†††
Studio Hamburg (a.k.a. Rahlstedt/Wandsbek), Hamburg, Germany 05/24/62 & 06/07/62†

Sweet Georgia Brown [revised lyric version†] (B. Bernie-M. Pinkard-K. Casey [revised lyrics by: P. Murphy†]) 2:04 (2-11) (04/08/64)
Additionally: **George Harrison: B. Vocals**; **Paul McCartney: Arrangement & B. Vocals**; **John Lennon: Guitar & B. Vocals**; Roy Young: Piano; Tony Sheridan: Lead Vocals (only)†††
Studio Hamburg (a.k.a. Rahlstedt/Wandsbek), Hamburg, Germany 05/24/62 & 01/03/64†††

Sweet Georgia Brown [revised lyric version† with guitar & drumming overdub††] (B. Bernie-M. Pinkard-K. Casey [revised lyrics by: P. Murphy†]) 2:04 (1-12) (06/01/64)
Additionally: **George Harrison: B. Vocals**; **Paul McCartney: Arrangement & B. Vocals**; **John Lennon: Guitar & B. Vocals**; Roy Young: Piano; Tony Sheridan: Lead Vocals (only)†; Bernard Purdie: (probable) Overdubbed Drums; Cornell Dupree: (probable) Overdubbed Guitar
Studio Hamburg (a.k.a. Rahlstedt/Wandsbek), Hamburg, Germany & probably Atlantic Studios, New York, NY†† 05/24/62, 01/03/64† & early-mid/xx/64††

Take Out Some Insurance On Me, Baby [a.k.a. If You Love Me Baby] [original lyric version] (C. Singleton-W. Hall) 2:54 (2-9) (02/xx/64)
Additionally: **John Lennon: (possible) Rhythm Guitar**

Take Out Some Insurance On Me, Baby [a.k.a. If You Love Me Baby] [overdubbed & edited version††]* (C. Singleton-W. Hall) 2:52 (1-13) (06/01/64)
Additionally: **John Lennon: (possible) Rhythm Guitar**; Bernard Purdie: (probable) Overdubbed Drums; Cornell Dupree: (probable) Overdubbed Guitar
Overdubbing probably at Atlantic Studios, New York, NY†† overdubs & edit early to mid/xx/64

Why (Can't You Love Me Again) (T. Sheridan-B. Compton) 2:58 (2-6)
(04/xx/62)
Additionally: **John Lennon: B. Vocals**

Chantal Meets Tony Sheridan: A Beatles Story
Blueswan/Zounds-27000 60038 (Audiophile Edition Vol. 8) (Germany) (10/xx/04)
Producer: Michael Hofmann-von der Weiden
Tony Sheridan: Lead Vocals & Guitar; Michael Hofmann-von der Weiden: 12-String Guitar & Arranger; Gabriele-von der Weiden: Harp; Ralf Gauck: Bass; Peter Götzmann: Drums; Petra Erdmann: Flute: Norma Lukoschek: Bass Recorder; Jeanine Krause: Oboe; Lilli Palm: Violin; Peter Breitmann: Keyboards; Ede Janson: Electric Guitar
Festspielhaus Worms, Germany 02/29/04

Tell Me If You Can [live] (**P. McCartney**-T. Sheridan) 3:28 (6)
[Also available on Blueswan/Zounds Music - 27150 00013 (5) (DVD PAL only) 11/xx/04]

Tony Sheridan was born Anthony Esmond

Sheridan McGinnity on May 21, 1940 in Norwich, England. He sang in his church choir, and played violin in grade school but switched to the guitar. He was soon in demand as a session player, was in several bands, including The Saints in 1955, Vince Taylor And The Playboys in 1959 and the Jets in 1960, and had appeared on BBC TV.

The Beatles first met Sheridan in November 1960 at the Top Ten Club in Hamburg, Germany where he and the Jets were the headline act. The Beatles then consisted of Liverpool, England natives John Lennon, born on October 9, 1940 on rhythm guitar, James Paul McCartney, born on June 18, 1942 on piano and guitar, and George Harrison, born on February 25, 1943 on lead guitar. Their bassist was Stuart Sutcliffe, born on June 23, 1940 in Edinburgh, Scotland and their drummer was Pete Best, born on November 24, 1941 in Madras, India. When The Beatles returned to Hamburg for an engagement at the Top Ten Club between April 1 and July 1, 1961 they bunked with Sheridan who was being backed by a number of house bands. The Beatles and Sheridan's band alternated sets, and before long they were backing Sheridan. Tony says, "I don't believe in accidents or coincidences, I believe we were brought together by fate. What impressed me most about them was that they were as obsessed with the whole rock 'n' roll thing as I was. When obsession meets obsession something mystical happens. There was an immediate chemistry among us – the sort that makes things rather effortless. We became very creative, probably for the first time, and didn't copy the records but did our own versions." Shortly after The Beatles arrived in Germany in 1961, Sutcliffe left the group to study art and spend more time with his German fiancée, Astrid Kirchherr.

German rock star Tommy Kent saw Sheridan performing with The Beatles at the Top Ten Club in early May 1961 and suggested them to his producer Berthold "Bert" Kaempfert. Bert, born October 16, 1923 in Hamburg, Germany, was an internationally known composer, musician, orchestra leader and Polydor Record's A&R Manager. The following night the two went to see them perform. Kent got up onstage and sang *Be-Bop-A-Lula* with them. Bert was equally impressed, and signed The Beatles and Sheridan to a one-year exclusive contract with Bert Kaempfert Productions, which took effect on July 1, 1961. Kaempfert arranged for Deutsche Grammophone Gesellschaft's Polydor Records label to release their recordings.

The most reliable information regarding these recordings are the notes (based on Hans Gottfridsson's 1997 book *The Beatles From Cavern To Star-Club*) accompanying the 2001 Bear Family release *Beatle Bop-Hamburg Days (Once Upon A Time In Germany)*, which is the most comprehensive release. Polydor's documents concerning these recordings are based on information given to them by Bert Kaempfert Productions making it secondhand information. These documents state the first recording sessions with Sheridan and The Beatles produced by Bert took place on June 22-23 1961 at Friedrich-Ebert-Halle (a concert hall in a community center and school in the Hamburg area which Tony says was a makeshift radio station British Forces set up after the war that was later used by German radio. They recorded *My Bonnie*, *Nobody's Child*, *When The Saints Go Marching In*, *Why*, *Take Out Some Insurance On Me, Baby*, *Ain't She Sweet* and *Cry For A Shadow*. They represent the first professional recordings The Beatles ever made. Tony didn't participate in The Beatles' recordings of *Ain't She Sweet* sung by Lennon, or the instrumental *Cry For A Shadow* (tentatively titled *Beatle Bop*) composed by Harrison and Lennon as a parody of *Apache* by Cliff Richards and The Shadows. The Beatles and Sheridan were performing all of these songs in their live set at the time.

The first few releases by Polydor with backing from The Beatles are credited as Tony Sheridan & The Beat Brothers. Some claim Bert used The Beat Brothers in lieu of The Beatles, because Beatles sounded like "peedles" — German slang for penis. Tony says he choose The Beat Brothers because Germans had difficulty pronouncing Beatles. He used the name, regardless of band members, until 1964. Following The Beatles' success Polydor, and other record companies, began crediting these recordings as Tony Sheridan & The Beatles. Later, they were credited as The Beatles with Tony Sheridan. Albums were often padded out with recordings by Tony Sheridan and The Beat Brothers to which The Beatles didn't contribute, creating much confusion. Tony says, "Those record companies did a lot of misleading and unethical things with those recordings over the years."

The first commercially released record that The Beatles ever appeared on was the single *My Bonnie / When The Saints Go Marching In* (Polydor-24 673) issued in Germany in October 1961 by Tony Sheridan & The Beat Brothers. *My Bonnie* is a traditional Scottish folk song that is often credited as being composed by

Charles Pratt but this has never been verified. Tony says, "I had backed Gene Vincent and was inspired by his arrangement of *My Bonnie*, so I did an arrangement of it, and *The Saints* that was inspired by an arrangement by Jerry Lee Lewis*." *My Bonnie* had about a half-minute spoken introduction in German, which Sheridan says Bert helped him with and thus snuck his name in the arrangement credits. This is the record that purportedly alerted Brian Epstein to The Beatles. As their manager, Brian persuaded Polydor to substitute The Beatles' name when the single was released in the UK with an English introduction in January 1962, and in Germany where it was a Top 40 hit. [After 1963 it was usually issued without any spoken introduction.] Brian used the single in helping The Beatles find a recording contract in the UK. [Once The Beatles were famous, Epstein objected to Polydor's continuous issuing of The Beatles recordings with Sheridan.] Polydor first issued *Why* and *Cry For A Shadow* in April 1962 on the French EP *Mr. Twist* (titled *My Bonnie* when later released in Germany and the UK).

Some have asserted that McCartney couldn't have played bass on these recordings because he'd only recently switched to playing it after Stuart had left the group. Tony says, "That's nonsense, Paul was a natural bass player. One told him what was needed and he did it — and more. Stuart and his girlfriend Astrid attended the sessions but only participated as creative personalities. Much of the rhythm [Paul's bass, and George and John's guitars] was meant to compensate for the lack of drive and punch from [Pete Best] the drums. I played most all of the lead guitar, which was pretty much improvised on the spot, including my shitty lead on *Take Out Some Insurance On Me, Baby*. I told Bert, 'You can't let that go out,' but he thought it was really good and wouldn't let me do it again. It was once voted one of the worst solos of all times, and poor George got the credit for it!" *Take Out Some Insurance On Me, Baby* and *Nobody's Child* were first released in February 1964. Tony (and others present) says all of the songs with The Beatles were recorded essentially "live" without any overdubbing. There is one other guitar on *Take Out Some Insurance On Me, Baby*, so it's unclear whether George or John plays it, but the Bear Family release credits George. [Harrison recorded a version of *Nobody's Child* with the Traveling Wilburys released in 1990.]

Sheridan and Top Ten Club owner Peter Eckhorn went to Liverpool in late December 1961 to book The Beatles for another engagement but couldn't reach an agreement with their new manager Brian Epstein. During the visit, Sheridan persuaded Rory Storm & The Hurricane's* drummer Ringo Starr to join his backing band The Beat Brothers in Hamburg, but by March 1962 Starr had rejoined The Hurricanes. The Beat Brothers' keyboardist Roy Young (see Cliff Bennett And The Rebel Rousers) thinks Ringo may play drums on their recording of *Ya Ya (Part 1 & 2)* but it doesn't sound like Ringo's drumming. The 1985 Polydor CD *The Beatles First* lists it as being recorded on August 28, 1962 and Gottfridsson's book lists October 18, 1962. If either date is correct, it rules out Ringo as he was in Liverpool and playing with The Beatles. Perhaps Roy is mistaken, or is referring to live performances of the song, or another (unreleased) version. Tony says Roy played organ and Johnny Watson played drums, and that Ringo didn't contribute to it or any of his recordings. Gottfridsson has also concluded that Ringo didn't contribute to any of Tony's recordings.

When The Beatles returned to Hamburg for an engagement between April 13 and May 31, 1962 to help open the new Star-Club they were met by Astrid, who informed them that Stuart Sutcliffe had died suddenly of a brain hemorrhage on April 10, 1962. Epstein (on the verge of being offered a recording contract for The Beatles with EMI in the UK), per the terms of their contract with Kaempfert, sought an early release due to expire on June 30, 1962. Bert agreed to release The Beatles but wanted to use them for one additional recording session for Sheridan. Brian agreed, and additionally booked May 28 and 29 with Bert for The Beatles to record 12 of their own songs to be paid for by Epstein, apparently in case they weren't offered a contract with EMI. Those sessions were cancelled when EMI offered them a contract. However, The Beatles' sessions for Sheridan did take place. Polydor's documents show that Bert produced recordings of *Sweet Georgia Brown* and *Swanee River* by Tony Sheridan and The Beat Brothers on May 24, 1962 at the newly opened, professional Studio Hamburg, and list McCartney as arranging *Sweet Georgia Brown*. On one of these documents the name Beat Brothers is crossed out and replaced with The Beatles. The following day The Beatles and Kaempfert terminated their contract. Polydor's failure for years to acknowledge The Beatles taking part in these sessions in 1962 may have been done to avoid legal conflicts with EMI. However, Tony says he didn't record anything with The Beatles in 1962 because he was being backed by The Beat Brothers, which included Roy Young. He maintains that *Sweet Georgia*

Brown with backing by The Beatles was recorded in June 1961. *Sweet Georgia Brown* is the only song The Beatles backed Tony on that features a piano. According to Roy (and Tony) he (not McCartney, as is often assumed) plays piano on *Sweet Georgia Brown.* It certainly sounds like Roy's style of playing. Roy joined The Beat Brothers in December 1961, ruling out his involvement in the June 1961 sessions. Tony thinks Roy's piano must have been overdubbed later. Roy says, "I don't recall dubbing the piano, I seem to remember recording it all together." Gunther Sorensen, a technician and recording engineer for Polydor, recalls a session with Sheridan and The Beatles in May of 1962. He says The Beatles recorded two songs, *Sweet Georgia Brown* and *Swanee River,* in one take without playback. If correct, it supports Roy's recollections. If there were no overdubs and McCartney plays piano, then someone else plays bass. If Roy's piano wasn't overdubbed, then the version of *Sweet Georgia Brown* with The Beatles was almost certainly recorded in the spring of 1962. Pete Best recalls in his autobiography *Beatle!* that they recorded *Sweet Georgia Brown* and *Skinny Minny* at a latter session when Epstein was involved, which would place it in 1962. *Mersey Beat* magazine reported in May 1962 that they recorded *Sweet Georgia Brown* and *Swanee River.* This has led to debate about whether The Beatles contributed to *Skinny Minny* and, or *Swanee River.* There's no evidence, other than Best's claim, that any of The Beatles contributed to Tony's versions of *Skinny Minny.* Tony insists he never recorded any versions of it or *Swanee River* with The Beatles. It seems unlikely that Bert would record The Beatles and Tony separately for his recordings. Tony would likely have been present to at least provide a rough vocal guide for them. However, Polydor's documents indicate that Tony recorded vocal overdubs on June 7, 1962 on *Sweet Georgia Brown* and *Swanee River* recorded on May 24 by The Beatles. Perhaps this is when Roy played piano. This would lend credibility to Tony's contentions regarding both songs, and Roy. [Polydor's documents also indicate Tony and The Beat Brothers had previously recorded a version *Swanee River* and *Sweet Georgia Brown* on December 21, 1961 excluding any involvement by The Beatles. Bert could have used these recordings as a reference for The Beatles' backing tracks. Unfortunately this earlier recording is the only version of *Swanee River* by Sheridan known to exist.] Polydor's documents indicate that the May 24 versions of *Sweet Georgia Brown* and *Swanee River* were to be issued as a single, but why Polydor never released it, or The Beatles' version of *Swanee River,* if it exists, remains a mystery. Even more perplexing is why they recorded two songs that Tony had already recorded and would release several weeks later. Tony says, "I only ever recorded and sang on one version of *Swanee River,* and it wasn't with The Beatles, though I wish it had been!" It's unlikely that The Beatles provided any lead vocals for it, so perhaps if Polydor only had a backing track with The Beatles they scrapped the tapes. Tony speculates that Polydor's documentation, provided by Kaempfert Productions, incorrectly lists the December 1961 recording of *Swanee River* on their May 24 recording documents with *Sweet Georgia Brown* because the two songs were scheduled to be released on a single, giving the impression that The Beatles recorded it that day. This would certainly explain why no version of *Swanee River* with backing by The Beatles has ever surfaced. Roy says Epstein asked him to join The Beatles following his performances with them onstage during their spring 1962 engagement at the Star-Club, making his involvement in recordings with them all the more plausible. Roy turned down the offer because of his more lucrative arrangement with the Star-Club at the time.

Sweet Georgia Brown with The Beatles' backing was first issued on the German EP *Ya Ya* in October 1962 (five months after the release of Tony's version recorded without them in December 1961) adding further credence that it was recorded in May 1962. Nearly all subsequent releases of *Sweet Georgia Brown* with The Beatles feature vocals re-recorded by Sheridan at Studio Hamburg in January 1964, with revised lyrics written by Liverpool native Paul Murphy (see Fred & Horst Fascher) who was a friend of The Beatles and Epstein. Murphy was Sheridan's producer, and Polydor Record's A&R Manager and Producer who was put in charge of re-mixing Sheridan and The Beatles' recordings for re-release by Polydor in 1964. Tony's original vocals must have been overdubbed on a separate track, as Polydor's June 1962 documents indicate, in order for the vocals to be re-recorded with revised lyrics. In the revised lyrics Sheridan sings about The Beatles' hair, their fan club, sounding marvelous with a piano and warning them not to be too commercial. Obviously, it was intended to capitalize on The Beatles' massive popularity in 1964. Sheridan says, "The new lyrics were a joke without malice," though he admits they bore some truth. Many felt The Beatles had become too commercial in sound and looks after Epstein's takeover in late 1961.

Various publications have claimed Sheridan

and The Beatles may also have recorded *What'd I Say* and *Hully Gully* during sessions for Kaempfert. Pete Best claims in his book that The Beatles also auditioned some Lennon and McCartney compositions during the initial recording sessions, but that Bert didn't seem impressed. In an article in *NME* magazine, Lennon seemed to recall that they may have recorded *Kansas City*, *Some Other Guy* and *Rock And Roll Music* then. All of these songs were regularly performed by The Beatles and Tony at the time. Tony doesn't recall recording any of these songs with them. Some of these numbers were recorded and released by Sheridan and The Beat Brothers, but none involve The Beatles. Most likely, Sheridan and The Beatles used some of these songs as warm-ups or sound checks before the start of proper recordings. Like *Swanee River*, it seems inconceivable, given how Polydor has perpetually capitalized on Sheridan's recordings with The Beatles, that they wouldn't release other recordings by them if they existed.

In a bizarre postscript, four of these recordings, released by Atco (Atlantic) Records in the US have edits and overdubs. The revised lyric version of *Sweet Georgia Brown* has overdubs of guitar and drums. *Take Out Some Insurance On Me, Baby* has drums, harmonica and guitar overdubs and Tony's "goddamn" expletive was omitted, along with a minute of *Nobody's Child*. [*Ain't She Sweet* was also sweetened with additional drums.] Odds are the guitarist is Cornell Dupree and the drummer is Bernard Purdie, veteran session players who worked extensively for Atlantic then. Purdie has long maintained that he was contracted to overdub drums on nearly two dozen early Beatles' recordings. His seemingly outrageous claims weren't initially taken seriously because they were vague and filled with obvious inaccuracies. However, some of his claims ring true. He recalls guitar overdubs, and being paid to keep quiet about his involvement. Atlantic, trying to capitalize on The Beatles' popularity then, probably felt a little musical updating might produce a hit, but that if Polydor or The Beatles found out they might be faced with a lawsuit.

Sheridan wrote *Tell Me If You Can* with McCartney in Hamburg in 1962. Tony recalls, "It was a song that developed when Paul and I were sitting down with guitars and having a few beers. I kept the song for years, and never recorded it because I didn't feel it would be right to try to make a buck out of it or offend Paul. I performed a bit of it during a radio interview many years later and people started encouraging me to record it. I was going to record it for my 2002 album *Vagabond* but I wanted to get Paul's blessing, so I wrote him. When he didn't respond right away my producer thought Paul didn't want me to do it, so we didn't record it. Then Paul got back and said he had no problem with me doing it. I saw Paul a few years later when he was doing a concert in Hamburg and he said, 'By the way, what happened to that song *Tell Me If You Can*?' I said, 'Oh well, it was a shitty song anyway,' and forgot about doing it. Then Chantal [Chantal is a German instrumental group known for their covers of The Beatles' songs] approached me about doing it with them. I wasn't too keen but I did it with them live just to get it down. I told them that to do it properly we should record it at Abbey Road Studios. I wrote a juicy introduction for it, which we recorded there, but I think the money ran out – the studio time, so it's just a demo – and then they released it just to make a buck! There's lots of 'music' in it that Paul might like but it's nothing I'd really like to play to him. I still may record it properly one day." Tony's live version of it with Chantal was released on *Chantal Meets Tony Sheridan: A Beatles Story* in the fall of 2004. Their over six minute version of it recorded at Abbey Road Studios in April 2004 was released on a CD single (Zounds-27000 60053) in Germany in mid-2005.

Bert Kaempfert, who died on June 21, 1980, will probably be remembered most for composing and recording such easy listening songs (many that were hits for other artists) as *Wonderland By Night*, *Spanish Eyes* (Al Martino), *Danke Shoen* (Wayne Newton), *Wooden Heart* (Elvis Presley, Joe Dowell) and *Strangers In The Night* that revived Frank Sinatra's career. John Lennon was murdered on December 8, 1980. *My Bonnie*, *Cry For A Shadow* and *Ain't She Sweet* became part of The Beatles' official catalogue in 1995 with their inclusion on *Anthology 1*. George Harrison died on November 29, 2001. Tony Sheridan still resides in the Hamburg area. He, Roy Young and Howie Casey (see Freddie Starr) have reunited The Beat Brothers on occasion, and have been guests at conventions and festivals for fans of The Beatles. For more information go to www.tony-sheridan.de, www.kaempfert.de

Pete Best, White's Bar, Saginaw, MI May 21, 2005.
© and photo by Kristofer Engelhardt

Roy Young and Kristofer Engelhardt "Boogie Woogie Christmas," Windsor, Ontario, Canada December 6, 2001. Photo by Jodi Patterson, © Kristofer Engelhardt.

Shorrock-Starr Band

[None]
[Unreleased]
Producer: Martin Benge
Ringo Starr: Drums & B. Vocals; Barbara Bach: Handclaps; Michael Parkinson: Handclaps; Glenn Shorrock: Vocals; Kirk Lorange: Guitar; Marc Kennedy: Drums; Greg Lyon: Bass; Mario Millo: Guitar; Alan Mansfield: Keyboards
ABC Channel Ten Studios, Sydney, Australia 09/28/82; airdate: 10/08/82

Medley: Honey Don't/Blue Suede Shoes [live] (C. Perkins) (5:26)

Glenn Shorrock was born on June 30, 1944 in Chatham, England but has spent most of his life in Australia. He gained notice as a singer in The Twilights, a band popular in Australian during the second half of the 1960s. The Twilights recorded at Abbey Road Studios while The Beatles were recording their album *Sgt. Pepper's Lonely Hearts Club Band* but Glenn says there wasn't any interaction. Later, The Twilights would perform that entire Beatles' album live. Following The Twilights' breakup in 1969, Shorrock joined Axiom, Esperanto, and Mississippi who changed their name to the Little River Band. As their lead singer between 1977 and 1982 they had the Top Five hit *Reminiscing*, Top 10 hits with *Lonesome Loser*, *Lady*, *Cool Change*, *Night Owls* and *Take It Easy On Me*, and Top 20 hits with *Help Is On Its Way*, *Happy Anniversary* and *Man On Your Mind*.

Glenn launched his solo career in 1982. The Glenn Shorrock Band appeared on Michael Parkinson's TV show *Parkinson In Australia* taped on September 28, 1982. Shorrock's band member Kirk Lorange recalls, "Ringo was on the show with his wife Barbara. We were on the show promoting Glenn's new single. An extra studio drum kit had been set up for our jam at the end of the show but we weren't sure if Ringo would join in with us — but he did! They were quite 'happy' because they'd been on a Sydney Harbor cruise drinking wine." The band, with Ringo assisting on drums and vocals, performed a medley of *Honey Don't* and *Blue Suede Shoes*. Parkinson dubbed them the Shorrock-Starr Band.

Glenn has released several solo albums and appeared in numerous stage shows. He rejoined the Little River Band between 1988 and 1996. Since that time, he has continued to write, record and tour, and has teamed up with former Little River Band founding members Beeb Birtles and Graeham Goble as Birtles Shorrock Goble: The Original Voices of The Little River Band because they don't own the Little River Band name. For more information go to www.birtlesschorrockgoble.com

The Silkie

Lennon & McCartney Songbook
Connoisseur Collection-VSOP CD 150 (UK/EEC) (07/02/90)
Producer: John Lennon & Paul McCartney
Paul McCartney: Electric Guitar & Vocal Arrangement; **George Harrison: Guitar Taps & Tambourine**; Sylvia Tatler: Vocals; Mike Ramsden: Vocals & Guitar; Ivor Aylesbury: Vocals & Guitar; Kevin Cunningham: Bass
IBC Studios, London, UK 08/09/65

You've Got To Hide Your Love Away (J. Lennon-P. McCartney) 2:09 (24) (09/10/65)

The Silkie was England's answer to American folk groups like Peter, Paul and Mary. The members were UK natives Michael Ramsden, Kevin Cunningham, Ivor Aylesbury and Sylvia Tatler. Sylvia is the only surviving member. They formed their group while students at Hull University. Sylvia recalls, "Kevin was from Liverpool and wrote to Brian Epstein inquiring why he was booking American folk groups when England had great folk groups like us. Brian requested a tape of us. After hearing it he offered to manage us. We occasionally ran into The Beatles in Brian's office in London. They offered us a demo of the song *One And One Is Two* [see The Strangers with Mike Shannon, The Fourmost, Billy J. Kramer with The Dakotas], which Paul sang. Being a bit cheeky, we rejected it!

"When it was time to make a single, Paul McCartney offered to help us record their [*Help!*] album track *You've Got To Hide Your Love Away.* They booked the studio and arranged the whole session with an engineer, which was very generous of them. John Lennon wanted to play around with the controls in the box. He brought some new electric keyboard with him that he was excited about and played, but didn't play it on the recording. Paul worked out the harmony arrangement with us and played electric guitar on the recording, but he was also involved in the production with John. George Harrison tapped out rhythm on the back of a guitar and played my tambourine on the recording. Somebody broke a guitar string, so George walked to a nearby music shop and ended up getting heavily mobbed by fans. He was pale and pretty shaken when he returned. I invited my sister, who took a cab to the studio. When she arrived she tapped on the back of the person sitting at the controls, which was John, and asked if he could pay her cab fare, which he did! When we were finished, John called Brian and played him our recording." Sylvia says Paul didn't play piano or sing on the recording as has been reported, and that The Beatles didn't contribute to any other recordings of theirs. Sylvia laments, "Our record company, which competed with The Beatles' record company, wanted control over us. They took exception to Brian and The Beatles' involvement and weren't very supportive in promoting the single in the UK." The Silkie's cover of *You've Got To Hide Your Love Away* was a Top 10 hit. The group broke up in 1966. Mike and Sylvia married, and carried on performing until a few years before Mike's death in 2004.

Carly Simon

Playing Possum
Elektra-1033-2 (10/25/90) (04/21/75)
Producer: Richard Perry
Ringo Starr: Drums; Carly Simon: Lead Vocals; Klaus Voormann: Bass; Dr. John: Piano; Alvin Robinson: Guitar; Jeff Baxter: Guitar; Freddie Staehle: Percussion; Richard Perry: Tambourine; Maxine Willard: B. Vocals; Julia Tillman: B. Vocals; Carolyn Willis: B. Vocals
Crystal Studios, Los Angeles, CA probably summer-fall/xx/74

More And More (M. Rebennack-A. Robinson) 4:02 (4)

No Secrets
Elektra-75049-2 (10/25/90) (11/03/72)
Producer: Richard Perry
Paul McCartney: B. Vocals†; Carly Simon: Lead Vocals; Nicky Hopkins: Piano; Jim Keltner: Drums; Klaus Voormann: Bass; Jimmy Ryan: Electric Guitar; Ray Cooper: Congas; Bobby Keys: Tenor Saxophone; Bonnie Bramlett: B. Vocals; Doris Troy: B. Vocals; Linda McCartney: B. Vocals
Trident & AIR Studios, London, UK 10/xx/72

Night Owl (J. Taylor) 3:47 (9)

Carly Simon was born on June 25, 1945 in New York, New York. Her father was the co-founder of Simon & Schuster Publishers, and an accomplished piano player. Her sisters Joanna and Lucy were singers. Carly and Lucy formed The Simon Sisters, and had a minor hit with the song *Winken, Blinken And Nod* in 1964 before Lucy's marriage ended her career. By 1967 Carly was managed by Albert Grossman who arranged for her to work with his other clients, including Bob Dylan* and members of The Band*, but nothing was released. The following year she worked briefly with Elephant's Memory*. Her self-titled debut album in 1971 yielded the Top 10 hit *That's The Way I've Always Heard It Should Be*. She also had a Top 20 hit with the title track of her 1971 album *Anticipation*.

Simon topped the charts with her 1972 album *No Secrets* and its song *You're So Vain*. The album also includes *Night Owl* with backing vocals from Paul and Linda McCartney*. Its producer Richard Perry says the backing tracks were recorded at Trident Studios but the vocals were recorded at George Martin's* AIR Studios in London in October 1972. The McCartneys were at AIR then recording *Live And Let Die* and dropped in on Carly's sessions. Carly would soon marry the song's composer, James Taylor*. The two would have a Top Five hit with the song *Mockingbird* in 1974.

Carly's 1975 album *Playing Possum*, also produced by Perry, features Ringo Starr playing drums on *More And More*. Perry had recently produced two albums for Ringo. Perry says Ringo's contribution was recorded at Crystal Studios in Los Angeles sometime between late summer and late fall of 1974.

Simon had Top 10 songs with *Nobody Does It Better*, the theme to the James Bond film *The Spy Who Loved Me* (co-starring Barbara Bach — future wife of Ringo Starr), in 1977 and *You*

Belong To Me in 1978. In 1980 she topped the charts with the song *Jesse*. Simon and Taylor were divorced in 1983. Simon had the Top 20 hit song *Coming Around Again* in 1986. She won a Grammy, Oscar and Golden Globe Award in the late 1980s for her song *Let The River Run* from the film *Working Girl*. Carly Simon has spent the last three decades raising her children, composing, recording, touring and writing children's books. For more information go to www.carlysimon.com

Paul Simon & George Harrison

1976-1977 SNL The Complete Second Season Universal/Broadway Video-61001030 (DVD) (12/04/07)
Producer: Lorne Michaels
George Harrison: Vocals & Guitar; Paul Simon: Vocals & Guitar
NBC TV Studio 8-H, 30 Rockefeller Plaza, New York, NY 11/19/76; AirdateL 11/20/76

Homeward Bound (P. Simon) 2:53 (3-[2]-9)
Also available on Nobody's Child, Warner Bros.-9 26280-2 (07/24/90) 2:38 (5)[

Paul Simon was born on October 13, 1941 in Newark, New Jersey. His father was a professional musician known as Lee Sims. Paul and Art Garfunkel were classmates in grade school, and in high school when they formed the folk duo Tom & Jerry, and began writing songs. Their minor hit song, *Hey, Schoolgirl* in 1957, earned them a spot on Dick Clark's *American Bandstand* show on ABC TV. Following high school they pursued solo careers but got together briefly in 1964 to record the album *Wednesday Morning, 3 A.M.* When its song *The Sounds Of Silence*, with overdubbed drums and electric guitar, was later released as a single it topped the charts, and Simon & Garfunkel reformed in the wake of its success. Some of their many hits written by Simon include *Homeward Bound, I Am A Rock, A Hazy Shade Of Winter, At The Zoo, Mrs. Robinson, Cecilia, The Boxer* and *Bridge Over Troubled Water.* They broke up in 1970 but since that time have re-united on a number of occasions for concerts and guest spots on each other's recordings. Art has pursued acting and had a few hits. Between 1970 and 1980 Simon wrote and recorded the hit songs *Mother And Child Reunion, Me And Julio Down By The School Yard, Kodachrome, Loves Me Like A Rock, 50 Ways To Leave Your Lover, Slip Slidin' Away* and *Late In The Evening.*

George Harrison recorded a portion of *Bridge Over Troubled Water* during sessions for his 1970 album *All Things Must Pass. Melody Maker* magazine reported in March 1971 that Harrison was in the studio with Simon, though there's no evidence he contributed to any of Simon's recordings then. Paul McCartney wrote a review of Simon's album *The Songs Of Paul Simon Songbook* for the August 8, 1973 issue of *Punch* magazine. In 1974 Simon & Garfunkel were invited to a recording session John Lennon was producing in New York for Harry Nilsson's* album *Pussy* Cats. A 95 minute tape exists, and reportedly includes such titles as *Rock Island Line, Midnight Special, Wake Up Little Susie, Railroad Bill, Everyday, Maybe Baby, Let The Good Times Roll, Send Me Some Lovin', Baby, Let's Play House, Give Me Head, You Can't Catch Me, That's All Right, Mama, Well Alright, Do You Wanna Dance, Dance All Night, Can't Get It Right, Having A Party, Keep Your Hands Off My Baby, Stand By Me, Groupie Talk, Goodnight, Baby, Johnny B. Goode, Slippin' And Slidin', Whole Lotta Shakin' Goin' On, Mean Woman Blues, Be-Bop-A-Lula, Tossin' And Turnin'* and others including a song Harry Nilsson and Ringo Starr wrote called *I Want You To Sit On My Face*. Unfortunately, Lennon, who was playing guitar and doing some singing, and Nilsson, who was playing drums and doing some singing, were so intoxicated that the session soon turned into a shouting match, and Simon & Garfunkel's contributions were never used. Noted Nilsson authority, Curtis Armstrong says Garfunkel remained in the playback booth during their visit and didn't contribute to the recordings, and that Peter Wolf also contributed to the session. Simon was apparently left with enough respect for Lennon to write *The Late Great Johnny Ace*, partly in tribute to John, shortly after his death.

Simon and Harrison were the musical guests on TV's *Saturday Night Live* on November 20, 1976. The music videos for *Crackerbox Palace* and *This Song*, from Harrison's new album *Thirty-Three & 1/3*, were aired. A rehearsal, and taping for a Harrison and Simon musical duet took place the previous day with full or partial renditions of *Dark Horse, Don't Let Me Wait Too Long, That's All Right (Mama), Yesterday, 50 Ways To Leave Your Lover, The Boxer, Bridge Over Troubled Water, Bye Bye Love, Rock Island Line, Flight Of The Valkyries, Here Comes The Sun* and *Homeward Bound.* Only the latter two songs were broadcast, and later released. *Homeward*

Bound was included on the *Nobody's Child - Romanian Angel Appeal* charity album conceived by Harrison and his wife Olivia, along with Ringo's wife Barbara Bach, Yoko Ono* and Linda McCartney*, to aid Romanian orphans. It is also available on the DVD *1976-1977 SNL the Complete Second Season. Bye Bye Love* and *Rock Island Line* are available on unauthorized releases, but aren't considered Harrison contributions to a Simon song.

Simon's *Graceland* earned a Grammy Award for Album Of The Year in 1986 and the title track earned a Grammy Award for Song Of The Year in 1987. Simon & Garfunkel were inducted into the Rock and Roll Hall of Fame in 1990, and Simon was separately inducted in 2001. On June 13, 2001 McCartney joined Simon onstage at the Greek Theatre in Los Angeles doing a duet on McCartney's Beatles' song *I've Just Seen A Face*. They did the same the following night at the Adopt-A-Minefield gala at the Regent Beverly Wilshire Hotel. Paul Simon continues to write, record and tour. For more information go to www.paulsimon.com, www.simonandgarfunkel.com

Peter Skellern

Hard Times
Island-ILPS 9352 (album 12") (UK) (09/26/75)
Producer: Meyer Shagaloff
George Harrison: Guitar; Peter Skellern: Lead Vocals & Keyboards; Rob Townsend: Drums; George Ford: Bass; Madeline Bell: B. Vocals; Joy Yates: B. Vocals; Joanne Williams: B. Vocals
Mayfair Sound Studios, London, UK probably 08/xx/75

Make Love, Not War (P. Skellern-J. Burrows-J. Harding) 3:16 (2/2)

Peter Skellern was born on March 14, 1947 in Bury, England. He played in school bands, and graduated with honors from the prestigious Guildhall School Of Music And Drama in 1968. He played piano with Billy Fury (see Various Artists - Without You – A Billy Fury Tribute), and later gained a following writing songs in a style reminiscent of Hoagy Carmichael and the brass band sound of the 1930s. He had hit songs with *You're A Lady* and *Hold On To Love* in the UK in the 1970s. In the early 1980s he performed the autobiographical program *Happy Endings* and hosted the talk show *Private Lives* on UK TV. In 1984 he formed Oasis with Julian Lloyd Webber, Mary Hopkin* and Bill Lovelady. Skellern continues to record, especially choral music, and work in theater and on TV.

Skellern's 1975 album *Hard Times* includes the song *Make Love, Not War* from the musical revue *Loud Reports* by John Burrows, John Harding and Skellern. The song features George Harrison on guitar. Ringo Starr covered the album's title track on his 1978 album *Bad Boy*.

"Legs" Larry Smith

HandMade Films The 10th Anniversary
AVM / [matrix #] AVM 1126859 (promotional only) (UK) (probably 11/xx/88)
Producer: [George Harrison] Ray Cooper & "Legs" Larry Smith
George Harrison: B. Vocals; "Legs" Larry Smith: Lead Vocals; Ray Cooper (probable) Percussion
London, UK probably xx/xx/82 &/or xx/xx/83

Bullshot (Theme To The Motion Picture "Bullshot") ([**G. Harrison**] J. Du Prez-D. Clement-A. Shearman-R. House) 2:21 (8)

"Legs" Larry Smith was born on January 18, 1944 in Oxford, England. He was the drummer, singer and tap dancer with The Bonzo Dog Band*. Smith and George Harrison became close friends. Smith says, "For some mad reason George, who I hardly knew, invited me to Trident Studios in London where he was recording *My Sweet Lord*. George had a very wicked, dry sense of humor and I seemed to make him laugh. There was a chemistry between us, so from that day on George and I became very close chums. Peter Sellers [see Peter Sellers, Terry Southern & Ringo Starr] would come over to George's house often and introduced him to the film *The Producers*. It was a favorite of his and we spent a lot of time watching it and laughing. George named several of his companies after one-liners from the film. He and I would sit up all night at my place doodling art masterpieces. George loved my artwork. I did the artwork for his [1982] album *Gone Troppo.* George loved my dad, so he had him write some of the album's inner sleeve notes – the bizarre ones about cleaning a cement mixer.

"George and I wrote a couple of mad songs together in his grand kitchen on his harmonium – just funny stuff. He would tell me he wanted to put The Beatles, The Bonzo Dog Band, Monty Python* and The Rutles together in one huge band. We also did a bit of late night jamming in his studio on occasion. He invited me to his home for dinner once, and began playing his Steinway piano and said, 'This is for you Larry,' and out came *His Name Is Legs (Ladies & Gentlemen)* from start to finish. I was honored beyond words and very impressed by this great little ditty with great lyrics. He said, 'I'm going to put it on my new album [1975's *Extra Texture (Read All About It)*]. When he recorded it, he asked me to do some madness in the middle of it, to which I duly obliged. That was the first time we seriously recorded together.

"The next time we recorded together was when George wanted me to sing the title track for HandMade Films' *Bullshot* in 1983, which was a singing style similar to my singing in the Bonzo's. It was pretty cool having a Beatle sing backing vocals with me on the song. As I recall, the backing track was already recorded but Ray Cooper was there. We recorded the vocals at a studio in London. I also appeared in the movie." The song is only available on the in-house, promotional CD *HandMade Films The 10th Anniversary*, and on the DVD release of *Bullshot* (BP-484).

Smith says, "I was recording a Bonzo tribute album with producer Gus Dudgeon and was interested in doing a new version of the Bonzo's song *Jollity Farm.* I asked George to come over to my home studio at the old vicarage, and play his ukulele, which he carried everywhere and loved to play. The song, which I call *Jollity Farm (The Laboratory Mix),* is really built around George's beautiful ukulele playing. He asked me what else he could do to help. I told him I thought Ringo would be perfect to sing the lead vocals, so George called Ringo and he promised to sing on it. Then George wrote the song *Doin' The Bonzo Dog* with Jim Capaldi*, but tragically George died, and then Gus and his wife were killed in a car crash, and the album was never finished. It still upsets me when I think about losing all of these wonderful people. George was a prince of a man, and very kind and generous. I've written a tribute song to him called *Oh, Keoki.* I'm now working with another producer and hope to have the album out soon. It's titled *It Was A Great Party...Until Somebody Found A Hammer.* I'm still hoping to have Ringo sing on *Jollity Farm.*" For more information go to www.legslarrysmith.co.uk

The Smokin' Mojo Filters

Come Together [Various Artists]
Go! Discs-GOD CD 136 (single) (UK) (12/04/95) (09/09/95)
Producer: Brendan Lynch
Paul McCartney: Guitar, Keyboards & B. Vocals; Paul Weller: Lead Vocals & Guitar; Noel Gallagher: Guitar; Steve White: Drums; Carleen Anderson: B. Vocals; Steve Craddock: Guitar; Damon Minchella: Bass
EMI-Abbey Road Studios, London, UK 09/04/95

Come Together (J. Lennon-P. McCartney) 3:33 (1)

The Smokin' Mojo Filters was a Paul Weller project. He was born John Weller on May 25, 1958 in Woking, England. Weller was greatly influenced by The Beatles and took up guitar as a teenager. He gained fame in The Jam who had over a dozen UK hits in the late 1970s and early 1980s, including the chart toppers *Going Underground, Start, Town Called Malice* and *Beat Surrender.* In 1983 Weller and keyboardist Mick Talbot formed the basis of Style Council who also had a dozen UK hits, including *Speak Like A Child, Long Hot Summer, My Ever Changing Moods, Groovin', Shout To The Top, The Walls Come Tumbling Down* and *It Didn't Matter.* Since 1990 Weller has been primarily a solo act and has covered a number of The Beatles' songs throughout his career.

In 1995 Weller enlisted the help of his friend Mary in getting her father Paul McCartney to contribute to a cover recording of John Lennon's Beatles' song *Come Together,* included on the War Child Charity album *Help,* which aided child victims of war, specifically those of the conflict in the former Yugoslavian Republics. The album's concept, which includes a variety of artists, was borrowed from Lennon's single *Instant Karma* as an example of how quickly a record could be written, recorded and released in response to a given situation. McCartney added backing vocals, guitar and keyboards to the recording. The recording also features Noel Gallagher from Oasis, often cited as a contemporary version of The Beatles. The session was filmed and included in the *Help* documentary on the making of the album. McCartney reportedly later had the assembled band back him on a song he had written the night before, though apparently there wasn't time to record it. When *Come Together* was issued as a single it was credited as The Smokin' Mojo Filters (Featuring Paul Weller, Paul McCartney and Noel Gallagher). The single's credits also include a quote from the late John Lennon about his *Instant Karma* record concept. For more information go to www.paulweller.com or www.warchildmusic.com

Phil Spector

The Harri-Spector Show
Strawberry-STR 022 (EEC) [unauthorized release] (xx/xx/01)
Producer: George Harrison & Phil Spector
George Harrison: Acoustic Guitar & B. Vocals; Phil Spector: Lead Vocals & Acoustic Guitar [unless noted otherwise]
Probably one of the following: Apple, EMI-Abbey Road, Trident or Olympic Studios, London, UK probably 02/xx/71

Bluebirds Over The Mountain (E. Hickey) 0:41 (4b)

Bring It On Home To Me 0:13 (S. Cooke) (2a)

God (J. Lennon) 0:10 (2b)
Additionally: **George Harrison: B. Vocals** (only)

I Hear You Knockin' (D. Bartholmew) 1:18 (4f)
Additionally: **George Harrison: Duet Vocals**

I'll Be Your Baby Tonight (B. Dylan) 1:05 (1a)

I Went To Your Wedding/The Great Pretender (J. Robinson/B. Ram) 3:05 (3b-3c)

Let's Work Together (W. Harrison) 0:39 (4g)

Money Honey (J. Stone) 2:02 (2d)
Additionally: (probably) Ronnie Spector: B. Vocals

River Deep-Mountain High (J. Berry-E. Greenwich-P. Spector) 3:32 (1b)

Save The Last Dance For Me (D. Pomus-M. Shuman 2:23 (1c)

That'll Be The Day (J. Allison-B. Holly-N. Petty) 0:55 (5a)

Tonight's The Night (L. Dixon-S. Owens) 0:51(2e)
Additionally: (probably) Ronnie Spector: B. Vocals

You Better Move On (A. Alexander) 1:34 (2f)

Your Cash Ain't Nothin' But Trash (C. Calhoun) 0:55 (2c)

Let's Have A Party [John Lennon]
Quality Compact Productions-QCP 72003 (Korea) [unauthorized release] (xx/xx/89)
Producer: probably **John Lennon** & Phil Spector
John Lennon: B. Vocals & Guitar; **Ringo Starr: B. Vocals & (probable) Percussion**; Phil Spector: Lead Vocals & Guitar; Allen Ginsberg: B. Vocals & (probable) Percussion; Elliot Mintz: B. Vocals; Nicky Hopkins: B. Vocals; Klaus Voormann: B. Vocals; Jim Keltner: B. Vocals & (probable) Percussion; Eric Clapton: Guitar & B. Vocals; Mal Evans: B. Vocals; Neil Aspinall: B. Vocals; May Pang: B. Vocals; Maureen Starkey: B. Vocals; Yoko Ono: B. Vocals
[Hotel Syracuse, Syracuse, NY 10/09/71

Crippled Inside [take one] (**J. Lennon**) 0:56 (15)

Crippled Inside [take two] (**J. Lennon**) 0:32 (17)

Tandoori Chicken (**G. Harrison**-P. Spector) 2:11 (9)

Tandoori Chicken
Apple (7" acetate single) (UK) [unreleased]
Producer: George Harrison & Phil Spector
EMI-Abbey Road &/or Trident Studios, London, UK 02 &/or 03/xx/71

Tandoori Chicken (**G. Harrison**-P. Spector) 2:14 (1/1)
George Harrison: Guitar; Phil Spector: Lead Vocals & Keyboards; Leon Russell: Keyboards; Klaus Voormann: Bass; Jim Gordon: Drums; John Lennon: B. Vocals; The Apple Scruffs (Cathy, Lucy & Carol): B. Vocals

Unbootlegged 08 – Get That Fly [John Lennon]
No Label Records-NLR 0402 (CD-R) [unauthorized release] (xx/xx/04)
Producer: probably **John Lennon** & Phil Spector

John Lennon: B. Vocals & Guitar; **Ringo Starr: B. Vocals & (probable) Percussion**; Phil Spector: Lead Vocals & Guitar; Allen Ginsberg: B. Vocals & (probable) Percussion; Elliot Mintz: B. Vocals; Nicky Hopkins: B. Vocals; Klaus Voormann: B. Vocals; Jim Keltner: B. Vocals & (probable) Percussion; Eric Clapton: Guitar & B. Vocals; Mal Evans: B. Vocals; Neil Aspinall: B. Vocals; May Pang: B. Vocals; Maureen Starkey: B. Vocals; Yoko Ono: B. Vocals
[Hotel Syracuse, Syracuse, NY 10/09/71

Imagine (J. Lennon-[Y. Ono]) (0:56) (32)

Oh Yoko! (J. Lennon) (1:22) (33)

Harvey Phillip Spector was born on December 26, 1939 in New York, New York but spent most of his life in Los Angeles, California. Phil was attracted to R&B and learned to play several musical instruments. In 1958 Spector wrote, arranged, produced and performed on his group The Teddy Bears' song *To Know Him Is To Love Him*. [The song became a regular in The Beatles' early repertoire. They performed it during their audition for Decca Records in early 1962 and live on BBC radio.] Phil returned to New York writing songs in the Brill Building with Gerry Goffin, Carole King, Barry Mann, Cynthia Weil, Jeff Barry, Ellie Greenwich and others. He helped form Philles Records in 1961, and was soon a highly successful songwriter and producer. He was greatly admired and emulated by his contemporaries, particularly Brian Wilson* and The Beatles.

On February 7, 1964 Phil, in the UK with his group The Ronettes, and there working with The Rolling Stones*, arranged to be on the same flight to New York as The Beatles in an attempt to form a friendship and musical relationship with them. In 1964 Phil produced and co-wrote, along with Pete (Andreoli) Anders and Vinnie Poncia, the novelty record *Ringo, I Love You* by Bonnie Jo Mason, a.k.a. Cher. [Poncia and Ringo Starr became good friends and collaborators in the 1970s.] The Beatles' and Spector's paths crossed occasionally during the next few years, but in spite of their great admiration, they had remained loyal to their producer George Martin* until 1970.

By the mid-1960s Spector had also produced hits for Gene Pitney, The Crystals, Darlene Love, The Righteous Brothers (see Bobby Hatfield) and Ike & Tina Turner* among others. His legendary "wall of sound" utilizing many session players, dubbed the "wrecking crew," included Glen Campbell, Leon Russell*, Larry Knechtel, Hal Blaine, Sonny & Cher and scores of others. Phil earned a reputation for being eccentric, temperamental, and obsessed with security and secrecy, but his productions were nearly always chart successes or rock 'n' roll classics. Spector's last production for Philles Records was Ike & Tina Turner's 1966 recording of his song *River Deep-Mountain High*. When it failed in the US charts, Phil shut down the label, withdrew from the music world for several years and suffered from mental disorders.

In late 1969 Allen Klein, a long-time acquaintance of Spector's, helped musically unit Phil with The Beatles. In January 1970 John Lennon, eager to record quickly, grabbed Spector to produce his single *Instant Karma*. Lennon was sufficiently impressed to ask Spector to re-produce The Beatles' year-old, rough and unfinished *Let It Be* album recordings initially produced by George Martin (with considerable help from Glyn Johns). Phil overdubbed a touch of his trademark "wall of sound" to what The Beatles originally intended to be a "live" studio album without any overdubs. Most of The Beatles, in the midst of breaking up, were pleased with the results, but Paul McCartney later cited Phil's overdubs of an orchestra and chorus to his song *The Long And Winding Road* as examples of the group's efforts to sabotage his music.

Harrison hired Phil to co-produce his first genuine solo album, *All Things Must Pass*, in 1970 and to help record *The Concert For Bangla Desh* in 1971. Phil and George also worked on recordings for Phil's wife Ronnie Spector*. During the sessions, George and Phil wrote, and recorded the song *Tandoori Chicken*. [An unreleased version with Phil on lead vocals exists on Apple acetates.] An unauthorized release of an Apple Studios acetate titled *The Harri-Spector Show* feature Phil and George jamming on acoustic guitars, mostly on oldies. George mainly sings *Leaning On The Lamppost*, *Ob La Di, Ob La Da*, *Down In The Valley*, *Baby Let's Play House*, *Let It Down* and *Hokey Pokey*. Phil sings the remainder of the songs to which Harrison contributed. Judging from the song selection, and what sounds like Ronnie on backing vocals, these recording were probably made during the time George and Phil were producing recordings for her.

Phil attended the opening of Yoko Ono's* one woman art show *This Is Not Here* in Syracuse, New York on October 9, 1971 and John Lennon's 31st birthday. Later, at a local hotel, Phil joined John, Ringo, Allen Ginsberg*, Nicky Hopkins*, Klaus Voormann*, Jim Keltner (see Attitudes), Eric Clapton*, May Pang, Mal Evans, Neil Aspinall, and their wives, girlfriends and others for a jam session. Portions of it are available on the unauthorized releases *John Lennon-Let's Have A Party* and *John Lennon: Unbootlegged 08 – Get That Fly*. Phil is clearly the ringleader and the loudest vocalist on many of the songs, but only those on which he mostly sings lead vocals, such as *Tandoori Chicken*, and especially those he'd recently produced for John, such as *Crippled Inside*, *Imagine* and *Oh Yoko*, are noted as contributions. A number of the songs were oldies that Phil would produce two years later for John's *Rock 'N' Roll* album. Phil also helped produce most of the Lennons' recordings between 1970 and 1973, including John's albums *John Lennon/Plastic Ono Band*, *Imagine* and *Some Time In New York City*. *Rock 'N' Roll* was the most infamous production of Spector's career. It was recorded at the height of John and Phil's excessive and eccentric behavior, and the results reflected it. Phil's attempt to reassemble his "wall of sound" was thwarted by the intoxication of many of the participants, and Phil was reportedly firing a gun in the studio. He disappeared with the master tapes a short time later. John said that when he tried to resume work and recover the tapes, Spector made the outrageous claim that he was too busy because he'd been hired to decipher President Nixon's White House (Watergate) tapes. Lennon obtained the tapes nearly a year later, but considered them so unusable that he re-recorded most of the tracks. Some of the last recordings Phil produced were for Yoko's 1981 album *Season Of Glass*, recorded shortly after John's murder. Yoko later released some of John's previously unreleased recordings on the albums *Live In New York City* and *Menlove Avenue*, which include production assistance from Phil, including *To Know Her [Him] Is To Love Her* and the only known Lennon-Spector composition, *Here We Go Again*.

Phil Spector was inducted into the Rock and Roll Hall of Fame in 1989. Unfortunately, Spector's eccentric behavior and obsession with guns caught up with him in 2009 when he was convicted of the shooting death of actress Lana Clarkson at his home on February 3, 2003. For more information go to www.philspector.com

Ronnie Spector

I Love Him Like I Love My Very Life [takes 1, 2, 3, 7 & 8]
Apple-RS1/RS2/RS3/RS7/RS8 (12" acetate) (UK) [unreleased]
Producer: probably **George Harrison** & Phil Spector
George Harrison: Slide Guitar & (probable) Acoustic Guitar; **Ringo Starr: (possible) Percussion**; Ronnie Spector: Lead Vocals; Jim Gordon: (probable) Drums; Phil Spector: (possible) Keyboards; Leon Russell: (probable) Keyboards; Klaus Voormann or Carl Radle: (probable) Bass
Probably EMI-Abbey Road, Island &/or Trident Studios, London, UK probably 02/xx/71

I Love Him Like I Love My Very Life [takes 1, 2, 3, 7 & 8] [a.k.a. I Loved You Like I Loved My Very Life] (T. Wine-I. Levine-P. Spector) 14:38 combined time (1/1)

I Love Him Like I Love My Very Life [takes 9, 10, 16, 17 & 18]
Apple-RS9/RS10/RS16/RS17/RS18 (12" acetate) (UK) [unreleased]
Producer: probably **George Harrison** & Phil Spector
George Harrison: Slide Guitar & (probable) Acoustic Guitar; Ringo Starr: (possible) Percussion; Ronnie Spector: Lead Vocals; Jim Gordon: (probable) Drums; Phil Spector: (possible) Keyboards; Leon Russell: (probable) Keyboards; Klaus Voormann or Carl Radle: (probable) Bass
Probably EMI-Abbey Road, Island &/or Trident Studios, London, UK probably 02/xx/71

I Love Him Like I Love My Very Life [takes 9, 10, 16, 17 & 18] [a.k.a. I Loved You Like I Loved My Very Life] (T. Wine-I. Levine-P. Spector) 13:41 combined time (1/1)

Lovely La-De-Day
Apple-RS3 (7" acetate single) (UK) [unreleased]
George Harrison: (probable) Acoustic Guitar; **Ringo Starr: (possible) Percussion;** Ronnie Spector: Lead Vocals; probably one or more of the following: Jim Gordon: Drums; Leon Russell: Keyboards; Klaus Voormann: Bass; Carl Radle: Bass; Phil Spector: (possible) Keyboards; Peter Kirtley: Guitar
Producer: probably **George Harrison** & Phil Spector
Probably EMI-Abbey Road, Island &/or Trident Studios, London, UK 02/xx/71

Lovely La-De-Day [A.K.A. Loverly Laddy Day]3:00 (1/1)

Try Some, Buy Some / Tandoori Chicken
Apple-1832 (7" single) (04/19/71) (04/16/71)
Producer: George Harrison & Phil Spector
EMI-Abbey Road &/or Trident Studios, London, UK probably 02/xx/71

Tandoori Chicken (**G. Harrison**-P. Spector) 2:14 (2/1)
George Harrison: Guitar; **John Lennon: B. Vocals**; Ronnie Spector: Lead Vocals; Phil Spector: Keyboards; Leon Russell: Keyboards; Klaus Voormann: Bass; Jim Gordon: Drums; The Apple Scruffs (Cathy, Lucy & Carol): B. Vocals

Try Some, Buy Some (**G. Harrison**) 4:08 (1/1)
George Harrison: Guitar; Ronnie Spector: Lead Vocals; Gary Wright: Keyboards: Leon Russell: Keyboards; Klaus Voormann: Bass; Jim Gordon: Drums; John Barham: Orchestral & String Arrangements; Pete Ham: (probable) Guitar

You [take 1]
Apple-RS1 (7" acetate single) (UK) [unreleased]
Producer: probably **George Harrison** & Phil Spector
George Harrison: Guitar; Leon Russell: Piano; Jim Gordon: Drums; Carl Radle: Bass; Gary Wright: Electric Piano
Probably EMI-Abbey Road, &/or Trident &/or Island Studios, London, UK 02/09/71

You [take 1] (**G. Harrison**) 3:48 (1/1)

You [take 2]
Apple-RS2 (7" acetate single) (UK) [unreleased]
Producer: probably **George Harrison** & Phil Spector
George Harrison: Guitar; Leon Russell: Piano; Jim Gordon: Drums; Carl Radle: Bass; Gary Wright: Electric Piano
Probably EMI-Abbey Road, &/or Trident &/or Island Studios, London, UK 02/09/71

You [take 2] (**G. Harrison**) 4:01 (1/1)

Ronnie Spector was born Veronica Bennett on August 10, 1943 in New York, New York. Ronnie, her sister Estelle and their cousin Nedra Talley formed The Ronettes. Phil Spector* signed the group to his label, Philles Records. Together they turned out such classic early 1960's hits as *Be My Baby*, *Baby I Love You* and *Walking In The Rain.*

During The Ronettes' UK tour in January 1964 they met The Beatles, who apparently showed more than musical interest in the girls, particularly John Lennon, who was attracted to Ronnie. Both groups were scheduled to be on the same flight to New York on February 7, but Phil put The Ronettes on an earlier flight and used their seats to be with The Beatles. The Ronettes visited The Beatles at their hotel in New York during this historic visit. They would offer The Ronettes billing on their tours, but Phil wouldn't consent until 1966, and then only with a stand-in for Ronnie. Ronnie and Phil were married in 1968.

According to Ronnie, Phil was hired as the unofficial A&R manager at Apple (he was never on their staff) in 1970 on the condition that he allowed her to sign with the label. [It also afforded Phil the opportunity to re-release his legendary Christmas album on Apple.] Phil and George Harrison began working on an album for Ronnie. During the sessions in early 1971 George and Phil wrote, and recorded the song *Tandoori Chicken* with Lennon on backing vocals. [An unreleased version with Phil on lead vocals exists on Apple acetates.] It was released as the B-side of *Try Some, Buy Some*, Ronnie's only release on Apple because she wasn't comfortable with the style and direction the recordings were taking. Several other songs were recorded including *You*, *Lovely La-De-Day* (a.k.a. *Loverly Laddy Day*) and *I Love Him Like I Love My Very Life* (a.k.a. *I Loved You Like I Loved My Very Life* when first issued by Carla Thomas in 1970 and when Phil later produced a version of it for Darlene Love). There is the possibility that Ringo may have contributed to some of Ronnie's recording sessions for Apple as well. Ten slightly different takes of *I Loved Him Like I Love My Very Life* exist on Apple acetates, which feature Harrison's distinctive slide guitar. Ronnie (along with Leon Russell* and Cilla Black*) reportedly also attempted Harrison's composition *I'll Still Love You* (a.k.a. *When Every Song Is Sung*). Harrison likely helped Phil with the production of these songs. The Apple acetate (RS 1&2) of *You* are backing tracks without vocals. Several years later, Harrison released *Try Some, Buy Some* and *You*, removing Ronnie's vocal track, substituting his voice, and adding a few instrumental overdubs to the original backing tracks.

Phil and Ronnie divorced in 1974. Ronnie restarted her career with a new lineup of Ronettes and made appearances with Bruce Springsteen, and Eddie Money singing on his Top 10 hit *Take Me Home Tonight*. She has released several solo records, and detailed a far from harmonious marriage to Phil in her 1990 autobiography *Be My Baby: How I Survived Mascara, Miniskirts, and Madness, or My Life as a Fabulous Ronette*. The Ronettes were inducted into the Rock and Roll Hall of Fame in 2007. For more information go to www.ronniespector.com

Spirit Choir

Every Man Has A Woman [Various Artists]
Polydor-823 490-2 (Germany) (09/13/84)
Producer: John Lennon & Yoko Ono
John Lennon: Guitar; Spirit Choir: Vocals†; Gary Van Scyoc: Bass; Adam Ippolito: Organ & Harmonium; Richard Frank Jr.: Drums & Percussion; Stan Bronstein: Saxophone; George Young: Saxophone; Wayne Tex Gabriel: Guitar
Record Plant Studios & probably Hit Factory†, New York, NY 10-11/xx/72 & xx/xx/84†

Now Or Never (Y. Ono) 3:44 (10)

The *Every Man Has A Woman* album, featuring well-known artists covering Yoko Ono's* songs, was apparently conceived by John Lennon as a gift to Yoko for her 50th birthday. Following John's murder in 1980, others decided to complete the project, which includes musical contributions from Elvis Costello*, Harry Nilsson*, Klaus Voormann's* group Trio, Eddie Money, Rosanne Cash, Roberta Flack, Alternating Boxes, the Lennons' son Sean and a recording of the title track sung by John several months before his murder. The album's song *Now Or Never* was recorded by Yoko with John and Elephant's Memory*, and included on her 1973 album *Approximately Infinite Universe*. An edited version of the original backing was used with new vocals by Spirit Choir.

Spirit Of Play

Children In Need / Children In Need (Instrumental)
Release-KIDS 1988 (7" single) (UK) (11/xx/88)
Producer: Paul McCartney & Spirit Of Play
Paul McCartney: Bass; Ken Wilson: Lead Guitar; Paul Fink: Guitar; Greenfields School Choir: Chorus; Andrew Skirrow: French Horn; London String Quartet: Strings; Woody Woodmansey: Drums; Nicky Hopkins: Piano & Keyboards [unless noted otherwise]
Hog Hill Mill Studios, Sussex, UK xx/xx/88

Children In Need (C. Mathieson-N. Hopkins) 4:45 (1/2)
Additionally: Craig Mathieson: Lead Vocals

Children In Need (Instrumental) (C. Mathieson-N. Hopkins) 4:45 (2/1)

Spirit Of Play were Craig Mathieson, Woody Woodmansey, born Mick Woodmansey in 1951 in Driffield, England and Nicky Hopkins*. Woody first gained notice as a member of David Bowie's* band The Spiders From Mars in the early 1970s. Their song *Children In Need* was recorded at Paul McCartney's private studio, probably during the period when Hopkins contributed to *That Day Is Done* on McCartney's album *Flowers In The Dirt*. Proceeds from the sale of the record went to the BBC's Children In Need Appeal in 1988. McCartney, long a supporter, performed at a benefit for the charity in 2009. The B-side is the same as the A-side minus the vocals. For more information go to www.woodywoodmansey.co.uk

Spirit Of The Forest

Spirit Of The Forest
Virgin-0-96551 (12" single) (06/05/89)
Producer: Gentlemen Without Weapons
Ringo Starr: Vocals†; Chris Rea: Vocals; Mr. Mister: Vocals; XTC (probably Andy Partridge, Colin Moulding & David Gregory): Vocals; Dave Gilmour: Vocals; Brian Wilson: Vocals; Joni Mitchell: Vocals; Fish (probably Tarjei van Ravens & Halvor Holter): Vocals; Belinda Carlisle: Vocals; Debbie Harry: Vocals; Bonnie Raitt: Vocals; Kate Bush: Vocals; Little Steven Van Zandt: Vocals; Jon Anderson: Vocals; Sam Brown: Vocals; Escape Club (probably Trevor Steel, John Holliday & Johnny Christo): Vocals; Olivia Newton-John: Vocals; Louise Goffin: Vocals; LL. Cool J: B. Vocals; Afrika Bambaata: B. Vocals; B-52's (probably Cindy Wilson, Fred Schneider, Kate Pierson & Keith Strickland): B. Vocals; Plasmatics (probably Wendy O. Williams): B. Vocals; Shikisha: B. Vocals; Fleetwood Mac (probably Rick Vito, Billy Burnette, Stevie Nicks & Christine McVie): B.

Vocals; Kenny Young: B. Vocals; Vic Coppersmith-Heaven: B. Vocals; Nick Glennie-Smith: B. Vocals; Amy Sky: B. Vocals; Dolette McDonald: B. Vocals; Big Country (probably Stuart Adamson, Tony Butler & Bruce Watson): B. Vocals; It Bites (probably Francis Dunnery): B. Vocals; Michael des Barres: B. Vocals; Marc Jordan: B. Vocals; Lisa Bonet: B. Vocals; Lenny Kravitz: B. Vocals; Andy Fairweather Low: B. Vocals; Jungle Brothers (probably Michael Small, Nathaniel Hall & Sammy Burwell): B. Vocals; Raging Hormones: B. Vocals; Johnny Warman: B. Vocals; Bruce Foxton: B. Vocals; David Clayton Thomas: B. Vocals
One or more of the following studios: Great Linford Manor, Gt. Linford; Sarm West†, Snake Ranch & Eden, London, UK; Complex, Los Angeles, CA &/or RCA, New York, NY 03/05/89†

Spirit Of The Forest (K. Young) 5:18 (1/1)

[Also available on Virgin-PRCD2795 (promotional only) (1)]

Spirit Of The Forest was organized by the group Gentlemen Without Weapons (Kenny Young, Vic Coppersmith-Heaven and Nick Glennie-Smith) for the Earth Love Fund-Rainforest Appeal to help bring attention to the destruction of the world's rain forests. An all-star cast, including Ringo Starr, was assembled at several locations to record several variations of the song *Spirit Of The Forest*. Ringo also appears in the promotional video for the song. Only the 12" single and a promotional CD include the full-length version with Ringo. An edited version (4:50) with Ringo was issued on the CD *Earthrise-The Rainforest Album* (Pyramid- R2 71830) in 1994, which also includes *How Many People* by Paul McCartney and *Saltwater* by Julian Lennon*. For more information go to www.earthlovefund.co.uk

Splinter

Harder To Live
Dark Horse-SP 22006 (album 12") (10/06/75)
FPSHOT, London, UK xx/xx/73

After Five Years (R. Purvis) 3:08 (2/2)
George Harrison: (possible) Guitar; Bill Elliott: Vocals; Bob Purvis: Vocals; probably one or more of the following: Chris Spedding: Guitar; Bill Dickinson: Bass; Klaus Voormann: Bass; Mike Kelly: Drums; Willie Weeks: Bass; Gary Wright: Keyboards; John Taylor: Keyboards; Earl Palmer: Drums; Jim Keltner: Drums; Bill Nuttycombe: String Concertmaster
Producer: probably **George Harrison** & Tom Scott

Lonely Man (From the film "Little Malcolm And His Struggle Against The Eunuchs") (R. Purvis-M. Evans) 5:29 (2/4)
George Harrison: Guitar; Bill Elliott: Vocals; Bob Purvis: Vocals; Billy Preston: Organ; Jim Keltner: Drums; Bill Dickinson: Bass; John Taylor: Fender Rhodes
Producer: George Harrison & Tom Scott

Lonely Man [sung in Japanese] / Lonely Man
Dark Horse-CM 2006 (7" single) (Japan) (05/21/76)
Producer: George Harrison & Tom Scott
George Harrison: Guitar; Bill Elliott: Vocals; Bob Purvis: Vocals; Billy Preston: Organ; Jim Keltner: Drums; Bill Dickinson: Bass; John Taylor: Fender Rhodes
FPSHOT, UK xx/xx/73 & xx/xx/76†

Lonely Man [sung in Japanese†] (M. Nakamura (translator)-M. Evans-[R. Purvis]) 4:15 (1/1)

The Place I Love
Dark Horse-SP 22001 (album 12") (09/25/74) (09/20/74)
Producer: George Harrison
Bill Elliott: Vocals; Bob Purvis: Vocals; Klaus Voormann: Bass; Mike Kelly: Drums [unless noted otherwise]
FPSHOT, UK xx/xx/73 or xx/xx/74

China Light (R. Purvis-W. Elliott) 4:35 (1/3)
Additionally: **George Harrison: Acoustic Guitar, Mandolin & Arrangement;** Bob Purvis: Guitar; Willie Weeks: Bass; Gary Wright: Piano; Billy Preston: Organ; Note: Klaus Voormann doesn't perform on this recording

Costafine Town (R. Purvis-W. Elliott) 3:10 (2/1) (09/13/74)
Additionally: **George Harrison: Bass, Harmonium & Hand Claps**; Gary Wright: Piano; Graham Maitland: Accordion; Note: Klaus Voormann doesn't perform on this recording

Drink All Day (Got To Find Your Own Way Home) (R. Purvis) 3:20 (1/2)
Additionally: **George Harrison: Harmonium,**

Jew's Harp, Percussion, Guitars & Dobro Guitar; Bob Purvis: Guitar; Jim Keltner: Drums; Note: Mike Kelly doesn't perform on this recording

Elly-May (R. Purvis) 2:43 (2/4) (09/13/74)
Additionally: **George Harrison: Guitar & Synthesizer**; Gary Wright: Piano

Gravy Train (R. Purvis) 4:50 (1/1)
Additionally: **George Harrison: Guitar**; Alvin Lee: Guitar; Mel Collins: Horn Arrangements; Billy Preston: Electric Piano

Haven't Got Time (R. Purvis) 3:55 (2/5)
Additionally: **George Harrison: Guitar & Percussion**; Alvin Lee: Guitar; Mel Collins: Horn Arrangements

The Place I Love (R. Purvis) 4:25 (2/2)
Additionally: **George Harrison: Percussion & Guitars**; Gary Wright: Electric Piano

Situation Vacant (R. Purvis) 4:00 (2/3)
Additionally: **George Harrison: Guitars & B. Vocals**; Bob Purvis: Guitar; Willie Weeks: Bass; Jim Keltner: Drums; Gary Wright: Piano; Mel Collins: Horn Arrangements; Note: Klaus Voormann & Mike Kelly don't perform on this recording

Somebody's City (R. Purvis) 5:20 (1/4)
Additionally: **George Harrison: Percussion & Guitars**; Bob Purvis: Guitar; Gary Wright: Piano; Mel Collins: Horn Arrangements; Alvin Lee: Guitar

Two Man Band
Dark Horse-DH 3073 (album 12") (10/03/77)
Producer: Norbert Putnam
FPSHOT, UK mid/xx/77

New York City (Who Am I) (R. Purvis) 3:49 (2/1)
George Harrison: (probable) Acoustic Guitar; Bill Elliott: Vocals; Bob Purvis: Vocals & Guitar; Norbert Putnam: Bass; Kenny Buttrey: Drums & Percussion; David Briggs: String Arrangement; (probably) The Memphis Horns

Round & Round (P. McGee) 3:13 (1/2) (09/06/77)
George Harrison: Slide Guitar; Bill Elliott: Vocals; Bob Purvis: Vocals; Norbert Putnam: Bass; Kenny Buttrey: Drums & Percussion; Steve Gibson: Guitar; Rod Argent (probable) Keyboards

Splinter was Newcastle-upon-Tyne, England natives Bob Purvis, born on May 31, 1950 and Bill Elliott*, born on July 6, 1950. They attended the same school and were playing music together by age 18. Mal Evans received demos of Purvis and Elliott's group Halfbreed. Apple was interested in Elliott as a singer and Purvis as a songwriter. In 1971 Elliott was recruited by Apple to sing lead vocals on *God Save Us* (see Bill Elliott And Elastic Oz Band). Purvis departed Halfbreed and Elliott formed the band Truth, which briefly included Purvis. Purvis (managed by Evans) reunited with Elliott and formed Splinter in August 1972. They rehearsed at Apple Studios where they met George Harrison who, along with Pete Ham (see Badfinger), helped them record the song *Another Chance That I Let Go* (Purvis still has an acetate). This incomplete recording (later re-titled *Lonely Man*) was featured in the Apple film *Little Malcolm And His Struggle Against The Eunuchs*, of which Harrison was executive producer. Harrison produced a completed version of *Lonely Man* for Splinter at FPSHOT, and Purvis says a video, featuring Harrison playing with them, was made. [*Lonely Man* was included on Splinter's 1975 album *Harder To Live*.]

The sessions for *Lonely Man* evolved into the album *The Place I Love*, which helped launch Dark Horse. Purvis says, "I have a demo where Bill and I are playing the songs that we're going to put on the album, and George is jamming away in the background. George spent more time on our album than he did on his album! He really put himself out for us." The September 9, 1974 edition of London's newspaper *The Sun* quotes Harrison saying of Splinter, "They are good, honest boys who make good, simple records, and it is a joy for me to help them." The album greatly benefits from Harrison's considerable contributions under the thinly veiled pseudonyms Hari Georgeson, Jai Raj Harisein and P. Roducer. Purvis proudly admits that he and Elliott were essentially composers and singers for what was somewhat of a Harrison album. Purvis says his rhythm guitar playing on most of the album wasn't credited because it was all but mixed out. Peter Sellers (see Peter Sellers, Terry Southern & Ringo Starr) took photos of them intended for the album's jacket but Purvis says, "We were feelin' rough and didn't want our photos taken. Peter took them away and never brought them back." The photos used were taken at Harrison's home (as was the photo on the *Harder To Live* album's back jacket). Harrison played the album through the public address system at venues, prior to performing, during his 1974 US tour. Splinter's debut single *Costafine Town* was a Top 20 hit in the UK. Their follow-up single *Drink All Day* was banned by the BBC and replaced with *China Light*, which like all of their successive singles, failed in the charts.

Splinter's 1975 album *Harder To Live* was produced by Tom Scott* because Harrison was away at the time. Scott says *Lonely Man* was already finished, and that he really didn't add anything to it, although he and Harrison are credited as the producers. He's quite sure that Harrison didn't make any other contributions to *Harder To Live*. However, Purvis is sure that the backing for *After Five Years* was recorded during the sessions for *The Place I Love* album and thus, would have been produced by Harrison. Purvis can't decide if Harrison plays guitar on the song, but was certain Chris Spedding did. He says they also recorded several versions of *After Five Years* in Japanese. Purvis suspects these, and the Japanese version of *Lonely Man*, using the original backing tracks that Harrison contributed to, were recorded at the same time. Noted Japanese singer and actor, Masatoshi Nakamura translated the lyrics into Japanese. The duo had several other Japanese-only releases because they were intrigued by the culture and very popular there, but Harrison didn't contribute to them.

Splinter's 1977 album *Two Man Band* doesn't have specific musical credits. Parker McGee is credited as playing guitar but Purvis doesn't recall him playing on anything. *I'll Bend For You*, the B-side of the single *Round & Round*, wasn't included on the album. Like the album, it lists Norbert Putnam as producer, and George Harrison and Dennis Morgan as executive producers. Purvis says, "George did come in and have his say on a few things on certain tracks. He plays guitar on *Round & Round*, and I think acoustic guitar on *New York City (Who Am I)*." Purvis also recalls Harrison playing guitar on the Splinter demos *Dreaming*, *Rush Of Daily Life* and *Domingo Bay*, which he thinks were recorded by Phil McDonald at the offices of Dark Horse in London around 1976.

Splinter struck out with their three tuneful and well-crafted albums for Dark Horse. Purvis laments, "We left George and Dark Horse under a cloud. I had a chip on my shoulder. If I could change any period of time in my life, I would change that period because of the things I said and did, and because George was a really terrific person. I wish I could turn back the clock and tell him that I've grown up. Few know what he was like in the studio and his dedication, and how good he is on the guitar; he had this incredible nature that drew people to him." Splinter released two more albums after they left Dark Horse. They broke up in 1984 when Elliott changed occupations and relocated. Purvis continues to write, record and perform.

Bruce Springsteen

Together At The Rock And Roll Hall Of Fame [Various Artists]
Living Legend-LLRCD 101(Italy) [unauthorized release] (xx/xx/93)
Producer: [unknown]
George Harrison: Guitar & Vocals; Ringo Starr: Drums; Bruce Springsteen: Lead Vocals & (probable) Tambourine; Bob Dylan: Vocals & Guitar; Paul Shaffer: Keyboards; Billy Joel: Keyboards & Vocals; probably one or more of the following: Mike Love: Percussion & B. Vocals; Bruce Johnston: B. Vocals & Handclaps; Little Richard: Handclaps; Elton John: Keyboards; Anton Fig: Drums; Dave Edmunds: Guitar; Les Paul: Guitar; Jeff Beck: Electric Guitar; Mick Jagger: Percussion, B. Vocals; Mary Wilson: B. Vocals; Carl Wilson: Handclaps; Brian Wilson: Handclaps; Yoko Ono: Handclaps; Sean Lennon: Handclaps; Sid McGinnis: Guitar; Ben E. King: B. Vocals & Handclaps; John Fogerty: Handclaps; Arlo Guthrie: Handclaps; Peter Wolf: Handclaps; Johnny Moore: Handclaps; Joe Blunt: Handclaps; Clyde Brown: Handclaps; Julian Lennon: Handclaps; Bill Pinkney: Handclaps; Charlie Thomas: Handclaps; Max Weinberg: Handclaps; Will Lee: Bass; Patti Scialfa: Handclaps & B. Vocals
Grand Ballroom Waldorf-Astoria Hotel, New York, NY 01/20/88
Twist And Shout (P. Medley-B. Russell) 3:14 (3)

With A Little Help To My Friends [Ringo Starr]
No Label Records-NLR 9904 (CD-R) [unauthorized release] (xx/xx/99)
Ringo Starr: Drums & B. Vocals; Bruce Springsteen: Lead Vocals & Guitar; Billy Preston: Keyboards & Vocals; Jim Keltner: Drums; Levon Helm: Drums; Nils Lofgren: Guitar & B. Vocals; Joe Walsh: Guitar; Rick Danko: Bass; Clarence Clemons: Saxophone; Dr. John: Keyboards
Garden State Arts Center, Holmdel, NJ 08/11/89

Get Back [live] (J. Lennon-P. McCartney) 4:17 (6)

Long Tall Sally [live] (E. Johnson-R. Blackwell-R. Penniman) 3:10 (7)

Bruce Springsteen was born on September 23, 1949 in Long Branch, New Jersey but grew up in nearby Freehold. By the time he was a teenager he was playing guitar and writing songs. He was in several bands in the mid-1960s and early '70s playing clubs and bars. During this period he met Steve Van Zandt (see Artists United Against Apartheid) and Clarence Clemons* who would later be a part of Bruce's E Street Band along with Nils Lofgren*, drummer Max Weinberg and others. Bruce signed with Columbia Records in 1972. His first two albums were praised by the critics but weren't initially successful, though he drew huge crowds with his energetic performances. His third album, and the title track *Born To Run*, launched him into superstardom in 1975. During the next 10 years he would have Top Five hits with *Hungry Heart*, *Dancing In The Dark* and *Glory Days*, and Top 10 hits with *Cover Me*, *Born In The USA*, *I'm On Fire*, *I'm Goin' Down* and *My Hometown*. Bruce reached the top of the charts via his compositions *Blinded By The Light* by Manfred Mann's Earth Band (see Paul Jones).

Bruce was part of the all-star jam with George Harrison and Ringo Starr when The Beatles were inducted into the Rock and Roll Hall of Fame on January 20, 1988 at New York's Waldorf Astoria Hotel, portions of which are available on unauthorized releases. He appeared with Ringo Starr's All-Starr Band, which included Nils Lofgren and Clarence Clemons, at the Garden State Arts Center in Holmdel, New Jersey on August 11, 1989. He played guitar while Ringo performed *Photograph* and *With A Little Help From My Friends*. He also played guitar, and sang lead vocals on *Long Tall Sally* and *Get Back* with backing from Ringo on drums. These performances are available on unauthorized releases. [Bruce's drummer, Max Weinberg, a good friend of Ringo's, has sat in with Ringo Starr's All-Starr Band on a number of occasions.] Bruce was inducted into the Rock and Roll Hall of Fame in 1999. Bruce Springsteen continues to write, record and tour. For more information go to www.brucespringsteen.net

Billy Squier

Ringo Starr & His All Starr Band Live 2006
Koch-KOC-DV-4543 (DVD) (07/08/08)
Producer: Brent Carpenter; Executive Producer: Ringo Starr
Ringo Starr: Drums; Billy Squier: Electric Guitar & Lead Vocals; Sheila Escovedo: Drums; Hamish Stuart: Bass; Rod Argent: Keyboards; Edgar Winter: Saxophone & B. Vocals; Richard Marx: Electric Guitar & B. Vocals
Mohegan Sun, Uncasville, CT 07/16/06

Everybody Wants You [live] (B. Squier) 5:20 (5)
Additionally: Hamish Stuart: B. Vocals; Rod Argent: B. Vocals; Edgar Winter: Keyboards
[Also available on Koch-KOC-CD-4542-2 (4) (07/08/08)]

Rock Me Tonight [live] (B. Squier) 6:21 (23)
[Also available on Koch-KOC-CD-4542-2 (15) (07/08/08)]

William "Billy" Squier was born on May 12, 1950 in Boston, Massachusetts. He took piano lessons as a youngster for several years before switching to guitar. He formed a band in high school. By 1968 he was a member of the house band at the Psychedelic Supermarket club in Boston, and several other bands over the next few years. In 1976 he formed the band Piper whose two albums for A&M Records were praised by the critics. By 1980 Squier was a solo artist for Capitol. His second album *Don't Say No*, which was a Top Five hit in 1981, produced the Top 20 hit *The Stroke*, and the hits *In The Dark*, *My Kinda Lover* and *Lonely Is The Night*. Squier says he dedicated the album's song *Nobody Knows* to John Lennon because it was inspired by a chance encounter with John, and recorded in New York the night he was murdered. In 1982 another Top Five hit album, *Emotions In Motion*, included the Top 40 hit *Everybody Wants You* (a number one hit on Billboard's Hot Mainstream Rock Tracks charts). His last Top 20 hit was *Rock Me Tonight* in 1984.

Squier was a member of Ringo Starr's All-Starr Band in 2006 performing *Everybody Wants You* and *Rock Me Tonight*, and again in 2008 performing *Lonely Is The Night* and *The Stroke*, all with backing from Ringo on drums. Squier recalls, "Being in the All-Starr Band was one of the great musical experiences of my life. Ringo had initially asked me to be in the 2000 lineup. I was incredibly flattered, but didn't do it because I wanted to spend the summer with my two young godchildren. I didn't feel that turning

Left to right: Kathryn Bunting, Billy Squier and Kristofer Engelhardt, Showboat Amphitheater, Chesaning, MI July 14, 2009. © Kristofer Engelhardt.

down a Beatle was a terribly smart thing to do, and didn't expect to be asked again, so I felt pretty lucky when he asked me again in 2006. Aside from actually being able to play with Ringo, I felt it gave me a great opportunity to be recognized as a lead guitarist, which is a part of my profile that tends to be overlooked. Ringo likes a good laugh and is a bit of a raconteur, which is not surprising given the life he's lived. He's very sharp and witty, and has a great generosity of spirit.

"Band members pick the songs they want to do, but since the show is designed to be something of a hit parade, certain songs are obligatory. Ringo insists on being part of the band. He makes clear what he wants on his songs, and takes direction from the other band members on their numbers. He's very comfortable in a band situation, and loves to sit back and play his drums. He has an exquisite balance between ego and humility. He can be very direct and forthright without being cocky or arrogant. He doesn't talk down to people or assert himself as a 'Beatle'— but he is who he is, so he naturally commands all of our respect. I think that's why the All-Starr Band concept has been so successful.

"With only about nine days to rehearse before a tour, it's a bit like boot camp! There's a lot to absorb, not to mention the underlying pressure of wanting to measure up to your peers. After the first week in '06, I was feeling a bit overwhelmed. My wife suggested that perhaps I wasn't the only one, so I got up my courage and mentioned to Edgar Winter* how nervous I was. He said, 'I'm so glad you said that because I'm peeing in my pants!' I got the same response from Rod Argent*. If they were nervous, I was in good company. Knowing we were all in the same boat brought us a lot closer together.

"Most of the feedback suggests that the '08 band was better than the '06 band but I think they were equally great. The '08 band benefited from having a core group of players who already knew the drill, and it was great to get Hamish Stuart* down front on his Average White Band tunes. I was a fan of The Zombies as a kid, so playing with Rod Argent in the '06 band was a really cool experience. I had no idea just how spectacular a player he is, and he's a very lovely guy. I knew Richard Marx* was an accomplished songwriter but felt his music was a bit 'lightweight,' so I was initially skeptical about him being in the band – but he really turned me around. He brought in two great rock songs and delivered on both of them. He's very passionate about what he does. His contributions really surprised me, and we ended up becoming good friends. Colin Hay*, who took over Richard's slot in '08, is a real sound craftsman. He added a different element and dimension to the band, which I really liked. Both of these guys are a joy to work with. Edgar's an extraordinary talent and a very sincere, dedicated musician. At the Greek Theatre, during the only show we recorded on the '08 tour, he had a major malfunction with his keyboards in the middle of his signature song *Frankenstein*. It wasn't his fault, but he was devastated and felt he'd let the band down. Edgar, you never let us down! Of all the great moments I've had with all of these great players, one night in '06 stands out. Sheila E's* a fiercely energetic performer, and near the end of a very hot and humid outdoor show in Florida she collapsed from heatstroke. I sensed that Ringo was hesitant about finishing the show without her. I'm speculating, because I have this tendency myself, but I think Ringo sometimes sells himself short as a player. He likes to have another accomplished drummer up there with him who he can collaborate with. The next song in the set was Rod's *Hold Your Head Up*. When Rod took off on his organ solo, those of us who were mobile congregated around Ringo's drum riser in a show of support. As the solo progressed, whatever trepidation he may have had evaporated, and Ringo proceeded to blow us away with his drumming. He was spectacular! It was a magical moment for all of us. Ringo's given me a great gift by making me one of the All-Starrs. It means a lot to me and the best part is — we all have so much fun! I'd play for him anytime." Squier contributed to Ringo's 2010 album *Y Not*. Billy Squier continues to write, record and tour. For more information go to www.billysquier.com

Freddie Starr

The Wanderer
Dover/Chrysalis-CCD17 (UK) (11/01/90)
Producer: Bruce Baxter & Mike Cooper
Paul McCartney: B. Vocals; Freddie Starr: Lead Vocals
Probably InterTel Studios, Stonebridge House, London, UK probably xx/xx/77 &/or xx/xx/78

You've Lost That Lovin' Feelin' (B. Mann-C. Weil-P. Spector) 5:08 (9) (05/19/78)

Freddie Starr was born Frederick Fowell in Liverpool, England on January 9, 1943. He won first prize for his singing and impersonations in a talent contest when he was nine years old. He was a member of the song and comedy act The Hilda Fallon Road Show from 1954 to 1958. He appeared in the 1958 film *Violent Playground*. In 1961 Freddie joined Howie Casey And The Seniors, a popular Liverpool band previously known as Derry And The Seniors, who were the first of many Liverpool bands to perform in Hamburg, Germany. [Casey embarrassingly admits he pleaded with The Beatles' booking agent Allan Williams not to send The Beatles to Hamburg, because they were lousy and would spoil it for other Liverpool groups.] Howie Casey And The Seniors disbanded in mid-1962. [Casey was part of the horn section for Wings' tours in 1975, 1976 and 1979, and contributed to most of Paul McCartney and Wings' albums released between 1974 and 1981.] Freddie adopted the stage name Starr (after another famous Liverpudlian whose first name is Ringo), and formed The Ventures, but soon left to form Freddie Starr And The Midnighters. These bands were on bills with The Beatles and briefly signed to NEMS before breaking up in 1964. Freddie released three unsuccessful singles for Decca Records, and fronted various groups during the mid-1960s, but became better known as an impersonator (including Elvis) in a variety of comedy acts. He had UK Top 10 hits with *It's You* in 1974 and *White Christmas* in 1975.

The 1978 album *Freddie Starr* gives "special thanks to Paul McCartney for his assistance with vocals." According to Starr, McCartney was at the studio in Wembley where he was recording, and added backing vocals to the album's song *You've Lost That Lovin' Feelin*. Perhaps Paul was returning an old favor, or his involvement had something to do with the album including a cover of a Buddy Holly song, whose publishing catalogue McCartney owns. Starr has also recorded covers of The Beatles' songs. Freddie was the star of ITV's *Who Do You Do* and BBC TV's *The Freddie Starr Show* in the 1990s. Freddie Starr still performs in the UK but remains virtually unknown in the US. For more information go to www.freddiestarr.com

Roadsinger (To Warm You Through The Night)
Island-2705149 + (DVD) (05/04/09)
LC0407.00602527053226 (Malaysia)
Producer: Yusuf Islam (audio); Carol Cohen (video)
Paul McCartney: B. Vocals†, Yusuf Islam: Lead Vocals, Guitar & Dobro; Dolly Parton: B. Vocals; Terry Sylvester: B. Vocals; Allison Krauss: B. Vocals; Gunnar Nelson: B. Vocals; Covent Garden Opera Singers: B. Vocals; Kenny Passarelli: Bass; Kristoffer Sonne: Drums & Tambourine; David Davidson: Violin; David Angell: Violin; Martin Terefe: Electric Guitar; Kenny Vaughn: Electric Guitar; Paul Franklin: Steel Guitar; Bryan Sutton: Acoustic Guitar & Mandolin; Jennifer Kumer: French Horn
Kensaltown Studio 12/06/07, 07/08/08 & 08/02/08, Angel Studio 09/04/08 & Soho Studio 07/29/08†, London, UK; Bluebird Studio 12/06/07 & Iris Studio 07/17/08 Nashville, TN; Jamal Records Studio, Dubai 08/19/08 & House Of Blues Studio, Encino, CA 11/08/08

Boots And Sand (Y. Islam) 3:40 (2-1)

Sink In The Can
Shottebel MYR 640707 (CD-R) [unauthorized release] (probably xx/xx/00)
Producer: Dave Kirshenbaum
Ringo Starr: Drums; Cat Stevens: Lead Vocals & (probable) Guitar; Jean Roussel: Keyboards; Bruce Lynch: Bass
Sweet Silence Studios, Copenhagen, Denmark 09/30/76

Baby, I Have Some Love For You 1:18 (17)

Blue Monday [take one] (A. Domino-D. Bartholomew) 3:08 (7)

Blue Monday [take 2 & 3] (A. Domino-D. Bartholomew) 4:13 (10 &11)

If I Have To Work For You 3:03 (8)

I Just Want To Make Love To You (W. Dixon) 4:31 (13)

Looking For The Sailor 8:16 (18)

Working In The Coal Mine [take one] (A. Toussaint) (4:18) (14)

Working In The Coal Mine [take two] (A. Toussaint) (4:36) (16)

Cat Stevens was born Steven Georgiou on July 21, 1948 in London, England. He developed a love for art and music but, seeing The Beatles' success, pursued a career in music. In 1966 he adopted the name Cat, in part, because of peoples' love for animals, and had a UK Top 40 hit with *I Love My Dog*. In 1967 his songs *Matthew And Son* and *I'm Gonna Get Me A Gun* were UK Top 10 hits, as was *Lady D'Arbanville* in 1970. Between 1971 and 1975 Cat had Top 10 hits with *Peace Train*, *Morning Has Broken*, *Another Saturday Night* and *Oh Very Young*, and Top 20 hits with *Wild World* and *Sitting*.

When Ringo Starr was promoting his album *Rotogravure* in early fall of 1976 he met Cat at a hotel in Copenhagen, Denmark. Cat invited Ringo to his recording sessions there at Sweet Silence Studios for his album *Izitso*. He recalls that the party atmosphere of the sessions led to a jam of him singing several takes of *Blue Monday*, *I Just Want To Make Love To You*, *Working In The Coal Mine* and several other songs, with Ringo joining in on drums. He says the tracks were not proper takes, so they weren't used (though they are available on unauthorized releases). He seems quite sure Ringo didn't play on any of the tracks used on *Izitso*. [Russ Ballard produced some recordings for Ringo at Sweet Silence Studios in July 1978.]

Cat's last Top 40 hit was *(Remember The Days Of The) Old School Yard* in 1977. Soon after, he converted to the Islamic religion, changed his name to Yusuf Islam and retired from the music business. He devoted much of his time and resources to the religion, education, and to peace and charitable organizations. In 1995 he began releasing several Islamic-based recordings and by 2003 was again making secular recordings.

Yusuf was a keynote speaker and performer at the Adopt-A-Minefield gala in Düsseldorf, Germany on May 28, 2005. Paul McCartney and Heather Mills* (major supporters of the organization) were in attendance. Paul joined Yusuf onstage for his rendition of The Beatles' songs *All You Need Is Love* and, with Yusuf on guitar and Paul on piano, *Let It Be*. In 2006 Yusuf released *An Other Cup*, his first album of pop songs since 1978. In 2008 he recorded the song *Boots & Sand* about his being refused admittance by US Immigration, which features backing vocals by McCartney. It was included on the bonus DVD with Yusuf's 2009 album *Roadsinger To Warm You Through The Night.* That year Yusuf recorded covers of George Harrison's songs *The Day The World Gets 'Round* and *All Things Must Pass* for Klaus Voormann's* album *A Sideman's Journey*. For more information go to www.yusufislam.com

John Stewart

I Gotta Blues [Ringo Starr]
Pebbles P-02005 [unauthorized release] (xx/xx/02)
Producer: Joe Hamilton
Ringo Starr: B. Vocals; John Stewart: Lead Vocals & Guitar; Tom Smothers: B. Vocals; Dick Smothers: B. Vocals; Pat Paulsen: B. Vocals; Bob Einstein: B. Vocals; Steve Martin: B. Vocals; Lilly Tomlin: B. Vocals; Don Novello: B. Vocals
NBC TV Studios, Burbank, CA probably 04/20/75; airdate: 04/28/75

Survivors (Can You Hear Me?) (J. Stewart) 1:17 (5)

John Stewart was born on September 5, 1939 in San Diego, California. He had an interest in music from an early age. By the mid-1950s he'd formed Johnny Stewart and The Furies, who performed around Southern California for several years, and released one single. John then became part of The Cumberland Three. They were patterned after the Kingston Trio, who John became a member of from 1961 until their breakup in 1967, though they reformed on numerous occasions with varying members. During John's tenure with the Kingston Trio they had a Top 10 hit with *The Reverend Mr. Black*, and Top 40 hits with *Where Have All The Flowers Gone?* and *Greenback Dollar*. They also covered songs by The Beatles. Stewart continued to develop his songwriting skills, and composed *Daydream Believer*, which became a huge hit for The Monkees in 1967, and later for Anne Murray. His 1969 solo album *California Bloodline* was praised by the critics.

In 1975 Stewart performed his song *Survivors* on NBC TV's *Smothers Brothers Show*. Joining him on backing vocals were most of the show's guests, including Ringo Starr who performed *No No Song* on the show. Both songs are available on unauthorized releases. [The Beatles were fans of CBS TV's *Smothers Brothers Comedy Hour* in the late 1960s. George Harrison made a cameo on the show, broadcast on November 17, 1968. The previous month, the show premiered The Beatles' music videos for *Hey Jude* and *Revolution* in the US. John Lennon recruited Tom Smothers for his initial recording of *Give Peace A Chance* in 1969.] When *Survivors* was issued as a single (RCA JB-10268) the picture sleeve featured a photo, including Ringo, of Stewart's performance of *Survivors* on the *Smothers Brothers Show* leading some to mistakenly believe that Ringo contributed to the single's studio recording.

Stewart found commercial success with his 1979 album *Bombs Away Dream Babies*, which includes the Top Five hit *Gold*, and the Top 40 hits *Midnight Wind* and *Lost Her In The Sun*. John Stewart continued to perform until his death on January 19, 2008. For more information go to www.chillywinds.com

Rod Stewart

Oriental Nightfish
Reading Railroad-HAR 169 (album 12") [unauthorized release]
Producer: [unknown-audience recording]
Paul McCartney: B. Vocals; Rod Stewart: Lead Vocals; Ron Wood: Guitar; Ian McLagan: Keyboards; Tetsu Yamauchi: Bass; Kenney Jones: Drums; Linda McCartney: B. Vocals
Odeon Cinema Theatre, Lewisham, UK 11/18/74

Mine For Me [live] (**P. McCartney**) 0:29 (1/4/1)

Smiler
Universal-558063 (10/25/05) (09/27/74)
Producer: Rod Stewart
Paul McCartney: B. Vocals; Rod Stewart: Lead Vocals; Ron Wood: Guitar; Martin Quittenton: Guitar; Ian McLagan: Organ; Spike Heatley: Bass; Kenney Jones: Drums; Ray Cooper: Percussion; The Tropic Isle Steel Band: Steel Drums
Morgan Studios, London, UK 01 or 02/xx/74

Mine For Me (**P. McCartney**) 4:02 (12)

Roderick "Rod" Stewart was born on January 10, 1945 in London, England. He began playing guitar as a youngster and joined a skiffle band. He didn't begin his musical career in earnest until 1961, after giving up as a professional soccer player and tiring as a grave digger. He spent several years honing his solo act, and was signed to a couple of record labels while dropping in and out of bands, including The Shotgun Express, The Jeff Beck Group and finally The Faces (see Kenney Jones, Ron Wood). Rod's breakthrough came in 1971 with the number one hit *Maggie May*.

Rod reportedly contacted Paul McCartney after hearing him say he wrote a song for Ringo because he was a friend and would write a song for Rod Stewart if he asked. McCartney contributed his composition *Mine For Me*, along with backing vocals, to Rod's 1974 album *Smiler*. Paul and Linda McCartney* joined Rod onstage at the Odeon Cinema Theatre in Lewisham, England on November 18, 1974 (not November 27) to sing *Mine For Me*. The performance was broadcast on April 25, 1975 on the NBC TV show *Midnight Special* and is available on unauthorized releases.

During the second half of 1970s Stewart became an international star but the Faces disintegrated, in part, due to Rod's successful solo career. Since that time he's had number one hits with *Tonight's The Night (Gonna Be Alright)*, *Da Ya Think I'm Sexy* and *All For* Love, and Top Five hits with *You're In My Heart (The Final Acclaim)*, *Passion*, *Young Turks*, *My Heart Can't Tell You No*, *Downtown Train*, *Rhythm Of My Heart* and *Have I Told You Lately*. Rod has recorded covers of The Beatles' songs and had a UK Top 20 hit with *Get Back*. He was inducted into the Rock and Roll Hall of Fame in 1994. Rod Stewart has recently had success recording classic American songs from the 1930s and '40s, and is still a huge concert draw. For more information go to www.rodstewart.com

Stephen Stills

Stephen Stills
Atlantic/WEA-82809-2(12/05/95) (11/16/70)
Producer: Stephen Stills & Bill Halverson
Island Studios, London, UK probably 03/xx/70

To A Flame (S. Stills) 3:10 (7)
Ringo Starr: Drums; Stephen Stills: Lead Vocals, Guitar, Arrangement & Piano; Arif Mardin: Arrangement & Conductor

We Are Not Helpless (S. Stills) 4:17 (10)
Ringo Starr: Drums; Stephen Stills: Lead Vocals, Guitar, Keyboards & Bass; Rita Coolidge: B. Vocals; Priscilla Coolidge-Jones: B. Vocals; Claudia Lennear: B. Vocals; John Sebastian: B. Vocals; Cass Elliot: B. Vocals; David Crosby: B. Vocals; Graham Nash: B. Vocals; Shirley Matthews: B. Vocals; Booker T. Jones: (probable) B. Vocals

Stills
Sony-SRCS 6189 (Japan) (01/26/93) (06/17/75)
Producer: Stephen Stills, Bill Halverson, Ron Albert & Howie Albert
Island Studios, London, UK (probably 03/xx/70 & early/xx/74

As I Come Of Age (S. Stills) 2:36 (9)
Ringo Starr: Drums; Stephen Stills: Lead Vocals; Piano, Bass & Organ; Donnie Dacus: Guitar; Graham Nash: B. Vocals; David Crosby: B. Vocals

Stephen Stills was born on January 3, 1945 in Dallas, Texas. He spent much of his youth in various foreign and domestic locations due to his father's military service, and developed an interest in music. He was in several bands including The Continentals with Don Felder who later became a member of The Eagles. In the early 1960 Stills, like many of his contemporaries, played in the folk clubs of New York's Greenwich Village, where he met Richie Furay. The two moved to California. Stills auditioned for The Monkees, but recommended his former roommate Peter "Tork" Torkelson who got the job.

Stills and Furay teamed up with Neil Young* to form the core of Buffalo Springfield. Their recording of Stills' song *For What It's Worth* was a Top 10 hit in 1967 and a counterculture anthem about the turbulent '60s. The jacket of the album *Buffalo Springfield Again* thanks, among others, The Nerk Twins [John Lennon and Paul McCartney] and George Harrison and Ringo Starr, though The Beatles didn't contribute to any of their recordings. The group soon disintegrated, in part, due to conflicts between Stills and Young.

Stills had recently worked with David Crosby who was leaving The Byrds. [The Byrds and The Beatles greatly admired each other. George and Paul attended one of The Byrds' recording sessions in Los Angeles in August 1965 but their producer Terry Melcher said they didn't contributed to any of their recordings. The Beatles included a brief portion of The Byrds' music in their 1996 *Anthology* film.] In the spring of 1968

Crosby introduced Stills to Graham Nash of The Hollies. [The Beatles had long been acquainted with The Hollies, and Nash who sang on their recording of *All You Need Is Love*.] Peter Asher (see Peter & Gordon) says he and Harrison went to Peter Tork's house in California in June 1968, and had a jam session along with Crosby, Stills and probably drummer Russ Kunkel (other reports claim Ringo, who accompanied Harrison to California, also attended), but nothing was recorded. Asher recalls that most of the participants (Harrison excluded) were naked. Later, Nash, with Stills and Crosby, returned to the UK and announced his departure from The Hollies. There the three rehearsed and auditioned for several record labels, including Apple, who rejected them! During this period Stills wrote, but apparently never recorded, the song *The Doctor Will See You Now Mr. L* about Lennon. They were finally signed to Atlantic who released their debut album *Crosby, Stills & Nash* in 1969. Their second album *Déjà vu* added the name (Neil) Young, but their chemistry has been as delicate as their harmonies, so solo projects have often taken priority over group efforts over the years. Members of Crosby, Stills and Nash have recorded covers of The Beatles' songs.

In late 1969 Stills bought Ringo Starr's home in the UK, formerly owned by Peter Sellers (see Peter Sellers, Terry Southern & Ringo Starr). While in the UK Stills contributed to Doris Troy's* album for Apple and recorded his first solo album *Stephen Stills*. It spawned the Top 20 hit *Love The One You're With*, and includes Ringo, under the name Richie, drumming on *To A Flame* and *We Are Not Helpless*. The 1975 album *Stills* includes Ringo, under the name English Richie, drumming on *As I Come Of Age*. [Ringo didn't contribute to the alternate version of *As I Come Of Age* included on the 1991 Crosby, Stills & Nash retrospective box set.] Many reliable publications, including the *Stills* credits, list *As I Come Of Age* as being recorded in 1971 with overdubs probably recorded in early 1974. *To A Flame* and *We Are Not Helpless* are usually listed as being recorded in London in June or July 1970, but Stills was touring the US then. The majority of *Stephen Stills* was recorded in March 1970, which is probably when all of the sessions with Ringo took place. Stills contributed to Ringo's 1981 album *Stop And Smell The Roses*. Stills continues to record and tour with, and without, Crosby, Stills & Nash and occasionally Young, who along with Buffalo Springfield were inducted into the Rock and Roll Hall of Fame in 1997. For more information go to
www.stephenstills.com, www.csny.com

Rory Storm & The Hurricanes

Liverpool 1963-1968 Volume One [Various Artists]
See For Miles-SEECD 370 (UK) (09/27/94)
Producer: Brian Epstein
EMI-Abbey Road, London, UK 09/30/64

America (L. Bernstein-S. Sondheim) 2:32 (7) (11/13/64)
Ringo Starr: Percussion & B. Vocals; Rory Storm: Lead Vocals; Shane Fenton (a.k.a. Alvin Stardust): Percussion & B. Vocals; Iris Caldwell, B. Vocals; Lou Walters: Bass & B. Vocals; Ty Brian: Guitar & B. Vocals; Johnny Guitar: Guitar & B. Vocals; Jimmy Tushingham: Drums & B. Vocals

Summertime/Fever/September Song / [commercial for various leather goods]
Akustik (single 10") (Germany) [unreleased]
Executive Producer: Allan Williams
Akustik Studio, Hamburg, Germany 10/15/60

Fever (J. Davenport [a.k.a. O. Blackwell]-E. Cooley) (1/2)
John Lennon: (possible) Guitar; **George Harrison: (possible) Guitar**; **Ringo Starr: Drums**; **Paul McCartney: (probable) Guitar**; Lou Walters: Lead Vocals & Bass; Ty Brian: (possible) Guitar

September Song (M. Anderson-K. Weill) (1/3)
John Lennon: (possible) Guitar; **George Harrison: (possible) Guitar**; **Ringo Starr: Drums**; **Paul McCartney: (possible) Guitar**
Lou Walters: Lead Vocals & Bass

Summertime (G. Gershwin-I. Gershwin-D. Heyward) (1/1)
John Lennon: Guitar; **Paul McCartney: Guitar**; **George Harrison: Guitar**; **Ringo Starr: Drums**; Lou Walters: Lead Vocals & Bass

Rory Storm & The Hurricanes were a popular group in Liverpool, England in the late 1950s and early '60s. They were first known as Al Caldwell's Texans, and then The Raving Texans and were influenced by skiffle, and country & western music. Their members (among others) were lead singer Rory Storm, born Alan Caldwell on September 21, 1939 in Liverpool; Lou "Wally" Walters, born Walter Eymond, on bass; Ty Brian, born Charles O'Brien, on guitar; Johnny "Guitar" Byrne, born on December 4, 1939 in Liverpool, on guitar; and drummer Richard Starkey, born on July 7, 1940 in Liverpool, who joined the group in March 1958. [Richard had been in The Eddie Clayton Skiffle Group and then Darktown Skiffle.] All of the members were adopting stage names, so Richard chose Ringo Starr. One of the most popular portions of The Hurricanes' live act was "Ringo Starrtime," featuring Ringo on half-a-dozen numbers. Storm was known for his outlandish outfits, stage acrobatics and a persistent stutter. Band members often sat in with other Liverpool groups, including Derry And The Seniors (see Freddie Starr) and The Beatles.

Rory Storm & The Hurricanes, like The Beatles, had engagements at several of Hamburg, Germany's music clubs and also backed Tony Sheridan there. On October 15, 1960 Wally cut a record in a small rudimentary studio near Hamburg's central rail station to demonstrate his vocal talents. Allan Williams says in his book *The Man Who Gave The Beatles Away* that Wally, backed by John Lennon, Paul McCartney, George Harrison and The Hurricanes' drummer Ringo, recorded *Summertime* and *Fever*. Allan recalls that The Beatles also wanted to record a song, but that there wasn't time. The initial record was cut at 78 RPM, with a leftover radio commercial on the other side. Allan thought four additional discs were cut. In an interview conducted by Mark Lewisohn in 1984, Wally maintained that the three Beatles and Ringo back him on *Summertime*, and that only Ty Brian, Johnny Byrne and Ringo backed him on *Fever* and *September Song*. Wally thought that nine discs were cut. Byrne said he went along to the sessions, but after consideration, didn't think he or Brian played on any of the recordings, even though he stated in previous interviews that he thought Brian might have been involved. He recalled Lennon and Harrison playing guitar, Ringo playing drums, and seemed sure McCartney was playing bass while Wally sang *Summertime* and *September Song*. He said that only McCartney and Ringo backed Wally on *Fever*. Byrne thought six discs were cut and said, "I never got a copy because I didn't play on the recordings." One copy supposedly exists but determining who is involved is difficult because the recordings have never surfaced. The musical credits listed for these songs are based on a composite of the available information, and some deductions. The recordings had no producer in the technical sense, other than the group and the studio engineer. Williams, who represented The Beatles at the time, paid for the sessions, so he is credited as executive producer. [McCartney covered *Summertime* on his 1988 album *Choba B. CCCP*.]

The Beatles and Storm were linked by more than similar interests and background. Storm's sister Iris had dated Harrison and was the steady girlfriend of McCartney during the early '60s. [Iris later married Shane Fenton (a.k.a. Alvin Stardust).] Ringo's drumming and deadpan humor won him the friendship of The Beatles, who occasionally used him as a substitute when their drummer Pete Best was unavailable. On August 16, 1962 Brian Epstein informed Best that The Beatles were replacing him with Starr. Storm was reportedly no happier about it than Best. Ringo was replaced by Gibson Kemp (see The Escorts, Paul Jones), and later others, including Keef Hartley and Jimmy Tushingham.

The Beatles rose to stardom shortly after Starr joined them, while Rory Storm & The Hurricanes languished in Liverpool. According to Byrne, by 1964 Epstein was feeling guilty about them losing Ringo, and offered to make the arrangements, pay the costs, and produce a recording for them, which was the *West Side Story* hit *America*. On hand to help out was Ringo. Byrne said, "Ringo played tambourine or maracas — some kind of percussion like that. He probably sang backing vocals, because all the musicians sang in the chorus." Some reference books claim Ringo was clapping in the background. The 1995 CD release of *Rory Storm & The Hurricanes' The Complete Works* (Street Records-RS01) makes the first claim that Epstein also sings backing vocals on *America*, but Byrne disputes this. Ray Coleman's biography of Epstein says *America* was recorded at IBC Studios in London. Bill Harry also lists IBC Studios in his books on The Beatles (Coleman's book probably being his source). Byrne said, "I'm certain *America* was recorded in at Abbey Road studios." This seems more likely as he said it was recorded on September 30, 1964, a day when The Beatles were recording at Abbey Road. He said it was released as a single (Parlophone R-5197) on a Friday, November 13 (the date most sources list). Harry also initially listed this date but in later books lists December 20. The Beatles' *I Feel Fine* single (Parlophone R-5200) was released on November 27. These catalogue numbers seem to indicate that *America* was released on November 13. The song didn't chart and Epstein never produced another recording.

The band disintegrated after the death of Ty Brian in 1967. On September 28, 1972, following the death of his father, Rory and his mother were found dead in their home. Though a double suicide was suspected, there was evidence to suggest that Rory died of an accidental overdose, prompting his mother to take her life after finding him dead. Ringo didn't attend the funeral, reportedly saying, in his typical deadpan humor, that he wasn't present at his birth either.

Iris reportedly found a tape identified as containing rehearsals and live recordings of Rory Storm & The Hurricanes (with Ringo) at the Cavern Club and the Jive Hive in Liverpool in 1962, but Byrne said something else was recorded over the entire contents. Byrne formed Johnny Guitar & The Hurricanes in the 1990s. He died on August 18, 1999. The 2003 UK CD *My Liverpool Home Volume 2-Merseybeat Mania!* (Mastersound MS CD 529) includes *I Can Tell* by Rory Storm & The Hurricanes, claiming it was recorded in 1961, which would include Ringo, but Mark Lewisohn says it was recorded at the Rialto Ballroom in Liverpool in 1963, after Ringo had joined The Beatles.

The Strangers with Mike Shannon

Lennon & McCartney Song Book Volume 2
Connoisseur Collection-VSOP CD 162 (UK/EEC) (05/31/91)
Mike Shannon: Lead Vocals
03/20/64

One And One Is Two (J. Lennon-**P. McCartney**) 2:11 (17) (05/08/64)

The Strangers with Mike Shannon were the first group to release the Lennon-McCartney composition *One And One Is Two*, which was one of the few chart failures by that songwriting team. It was written by Paul McCartney, and first attempted by Billy J. Kramer with The Dakotas*, and then The Fourmost* but neither version was released. Mike Shannon and The Strangers seem to be just that! There is virtually no information available on them. They were apparently a Liverpool band, but reportedly broke up over a year before *One And One Is Two* was reported to have been recorded and released. Other reports claim the group was from Birmingham, England. Shannon was apparently from South Africa.

Hamish Stuart

Nashville Diary
Quarter Apple-PCS 7304/5 [unauthorized release] (xx/xx/01)
Hamish Stuart: Vocals; Robbie McIntosh: Guitar
Crowne Plaza Hotel Meadowlands, Secaucus, NJ 03/17/01

Is It Raining In London? 4:48 (**P. McCartney**-H. Stuart) (2-24)

Hamish Stuart was born on October 8, 1949 in Glasgow, Scotland. He was in the Dream Police before gaining notice as the falsetto singer, bassist, guitarist, composer and producer for the jazz, funk and R&B-oriented Average White Band who formed in the early 1970s. Their 1974 album *AWB*, and the song *Pick Up The Pieces* from it, topped the charts. The group broke up in the early 1980s. Stuart later worked with David Sanborn, Aretha Franklin* and others, and has written songs covered by Diana Ross, George Benson*, Chaka Khan (co-composing her 1981 hit *What Cha' Gonna Do For Me?*) and Atlantic Starr (composing her 1986 hit *If Your Heart Isn't In It*).

When the Average White Band decided to regroup in 1988, Stuart was unavailable having become part of Paul McCartney's backing band for his albums *Flowers In The Dirt* in 1989 and *Off The Ground* in 1993. He helped McCartney write the songs *The First Stone*, *Party Party*, *Keep Coming Back To Love*, *Inner City Madness* and *Together*. Stuart says, "Paul has so much studio stuff – including lovely little bits and pieces of inspiration we did — that we would go through looking for ideas, which probably won't see the light of day." Stuart was also a member of McCartney's touring band during this period, which resulted in the early 1990's albums *Tripping The Live Fantastic*, *Unplugged (The Official Bootleg)* and *Paul Is Live*. Stuart admits, "Playing with Paul made me realize how much I missed playing guitar and playing live because I hadn't done much of either since the Average White Band had broken up. The Liverpool and Rio [184,000 estimated attendance] shows were real highlights, but I enjoyed the [MTV] *Unplugged* experience most because it was so natural — like playing off in the corner. It was very naked and there was no room for mistakes. It was lovely playing some of those songs and doing a duet with Paul on *And I Love Her*."

In late fall 1992 Stuart and McCartney wrote, and began recording the song *Is It Raining In London?* Stuart says, "I had the first verse and most of the chords when I went to Paul's place in St. John's Wood, where we finished it off in a couple of hours. It was intended to be on the *Off The Ground* album, which we approached more as a band album. I was singing the lead vocals and Paul did a beautiful middle harmony section. We only took one stab at the rhythm track, so we didn't really get it right. It wasn't strong enough and I couldn't think of a solution. Angelo Badalamenti did a phenomenal string arrangement for it, which we overdubbed onto it at Abbey Road Studios [included on the McCartney video special *Movin' On*]. The basic track needed re-cutting, but it never happened and it got lost in the shuffle, which is a shame. I always thought it would be nice to revisit it and recreate a different track underneath it. I produced the Russian band Time Machine in 2007, and we talked about doing the song, and I spoke to Paul about it, but in the end they wanted to do their own material. It languishes in nowhere land at the moment but I'm working on a way to get it finished. Robbie McIntosh and I played it just one time at a festival for fans of The Beatles." That rendition, at the Crowne Plaza Hotel in Secaucus, New Jersey on March 17, 2001, is available on the unauthorized release *Nashville Diary*.

Stuart says, "I met Ringo at the airport in Los Angeles the first time I came over with Paul. When I told him I was there to work with Paul he said, 'I hope he's flying you first class!' Ringo's humor is great. Mark Hudson* was supposed to be a part of Ringo Starr's All-Starr Band in 2006 but that fell through, so about six weeks before the tour I was asked if I would be interested in joining. I immediately agreed and started learning the songs. They pretty much had everything down, so we didn't do any of my songs the first time around, which was fine with me because I also love being the sideman, not having to play guitar and sing all night, and just be in the rhythm section playing with the drummer. So, it was a big kick for me playing with Ringo and Sheila E — and Gregg Bissonette in 2008. Rehearsals are about 10 days solid. Each band has a slightly different character because of the different players but Ringo is the unifying force. I really enjoyed playing Rod Argent's* songs. It's nice playing songs you're familiar with. I came to the 2008 tour with much more familiarity, and mostly played the same songs but it's nice to be able to play different musician's songs each time around. On the 2008 tour I performed *Pick Up The Pieces* and *Work To Do*, and Ringo tore into them playing great! Ringo's a really nice human being — I like him immensely." Hamish Stuart continues to work with other artists, produce, write, perform and record with the Hamish Stuart Band, and Jim Jam who have released several albums.

Super Furry Animals

Rings Around The World
XL-EXL026 (03/19/02) (07/23/01)
Producer: Chris Shaw & Super Furry Animals
Paul McCartney: Carrot & Celery Sounds; Gruff Rhys: Lead Vocals & Guitar; Huw Bunford: Guitar & Vocals; Guto Pryce: Bass; Cian Ciaran: Keyboards & Electronics; Dafydd Ieuan: Drums; Tony Robinson: Trombone, Trumpet & Flugelhorn; Matt Sibley: Saxophone; Gary Alesbrook: Trumpet
Monnow Valley Studios, Monmouth, Wales, UK & Bearsville Studios, Bearsville, NY 04-10/xx/00

Receptacle For The Respectable (G. Rhys-H. Bunford-G. Pryce-C. Ciaran-D. Ieuan) 4:32 (1-5)

Super Furry Animals are Welsh natives Gruffydd "Gruff" Rhys, born on July 18, 1970 in Haverfordwest; Huw Bunford, born on September 15, 1967 in Cardiff; Guto Pryce, born on September 4, 1972 in Cardiff; Cian Ciaran, born on June 16, 1976 in Bangor and Dafydd Ieuan, born on March 1, 1969 in Bangor. They formed in 1993 and had a couple of regional singles sung in Cymraeg (Welsh). By the mid-1990s, with growing popularity, they began singing most of their songs in English. With their unique fusion of techno, punk, pop and psychedelic sounds, they were able to land a record contract. Between 1996 and 2004 they had UK Top 20 hits with *Something 4 The Weekend, If You Don't Want Me To Destroy You, The Man Don't Give A Fuck, Northern Lites, Do Or Die, Juxtapozed With U* and *Golden Retriever.* Seven of their albums have reached the UK Top 20.

The band bumped into Paul McCartney at the *NME* Awards in London in 2000 and by evening's end McCartney offered them some previously unreleased recordings by The Beatles to remix. Rhys recalls in an article by MTV News and VH1 in 2001, "Within two weeks four boxes of original Beatles' master tapes arrived in our office in Cardiff. We sampled chunks of John and Paul chatting, and we made loops of George's guitar and Ringo's drums. That was extremely surreal. We mixed it for an album [Paul was producing] called *Liverpool Sound Collage* and figured he owed us one [for the album *Rings Around The World*]. He was always going to fashion shows in Paris and was always canceling on us. Also, there was a lot of security involved. It was like trying to make a record with the Pope. We really didn't know what we wanted him to do [on the song *Receptacle For The Respectable*], so it came down to getting him to munch carrots and celery [as McCartney had reportedly done on The Beach Boys'* song *Vegetables*]. He claims that was his favorite moment of last year – chewing the celery and carrots to the beat. We just didn't want him to strain his voice, and we didn't want him to play bass because he's done that so many times in his life. He's probably sick of singing cameo roles." The Super Furry Animals continue to write and record. For more information go to www.superfurry.com

Bernie Taupin

[None]
Rocket [unreleased]
Producer: Robert Appere
Ringo Starr: Vocals; Bernie Taupin: Vocals
Probably Eastern Studios, Toronto, Ontario Canada 11/1-14/76

Cryin' Time (B. Owens)

Bernard "Bernie" Taupin was born on May 22, 1950 near Sleaford, England. In 1967 Elton John* failed an audition for Ray Williams of Liberty Records, but Williams gave Elton lyrics sent to him by Taupin. John corresponded with Taupin, setting in motion what has become one of the most successful songwriting teams in history.

Taupin released a book in 1976 of his lyrics titled *The One Who Writes The Words For Elton John*, edited by Alan Aldridge, which includes illustrations by John Lennon and Ringo Starr. [Aldridge also edited and Illustrated the books *The Beatles Illustrated Lyrics* and *The Beatles Illustrated Lyrics 2.*] In late 1976 Taupin began work on a solo album planned for release on Elton's Rocket Record label. Around the same time, John started making some career changes and began working with lyricist Gary Osborne. Taupin's untitled solo album was to include a duet vocal with Ringo Starr of the Buck Owens' song *Cryin' Time* but it was never released.

By 1980 John and Taupin had reunited in a partnership that has lasted ever since. Taupin continues to involve himself with side projects that have included owning a restaurant, recording several solo albums, forming the band Farm Dogs, producing, painting, and writing lyrics for other artists such as Courtney Love, Brian Wilson* Alice Cooper, Starship (*We Built This City*) and Heart (*These Dreams*). For more information go to www.berniejtaupin.com

John Tavener

The Whale
Apple-CD SAPCOR 15 (UK) (10/19/92) (09/25/70)
Producer: Michael Bremner
Ringo Starr: Dialogue & Percussion; Anna Reynolds: Vocals; Raimund Herincx: Vocals; Alvar Lidell: Vocals; John Tavener: Keyboards; The London Sinfonietta: Orchestra; The London Sinfonietta Chorus: Chorus; David Atherton: Conductor
Church Of St. John The Evangelist, Islington, London, UK 07/22-24/70

The Whale (Part One) (J. Tavener) 18:23 (1)

The Whale (Part Two) (J. Tavener) 13:15 (2)

John Tavener was born on January 28, 1944 in London, England. Tavener attended the Royal Academy of Music. He is a classical composer, conductor and keyboardist. Over the years his compositions have been widely recorded and favorably received, including *The Akathist Of Thanksgiving*, *The Lamb*, *Innocence* and *Prayer To The Holy Trinity*. Tavener was knighted in 2000.

In 1966 Tavener wrote *The Whale*, which was first performed on January 24, 1968 and recorded for broadcast by the BBC on March 8, 1968. In 1969 Tavener met John Lennon and Yoko Ono*. Lennon, exposed to avant-garde and experimental music by Yoko, was looking to broaden Apple's repertoire and offered Tavener a contract. Ringo Starr ended up in charge of Tavener, and was present during the recording of Tavener's first Apple album *The Whale*, lending his voice, along with noises and percussion. 1971's *Celtic Requiem* was Tavener's second and last album for Apple. According to Tavener, Ringo was present but didn't contribute to the recording. Tavener was surprised to learn that some of his music was used for the film *Son Of Dracula* starring Harry Nilsson* and Ringo Starr. *The Whale* was rereleased on Ring O'Records in 1978.

At Tavener's request, on May 4, 2000 Paul McCartney read the poem *In The Month Of Athyr* by Constantine Cavafy, set to music by Tavener, performed by the Tallis Scholars choir directed by Peter Phillips at the Church of St. Ignatius Loyola in New York. The performance was broadcast live on WNYC's *New Sounds Live* radio program.

James Taylor

James Taylor
Apple-CDP 7975772 (Germany) (11/19/91) (12/06/68)
Producer: Peter Asher
Paul McCartney: Bass; **George Harrison (supposed) B. Vocals**; James Taylor: Lead Vocals & Guitar; Mick Wayne: Guitar; Peter Asher: Tambourine & B. Vocals; Freddie Redd: Organ; Joel "Bishop" O'Brien: Drums; Richard Hewson: String Arrangement & Conductor
Trident Studios, London, UK 07-10/xx/68

Carolina In My Mind (J. Taylor) 3:37 (7)

Walking Man
Warner Bros.-2794-2 (xx/xx/88) (06/28/74)
Producer: David Spinozza
Hit Factory, New York, NY 01-04/xx/74

Let It Fall Down (J. Taylor) 3:30 (3)
Paul McCartney: B. Vocals; James Taylor: Lead Vocals & Acoustic Guitar; Rick Marotta: Drums; Andy Muson: Bass; Hugh McCracken: Electric Guitar; Ralph MacDonald: Percussion; Kenny Ascher: Electric Piano; Linda McCartney: B. Vocals; Carly Simon: B. Vocals

Rock 'N' Roll Is Music Now (J. Taylor) 3:25 (2)
Paul McCartney: B. Vocals; James Taylor: Lead Vocals & Acoustic Guitar; Rick Marotta: Drums & B. Vocals; Andy Muson: Bass; Hugh McCracken: Electric Guitar; David Spinozza: Electric Piano; Kenny Ascher: Piano; Linda McCartney: B. Vocals; Carly Simon: B. Vocals; Howard Johnson: Tuba; Kenny Berger: Baritone Saxophone; Barry Rogers: Trombone; Michael Brecker: Tenor Saxophone; George Young: Alto Saxophone; Alan Rubin: Trumpet; Randy Brecker: Trumpet

James Taylor was born on March 12, 1948 in Boston, Massachusetts but spent his formative years on the nearby island of Martha's Vineyard, and near the University of North Carolina where his father taught. His mother encouraged him, and siblings Alex, Livingston and Kate to pursue music. All would eventually find some musical success, especially James. Taylor met guitarist Danny Kortchmar (see Attitudes) and they formed a long musical association. In 1964 James joined Alex's band, and later moved to New York to join Kortchmar's band The Flying Machine.

Taylor moved to the UK in 1968. Kortchmar urged James to send his friend Peter Asher (see Peter & Gordon), Apple's A&R Manager, a tape of his music. Asher persuaded Paul McCartney to sign Taylor to Apple for whom Asher produced the album *James Taylor*. It includes *Carolina In My Mind* featuring McCartney on bass. Taylor has stated that George Harrison does backing vocals on the song. Asher, who sings backing vocals on it says, "I've read that too, but I'm certain it isn't true!" Richard Hewson, the string arranger and conductor for the song, also doesn't recall Harrison being present. A line in the song about "a holy host of others" apparently refers to The Beatles. The album's song *Something In The Way She Moves* was part of the lyrics and inspiration for Harrison's song *Something*.

Shortly after the album's release, Taylor returned to the US along with Asher who left Apple to become his full-time manager and producer. Taylor signed with Warner Bros., who released the album *Sweet Baby James* in 1970 that included the song *Fire And Rain*, which launched Taylor to stardom. [An early version of the song was recorded for Taylor's Apple album but he and Asher rejected it.] Taylor met Carly Simon* in 1971 and they married the following year. They contributed to each other's recordings. [They were divorced in 1983.]

Paul and Linda McCartney* sang backing vocals on two songs from Taylor's 1974 album *Walking Man*. McCartney inducted Taylor into the Rock and Roll Hall of Fame in 2000, and on June 15 that year joined Taylor, Ben E. King* and others singing *Stand By Me* and *Kansas City* at Taylor's induction ceremonies for the Songwriters Hall of Fame at the Sheraton New York Hotel & Towers. Taylor sang with McCartney at the *Concert For New York City* on October 20, 2001 at Madison Square Garden. On September 23, 2003 Taylor joined McCartney on his Beatles' song *Two Of Us* at the Adopt-A-Minefield gala at the Beverly Hills Hilton in Los Angeles. Taylor proved to be Apple's most successful discovery, and retains a solid following, especially on the concert circuit performing such hits as *Don't Let Me Be Lonely Tonight*, *You've Got A Friend*, *Country Road*, *How Sweet It Is (To Be Loved By You)*, *Shower The People*, *Her Town Too*, *Night Owl* and *Fire And Rain*. For more information go to www.jamestaylor.com

10cc (& Eric Stewart*)

Do Not Bend [Eric Stewart*]
Strawberry Soundtracks-STRSCD 20031/2 (UK) (08/12/03) **Paul McCartney: Liner Notes**
Producer: Eric Stewart
Paul McCartney: Electric Piano, Bass & String Pad†; Eric Stewart: Lead Vocals & Electric Guitar
Eric Stewart's home studios in Wittersham† & Bethersden, UK fall/xx/87† & 03/xx/89

Code Of Silence (Original Demo Version) (E. Stewart-**[P. McCartney]**) 6:30 (2-4)

Meanwhile
Polydor-513279-2 (UK) (05/11/92)
Producer: Gary Katz & 10cc
Eric Stewart: Lead Vocals & Keyboards; Graham Gouldman: Electric & Acoustic Guitars; Jeff Porcaro: Drums & Percussion; Freddie Washington: Bass; Michael Landau: Lead Guitar; David Paich: String Synthesizer
River Sound, New York, & Bearsville Sound, Bearsville, NY & Village Recorders, Los Angeles, CA 02-03/xx/91

Don't Break The Promises (E. Stewart-**P. McCartney**-G. Gouldman) 6:22 (10)

Mirror Mirror
AVEX/ZYX-ZYX 20350-2 (Germany) (06/xx/95)
Producer: Eric Stewart & Adrian Lee

Code Of Silence (E. Stewart-**[P. McCartney]**) 5:41 (2) (03/28/95)
Paul McCartney: String Pad, Bass, Electric Piano, Frog Crickets & Percussion†; Eric Stewart: Lead Vocals, Lead Guitar & Percussion; Adrian Lee: Programming
Eric Stewart's home studios in Wittersham† & Bethersden UK & Templar Studios, Lot et Garonne, France fall/xx/87†, 03/xx/89 & xx/xx/94

Yvonne's The One (**P. McCartney**-E. Stewart) 4:26 (1)
Eric Stewart: Lead Vocals, Guitars, Keyboards & Percussion; Adrian Lee: Bass, Programming & Arrangements
Templar Studios, France xx/xx/93

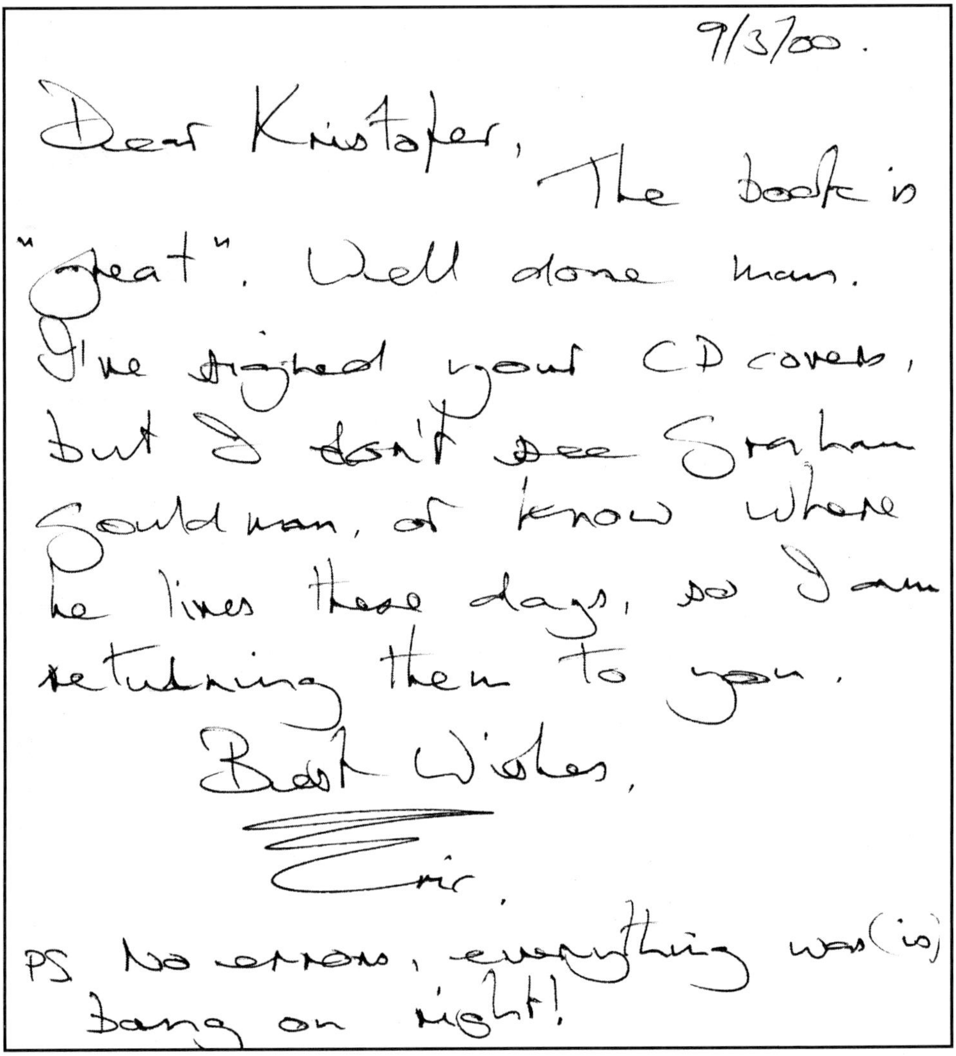

9/3/00.

Dear Kristofer,
The book is "great". Well done man.
I've signed your CD covers, but I don't see Graham Gouldman, or know where he lives these days, so I am returning them to you.

Best Wishes,

Eric.

PS No errors, everything was (is) bang on right!

Letter from Eric Stewart to Kristofer Engelhardt.

10cc initially consisted of Manchester, England area natives Kevin Godley, born on October 7, 1945; Lawrence "Lol" Creme (see Godley & Creme); Graham Gouldman, born on May 10, 1946; and Eric Stewart, born on January 20, 1945. All but Stewart were schoolmates. Eric was a member of Wayne Fontana & The Mindbenders when they performed their number one hit *The Game Of Love* at *NME* magazine's Poll-Winners' Award at Empire Pool, Wembley (London) on April 11, 1965. It was there that he met The Beatles. Fontana left the group before The Mindbenders' 1966 Top Five hit *Groovy Kind Of Love*, which Eric sang. Though not a member, Graham sat in with The Mindbenders briefly before their breakup in 1968. Graham had found success as a songwriter of such Top 10 hits as *For Your Love* and *Heart Full Of Soul* (The Yardbirds), *Look Through Any Window* and *Bus Stop* (The Hollies), and *No Milk Today* (Herman's Hermits). Eric, Kevin and Lol formed the band Hotlegs, who had a hit with *Neanderthal Man* in 1970. Hotlegs teamed up with Gouldman and renamed themselves 10cc (1cc more than the amount in a typical male ejaculation) indicating they were above average. 10cc's first hit was *Donna*, a UK Top Five in 1972, which some compare to The Beatles' song *Oh! Darling*. [Apple had considered signing them but they were apparently turned down by Ringo.] Their critically acclaimed mid-1970's albums and Top

Five hits *I'm Not In Love* and *The Things We Do For Love*, earned them a cult following. Godley and Creme left 10cc in 1976 to concentrate on inventing new musical devices, including the "Gizmo," and later became pioneers in music video production.

The "Gizmo" or "Gysmorchestra" as it was apparently called in 1974, was used on the Mike **McGear** album recorded at 10cc's Strawberry Studios, so named because of Eric's love of The Beatles' song *Strawberry Fields Forever*. Helping out were members of 10cc, who were there recording their album *Sheet Music*. Eric and Graham recall having the studio during the day and Paul having it at night, and sharing equipment, but say that Paul didn't contribute to any of their recordings then.

Eric began working with McCartney in early 1981 for what became Paul's 1982 album *Tug Of War*. By 1983 10cc had disintegrated. Eric essentially became a member of McCartney's band through 1986 working on the albums *Pipes Of Peace*, *Give My Regards To Broad Street* (and appearing in the film), and *Press To Play* for which he wrote many songs and was given a "special contribution" credit for helping in the production.

In 1991Eric and Graham reunited, and recorded the 10cc album *Meanwhile*, which includes guest appearances by Godley and Creme, and gives special thanks to McCartney. The album contains *Don't Break The Promises* originally written by Paul and Eric during the *Press To Play* period, and later rewritten by Graham. Eric says Paul didn't play guitar on the song as reported. [Paul featured a portion of his and Eric's reggae-styled demo of it, along with 10cc's version, on his 1995 radio series *Oobu Joobu*. Paul released the full version of the demo titled *Don't Break The Promise* in 1997.]

10cc toured (performing some Beatles' songs) to support their 1995 album *Mirror Mirror*. The album includes *Code Of Silence* to which McCartney contributed. Eric says, "In the fall of 1987 I was living in Wittersham, not far from Paul's residence. After lunch, and a couple of bottles of good wine with Paul, he felt like doing some recording in my home studio and we ended up with the backing track of *Code Of Silence*, which is pure McCartney. He played some cricket sounds and things like that; it was all Midi instruments. I was really excited about the song and wrote lyrics for it. In March of '89 I was living in Bethersden, and Paul dropped in and had a try at singing my lyrics and melody, but he felt it wasn't working for him, and I agreed. No version of this attempt exists. With Paul's blessing, I continued developing the song at my next studios in Dorset and France in '91 and '92. We never used the song on anything at the time, so I used the backing for the *Mirror Mirror* album and recorded new vocals at my home studio in France. I told Paul I was going to release *Code Of Silence*, and asked him if he wanted a credit with me for writing most of the backing track, but he said, 'No, I think the song is yours.' Paul could have done justice to *Code Of Silence*. [Initial copies of Stewart's third solo album, *Do Not Bend* released in 2003, include a bonus disc with the original demo version of *Code Of Silence*.] Many foreign versions of *Mirror Mirror* also include *Yvonne's The One*, also written by Paul and Eric during the *Press To Play* period. Eric says Paul didn't play guitar (as credited) on 10cc's recording of *Yvonne's The One*. Paul and Eric's recording of it is available on unauthorized releases. Eric says he hasn't worked with Paul in a number of years but that they still keep in touch. He says, "I had a terrific jam session with George Harrison, which unfortunately wasn't recorded, at the home of Maclaren Formula 1 auto designer Gordon Murray, not too long before George passed away, which made me very sad. George was a lovely man." For more information go to www.ericstewart.uk.com, www.gg06.co.uk, www.10ccworld.com

Guthrie Thomas

Hobo Eagle Thief
Sawdust/Line-SDCD 9.00915 (Germany) (xx/xx/90) (xx/xx/85)
Producer: Guthrie Thomas & Larry Hirsch
Guthrie Thomas: Lead Vocals & Acoustic Guitars; Lee Montgomery: B. Vocals; Sonny Garrish: Pedal Steel Guitar; Jesse Ed Davis: Guitar [unless noted otherwise]
Probably Cherokee or possibly Paramount Studios, Los Angeles, CA probably xx/xx/77

Captain Jack (G. Thomas) 4:19 (2)
Additionally: **Ringo Starr: Drums**; Marc Edelsen: Guitar & B. Vocals; Mark Dawson: Harmonica & B. Vocals; Byron Berline: Mandolin; Jim Keltner (probable) Drums; Lyle Ritz or Bob Glob: Bass; David Foster: Organ; Larry Hirsch: Percussion, or Celeste or Glockenspiel; Note: Jesse Ed Davis doesn't perform on this recording

Carolyn And Benjamin (G. Thomas-M. Edelsen) 3:56 (1)
Additionally: **Ringo Starr: (probable) Drums;**

Marc Edelsen: Vocals; Byron Berline: Mandolin; Jim Keltner (probable) Drums; Lyle Ritz or Bob Glob: Bass; Larry Hirsch: Synthesizer

If You Want Me To (G. Thomas) 4:05 (8)
Additionally: **Ringo Starr: (possible) Drums**; Marc Edelsen: Rhythm Guitar & B. Vocals; Mark Dawson: Harmonica; Jim Keltner: Drums; Lyle Ritz: Bass; Bob Glob: Bass; Skip Conover: Dobro Guitar; Note: Lee Montgomery doesn't perform on this recording

Ship Of Fools (G. Thomas) 3:59 (4)
Additionally: **Ringo Starr: Drums**; Marc Edelsen: Rhythm Guitar & B. Vocals; Mark Dawson: Harmonica & B. Vocals; John Hartford: Fiddle; Byron Berline: Fiddle; Jim Keltner: Drums; Lyle Ritz: Bass; Bob Glob: Bass; David Paich: Piano; Nicolette Larson: B. Vocals

Wake Up (G. Thomas-M. Edelsen) 4:11 (3)
Additionally: **Ringo Starr: Drums**; Marc Edelsen: (probable) B. Vocals; Mark Dawson: (probable) B. Vocals; Jim Keltner: (probable) Drums; Lyle Ritz or Bob Glob: Bass; David Paich &/or David Foster: Keyboards; Tom Cherry: Tenor Saxophone; Note: Sonny Garrish doesn't perform on this recording

Lies And Alibis
Capitol-ST-11519 (album 12") (05/03/76)
Producer: Guthrie Thomas & John Carter
Guthrie Thomas: Lead Vocals & Acoustic Guitar; Jim Keltner: Drums; David Paich: Keyboards; Lyle Ritz: Bass; David Foster: Keyboards; Lee Montgomery: B. Vocals; Roger Johnson: Electric Guitar; John Hartford: Fiddle [unless noted otherwise]
Capitol Records Studios, Los Angeles, CA 02/xx/76

Band Of Steel (R. Starkey) 5:20 (1/3)
Additionally: **Ringo Starr: Drums & B. Vocals**; Steve Cropper: B. Vocals; Tom Brumley: Pedal Steel; Note: Dave Foster doesn't perform on this recording

Fifty-Five (G. Thomas-M. Edelsen) 3:55 (1/1)
Additionally: **Ringo Starr: Drums**; Mark Dawson: Harmonica & B. Vocals; Marc Edelsen: Acoustic Guitar; Renee Armand: B. Vocals; Brooks Cropper: B. Vocals

For Awhile (G. Thomas) 4:42 (1/4)
Additionally: **Ringo Starr: (probable) Drums**; Mark Dawson: Harmonica; Marc Edelsen: Acoustic Guitar; Renee Armand: B. Vocals; Brooks Cropper: B. Vocals; Note: John Hartford doesn't perform on this recording

Good Days Are Rollin' In (G. Thomas) 3:24 (2/2)
Additionally: **Ringo Starr: Drums**; Marc Edelsen: Acoustic Rhythm Guitar; Mark Dawson: B. Vocals; Brooks Cropper: B. Vocals; Renee Armand: B. Vocals; Note: Lee Montgomery & John Hartford don't perform on this recording

Ramblin' Cocaine Blues (L. Jordan-G. Thomas) 4:42 (2/5)
Additionally: **Ringo Starr: Drums & B. Vocals**; Mark Dawson: B. Vocals; Nicolette Larson: B. Vocals; Bill Herring: B. Vocals; David Jackson: B. Vocals; Denny Brooks: B. Vocals; Ginny Vick: B. Vocals

Yesterdays & Tomorrows (G. Thomas) 3:38 (2/2)
Additionally: **Ringo Starr: Drums**; Mark Dawson: Harmonica; Ginny Vick: Tambourine; Tom Brumley: Pedal Steel Guitar; Note: David Paich, Lee Montgomery & Roger Johnson don't perform on this recording

Folk and country singer Guthrie Thomas was born on January 6, 1952 in Wichita Falls, Texas but was raised in Oklahoma. Thomas began making guitars at the age of 15. His heroes were Woody Guthrie and Dylan Thomas, so he adopted their names. Later, Thomas was the musical director for the film *Bound For Glory*, about the life of Woody Guthrie, and played Guthrie's brother in the film.

Thomas met Ringo Starr in Los Angeles in 1975 during the taping of his friend Hoyt Axton's TV special. Guthrie handed Ringo a copy of his album *Sittin' Crooked* following the taping. Subsequently, Arlo Guthrie (Woody's son) and Axton put in a good word to Ringo about Thomas. Within weeks Ringo contacted Capitol and arranged for Thomas to be signed to the label. The two became good friends and Thomas became a regular guest at Ringo's home in Los Angeles. Thomas says his album *Guthrie Thomas I* wouldn't have been possible without Ringo, who was given special thanks in the credits, though he didn't perform on it.

Ringo was also given thanks on Thomas' second Capitol album *Lies And Alibis* and is credited contributing to *Band of Steel*, *Good Days Are Rollin' In* and *Ramblin' Cocaine Blues*. Though not credited, Thomas says Ringo also plays drums on *Yesterdays & Tomorrows* and probably on *For Awhile*, and sings backing vocals on *Ramblin' Cocaine Blues*. *Band Of Steel*, written by Ringo, was originally intended for Starr's album *Beaucoups Of Blues*. [A limited CD of the album was issued in Japan on Toshiba-EMI in 1998.]

Ringo also contributed to Thomas' album *Hobo Eagle Thief* (a.k.a. *Like No Other* and *Once In Awhile* in some countries). Though specific musical credits for each song aren't given, Guthrie seems quite certain Ringo drums on *Captain Jack*, *Ship Of Fools*, *Wake Up*, and probably *Carolyn And Benjamin* and *If You Want Me To*. Ringo is also thanked on Thomas' albums *Kidnapped* and *This One's For Sarah,* but Thomas says he didn't play on these albums, and is thanked for his support and friendship over the years. Thomas says, "One of the nicest people I ever met in the business, and certainly the most generous, was Richard Starkey." Thomas self-depreciatingly refers to himself as a dumb Okie but he's also a practicing pharmacologist. He continues to write, record and tour. For more information go to www.guthriethomas.com

Thornton, Fradkin & Unger And The Big Band

Godz Bless California
ESP-DISK/ZYX-Music-ESP 3019-2 (Germany) (probably xx/xx/93) (06/17/74)
Producer: Randy Edelman & Leslie Fradkin
Paul McCartney: Bass & B. Vocals†; Leslie Fradkin: Lead Vocals, Mellotron & Guitars; Randy Edelman: Piano & B. Vocals; Denny Seiwell: Drums; Don Thomas: Lead Guitar; Linda McCartney: B. Vocals; Dorthea Joyce: B. Vocals; Gail Kantor: B. Vocals; Dick Williams: B. Vocals; Corky Hale: Upright Harp; Michael Leonard & Les Fradkin: Orchestrations
Sound Exchange Studios, A&R Studios†, Mercury Studios & A-1 Sound Studios New York, NY probably 12/xx/70 & 01/xx/71† & xx/xx/72-73

God Bless California (L. Fradkin) 3:36 (1)

Godzology
Renaissance-RMED00132 (07/11/00)
Producer: Randy Edelman & Leslie Fradkin
Paul McCartney: Bass & B. Vocals†; Leslie Fradkin: Lead Vocals, Mellotron & Guitars; Randy Edelman: Piano & B. Vocals; Denny Seiwell: Drums; Don Thomas: Lead Guitar; Linda McCartney: B. Vocals; Dorthea Joyce: B. Vocals; Gail Kantor: B. Vocals; Dick Williams: B. Vocals; Corky Hale: Upright Harp; Michael Leonard & Les Fradkin: Orchestrations
Sound Exchange Studios, A&R Studios†, Mercury Studios & A-1 Sound Studios New York, NY probably 12/xx/70 & 01/xx/71† & xx/xx/72-73

Black Gypsy (L. Fradkin) 2:49 (10)

God Bless California (Version #5/Alternate Take) (L. Fradkin) 3:36 (9)
Additionally: Les Fradkin: 12-String Effects
Additionally: Parker, CO xx/xx/00

Leslie Fradkin was born on January 15, 1951 in New York, New York. His mother, a former concert pianist, taught him to play piano as a youngster. Inspired by The Beatles and others, Les taught himself to play guitar, began writing songs and took an interest in record production. He has recorded for Laurie Records and other labels since the early 1970s. He composed the French hit *La Chanson Des Souvenirs* (a.k.a. *Song Of A Thousand Voices*) by Mirielle Mathieu. Fradkin was a member of the 1970's group Godz and David Peel's* Apple Band. He played George Harrison in the original cast of the Broadway stage musical *Beatlemania* in the late 1970s.

In early 1971 Paul McCartney was in New York recording his album *Ram*. He held auditions for some of the city's top studio musicians, among them drummer Denny Seiwell. According to Fradkin, Seiwell was also playing then on sessions he was cutting for MGM Records. Fradkin says, "I needed some overdubs done, so I went to A&R Studios. McCartney was there recording his album *Ram*, which is when I asked Paul and Linda to dub their bits on my recordings of *God Bless California* and *Black Gypsy*. Paul was very professional. He has great confidence in the studio. He had many ideas (and he's come up with many good ones) and he wanted me to listen to them. I didn't want to get in the way of that because I wanted to see what he'd come up with. In those days record companies were highly territorial about the artists signed to them. When it came time to release those recordings I knew there was no way that Paul's record label would allow me to use the name McCartney on another label's release, so I didn't list his last name, but everybody knew who the Paul and Linda were. I also wanted to create a bit of mystery, and let the rumors spread without confirming or denying their involvement." *God Bless California* was first released in 1974 on the obscure album *Pass On This Side* (ESP-DISK-ESP 63019) by Thornton, Fradkin & Unger And The Big Band. *Black Gypsy* was first released on the Thornton & Fradkin album *Godzology* in 2000, which also includes *God Bless California* with additional overdubs recorded in 2000. Leslie Fradkin has been a proponent and player of synthesized guitars since the early 1980s. For more information go to www.lesfradkin.com

Tibetan Chants

[None]
Apple [unreleased]
Producer: John Lennon
Record Plant Studios, New York, NY 12/16/71

Tantric Lamas Part I (probably: Tibetan Chants)
Tibetan Chants: Vocals

Tantric Lamas Part II (probably: Tibetan Chants)
Tibetan Chants: Vocals

Tibetan Chants is listed as the artist on a box of unreleased recordings found in the tape library from the old Record Plant Studios in New York with John Lennon's name listed on it as producer. The client is listed as Apple. Dennis Ferrante, the recording engineer for these sessions, thinks they are an outgrowth of sessions for David Peel's* album *The Pope Smokes Dope* produced by John and Yoko Ono*. He says Tibetan Chants consisted of a group of about 25 people that Peel brought into the studio off the streets of New York to sing chants. Peel disputes all of this and knows nothing of Tibetan Chants. These recordings are marked as outtakes and may be nothing more than incidental sounds for possible use on Peel's album or another of the Lennons' projects for Apple. Other tapes marked "David Peel Talk Tracks" and "David Peel Laugh Tracks" were also discovered in the same tape library. Lenny Mars, who plays on much of Peel's album, remembers a recording engineer spending a day wandering around the streets of New York trying to get traffic sounds for use on Peel's album. According to May Pang the Lennons put their names to many things during this period that they didn't have hands-on involvement in producing (see Indian Mosk).

Timon (a.k.a. Tymon Dogg)

Something New Every Day
Apple (acetate) (UK) [unreleased]
Producer: Peter Asher
Paul McCartney: Piano; Timon: Lead Vocals & Acoustic Guitar; James Taylor: Electric Guitar; Joel "Bishop" O'Brien: Drums; Louis Cennamo: Bass
Trident Studios, London, UK probably 05 or 06 & 08/xx/68

Something New Every Day (T. Dogg)

Timon was born Stephen Murray on May 26, 1950 in Formby (Liverpool), England. He plays numerous instruments (primarily violin), writes songs and is a poet. By the age of 14 he was playing clubs such as the Cavern in Liverpool. He began billing himself as Timon. His first single, *The Bitter Thoughts Of Little Jane* released in early 1968, features John Paul Jones and Jimmy Page of Led Zeppelin fame.

Paul McCartney liked the song and some months later Timon was auditioning for Apple's A&R Manager Peter Asher (see Peter & Gordon). Paul wanted to produce a new recording of the song for Apple but Timon, more interested in recording newer material, turned down [illegible]. He suspects Paul's recent breakup with Asher's sister Jane may have sparked his interest in the song. Timon recalls, "I went to Trident Studios in the summer of 1968 hearing that Apple wanted to sign artists and make music that the big records companies wouldn't make. Paul was there and played me *Hey Jude*, which The Beatles had recently recorded. I recorded three songs produced by Asher including *Something New Every Day*, on which Paul plays piano, and James Taylor* plays John Lennon's electric guitar (the one he later used on the Apple rooftop performance) along with his backing band. Mike Vickers did some orchestral arrangements that were later added to the song, but it tended to obscure Taylor and McCartney's really nice playing — I still have the acetate. Apple was signing songwriters and giving their songs to other Apple artists. They offered me *Golly Miss Pringle*, a very commercial sort of children's song, though Paul didn't write it as was reported. I was under Paul's wing and he wanted to make very commercial, pop records. They offered me a publishing contract but I never signed it. I was a serious songwriter. I wanted to make a proper album, but they only wanted me to make a single, and be a commercial pop star, which isn't what I wanted to do or be, so I went elsewhere."

Timon signed with Threshold Records in 1969

and soon changed his professional name to Tymon Dogg. He began working with John Mellor (a.k.a. Joe Strummer), leading to his work with The Clash, Ian Hunter* and others. In 2000 he joined The Mescaleros, Strummer's band until his death in 2002. Tymon Dogg continues to compose, record and make public appearances. For more information go to www.tymondogg.net

TOTO And Friends

The Jeff Porcaro Tribute Concert
Flac-12141992 [unauthorized release]
Producer: Dirk Shubert
George Harrison: Guitar; Steve Lukather: Guitar & Vocals; David Paich: Keyboards & Vocals; Mike Porcaro: Bass; Simon Phillips: Drums; John James: Vocals; Paulette Browne: Vocals; Jackie Mahgee: Vocals; Jenny Douglas McRae: Vocals; Donna McDaniels: Vocals; Sheryl Crow: Vocals; Steve Porcaro: Keyboards; Chris Trujillo: Percussion; Lenny Castro: Percussion; Michael McDonald: Keyboards & Vocals; Don Henley: Drums & Vocals; Donald Fagen: Keyboards & Vocals; Denny Dias: Guitar; Eddie Van Halen: Guitar; David Crosby: Guitar & Vocals; Boz Scaggs: Guitar & Vocals; James Newton Howard: Keyboards
Universal Amphitheater, Los Angeles, CA
12/14/92

With A Little Help From My Friends [live] (J. Lennon-P. McCartney) 5:59 (3-12)

The band TOTO included Jeff Porcaro who was born on April 1, 1954 in Hartford, Connecticut. His father Joe, a noted percussionist, was instrumental in helping Jeff become a drummer. By age 17 Jeff was drumming in Sonny & Cher's tour band. In 1977 Jeff, his brother Steve, old high school musician friends David Paich and Steve Lukather, and David Hungate and Bobby Kimball formed TOTO. Their 1978 self-titled, debut album was certified Multi-Platinum and yielded the Top Five hit *Hold The Line*. Their follow-up album in 1979 was certified Gold and included the hit *99*. Their 1982 Multi-Platinum album *TOTO IV* earned six Grammy Awards including Album of the Year, and Record of the Year for the song *Rosanna*. The album also produced the Top 10 hit *I Won't Hold You Back* and their number one hit *Africa*. The band underwent personnel changes over the next few years, including the departure of Kimball, and Hungate who was replaced by Jeff's brother Mike. Their last Top 20 hit was *I'll Be Over You* in 1986. Kimball rejoined the group as lead singer in 1998.

TOTO's members have frequently pursued solo projects and been sought for session work. Guitarist Steve Lukather recalls one very special session. "In 1992 Jeff Porcaro and I got a call to work with Quincy Jones on Michael Jackson's* *Thriller* album. We were told that Paul McCartney and George Martin (and Geoff Emerick) were going to be there. They were my heroes — and Jackson was huge then. We were pretty excited. The Beatles changed my life! When I saw them on *The Ed Sullivan Show* I wanted to be George Harrison. My parents gave me a guitar and a copy of *Meet The Beatles* for my seventh birthday. I practiced playing George's guitar solos over and over, and wore that album out. They reinvented the wheel with every album. Their music has stood the test of time and set a standard that has yet to be topped. Nobody makes music that good today. Some of their albums were recorded in a few days. They didn't have Pro Tools then or punch in every note. I'd like to see bands today do that!

"Paul and Linda McCartney* took a shine to us at that session, which turned out to be for *The Girl Is Mine*. They invited us to London to be a part of their *Give My Regards To Broadstreet* film project. I was told not to play any Beatles' songs in front of Paul, so of course the first thing I did was play *Please Please Me*, but he dug it and started telling me Beatles' stories. Later, I started playing *Strawberry Fields Forever* on their Mellotron and Paul started cracking up because I had played it right. I ended up having to wear one of those ridiculous monkey outfits in the film, but Paul wore one, so if it was good enough for him, it was good enough for me! We spent about two weeks hanging out at the studio playing live during filming. Paul and Linda (who was an absolute sweetheart) were very kind, wonderful and gracious people. They defined cool. They were two of the most famous people in the world, but they didn't have bodyguards or jive-ass, paparazzi bullshit around them — just their kids. They were great parents. They didn't raise preten-

Left to right: Steve Lukather, Elissa Perry (Joe's ex) and Kristofer Engelhardt, The Baked Potato, Los Angeles, CA February 15, 2006. © Kristofer Engelhardt.

tious kids who were in the tabloids and doing fucked up shit."

Jeff Porcaro died suddenly on August 5, 1992. TOTO reluctantly decided to carry on asking Simon Phillips to play drums. On December 14, 1992 *The Tribute To Jeff Porcaro Concert* was held in Los Angeles in memory of the life of the renowned drummer who'd worked with countless artists including Eric Clapton*, Paul Simon*, Bruce Springsteen* and Elton John*. Lukather recounts a very special moment during the tribute concert. "I had run into George Harrison three days before the tribute. I used my working with Paul as an excuse to introduce myself to him. He actually knew who I was! He liked my sense of humor and I didn't lick his ass too hard, so we got on. I really connected with him. He was such a cool cat. I told him about the concert we were doing for our dear departed 'bro' Jeff and invited him to play. I told him about the many musicians that Jeff had worked with who'd be there to play, and that the money was going to charity. Just before the finale of *With A Little Help For My Friends*, which TOTO had recently been doing in tribute to Jeff, I announced, 'I met this guy the other night; he's the reason we all play. Thank you very much — George Harrison!' The crowd lost their minds when he came out. I know Jeff was smiling. I'd only just met him, and he shows up and plays on *With A Little Help From My Friends*. He didn't sing on it but everyone else did.

"George befriended me. When he was in Los Angeles he'd invite me over to his hotel and play me things such as *Free As A Bird* before it was released. I was such a fan. I knew which solos he played on The Beatles' recordings. When he was at my house I asked him to sign something for me. He said, 'This is what the lads and I used to do,' and signed every Beatles' name exactly like their signatures! I drove George to Capitol in my Porsche once and there were these 100 foot cutouts of The Beatles to promote *The Beatles Anthology*. When he saw them he said, 'Dreadful.' He was mortified by his fame and didn't dig it at all. He'd rent cheap cars and wouldn't have bodyguards or anybody — just his son Dhani. He took me to Jeff Lynne's* place once. Bob Dylan* and Jim Keltner [see Attitudes] were also there and we all jammed. I went to a section on George's Beatles' song *I Want To Tell You* on my guitar, which was originally done on piano. George said, 'What is that – how do you play that?' I told him, 'It's your fuckin' song dude.' He was a great friend to me. He'd tell me about meditation saying I needed to relax. I feel honored and blessed, being a kid from the Valley, to hang out with legends like those guys — and McCartney. After George was stabbed we lost touch because he changed all of his numbers. I did get a few messages through Jim Keltner that he'd asked about me. I knew he was ill but I didn't know how ill. I miss him very much." TOTO released a cover of Harrison's Beatles' song *While My Guitar Gently Weeps* in 2002. In 2008 Lukather announced that TOTO, who'd sold over 30 million records in over 30 years, had disbanded. For more information go to www.toto99.com, www.stevelukather.net

T. Rex

Born To Boogie
Sanctuary/Sony BMG-06076-88414-9 (DVD) (06/07/05) (04/29/92)
Producer: Tony Visconti (music) [unless noted otherwise]; Ringo Starr: Production & Director (film)
Apple Studios, London, UK 05/xx/72 [unless noted otherwise]

Children Of The Revolution (M. Bolan) 3:40 (1-5)
Producer: [unknown]
Ringo Starr: Drums; Marc Bolan: Lead Vocals, Electric & Acoustic Guitar; Elton John: Piano; Steve Currie: Bass; Mickey Finn: Percussion; Bill Legend: Drums
[Also available on *Born To Boogie (The Soundtrack Album)*. Sanctuary-86382 (1-6) (06/07/05)]

I Looked To The Left (M. Bolan) 0:18 (1-6) (11/04/91)
Ringo Starr: B. Vocals; Marc Bolan: Lead Vocals & Acoustic Guitar
On location at Tittenhurst Park, Ascot, UK 03-05/xx/72
[Also available on *Born To Boogie (The Soundtrack Album)*. Sanctuary-86382 (1-7) (06/07/05)]

Tutti-Frutti (M. Bolan) 1:20 (1-4)
Producer: [unknown]
Ringo Starr: Drums; Marc Bolan: Lead Vocals & Electric Guitar; Elton John: Piano; Steve Currie: Bass; Mickey Finn: Percussion; Bill Legend: Drums
[Also available on *Born To Boogie (The Soundtrack Album)*. Sanctuary-86382 (1-5) (06/07/05)]

The glitter rock band T. Rex was the brainchild of Marc Bolan, born Mark Feld on September 30, 1947 in London, England. As a youngster he'd found bit acting parts, formed a skiffle band and did some modeling. By the mid-1960 he was writing songs and performing under several stage names before settling on Marc Bolan. He recorded for Decca Records and then EMI but without success. He was a brief member of John's Children before forming the poetic, folk-rock duo Tyrannosaurus Rex with Steve Took in 1968. They were produced by Tony Visconti but found little commercial success. Took was replaced by Michael "Mickey" Finn, born on June 3, 1947 in Thornton Heath, England. Marc shortened their name to T. Rex and added bassist Steve Currie, born on May 19, 1947 in Grimsby, England and drummer Bill Legend, born William Fifield on May 8, 1944 in Barking, England. Between 1970 and 1973 they topped the UK charts with their songs *Hot Love*, *Metal Guru*, *Telegram Sam* and *Get It On* (released in the US as *Bang A Gong* where it was their only Top 10), and had UK Top Five hits with *Ride A White Swan*, *Jeepster*, *Children Of The Revolution*, *Solid Gold Easy Action*, *20th Century Boy* and *The Groover*. The reaction they received from large crowds in the UK was termed "T. Rextasy."

The Beatles had taken notice of Bolan's paintings at their Apple Boutique in 1968. By the early 1970s Ringo Starr and Marc had become party buddies. The lyrics of Ringo's 1972 hit *Back Off Boogaloo* (not about Paul McCartney) were inspired in part by Marc. Ringo was Managing Director of Apple Films then and offered to document the Beatlemania-like "T. Rextasy." Starr produced, directed, helped shoot, appeared in and attended the premiere on December 14, 1972 of the resulting film *Born To Boogie*. It was released on VHS in 1992 by Apple Films and on DVD in 2005 with bonus footage including Ringo. The film includes a cameo by Keith Moon*, Ringo playing the part of a mouse, and jams of *Tutti-Frutti* and *Children Of The Revolution* at Apple Studio with Ringo on drums and Elton John* on keyboards. Most of the film was shot at a T. Rex concert at Wembley Empire Pool on March 18, 1972, and on the grounds of Tittenhurst Park (Ringo's residence, then owned by John Lennon before Ringo's purchase of it.) in Ascot.

Ringo is credited as taking the jacket photos of T. Rex's 1972 album *The Slider.* Tony Visconti insists, "I took those photos during a long day of shooting the Mad Hatter's tea party sequence [for *Born To Boogie*] at Lennon's house. Ringo was very busy organizing each new shot, so we had nothing to do and were bored. Marc was wearing his leather top hat and asked me to take some pictures of him from the front and back with his new Nikon camera. Ringo didn't go near Marc's Nikon that day — he was too busy. When the album came out with my photos on it [credited to Ringo] I confronted Marc about it but, always the opportunist, he conveniently 'remembered' Ringo taking the photos. He apologized but it was too late to change the credits. I'd be interested to hear Ringo's version." Bolan sings about Lennon on the album's track *Ballrooms Of Mars.* Several T. Rex albums thank Ringo, but Visconti (who produced most all of Marc's recordings during this period) says, "Marc was such an opportunist, he would have screamed it from the rooftops if Ringo played on his albums; it never happened!" Marc contributed guitar to *Have You Seen My Baby (Hold On)* on the 1973 album *Ringo.*

T. Rex's fame rapidly faded. Several personnel changes were made, including the addition of American soul singer Gloria Jones, who became Bolan's girlfriend until his death in a car she was driving on September 16, 1977. Ringo made an appearance in a 1993 TV retrospective on Marc's career. Steve Currie died on April 28, 1981. Mickey Finn died on January 11, 2003. Bill Legend still dabbles in music. For more information go to www.borntoboogie.net, www.bill-legend.com

Doris Troy

Doris Troy
Apple-CDP 7 98701 2 (06/30/92) (09/11/70)
Producer: possibly **George Harrison** & Doris Troy [unless noted otherwise]
One or more of the following studios: Trident, Apple &/or EMI-Abbey Road, London, UK 10/xx/69-07/xx/70 [unless noted otherwise]

Ain't That Cute (**G. Harrison**-D. Troy) 3:52 (1) (02/13/70)
Producer: George Harrison
George Harrison: Guitar; **Ringo Starr: (possible) Drums**; Doris Troy: Lead Vocals; Eric Clapton: (possible) Guitar; Bill Moody: (probable) Drums; Berry Morgan (possible) Drums; Daryl Runswick: (probable) Bass; Klaus Voormann: (possible) Bass; Bobby Keys: Saxophone; Jim Price: Trumpet; Reg Powell: Piano; Billy Preston: Keyboards & B. Vocals; Peter Frampton: Guitar; Delaney Bramlett: (probable) B. Vocals; Madeline Bell: (probable) B. Vocals; Eliza Strike: (probable) B. Vocals; Nanette Workman: (probable) B. Vocals
Trident & possibly Apple Studios, London, UK 10/xx/69

All That I've Got (D. Troy-B. Preston) 3:55 (14)
Ringo Starr: (probable) Drums; Doris Troy: Lead Vocals & (probable) Keyboards; probably one or more of the following: Billy Preston: Keyboards; Leon Russell: Keyboards; Gary Wright: Keyboards; Klaus Voormann: Bass; Carl Radle: Bass; Alan White: Drums; Jim Gordon: Drums

Dearest Darling (D. Troy) 2:50 (16)
George Harrison: (probable) Guitar; **Ringo Starr**; **(probable) Drums**; Doris Troy: Lead Vocals & (probable) Keyboards; probably one or more of the following: Alan White: Drums; Jim Gordon: Drums; Klaus Voormann: Bass; Carl Radle: Bass; Gary Wright: Keyboards; Leon Russell: Keyboards; Billy Preston: Keyboards; Bobby Keys: Saxophone; Jim Price: Horns

Don't Call Me No More (D. Troy-R. Schinnery) 2:05 (12)
George Harrison: Guitar; **Ringo Starr: Drums**; Doris Troy: Vocals & (probable) Keyboards; Ray Schinnery: Vocals; Eric Clapton: Guitar; Billy Preston (probable) Keyboards & B. Vocals; Klaus Voormann: Bass
Trident &/or Apple Studios, London, UK 10/xx/69

Exactly Like You (J. McHugh-D. Fields) 3:06 (10)
Doris Troy: Lead Vocals; Bill Moody: Drums; Reg Powell: Keyboards; Billy Preston: Keyboards; Bobby Keys: (probable) Saxophone; Jim Price: (probable) Horns; Daryl Runswick: Bass

Games People Play (J. South) 3:04 (5)
George Harrison: (probable) B. Vocals; Doris

Troy: Lead Vocals; Reg Powell: Keyboards; Billy Preston: Organ; Delaney Bramlett: (probable) B. Vocals; Bill Moody: Drums; Daryl Runswick: Bass; Madeline Bell (probable) B. Vocals; Eliza Strike (probable) B. Vocals; Nanette Workman: (probable) B. Vocals

Get Back (J. Lennon-P. McCartney) 3:06 (15) (08/28/70)
George Harrison: Guitar; **Ringo Starr: Drums**; Doris Troy: Lead Vocals; Eric Clapton: Guitar; Billy Preston: Keyboards; Klaus Voormann: Bass; Bobby Keys: Saxophone; Jim Price: Horns
One or more of the following studios: Trident, Apple &/or EMI-Abbey Road, London, UK 10/xx/69

Give Me Back My Dynamite (**G. Harrison**-D. Troy) 4:54 (3)
Producer: probably **George Harrison** & Doris Troy
George Harrison: Guitar; **Ringo Starr: Drums**; Doris Troy: Lead Vocals; Eric Clapton: Guitar; Billy Preston: Keyboards; Klaus Voormann: Bass
Trident &/or Apple Studios, London, UK 10/xx/69

Gonna Get My Baby Back (**G. Harrison-R. Starkey**-D. Troy-S. Stills) 2:17 (6)
Producer: probably **George Harrison** & Doris Troy
Ringo Starr: (probable) Drums; George Harrison: (probable) Guitar; Doris Troy: Lead Vocals; probably one or more of the following: Billy Preston: Keyboards; Klaus Voormann: Bass; Carl Radle: Bass; Jim Price: Horns; Bobby Keys: Saxophone; Peter Frampton: Guitar; Stephen Stills: Guitar

I've Got To Be Strong (J. Lomax-D. Troy) 2:34 (7)
George Harrison: Guitar; **Ringo Starr: Drums**; Doris Troy: Lead Vocals; Eric Clapton: Guitar; Billy Preston: Keyboards & B. Vocals; Gary Wright: Keyboards; Jim Price: (probable) Horns; Bobby Keys: Saxophone; Madeline Bell: (probable) B. Vocals; Eliza Strike: (probable) B. Vocals; Nanette Workman: (probable) B. Vocals
Trident &/or Apple Studios, London, UK 10/xx/69

Jacob's Ladder [a.k.a. Soldier Of The Cross] (Trad. Arr: **G. Harrison**-D. Troy) 2:57 (13) (08/28/70)
Producer: [George Harrison] & Doris Troy
George Harrison: Arrangement & (possible) Guitar; Doris Troy: Vocals & (probable) Keyboards; Delaney Bramlett: Vocals & (probable) Guitar; probably one or more of the following: Leon Russell: Piano; Billy Preston: Keyboards; Madeline Bell: B. Vocals; Eliza Strike: B. Vocals; Nanette Workman: B. Vocals; Klaus Voormann: Bass; Carl Radle: Bass; Jim Gordon: Drums; Bobby Keys: Saxophone

So Far (K. Voormann-D. Troy) 4:25 (9)
Producer: [George Harrison] & Doris Troy
Doris Troy: Lead Vocals & Keyboards; Eric Clapton: Guitar; Alan White: Drums; Carl Radle: Bass; John Barham: Orchestral Arrangements; Bobby Whitlock: Keyboards; Delaney Bramlett: B. Vocals; Rita Coolidge: B. Vocals

Special Care (S. Stills) 2:57 (2)
Ringo Starr: (probable) Drums; Doris Troy: Lead Vocals & (probable) Keyboards; probably one or more of the following: Stephen Stills: Guitar; Peter Frampton: Guitar; Jim Price: Horns; Bobby Keys: Saxophone; Leon Russell: Keyboards; Billy Preston: Keyboards & B. Vocals; Alan White: Drums; Jim Gordon: Drums; Klaus Voormann: Bass; Carl Radle: Bass

Vaya Con Dios (L. Russell-I. James-B. Pepper) 3:29 (18) (02/13/70)
George Harrison (supposed) Guitar & (possible) Bass; Doris Troy: Lead Vocals; Billy Preston: Keyboards; Bill Moody: Drums; Daryl Runswick: Bass; Reg Powell: Keyboards

What You Will Blues [a.k.a. Give Me Back My Dynamite] (D. Troy) 4:57 (17)
Producer: probably **George Harrison** & Doris Troy
George Harrison: Dialogue & Guitar; **Ringo Starr: Drums**; Doris Troy: Lead Vocals; Eric Clapton: Guitar; Billy Preston: Keyboards; Klaus Voormann: Bass

You Give Me Joy Joy (D. Troy-**G. Harrison-R. Starkey**-S. Stills) 3:38 (11)
Producer: probably **George Harrison** & Doris Troy
George Harrison: Guitar; **Ringo Starr: Drums**; Doris Troy: Lead Vocals & Keyboards; Eric Clapton: Guitar; Stephen Stills: Guitar; Peter Frampton: Guitar; Bobby Keys: Saxophone; Jim Price Horns; Klaus Voormann: Bass
Trident & possibly Apple Studios, London, UK 10/xx/69

Doris Troy was born Doris Higgensen in New York, New York on January 6, 1937. Her father was a well-known Pentecostal minister and Doris was soon singing in the choir. Later, she worked as an usherette at the famous Apollo Theater in New York. She sang with the Halos and worked as a backing singer for Dionne Warwick, Cissy Houston, The Drifters, Solomon Burke, Chuck Jackson and others. She changed her name to Troy (after Helen of Troy) joined Atlantic Records in 1963 where she co-wrote under the name Payne, and recorded the Top 10 hit *Just One Look*. [*Just One Look* was later a hit for The Hollies and Linda Ronstadt.]

On April 16, 1965 Troy appeared on the UK TV show *Ready, Steady, Goes Live!* and during the finale sang with guests John Lennon, George Harrison and Adam Faith*. Troy moved to the UK in 1969 and, along with Madeline Bell, Eliza Strike and Nanette Workman, was a highly sought after session singer. Doris appeared as a backing singer in the 1970 promotional video for Ringo Starr's *Sentimental Journey*.

Troy's involvement with Billy Preston* on his first Apple album, produced by Harrison, landed her a deal with Apple as a songwriter, producer and artist. Harrison and Ringo Starr began helping her record the album *Doris Troy* with many of the same musicians Harrison used on his album *All Things Must Pass*. When *Doris Troy* was released in 1970 it didn't include any musical credits but the CD release mentions contributions from Eric Clapton*, Leon Russell*, Peter Frampton*, Stephen Stills* and Delaney & Bonnie Bramlett*. Doris remembered Delaney's involvement, but didn't think Bonnie was present, nor does Bonnie. Troy said the background vocals were supplied by Bell, Strike and Workman, and the other musicians including Harrison. Drummer Alan White, who was also working with Lennon then, recalls drumming on numerous tracks for the album but is fairly sure Jim Gordon (see Derek And The Dominos) drummed on *Jacob's Ladder*. He recalls Gary Wright* and Klaus Voormann* playing on the sessions, and thinks Carl Radle played on a track. Troy wanted to record a Beatles' song and chose *Get Back*, which she thought Harrison probably plays on, as well as most of the tracks on the album. The CD and other sources also claim that Harrison plays guitar on *Get Back*, though it sounds like Eric playing both the lead and the rhythm break. It's possible that Harrison is buried in the mix or is doing a fairly good job of imitating Clapton. Doris recalled Klaus playing bass, Ringo playing drums and Billy playing keyboards on most of the songs on the album and Stills playing guitar on a few tracks. Mark Roberty's book *Eric Clapton The Complete Recording Sessions, 1963 – 1992* lists recordings at Apple and Trident Studios in London for the *Doris Troy* album as including Eric and George on guitar and Ringo on drums for the songs *Ain't That Cute*, *Give Me Back My Dynamite*, *I've Got To Be Strong*, *You Give Me Joy Joy*, *Don't Call Me No More* and *Get Back*. Eric's guitar, especially on *Give Me Back My Dynamite* (a.k.a. *What You Will Blues*), *I've Got To Be Strong* and *You Give Me Joy Joy*, is unmistakable. Harrison's guitar contributions are less identifiable. Jackie Lomax*, who's credited as composing *I've Got To Be Strong* with Troy, maintains he alone composed the song, originally titled *You've Got To Be Strong*, about Troy. The CD states Frampton plays guitar on the single *Ain't That Cute*, and Harrison plays guitar on the B-side, *Vaya Con Dios*, but only a bass guitar is audible on the B-side. It's possible that Harrison (known to play bass) played bass on it given that the A-side was co-written and produced by him. Frampton says, "I walked into the control room at Trident Studios and George looked me straight in the eye and said, 'Hello Pete.' It was my first meeting with a Beatle, and I was walking on air, but I was in The Herd and he knew who I was and said, 'Do you want to play?' He gave me a Les Paul guitar and I started playing rhythm on *Ain't That Cute*. He stopped me and said, 'Pete, you don't understand; I play rhythm, you play lead!' That's when I developed the lead riff for that; that's not Clapton, that's me! Eric wasn't there when I was. George played rhythm and I think it was Berry Morgan of Morgan Studios on drums, but I'm not sure." Frampton also recalls playing on about six other songs on the album, along with Voormann, at Trident including *You Give Me Joy Joy* and probably *Special Care*. Troy said Harrison's mother died during recordings for *Ain't That Cute*, so he left her to work on it and other songs for the album. However, *Ain't That Cute* was one of the first songs worked on and was released five months before Harrison's mother died. Troy said Bill Moody plays drums, Daryl Runswick plays bass and Reg Powell plays piano on *Ain't That Cute*, *Vaya Con Dios*, *Games People Play* and *Exactly Like You*. Moody's recollections leave little doubt that he and these other musicians play on the album. Marc Roberty's book makes no mention of these musicians, or Frampton on *Ain't That Cute*, and lists a completely different lineup. The CD states *Hurry* was previously recorded in the US, and Troy insisted that *You Tore Me Up Inside* was also recorded in the US, which would exclude involvement by any of The Beatles. An early backing track of *Give Me Back My Dynamite* is identified on the CD as the previously unreleased bonus track *What You Will Blues* casting doubt on the reliability of the CD's information. Harrison is clearly heard counting off the take, which is credited as being composed solely by Troy. Troy said Harrison only helped write a few of the lyrics to *Give Me Back*

Kristofer Engelhardt and Doris Troy, Beatlefest, Crowne Plaza Meadowlands Hotel, Secaucus, New Jersey March 28, 1999. Photo by asshole, © Kristofer Engelhardt.

My Dynamite. Klaus supplied the credits for his and Troy's composition *So Far* with his album *Voormann & Friends A Sideman's Journey*. Doris said that Ray Schinnery, who helped her compose *Don't Call Me No More*, sang duet vocals with her on it. Roberty's book doesn't list Schinnery, but does list Preston on backing vocals. Troy is credited as producing all of her recordings, except *Ain't That Cute* produced by Harrison, but said George had a hand in producing much of her album, specifically *Jacob's Ladder*. George likely helped produce the songs he had a hand in writing or on which he played. Doris said that Delaney provided the duet vocals on *Jacob's Ladder*, though it's difficult to tell their vocals apart. Delaney said he thought he sang on *Jacob's Ladder* and probably plays guitar because, "It's too sloppy to be Eric." [Delaney & Bonnie's version of *Soldier Of The Cross* (a.k.a. *Jacob's Ladder*), appears on their album *The Original Delaney & Bonnie-Accept No Substitute*, which had been scheduled for release on Apple in 1969.] The musicians' contributions (which aren't all-inclusive, or exclusive, for each song), including those by Harrison and Starr, to *Doris Troy* can't be verified with certainty. It's very likely that George and Ringo play on those tracks that they helped compose. Had the initial release of *Doris Troy* noted the musicians involved it probably would have been more successful. Perhaps rightfully, Harrison felt the music was more impressive than the musicians, or they remained anonymous to avoid contractual entanglements.

Doris sang backing vocals on Lennon's song *Power To The People* in 1971. Like most, she left Apple amidst the chaos and changes that were taking place. Troy carried on as a session singer, notably for The Rolling Stones* and on Pink Floyd's album *Dark Side Of The Moon*. She returned to the US in 1973, and worked extensively with Lola Falana in Las Vegas, where she lived and performed. She turned to acting appearing in films and on TV. In 1984 she began playing the role of her mother in the highly successful stage production of her life story *Mama I Want To Sing*, which was later made into a film. Doris Troy died on February 16, 2004.

Ike & Tina Turner

River Deep-Mountain High
A&M-SP-4178 (album 12") (09/13/69) **George Harrison message on sticker on album jacket**

Ike & Tina Turner were a popular husband and wife R&B act in the 1960s. Ike was born Izear Turner Jr. on November 5, 1931 in Clarksdale, Mississippi. His formative years in music were spent backing blues players such as Sonny Boy Williamson, Howlin' Wolf* and B.B. King*. He played on the 1951 record *Rocket 88*, often cited as the first rock 'n' roll song. Tina was born Anna Mae Bullock on November 26, 1939 in Nutbush (Brownsville), Tennessee. In 1956 Tina was at a club in St. Louis and started singing with Ike Turner and The Kings Of Rhythm. By 1958 she was calling herself Tina and fronting her new husband Ike's band. They had a Top 20 hit with *It's Gonna Work Out Fine* in 1961.

In 1966 Ike signed a production agreement with Phil Spector* who had Tina record his song *River Deep-Mountain High*. It barely charted, though it was a Top Five hit in the UK, prompting Spector to cancel their album of the same title. The Rolling Stones'* booked Ike & Tina Turner for several of their tours, which helped make them major stars in Europe. The *River Deep-Mountain High* album was finally released in 1969 on A&M Records with a jacket sticker that read "'River Deep-Mountain High' is a perfect record from start to finish. You couldn't improve on it – George Harrison."

Ike & Tina Turner had a Top Five hit in 1971 with their cover of Creedence Clearwater Revival's (see John Fogerty) *Proud Mary* and their last Top 40 hit in 1973 with *Nutbush City Limits* composed by Tina. Tina left Ike in 1976 and they were later divorced. Her 1984 Multi-Platinum certified album *Private Dancer* includes the Top Five hit *Better Be Good To Me*, the Top 10 hit *Private Dancer* and the number one hit *What's Love Got To Do With It?* It marked the beginning of her huge comeback. Tina has sung duets with a number of rock legends, including Mick Jagger*, David Bowie*, Eric Clapton*, Rod Stewart,* and Paul McCartney on the song *Get Back* at Wembley Arena for the annual *Prince's Trust All - Star Rock Concert* on June 20, 1986. Throughout her career she (and Ike) has recorded covers of The Beatles' songs. Ike & Tina Turner were inducted into the Rock and Roll Hall of Fame in 1991. Tina's autobiography was adapted into the successful motion picture *What's Love Got To Do With It* in 1993. Her last Top 10 hit was *I Don't Wanna Fight* co-composed by Billy Lawrie* and Lulu* in 1993. Tina Turner has been less active in recent years. Ike didn't have much success after Tina left him and Ike Turner died on December 12, 2007.

Ruby Turner

Unbootlegged Vol. 27 [Paul McCartney]
No Topo Records NTR-0801 (CD-R) [unauthorized release] (xx/xx/08)
Producer: Alison Howe & Jools Holland
Paul McCartney: B. Vocals; Ruby Turner: Lead Vocals; Lulu: B. Vocals; Kate Nash: B. Vocals; Kyle Minogue: B. Vocals; Eddie Floyd: B. Vocals; Mika (Michael Penniman Jr.): B. Vocals; Aiméé Duffy: B. Vocals; Seasick Steve: B. Vocals; Jools Holland: Keyboards; Gilson Lavis: Drums; Mark Flanagan: Guitar; Dave Swift: Bass; Christopher Holland: Keyboards; Louise Marshall: B. Vocals; Phil Veacock: Saxophone; Michael Rose: Saxophone; Lisa Grahame: Saxophone; Derek Nash: Saxophone; Nick Lunt: Saxophone; Winston Rollins: Trombone; Roger Goslyn: Trombone; Favyaz Virji: Trombone; Rico Rodriguez: Trombone; Jon Scott: Trumpet; Jason McDermid: Trumpet; Chris Storr: Trumpet
BBC Television Centre, London, UK 12/20/07

Up Above My Head [live] (trad.) 2:54

Ruby Turner was born on June 22, 1958 in Montego Bay, Jamaica but moved to Birmingham, England as a youngster. The gospel and R&B singer, and songwriter first gained notice in the mid-1980s as a member of Culture Club before embarking on a successful solo career. Ruby has released over a dozen albums and had several hit songs including, *If You're Ready (Come Go With Me)*, *I'd Rather Go Blind*, and the R&B chart topping song *It's Gonna Be Alright* in 1990. Ruby has also had a successful acting career. She has worked with a number of artists including Mick Jagger*, Zoot Money*, Steve Winwood (see Blind Faith), UB 40*, Brian

Ferry and Jools Holland.

Ruby closed Jools Holland's *Hootenanny*, an annual New Year's Eve show on BBC TV, with *Up Above My Head*. She was backed by Holland's Rhythm and Blues Orchestra and the show's other guests, including Paul McCartney on backing vocals. Ruby recalls, "We rehearsed *Up Above My Head* at the last moment because we were running out of time. Jools asked me to take the lead on it because I'd sung the song with his band in the past, so we were ready to fly when we closed the show with it. Everyone there joined in on the chorus. It was electrifying for us all to be singing this old spiritual number. It was like church that night. I'd met McCartney and Ringo Starr before, but having Paul there was awesome. He is a true musician. There's none of that show business nonsense with him. He's real 'old school' – he doesn't mess around. Sadly, that song was the only time so far that I've had a chance to work with a Beatle, but what a time we had." For more information go to www.rubyturner.com

Lon & Derrek Van Eaton

Black & White
IBW-398D (05/09/98)
Producer: Klaus Voormann [unless noted otherwise]
Sunset Sound Studios, Los Angeles, CA xx/xx/78 [unless noted otherwise]

Hold On (L. Van Eaton-D. Van Eaton) 3:19 (12)
Ringo Starr: Drums; Derrek Van Eaton: Lead Vocals; Klaus Voormann: Bass, Guitar & B. Vocals; Cynthia Webb: B. Vocals; Lon Van Eaton: Keyboards, B. Vocals & Guitar; Carlos de la Paz: Guitar

My World Is Empty Without You (B. Holland-L. Dozier-E. Holland) 2:41 (1-B)
Ringo Starr: Drums; Derrek Van Eaton: Lead Vocals; Klaus Voormann: Bass, Keyboards & Guitar; Lon Van Eaton: Keyboards & Guitar; Tom Seifert: Guitar

Ringo Ad (contains portions of: Sun Song/Maybe There's Another/Sweet Music) 0:60 (1-A)
Producer: Unknown
Ringo Starr: Dialogue, Drums & Tambourine; Derrek Van Eaton: Lead Vocals & Guitar; Jim Gordon: Drums; Mike Hugg: Harmonium; Peter Frampton: Guitar; Lon Van Eaton: Guitar, Saxophone, B. Vocals & Keyboards; Klaus Voormann: Bass
xx/xx/72

Brother
Apple-SMAS 3390 (album 12") (09/22/72)

Another Thought (L. Van Eaton-D. Van Eaton) 3:41 (2/5)
Producer: Klaus Voormann
Ringo Starr: Drums; Derrek Van Eaton: Lead Vocals; Klaus Voormann: Bass; T. J. Tindall: Guitar; Lon Van Eaton: Piano, Horn & String Arrangements
Apple Studios, London, UK 10-12/xx/71

Sweet Music (L. Van Eaton-D. Van Eaton) 3:41 (1/6) (03/06/72)
Producer: George Harrison
Ringo Starr: Drums & Tambourine; Derrek Van Eaton: Lead Vocals & Guitar; Jim Gordon: Drums; Mike Hugg: Harmonium; Peter Frampton: Guitar; Lon Van Eaton: Guitar, Saxophone, B. Vocals & Keyboards; Klaus Voormann: Bass
EMI-Abbey Road & Apple Studios, London, UK 09 &/or 10/xx/71

Give A Little Love (Boy Scouts Of America) [Various Artists]
Comin-CMN 1187-002 (12/xx/88)
Producer: Klaus Voormann
Ringo Starr: Drums & Percussion; Derrek Van Eaton: Lead Vocals & Vibra-Slap; Klaus Voormann: Bass & Sleigh Bells; Lon Van Eaton: Keyboards & Horns; Carlos de la Paz: Guitar
Sunset Sound Studios, Los Angeles, CA, xx/xx/78

Get Happy (L. Van Eaton-D. Van Eaton) 3:25 (4)

[None]
Apple [unreleased]
Producer: Klaus Voormann
Apple Studios, London, UK 10-12/xx/71 [unless noted otherwise]

Don't You Know That It's Over (L. Van Eaton-D. Van Eaton) 3:35
George Harrison: Slide Guitar; Derrek Van Eaton: Lead Vocals; Lon Van Eaton: Guitar & Keyboards; Klaus Voormann: Bass; Steve Moseley: Drums

Media Sound Studios, New York, NY xx/xx/72

The Sea (L. Van Eaton-D. Van Eaton-J. Tavener) 4:12
Ringo Starr: Drums; Derrek Van Eaton: Lead Vocals; John Tavener: Conductor, String & Horn Arrangements; Klaus Voormann: Bass; Lon Van Eaton: Keyboards

Warm Woman [alternate version] (L. Van Eaton-D. Van Eaton) 3:10
Ringo Starr: Drums; Derrek Van Eaton: Lead Vocals; Lon Van Eaton: Keyboards; Klaus Voormann: Bass

[None]
Portrait [unreleased]
Producer: Klaus Voormann
Sunset Sound Studios, Los Angeles, CA xx/xx/78

Bye Baby (L. Van Eaton-D. Van Eaton) 3:25
Ringo Starr: Drums; Derrek Van Eaton: Lead Vocals; Klaus Voormann: Bass & Guitar; Lon Van Eaton: Keyboards

Keep It Up (L. Van Eaton-D. Van Eaton) 3:23
Ringo Starr: Drums; Derrek Van Eaton: Lead Vocals; Klaus Voormann: Bass & Guitar; Lon Van Eaton: Keyboards; Carlos de la Paz: Guitar

Lon Van Eaton was born on March 12, 1948 and his brother Derrek was born on August 12, 1950, both in Trenton, New Jersey. They had been members of The Trees, and later Jacobs Creek who released an album on Columbia Records in 1969 but broke up in March 1971. Known simply as Lon & Derrek Van Eaton they submitted their music to many record companies including Apple. George Harrison and John Lennon loved their music. They met with Harrison while he was in New York working on *The Concert For Bangla Desh* project and signed a contract with Apple on September 15, 1971. On September 19 they flew to the UK and were escorted to Harrison's home, where he greeted them playing their songs on acoustic guitar. Within days Harrison was producing their first Apple single *Sweet Music* with Ringo on drums. Derrek believes Harrison decided to produce that track because it was similar in sound to what he was recording at the time. The remainder of the sessions were produced by Klaus Voormann*, but they say Harrison often dropped by, and that he and Ringo contributed to some unreleased recordings of theirs then, including an alternate version of *Warm Woman* and *The Sea* (with contributions from John Tavener*) with Ringo on drums. Harrison reportedly spared no expense on the duo's project. They lived at Harrison's home or Ringo's apartment during their three month stay in the UK. Their 1972 debut album *Brother* also features Ringo drumming on *Another Thought*. Their unreleased song *Don't You Know That It's Over* was recorded in New York in 1972 with Harrison on slide guitar.

Harrison suggested Lon & Derrek relocate to Los Angeles to improve their chances for success, and helped get them signed to A&M Records who released their album *Who Do You Out Do* in 1975. While in Los Angeles during the mid-1970s they contributed to Ringo's albums *Ringo* and *Goodnight Vienna*, and Harrison's song *Dark Horse*. Lon plays on Ringo's albums *Rotogravure* and *Ringo The 4th*, and was a member of Ringo's Roadside Attraction, a makeshift band he formed for his 1978 album *Bad Boy* and his TV special *Ringo*.

Ringo drums on Lon & Derrek's recordings of *Hold On*, *Get Happy*, *Bye Baby*, *Keep It Up* and *My World Is Empty Without You* for Portrait Records in 1978. *Get Happy* was released on the 1988 various artists album *Give A Little Love (Boy Scouts Of America)*. The album also features *Sweet Music* and a cover of The Beatles' song *Getting Better*. *Hold On* and *My World Is Empty Without You* were released on Lon & Derrek's 1998 album *Black & White*. It also includes a 60-second radio spot by Ringo, which was made for the *Brother* album, and the demo version of *Sweet Music* that was sent to Apple. Lon also contributed to the posthumously released 1998 album *John Lennon Anthology*.

Derrek has essentially left the music business. Lon owns and operates Angels Ranch Recordings Studios. He has been active in musical projects for a wide range of artists, such as Carly Simon* and Harry Nilsson*, and community and charitable organizations. For more information go to www.imagineabetterworld.com

Various Artists - Hurricane RELIEF

Come Together Now [Various Artists]
RIAA-CCD2-2311-2 (11/22/05)
Producer: Sharon Osbourne & Simon Cowell
Ringo Starr: Drums; Elton John: Vocals & Keyboards†; Rod Stewart: Vocals; Mary J. Blige: Vocals; Andrea Bocelli: Vocals†; Phil Collins: Vocals†; Robert Downey Jr.: Vocals; Josh Groban: Vocals; Katie Melua: Vocals; Kelly Osbourne: Vocals; Ozzy Osbourne: Vocals; Pink: Vocals††; Gavin Rossdale: Vocals; Robbie Williams: (probable) Vocals; Brian McFadden: (probable) Vocals; Nicky Byrne: (probable) Vocals; Kiam Egan: (probable) Vocals; Mark Feehily: (probable) Vocals; Shane Filan: (probable) Vocals; Will Young: (probable) Vocals; Gwen Stefani: Vocals; Steven Tyler: Vocals†††; Saul Hudson a.k.a. Slash: Guitar†; Matt Sorum: Drums†; Dave Kushner: Guitar†; Scott Weiland: Vocals†; Duff McKagan: Bass†; Mark Hudson: Vocals
Whitfield Street Studios, London, UK 01/20/04†; Los Angeles, CA 01/xx/04; New York, NY 01 or 02/xx/04††; Boston, MA 01 or 02/xx/04†††

Tears In Heaven (E. Clapton-W. Jennings) 4:20 (1-13)

Ozzy Osbourne's wife, Sharon, organized a number of all-star musicians to record a cover of Eric Clapton's* hit *Tears In Heaven* to raise relief money for the victims of the 2003 tsunami in Southeast Asia. The basic backing was recorded in London with Elton John, members of Velvet Revolver and others. Many of the guest vocals were recorded the following week in Los Angeles. The recordings were produced by Sharon, and Simon Cowell, a judge on TV's *American Idol*. Ringo Starr is seen playing drums in one of the videos for the recording of the song. The song wasn't available on record until Sharon included it on the album *Hurricane RELIEF Come Together Now* in late 2005 with proceeds also benefiting victims of Hurricanes Rita and Katrina. Mark Hudson* also appears in the video, though he's not listed in the album's credits, nor was Robbie Williams, Will Young or the group Westlife who were reported to be contributing vocals to the recording.

Various Artists - Mick Jagger, Bruce Springsteen And The Rock Hall Jam Band

Rock And Roll Hall Of Fame & Museum
Time Life-24943-X (Light My Fire Live) (24629-X) (Sweet Emotion Live 24630-X) (DVD) (10/20/09)
Producer: Bob Sarles & Christina Keating
Grand Ballroom Waldorf-Astoria Hotel, New York, NY 01/20/88

(I Can't Get No) Satisfaction [live] (M. Jagger-K. Richards) 4:04 (2-2)
George Harrison: Electric Guitar & B. Vocals; Ringo Starr: Drums; Mick Jagger: Lead Vocals; Bruce Springsteen: Vocals & Handclaps; Paul Shaffer: Keyboards; Jeff Beck: Electric Guitar; Jeff Lynne: Electric Guitar; Bruce Johnston: B. Vocals & Tambourine; Billy Joel: B. Vocals & Keyboards; John Fogerty: Electric Guitar & B. Vocals; Bob Dylan: Electric Guitar; Little Steven Van Zandt: Tambourine; Patti Scialfa: Handclaps & B. Vocals; Mary Wilson: B. Vocals & Handclaps; Al Jardine: Guitar & Percussion; Mike Love: B. Vocals & Tambourine; Dave Edmunds: Electric Guitar; Max Weinberg: Drums; Arlo Guthrie: Guitar; Ben E. King: Handclaps & B. Vocals; Sid McGinnis: Guitar; Will Lee: Bass; Nile Rodgers: Guitar; Johnny Moore: Handclaps; Joe Blunt: Handclaps; Clyde Brown: Handclaps; Bill Pinkney: Handclaps; Charlie Thomas: Handclaps

I Saw Her Standing There [live] (J. Lennon-P. McCartney) 2:55 (1-1)
George Harrison: Acoustic Guitar & B. Vocals; Ringo Starr: Drums; Billy Joel: Vocals & Keyboards; Dave Edmunds: Electric Guitar; Paul Shaffer: Keyboards, B. Vocals & Handclaps; Bob Dylan: Electric Guitar; Les Paul: Electric Guitar; Mick Jagger: Vocals & Tambourine; John Fogerty: Electric Guitar; Bruce Springsteen: Vocals & Tambourine; Bruce Johnston: B. Vocals; Jeff Beck: Electric Guitar; Mary Wilson: B. Vocals; Roy Bittan: Keyboards; Anton Fig: Drums; Peter Wolf: Handclaps; Arlo Guthrie: Guitar; Sid McGinnis: Guitar; Nile Rodgers: Guitar; Johnny Moore: Handclaps; Joe Blunt: Handclaps; Clyde Brown: Handclaps; Julian Lennon: Handclaps;

Bill Pinkney: Handclaps; Charlie Thomas: Handclaps; Max Weinberg: Handclaps; Will Lee: Bass; Sean Lennon: Handclaps; Yoko Ono: Handclaps

In 2009 Time Life released the *Rock And Roll Hall Of Fame & Museum* series on DVD in several configurations. Contained on the DVDs are a number of appearances and performances by members of The Beatles. The Beatles were inducted into the Rock and Roll Hall of Fame in 1988 along with The Beach Boys*, The Drifters, The Supremes, Bob Dylan*, Les Paul and others. Mick Jagger* inducted The Beatles. George Harrison and Ringo Starr were in attendance for the ceremonies. Yoko Ono* and John Lennon's two sons, Julian Lennon* and Sean Lennon were also in attendance to represent him. Paul McCartney didn't attend the ceremonies releasing the following statement to the press, "I was keen to go and pick up my award but after 20 years, The Beatles still have some business differences, which I had hoped would have been settled by now. Unfortunately, they haven't been, so I would feel like a complete hypocrite waving and smiling with them at a fake reunion." At the ceremonies Ringo said, "I've been nominated to say, 'Hi, and thank you.' Anyway, there were four of us in that band and there just seems to be George and I, Yoko, Sean and Julian here. So anyway, that's all I have to say – thank you, thank you, thank you – over to George." Harrison said, "I don't have much to say because I'm the quiet Beatle. It's got to be bigger than any of us expected, and it's certainly wonderful to be here and certainly a thrill. It is unfortunate Paul's not here 'cause he was the one that had the speech in his pocket. We all know why John can't be here, and I'm sure he would be. It's hard really to stand here supposedly representing The Beatles. Uh — it's what's left, I'm afraid. But we all loved him so much, and we all love Paul very much. Anyway, thank you all very much and on behalf of John – I'm sure that he is well-covered with Yoko, Sean and Julian – and thank you all very much — God bless." Yoko said of John, "He would have been here, you know. He would have come."

When Ringo was asked to join in the traditional all-star jam to take place following the inductions, he was reported to have said, "Absolutely not! There will be real musicians up there." However, Ringo, George and most of the inducted musicians on hand, with backing from Paul Shaffer's* band, Bruce Springsteen*, Billy Joel*, Elton John*, John Fogerty*, Jeff Lynne*, and other guests, jammed together on most of the 10 songs performed, including *I Saw Her Standing There* and *(I Can't Get No) Satisfaction* billed as Mick Jagger, Bruce Springsteen And The Rock Hall Jam Band, and *Stand By Me* by Ben E. King* included in the Time Life series. The remainder of the performance is available on unauthorized releases. The set also includes McCartney inducting Lennon in 1994, Paul accepting his induction in 1999 and his performance of several songs, including *What'd I Say* with Billy Joel, and Harrison's widow Olivia and son Dhani accepting George's induction in 2004.

Various Artists - Live Aid

Do They Know It's Christmas?
Mercury-0249869413 (single) (Canada) (11/29/04)
Producer: Will Shapland & Jeff Griffin
Paul McCartney: B. Vocals; David Bowie: Vocals; Bob Geldof: Vocals; George Michael: Vocals; Bono: Vocals; Sting: Vocals; Roger Daltrey: Vocals; Linda McCartney: B. Vocals; Pete Townshend: B. Vocals; Alison Moyet: B. Vocals; Howard Jones: B. Vocals; Elton John: B. Vocals; Francis Rossi: B. Vocals; Freddie Mercury: B. Vocals; probably the following in the chorus: Alan Lancaster, Pete Kircher, Andy Bown, Rick Parfitt, Mick Talbot, Paul Weller, Steve White, Dee C. Lee, Adam Ant, Marco Pirroni, Bogdan Wiczling, Chris Constantinou, Tony Hadley, Martin Kemp, Steve Norman, John Keeble, Nick Kershaw, Sade, Stuart Matthewman, Paul Denman, Andrew Hale, Paul Cook, Omar Hakim, Darryl Jones, Kenny Kirkland, Branford Marsalis, Dollette McDonald, Janice Pendarvis, Dave Gilmour, Brian Ferry, Guy Fletcher, The Edge, Larry Mullen Jr., John Illsley, Alan Clark, Terry Williams, Chris White, Roger Taylor, Brian May, John Deacon, Kenney Jones, John Entwistle, Davey Johnstone, Ray Cooper, Dee Murray, Nigel Olsson, Andrew Ridgeley, Paul Young, probably the following: Pete Briquette, Chris Cross &/or Adam Clayton: Bass; Midge Ure, Billy Currie &/or Johnny Fingers: Keyboards; Warren Cann &/or Simon Crowe: Drums; Garry Roberts &/or Gary Kemp: Guitar
Wembley Stadium, London, UK 07/13/85

Do They Know It's Christmas? [live] (B. Geldof-M. Ure) 4:29 (3)
[Also available on *20 Years Ago Today-Live Aid.*

Warner Strategic Marketing-R2 970451 (DVD) (42) (07/12/05)]

Bob Geldof and Midge Ure organized daylong concerts from Wembley Stadium in London, and John F. Kennedy Stadium in Philadelphia, Pennsylvania broadcast live on TV on July 13, 1985 as part of their Band Aid* concept to raise funds for famine relief in Ethiopia. Many of the biggest names in rock music performed including Paul McCartney, who closed the show in London singing *Let It Be* only to have his microphone fail. Paul and Linda McCartney* joined most of the other performers for the encore of *Do They Know It's Christmas?*

Various Artists - Sir Paul McCartney, Rod Stewart, Joe Cocker, Ladysmith Black Mambazo

Party At The Palace
BBC Opus Arte-OA 0857 D (DVD) (07/09/02)
Producer: Cerrie Frost
Paul McCartney: Vocals & Bass; Joe Cocker: Vocals; Rod Stewart: Vocals; Ladysmith Black Mambazo: Vocals; Eric Clapton: Lead Guitar; Paul Wickens: Keyboards; Phil Collins: Drums; Steve Winwood: Keyboards; Cliff Richard: B. Vocals; Brian May: Guitar; Brian Ray: Guitar; Ozzy Osbourne: B. Vocals; Rusty Anderson: Guitar & B. Vocals; Roger Taylor: Drums; Ray Cooper: Percussion; Brian Wilson: B. Vocals; The Royal Academy Of Music Symphony Orchestra & Jazz Horns
Buckingham Palace Garden, London, UK
06/03/02

All You Need Is Love [live] 3:28 (J. Lennon-P. McCartney) (37)
[Also available on Virgin-7243 8 12833 2 5 (20)]

The *Party At The Palace* was a concert held in the garden of Buckingham Palace on June 3, 2002 in commemoration of the Golden Jubilee of Queen Elizabeth II who ascended to the throne in 1952. The event, attended by 12,000 guests, and an estimated one million people outside the palace, featured some of the best of the UK's comedy, classical and pop performers including Paul McCartney and his band. McCartney also played piano and sang backing vocals on Eric Clapton's* rendition of *While My Guitar Gently Weeps*, and shared vocals with Rod Stewart*, Joe Cocker* and Ladysmith Black Mambazo on *All You Need Is Love*. Most of the performers, including Tony Bennett* and Brian Wilson*, joined McCartney on stage for the concert finale of *Hey Jude*.

Various Artists - (Adventure): Ring Of Fire (An Indonesian Odyssey)

(Adventure): Ring Of Fire (An Indonesian Odyssey): Spice Island Saga/Dance Of The Warriors/East Of Krakatoa/Dream Wanderers Of Borneo
Mystic Fire Video/MYS-76496 (DVDS) (10/30/07) (xx/xx/89)
Producer: Lawrence & Lorne Blair; Associate Producers: Ringo Starr & Hilary Gerrard
George Harrison: (possible) Incidental Music; Lawrence Blair: Narration; Lorne Blair: Narration; Mason Daring and the people of Indonesia
Indonesia mid-70s-mid-80s
In 1972 Ringo Starr, through Apple Films, put up the money for brothers Lorne and Lawrence Blair who were making a documentary on the Indonesian Archipelago that forms part of a region known as the Ring of Fire, due to its volcanic activity. At the time of Ringo's involvement, it was reported that George Harrison was contributing incidental music to the film. When the film was finally released in 1988 Ringo was given credit as associate producer, probably for his financial aid, but there was no mention of Harrison in the credits. What, if any, contribution by Harrison isn't known.

Various Artists - Shanghai Surprise

Shanghai Surprise
Lionsgate/MGM-21172 (DVD) (04/10/07) (03/04/87)
Producer: Malcolm Rose, Jeff Lynne & George Harrison (music); John Kohn (film)
Lee International Studios, Shepperton, UK, Shaw Studios, Hong Kong, & on location in Hong Kong & Macau (film) 01/20/86-03/xx/86; FPSHOT, De Lane Lea & EMI-Abbey Road Studios, London, UK; Village Recorders, Los Angeles, CA (music) 01-05/xx/86

Shanghai Surprise (Music-Score) (G. Harrison-M. Kamen) total film time 1hr. 33 min. (1)

HandMade Films, looking for its first major Hollywood, box office success, cast Sean Penn and his new bride, pop star Madonna (who would eventually rack up 12 number one hits) in the starring roles of *Shanghai Surprise*. Penn had recently had a string of successful and critically acclaimed films, and though Madonna had less acting experience her fame was a guaranteed box office draw. HandMade Films' Executive Producer George Harrison took a greater than usual interest in the film. Though he didn't contribute to other artists' music in the film, his efforts and contributions to it are considerable enough to qualify them as contributions to a project by others artists. He made a cameo in the film, wrote and recorded six songs for the soundtrack, and contributed to the film's score and incidental music with Michael Kamen and Ray Cooper. At the very least, this could be considered a contribution by Harrison to Cooper and Kamen's music. [Cooper was Harrison's primary percussionist for years. Kamen worked on a number of HandMade Films. Harrison appears in the early 1990's video documentary of Kamen's album *Concerto For Saxophone* (issued on DVD in 1999 on Pioneer Artists-PA-99-620-D), and is thanked for that appearance in the album's credits, though he never contributed to these or other recordings by Kamen.] Harrison sang the title theme with Vicki Brown*; which reportedly was originally intended to be sung with Madonna. He wrote *Zig Zag* for a scene in a club by that name, and *Someplace Else*, at the request of the film's producer, as the love song for Penn and Madonna. Another of his songs in the film was *Breath Away From Heaven*, which features Laurence Juber* on guitar. [These four songs are included on the *Cloud Nine* album included in the box set *George Harrison The Dark Horse Years 1976-1992*, though the last two songs are different versions from those in the film. The box set also includes a DVD with a video of Harrison recording *Shanghai Surprise*, *Someplace Else*, and a portion of *Hottest Gong In Town*, which Harrison performs in the club scene along with *Zig Zag*. The complete recording of *Hottest Gong In Town* is only officially available on a record with the expensive, limited edition book *Song By George Harrison 2* from Genesis Publications.] The sixth song Harrison contributed to the film is *Twelve Bar Bali*, which isn't even listed in the credits.

Penn was angered during filming by the press hounding him and his wife, who were fighting with each other and the crew, threatening the film's completion. Harrison flew to the filming location in Hong Kong trying to resolve the situation and later held a press conference with Madonna. *Shanghai Surprise* opened on August 29, 1986 to justifiably caustic reviews despite Harrison's efforts, and was HandMade's first unintentional "disaster film." It was a personal embarrassment, as well as a financial loss, to Harrison. Though Harrison defended the couple throughout the filming, his comments were more candid following the film's failure. The documentary film *HandMade In Hong Kong* features interviews with Harrison and footage of him recording the soundtrack music. The closing credits to *Shanghai Surprise* note that the original soundtrack album is available on Dark Horse, but no album was ever issued, no doubt due to the film's lack of success. *Shanghai Surprise* was released on DVD in 2007.

Various Artists - The Celebrity Selection Of Childrens Stories

The Celebrity Selection Of Childrens Stories
Warwick-STMP 9030 (UK) (album 12") (09/01/83) **Paul McCartney: Liner Notes**

Paul and Linda McCartney* penned some liner notes on the jacket of this children's record with proceeds going to the National Society for the Prevention of Cruelty to Children.

Various Artists - Time Bandits

Time Bandits
Anchor Bay-DV 10685 (DVD) (05/11/99) (02/21/95)
Producer: Ray Cooper (music); Terry Gilliam (Producer & Director) (film)
George Harrison: Songs & Additional Material
Lee International Studios and on location in the UK & Morocco (film); CTS Studios, London (music) xx/xx/80 &/or xx/xx/81

Time Bandits (Musical Score) (M. Moran)
1 hr: 56 min.

Time Bandits, a HandMade Films Production, which co-stars John Cleese and Michael Palin, was the brainchild of Terry Gilliam (see Monty Python). The 1981 film is loosely based on *The Wizard Of Oz*. Executive Producer George Harrison contributed his song *Dream Away* (later released on his 1982 album *Gone Troppo*) to play over the film's closing credits. A six track EP, including *Dream Away* and excerpts from the film's soundtrack, was planned but never released. The film's credits list Harrison's friends Ray Cooper as the musical producer, and Mike Moran as composing and orchestrating the musical score, but they also list "songs and additional material by George Harrison." These credits would seem to indicate that Harrison's involvement in the film's musical score wasn't limited to *Dream Away*, though what additional material he contributed isn't known.

Various Artists

Without You – A Billy Fury Tribute
Peaksoft-001 (UK) (01/26/03) **Paul McCartney: Liner Notes**

Billy Fury was born Ronald Wycherley on April 17, 1940 in Liverpool, England. He was primarily a vocalist and songwriter who was one of the first internationally famous rock stars from Liverpool. He sent a tape of his songs to promoter Larry Parnes, who soon had him performing under the name Billy Fury. He had UK Top 20 hits with *Colette*, *That's Love* and *A Thousand Stars* in 1960. Parnes held auditions that year for a new backing band for a tour. Among them were The Beatles (then newly named The Silver Beetles) who Parnes instead decided to use to back Johnny Gentle (see Darren Young) on a brief tour of Scotland. In the UK between 1961 and 1964 Fury had Top Five hits with *Halfway To Paradise*, *Jealousy*, *I'd Never Find Another You*, *Last Night Was Made For Love*, *Like I've Never Been Gone*, *When Will You Say: "I Love You?"* and *In Summer*. His last UK Top 10 hit was *In Thoughts Of You* in 1965. Fury never found chart success in the US. By the mid-1960s he'd become a teen idol singing ballads and appearing in films. During the second half of the 1960s Fury, plagued by heart problems most of his life, had all but vanished from the stage and the charts. In 1973 he returned to the big screen playing Stormy Tempest in *That'll Be The Day* co-starring Ringo Starr. Fury, in poor health, recorded for Polydor Records in the early 1980s and resumed making public appearances until his death on January 28, 1983.

Following Fury's death there was a drive to have a statue of him erected in Liverpool. Among the major financial contributors was Fury's friend and fan, Paul McCartney. McCartney also contributed liner notes to the album *Without You-A Billy Fury Tribute*. For more information go to www.billyfury.com

Michael Viner's Incredible Bongo Band

Bongo Rock
Mr. Bongo Records-MRBCD043 (UK)
(01/09/06)
Producer: Michael Viner & Perry Botkin Jr.;
John Lennon: Mixing (tracks unknown)
Ringo Starr: Drums &/or Percussion; probably one or more of the following: Jim Gordon: Drums &/or Percussion; King Errisson: Percussion; Michael Viner: Percussion & Bass; Bobbye Hall: Percussion; Hal Blaine: Drums
Los Angeles, CA xx/xx/74

Kiburi (Part 1) (M. Viner-K. Johnson) 2:15 (9) (xx/xx/74)

Michael Viner was born on February 27, 1944 in Washington, District of Columbia. By the early 1970s Viner had become an executive and staff producer for MGM Records period he was responsible for signing the Osmonds and helped produce *Candy Man* and *Mr. Bojangles* for Sammy Davis, Jr. Viner and Perry Botkin, Jr. conceived the Incredible Bongo Band on a lark and recorded two tracks, which ended up on the soundtrack album to the film *The Thing With Two Heads*. The songs were later released as a single, which eventually sold over two million copies. When studios weren't booked, they recruited available musicians to record because there was no actual Incredible Bongo Band.

According to the liner notes of the 2006 album *Michael Viner's Incredible Bongo Band*, "Ringo Starr dropped by one time," Viner reveals. "He worked on *Kiburi*. And John Lennon came by too, he helped us with mixing. Glen Campbell's somewhere in there. And there was also a guy who helped us called Don Coster, who was one of the really great arrangers of our time. Harry Nilsson as well – who Perry had discovered. All sorts of people came by and helped on a few tracks. It was really like an open house." [Viner, Harry Nilsson* and Starr were friends at the time and Viner reportedly help fund their short film *Harry & Ringo's Night Out*.] The album is a compilation of their only two albums, *Bongo Rock* and *Return Of The Incredible Bongo Band*. *Bongo Rock* was recorded in Vancouver, Canada and released in 1973, probably ruling out any involvement by Ringo, and certainly ruling out Lennon's involvement as he would not have left the US then due to a deportation order he was fighting. *Return Of The Incredible Bongo Band* was recorded in Los Angeles, released in 1974, and includes *Kiburi*, so the sessions for this album are almost certainly the ones in which Lennon and Ringo participated. The extent of Lennon's mixing contributions isn't known. Other songs on the album include *When The Bed Breaks Down, I'll Meet You In The Spring*, *Sing, Sing, Sing*, *Pipeline*, *Wipe Out*, *Hang Down Your Head Tom Dooley, Your Tie's Caught In Your Zipper*, *Topsey (Parts1-3)*, *Sharp Nine*, *(I Can't Get No) Satisfaction*, *Got The Sun In The Morning And The Daughter At Night* and *Ohkey Dokey*.

The Incredible Bongo Band's recording of the song *Apache* was sampled by hip hop artists, including Grandmaster Flash in the late 1970s, leading to other recordings of theirs being used in similar fashion. *Apache* was also used in a national advertisement for a car in 2001. Michael Viner died on August 8, 2009.

Voor De Vuist Weg Band

I Gotta Blues [Ringo Starr]
Pebbles P-02005 [unauthorized release]
(xx/xx/02)
Ringo Starr: Drums; Voor De Vuist Weg House Band
Amsterdam, Netherlands 10/05/76

[Instrumental] ([unknown]) 0:33 (7)

In early fall of 1976 Ringo was in Europe promoting his album *Rotogravure* and made an appearance on the AVRO NED2 TV program *Voor De Vuist Weg* hosted by Williem Duys. Ringo was interviewed on the show, which aired the promotional videos for his songs *Hey Baby* and *You Don't Know Me At All*, and played drums with the *Voor De Vuist Weg* house band on the show's closing theme song.

Klaus Voormann (Max Buskohl)

Voormann & Friends A Sideman's Journey [Max Buskohl]
Mercury/Universal-0 60257 068060 (+ DVD) (Germany) (07/17/09)
Producer: Christina & Klaus Voormann
Blue Palm Digital Studios, Los Angeles, CA & Zara Studio, Munich, Germany† 08/04/08 & 11/22/08†
Ringo Starr: Drums; Max Buskohl: Lead Vocals†; Carl Carlton: Slide Guitar†; Grant Geissman: Guitars; Jim Keltner: Drums; Klaus Voormann: Bass; Van Dyke Parks: Keyboards; Trevor Lawrence: Saxophone

You're Sixteen (R. Sherman-R. Sherman) 2:39 (8)

Klaus Voormann was born in Berlin, Germany on April 29, 1938. He took classical piano lessons as a youngster and later pursued a career in fine arts. He, and his girlfriend Astrid Kirchherr, first met The Beatles during their engagement at the Kaiserkeller Club in Hamburg, Germany in 1960. Astrid soon fell in love with The Beatles' bass player Stuart Sutcliffe. Klaus remained friends with The Beatles, and for a time moved into their London apartment shortly after they became world famous. He, along with Liverpool musicians Patty Chambers (see The Escorts) and Gibson Kemp (see Rory Storm & The Hurricanes) formed the short-lived trio Patty, Klaus & Gibson, who were briefly signed to NEMS. The Beatles commissioned Klaus to design the cover for their 1966 album *Revolver* for which he earned a Grammy Award. That year he became the bassist for Manfred Mann (see Paul Jones) who had a Top 10 hit with Bob Dylan's* song *The Mighty Quinn* in 1968 before breaking up the following year.

Klaus Voormann, Beatlefest, Hyatt Regency Hotel O'Hare, Rosemont (Chicago), IL August 18, 2001. © and photo by Kristofer Engelhardt.

Shortly thereafter, John Lennon recruited Klaus for membership in his makeshift Plastic Ono Band, and for most of John and Yoko Ono's* recordings through 1971. He also contributed to Lennon's albums *Walls And Bridges* in 1974, *Rock 'n' Roll* in 1975 and the posthumously released *John Lennon Anthology* in 1998. Klaus contributed to all of George Harrison's albums in the first half of the 1970s (except *Dark Horse*), and designed the picture sleeve for Harrison's 1988 single *When We Was Fab.* He contributed to all of Ringo Starr's albums between 1970 and 1976 (except *Beaucoups Of Blues*) including the lithographs with the album *Ringo.* He made an appearance in the film *Son Of Dracula* starring Harry Nilsson* and Ringo. Klaus served as part-time producer and defacto studio bassist for Apple until he relocated to the US in 1973. Klaus moved into a rented house in Los Angeles with Starr and Lennon in 1974. He has denied reports that he was asked to replace Paul McCartney when he left The Beatles.

Klaus continued to do session work throughout the 1970s for many other artists including Peter Frampton*, B.B. King*, Jerry Lee Lewis*, Harry Nilsson*, Billy Preston*, Carly Simon*, James Taylor*, Gary Wright* and Cynthia Webb* before returning to Germany in 1979. During the first half of the 1980s he produced the band Trio and their international hit *Da Da Da I Don't Love You You Don't Love Me Aha Aha Aha.* By the 1990s his graphics had graced the covers of over 100 records, or books including *Hamburg Days* with Astrid Kirchherr, with input from McCartney and a forward written by Harrison. In 1995 The Beatles commissioned Klaus to handle the artwork for their *Anthology* project. Klaus took part in the Harrison tribute *Concert For George* in 2002.

In 2009 Klaus released *Voormann & Friends A Sideman's Journey*, a concept album conceived and co-produced by his wife Christina. It retraces his long musical career with new recordings he'd originally played on as a sideman or session player with some of the original artists including, among others, Dr. John*, Don Nix*, Joe Walsh* and Bonnie Bramlett (see Delaney & Bonnie & Friends), and McCartney. Klaus recalls, "One evening at the Top Ten Club in Hamburg, Stuart stuck his bass in my hand and The Beatles said, 'Come on Klaus, you play now.' I had never played the bass before. One of the songs we did was *I'm In Love Again*, and Paul played piano, which is why we chose that song [for this album]." Paul sings lead vocals and plays most of the instruments, and Klaus plays a Hofner 333 bass (the model Stuart had first given him to play) on the recording. [McCartney also covered this Fats Domino* song on his 1988 album *Choba B CCCP*.] Ringo played drums on the recording at a later date, and on his hit *You're Sixteen*. Ringo didn't want to sing on it telling Klaus that he had eliminated the song from his shows because he felt it wasn't proper for a 60-year-old man to sing about his love for a 16-year-old girl. Klaus felt it was important to also include younger musicians on the album, so he asked family friend Max Buskohl, from the German band Empty Trash, to sing it. The album also includes covers, sung by Cat Stevens (Yusuf Islam)*, of *The Day The World Gets 'Round* and *All Things Must Pass* in tribute to Harrison, and for a charity project. Portions of McCartney's and Ringo's performances also appear on the album's bonus DVD. For more information go to www.klaus-voormann.com

John Waite

Ringo Starr & His All-Starr Band Tour 2003
Warner Music Vision-R2 970326 (DVD) (09/21/04)
Producer: (Mixer: Bruce Sugar; Re-recording: Elmo Ponsdomenech & Andre Perreault);
Executive Producer: Ringo Starr & David Fishof
Ringo Starr: Drums; John Waite: Lead Vocals & Electric Guitar; Colin Hay: Electric Guitar & B. Vocals; Paul Carrack: Keyboards; Sheila Escovedo: Drums; Mark Rivera: Bass & B. Vocals
Casino Rama, Rama, Ontario Canada 07/24/03

Missing You [live] (J. Waite-M. Leonard-C. Sandford) 4:40 (12)
Additionally: John Waite: Lead Vocals (only); Sheila Escovedo: B. Vocals;
Paul Carrack: B. Vocals
[Also available on Koch-KOC-CD-9549 (12) 4:03 (03/23/04)]

When I See You Smile [live] (D. Warren) 4:48 (6)
[Also available on Koch-KOC-CD-9549 (6) (03/23/04)]

John Waite was born on July 4, 1952 in Lancaster, England. He first gained notice in 1975 as the bassist and lead vocalist for The Babys. The Babys, who had the Top 20 hit *Isn't It Time* in 1977, broke up in 1980. Waite pursued a solo career and had a number one hit with his song *Missing You* in 1984. In 1988 Waite became the lead singer of Bad English, who had the number one hit *When I See You Smile* in 1989. They broke up in 1992.

Waite was a member of Ringo Starr's All-Starr Band in 2003 performing *Missing You*, *When I See You Smile* and *Isn't It Time* with Ringo backing him on drums. Waite recalls, "Ringo and his manager decided to film the opening night's show. I was already nervous as a cat. Ringo had been my hero since I was 10 years old and was a major reason I thought I could make it out of Northwest England to play music. It meant a lot to me to play with him. I felt I owed him a great deal and didn't want to fuck up. As the lights went down, and Sheila E. counted off the opening song, *It Don't Come Easy*, I looked down at my bass, and had an out-of-body experience turning into something I didn't even recognize or understand. Where was A or D? How did I ever think I could cut it playing bass again? It was just a block of wood with wires on it! Ringo walked onstage behind me to thunderous applause and shot me a big grin. I took a deep breath and dug in. It turned out to be a great gig." Waite continues to write, record and tour. For more information go to www.johnwaite.com

The Best Of Ringo Starr And His All-Starr Band...So Far
Image-ID0828RO (DVD) (10/23/01)
Producer: Ringo Starr (music); Michael Drumm; Jim Beach & Louise Velazquez (film); Executive Producer: Ringo Starr & David Fishof
Ringo Starr: Drums; Joe Walsh: L. Vocals & E. Guitar; Todd Rundgren: Electric Guitar & B. Vocals; Burton Cummings: Keyboards; Nils Lofgren: Electric Guitar; Dave Edmunds: Electric Guitar; Timothy B. Schmit: Bass & B. Vocals; Tim Cappello: Saxophone; Zak Starkey: Drums
Montreux Jazz Festival, Montreux, Switzerland 07/13/92

Rocky Mountain Way [live] (J. Walsh-J. Vitale-K. Passarelli-S. Grace)
6:18 (6) (probably 11/xx/93)

Ringo Starr And His All-Starr Band
Pioneer Artists-PA-090-007 (LD 12") (07/xx/90)
Tim Snow (video); Joe Walsh & Jim Nipar (music); Executive Producer: Ringo Starr & David Fishof
Greek Theatre, Los Angeles, CA 09/03/89

Life In The Fast Lane [live] (G. Frey-D. Henley-J. Walsh) 6:13 (1/12)
Ringo Starr: Drums; Joe Walsh: Lead Vocals & Guitar; Billy Preston: Keyboards & B. Vocals; Jim Keltner: Drums; Levon Helm: Drums & B. Vocals; Nils Lofgren: Guitar & B. Vocals; Rick Danko: Bass & B. Vocals; Clarence Clemons: Percussion, Saxophone & B. Vocals; Dr. John: Keyboards & B. Vocals
[Also available on *Ringo Starr And His All Starr Band The Anthology...So Far.* Koch-KOC-CD-8312 (1-10) (07/24/01) (02/05/01)]

Rocky Mountain Way [live] (J. Walsh-J. Vitale-K. Passarelli-S. Grace) 8:11 (2/6)
Ringo Starr: Drums; Joe Walsh: Lead Vocals & Guitar; Billy Preston: Keyboards; Jim Keltner: Drums; Levon Helm: Harmonica; Nils Lofgren: Guitar; Rick Danko: Bass; Clarence Clemons: Saxophone; Dr. John: Keyboards
[Also available on *Ringo Starr And His All-Starr Band.* Rykodisc-RCD 90190 (RCD-10190 & RCD5-1019) (2-3) (10/12/90)]

Joseph "Joe" Walsh was born on November 20, 1947 in Wichita, Kansas. He gained fame in 1969 as the guitarist in The James Gang, who were initially rejected by Apple, but left two years later. He had several successful recordings in the early 1970s including his song *Rocky Mountain Way.* Walsh joined The Eagles in 1976. In 1978 he had a hit with his song *Life's Been Good.*

Walsh made major contributions to Ringo Starr's 1983 album *Old Wave.* He covered the song *In My Car* from the album on his 1987 album *Got Any Gum?*, though Ringo didn't contribute to Walsh's version. Joe was a member of Ringo Starr's All-Starr Band tour in 1989 performing *Life In The Fast Lane* and *Rocky Mountain Way* with Ringo backing him on drums. Joe backed Ringo singing *I Call Your Name* as a contribution to *The John Lennon Scholarship Concert* held on May 5, 1990 in Liverpool, included on the 1991 LD *The World's Greatest Artists Sing LENNON A Tribute.* Joe's 1991 album *Ordinary Average Guy* lists Ringo as one of "The Ordinary Average Guys." He didn't contribute to the album but is mentioned because of his long association with Walsh. Joe joined George Harrison onstage during his Royal Albert Hall performance in London for the Natural Law Political Party's fund-raiser on April 6, 1992. Walsh was also a member of Ringo Starr's All-Starr Band tour in 1992, again performing *Rocky Mountain Way* with Ringo on drums. That year Ringo took part in Joe's charity concert at the China Club in New York on August 27. Ringo cleared the legal path for Joe's use of a sample of The Beatles' song *A Day In The Life* on the song *Decades* in 1992. His touring with The Eagles prevented him from joining Ringo Starr's All-Starr Band tour in 1995. However, he joined them for *With A Little Help From My Friends* at the Greek Theatre in Los Angeles on August 18, and again the following night there performing *Rocky Mountain Way.* He also joined them on *Photograph* and *With A Little Help From My Friends* at Six Flags Astro World in Houston on May 25, 1997. Joe contributed to Ringo's 1998 albums *Vertical Man,* and *VH1Storytellers* as a member of Ringo's band The Roundheads. He joined Ringo Starr's All-Starr Band at the Universal Amphitheater in Los Angeles on March 18, 2009 on *With A Little Help From My Friends.* Walsh also contributed to Ringo's 2010 album *Y Not.* He is married to Marjorie Bach, the sister of Ringo's wife Barbara. Joe Walsh remains a member of The Eagles, who were inducted into the Rock and Roll Hall of Fame in 1998, while maintaining a career as a solo artist, producer, songwriter and session player. For more information go to www.joewalsh.com

Cynthia Webb

[None]
[Unreleased]
Producer: Klaus Voormann & Cynthia Webb
Ringo Starr: Drums; Cynthia Webb: Lead Vocals & Piano; Klaus Voormann: Bass
Stronghold & Jimmy Webb's home studio, Los Angeles, CA 11-12/xx/74 & spring/xx/75

Changing (C. Webb)
Additionally: Lon Van Eaton: Guitar

Dream Baby (C. Webb)

I Am Sorry (C. Webb)
Additionally: Lon Van Eaton: Guitar

Let Go Of Love (C. Webb)
Additionally: Cynthia Webb: Lead Vocals (only); Gary Wright: (possible) Piano; Lon Van Eaton: Guitar

Secret (C. Webb)
Additionally: Gary Wright: (possible) Electric Piano

Take Your Love (C. Webb)

Window Blues (C. Webb)
Additionally: Klaus Voormann: Guitar

Cynthia Webb was born in 1943 and raised in the Los Angeles, California area. Her mother was a teacher who encouraged her interest in fine arts. As a child she studied dance, violin and piano. Cynthia wrote poems and put them to melodies she created as she grew older. In the mid-1960s Webb was performing in well-known rock clubs in the Los Angeles area.

Cynthia moved to the UK in the mid-1960s and later there formed a folk-rock trio with Karen Harvey and Nicole Tacot. George Harrison and Tony Meehan produced some demos of them for possible release on Apple, but Webb says nothing ever developed beyond that. Webb returned to the US in the early 1970s and met Klaus Voormann*. Being with Klaus put her in the company of George Harrison again, and John Lennon and Ringo Starr. In 1974 Webb contributed backing vocals to Ringo's album *Goodnight Vienna* and played maracas on Harry Nilsson's* album *Pussy Cats* produced by Lennon. Between the winter of 1974 and spring of 1975 Webb made some recordings with contributions from Ringo, Lon & Derrek Van Eaton*, Klaus and others, which remain unreleased. Cynthia and Klaus had a son, Otto born in 1975 but separated in the early 1980s. She continued to work in the entertainment and film industry until her retirement.

Jimmy Webb

Land's End
Collectors' Choice- CCM-06612 (04/04/06) (06/03/74)
Producer: Jimmy Webb
Ringo Starr: Drums; Jimmy Webb: Lead Vocals & Piano; Tom Scott: Saxophone; Fred Tackett: Guitar; Dee Murray: Bass
Trident Studios, London, UK 07-08 or fall/xx/73

Alyce Blue Gown (J. Webb) 4:58 (8)

Jimmy Webb was born August 15, 1946 in Elk City, Oklahoma. His father was a minister. With musical encouragement from his mother, he was playing keyboards in his father's church by the age of 12. Jimmy has worked as a producer and arranger, but he's primarily known as the songwriter of such hits as Glen Campbell's *By The Time I Get To Phoenix*, *Wichita Lineman* and *Galveston*, The 5th Dimension's *Up-Up And Away* and Richard Harris's *MacArthur Park*. His compositions have also been recorded by such diverse talents as Johnny Cash*, Joe Cocker*, The Everly Brothers* and Toto*.

By the 1970s Webb was recording his compositions, and released several solo albums, including *Land's End* recorded in London with help from Ringo Starr on one song. According to Webb, Ringo's involvement was the result of their mutual friendship with Harry Nilsson*. Webb recalls, "I was thrilled at the sight of Ringo and his drum kit in Trident Studio. I'd first met The Beatles there when they were recording their 'white' album [*The Beatles*]." Webb has vivid memories of the session because Ringo told him he hadn't played drums for a while, and the sound engineer felt the drums needed additional tuning and spent hours with Ringo trying to get the right sound. Meanwhile, Webb says he engaged Ringo in conversation fearing he would become discouraged and leave, but he says, "Ringo laid down the album's best sounding drum track on *Alyce Blue Gown*." Months later, Webb was hanging out with John Lennon, and Ringo who told him the drum tuning incident had shaken his confidence and intimidated him. Webb says he occasionally bumped into George Harrison at A&M Studios, and was a guest at several of Paul McCartney's parties, including the one held on the ocean liner Queen Mary in 1975. The Beatles' producer George Martin* has also worked with Webb. Jimmy Webb has been a Member of the Board of Directors of the Songwriter's Hall of Fame, and ASCAP. He continues to write, record and tour. For more information go to www.jimmywebb.com

Bobby Whitlock

Bobby Whitlock
Dunhill/ABC-DSX 50121 (12" album) (xx/xx/72) (07/xx/71)
Producer: Bobby Whitlock & Andy Johns
Olympic Studios, London, UK 01/xx/71

A Day Without Jesus (B. Whitlock-D. Nix) 3:22 (1/5)
George Harrison: Guitar; Bobby Whitlock: Lead Vocals & Keyboards; Carl Radle: Bass; Jim Gordon: Drums; Eric Clapton: Guitar; Delaney Bramlett: B. Vocals; Bonnie Bramlett: B. Vocals

Back In My Life Again (B. Whitlock) 3:30 (2/1)
George Harrison: Guitar; Bobby Whitlock: Lead Vocals & Keyboards; Eric Clapton: Guitar; Carl Radle: Bass; Jim Price: Horns; Bobby Keys: Saxophone; Jim Gordon: Drums

Where There's A Will There's A Way (B. Whitlock-B. Bramlett) 3:43 (1/1)
George Harrison: Guitar; Bobby Whitlock: Lead Vocals & Keyboards; Carl Radle: Bass; Jim Gordon: Drums; Eric Clapton: Guitar; Bobby Keys: Saxophone; Jim Price: Horns

Bobby Whitlock was born on March 18, 1948 in Memphis, Tennessee. He was playing piano on sessions at Stax Studios while still a teenager. Bobby was a member of Delaney & Bonnie & Friends* in the late 1960s. In 1970 he became a member of Derek And The Dominos*, who contributed to George Harrison's album *All Things Must Pass.*

Advertisements for the 1971 album *Bobby Whitlock* list Harrison as a contributor. Several of the songs from it, and Whitlock's album *Raw Velvet*, are essentially Derek And The Dominos tracks with Bobby on lead vocals. In Marc Roberty's book *Eric Clapton The Complete Recording Sessions 1963 – 1992* he lists Clapton as playing on the Whitlock tracks *Where There's A Will There's A Way*, *A Day Without Jesus*, *Back In My Life Again*, *The Scenery Has Slowly Changed*, *The Dreams Of A Hobo* and *Hello L.A., Bye-Bye-Birmingham* recorded at Olympic Studios in January 1971. Harrison is listed among the musicians but it isn't clear if he play on every song. To the best of Bobby's recollection, Harrison only plays on his recordings of *Where There's A Will There's A Way*, *A Day Without Jesus* and *Back In My Life Again*. He says Don Nix* didn't help him write *A Day Without Jesus* as credited. Whitlock continues to write, record and tour. For more information go to www.bobbywhitlock.com

John Williams

Filmtracks - The Best Of British Film Music
[Various Artists]
London-820 252-2 (820 253-2) (Germany) (07/xx/85) (12/19/83)
Producer: [Paul McCartney] Stanley Myers & Richard Harvey
Paul McCartney: Guitar; John Williams: Guitar
Olympic Studios, London, UK xx/xx/83

Paul McCartney's Theme From The Film "The Honorary Consul" (**P. McCartney**) 3:44 (1-2)

John Williams was born on April 24, 1941 in Melbourne, Australia. His father Leonard was a respected jazz guitarist. He bought John a guitar when he was four years old and taught him to play. Years later, John attended courses with Andres Segovia and studied at the Royal College of Music in London. He has become one of the world's most renowned classical guitarist, and prolific recording artists. He has collaborated with Julian Bream, Itzhak Perlman, Andre Previn, Cleo Laine, John Dankworth, Daniel Barenboim, and many pop musicians. *Travelling* and *Bridges* were UK Top 20 hit albums for him in the late 1970s. In 1979 he helped form the classical-jazz-rock fusion, instrumental group Sky, whose first four albums were also UK Top 20 hits. George Martin* produced John's 1998 cover of George Harrison's Beatles' song *Here Comes The Sun*.

Williams performed Paul McCartney's instrumental title theme for the 1984 film *The Honorary Consul* (a.k.a. *Beyond The Limit*). The film was directed by John McKenzie, who also directed the promotional video for Paul's song *Take It Away*, and was probably responsible for his contributing the theme. According to McCartney's fan club magazine *Club Sandwich* (Autumn 1993 issue No. 67) he also produced John's recording, and in Paul's 1989 World Tour Program, he states he also played guitar on it. Paul's demo and several takes by John with Paul's count-in are available on unauthorized releases. For more information go to www.johnwilliamsguitar.com

Nicol Williamson

Nicol Williamson was born on September 14, 1938 in Hamilton, Scotland. He is an accomplished Shakespearean actor who has appeared in many films including *Excalibur*, *The Goodbye Girl*, *I'm Dancing As Fast As I Can*, *Exorcist III*, and on TV, including an episode of *Columbo*.

According to keyboardist Roy Young (see Cliff Bennett And The Rebel Rousers, Tony Sheridan) he, George Harrison on guitar, Ringo Starr on drums, Klaus Voormann* on bass and Eric Clapton* on guitar, backed Nicol on his recordings of rock standards like *Shakin' All Over* and *Be-Bop-A-Lula* in London in the early 1970s. Young doesn't recall much about the festive sessions except that the results weren't suitable for release. Nicol, who was a good friend of Ringo's then recalls, "We did *All Shook Up* but I can't remember what else we recorded. George was not there, but Eric, Ringo, Roy and Klaus were there. It was a lot of fun. The stuff we did was pretty good as I recall, but I was recording a mixture of stuff for CBS. I was just having fun and dabbling in many different projects at the time. CBS wanted to do it. I was the 'hot' actor at the moment, but there was no real push or drive behind it. I did have a record with those recordings on it somewhere, probably a test pressing, but I don't know where it is now." Nicol thinks as many as five songs were recorded with Ringo. He says the songs were considered for his 1971 CBS album *Nicol Williamson*, which contains mostly orchestrated, easy listening music, but that none of them were ever used for any of his releases because they didn't fit in with the other material. For more information go to www.nicolwilliamson.com

Brian Wilson

Adopt-A-Minefield Live [Paul McCartney]
Birthday Records-BR-110 [unauthorized release] (xx/xx/04)
Paul McCartney: Duet Vocals; Brian Wilson: Duet Vocals & Keyboards; Jeffrey Foskett: Guitar & B. Vocals; Bob Lizik: Bass; Jim Hines: Drums & B. Vocals; Scott Bennett: Keyboards & Vocals; Paul Mertens: Horns; Taylor Mills: B. Vocals & Percussion; Darian Sahanaja: Keyboards & B. Vocals; Nick Walusko: Guitar & B. Vocals; Probyn Gregory: Guitar, Horns, Keyboards & B. Vocals
Century Plaza Hotel, Los Angeles, CA 09/18/02
God Only Knows [live] (B. Wilson-T. Asher) 3:57 (10)

Gettin' In Over My Head
Brimel/Rhino/Warner-R2 76471 (06/22/04)
Producer: Brian Wilson
Paul McCartney: Vocals & Acoustic Guitar†; Brian Wilson: Vocals & Piano; Carol Robbins: Harp; Paul Mertens: Saxophone & Harmonicas; Todd Sucherman: Drums & Percussion; Darian Sahanaja: Keyboards; Scott Bennett: Keyboards & Vibes; Amy Farris: Viola; Jeffrey Foskett: Guitar; Probyn Gregory: Guitar; Susan Jensen: Violin; Peter Kent: String Contractor & Violin; Bob Lizik: Bass; Michael Rhodes: Bass; Nick

Kristofer Engelhardt and Brian Wilson, Borders Books Novi (Detroit), Michigan November 1991. Photo by Mark Witzke, ©Kristofer Engelhardt.

Walusko: Guitar
Your Place Or Mine Recording & Cello Studio 2†, Los Angeles, CA 09/xx/03

A Friend Like You (B. Wilson-S. Kolinich) 3:37 (7)

Brian Wilson was born in Hawthorne (Los Angeles), California on June 20, 1942. He gained fame as the gifted songwriter, producer, bass player, keyboardist and falsetto singer of The Beach Boys*. In 1965, after several years of dizzying success and constant work, Brian suffered a nervous breakdown. He stopped touring with The Beach Boys to concentrate on songwriting, recording and side projects. Feeling competitive pressure from groups such as The Beatles, he attempted to outdo The Beach Boys' critically acclaimed 1966 album *Pet Sounds* with an elaborate concept album called *Smile* but abandoned the project shortly before its completion. His mental and physical health deteriorated, and he continued to withdraw from The Beach Boys and the public. During the latter half of the 1970s therapist Eugene Landy had some success in rehabilitating and returning Brian to his former role in The Beach Boys, but by 1983 his condition had worsened and Landy was again hired to intervene. He improved and in 1988 released his first solo album, *Brian Wilson*. However, Landy became so controlling of Wilson's personal and professional life that it required a court order in 1991 to end his involvement.

Brian contributed backing vocals to Ringo Starr's 1992 album *Time Takes Time*. That year Brian appeared in the TV documentary *The Making Of Sgt. Pepper* on The Beatles' 1967 album. He made a guest appearance on Paul McCartney's 1995 radio series *Oobu Joobu* performing a brief rendition of *Hey Jude*. Paul was thanked in the credits of the 1995 Brian Wilson retrospective film *I Just Wasn't Made For These Times*, though he didn't contribute to it or the soundtrack album. Brian says, "I thanked him for the inspiration, and his energy and enthusiasm about music — it's very contagious — it rubbed off on me." Brian and Ringo sang *Barbara Ann* at a birthday party for Ringo's wife Barbara on August 26, 1996. Brian contributed to Ringo's 1998 album *Vertical Man*. A promotional sampler of Brian's 1998 album *Imagination* includes an interview of him conducted by John Lennon and Yoko Ono's* son Sean.

Brian, who'd long disliked touring, began touring again in 1998 and released several live albums. On June 15, 2000 McCartney inducted Brian into the Songwriters Hall of Fame, which is included on the 2003 DVD *Brian Wilson On Tour* (Sanctuary-060768834897). Brian said being inducted by McCartney was the highest honor he'd ever had. On February 20, 2004 Brian premiered the *Smile* album (which he finally completed and released) at London's Royal Festival Hall with McCartney in attendance. The performance was released on the 2005 DVD *Smile* (Rhino-603497041527), which also includes the documentary *Beautiful Dreamer* with a cameo by McCartney.

Brian released the album *Gettin' In Over My Head* in 2004, which includes contributions from Eric Clapton*, Elton John* and McCartney. The album's cover art was done by Peter Blake who also did the cover for The Beatles' *Sgt. Pepper's Lonely Hearts Club Band* album. Quoting David Leaf from the album's liner notes: "*A Friend Like You* was written by Brian after he and Paul McCartney had spent time together at the Landmine Benefit [Paul sang *God Only Knows* with Brian, and Brian sang with Paul on *Let It Be* at the Adopt-A-Minefield gala at the Century Plaza Hotel in Los Angeles on September 18, 2002, which are available on unauthorized releases.], and backstage and onstage at the *Queens Jubilee* (the highlight of that event for me being the rehearsal of *All You Need Is Love* with just Sir Paul, Eric [Clapton], and Brian, who was seated at Paul's magic piano). Brian wrote this song out of his feelings for his friend, and Paul graciously and gracefully added a beautiful vocal on the chorus. At long last—Brian and Paul ... born two days apart ... the bass-playing melodic geniuses of their respective groups ... were on the same record." Wilson was reported to say that McCartney got it in three takes and that working with him was cool. Brian hasn't interacted much with The Beach Boys since the mid-1990s. He continues to tour and record with his band. He has also recorded with his daughters Wendy and Carnie, who along with Chynna Phillips (daughter of John and Michelle Phillips of the Mamas & the Papas) were part of the successful singing trio, Wilson Phillips in the early 1990s. For more information go to www.brianwilson.com

Mary Wilson

Together At The Rock And Roll Hall Of Fame [Various Artists]
Living Legend-LLRCD 101(Italy) [unauthorized release] (xx/xx/93)
Producer: [unknown]
George Harrison: (probable) Guitar & (probable) B. Vocals; Mary Wilson: Lead Vocals; Yoko Ono: B. Vocals; Mick Jagger: B. Vocals; probably one or more of the following: Paul Shaffer: Keyboards; Billy Joel: Keyboards & Vocals; Ben E. King: B. Vocals & Handclaps; Al Jardine: Guitar &/or Handclaps; Mike Love: Percussion; Bruce Johnston: Handclaps; Bruce Springsteen: Percussion; Little Richard: Handclaps; Elton John: Keyboards; Anton Fig: Drums; Bob Dylan: Electric Guitar; Dave Edmunds: Electric Guitar; Les Paul: Electric Guitar; Jeff Beck: Electric Guitar; Carl Wilson: Handclaps; Brian Wilson: Handclaps; Sean Lennon: Handclaps; Sid McGinnis: Guitar; John Fogerty: Electric Guitar; Arlo Guthrie: Handclaps &/or Guitar; Peter Wolf: Handclaps; Johnny Moore: Handclaps; Joe Blunt: Handclaps; Clyde Brown: Handclaps; Julian Lennon: Handclaps; Bill Pinkney: Handclaps; Charlie Thomas: Handclaps; Max Weinberg: Percussion; Will Lee: Bass; Roy Bittan: Keyboards; Nile Rodgers: Guitar; Patti Scialfa: Handclaps & B. Vocals
Grand Ballroom Waldorf-Astoria Hotel, New York, NY 01/20/88

Stop! In The Name Of Love [live] (L. Dozier-B. Holland-E. Holland) 3:22 (7)

Mary Wilson was born on March 6, 1944 in Greenville, Mississippi. Her family relocated to Detroit, Michigan in 1950. In 1959 she and fellow schoolmate Florence Ballard were recruited by The Primes (who later evolved into The Temptations) for a female version of them called The Primettes, along with Diana Ross and Betty McGlown. By1961 Betty had left the group, who was signed to Detroit's Motown Records and renamed The Supremes. They struggled in the charts until 1964 but within a year they had racked up consecutive number one hits with *Where Did Our Love Go*, *Baby Love*, *Come See*

Mary Wilson, Veterans Memorial Park, Bay City, MI August 6, 2004.
© and photo by Kristofer Engelhardt.

About Me, *Stop! In The Name Of Love* and *Back In My Arms Again*. They also had consecutive number one hits with *I Hear A Symphony*, *You Can't Hurry Love*, *You Keep Me Hangin' On*, *Love Is Here And Now You're Gone* and *The Happening* between 1965 and 1967. All of these number one hits were composed by the legendary songwriting team of Lamont Dozier, and brothers Brian and Edward Holland, Jr. In 1967 the group became known as Diana Ross & The Supremes, and Ballard was replaced by Cindy Birdsong. They had number one hits with *Love Child* in 1968, and the ironic *Someday We'll Be Together* in 1969 as Ross soon left the group for a successful solo career and the original members would never perform together again. Jean Terrell replaced Ross, and Wilson, the only original member, assumed leadership of the group who again became known as The Supremes. In 1970 they had Top 10 hits with *Up The Ladder To The Roof* and *Stoned Love*. Their final Top 20 hit was *Floy Joy* in 1972.

Since the group's breakup in 1977 Wilson has released several albums and singles, toured extensively, starred in a number of stage musicals, done motivational speaking, and has been recognized for her charitable work. Having battled over the rights to use The Supremes' name, and an advocate for the group's legacy, she has become active in the passage of legislation to protect the rights of artists. Mary has also written the best-selling books *Dreamgirl: My Life As A Supreme* and *Supreme Faith: Someday We'll Be Together.*

The Supremes were inducted into the Rock and Roll Hall of Fame in 1987 along with The Beatles, who were represented by Ringo Starr, George Harrison and Yoko Ono*. Mary was the only original member of The Supremes to attend the induction ceremonies. She was onstage for the entire ending jam session with the other inductees and guests, and performed *Stop! In The Name Of Love*. She recalls Harrison being onstage during her performance but isn't sure if he played guitar, but seems fairly sure Ringo was off stage at the time. She laments, "It was one of the most embarrassing moments of my life because I didn't know Paul Shaffer* was going play the song in the key Diana Ross sang it in on the record, which made it difficult for me to sing." Mary Wilson continues to record and tour. For more information go to www.marywilson.com

Edgar Winter

Ringo Starr & His All Starr Band Live 2006
Koch-KOC-DV-4543 (DVD) (07/08/08)
Producer: Brent Carpenter; Ringo Starr Executive Producer
Ringo Starr: Drums; Edgar Winter: Lead Vocals & Keyboards; Rod Argent: Keyboards & B. Vocals; Sheila Escovedo: Drums & B. Vocals; Richard Marx: Electric Guitar; Billy Squier: Electric Guitar; Hamish Stuart: Bass
Mohegan Sun, Uncasville, CT 07/16/06

Free Ride [live] (D. Hartman) 4:41 (6)
[Also available on *Ringo Starr and his All Starr Band 2006*. Koch-KOC-CD-4542-2 (5) (07/08/08)]

Edgar Winter was born on December 28, 1946 in Beaumont, Texas. His parents were musicians. He, and his brother Johnny Winter*, had an interest in music as youngsters. Edgar became an

Kristofer Engelhardt and Edgar Winter, Soaring Eagle Casino, Mt. Pleasant, MI December 28, 2007. © Kristofer Engelhardt.

accomplished instrumentalist, particularly on keyboards, saxophone and percussion. The brothers were greatly influenced by The Beatles and frequently performed their songs. Edgar formed the group White Trash in 1971 who released two albums. In 1972 he formed the Edgar Winter Group. Their 1973 Multi-Platinum certified album *They Only Come Out At Night* pioneered the use of the synthesizer as the lead instrument on the song *Frankenstein* that topped the charts. The album also includes the Top 20 hit *Free Ride*.

Winter was a member of Ringo Starr's All-Starr Band in 2006 and 2008. Edgar recalls, "I don't know how or why I was initially chosen, but you do have to have several recognizable hits to be considered. In my case they were *Frankenstein* and *Free Ride*. When my manager called me and asked if I was up for the Ringo tour I said, 'Oh, man am I ever!' I'd always wanted to be in the All-Starr Band because it's such a cool concept. Because I had other dates booked, I told my manager, 'Do what you have to do, but I want to be on that tour!'

"I'd never met Ringo before the 2006 tour. Ringo set the tone by making everyone feel very comfortable and rehearsing us on the stage at the remote Casino Rama, north of Toronto, where we were to open the tour. That was a very intelligent way to start things out. The best leader is one who leads by example and that's what Ringo did. He was there to have fun, but he was also serious about it and played with us all of the time. He scheduled plenty of time to rehearse – nine to six with a break for lunch — for about 12 days, and made everybody feel like it was normal. He wanted it to be good. The group's musical diversity made it interesting and better. Everyone was very supportive of each other and checked their egos at the door. Much of that is due to the way Ringo handles things. Both bands more than rose to the task on *Frankenstein*, which is complex. I performed several other songs including *Free Ride*, the only song of mine on which Ringo played drums.

"I would wake up each morning on the tour and think, "Wow! Tonight I'm going to be playing with one of The Beatles — my musical heroes — along with other great people in the band. Ringo was so humorous. It's one of the most positive and fun things I've ever done with a group of celebrity players. Everybody loved it. I was so inspired working with Ringo that I wrote and recorded the song *Peace And Love* [a favorite expression of Ringo's], and dedicated it to him and the other Beatles. Playing with Ringo is hard to explain because The Beatles meant so much to me. They wrote about everything – from *Help!* to *Revolution* and made us think, wonder, dream and believe. They opened us up to possibilities of freedom and change as they changed, and took us with them. They changed my life. They're in a musical category unto themselves — the greatest band in the world!" Winter contributed to Ringo's 2010 album *Y Not*. Edgar continues to write, record and tour. For more information go to www.edgarwinter.com

Johnny Winter

Saints & Sinners-John Dawson Winter III
BGO/BGOCD766 (UK) (09/18/07)
Producer: Shelly Yakus
Johnny Winter: Lead Vocals & Guitar; Randy Jo Hobbs: Bass & Percussion; Richard Hughes: Drums & Percussion
Record Plant Studios, New York, NY probably 08-09/xx/74

Rock & Roll People (J. Lennon) 2:44 (12) (11/25/74)

John Dawson Winter III was born on February 23, 1944 in Beaumont, Texas. His parents were musicians. He, and his brother Edgar Winter*, had an interest in blues and rock music as youngsters. By the late 1960s both had become rock stars.

The 1974 album *John Dawson Winter III* includes the John Lennon composition *Rock & Roll People*. The album was recorded at Record Plant Studios in New York and produced by Shelly Yakus, who helped engineer many of Lennon's recordings at that studio. Yakus felt that Lennon's then unreleased song *Rock & Roll People* (recorded during sessions for Lennon's album *Mind Games*) was perfect for Winter, and Lennon agreed. Johnny recalls, "John and I were recording at the same studio. My manager asked him if he had anything we could use. He played us a tape of *Rock & Roll People*, which I really liked and recorded. John liked my recording of it." Lennon's recording of *Rock & Roll People* appears on his posthumous album *Menlove Ave* released in 1986. Johnny Winter continues to write, record and tour. For more information go to www.johnnywinter.net

Stevie Wonder

A Time To Love
Motown-B0002402-02 (10/18/05)
Producer: Stevie Wonder
Paul McCartney: Acoustic & Electric Guitar†; Stevie Wonder: Piano, Moog Bass & Drums; Francis Awe: Talking Drum; Swapan Chaudhuri: Tabla; Richie Gajate-Garcia: Congas & Hand Percussion; D. Munyungo Jackson: Tan Tan, Shekere & Hand Percussion; Abbos Kosimov: Doira; Amir Sofi: Darbuka/Arbic Tabla; Jeffery Coprich: Leader of The Los Angeles Inner City Mass Choir (Joy Carter, Ayranna Cerant, Brianna Ford, Anthony Gates, Daronn Gooden, Timothy Hall, Accalra Johnson, Unique Johnson, Chatoya Jones, Jabbarri Jones, Jamelle Jones, Brijee McDowell, Midori Norris, Sherman B. Wilson, Lalynda Winfield, LaShanea Winfield, LaShanique Winfield, Johniesha White, Joshlyn White & Sebastian Mego); Rob Arbittier: Drums & Digital Editing; Rickey Minor: String Arrangement & Orchestra Supervisor; Andy Weiner: String Arrangement & Orchestra Conducting
London, UK†; Westlake Recording, O'Henry & Wonderland Studios, Los Angeles, CA probably xx/xx/03 or 04

A Time To Love (S. Wonder-I. Arie) 9:16 (15)

A Toot And A Snore In '74
Mistral Music-MM9225 [unauthorized release] (xx/xx/92)
John Lennon: Guitar & Dialogue; Paul McCartney: Drums & B. Vocals; Stevie Wonder: Lead Vocals & Keyboards; Linda McCartney: Keyboards; May Pang &/or Mal Evans: Tambourine; Jesse Ed Davis: Guitar; Harry Nilsson: B. Vocals; Ed Freeman: Bass; Bobby Keys: Saxophone; Danny Kortchmar: Guitar
Burbank Studios, Los Angeles, CA 03/28/74

Medley: Cupid/Chain Gang/Take This Hammer (S. Cooke-C. Cooke/S. Cooke/trad.) 3:10 (9)

Stevie Wonder was born Steveland Hardaway Judkins (later changed to Morris – his mother's maiden name) on May 13, 1950 in Saginaw, Michigan but grew up in Detroit, Michigan. He became blind soon after birth. By the age of 10 he was proficient on piano, harmonica and drums. He was signed to Detroit's burgeoning Motown Records and billed as Little Stevie Wonder, the 12-year-old genius on the harmonica. In 1963 he had his first of many number one hits with *Fingertips (Pt. 2)*. Since that time, he's had over 30 Top 10 hits, nine of which topped the charts, 150 million album units sold and two dozen Grammy Awards. Some of his many hits include *Uptight (Everything's Alright)*, *I Was Made To Love Her*, *For Once In My Life*, *My Cherie Amour*, *Signed, Sealed, Delivered I'm Yours*, *Superstition*, *You Are The Sunshine Of My Life*, *I Wish*, *Sir Duke*, *I Just Called To Say I Love You* and *Part-Time Lover*. He also had a Top 20 hit with a cover of The Beatles' song *We Can Work It Out* in 1971. Wonder has worked with many artists including The Beach Boys*, Carly Simon*, James Taylor*, Tony Bennett*, Elton John*, Billy Preston*, Rod Stewart and Michael Jackson*.

All of The Beatles greatly admired Stevie Wonder. He was on the bill at the *John Sinclair Freedom Rally* benefit concert headlined by John Lennon and Yoko Ono* on December 10, 1971, and again on August 30, 1972 at their *One To One* benefit concerts and joined them during their encore of *Give Peace A Chance*. On the back of Paul McCartney and Wings' 1973 album *Red Rose Speedway* was a message of love in brail reportedly to Wonder. On March 28, 1974 Wonder took part in a late night jam with Lennon and McCartney at Burbank Studios in Los Angeles where Lennon was producing the album *Pussy Cats* for Harry Nilsson*. The recordings are available on the unauthorized release *A Toot And A Snore In '74*. Wonder sang a medley of *Cupid/Chain Gang/Take This Hammer*. In February 1981 McCartney invited Wonder to Montserrat where he was recording his album *Tug Of War*. The results were a song Paul and Stevie wrote and played on called *What's That You're Doing?*, and Stevie's duet vocals and keyboards on the number one hit *Ebony And Ivory*, which McCartney wrote about racial harmony. The two also appeared in the video for the song. McCartney provided a videotaped introduction of Wonder on ABC TV's American Music Awards on January 25, 1982. In the liner notes of Wonder's 2005 album *A Time To Love* he says, "To Sir Paul – I called and you answered; you call and I'll forever be there!" McCartney overdubbed some guitar for the album's title track in the UK.

Wonder was inducted into the Rock and Roll Hall of Fame in 1989. He performed Lennon's song *Imagine* during the closing ceremony of the 1996 Olympic Games in Atlanta, Georgia. Stevie Wonder is still touring, writing, recording and producing for Motown. For more information go to www.steviewonder.net

Ron Wood (The New Barbarians)

I've Got My Own Album To Do
Warner Bros.-2-45692 (09/13/94) (09/23/74)

Far East Man (**G. Harrison**-R. Wood) 4:40 (2)
Producer: Ron Wood & Gary Kellgren
George Harrison: Guitar & B. Vocals; Ron Wood: Lead Vocals & Guitar; Willie Weeks: Bass; Ian McLagan: Keyboards; Jean Rousseu: Keyboards; Andy Newmark: Drums
FPSHOT, UK 10/xx/73

Take A Look At The Guy ([possibly P. McCartney] R. Wood) 2:33 (4)
Producer: probably **Paul McCartney**, Ron Wood & Gary Kellgren
Ron Wood: Lead Vocals & (probable) Guitar; probably one or more of the following: Rod Stewart: B. Vocals; Willie Weeks: Bass; Ian McLagan: Keyboards; Andy Newmark: Drums; **Paul McCartney: (possible) B. Vocals**
The Wick (Ron Wood's home studio), Richmond Hill, UK 07/xx/74

With A Little Help To My Friends (The New Barbarians*) [Ringo Starr]
No Label Records-NLR 9904 (CD-R) [unauthorized release] (xx/xx/99)
Producer: Burt Sugarman
Ringo Starr: Drums; Ron Wood: Lead Vocals & Guitar; Pops Powell: Bass; Ian McLagan: Keyboards & B. Vocals; Bobby Keys: Saxophone
NBC TV Studios, Burbank, CA airdate: 06/08/79

Buried Alive [live] (R. Wood) 4:39 (1)

Ronald "Ronnie" Wood was born on June 1, 1947 in London, England. He began his music career as a guitarist in The Birds, before joining Rod Stewart* in the Jeff Beck Group. In June 1969 he joined The Faces, which had formed from the Small Faces (see Kenney Jones, Ian McLagan). In April 1975 The Rolling Stones* asked Wood to fill in for the departed Mick Taylor on their tour. By the end of the year, The Faces had disintegrated and Wood became a permanent member of The Rolling Stones.

When preparing his first solo album *I've Got My Own Album To Do* in 1974 Wood asked George Harrison to help him finish the lyrics to the song *Far East Man* on which the two had previously worked. Harrison came up with some lyrics on his way to Wood's home, and wrote the middle eight and more lyrics during the song's rehearsal. In the June 21, 1996 issue of *Goldmine* magazine, Ian McLagan claims that he also helped write *Far East Man* but Wood discounts this. Though un-credited, Harrison also shares the vocals and guitar work on *Far East Man.* Harrison's involvement was largely ignored when he released his version of *Far East Man* a short time later on his album *Dark Horse* to which Wood also contributed. Wood says, "Paul McCartney helped shape up the song *Take A Look At The Guy* on *I Got My Own Album To Do.*" He didn't elaborate on the shaping up but it likely involves production, composition or possibly performing on it.

Wood says none of The Beatles contributed to his 1979 album *Gimme Some Neck*. Ringo did play drums with Wood's band The New Barbarians during their performance of *Buried Alive* from *Gimme Some Neck* on NBC TV's *Midnight Special* in 1979, which is available on unauthorized releases. Wood contributed to Ringo's 1981 album *Stop And Smell The Roses*. Wood maintains a solo career and membership in The Rolling Stones. For more information go to www.ronniewood.com

Gary Wright

Benjamin (The Original Soundtrack Of Willy Bogner's Motion Picture)
Ariola-C 86 405 IT (12" album) (Germany) (xx/xx/72)
Producer: Gary Wright
George Harrison: Guitar; Gary Wright: Lead Vocals & Keyboards; Mick Jones: Guitar; Bryson Graham: Drums; Tom Duffy: Bass
Probably Apple Studios or possibly Olympic Studios London, UK xx/xx/72

Goodbye Sunday (G. Wright) 2:59 (1/1)

The Best Of The Dream Weaver
Warner Archives/Rhino-R2 75565 (09/15/98)

Stand For Our Rights (G. Wright) 3:32 (3) (05/28/71)
Producer: [George Harrison] & Gary Wright
George Harrison: Guitar; Gary Wright: Lead Vocals; Jim Keltner: Drums; Jim Gordon: Drums;

Hugh McCracken: Guitar; Jerry Donahue: Guitar; Klaus Voormann: Bass; King Curtis: Saxophone†; Bobby Keys: Tenor Saxophone; Jim Price: Trumpet & Trombone; Doris Troy: B. Vocals; Nannette Workman: B. Vocals; Madeline Bell: B. Vocals; Barry St. John: B. Vocals; Pat Arnold: B. Vocals; Liza Strike: B. Vocals; Jimmy Thomas: B. Vocals; Colin Allen: Percussion; Alan White: Percussion; Nicky Hopkins: (possible) Harpsichord
Olympic Studios, London, UK & New York, NY†
probably 04-05/xx/71

Two Faced Man (G. Wright) 3:40 (4) (11/01/71)
Producer: Gary Wright
George Harrison: Slide Guitar; Gary Wright: Lead Vocals & Keyboards; Alan White: Drums; Hugh McCracken: Guitar; Klaus Voormann: Bass; John Barham: String Arrangements
Olympic Studios, London, UK xx/xx/70 &/or xx/xx/71

The Dick Cavett Show/Rock Icons
Shout!/Sony BMG-D3D 33030 (DVD) (08/01/06)
Producer: Judy Englander
George Harrison: Slide Guitar; Gary Wright: Lead Vocals & Acoustic Guitar; Mick Jones: Electric Guitar & B. Vocals; Bryson Graham: Drums; Archie Legget: Bass
ABC TV Studios, New York, NY 11/23/71

Two Faced Man [live] (G. Wright) 3:49 (3-2)

First Signs Of Life
Acadia-ACAM 8153 (+DVD) (UK) (05/28/07) (04/25/95)
Producer: Gary Wright
George Harrison: B. Vocals; Gary Wright: Lead Vocals & Keyboards; Terry Bozzio: Drums; Jimmy Haslip: Bass; Steve Farris: Guitar
High Wave Studios, Los Angeles, CA 07/xx/94

Don't Try To Own Me (G. Wright-D. Hitchings) 4:18 (1-6)

Who I Am
Cypress-YD0111/DIDX 003275 (09/21/88)
Producer: Wyn Davis & Gary Wright
George Harrison: Solo Guitar; Gary Wright: Lead Vocals, Keyboards & Arrangement; Steve Farris: Rhythm Guitar; Bruce Gaitsch: Arrangement & Rhythm Guitar; Jimmy Johnson: Bass; Terry Bozzio: Drum Machine Programming; Mindy Lee: B. Vocals
High Wave Studios, Los Angeles, CA probably 03/xx/87

(I Don't Wanna) Hold Back (R. Brookins-G. Wright) 4:12 (8)

Gary Wright was born on April 26, 1943 in Englewood, New Jersey but grew up in nearby Cresskill. Wright was a child actor on the *Captain Video* TV show and appeared in commercials. He was a cast member of the Broadway play *Fanny* leading to an appearance on *The Ed Sullivan Show*. He played keyboards in several rock bands in his teens. He attended college in Berlin, Germany planning a career in psychology, but instead joined the UK band Art, who renamed themselves Spooky Tooth in 1967. He left the band between 1970 and 1973 to pursue a solo career.

He contributed to George Harrison's 1970 album *All Things Must Pass*, and the two became lifelong friends. Gary says George (under the pseudonym George O'Hara) plays guitar on *Two Faced Man* and *Stand For Our Rights* and helped produce the latter song from his 1971 album *Footprint*. Later that year he formed Gary Wright's Wonderwheel. Harrison joined Wonderwheel on ABC TV's *The Dick Cavett Show* on November 23, 1971 playing guitar on *Two Faced Man*. Wonderwheel's first album, reportedly to be titled *Ring Of Changes* or *Wright's Wonderwheel*, was recorded in part at Apple Studios in London in 1972. Apple acetates of the album exist. It was scheduled for release that July on A&M Records (AMLH 64362) but was cancelled, though Gary has no idea why. He says Harrison's sole contribution to it was playing guitar on the song *Goodbye Sunday*. The recording was produced by Gary and included on *Benjamin (The Original Soundtrack Of Willy Bogner's Motion Picture)* and also released as a single in 1972. Gary says George invited him on a trip to India in 1972 and was his spiritual mentor. Around this time they wrote the unreleased song *To Discover Your Self*.

In 1973 Gary rejoined Spooky Tooth who had been undergoing numerous personnel changes. Henry McCullough was briefly a member before he joined Wings. Spooky Tooth broke up in 1974. [Spooky Tooth regrouped in the late 1990s and Wright rejoined them for a time in 2004.] Wright's 1975 album *Dream Weaver* was certified Platinum. The title track, inspired by some Indian writings Harrison gave him, along with the song *Love Is Alive*, were Top Five hits. Gary has worked with many artists during his long career including Eric Clapton*, Elton John* and Jeff Lynne*, but contrary to rumors, he says he didn't contribute to any of John Lennon's recordings.

Wright also plays on Harrison's 1970's albums *Living In The Material World*, *Dark Horse*, *Extra*

Texture (Read All About It), *Thirty-Three & 1/3*, *George Harrison*, and *Cloud Nine* in 1987. Contrary to reports, he didn't appear in Harrison's music video for *When We Was Fab*. Harrison plays on the song *(I Don't Wanna) Hold Back* on Wright's 1988 album *Who I Am*, and sings backing vocals on *Don't Try To Own Me* from Wright's 1995 album *First Signs Of Life*. Some issues include a bonus DVD with Harrison singing in the video for the song.

Wright contributed keyboards to Ringo's songs *It Don't Come Easy*, *Back Off Boogaloo* and *Down And Out* in the early 1970s. He was a member of Ringo Starr's All-Starr Band in 2008 performing *Dream Weaver* and *Love Is Alive* with Ringo on drums. Wright recalls, "I had known and worked with Ringo, initially through George, in the early 1970s. Ringo and I kind of lost contact when I moved back to the US. I was thrilled when I got the call to work with him again because he's a terrific person. It was a very special moment for me during rehearsals in Canada when I was doing *Dream Weaver* and I turned around to see Ringo drumming on it. Edgar Winter*, who's a fantastic musician, was the only other person in the band I'd worked with before. I love playing his stuff. I love playing Billy Squier* and Colin Hay's* stuff too. Hamish Stuart* was the only dark horse for me because when I first got his Average White Band songs I knew they were going to be hard to play. I had to struggle to learn all the parts, but I did and his songs went down really well. There were never any bad vibes with anyone. The chemistry among all of these great musicians was fantastic. Everyone respected each other. The vibe touring with Ringo is fantastic. It's touring deluxe style! I got to see a side of Ringo I'd never seen before. It's not just his singing and drumming, which is great, but the fantastic way he communicates with his audience, which is part of his artistry. He's very funny onstage. My only regret is that the tour didn't last longer." He contributed to Ringo's 2010 album *Y Not* and Ringo plays drums on Gary's 2010 album *Connected*. Gary continues to write, record and tour. For more information go to www.thedreamweaver.com

Bill Wyman's Rhythm Kings

Double Bill
Velvel/Koch-KOC CD 8287 (06/26/01)
Producer: Bill Wyman & Terry Taylor
George Harrison: Slide Guitar; Beverley Skeete: Lead & B. Vocals; Graham Broad: Drums; Bill Wyman: Bass; Dave Hartley: Piano; Georgie Fame: Organ; Tommy Emmanuel: Guitar; Terry Taylor: Guitar; Frank Ricotti: Percussion; Janice Hoyte: B. Vocals
Snake Ranch Studio, London & FPSHOT†, UK
11/14/00 & 12/19/00†

Love Letters (E. Heyman-V. Young) 3:33 (1-4) (04/23/01)

Bill Wyman was born William Perks on October 24, 1936 in Lewisham (London), England. He is best known as the bassist for The Rolling Stones* from 1962 until he officially quit the group in 1992. He studied piano for several years as a youngster and was later in the band The Cliftons. He adopted the surname Wyman from a good friend. While a member of The Rolling Stones he cultivated a solo career releasing three albums and a few singles but without much success. He has also scored the music for several films, written books, opened a rock 'n' roll-themed restaurant, produced and managed rock groups, and sponsored a line of metal detectors.

Wyman joined Ringo Starr, Kiki Dee,* Dave Mason*, Todd Rundgren* and others in a band that performed on the *Jerry Lewis Muscular Dystrophy Telethon* airing on September 3, 1979. In 1985 Wyman formed the group Willie & The Poor Boys with Ron Wood*, Charlie Watts, Kenney Jones*, Jimmy Page, Andy Fairweather Low and others. Ringo makes a cameo as the Janitor in the 1985 charity video *Willie And The Poor Boys Live* released in 2004 in the UK on DVD (Classic Pictures -7092X0). Wyman was a co-owner with Ringo of the London Brasserie in Atlanta's Peachtree Center in the late 1980s.

In 1997 Wyman formed Bill Wyman's Rhythm Kings, not unlike Ringo Starr's All-Starr Band, which has included among other guest musicians and members, Gary Brooker*, Peter Frampton*, Eric Clapton*, Albert Lee, Martin Taylor, Mike Sanchez, Georgie Fame, and George Harrison on the song *Love Letters*. Bill Wyman's Rhythm Kings contributed a cover of *Taxman* for the 2003 album *Songs From The Material World: A Tribute To George Harrison*. The Rhythm Kings have released half-a-dozen albums and continue to tour. For more information go to www.billwyman.com

Darren Young (with John Barry and His Orchestra)

John Berry-The Hits & The Misses [Various Artists]
Play It Again-PLAY 007 (UK) (07/07/98)
Producer: Norman Newell & John Burgess
Darren Young: Lead Vocals; John Barry: Conductor & Arranger and His Orchestra
EMI-Abbey Road Studios, London, UK 04/xx/62

I've Just Fallen For Someone (**[J. Lennon]**-J. Askew**)** 1:50 (2-2) (07/xx/62)

Darren Young was born John Askew on December 8, 1936 in Liverpool, England. He performed under the name Johnny Gentle in the late 1950s, and was a regular on the UK pop music TV shows *Oh Boy* and *Drumbeat*. His manager, promoter Larry Parnes, hired a band who'd recently become known as The Silver Beetles, which included John Lennon, Paul McCartney, George Harrison, Stu Sutcliffe and Tommy Moore on drums, to back up Gentle on a brief tour of Scotland in May 1960. He also appeared with them at the Grosvenor Ballroom in Liscard on July 2. He tried (unsuccessfully) to get Parnes to sign them to a long-term contract. Askew says, "I met The Beatles just before they first backed me. The chemistry between us was great and we didn't have a bad show. During the tour I was having problems with the middle eight of a song I was writing called *I've Just Fallen For Someone*. John played something he had written that he thought would fit the song, and I liked it, so I used it. It's the part 'We know that we'll get by, just wait and see, just like the song tells us, the best things in life are free.'" The song was issued as the B-side of the Parlophone single (R 4919) *My Tears Will Turn To Laughter* by Darren Young, Askew's pseudonym by then. Lennon wasn't credited as a composer on the label, and the song wasn't a hit. However, the song was first issued months earlier by Adam Faith* using the same conductor and arranger, and probably recorded at the same studio with the same producer. No doubt a version by Young was referenced by Faith. However, because Lennon wrote the song with Askew it's also considered a contribution to Young's recording. By the late 1960s Askew had retired from show business. For more information go to www.johnnygentle.co.uk

Neil Young

Paul McCartney & Neil Young Together On Stage 2004 [Paul McCartney]
Piccadilly Circus-PCCD 029/030 [unauthorized release] (12/xx/04)
Paul McCartney: Vocals & Guitar; Neil Young: Vocals & Guitar; Rusty Anderson: Guitar; Brian Ray: Bass; Abe Laboriel Jr. Drums; Paul Wickens: Keyboards
Century Plaza Hotel, Los Angeles, CA 10/15/04

Only Love Can Break Your Heart [live] (N. Young) 4:02 (2-8)

Neil Young was born on November 12, 1945 in Toronto, Ontario but spent his teenage years in Winnipeg, Manitoba Canada. He was in several bands in high school including the Squires who had a local hit. He dropped out of high school, and hit the road making friends with Stephen Stills*, Randy Bachman* and Joni Mitchell, and began actively writing songs. By the mid-1960s he was in the band The Mynah Birds fronted by Rick James, who were contracted to Motown Records but broke up before releasing anything. Young and the band's bass player Bruce Palmer headed for Los Angeles, and teamed up with Stills, Richie Furay and Dewey Martin forming the critically acclaimed group Buffalo Springfield in 1966. They had the Top 10 hit *For What It's Worth* in 1967. Unfortunately the group, fraught with musical differences and personal problems, broke up within two years. [They were inducted into the Rock and Roll Hall of Fame in 1997.]

Young, with and without the group Crazy Horse, launched a solo career. He has seen far more chart success with his Platinum certified albums *Everybody Knows This Is Nowhere* in 1969, *After The Gold Rush* in 1970, *Harvest* in 1972 and *Harvest Moon* in 1992, than with the classic songs they contain such as *Cinnamon Girl*, *Down By The River*, *Only Love Can Break Your Heart*, *Old Man*, *Southern Man*, *Alabama* and his only number one hit *Heart Of Gold* in 1972. Young has also been a part-time member of the highly successful group Crosby, Stills & Nash (& Young) since 1969. Neil has explored many musical styles throughout his career working with a wide range of artists including Nils Lofgren*, James Taylor*, Rick Danko*, Levon Helm*, Willie Nelson, Pearl Jam, Sonic Youth, Phish and others. Neil has also been involved in a number of causes such as Farm Aid (see The New Maroons, Lyle Lovett). Neil Young was inducted into the Rock and Roll Hall of Fame in 1995. He performed John Lennon's song *Imagine* for the *Telethon America: A Tribute To Heroes* in support of victims of the attacks on September 11, 2001.

Paul, (and particularly his late wife Linda McCartney*), has been a huge Neil Young fan. In 1999 Young inducted Paul McCartney into the Rock and Roll Hall of Fame saying McCartney was one of the world's greatest songwriters and that the first song he learned to play was from a Beatles' record. On October 15, 2004 Neil performed at the annual Adopt-A-Minefield gala held at the Century Plaza Hotel in Los Angeles. Adopt-A-Minefield is an organization heavily supported by McCartney's then wife, Heather Mills*. Young sang *Only Love Can Break Your Heart* with McCartney and his band, and joined them on *Hey Jude*. McCartney and his band returned the favor some days later by performing the same songs together at Young's annual *Bridge School Benefit Concert* for developmentally disabled children on October 23 and 24 at the Shoreline Amphitheatre in Mountain View, California. All three performances are available on unauthorized releases. McCartney joined Young on backing vocals and vibraphone during Neil's performance of *A Day In The Life* at the *Hard Rock Calling* festival in Hyde Park in London on June 27, 2009. Neil Young continues to write, record and perform. For more information go to www.neilyoung.com

Frank Zappa And The Mothers

Playground Psychotics
Barking Pumpkin-D2 74244 (11/03/92)
Producer: Frank Zappa
Fillmore East Theater, New York, NY 06/06/71

A Small Eternity With Yoko Ono [live] [a.k.a. Au] (J. Lennon-Y. Ono) 6:11 (1-26)
John Lennon: Dialogue & Feedback Guitar; Yoko Ono: Dialogue, Lead Vocals & Tambourine; Frank Zappa: Dialogue & Feedback Guitar; Don Preston: Mini Moog; Ian Underwood: Keyboards

Aaawk [live] [a.k.a. Jamrag] (J. Lennon-Y. Ono-F. Zappa) 2:59 (1-24)
John Lennon: Guitar; Yoko Ono: Lead Vocals; Frank Zappa: Guitar; Mark Volman: Tambourine; Howard Kaylan: Tambourine; Ian Underwood: Keyboards; Aynsley Dunbar: Drums; Jim Pons: Bass; Bob Harris: Keyboards

Say Please [live] [a.k.a. Jamrag] (**J. Lennon**-Y. Ono-F. Zappa) 0:57 (1-23)
John Lennon: Dialogue, B. Vocals & Guitar; Yoko Ono: Lead Vocals; Frank Zappa: Dialogue & Guitar; Mark Volman: B. Vocals; Howard Kaylan: B. Vocals; Ian Underwood: keyboards; Aynsley Dunbar: Drums; Jim Pons: Bass

Frank Zappa was born on December 21, 1940 in Baltimore, Maryland but spent most of his life in Southern California. Frank played in his high school orchestra and formed the band the Blackouts in the late 1950s, already demonstrating his bizarre brand of humor. By the early 1960s he'd been in several groups, was scoring music for other artists and films, and appeared on TV's *The Steve Allen Show* performing a *Bicycle Concerto* by blowing through the handlebars and plucking the spokes. His music was a mixed bag of free-form jazz, avant-garde classical, R&B, doo-wop, and hard rock fused with political satire and bizarre, sexually oriented comedy. Though a renowned guitarist, Zappa never craved, or achieved much chart success, though his albums were consistent sellers and usually received high critical praise. Paul McCartney cited Zappa and his band The Mothers Of Invention's 1966 album *Freak Out* as influencing The Beatles' *Sgt. Pepper's Lonely Hearts Club Band* album. The jacket for their 1968 album *We're Only In It For The Money* parodied that of *Sgt. Pepper's Lonely Hearts Club Band*.

In 1970 The Mothers included the vocal and comedy talents of Mark Volman and Howard Kaylan (The Phlorescent Leech and Eddie, a.k.a. Flo & Eddie), founding members of The Turtles. [On April 14, 1974 Ringo Starr and Keith Moon were guests on Flo & Eddie's radio show on KROQ in Los Angeles. Unfortunately, Ringo's repeated use of profanity over the airwaves later resulted in the show being cancelled. A portion of Ringo's appearance is included on the 1983 album *The History Of Flo & Eddie And the Turtles* (Rhin-RNTA 1998). Flo & Eddie were considered for Ringo Starr's All-Starr Band tour in 1995.]

On June 6, 1971 John Lennon and Yoko Ono* joined Frank Zappa And The Mothers onstage during their performance at New York's Fillmore East Theater. The performance was a combination of John's, and particularly Yoko's, experimental music fused with Zappa and The Mothers' free-form jazz and comedy. Reportedly, Allen Klein wouldn't allow Zappa permission to use the Lennons' portion of the show for his release, and what Zappa turned over to the Lennons didn't include much of The Mothers' backing. Zappa stated in a *Rolling Stone* magazine interview in February 1988, "The deal I made with John and Yoko was that we were both to have access to the tapes, and could deploy them any way we wanted. They got a duplicate copy of the master, and they mixed it their way. I had a copy of the master, and I was gonna mix it and put it out as part of The Mothers' album. They put out this record that took *King Kong* – which obviously has a tune, and a rhythm and chord changes – and they called it *Jamrag*, and accredited the writing and publishing to themselves." Zappa eventually released his mix and edit of the performance on his 1992 album *Playground Psychotics*. He recounts in the album's liner notes: "Some of you might have heard another version of this material on the John and Yoko album *Some Time In New York City*. When they sat in with us that night, we were in the process of recording the *Live At The Fillmore East, June 1971* album, and all of this insanity was captured on tape. After the show, John and I agreed we would each put out our own version of the performance, and I gave him a copy of the 16 track master tape. Here is our version ... a substantially different mix from what they released [in 1972]." Due to the nature of the jam, song times (and titles) vary widely from release to release, and are an approximation. For example, the song *Well*, sung by John, has a longer introduction and is about 20-seconds longer on the fadeout. [The complete performance of the song was over seven minutes.] The only song on Zappa's release that is edited down (about 1:30) from the Lennons' release is *Jamrag*, which is divided into the more appropriate new titles of *Say Please* and *Aaawk*. Zappa justifiably took credit for composing much of *Jamrag*, which consists of well-known Zappa compositions, including *King Kong*. *Scumbag*, which John also sings, restores the full backing band, including Flo & Eddie's vocals, which were mixed out on the Lennons' release. Zappa also re-titled the final song *Au*, to *A Small Eternity With Yoko Ono*. Though it may appear from differing times (some releases include the tail end of *Scumbag* in the timing of *Au*) on the Lennons' release that almost two minutes of this song were edited out by Zappa, it's the same length, except for a much longer audience fadeout. What Zappa rightfully presented on *Playground Psychotics* is his and The Mothers' performance, which includes a guest appearance by the Lennons. What the Lennons and producer Phil Spector* released is a sparse Plastic Ono Band sound with Frank Zappa And The Mothers' backing all but eliminated from the mix. They used the album jacket design of *The Mothers' Fillmore East, June 1971*, which didn't include their performance, as the inner sleeve for *Some Time In New York City*, defacing and inserting their credits with a red marker. Mark Volman says, "There was a battle over the tapes. Frank was never happy about the way Lennon released our portion of the record, and he didn't like the way John changed the [Mothers'] album design."

Zappa and The Mother's film *200 Motels*, which premiered on November 10, 1971, features Keith Moon* playing a nun and Ringo Starr playing Larry The Dwarf who impersonates Frank Zappa. Ringo's chauffeur Martin Lickert also ended up with a role in the film. The film was released in 1988 on VHS (MGM/UA-M200423).

In December 1971 an audience member pushed Zappa off the stage during the group's encore (a rendition of The Beatles' *I Want To Hold Your Hand*) seriously injuring him. Following his lengthy recovery Zappa disbanded The Mothers and used top session musicians to tour and record until his death on December 4, 1993. Frank Zappa was inducted into the Rock and Roll Hall of Fame in 1995. For more information go to www.zappa.com

Is This It?

Despite my 10 years of exhaustive efforts to discover every contribution any of The Beatles made to other artists' records and recordings, I undoubtedly missed a few, and more will surely be discovered. Who knows, perhaps recordings exist of George Harrison's two performances with The Four Bests during a visit to see his sister in Illinois in September 1963. One thing is certain, the surviving Beatles will continue to work with other artists and contribute to their recordings.

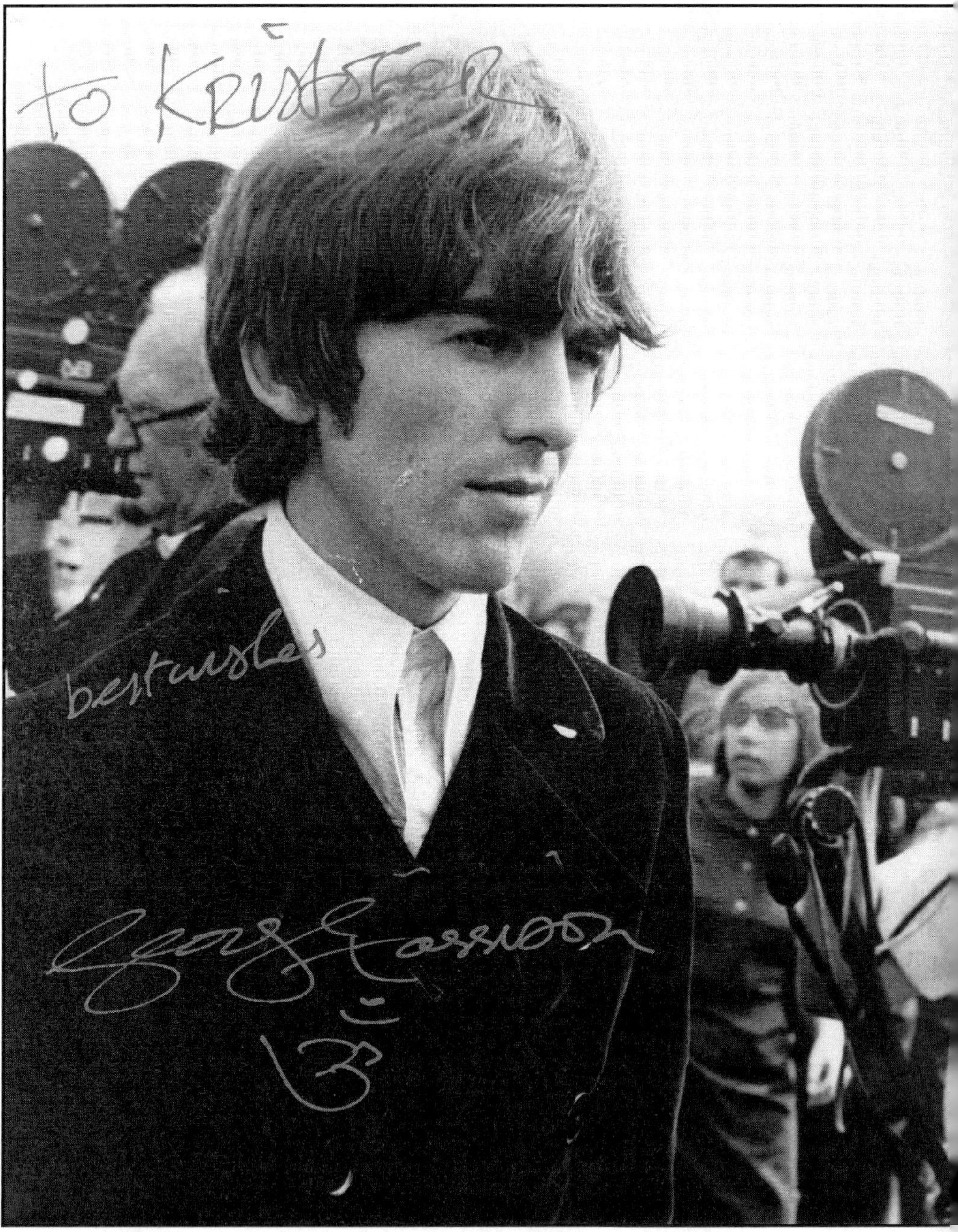

George Harrison arriving with The Beatles on August 11, 1966 at Boston's Logan Airport for the beginning of their final tour. ©Photo courtesy of Guy Greve

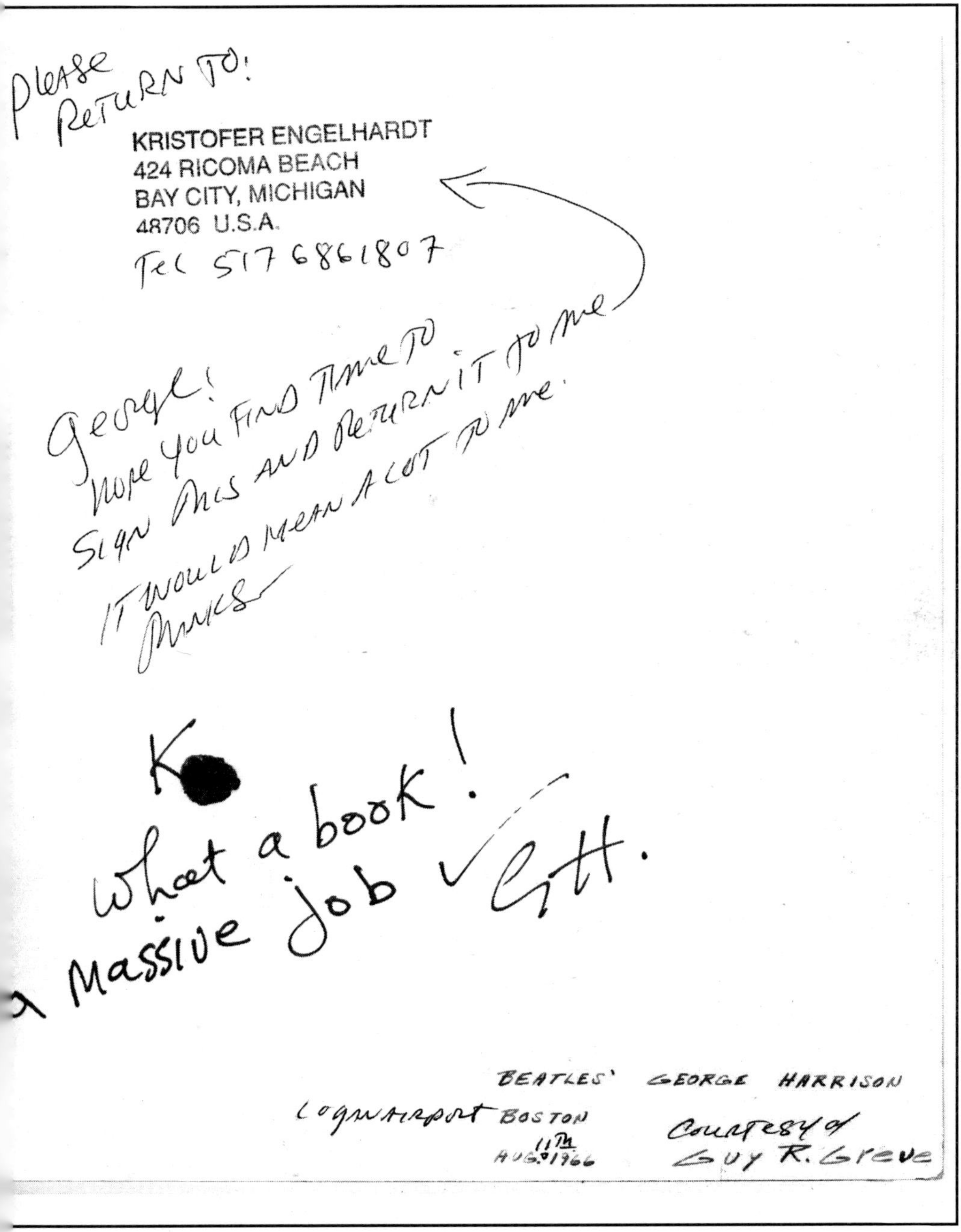

PLEASE RETURN TO!

KRISTOFER ENGELHARDT
424 RICOMA BEACH
BAY CITY, MICHIGAN
48706 U.S.A.
TEL 517 6861807

GEORGE!
HOPE YOU FIND TIME TO
SIGN THIS AND RETURN IT TO ME
IT WOULD MEAN A LOT TO ME.
THANKS

K[redacted]
What a book!
A MASSIVE JOB ✓ GH.

BEATLES' GEORGE HARRISON
LOGAN AIRPORT BOSTON
11TH AUG. 1966
COURTESY OF
GUY R. GREVE

George Harrison's note to the author of the book "Beatles Undercover" on the back of the photo on the previous page.

About The Author

Kristofer Karl Engelhardt's first appearance was at Mercy Hospital (6 years before Madonna) on January 20, 1952 in Bay City, Michigan. His passion for music found him frantically fiddling with the antenna of his TV set on February 9, 1964 to watch The Beatles on *The Ed Sullivan Show*. Seeing both of The Beatles' performances at Olympia Stadium in Detroit in 1966 inspired him to begin seriously collecting and cataloging their work. He is considered the leading expert on the subject of The Beatles' musical contributions to other artists' recordings. He has also authored the books *Beatles Undercover* (Collector's Guide Publishing 1998, ISBN 1-896522-43-2) and *From Grand Funk To Grace (The Authorized Biography of Mark Farner)* (Collector's Guide Publishing 2001, ISBN 1-896522-74-2) and is nearing completion on another biography on a rock group. He has been a guest at conventions and festivals for fans of The Beatles, on numerous national TV and radio shows, and was the "Magical Mr. E" who hosted WMJT FM's *Breakfast With The Beatles* in the early 1990s.